Texas
Civil Practice and Remedies Code

2022 Edition
[Supersedes 2020 Edition]

WITH TABLES
AND INDEX

THOMSON REUTERS™

Mat #42706651

ISBN 978-1-539-22198-2

PREFACE

Designed for use in the office or courtroom, this pamphlet brings together in one convenient publication the complete Texas Civil Practice & Remedies Code.

WHAT'S NEW

This product brings up to date statutes through the 2021 Third Called Session of the 87th Legislature.

This pamphlet includes new enactments or important amendments relating to:

- Trial, Judgments and Appeals
- Extraordinary Remedies
- Tort Liability
- Alternate Methods of Dispute Resolution

CONTACT US

For additional information or research assistance, contact the Reference Attorneys at 1-800-REF-ATTY (1-800-733-2889) or by Live Chat: Access via Westlaw. Contact our U.S. legal editorial department directly with your questions and suggestions by e-mail at editors.us-legal@tr.com.

Thank you for subscribing to this product. Should you have any questions regarding this product, please contact Customer Service at 1-800-328-4880 or by fax at 1-800-340-9378. If you would like to inquire about related publications, or to place an order, please contact us at 1-888-728-7677 or visit us at legalsolutions.thomsonreuters.com.

THE PUBLISHER

November, 2021

EFFECTIVE DATES

The following table shows the date of adjournment and the effective date of ninety day bills enacted at sessions of the legislature beginning with the year 1945:

Year	Leg.	Session	Adjournment Date	Effective Date
1945	49	Regular	June 5, 1945	September 4, 1945
1947	50	Regular	June 6, 1947	September 5, 1947
1949	51	Regular	June 6, 1949	September 5, 1949
1951	52	Regular	June 8, 1951	September 7, 1951
1953	53	Regular	May 27, 1953	August 26, 1953
1954	53	1st C.S.	May 13, 1954	August 12, 1954
1955	54	Regular	June 7, 1955	September 6, 1955
1957	55	Regular	May 23, 1957	August 22, 1957
1957	55	1st C.S.	November 12, 1957	February 11, 1958
1957	55	2nd C.S.	December 3, 1957	March 4, 1958
1959	56	Regular	May 12, 1959	August 11, 1959
1959	56	1st C.S.	June 16, 1959	September 15, 1959
1959	56	2nd C.S.	July 16, 1959	October 15, 1959
1959	56	3rd C.S.	August 6, 1959	November 5, 1959
1961	57	Regular	May 29, 1961	August 28, 1961
1961	57	1st C.S.	August 8, 1961	November 7, 1961
1961	57	2nd C.S.	August 14, 1961	November 13, 1961
1962	57	3rd C.S.	February 1, 1962	May 3, 1962
1963	58	Regular	May 24, 1963	August 23, 1963
1965	59	Regular	May 31, 1965	August 30, 1965
1966	59	1st C.S.	February 23, 1966	*
1967	60	Regular	May 29, 1967	August 28, 1967
1968	60	1st C.S.	July 3, 1968	*
1969	61	Regular	June 2, 1969	September 1, 1969
1969	61	1st C.S.	August 26, 1969	*
1969	61	2nd C.S.	September 9, 1969	December 9, 1969
1971	62	Regular	May 31, 1971	August 30, 1971
1971	62	1st C.S.	June 4, 1971	September 3, 1971
1972	62	2nd C.S.	March 30, 1972	June 29, 1972
1972	62	3rd C.S.	July 7, 1972	*
1972	62	4th C.S.	October 17, 1972	January 16, 1973
1973	63	Regular	May 28, 1973	August 27, 1973
1973	63	1st C.S.	December 20, 1973	*
1975	64	Regular	June 2, 1975	September 1, 1975
1977	65	Regular	May 30, 1977	August 29, 1977
1977	65	1st C.S.	July 21, 1977	*
1978	65	2nd C.S.	August 8, 1978	November 7, 1978
1979	66	Regular	May 28, 1979	August 27, 1979
1981	67	Regular	June 1, 1981	August 31, 1981

EFFECTIVE DATES

Year	Leg.	Session	Adjournment Date	Effective Date
1981	67	1st C.S.	August 11, 1981	November 10, 1981
1982	67	2nd C.S.	May 28, 1982	*
1982	67	3rd C.S.	September 9, 1982	*
1983	68	Regular	May 30, 1983	August 29, 1983
1983	68	1st C.S.	June 25, 1983	September 23, 1983
1984	68	2nd C.S.	July 3, 1984	October 2, 1984
1985	69	Regular	May 27, 1985	August 26, 1985
1985	69	1st C.S.	May 30, 1985	August 29, 1985
1986	69	2nd C.S.	September 4, 1986	December 4, 1986
1986	69	3rd C.S.	September 30, 1986	December 30, 1986
1987	70	Regular	June 1, 1987	August 31, 1987
1987	70	1st C.S.	June 3, 1987	September 2, 1987
1987	70	2nd C.S.	July 21, 1987	October 20, 1987
1989	71	Regular	May 29, 1989	August 28, 1989
1989	71	1st C.S.	July 19, 1989	October 18, 1989
1989	71	2nd C.S.	December 12, 1989	*
1990	71	3rd C.S.	March 28, 1990	*
1990	71	4th C.S.	May 1, 1990	*
1990	71	5th C.S.	May 30, 1990	*
1990	71	6th C.S.	June 7, 1990	September 6, 1990
1991	72	Regular	May 27, 1991	August 26, 1991
1991	72	1st C.S.	August 13, 1991	November 12, 1991
1991	72	2nd C.S.	August 25, 1991	November 24, 1991
1992	72	3rd C.S.	January 8, 1992	April 8, 1992
1992	72	4th C.S.	December 3, 1992	*
1993	73	Regular	May 31, 1993	August 30, 1993
1995	74	Regular	May 29, 1995	August 28, 1995
1997	75	Regular	June 2, 1997	September 1, 1997
1999	76	Regular	May 31, 1999	August 30, 1999
2001	77	Regular	May 28, 2001	September 1, 2001
2003	78	Regular	June 2, 2003	September 1, 2003
2003	78	1st C.S.	July 28, 2003	*
2003	78	2nd C.S.	August 26, 2003	*
2005	79	2nd C.S.	August 19, 2005	November 18, 2005
2006	79	3rd C.S.	May 16, 2006	August 15, 2006
2007	80	Regular	May 28, 2007	August 27, 2007
2009	81	Regular	June 1, 2009	August 31, 2009
2009	81	1st C.S.	July 2, 2009	*
2011	82	Regular	May 30, 2011	August 29, 2011
2011	82	1st C.S.	June 29, 2011	September 28, 2011**
2013	83	Regular	May 27, 2013	August 26, 2013
2013	83	1st C.S.	June 25, 2013	September 24, 2013**
2013	83	2nd C.S.	July 30, 2013	October 29, 2013**
2013	83	3rd C.S.	August 5, 2013	*
2015	84	Regular	June 1, 2015	August 31, 2015

EFFECTIVE DATES

Year	Leg.	Session	Adjournment Date	Effective Date
2017	85	Regular	May 29, 2017	August 28, 2017
2017	85	1st C.S.	August 15, 2017	November 14, 2017
2017	85	1st C.S.	August 15, 2017	November 14, 2017
2019	86	Regular	May 27, 2019	August 26, 2019
2021	87	Regular	May 31, 2021	August 30, 2021
2021	87	1st C.S.	August 6, 2021	*
2021	87	2nd C.S.	September 2, 2021	December 2, 2021
2021	87	3rd C.S.	October 19, 2021	January 18, 2022

* No legislation for which the ninety day effective date is applicable.

** Legislation effective on the 91st day after session.

DISPOSITION TABLE

Showing where provisions of former articles of the Civil Statutes and sections of the Education Code are covered in the Civil Practice and Remedies Code as originally enacted.

Civ.Stat. Article		Civil Practice and Remedies Code Section
1		5.001
1a		74.001
		74.002
1b,	§ 1	75.002
	§ 2	75.003
	§ 3	75.003
	§ 4	75.003
	§ 5	75.003
	§ 6	75.001
1d		124.001
275		61.001
1		61.002
		61.021
		61.022
276		61.001
277		61.003
278		61.004
279		61.022
		61.023
279a		6.001
281		61.005
		61.023
282		61.023 note
287		61.044 note
288		61.041
290		61.042
291		61.044
300		61.061
301		61.062
302		61.063
320c		7.011
941		51.002
960		51.011
1070.1		78.001
1840–A		30.003 note
		21.031
1970–325,	§ 1	21.031 note
	§ 2	21.031
	§ 3	21.032
1975		17.003
1976		17.003
		17.003 note
1982		17.002
1986		17.001
1987		17.001
1991		7.021
1995,	§ 1	15.001
	§ 2(a)	15.011
	§ 2(b)	15.012
	§ 2(c)	15.013
	§ 2(d)	15.014
	§ 2(e)	15.015
	§ 2(f)	15.016
	§ 2(g)	15.017
	§ 3(a)	15.031
	§ 3(b)	15.032
	§ 3(c)	15.033
	§ 3(d)	15.034
	§ 3(e)	15.035
	§ 3(f)	15.036
		15.037
	§ 3(h)	15.038
	§ 3(i)	15.039
	§ 3(j)	15.040
	§ 4(a)	15.061
	§ 4(b)	15.062
	§ 4(c)	15.063
	§ 4(d)	15.064
1996		15.065
2027		17.024
2028,	§ 1	17.024
	§ 2	17.024
2029		17.023
2030		64.076
2031b,	§ 1	17.044
	§ 2	17.043
		17.045
	§ 3	17.044
	§ 4	17.042
	§ 5	17.045
	§ 6	17.044
		17.045
	§ 7	17.045 note
2032		17.093
2033		17.022
2033a		17.092
2033b		17.021
2033c		17.021
2039a,	§ 1	17.062
		17.063
		17.064
	§ 2	17.063
		17.065
	§ 3	17.066
	§ 4	17.069
	§ 5	17.063
		17.067
	§ 6	17.068
2039b		17.091
2040		17.004
		17.004 note
2041a,	§ 1	17.005
2041b		17,025
2072		6.001
		6.002
2072a		6.001

DISPOSITION TABLE

Civ.Stat. Article		Civil Practice and Remedies Code Section
2088		17.001
2090		17.093 note
2168a		30.003
2212		32.001
		32.002
		32.003
2212a,	§ 1	33.001
	§ 2(a)	33.001
	§ 2(b)	33.012
	§ 2(c)	33.013
	§ 2(d)	33.014
	§ 2(e)	33.015
	§ 2(f)	33.016
	§ 2(g)	33.017
	§ 2(h)	33.017 note
2212b,	§ 1	127.002
	§ 2	127.003
	§ 3	127.001
	§ 4(a)	127.001
		127.004
	§ 4(b)	127.006
		127.007
	§ 4(c)	127.005
		127.008
	§ 4(d)	note
	§ 5	127.008
2214		31.001
2218a		31.006 note
2218b		31.006 note
2223		31.003
2224		30.001
2226		38.001
		38.002
		38.003
		38.004
		38.005
		38.006
2226a,	§ 1	31.004
	§ 2	31.005
2226b,	§ 1	105.001
	§ 2	105.002
		105.003
	§ 3	105.003
	§ 4	105.002
	§ 5	105.004
2248		30.002
2249		51.012
2250		51.014
2251		51.014
2255		51.013
2276		6.001
		6.003 note
2276a		6.003
2286a		17.093 note
2287		7.001
2290		7.002
2293		64.001
	§ 5	126.001
2293a,	§ 1	126.002
	§ 6	126.002
2294		64.021
2294a		126.003
2295		64.075
2296		64.022
2297		64.031

Civ.Stat. Article		Civil Practice and Remedies Code Section
2297a		126.004
2298		64.034
2299		64.051
2300		64.052
		64.056
2301		64.055
2302		64.054
		64.056
2303		64.056
2304		64.052
2305		64.056
2306		64.056
2307		64.056
2308		64.092 note
2309		64.035
2310		64.033
		64.052
		64.053
2311		64.052
		64.076
2312		64.071
2313		64.003
2314		64.032
2315		64.073
2316		64.074
2317		64.072
2318		64.002
2319		64.004
2320a		64.092 note
2320b		64.091
2320c		64.092
2328b–5,	§ 1	35.001
	§ 2	35.003
	§ 3(a)	35.004
	§ 3(b)	35.004
		35.005
	§ 4	35.006
	§ 5	35.007
	§ 6	35.008
	§ 7	35.008 note
	§ 8	35.002
2328b–6,	§ 1	36.003
	§ 2	36.001
	§ 3	36.002
	§ 4	36.004
	§ 5	36.005
	§ 6	36.006
	§ 7	36.007
	§ 8	36.008
	§ 9	36.008 note
	§ 10	36.002
2390		15.081
		15.082
		15.087
	Subd. 1	15.084
	Subd. 2	15.085
	Subd. 3	15.086
	Subd. 4	15.092
	Subd. 5	15.091
	Subd. 6	15.093
	Subd. 7	15.089
	Subd. 8	15.008
	Subd. 9	15.090
	Subd. 10	15.094
	Subd. 11	15.095

DISPOSITION TABLE

Civ.Stat. Article		Civil Practice and Remedies Code Section
	Subd. 12	15.097
	Subd. 13	15.096
		15.098
2391		15.083
2392		15.099
2393		15.100
2451		34.001
2454		51.001
2455		51.001
		51.002
2455–1		51.001
		51.002
2460		51.002
2524–1,	§ 1	37.003
	§ 2	37.004
	§ 3	37.004
	§ 4	37.005
	§ 5	37.003
	§ 6	37.008
	§ 7	37.010
	§ 8	37.011
	§ 9	37.007
	§ 10	37.009
	§ 11	37.006
	§ 12	37.002
	§ 13	37.001
	§ 14	37.011 note
	§ 15	37.002
	§ 16	37.002
3708		22.001
3710		22.011
3712a(a)		21.001
		21.002
		21.003
3712a(b)		21.004
3712a(c)		21.005
		21.008
3712a(d)		21.006
3712a(e)		21.007
3733		18.031
3737d–1,	§ 1	21.021
		21.022
		21.023
		21.023 note
	§ 2	21.022
3737h		18.001
3746		20.001
3748		20.002 note
3757		20.002 note
3769a		20.002
3769b		20.002 note
3773		34.001
3775		34.002
3785		34.063
3786		34.005
3787		34.062
3792		34.004
3798		34.044
3799		34.061
3799a,	§ 1	7.003
	§ 2	7.003
3799a,	§ 3(a)	34.021
	§ 3(b)	34.022
3800		34.047
3805		34.041

Civ.Stat. Article		Civil Practice and Remedies Code Section
3806		34.042
3807		34.043
3816		34.045
3817		34.045
3818		34.046
3819		34.066
3820		34.048
3824		34.047
		34.067
3825		34.065
3826		34.064
3827		34.047
3827a		31.002
3829		34.003
3830		34.002
4076		63.001
		63.002
4084		63.003
		63.005 note
4093		63.005 note
4096		63.005
4099		63.004
4331a		126.002
		126.011
		126.012
		126.013
4476–5c,	§ 1	76.002
	§ 2	76.001
		76.003
	§ 3	76.004
4590–3,	§ 1	77.002
	§ 2	77.001
		77.003
	§ 3	77.004
4642		65.011
		65.021
		65.022
4643		65.022
4644		65.012
4645		65.013
4646		65.014
4646a		65.015
4656		65.023
4660		65.031
4662		51.014
4663		65.001
4664		125.001
		125.001 note
4665		125.004
4666		125.002
		125.003
4667(a)		125.021
		125.022
4667(b)		125.022
4671		71.001
		71.002
		71.003
		71.007
4672		71.003
4673		71.009
4674		71.006
4675		71.004
		71.011
4675a		71.005
4676		71.008

DISPOSITION TABLE

Civ.Stat. Article		Civil Practice and Remedies Code Section
4677		71.010
4678		71.031
5207b(a)		122.001
5207b(b)		122.001
5207b(c)		122.002
5207b(d)		122.003
5430		73.001
5431		73.003
		73.005
5432		73.002
5433		73.006
5433a		73.004
5507		16.024
5508		16.021
5509		16.025
5510		16.026
5511		16.031
5512		16.032
5513		16.030
5514		16.021
5515		16.021
5516		16.023
5517		16.030
		16.061
5518		16.022
		16.027
5519		16.028
5519a		16.029
5520		16.035
		16.036
		16.037
5522		16.036
		16.037
5523a		16.033
5523b		16.034
5524		16.002
5525		71.021
5526		16.003
5526a		16.005
5526b		16.006
5527		16.004
5528		16.004
5529		16.051
5530		16.066
5531		16.004
5532		31.006
5533		16.007
5534		16.072 note
5535		16.001
5536		16.072 note
5536a,	§ 1	16.008
	§ 2	16.009
5537		16.063
5538		16.062
5539		16.065
5539a		16.064
5539b		16.068
5539c		16.069
5539d		16.072
5542		16.067
5543		16.067
5544		16.001
5545		16.070
5546		16.071
5923b,	§ 1	129.001

Civ.Stat. Article		Civil Practice and Remedies Code Section
	§ 2	129.002
	§ 4	129.003
6252–16,	§ 1	106.001
	§ 2	106.002
	§ 3	106.003
		106.003
	§ 4	note
6252–19,	§ 1	101.002
	§ 2	101.001
	§ 3(a)	101.001
	§ 3(b)	101.001
		101.021
		101.023
		101.024
	§ 4	101.025
	§ 5	101.102
	§ 6	101.003
		101.109
		note
		101.109
	§ 7	note
	§ 8	101.102
	§ 9	101.027
		101.103
		101.104
	§ 10	101.105
	§ 11	101.107
		101.108
	§ 12(a)	101.106
	§ 12(b)	101.027
		101.109
	§ 13	note
	§ 14(1)	101.061
	§ 14(2)	101.052
	§ 14(3)	101.053
	§ 14(4)	101.053
	§ 14(5)	101.055
	§ 14(6)	101.054
	§ 14(7)	101.056
	§ 14(8)	101.055
	§ 14(9)	101.055
		101.057
	§ 14(10)	101.057
	§ 14(11)	101.059
	§ 14(12)	101.060
	§ 15	101.026
	§ 16	101.101
	§ 17	101.109
	§ 18(a)	101.001
		101.058
	§ 18(b)	101.022
	§ 19	101.028
	§ 19A	101.051
		101.109
	§ 20	note
		101.109
	§ 21	note
		101.109
	§ 22	note
6252–19b,	§ 1	102.001
	§ 2(a)	102.001
		102.002
	§ 2(b)	102.002
		102.003
		102.006

DISPOSITION TABLE

Civ.Stat. Article		Civil Practice and Remedies Code Section
	§ 3(a)	102.004
	§ 3(b)	102.004
	§ 3(c)	102.005
		102.006
	§ 5	note
		103.007
6252–25,	§ 1	note
	§ 2	103.001
	§ 3(c)	103.002
	§ 4	103.003
		103.004
	§ 5	103.005
	§ 6	103.006
	§ 7	103.007
6252–26,	§ 1(a)	104.001
		104.002
	§ 1(b)	104.003
		104.008
		104.008
	§ 2	note
	§ 3(a)	104.004
		104.005
	§ 3(b)	104.006
	§ 4	104.007
	§ 5	104.001
6253		66.001
		66.002
6257		66.003
6582		19.001
		19.002
6583		19.003
		19.004
		19.007
6584		19.005
6585		19.003
		19.004
		19.005
6586		19.006
6587		19.009
6588		19.008
6589		19.006
6602		121.001
6602a		121.002
6603		121.004
6604		121.005
6606		121.004
6607		121.007
6607a,	§ 1	121.006
		121.008
	§ 2	121.006
	§ 3	121.008
	§ 4	121.006
6609		121.009
6610		121.009

Civ.Stat. Article		Civil Practice and Remedies Code Section
6611		121.010
6612		121.011
6613		121.011
6614		121.011
6615		121.011
6616		121.003
6617		121.013
6618		121.013
6619		121.012
6620		121.012
6621		121.012
6622		121.012
6623		121.014
6662		61.043
6701b,	§ 1(a)	72.001
	§ 1(b)	72.003
	§ 1(c)	72.004
	§ 2	72.003
6840,	§ 1(a)	62.001
		62.002
		62.021
	§ 1(b)	62.001
	§ 1(c)	62.001
	§ 1(d)	62.001
	§ 1(e)	62.001
	§ 2	62.022
	§ 3(a)	62.041
	§ 3(b)	62.042
		62.043
	§ 3(c)	62.043
		62.044
	§ 3(d)	62.045
	§ 3(e)	62.041
	§ 4	62.023
6844		62.003
6846		62.061
6847		62.062
6848		62.063
6858		62.046
9019,	§ 1	123.001
	§ 2(a)	123.002
	§ 2(b)	123.004
	§ 2(c)	123.003
	§ 2(d)	123.002
		123.004
	§ 3	note
9207,	§ 1	79.001
		79.002
	§ 2	79.002

Education Code Section	Civil Practice and Remedies Code Section
65.42	104.001

DERIVATION TABLE

Showing where provisions of the Civil Practices and Remedies Code as originally enacted were formerly covered in Vernon's Civil Statutes or the Education Code.

Civil Practice and Remedies Code Section	Vernon's Civ.St. Article
5.001	1
6.001	279a
	2072
	2072a
	2276
6.002	2072
6.003	2276a
7.001	2287
7.002	2290
7.003	3799a, §§ 1, 2
7.011	302c
7.021	1991
15.001	1995, § 1
15.011	1995, § 2(a)
15.012	1995, § 2(b)
15.013	1995, § 2(c)
15.014	1995, § 2(d)
15.015	1995, § 2(e)
15.016	1995, § 2(f)
15.017	1995, § 2(g)
15.031	1995, § 3(a)
15.032	1995, § 3(b)
15.033	1995, § 3(c)
15.034	1995, § 3(d)
15.035	1995, § 3(e)
15.036	1995, § 3(f)
15.037	1995, § 3(g)
15.038	1995, § 3(h)
15.039	1995, § 3(i)
15.040	1995, § 3(j)
15.061	1995, § 4(a)
15.062	1995, § 4(b)
15.063	1995, § 4(c)
15.064	1995, § 4(d)
15.065	1996
15.081	2390
15.082	2390
15.083	2391
15.084	2390, Subd. 1
15.085	2390, Subd. 2
15.086	2390, Subd. 3
15.087	2390
15.088	2390, Subd. 8
15.089	2390, Subd. 7
15.090	2390, Subd. 9
15.091	2390, Subd. 5
15.092	2390, Subd. 4
15.093	2390, Subd. 6
15.094	2390, Subd. 10
15.095	2390, Subd. 11
15.096	2390, Subd. 13

Civil Practice and Remedies Code Section	Vernon's Civ.St. Article
15.097	2390, Subd. 12
15.098	2390, Subd. 13
15.099	2392
15.100	2393
16.001	5535
	5544
16.002	5524
16.003	5526
16.004	5527
	5528
	5531
16.005	5526a
16.006	5526b
16.007	5533
16.008	5536a, § 1
16.009	5536a, § 2
16.021	5508
	5514
	5515
16.022	5518
16.023	5516
16.024	5507
16.025	5509
16.026	5510
16.027	5518
16.028	5519
16.029	5519a
16.030	5513
	5517
16.031	5511
16.032	5512
16.033	5523a
16.034	5523b
16.035	5520
16.036	5520
	5522
16.037	5520
	5522
16.051	5529
16.061	5517
16.062	5538
16.063	5537
16.064	5539a
16.065	5539
16.066	5530
16.067	5542
	5543
16.068	5539b
16.069	5539c
16.070	5545
16.071	5546

DERIVATION TABLE

Civil Practice and Remedies Code Section	Vernon's Civ.St. Article
16.072	5539d
17.001	1986
	1987
	2088
17.002	1982
17.003	1975
	1976
17.004	2040
17.005	2041a, § 1
17.021	2033b
	2033c
17.022	2033
17.023	2029
17.024	2027
	2028
17.025	2041b
17.042	2031b, § 4
17.043	2031b, § 2
17.044	2031b, §§ 1, 3, 6
17.045	2031b, §§ 2, 5, 6
17.062	2039a, § 1
17.063	2039a, §§ 1, 2, 5
17.064	2039a, § 1
17.065	2039a, § 2
17.066	2039a, § 3
17.067	2039a, § 5
17.068	2039a, § 6
17.069	2039a, § 4
17.091	2039b
17.092	2033a
17.093	2032
18.001	3737h
18.031	3733
19.001	6582
19.002	6582
19.003	6583
	6585
19.004	6583
	6585
19.005	6584
	6585
19.006	6586
	6589
19.007	6583
19.008	6588
19.009	6587
20.001	3746
20.002	3769a
21.001	3712a(a)
21.002	3712a(a)
21.003	3712a(a)
21.004	3712a(b)
21.005	3712a(c)
21.006	3712a(d)
21.007	3712a(e)
21.008	3712a(c)
21.021	3737d–1, § 1
21.022	3737d–1
21.023	3737d–1, § 1
21.031	1970–325, §§ 1, 2
21.032	1970–325, § 3
22.001	3708
22.011	3710
30.001	2224
30.002	2248
30.003	2168a
31.001	2214
31.002	3827a
31.003	2223
31.004	2226a, § 1
31.005	2226a, § 2
31.006	5532
32.001	2212
32.002	2212
32.003	2212
33.001	2212a, § 1
33.011	2212a, § 2(a)
33.012	2212a, § 2(b)
33.013	2212a, § 2(c)
33.014	2212a, § 2(d)
33.015	2212a, § 2(e)
33.016	2212a, § 2(f)
33.017	2212a, § 2(g)
34.001	2451
	3773
34.002	3775
	3830
34.003	3829
	3792
34.005	3786
34.021	3799a, § 3(a)
34.022	3799a, § 3(b)
34.041	3805
34.042	3806
34.043	3807
34.044	3798
34.045	3816
	3817
34.046	3818
34.047	3800
	3824
	3827
34.048	3820
34.061	3799
34.062	3787
34.063	3785
34.064	3826
34.065	3825
34.066	3819
34.067	3824
35.001	2328b–5, § 1
35.002	2328b–5, § 8
35.003	2328b–5, § 2
35.004	2328b–5, § 3
35.005	2328b–5, § 3(b)
35.006	2328b–5, § 4
35.007	2328b–5, § 5
35.008	2328b–5, § 6
36.001	2328b–6, § 2
36.002	2328b–6, §§ 3, 10
36.003	2328b–6, § 1
36.004	2328b–6, § 4
36.005	2328b–6, § 5
36.006	2328b–6, § 6
36.007	2328b–6, § 7
36.008	2328b–6, § 8
37.001	2524–1, § 13
37.002	2524–1, §§ 12, 15, 16

DERIVATION TABLE

Civil Practice and Remedies Code Section	Vernon's Civ.St. Article
37.003	2524–1, §§ 1, 5
37.004	2524–1, §§ 2, 3
37.005	2524–1, § 4
37.006	2524–1, § 11
37.007	2524–1, § 9
37.008	2524–1, § 6
37.009	2524–1, § 10
37.010	2524–1, § 7
37.011	2524–1, § 8
38.001	2226
38.002	2226
38.003	2226
38.004	2226
38.005	2226
38.006	2226
51.001	2454
	2455
	2455–1
51.002	941
	2455
	2455–1
	2460
51.011	960
51.012	2249
51.013	2255
51.014	2250
	2251
	4662
61.001	275
	276
61.002	275
61.003	277
61.004	278
61.005	281
61.021	275
61.022	275
	279
61.023	279
	281
61.041	288
61.042	290
61.043	6662
61.044	291
61.061	300
61.062	301
61.063	302
62.001	6840, § 1
62.002	6840, § 1(a)
62.003	6844
62.021	6840, § 1(a)
62.022	6840, § 2
62.023	6840, § 4
62.041	6840, § 3(a), (e)
62.042	6840, § 3(b)
62.043	6840, § 3(b), (c)
62.044	6840, § 3(c)
62.045	6840, § 3(d)
62.046	6858
62.061	6846
62.062	6847
62.063	6848
63.001	4076
63.002	4076
63.003	4084

Civil Practice and Remedies Code Section	Vernon's Civ.St. Article
63.004	4099
63.005	4096
64.001	2293
64.002	2318
64.003	2313
64.004	2319
64.021	2294
64.022	2296
64.023	2296
64.031	2297
64.032	2314
64.033	2310
64.034	2298
64.035	2309
64.051	2299
64.052	2300
	2304
	2310
	2311
64.053	2310
64.054	2302
64.055	2301
64.056	2300
	2302
	2303
	2305
	2306
	2307
64.071	2312
64.072	2317
64.073	2315
64.074	2316
64.075	2295
64.076	2030
	2311
64.091	2320b
64.092	2320c
65.001	4663
65.011	4642
65.012	4644
65.013	4645
65.014	4646
65.015	4646a
65.021	4642
65.022	4642
	4643
65.023	4656
65.031	4660
66.001	6253
66.002	6253
66.003	6257
71.001	4671
71.002	4671
71.003	4671
	4672
71.004	4675
71.005	4675a
71.006	4674
71.007	4671
71.008	4676
71.009	4673
71.010	4677
71.011	4675
71.021	5525

Civil Practice and Remedies Code Section	Vernon's Civ.St. Article
71.031	4678
72.001	6701b, § 1(a)
72.003	6701b, § 1(b), 2
72.004	6701b, § 1(c)
73.001	5430
73.002	5432
73.003	5431
73.004	5433a
73.005	5431
73.006	5433
74.001	1a
74.002	1a
75.001	1b, § 6
75.002	1b, § 1
75.003	1b, §§ 2 to 5
76.001	4476–5c, § 2
76.002	4476–5c, § 1
76.003	4476–5c, § 2
76.004	4476–5c, § 3
77.001	4590–3, § 2
77.002	4590–3, § 1
77.003	4590–3, § 2
77.004	4590–3, § 3
78.001	1070.1
79.001	9207, § 1
79.002	9207
101.001	6252–19, §§ 2, 3, 18(a)
101.002	6252–19, § 1
101.003	6252–19, § 6
101.021	6252–19, § 3(b)
101.022	6252–19, § 18(b)
101.023	6252–19, § 3(b)
101.024	6252–19, § 3(b)
101.025	6252–19, § 4
101.026	6252–19, § 15
101.027	6252–19, §§ 9, 12(b)
101.028	6252–19, § 19
101.051	6252–19, § 19A
101.052	6252–19, § 14(2)
101.053	6252–19, § 14(3), (4)
101.054	6252–19, § 14(6)
101.055	6252–19, § 14(5), (8), (9)
101.057	6252–19, § 14(9), (10)
101.058	6252–19, § 18(a)
101.059	6252–19, § 14(11)
101.060	6252–19, § 14(12)
101.061	6252–19, § 14(1)
101.101	6252–19, § 16
101.102	6252–19, §§ 5, 8
101.103	6252–19, § 9
101.104	6252–19, § 9
101.105	6252–19, § 10
101.106	6252–19, § 12(a)
101.107	6252–19, § 11
101.108	6252–19, § 11
101.109	6252–19, § 17
102.001	6252–19b, §§ 1, 2(a)
102.002	6252–19b, § 2
102.003	6252–19b, § 2(b)
102.004	6252–19b, § 3(a), (b)
102.005	6252–19b, § 3(c)
102.006	6252–19b, § 2(b)
103.001	6252–25, § 2
103.002	6252–25, § 3
103.003	6252–25, § 4
103.004	6252–25, § 4
103.005	6252–25, § 5
103.006	6252–25, § 6
103.007	6252–25, § 7
104.001	6252–26, §§ 1(a), 5
	Educ.C. § 65.42
104.002	6252–26, § 1(a)
104.003	6252–26, § 1(b)
104.004	6252–26, § 3(a)
104.005	6252–26, § 3(a)
104.006	6252–26, § 3(b)
104.007	6252–26, § 4
104.008	6252–26, § 1(b)
105.001	2226b, § 1
105.002	2226b, §§ 2, 4
105.003	2226b, §§ 2, 3
105.004	2226b, § 5
106.001	6252–16, § 1
106.002	6252–16, § 2
106.003	6252–16, § 3
121.001	6602
121.002	6602a
121.003	6616
121.004	6603
	6606
121.005	6604
121.006	6607a, §§ 1, 2, 4
121.007	6607
121.008	6607a, §§ 1, 3
121.009	6609
	6610
121.010	6611
121.011	6612
	6613
	6614
	6615
121.012	6619
	6620
	6621
	6622
121.013	6617
	6618
121.014	6623
122.001	5207b(a), (b)
122.002	5207b(c)
122.003	5207b(d)
123.001	9019, § 1
123.002	9019, § 2(a), (d)
123.003	9019, § 2(c)
123.004	9019, § 2(b)
124.001	1d
125.001	4664
125.002	4666
125.003	4666
125.004	4665
125.021	4667(a)
125.022	4667
126.001	2293, § 5
126.002	2293a, §§ 1, 6
	4331a
126.003	2294a
126.004	2297a
126.011	4331a
126.012	4331a
126.013	4331a
127.001	2212b, §§ 3, 4(a)

DERIVATION TABLE

Civil Practice and Remedies Code Section	Vernon's Civ.St. Article
127.002	2212b, § 1
127.003	2212b, § 2
127.004	2212b, § 4(a)
127.005	2212b, § 4(c)
127.006	2212b, § 4(b)
127.007	2212b, § 4(b)
127.008	2212b, § 5
129.001	5923b, § 1
129.002	5923b, § 2
129.003	5923b, § 4

CIVIL PRACTICE AND REMEDIES CODE
TABLE OF SECTIONS AFFECTED
BY THE 87TH LEGISLATURE, REGULAR SESSION

Sec.	Effect	Acts 2021 Ch.	Sec.
12.005(a)	Amended	472	4.01
12.005(b)	Repealed	472	5.01(a)(1)
12.005(d)	Repealed	472	5.01(a)(1)
16.0045(a)	Amended	221	2.01
16.008(a)	Amended	484	1
16.008(a–1)	Added	484	1
16.008(c)	Amended	484	1
16.008 note	–	484	3(a) 3(b)
16.009(a)	Amended	484	2
16.009(a–1)	Added	484	2
16.009(c)	Amended	484	2
16.009(d)	Amended	484	2
16.009 note	–	484	4(a) 4(b)
16.013	Added	328	1
16.013 note	–	328	2
16.025(b)	Amended	94	1
16.025 note	–	94	3
21.051	Repealed	472	5.01(a)(2)
27.010(a)	Amended	915	3.001
30.014(a)	Amended	521 576	1 1
30.014 note	–	521	72(a)
30.022	Added	62	4
33.013(b)	Amended	221 837	2.02 4
38.001	Amended	665	1
38.001 note	–	665	2
38.0015	Added	1015	1
38.0015 note	–	1015	2
41.008(c)	Amended	221 837	2.03 5
51.014(a)	Amended	167 528 813	1 1 1
51.014 note	–	167	4
61.0021(a)	Amended	221	2.04
64.101(c)	Amended	934	9.01
Ch. 72 Subch. A heading	Added	785	2
Ch. 72 heading	Amended	785	1
72.001 note	–	785	6
72.002	Amended	785	3
72.003	Amended	785	3
72.051	Added	785	4
72.052	Added	785	4
72.053	Added	785	4
72.054	Added	785	4
72.055	Added	785	4
74.155	Added	528	2
74.155 note	–	528	4(a) 4(b) 4(c) 5(a)

		Acts 2021	
Sec.	Effect	Ch.	Sec.
74.155 note (Cont'd)	– (Cont'd)	528 (Cont'd)	5(b)
74.351(a)	Amended	167	2
74.351(c)	Amended	167	2
74.353	Added	167	3
Ch. 87 heading	Amended	219	1
87.001(1)	Amended	219	2
87.001(2–a)	Amended	219	2
87.001(2–b)	Added	219	2
87.001(3)	Amended	219	2
87.001(4)	Amended	219	2
87.001(5)	Amended	219	2
87.001(6–a)	Amended	219	2
87.001(9)	Amended	219	2
87.001 note	–	219	6
87.0021	Added	219	3
87.003	Amended	219	4
87.004	Amended	219	4
87.005(a)	Amended	219	5
87.005(b)	Amended	219	5
87.005(c)	Amended	219	5
91B.001	Added	827	1
91B.001 note	–	827	3
91B.002	Added	827	1
91B.003	Added	827	1
98.007	Added	807	4
98.007 note	–	807	63(b)
			63(d)
110.001(a)(3)	Added	799	1
110.001(a)(4)	Added	799	1
110.001 note	–	799	5
110.002(d)	Added	799	2
110.0031	Added	799	3
110.0031 note	–	799	5
110.004	Amended	799	4
112.001	Amended	1026	1
112.001(a)	Amended	1026	2
112.001(b)	Amended	1026	2
112.001(c)	Amended	1026	2
112.001 note	–	1026	11
125.001 note	–	807	63(c)
125.0015(a)	Amended	79	5
		221	2.05
		807	33
		942	6
125.0017	Amended	807	5
	Repealed	807	62(1)
125.002(f–1)	Amended	280	3
125.0025(b)	Amended	807	6
125.003(d)	Repealed	807	62(2)
125.004(a–1)	Amended	807	7
125.004(a–2)	Amended	807	7
125.004(a–3)	Amended	807	8
	Repealed	807	62(3)
125.005	Added	807	9
125.068	Repealed	807	62(4)
125.070(d)	Amended	807	10
126.012	Repealed	472	5.01(a)(2)
127A.001	Added	903	1
127A.001 note	–	903	2
127A.002	Added	903	1
127A.003	Added	903	1

Sec.	Effect	Acts 2021 Ch.	Sec.
127A.004	Added	903	1
Ch. 130 heading	Amended	686	1
		838	2
130.002(c)	Added	686	2
130.002(d)	Added	686	2
130.002(e)	Added	686	2
130.002(f)	Added	686	2
130.002 note	–	686	5(a) 5(b)
130.0021	Added	686	3
		838	3
130.0021 note	–	686	5(b)
130.004	Amended	686	4
		838	4
140A.001 note	–	807	63(c)
140A.002	Amended	807	11
140A.102(b)	Amended	807	12
140A.104(d)	Amended	807	13
144.010	Repealed	915	3.002
148.001	Added	528	3
148.001 note	–	528	4(c) 5(a)
148.002	Added	528	3
148.003	Added	528	3
148.004	Added	528	3
148.005	Added	528	3
150C.001	Added	658	1
150C.002	Added	658	1
152.004	Repealed	472	5.01(a)(3)
152.005	Repealed	472	5.01(a)(3)

CIVIL PRACTICE AND REMEDIES CODE
TABLE OF SECTIONS AFFECTED
BY THE 87TH LEGISLATURE, SECOND CALLED SESSION

		Acts 2021	
Sec.	Effect	Ch.	Sec.
143A.001	Added	3	7
143A.001 note	–	3	9
143A.002	Added	3	7
143A.003	Added	3	7
143A.004	Added	3	7
143A.005	Added	3	7
143A.006	Added	3	7
143A.007	Added	3	7
143A.008	Added	3	7

TABLE OF CONTENTS

CIVIL PRACTICE AND REMEDIES CODE

Section Analysis, see beginning of each Chapter.

TITLE 1. GENERAL PROVISIONS

TITLE 2. TRIAL, JUDGMENT, AND APPEAL
SUBTITLE A. GENERAL PROVISIONS

SUBTITLE B. TRIAL MATTERS

SUBTITLE C. JUDGMENTS

TABLE OF CONTENTS

TABLE OF CONTENTS

TITLE 5. GOVERNMENTAL LIABILITY

TABLE OF CONTENTS

TITLE 6. MISCELLANEOUS PROVISIONS

TABLE OF CONTENTS

TITLE 7. ALTERNATE METHODS OF DISPUTE RESOLUTION

INDEX

CIVIL PRACTICE AND REMEDIES CODE

Enactment

The Civil Practice and Remedies Code was enacted by Acts 1985, 69th Leg., ch. 959, § 1, effective September 1, 1985.

TITLE 1. GENERAL PROVISIONS

CHAPTER 1. GENERAL PROVISIONS

§ 1.001. Purpose of Code

(a) This code is enacted as a part of the state's continuing statutory revision program, begun by the Texas Legislative Council in 1963 as directed by the legislature in Chapter 323, Government Code. The program contemplates a topic-by-topic revision of the state's general and permanent statute law without substantive change.

(b) Consistent with the objectives of the statutory revision program, the purpose of this code is to make the law encompassed by this code more accessible and understandable, by:

(1) rearranging the statutes into a more logical order;

(2) employing a format and numbering system designed to facilitate citation of the law and to accommodate future expansion of the law;

(3) eliminating repealed, duplicative, unconstitutional, expired, executed, and other ineffective provisions; and

(4) restating the law in modern American English to the greatest extent possible.

Acts 1985, 69th Leg., ch. 959, § 1, eff. Sept. 1, 1985. Amended by Acts 1987, 70th Leg., ch. 167, § 3.01, eff. Sept. 1, 1987.

§ 1.002. Construction of Code

The Code Construction Act (Chapter 311, Government Code) applies to the construction of each provision in this code, except as otherwise expressly provided by this code.

Acts 1985, 69th Leg., ch. 959, § 1, eff. Sept. 1, 1985. Amended by Acts 1987, 70th Leg., ch. 167, § 3.02, eff. Sept. 1, 1987.

§ 1.003. Internal References

In this code:

(1) a reference to a title, chapter, or section without further identification is a reference to a title, chapter, or section of this code; and

(2) a reference to a subtitle, subchapter, subsection, subdivision, paragraph, or other numbered or lettered unit without further identification is a reference to a unit of the next larger unit of this code in which the reference appears.

Acts 1985, 69th Leg., ch. 959, § 1, eff. Sept. 1, 1985.

TITLE 2. TRIAL, JUDGMENT, AND APPEAL

SUBTITLE A. GENERAL PROVISIONS

CHAPTER 5. RULE OF DECISION

§ 5.001. Rule of Decision

(a) The rule of decision in this state consists of those portions of the common law of England that are not inconsistent with the constitution or the laws of this state, the constitution of this state, and the laws of this state.

(b) In any action governed by the laws of this state concerning rights and obligations under the law, the American Law Institute's Restatements of the Law are not controlling.

Acts 1985, 69th Leg., ch. 959, § 1, eff. Sept. 1, 1985. Amended by Acts 2019, 86th Leg., ch. 845 (H.B. 2757), § 1, eff. Sept. 1, 2019.

CHAPTER 6. GOVERNMENTAL EXEMPTION FROM BOND AND SECURITY REQUIREMENTS

§ 6.001. State and Federal Agencies Exempt From Bond for Court Costs or Appeal

(a) A governmental entity or officer listed in Subsection (b) may not be required to file a bond for court costs incident to a suit filed by the entity or officer or for an appeal or writ of error taken out by the entity or officer and is not required to give a surety for the issuance of a bond to take out a writ of attachment, writ of sequestration, distress warrant, or writ of garnishment in a civil suit.

(b) The following are exempt from the bond requirements:

(1) this state;

(2) a department of this state;

(3) the head of a department of this state;

(4) a county of this state;

(5) the Federal Housing Administration;

(6) the Federal National Mortgage Association;

(7) the Government National Mortgage Association;

(8) the Veterans' Administration;

(9) the administrator of veterans affairs;

(10) any national mortgage savings and loan insurance corporation created by an act of congress as a national relief organization that operates on a statewide basis; and

(11) the Federal Deposit Insurance Corporation in its capacity as receiver or in its corporate capacity.

(c) Notwithstanding Subsection (a), a county or district attorney is not exempted from filing a bond to take out an extraordinary writ unless the commissioners court of the county approves the exemption in an action brought in behalf of the county or unless the attorney general approves the exemption in an action brought in behalf of the state.

Acts 1985, 69th Leg., ch. 959, § 1, eff. Sept. 1, 1985. Amended by Acts 1987, 70th Leg., ch. 167, § 3.03(a), eff. Sept. 1, 1987.

§ 6.002. Cities Exempt From Security for Court Costs

(a) Security for costs may not be required of an incorporated city or town of this state in an action, suit, or proceeding.

(b) A municipality may institute and prosecute suits without giving security for cost and may appeal from judgment without giving supersedeas or cost bond.

Acts 1985, 69th Leg., ch. 959, § 1, eff. Sept. 1, 1985. Amended by Acts 1987, 70th Leg., ch. 149, § 21, eff. Sept. 1, 1987; Acts 2001, 77th Leg., ch. 625, § 1, eff. Sept. 1, 2001.

§ 6.003. Water Districts Exempt From Appeal Bond

(a) A governmental entity listed in Subsection (b) may not be required to give bond on an appeal or writ of error taken in a civil case that the entity is prosecuting or defending in its official capacity.

(b) The following are exempt from the appeal bond requirements:

(1) a water improvement district, a water control and improvement district, an irrigation district, a conservation and reclamation district, or a water control and preservation district organized under state law;

(2) a levee improvement district organized under state law;

(3) a drainage district organized under state law; and

(4) an entity created under Section 52, Article III, or Section 59, Article XVI, Texas Constitution.

Acts 1985, 69th Leg., ch. 959, § 1, eff. Sept. 1, 1985. Amended by Acts 1997, 75th Leg., ch. 1070, § 46, eff. Sept. 1, 1997.

§ 6.004. School Districts Exempt From Security for Court Costs and Appeal Bond

A school district may institute and prosecute suits without giving security for cost and may appeal from judgment without giving supersedeas or cost bond.

Added by Acts 2011, 82nd Leg., ch. 243 (H.B. 942), § 1, eff. Sept. 1, 2011.

CHAPTER 7. LIABILITY OF COURT OFFICERS

SUBCHAPTER A. LIABILITY OF OFFICER

§ 7.001. Liability for Refusal or Neglect in Performance of Official Duties

(a) A clerk, sheriff, or other officer who neglects or refuses to perform a duty required under the Texas Rules of Civil Procedure or under a provision of this code derived from those rules is liable for actual damages only in a suit brought by a person injured by the officer's neglect or refusal.

(b) The officer may be punished for contempt of court for neglect or refusal in the performance of those duties. The court shall set the fine at not less than $10 or more than $100, with costs. The officer must be given 10 days' notice of the motion.

(c) This section does not create a cause of action for an action that can otherwise be brought under Chapter 34. A party may seek actual damages under this section or Chapter 34, or the party may seek contempt sanctions, but the party may not seek both damages and contempt.

(d) An action or motion brought under this section must comply with and is subject to the provisions in Sections 34.068, 34.069, 34.070, and 34.074, except that a motion brought under Subsection (b) need not comply with Section 34.068(b).

Acts 1985, 69th Leg., ch. 959, § 1, eff. Sept. 1, 1985. Amended by Acts 2007, 80th Leg., ch. 421, § 1, eff. Sept. 1, 2007.

§ 7.002. Liability for Deposits Pending Suit

(a) An officer who has custody of a sum of money, a debt, an instrument, or other property paid to or deposited with a court pending the outcome of a cause of action shall seal the property in a secure package in a safe or bank vault that is accessible and subject to the control of the court.

(b) The officer shall keep in his office as part of his records an itemized inventory of property deposited with the court. The inventory must list the disposition of the property and the account for which the property was received.

(c) At the expiration of the officer's term, the officer shall transfer all deposited property and the inventory to the officer's successor in office. The successor shall give a receipt for the transferred property and the inventory.

(d) This section does not exempt an officer or the officer's surety from liability on the officer's bond due to neglect or other default in regard to the deposited property.

Acts 1985, 69th Leg., ch. 959, § 1, eff. Sept. 1, 1985.

§ 7.003. Liability Regarding Execution of Writs

(a) Except as provided by Section 34.061, an officer is not liable for damages resulting from the execution of a writ issued by a court of this state if the officer in good faith executes or attempts to execute the writ as provided by law and by the Texas Rules of Civil Procedure.

(b) An officer shall execute a writ issued by a court of this state without requiring that bond be posted for the indemnification of the officer.

(c) An officer shows that the officer acted in good faith when the officer shows that a reasonably prudent officer, under the same or similar circumstances, could have believed that the officer's conduct was justified based on the information the officer possessed when the conduct occurred.

Acts 1985, 69th Leg., ch. 959, § 1, eff. Sept. 1, 1985. Amended by Acts 2007, 80th Leg., ch. 421, § 2, eff. Sept. 1, 2007.

SUBCHAPTER B. LIABILITY OF ATTORNEY

§ 7.011. Attorney's Liability for Costs

An attorney who is not a party to a civil proceeding is not liable for payment of costs incurred by a party to the proceeding.

Acts 1985, 69th Leg., ch. 959, § 1, eff. Sept. 1, 1985.

SUBCHAPTER C. SUIT ON OFFICIAL BONDS

§ 7.021. Suit on Official Bonds

Suit may be brought in the name of this state alone on an official bond for the benefit of all the parties entitled to recover on the bond if:

(1) the bond is made payable to this state or to an officer of this state; and

(2) a recovery on the bond is authorized by or would inure to the benefit of parties other than this state.

Acts 1985, 69th Leg., ch. 959, § 1, eff. Sept. 1, 1985.

CHAPTER 8. STATE EXEMPTION FROM CERTAIN FEES: FEES PAID BY OPPOSING PARTY

Section

§ 8.01. State Exemption

The state is exempt from the payment of the filing fee imposed by Section 51.701, Government Code.

Added by Acts 1989, 71st Leg., ch. 2, § 4.01(a), eff. Aug. 28, 1989.

§ 8.02. Fee Paid by Opposing Party

If the state prevails in a lawsuit, the opposing party shall pay the entire amount of any filing fee attributable to the state, including any amount exempted under Section 8.01.

Added by Acts 1989, 71st Leg., ch. 2, § 4.01(a), eff. Aug. 28, 1989.

CHAPTER 9. FRIVOLOUS PLEADINGS AND CLAIMS

SUBCHAPTER A. GENERAL PROVISIONS

Section

SUBCHAPTER B. SIGNING OF PLEADINGS

SUBCHAPTER A. GENERAL PROVISIONS

§ 9.001. Definitions

In this chapter:

(1) "Claimant" means a party, including a plaintiff, counterclaimant, cross-claimant, third-party plaintiff, or intervenor, seeking recovery of damages. In an action in which a party seeks recovery of damages for injury to another person, damage to the property of another person, death of another person, or other harm to another person, "claimant" includes both that other person and the party seeking recovery of damages.

(2) "Defendant" means a party, including a counterdefendant, cross-defendant, or third-party defendant, from whom a claimant seeks relief.

(3) "Groundless" means:

(A) no basis in fact; or

(B) not warranted by existing law or a good faith argument for the extension, modification, or reversal of existing law.

(4) "Pleading" includes a motion.

Added by Acts 1987, 70th Leg., 1st C.S., ch. 2, § 2.01, eff. Sept. 2, 1987.

§ 9.002. Applicability

(a) This chapter applies to an action in which a claimant seeks:

(1) damages for personal injury, property damage, or death, regardless of the legal theories or statutes on the basis of which recovery is sought, including an action based on intentional conduct, negligence, strict tort liability, products liability (whether strict or otherwise), or breach of warranty; or

(2) damages other than for personal injury, property damage, or death resulting from any tortious conduct, regardless of the legal theories or statutes on the basis of which recovery is sought, including libel, slander, or tortious interference with a contract or other business relation.

(b) This chapter applies to any party who is a claimant or defendant, including but not limited to:

(1) a county;

(2) a municipality;

(3) a public school district;

(4) a public junior college district;

(5) a charitable organization;

(6) a nonprofit organization;

(7) a hospital district;

(8) a hospital authority;

(9) any other political subdivision of the state; and

(10) the State of Texas.

(c) In an action to which this chapter applies, the provisions of this chapter prevail over all other law to the extent of any conflict.

Added by Acts 1987, 70th Leg., 1st C.S., ch. 2, § 2.01, eff. Sept. 2, 1987.

§ 9.003. Texas Rules of Civil Procedure

This chapter does not alter the Texas Rules of Civil Procedure or the Texas Rules of Appellate Procedure.

Added by Acts 1987, 70th Leg., 1st C.S., ch. 2, § 2.01, eff. Sept. 2, 1987.

§ 9.004. Applicability

This chapter does not apply to the Deceptive Trade Practices-Consumer Protection Act (Subchapter E, Chapter 17, Business & Commerce Code)[1] or to Chapter 21, Insurance Code.

Added by Acts 1987, 70th Leg., 1st C.S., ch. 2, § 2.01, eff. Sept. 2, 1987.

[1] V.T.C.A., Bus. & C. Code § 17.41 et seq.

SUBCHAPTER B. SIGNING OF PLEADINGS

§ 9.011. Signing of Pleadings

The signing of a pleading as required by the Texas Rules of Civil Procedure constitutes a certificate by the signatory that to the signatory's best knowledge, information, and belief, formed after reasonable inquiry, the pleading is not:

(1) groundless and brought in bad faith;

(2) groundless and brought for the purpose of harassment; or

(3) groundless and interposed for any improper purpose, such as to cause unnecessary delay or needless increase in the cost of litigation.

Added by Acts 1987, 70th Leg., 1st C.S., ch. 2, § 2.01, eff. Sept. 2, 1987.

§ 9.012. Violation; Sanction

(a) At the trial of the action or at any hearing inquiring into the facts and law of the action, after reasonable notice to the parties, the court may on its own motion, or shall on the motion of any party to the action, determine if a pleading has been signed in violation of any one of the standards prescribed by Section 9.011.

(b) In making its determination of whether a pleading has been signed in violation of any one of the standards prescribed by Section 9.011, the court shall take into account:

(1) the multiplicity of parties;

(2) the complexity of the claims and defenses;

(3) the length of time available to the party to investigate and conduct discovery; and

(4) affidavits, depositions, and any other relevant matter.

(c) If the court determines that a pleading has been signed in violation of any one of the standards prescribed by Section 9.011, the court shall, not earlier than 90 days after the date of the determination, at the trial or hearing or at a separate hearing following reasonable notice to the offending party, impose an appropriate sanction on the signatory, a represented party, or both.

(d) The court may not order an offending party to pay the incurred expenses of a party who stands in opposition to the offending pleading if, before the 90th day after the court makes a determination under Subsection (a), the offending party withdraws the pleading or amends the pleading to the satisfaction of the court or moves for dismissal of the pleading or the offending portion of the pleading.

(e) The sanction may include one or more of the following:

(1) the striking of a pleading or the offending portion thereof;

(2) the dismissal of a party; or

(3) an order to pay to a party who stands in opposition to the offending pleading the amount of

the reasonable expenses incurred because of the filing of the pleading, including costs, reasonable attorney's fees, witness fees, fees of experts, and deposition expenses.

(f) The court may not order an offending party to pay the incurred expenses of a party who stands in opposition to the offending pleading if the court has, with respect to the same subject matter, imposed sanctions on the party who stands in opposition to the offending pleading under the Texas Rules of Civil Procedure.

(g) All determinations and orders pursuant to this chapter are solely for purposes of this chapter and shall not be the basis of any liability, sanction, or grievance other than as expressly provided in this chapter.

(h) This section does not apply to any proceeding to which Section 10.004 or Rule 13, Texas Rules of Civil Procedure, applies.

Added by Acts 1987, 70th Leg., 1st C.S., ch. 2, § 2.01, eff. Sept. 2, 1987. Amended by Acts 1999, 76th Leg., ch. 1111, § 1, eff. Sept. 1, 1999.

§ 9.013. Report to Grievance Committee

(a) If the court imposes a sanction against an offending party under Section 9.012, the offending party is represented by an attorney who signed the pleading in violation of any one of the standards under Section 9.011, and the court finds that the attorney has consistently engaged in activity that results in sanctions under Section 9.012, the court shall report its finding to an appropriate grievance committee as provided by the State Bar Act (Article 320a–1, Vernon's Texas Civil Statutes) or by a similar law in the jurisdiction in which the attorney resides.

(b) The report must contain:

(1) the name of the attorney who represented the offending party;

(2) the finding by the court that the pleading was signed in violation of any one of the standards under Section 9.011;

(3) a description of the sanctions imposed against the signatory and the offending party; and

(4) the finding that the attorney has consistently engaged in activity that results in sanctions under Section 9.012.

Added by Acts 1987, 70th Leg., 1st C.S., ch. 2, § 2.01, eff. Sept. 2, 1987.

§ 9.014. Pleadings not Frivolous

(a) A general denial does not constitute a violation of any of the standards prescribed by Section 9.011.

(b) The amount requested for damages in a pleading does not constitute a violation of any of the standards prescribed by Section 9.011.

Added by Acts 1987, 70th Leg., 1st C.S., ch. 2, § 2.01, eff. Sept. 2, 1987.

CHAPTER 10. SANCTIONS FOR FRIVOLOUS PLEADINGS AND MOTIONS

§ 10.001. Signing of Pleadings and Motions

The signing of a pleading or motion as required by the Texas Rules of Civil Procedure constitutes a certificate by the signatory that to the signatory's best knowledge, information, and belief, formed after reasonable inquiry:

(1) the pleading or motion is not being presented for any improper purpose, including to harass or to cause unnecessary delay or needless increase in the cost of litigation;

(2) each claim, defense, or other legal contention in the pleading or motion is warranted by existing law or by a nonfrivolous argument for the extension, modification, or reversal of existing law or the establishment of new law;

(3) each allegation or other factual contention in the pleading or motion has evidentiary support or, for a specifically identified allegation or factual contention, is likely to have evidentiary support after a reasonable opportunity for further investigation or discovery; and

(4) each denial in the pleading or motion of a factual contention is warranted on the evidence or, for a specifically identified denial, is reasonably based on a lack of information or belief.

Added by Acts 1995, 74th Leg., ch. 137, § 1, eff. Sept. 1, 1995.

§ 10.002. Motion for Sanctions

(a) A party may make a motion for sanctions, describing the specific conduct violating Section 10.001.

(b) The court on its own initiative may enter an order describing the specific conduct that appears to violate Section 10.001 and direct the alleged violator to show cause why the conduct has not violated that section.

(c) The court may award to a party prevailing on a motion under this section the reasonable expenses and attorney's fees incurred in presenting or opposing the motion, and if no due diligence is shown the court may award to the prevailing party all costs for inconvenience, harassment, and out-of-pocket expenses incurred or caused by the subject litigation.

Added by Acts 1995, 74th Leg., ch. 137, § 1, eff. Sept. 1, 1995.

§ 10.003. Notice and Opportunity to Respond

The court shall provide a party who is the subject of a motion for sanctions under Section 10.002 notice of the allegations and a reasonable opportunity to respond to the allegations.

Added by Acts 1995, 74th Leg., ch. 137, § 1, eff. Sept. 1, 1995.

§ 10.004. Violation; Sanction

(a) A court that determines that a person has signed a pleading or motion in violation of Section 10.001 may impose a sanction on the person, a party represented by the person, or both.

(b) The sanction must be limited to what is sufficient to deter repetition of the conduct or comparable conduct by others similarly situated.

(c) A sanction may include any of the following:

(1) a directive to the violator to perform, or refrain from performing, an act;

(2) an order to pay a penalty into court; and

(3) an order to pay to the other party the amount of the reasonable expenses incurred by the other party because of the filing of the pleading or motion, including reasonable attorney's fees.

(d) The court may not award monetary sanctions against a represented party for a violation of Section 10.001(2).

(e) The court may not award monetary sanctions on its own initiative unless the court issues its order to show cause before a voluntary dismissal or settlement of the claims made by or against the party or the party's attorney who is to be sanctioned.

(f) The filing of a general denial under Rule 92, Texas Rules of Civil Procedure, shall not be deemed a violation of this chapter.

Added by Acts 1995, 74th Leg., ch. 137, § 1, eff. Sept. 1, 1995.

§ 10.005. Order

A court shall describe in an order imposing a sanction under this chapter the conduct the court has determined violated Section 10.001 and explain the basis for the sanction imposed.

Added by Acts 1995, 74th Leg., ch. 137, § 1, eff. Sept. 1, 1995.

§ 10.006. Conflict

Notwithstanding Section 22.004, Government Code, the supreme court may not amend or adopt rules in conflict with this chapter.

Added by Acts 1995, 74th Leg., ch. 137, § 1, eff. Sept. 1, 1995.

CHAPTER 11. VEXATIOUS LITIGANTS

SUBCHAPTER A. GENERAL PROVISIONS

Chapter 11, Vexatious Litigants, consisting of §§ 11.001 to 11.104, was added by Acts 1997, 75th Leg., ch. 806, § 1.

Another Chapter 11, Liability Related to a Fraudulent Court Record or a Fraudulent Lien or Claim Filed Against Real or Personal Property, consisting of §§ 11.001 to 11.007, as added by Acts 1997, 75th Leg., ch.

189, § 16, was renumbered as Chapter 12, consisting of §§ 12.001 to 12.007 by Acts 1999, 76th Leg., ch. 62, § 19.01(3).

SUBCHAPTER A. GENERAL PROVISIONS

§ 11.001. Definitions

In this chapter:

(1) "Defendant" means a person or governmental entity against whom a plaintiff commences or maintains or seeks to commence or maintain a litigation.

(2) "Litigation" means a civil action commenced, maintained, or pending in any state or federal court.

(3) Repealed by Acts 2013, 83rd Leg., ch. 1224 (S.B. 1630), § 10.

(4) "Moving defendant" means a defendant who moves for an order under Section 11.051 determining that a plaintiff is a vexatious litigant and requesting security.

(5) "Plaintiff" means an individual who commences or maintains a litigation pro se.

Added by Acts 1997, 75th Leg., ch. 806, § 1, eff. Sept. 1, 1997. Amended by Acts 2011, 82nd Leg., 1st C.S., ch. 3 (H.B. 79), § 9.01, eff. Jan. 1, 2012; Acts 2013, 83rd Leg., ch. 1224 (S.B. 1630), §§ 1, 10, eff. Sept. 1, 2013.

§ 11.002. Applicability

(a) This chapter does not apply to an attorney licensed to practice law in this state unless the attorney proceeds pro se.

(b) This chapter does not apply to a municipal court.

Added by Acts 2013, 83rd Leg., ch. 1224 (S.B. 1630), § 2, eff. Sept. 1, 2013.

§§ 11.003 to 11.007. Renumbered as V.T.C.A., Civil Practice & Remedies Code §§ 12.003 to 12.007 by Acts 1999, 76th Leg., ch. 62, § 19.01(3), eff. Sept. 1, 1999

SUBCHAPTER B. VEXATIOUS LITIGANTS

§ 11.051. Motion for Order Determining Plaintiff a Vexatious Litigant and Requesting Security

In a litigation in this state, the defendant may, on or before the 90th day after the date the defendant files the original answer or makes a special appearance, move the court for an order:

(1) determining that the plaintiff is a vexatious litigant; and

(2) requiring the plaintiff to furnish security.

Added by Acts 1997, 75th Leg., ch. 806, § 1, eff. Sept. 1, 1997.

§ 11.052. Stay of Proceedings on Filing of Motion

(a) On the filing of a motion under Section 11.051, the litigation is stayed and the moving defendant is not required to plead:

(1) if the motion is denied, before the 10th day after the date it is denied; or

(2) if the motion is granted, before the 10th day after the date the moving defendant receives written notice that the plaintiff has furnished the required security.

(b) On the filing of a motion under Section 11.051 on or after the date the trial starts, the litigation is stayed for a period the court determines.

Added by Acts 1997, 75th Leg., ch. 806, § 1, eff. Sept. 1, 1997.

§ 11.053. Hearing

(a) On receipt of a motion under Section 11.051, the court shall, after notice to all parties, conduct a hearing to determine whether to grant the motion.

(b) The court may consider any evidence material to the ground of the motion, including:

(1) written or oral evidence; and

(2) evidence presented by witnesses or by affidavit.

Added by Acts 1997, 75th Leg., ch. 806, § 1, eff. Sept. 1, 1997.

§ 11.054. Criteria for Finding Plaintiff a Vexatious Litigant

A court may find a plaintiff a vexatious litigant if the defendant shows that there is not a reasonable probability that the plaintiff will prevail in the litigation against the defendant and that:

(1) the plaintiff, in the seven-year period immediately preceding the date the defendant makes the motion under Section 11.051, has commenced, prosecuted, or maintained at least five litigations as a pro se litigant other than in a small claims court that have been:

(A) finally determined adversely to the plaintiff;

(B) permitted to remain pending at least two years without having been brought to trial or hearing; or

(C) determined by a trial or appellate court to be frivolous or groundless under state or federal laws or rules of procedure;

(2) after a litigation has been finally determined against the plaintiff, the plaintiff repeatedly relitigates or attempts to relitigate, pro se, either:

(A) the validity of the determination against the same defendant as to whom the litigation was finally determined; or

(B) the cause of action, claim, controversy, or any of the issues of fact or law determined or concluded by the final determination against the same defendant as to whom the litigation was finally determined; or

(3) the plaintiff has previously been declared to be a vexatious litigant by a state or federal court in an action or proceeding based on the same or substantially similar facts, transition, or occurrence.

Added by Acts 1997, 75th Leg., ch. 806, § 1, eff. Sept. 1, 1997. Amended by Acts 2013, 83rd Leg., ch. 1224 (S.B. 1630), § 3, eff. Sept. 1, 2013.

§ 11.055. Security

(a) A court shall order the plaintiff to furnish security for the benefit of the moving defendant if the court, after hearing the evidence on the motion, determines that the plaintiff is a vexatious litigant.

(b) The court in its discretion shall determine the date by which the security must be furnished.

(c) The court shall provide that the security is an undertaking by the plaintiff to assure payment to the moving defendant of the moving defendant's reasonable expenses incurred in or in connection with a litigation commenced, caused to be commenced, maintained, or caused to be maintained by the plaintiff, including costs and attorney's fees.

Added by Acts 1997, 75th Leg., ch. 806, § 1, eff. Sept. 1, 1997.

§ 11.056. Dismissal for Failure to Furnish Security

The court shall dismiss a litigation as to a moving defendant if a plaintiff ordered to furnish security does not furnish the security within the time set by the order.

Added by Acts 1997, 75th Leg., ch. 806, § 1, eff. Sept. 1, 1997.

§ 11.057. Dismissal on the Merits

If the litigation is dismissed on its merits, the moving defendant has recourse to the security furnished by the plaintiff in an amount determined by the court.

Added by Acts 1997, 75th Leg., ch. 806, § 1, eff. Sept. 1, 1997.

SUBCHAPTER C. PROHIBITING FILING OF NEW LITIGATION

§ 11.101. Prefiling Order; Contempt

(a) A court may, on its own motion or the motion of any party, enter an order prohibiting a person from filing, pro se, a new litigation in a court to which the order applies under this section without permission of the appropriate local administrative judge described by Section 11.102(a) to file the litigation if the court finds, after notice and hearing as provided by Subchapter B,[1] that the person is a vexatious litigant.

(b) A person who disobeys an order under Subsection (a) is subject to contempt of court.

(c) A litigant may appeal from a prefiling order entered under Subsection (a) designating the person a vexatious litigant.

(d) A prefiling order entered under Subsection (a) by a justice or constitutional county court applies only to the court that entered the order.

(e) A prefiling order entered under Subsection (a) by a district or statutory county court applies to each court in this state.

Added by Acts 1997, 75th Leg., ch. 806, § 1, eff. Sept. 1, 1997. Amended by Acts 2011, 82nd Leg., 1st C.S., ch. 3 (H.B. 79), § 9.02, eff. Jan. 1, 2012; Acts 2013, 83rd Leg., ch. 1224 (S.B. 1630), § 4, eff. Sept. 1, 2013.

[1] V.T.C.A., Civil Practice & Remedies Code § 11.051 et seq.

§ 11.102. Permission by Local Administrative Judge

(a) A vexatious litigant subject to a prefiling order under Section 11.101 is prohibited from filing, pro se, new litigation in a court to which the order applies without seeking the permission of:

(1) the local administrative judge of the type of court in which the vexatious litigant intends to file, except as provided by Subdivision (2); or

(2) the local administrative district judge of the county in which the vexatious litigant intends to file if the litigant intends to file in a justice or constitutional county court.

(b) A vexatious litigant subject to a prefiling order under Section 11.101 who files a request seeking permission to file a litigation shall provide a copy of the request to all defendants named in the proposed litigation.

(c) The appropriate local administrative judge described by Subsection (a) may make a determination on the request with or without a hearing. If the judge determines that a hearing is necessary, the judge may require that the vexatious litigant filing a request under Subsection (b) provide notice of the hearing to all defendants named in the proposed litigation.

(d) The appropriate local administrative judge described by Subsection (a) may grant permission to a vexatious litigant subject to a prefiling order under Section 11.101 to file a litigation only if it appears to the judge that the litigation:

(1) has merit; and

(2) has not been filed for the purposes of harassment or delay.

(e) The appropriate local administrative judge described by Subsection (a) may condition permission on the furnishing of security for the benefit of the defendant as provided in Subchapter B.[1]

(f) A decision of the appropriate local administrative judge described by Subsection (a) denying a litigant permission to file a litigation under Subsection (d), or conditioning permission to file a litigation on the furnishing of security under Subsection (e), is not grounds for appeal, except that the litigant may apply for a writ of mandamus with the court of appeals not later than the 30th day after the date of the decision. The denial of a writ of mandamus by the court of appeals is not grounds for appeal to the supreme court or court of criminal appeals.

Added by Acts 1997, 75th Leg., ch. 806, § 1, eff. Sept. 1, 1997. Amended by Acts 2011, 82nd Leg., 1st C.S., ch. 3 (H.B. 79), § 9.03, eff. Jan. 1, 2012; Acts 2013, 83rd Leg., ch. 1224 (S.B. 1630), § 5, eff. Sept. 1, 2013.

[1] V.T.C.A., Civil Practice & Remedies Code § 11.051 et seq.

§ 11.103. Duties of Clerk

(a) Except as provided by Subsection (d), a clerk of a court may not file a litigation, original proceeding, appeal, or other claim presented, pro se, by a vexatious litigant subject to a prefiling order under Section 11.101 unless the litigant obtains an order from the appropriate local administrative judge described by Section 11.102(a) permitting the filing.

(b) Repealed by Acts 2013, 83rd Leg., ch. 1224 (S.B. 1630), § 10.

(c) If the appropriate local administrative judge described by Section 11.102(a) issues an order permitting the filing of the litigation, the litigation remains stayed and the defendant need not plead until the 10th day after the date the defendant is served with a copy of the order.

(d) A clerk of a court of appeals may file an appeal from a prefiling order entered under Section 11.101 designating a person a vexatious litigant or a timely filed writ of mandamus under Section 11.102.

Added by Acts 1997, 75th Leg., ch. 806, § 1, eff. Sept. 1, 1997. Amended by Acts 2011, 82nd Leg., 1st C.S., ch. 3 (H.B. 79), § 9.04, eff. Jan. 1, 2012; Acts 2013, 83rd Leg., ch. 1224 (S.B. 1630), §§ 6, 7, 10, eff. Sept. 1, 2013.

§ 11.1035. Mistaken Filing

(a) If the clerk mistakenly files litigation presented, pro se, by a vexatious litigant subject to a prefiling order under Section 11.101 without an order from the appropriate local administrative judge described by Section 11.102(a), any party may file with the clerk and serve on the plaintiff and the other parties to the litigation a notice stating that the plaintiff is a vexatious litigant required to obtain permission under Section 11.102 to file litigation.

(b) Not later than the next business day after the date the clerk receives notice that a vexatious litigant subject to a prefiling order under Section 11.101 has filed, pro se, litigation without obtaining an order from the appropriate local administrative judge described by Section 11.102(a), the clerk shall notify the court that the litigation was mistakenly filed. On receiving notice from the clerk, the court shall immediately stay the litigation and shall dismiss the litigation unless the plaintiff, not later than the 10th day after the date the notice is filed, obtains an order from the appropriate local administrative judge described by Section 11.102(a) permitting the filing of the litigation.

(c) An order dismissing litigation that was mistakenly filed by a clerk may not be appealed.

Added by Acts 2013, 83rd Leg., ch. 1224 (S.B. 1630), § 8, eff. Sept. 1, 2013.

§ 11.104. Notice to Office of Court Administration; Dissemination of List

(a) A clerk of a court shall provide the Office of Court Administration of the Texas Judicial System a copy of any prefiling order issued under Section 11.101 not later than the 30th day after the date the prefiling order is signed.

(b) The Office of Court Administration of the Texas Judicial System shall post on the agency's Internet website a list of vexatious litigants subject to prefiling orders under Section 11.101. On request of a person designated a vexatious litigant, the list shall indicate whether the person designated a vexatious litigant has filed an appeal of that designation.

(c) The Office of Court Administration of the Texas Judicial System may not remove the name of a vexatious litigant subject to a prefiling order under Section 11.101 from the agency's Internet website unless the office receives a written order from the court that entered the prefiling order or from an appellate court. An order of removal affects only a prefiling order entered under Section 11.101 by the same court. A court of appeals decision reversing a prefiling order entered under Section 11.101 affects only the validity of an order entered by the reversed court.

Added by Acts 1997, 75th Leg., ch. 806, § 1, eff. Sept. 1, 1997. Amended by Acts 2011, 82nd Leg., 1st C.S., ch. 3 (H.B. 79), § 9.05, eff. Jan. 1, 2012; Acts 2013, 83rd Leg., ch. 1224 (S.B. 1630), § 9, eff. Sept. 1, 2013.

CHAPTER 12. LIABILITY RELATED TO A FRAUDULENT COURT RECORD OR A FRAUDULENT LIEN OR CLAIM FILED AGAINST REAL OR PERSONAL PROPERTY

Section

Acts 1999, 76th Leg., ch. 62, § 19.01(3) renumbered Chapter 11, Liability Related to a Fraudulent Court Record or a Fraudulent Lien or Claim Filed Against Real or Personal Property, as added by Acts 1997, 75th Leg., ch. 189, § 16, as Chapter 12.

§ 12.001. Definitions

In this chapter:

(1) "Court record" has the meaning assigned by Section 37.01, Penal Code.

(2) "Exemplary damages" has the meaning assigned by Section 41.001.

(2–a) "Filing office" has the meaning assigned by Section 9.102, Business & Commerce Code.

(2–b) "Financing statement" has the meaning assigned by Section 9.102, Business & Commerce Code.

(2–c) "Inmate" means a person housed in a secure correctional facility.

(3) "Lien" means a claim in property for the payment of a debt and includes a security interest.

(4) "Public servant" has the meaning assigned by Section 1.07, Penal Code, and includes officers and employees of the United States.

(5) "Secure correctional facility" has the meaning assigned by Section 1.07, Penal Code.

Added by Acts 1997, 75th Leg., ch. 189, § 16, eff. May 21, 1997. Renumbered from V.T.C.A., Civil Practice & Remedies Code § 11.001 by Acts 1999, 76th Leg., ch. 62, § 19.01(3), eff. Sept. 1, 1999; Acts 2007, 80th Leg., ch. 895, § 1, eff. Sept. 1, 2007.

§ 12.002. Liability

(a) A person may not make, present, or use a document or other record with:

(1) knowledge that the document or other record is a fraudulent court record or a fraudulent lien or claim against real or personal property or an interest in real or personal property;

(2) intent that the document or other record be given the same legal effect as a court record or document of a court created by or established under the constitution or laws of this state or the United States or another entity listed in Section 37.01, Penal Code, evidencing a valid lien or claim against real or personal property or an interest in real or personal property; and

(3) intent to cause another person to suffer:

(A) physical injury;

(B) financial injury; or

(C) mental anguish or emotional distress.

(a–1) Except as provided by Subsection (a–2), a person may not file an abstract of a judgment or an instrument concerning real or personal property with a court or county clerk, or a financing statement with a filing office, if the person:

(1) is an inmate; or

(2) is not licensed or regulated under Title 11, Insurance Code, and is filing on behalf of another person who the person knows is an inmate.

(a–2) A person described by Subsection (a–1) may file an abstract, instrument, or financing statement described by that subsection if the document being filed includes a statement indicating that:

(1) the person filing the document is an inmate; or

(2) the person is filing the document on behalf of a person who is an inmate.

(b) A person who violates Subsection (a) or (a-1) is liable to each injured person for:

(1) the greater of:

(A) $10,000; or

(B) the actual damages caused by the violation;

(2) court costs;

(3) reasonable attorney's fees; and

(4) exemplary damages in an amount determined by the court.

(c) A person claiming a lien under Chapter 53, Property Code, is not liable under this section for the making, presentation, or use of a document or other record in connection with the assertion of the claim unless the person acts with intent to defraud.

Added by Acts 1997, 75th Leg., ch. 189, § 16, eff. May 21, 1997. Renumbered from V.T.C.A., Civil Practice & Remedies Code § 11.002 by Acts 1999, 76th Leg., ch. 62, § 19.01(3), eff. Sept. 1, 1999; Amended by Acts 2007, 80th Leg., ch. 895, § 2, eff. Sept. 1, 2007; Acts 2009, 81st Leg., ch. 1260, § 1, eff. Sept. 1, 2009.

§ 12.003. Cause of Action

(a) The following persons may bring an action to enjoin violation of this chapter or to recover damages under this chapter:

(1) the attorney general;

(2) a district attorney;

(3) a criminal district attorney;

(4) a county attorney with felony responsibilities;

(5) a county attorney;

(6) a municipal attorney;

(7) in the case of a fraudulent judgment lien, the person against whom the judgment is rendered; and

(8) in the case of a fraudulent lien or claim against real or personal property or an interest in real or personal property, the obligor or debtor, or a person who owns an interest in the real or personal property.

(b) Notwithstanding any other law, a person or a person licensed or regulated by Title 11, Insurance Code (the Texas Title Insurance Act), does not have a duty to disclose a fraudulent, as described by Section 51.901(c), Government Code, court record, document, or instrument purporting to create a lien or purporting to assert a claim on real property or an interest in real property in connection with a sale, conveyance, mortgage, or other transfer of the real property or interest in real property.

(c) Notwithstanding any other law, a purported judgment lien or document establishing or purporting to establish a judgment lien against property in this state, that is issued or purportedly issued by a court or a purported court other than a court established under the laws of this state or the United States, is void and has no effect in the determination of any title or right to the property.

Added by Acts 1997, 75th Leg., ch. 189, § 16, eff. May 21, 1997. Renumbered from V.T.C.A., Civil Practice & Remedies Code § 11.003 by Acts 1999, 76th Leg., ch. 62, § 19.01(3), eff. Sept. 1, 1999. Amended by Acts 2005, 79th Leg., ch. 728, § 11.104, eff. Sept. 1, 2005.

§ 12.004. Venue

An action under this chapter may be brought in any district court in the county in which the recorded document is recorded or in which the real property is located.

Added by Acts 1997, 75th Leg., ch. 189, § 16, eff. May 21, 1997. Renumbered from V.T.C.A., Civil Practice & Remedies Code § 11.004 by Acts 1999, 76th Leg., ch. 62, § 19.01(3), eff. Sept. 1, 1999.

§ 12.005. Filing Fees

Text of (a) effective until January 1, 2022

(a) The fee for filing an action under this chapter is $15. The plaintiff must pay the fee to the clerk of the court in which the action is filed. Except as provided by Subsection (b), the plaintiff may not be assessed any other fee, cost, charge, or expense by the clerk of the court or other public official in connection with the action.

Text of (a) effective January 1, 2022

(a) The fee for filing an action under this chapter is the fee that generally applies to the filing of a civil case.

(b) The fee for service of notice of an action under this section charged to the plaintiff may not exceed:

(1) $20 if the notice is delivered in person; or

(2) the cost of postage if the service is by registered or certified mail.

(c) A plaintiff who is unable to pay the filing fee and fee for service of notice may file with the court an affidavit of inability to pay under the Texas Rules of Civil Procedure.

(d) If the fee imposed under Subsection (a) is less than the filing fee the court imposes for filing other similar actions and the plaintiff prevails in the action, the court may order a defendant to pay to the court the differences between the fee paid under Subsection (a) and the filing fee the court imposes for filing other similar actions.

Added by Acts 1997, 75th Leg., ch. 189, § 16, eff. May 21, 1997. Renumbered from V.T.C.A., Civil Practice & Remedies Code § 11.005 by Acts 1999, 76th Leg., ch. 62, § 19.01(3), eff. Sept. 1, 1999. Amended by Acts 2021, 87th Leg., ch. 472 (S.B. 41), §§ 4.01, 5.01(a)(1), eff. Jan. 1, 2022.

Repeal of (b) and (d)

Acts 2021, 87th Leg., ch. 472 (S.B. 41), § 5.01(a)(1) repeals (b) and (d) effective Jan. 1, 2022.

§ 12.006. Plaintiff's Costs

(a) The court shall award the plaintiff the costs of bringing the action if:

(1) the plaintiff prevails; and

(2) the court finds that the defendant, at the time the defendant caused the recorded document to be recorded or filed, knew or should have known that the recorded document is fraudulent, as described by Section 51.901(c), Government Code.

(b) For purposes of this section, the costs of bringing the action include all court costs, attorney's fees, and related expenses of bringing the action, including investigative expenses.

Added by Acts 1997, 75th Leg., ch. 189, § 16, eff. May 21, 1997. Renumbered from V.T.C.A., Civil Practice & Remedies Code § 11.006 by Acts 1999, 76th Leg., ch. 62, § 19.01(3), eff. Sept. 1, 1999.

§ 12.007. Effect on Other Law

This law is cumulative of other law under which a person may obtain judicial relief with respect to a recorded document or other record.

Added by Acts 1997, 75th Leg., ch. 189, § 16, eff. May 21, 1997. Renumbered from V.T.C.A., Civil Practice & Remedies Code § 11.007 by Acts 1999, 76th Leg., ch. 62, § 19.01(3), eff. Sept. 1, 1999.

CHAPTER 13. AFFIDAVIT OF INABILITY TO PAY COSTS

Section

§ 13.001. Dismissal of Action

(a) A court in which an affidavit of inability to pay under Rule 145, Texas Rules of Civil Procedure, has been filed may dismiss the action on a finding that:

(1) the allegation of poverty in the affidavit is false; or

(2) the action is frivolous or malicious.

(b) In determining whether an action is frivolous or malicious, the court may consider whether:

(1) the action's realistic chance of ultimate success is slight;

(2) the claim has no arguable basis in law or in fact; or

(3) it is clear that the party cannot prove a set of facts in support of the claim.

(c) An action may be dismissed under Subsection (a) as frivolous or malicious either before or after service of process.

Added by Acts 1987, 70th Leg., ch. 976, § 1, eff. June 19, 1987.

§ 13.002. Judgment

Judgment may be rendered for costs at the conclusion of the action as in other cases, but the state is not liable for any of those costs.

Added by Acts 1987, 70th Leg., ch. 976, § 1, eff. June 19, 1987.

§ 13.003. Free Transcript of Statement of Facts on Appeal

(a) Subject to Subsection (c), a court reporter shall provide without cost a statement of facts and a clerk of a court shall prepare a transcript for appealing a judgment from the court only if:

(1) an affidavit of inability to pay the cost of the appeal has been filed under the Texas Rules of Appellate Procedure; and

(2) the trial judge finds:

(A) the appeal is not frivolous; and

(B) the statement of facts and the clerk's transcript is needed to decide the issue presented by the appeal.

(b) In determining whether an appeal is frivolous, a judge may consider whether the appellant has presented a substantial question for appellate review.

(c) The trial judge may order a clerk of a court to prepare a transcript, or any part of the transcript, necessary for making the determination required by Subsection (a)(2).

Added by Acts 1993, 73rd Leg., ch. 861, § 1, eff. Sept. 1, 1993. Amended by Acts 1997, 75th Leg., ch. 467, § 1, eff. Sept. 1, 1997.

§ 13.004. Inapplicability to Certain Claims

This chapter does not apply to a claim governed by Chapter 14.

Added by Acts 1995, 74th Leg., ch. 378, § 3, eff. June 8, 1995.

CHAPTER 14. INMATE LITIGATION

Section

§ 14.001. Definitions

In this chapter:

(1) "Claim" means a cause of action governed by this chapter.

(2) "Department" means the Texas Department of Criminal Justice.

(3) "Inmate" means a person housed in a secure correctional facility.

(4) "Secure correctional facility" has the meaning assigned by Section 1.07, Penal Code.

(5) "Trust account" means an inmate's trust account administered by the department under Section 501.014, Government Code, by a facility under contract with the department, or by a jail.

(6) "Unsworn declaration" means a document executed in accordance with Chapter 132.

Added by Acts 1995, 74th Leg., ch. 378, § 2, eff. June 8, 1995.

§ 14.002. Scope of Chapter

(a) This chapter applies only to an action, including an appeal or original proceeding, brought by an inmate in a district, county, justice of the peace, or small claims court or an appellate court, including the supreme court or the court of criminal appeals, in which an affidavit or unsworn declaration of inability to pay costs is filed by the inmate.

(b) This chapter does not apply to an action brought under the Family Code.

Added by Acts 1995, 74th Leg., ch. 378, § 2, eff. June 8, 1995. Amended by Acts 2011, 82nd Leg., 1st C.S., ch. 3 (H.B. 79), § 12.01, eff. Jan. 1, 2012.

§ 14.003. Dismissal of Claim

(a) A court may dismiss a claim, either before or after service of process, if the court finds that:

(1) the allegation of poverty in the affidavit or unsworn declaration is false;

(2) the claim is frivolous or malicious; or

(3) the inmate filed an affidavit or unsworn declaration required by this chapter that the inmate knew was false.

(b) In determining whether a claim is frivolous or malicious, the court may consider whether:

(1) the claim's realistic chance of ultimate success is slight;

(2) the claim has no arguable basis in law or in fact;

(3) it is clear that the party cannot prove facts in support of the claim; or

(4) the claim is substantially similar to a previous claim filed by the inmate because the claim arises from the same operative facts.

(c) In determining whether Subsection (a) applies, the court may hold a hearing. The hearing may be held before or after service of process, and it may be held on motion of the court, a party, or the clerk of the court.

(d) On the filing of a motion under Subsection (c), the court shall suspend discovery relating to the claim pending the hearing.

(e) A court that dismisses a claim brought by a person housed in a facility operated by or under contract with the department may notify the department of the dismissal and, on the court's own motion or the motion of any party or the clerk of the court, may advise the department that a mental health evaluation of the inmate may be appropriate.

Added by Acts 1995, 74th Leg., ch. 378, § 2, eff. June 8, 1995.

§ 14.004. Affidavit Relating to Previous Filings

(a) An inmate who files an affidavit or unsworn declaration of inability to pay costs shall file a separate affidavit or declaration:

(1) identifying each action, other than an action under the Family Code, previously brought by the person and in which the person was not represented by an attorney, without regard to whether the person was an inmate at the time the action was brought; and

(2) describing each action that was previously brought by:

(A) stating the operative facts for which relief was sought;

(B) listing the case name, cause number, and the court in which the action was brought;

(C) identifying each party named in the action; and

(D) stating the result of the action, including whether the action or a claim that was a basis for the action was dismissed as frivolous or malicious under Section 13.001 or Section 14.003 or otherwise.

(b) If the affidavit or unsworn declaration filed under this section states that a previous action or claim was dismissed as frivolous or malicious, the affidavit or unsworn declaration must state the date of the final order affirming the dismissal.

(c) The affidavit or unsworn declaration must be accompanied by the certified copy of the trust account statement required by Section 14.006(f).

Added by Acts 1995, 74th Leg., ch. 378, § 2, eff. June 8, 1995. Amended by Acts 2011, 82nd Leg., 1st C.S., ch. 3 (H.B. 79), § 12.02, eff. Jan. 1, 2012.

§ 14.005. Grievance System Decision; Exhaustion of Administrative Remedies

(a) An inmate who files a claim that is subject to the grievance system established under Section 501.008, Government Code, shall file with the court:

(1) an affidavit or unsworn declaration stating the date that the grievance was filed and the date the written decision described by Section 501.008(d), Government Code, was received by the inmate; and

(2) a copy of the written decision from the grievance system.

(b) A court shall dismiss a claim if the inmate fails to file the claim before the 31st day after the date the inmate receives the written decision from the grievance system.

(c) If a claim is filed before the grievance system procedure is complete, the court shall stay the proceeding with respect to the claim for a period not to exceed 180 days to permit completion of the grievance system procedure.

Added by Acts 1995, 74th Leg., ch. 378, § 2, eff. June 8, 1995.

§ 14.006. Court Fees, Court Costs, Other Costs

(a) A court may order an inmate who has filed a claim to pay court fees, court costs, and other costs in accordance with this section and Section 14.007. The clerk of the court shall mail a copy of the court's order and a certified bill of costs to the department or jail, as appropriate.

(b) On the court's order, the inmate shall pay an amount equal to the lesser of:

(1) 20 percent of the preceding six months' deposits to the inmate's trust account; or

(2) the total amount of court fees and costs.

(c) In each month following the month in which payment is made under Subsection (b), the inmate shall pay an amount equal to the lesser of:

(1) 10 percent of that month's deposits to the trust account; or

(2) the total amount of court fees and costs that remain unpaid.

(d) Payments under Subsection (c) shall continue until the total amount of court fees and costs are paid or until the inmate is released from confinement.

(e) On receipt of a copy of an order issued under Subsection (a), the department or jail shall withdraw money from the trust account in accordance with Subsections (b), (c), and (d). The department or jail shall hold the money in a separate account and shall forward the money to the court clerk on the earlier of the following dates:

(1) the date the total amount to be forwarded equals the total amount of court fees and costs that remains unpaid; or

(2) the date the inmate is released.

(f) The inmate shall file a certified copy of the inmate's trust account statement with the court. The statement must reflect the balance of the account at the time the claim is filed and activity in the account during the six months preceding the date on which the claim is filed. The court may request the department or jail to furnish the information required under this subsection.

(g) An inmate may authorize payment in addition to that required by this section.

(h) The court may dismiss a claim if the inmate fails to pay fees and costs assessed under this section.

(i) An inmate may not avoid the fees and costs assessed under this section by nonsuiting a party or by voluntarily dismissing the action.

Added by Acts 1995, 74th Leg., ch. 378, § 2, eff. June 8, 1995.

§ 14.007. Other Costs

(a) An order of a court under Section 14.006(a) shall include the costs described by Subsection (b) if the court finds that:

(1) the inmate has previously filed an action to which this chapter applies; and

(2) a final order has been issued that affirms that the action was dismissed as frivolous or malicious under Section 13.001 or Section 14.003 or otherwise.

(b) Costs under Subsection (a) shall include, as costs of court, expenses incurred by the court or by the department, jail, or private facility operator, in connection with the claim and not otherwise charged to the inmate under Section 14.006, including:

(1) expenses of service of process;

(2) postage; and

(3) transportation, housing, or medical care incurred in connection with the appearance of the inmate in the court for any proceeding.

Added by Acts 1995, 74th Leg., ch. 378, § 2, eff. June 8, 1995. Amended by Acts 2011, 82nd Leg., 1st C.S., ch. 3 (H.B. 79), § 12.03, eff. Jan. 1, 2012.

§ 14.008. Hearing

(a) The court may hold a hearing under this chapter at a jail or a facility operated by or under contract with the department or may conduct the hearing with video communications technology that permits the court to see and hear the inmate and that permits the inmate to see and hear the court and any other witness.

(b) A hearing conducted under this section by video communications technology shall be recorded on videotape. The recording is sufficient to serve as a permanent record of the hearing.

Added by Acts 1995, 74th Leg., ch. 378, § 2, eff. June 8, 1995.

§ 14.009. Submission of Evidence

(a) The court may request a person with an admissible document or admissible testimony relevant to the subject matter of the hearing to submit a copy of the document or written statement stating the substance of the testimony.

(b) A written statement submitted under this section must be made under oath or made as an unsworn declaration under Section 132.001.

(c) A copy of a document submitted under this section must be accompanied by a certification executed under oath by an appropriate custodian of the record stating that the copy is correct and any other matter relating to the admissibility of the document that the court requires.

(d) A person submitting a written statement or document under this section is not required to appear at the hearing.

(e) The court shall require that the inmate be provided with a copy of each written statement or document not later than 14 days before the date on which the hearing is to begin.

Added by Acts 1995, 74th Leg., ch. 378, § 2, eff. June 8, 1995.

§ 14.010. Dismissal of Claim

(a) The court may enter an order dismissing the entire claim or a portion of the claim under this chapter.

(b) If a portion of the claim is dismissed, the court shall designate the issues and defendants on which the claim may proceed, subject to Sections 14.006 and 14.007.

(c) An order under this section is not subject to interlocutory appeal by the inmate.

Added by Acts 1995, 74th Leg., ch. 378, § 2, eff. June 8, 1995.

§ 14.011. Effect on Other Claims

(a) Except as provided by Subsection (b), on receipt of an order assessing fees and costs under Section 14.006 that indicates that the court made the finding described by Section 14.007(a), a clerk of a court may not accept for filing another claim by the inmate until the fees and costs assessed under Section 14.006 are paid.

(b) A court may allow an inmate who has not paid the fees and costs assessed against the inmate to file a claim for injunctive relief seeking to enjoin an act or failure to act that creates a substantial threat of irreparable injury or serious physical harm to the inmate.

Added by Acts 1995, 74th Leg., ch. 378, § 2, eff. June 8, 1995.

§ 14.012. Questionnaire

To implement this chapter, a court may develop, for use in that court, a questionnaire to be filed by the inmate.

Added by Acts 1995, 74th Leg., ch. 378, § 2, eff. June 8, 1995.

§ 14.013. Review and Recommendation by Magistrates

(a) The supreme court shall, by rule, adopt a system under which a court may refer a suit governed by this chapter to a magistrate for review and recommendation.

(b) The system adopted under Subsection (a) may be funded from money appropriated to the supreme court or from money received by the supreme court through interagency contract or contracts.

(c) For the purposes of Section 14.014, the adoption of a system by rule under Subsection (a) does not constitute a modification or repeal of a provision of this chapter.

Added by Acts 1995, 74th Leg., ch. 378, § 2, eff. June 8, 1995.

§ 14.014. Conflict With Texas Rules of Civil Procedure

Notwithstanding Section 22.004, Government Code, this chapter may not be modified or repealed by a rule adopted by the supreme court.

Added by Acts 1995, 74th Leg., ch. 378, § 2, eff. June 8, 1995.

SUBTITLE B. TRIAL MATTERS

CHAPTER 15. VENUE

SUBCHAPTER A. DEFINITIONS; GENERAL RULES

SUBCHAPTER A. DEFINITIONS; GENERAL RULES

§ 15.001. Definitions

In this chapter:

(a) "Principal office" means a principal office of the corporation, unincorporated association, or partnership in this state in which the decision makers for the organization within this state conduct the daily affairs of the organization. The mere presence of an agency or representative does not establish a principal office.

(b) "Proper venue" means:

(1) the venue required by the mandatory provisions of Subchapter B[1] or another statute prescribing mandatory venue; or

(2) if Subdivision (1) does not apply, the venue provided by this subchapter or Subchapter C.[2]

Added by Acts 1995, 74th Leg., ch. 138, § 1, eff. Aug. 28, 1995.

[1] V.T.C.A., Civil Practice & Remedies Code § 15.011 et seq.
[2] V.T.C.A., Civil Practice & Remedies Code § 15.031 et seq.

§ 15.002. Venue: General Rule

(a) Except as otherwise provided by this subchapter or Subchapter B or C,[1] all lawsuits shall be brought:

(1) in the county in which all or a substantial part of the events or omissions giving rise to the claim occurred;

(2) in the county of defendant's residence at the time the cause of action accrued if defendant is a natural person;

(3) in the county of the defendant's principal office in this state, if the defendant is not a natural person; or

(4) if Subdivisions (1), (2), and (3) do not apply, in the county in which the plaintiff resided at the time of the accrual of the cause of action.

(b) For the convenience of the parties and witnesses and in the interest of justice, a court may transfer an action from a county of proper venue under this subchapter or Subchapter C to any other county of proper venue on motion of a defendant filed and served concurrently with or before the filing of the answer, where the court finds:

(1) maintenance of the action in the county of suit would work an injustice to the movant considering the movant's economic and personal hardship;

(2) the balance of interests of all the parties predominates in favor of the action being brought in the other county; and

(3) the transfer of the action would not work an injustice to any other party.

(c) A court's ruling or decision to grant or deny a transfer under Subsection (b) is not grounds for appeal or mandamus and is not reversible error.

Acts 1985, 69th Leg., ch. 959, § 1, eff. Sept. 1, 1985. Redesignated from V.T.C.A., Civil Practice & Remedies Code § 15.001 and amended by Acts 1995, 74th Leg., ch. 138, § 1, eff. Aug. 28, 1995.

[1] V.T.C.A., Civil Practice & Remedies Code § 15.011 et seq. or § 15.031 et seq.

§ 15.003. Multiple Plaintiffs and Intervening Plaintiffs

(a) In a suit in which there is more than one plaintiff, whether the plaintiffs are included by joinder, by intervention, because the lawsuit was begun by more than one plaintiff, or otherwise, each plaintiff must, independently of every other plaintiff, establish proper venue. If a plaintiff cannot independently establish proper venue, that plaintiff's part of the suit, including all of that plaintiff's claims and causes of action, must be transferred to a county of proper venue or dismissed, as is appropriate, unless that plaintiff, independently of every other plaintiff, establishes that:

(1) joinder of that plaintiff or intervention in the suit by that plaintiff is proper under the Texas Rules of Civil Procedure;

(2) maintaining venue as to that plaintiff in the county of suit does not unfairly prejudice another party to the suit;

(3) there is an essential need to have that plaintiff's claim tried in the county in which the suit is pending; and

(4) the county in which the suit is pending is a fair and convenient venue for that plaintiff and all persons against whom the suit is brought.

(b) An interlocutory appeal may be taken of a trial court's determination under Subsection (a) that:

(1) a plaintiff did or did not independently establish proper venue; or

(2) a plaintiff that did not independently establish proper venue did or did not establish the items prescribed by Subsections (a)(1)–(4).

(c) An interlocutory appeal permitted by Subsection (b) must be taken to the court of appeals district in which the trial court is located under the procedures established for interlocutory appeals. The appeal may be taken by a party that is affected by the trial court's determination under Subsection (a). The court of appeals shall:

(1) determine whether the trial court's order is proper based on an independent determination from the record and not under either an abuse of discretion or substantial evidence standard; and

(2) render judgment not later than the 120th day after the date the appeal is perfected.

(d) An interlocutory appeal under Subsection (b) has the effect of staying the commencement of trial in the trial court pending resolution of the appeal.

Added by Acts 1995, 74th Leg., ch. 138, § 1, eff. Aug. 28, 1995. Amended by Acts 2003, 78th Leg., ch. 204, § 3.03, eff. Sept. 1, 2003.

§ 15.004. Mandatory Venue Provisions Governs Multiple Claims

In a suit in which a plaintiff properly joins two or more claims or causes of action arising from the same transaction, occurrence, or series of transactions or occurrences, and one of the claims or causes of action is governed by the mandatory venue provisions of Subchapter B,[1] the suit shall be brought in the county required by the mandatory venue provision.

Added by Acts 1995, 74th Leg., ch. 138, § 1, eff. Aug. 28, 1995.

[1] V.T.C.A., Civil Practice & Remedies Code § 15.011 et seq.

§ 15.005. Multiple Defendants

In a suit in which the plaintiff has established proper venue against a defendant, the court also has venue of all the defendants in all claims or actions arising out of the same transaction, occurrence, or series of transactions or occurrences.

Added by Acts 1995, 74th Leg., ch. 138, § 1, eff. Aug. 28, 1995.

§ 15.006. Venue Determined by Facts Existing at the Time of Accrual

A court shall determine the venue of a suit based on the facts existing at the time the cause of action that is the basis of the suit accrued.

Added by Acts 1995, 74th Leg., ch. 138, § 1, eff. Aug. 28, 1995.

§ 15.007. Conflict With Certain Provisions

Notwithstanding Sections 15.004, 15.005, and 15.031, to the extent that venue under this chapter for a suit by or against an executor, administrator, or guardian as such, for personal injury, death, or property damage conflicts with venue provisions under the Estates Code, this chapter controls.

Added by Acts 1995, 74th Leg., ch. 138, § 1, eff. Aug. 28, 1995. Amended by Acts 2015, 84th Leg., ch. 1236 (S.B. 1296), § 20.001, eff. Sept. 1, 2015.

SUBCHAPTER B. MANDATORY VENUE

§ 15.011. Land

Actions for recovery of real property or an estate or interest in real property, for partition of real property, to remove encumbrances from the title to real property, for recovery of damages to real property, or to quiet title to real property shall be brought in the county in which all or a part of the property is located.

Acts 1985, 69th Leg., ch. 959, § 1, eff. Sept. 1, 1985. Amended by Acts 1995, 74th Leg., ch. 138, § 2, eff. Aug. 28, 1995.

§ 15.0115. Landlord-Tenant

(a) Except as provided by another statute prescribing mandatory venue, a suit between a landlord and a tenant arising under a lease shall be brought in the county in which all or a part of the real property is located.

(b) In this section, "lease" means any written or oral agreement between a landlord and a tenant that establishes or modifies the terms, conditions, or other provisions relating to the use and occupancy of the real property that is the subject of the agreement.

Added by Acts 1995, 74th Leg., ch. 138, § 2, eff. Aug. 28, 1995.

§ 15.012. Injunction Against Suit

Actions to stay proceedings in a suit shall be brought in the county in which the suit is pending.

Acts 1985, 69th Leg., ch. 959, § 1, eff. Sept. 1, 1985.

§ 15.013. Injunction Against Execution of Judgment

Actions to restrain execution of a judgment based on invalidity of the judgment or of the writ shall be brought in the county in which the judgment was rendered.

Acts 1985, 69th Leg., ch. 959, § 1, eff. Sept. 1, 1985.

§ 15.014. Head of State Department

An action for mandamus against the head of a department of the state government shall be brought in Travis County.

Acts 1985, 69th Leg., ch. 959, § 1, eff. Sept. 1, 1985.

§ 15.015. Counties

An action against a county shall be brought in that county.

Acts 1985, 69th Leg., ch. 959, § 1, eff. Sept. 1, 1985.

§ 15.0151. Certain Political Subdivisions

(a) Except as provided by a law not contained in this chapter, an action against a political subdivision that is located in a county with a population of 100,000 or less shall be brought in the county in which the political subdivision is located. If the political subdivision is located in more than one county and the population of each county is 100,000 or less, the action shall be brought in any county in which the political subdivision is located.

(b) In this section, "political subdivision" means a governmental entity in this state, other than a county, that is not a state agency. The term includes a municipality, school or junior college district, hospital district, or any other special purpose district or authority.

Added by Acts 1997, 75th Leg., ch. 733, § 1, eff. Sept. 1, 1997.

§ 15.016. Other Mandatory Venue

An action governed by any other statute prescribing mandatory venue shall be brought in the county required by that statute.

Acts 1985, 69th Leg., ch. 959, § 1, eff. Sept. 1, 1985.

§ 15.017. Libel, Slander, or Invasion of Privacy

A suit for damages for libel, slander, or invasion of privacy shall be brought and can only be maintained in the county in which the plaintiff resided at the time of the accrual of the cause of action, or in the county in which the defendant resided at the time of filing suit, or in the county of the residence of defendants, or any of them, or the domicile of any corporate defendant, at the election of the plaintiff.

Acts 1985, 69th Leg., ch. 959, § 1, eff. Sept. 1, 1985.

§ 15.018. Federal Employers' Liability Act

(a) This section only applies to suits brought under the federal Employers' Liability Act (45 U.S.C. Section 51 et seq.).

(b) All suits brought under the federal Employers' Liability Act shall be brought:

(1) in the county in which all or a substantial part of the events or omissions giving rise to the claim occurred;

(2) in the county where the defendant's principal office in this state is located; or

(3) in the county where the plaintiff resided at the time the cause of action accrued.

Added by Acts 1995, 74th Leg., ch. 138, § 2, eff. Aug. 28, 1995. Amended by Acts 2007, 80th Leg., ch. 203, § 1, eff. May 24, 2007.

§ 15.0181. Jones Act

(a) In this section:

(1) "Coastal county" means:

(A) a county in a coastal area, as defined by Section 33.004, Natural Resources Code; or

(B) a county having a United States Customs port through which waterborne freight is transported.

(2) "Coastal erosion" means the loss of land, marshes, wetlands, beaches, or other coastal features because of the actions of wind, waves, tides, storm surges, subsidence, or other forces.

(3) "Erosion response project" means an action intended to address or mitigate coastal erosion, including beach nourishment, sediment management, beneficial use of dredged material, creation or enhancement of a dune, wetland, or marsh, and construction of a breakwater, bulkhead, groin, jetty, or other structure.

(4) "Gulf Coast state" means Louisiana, Mississippi, Alabama, or Florida.

(5) "Inland waters" means the navigable waters shoreward of the navigational demarcation lines dividing the high seas from harbors, rivers, the Gulf Intracoastal Waterway, and other inland waters of Texas, Louisiana, Mississippi, Alabama, Arkansas, Tennessee, Missouri, Illinois, Kentucky, or Indiana or of Florida along the Gulf of Mexico shoreline of Florida from the Florida–Alabama border down to and including the shoreline of Key West, Florida. The term does not include the Great Lakes.

(b) This section applies only to suits brought under the Jones Act (46 U.S.C. Section 30104).

(c) Except as provided by this section, a suit brought under the Jones Act shall be brought:

(1) in the county where the defendant's principal office in this state is located;

(2) in the county in which all or a substantial part of the events or omissions giving rise to the claim occurred; or

(3) in the county where the plaintiff resided at the time the cause of action accrued.

(d) If all or a substantial part of the events or omissions giving rise to the claim occurred on the inland waters of this state, ashore in this state, or during the course of an erosion response project in this state, the suit shall be brought:

(1) in the county in which all or a substantial part of the events giving rise to the claim occurred; or

(2) in the county where the defendant's principal office in this state is located.

(e) If all or a substantial part of the events or omissions giving rise to the claim occurred on inland waters outside this state, ashore in a Gulf Coast state, or during the course of an erosion response project in a Gulf Coast state, the suit shall be brought:

(1) in the county where the defendant's principal office in this state is located if the defendant's principal office in this state is located in a coastal county;

(2) in Harris County unless the plaintiff resided in Galveston County at the time the cause of action accrued;

(3) in Galveston County unless the plaintiff resided in Harris County at the time the cause of action accrued; or

(4) if the defendant does not have a principal office in this state located in a coastal county, in the

county where the plaintiff resided at the time the cause of action accrued.

Added by Acts 2007, 80th Leg., ch. 203, § 2, eff. May 24, 2007. Amended by Acts 2009, 81st Leg., ch. 87, § 5.001, eff. Sept. 1, 2009.

§ 15.019. Inmate Litigation

(a) Except as provided by Section 15.014, an action that accrued while the plaintiff was housed in a facility operated by or under contract with the Texas Department of Criminal Justice shall be brought in the county in which the facility is located.

(b) An action brought by two or more plaintiffs that accrued while the plaintiffs were housed in a facility operated by or under contract with the Texas Department of Criminal Justice shall be brought in a county in which a facility that housed one of the plaintiffs is located.

(c) This section does not apply to an action brought under the Family Code.

Added by Acts 1995, 74th Leg., ch. 378, § 1, eff. June 8, 1995. Renumbered from V.T.C.A., Civil Practice and Remedies Code § 15.018 by Acts 1997, 75th Leg., ch. 165, § 31.01(3), eff. Sept. 1, 1997.

§ 15.020. Major Transactions: Specification of Venue by Agreement

(a) In this section, "major transaction" means a transaction evidenced by a written agreement under which a person pays or receives, or is obligated to pay or entitled to receive, consideration with an aggregate stated value equal to or greater than $1 million. The term does not include a transaction entered into primarily for personal, family, or household purposes, or to settle a personal injury or wrongful death claim, without regard to the aggregate value.

(b) An action arising from a major transaction shall be brought in a county if the party against whom the action is brought has agreed in writing that a suit arising from the transaction may be brought in that county.

(c) Notwithstanding any other provision of this title, an action arising from a major transaction may not be brought in a county if:

(1) the party bringing the action has agreed in writing that an action arising from the transaction may not be brought in that county, and the action may be brought in another county of this state or in another jurisdiction; or

(2) the party bringing the action has agreed in writing that an action arising from the transaction must be brought in another county of this state or in another jurisdiction, and the action may be brought in that other county, under this section or otherwise, or in that other jurisdiction.

(d) This section does not apply to an action if:

(1) the agreement described by this section was unconscionable at the time that it was made;

(2) the agreement regarding venue is voidable under Chapter 272, Business & Commerce Code; or

(3) venue is established under a statute of this state other than this title.

(e) This section does not affect venue and jurisdiction in an action arising from a transaction that is not a major transaction.

Added by Acts 1999, 76th Leg., ch. 84, § 1, eff. Aug. 30, 1999. Amended by Acts 2007, 80th Leg., ch. 885, § 2.10, eff. April 1, 2009.

SUBCHAPTER C. PERMISSIVE VENUE

§ 15.031. Executor; Administrator; Guardian

If the suit is against an executor, administrator, or guardian, as such, to establish a money demand against the estate which he represents, the suit may be brought in the county in which the estate is administered, or if the suit is against an executor, administrator, or guardian growing out of a negligent act or omission of the person whose estate the executor, administrator, or guardian represents, the suit may be brought in the county in which the negligent act or omission of the person whose estate the executor, administrator, or guardian represents occurred.

Acts 1985, 69th Leg., ch. 959, § 1, eff. Sept. 1, 1985.

§ 15.032. Insurance

Suit against fire, marine, or inland insurance companies may also be commenced in any county in which the insured property was situated. A suit on a policy may be brought against any life insurance company, or accident insurance company, or life and accident, or health and accident, or life, health, and accident insurance company in the county in which the company's principal office in this state is located or in the county in which the loss has occurred or in which the policyholder or beneficiary instituting the suit resided at the time the cause of action accrued.

Acts 1985, 69th Leg., ch. 959, § 1, eff. Sept. 1, 1985. Amended by Acts 1995, 74th Leg., ch. 138, § 3, eff. Aug. 28, 1995.

§ 15.033. Breach of Warranty by Manufacturer

A suit for breach of warranty by a manufacturer of consumer goods may be brought in any county in which all or a substantial part of the events or omissions giving rise to the claim occurred, in the county in which the manufacturer has its principal office in this state, or in the county in which the plaintiff resided at the time the cause of action accrued.

Acts 1985, 69th Leg., ch. 959, § 1, eff. Sept. 1, 1985. Amended by Acts 1995, 74th Leg., ch. 138, § 3, eff. Aug. 28, 1995.

§ 15.034. Repealed by Acts 1987, 70th Leg., 1st C.S., ch. 4, § 2, eff. Sept. 2, 1987

§ 15.035. Contract in Writing

(a) Except as provided by Subsection (b), if a person has contracted in writing to perform an obligation in a particular county, expressly naming the county or a definite place in that county by that writing, suit on or by reason of the obligation may be brought against him either in that county or in the county in which the defendant has his domicile.

(b) In an action founded on a contractual obligation of the defendant to pay money arising out of or based on a consumer transaction for goods, services, loans, or extensions of credit intended primarily for personal, family, household, or agricultural use, suit by a creditor on or by reason of the obligation may be brought against the defendant either in the county in which the defendant in fact signed the contract or in the county in which the defendant resides when the action is commenced. No term or statement contained in an obligation described in this section shall constitute a waiver of these provisions.

Acts 1985, 69th Leg., ch. 959, § 1, eff. Sept. 1, 1985.

§§ 15.036, 15.037. Repealed by Acts 1995, 74th Leg., ch. 138, § 10, eff. Aug. 28, 1995

§ 15.038. Other Permissive Venue

An action governed by any other statute prescribing permissive venue may be brought in the county allowed by that statute.

Acts 1985, 69th Leg., ch. 959, § 1, eff. Sept. 1, 1985.

§ 15.039. Transient Person

A transient person may be sued in any county in which he may be found.

Acts 1985, 69th Leg., ch. 959, § 1, eff. Sept. 1, 1985.

§ 15.040. Repealed by Acts 1995, 74th Leg., ch. 138, § 10, eff. Aug. 28, 1995

SUBCHAPTER D. GENERAL PROVISIONS

§ 15.061. Repealed by Acts 1995, 74th Leg., ch. 138, § 10, eff. Aug. 28, 1995

§ 15.062. Counterclaims, Cross Claims, and Third-Party Claims

(a) Venue of the main action shall establish venue of a counterclaim, cross claim, or third-party claim properly joined under the Texas Rules of Civil Procedure or any applicable statute.

(b) If an original defendant properly joins a third-party defendant, venue shall be proper for a claim arising out of the same transaction, occurrence, or series of transactions or occurrences by the plaintiff against the third-party defendant if the claim arises out of the subject matter of the plaintiff's claim against the original defendant.

Acts 1985, 69th Leg., ch. 959, § 1, eff. Sept. 1, 1985. Amended by Acts 1995, 74th Leg., ch. 138, § 4, eff. Aug. 28, 1995.

§ 15.063. Transfer

The court, on motion filed and served concurrently with or before the filing of the answer, shall transfer an action to another county of proper venue if:

(1) the county in which the action is pending is not a proper county as provided by this chapter;

(2) an impartial trial cannot be had in the county in which the action is pending; or

(3) written consent of the parties to transfer to any other county is filed at any time.

Acts 1985, 69th Leg., ch. 959, § 1, eff. Sept. 1, 1985.

§ 15.064. Hearings

(a) In all venue hearings, no factual proof concerning the merits of the case shall be required to establish venue. The court shall determine venue questions from the pleadings and affidavits. No interlocutory appeal shall lie from the determination.

(b) On appeal from the trial on the merits, if venue was improper it shall in no event be harmless error and shall be reversible error. In determining whether venue was or was not proper, the appellate court shall consider the entire record, including the trial on the merits.

Acts 1985, 69th Leg., ch. 959, § 1, eff. Sept. 1, 1985.

§ 15.0641. Venue Rights of Multiple Defendants

In a suit in which two or more defendants are joined, any action or omission by one defendant in relation to venue, including a waiver of venue by one defendant, does not operate to impair or diminish the right of any other defendant to properly challenge venue.

Added by Acts 1995, 74th Leg., ch. 138, § 5, eff. Aug. 28, 1995.

§ 15.0642. Mandamus

A party may apply for a writ of mandamus with an appellate court to enforce the mandatory venue provisions of this chapter. An application for the writ of mandamus must be filed before the later of:

(1) the 90th day before the date the trial starts; or

(2) the 10th day after the date the party receives notice of the trial setting.

Added by Acts 1995, 74th Leg., ch. 138, § 5, eff. Aug. 28, 1995.

§ 15.065. Watercourse or Roadway Forming County Boundary

If a river, watercourse, highway, road, or street forms the boundary line between two counties, the courts of each county have concurrent jurisdiction over the parts of the watercourse or roadway that form the boundary of the county in the same manner as if the watercourse or roadway were in that county.

Acts 1985, 69th Leg., ch. 959, § 1, eff. Sept. 1, 1985.

§ 15.066. Conflict With Rules of Civil Procedure

Subject to Section 22.004, Government Code, to the extent that this chapter conflicts with the Texas Rules of Civil Procedure, this chapter controls.

Added by Acts 1995, 74th Leg., ch. 138, § 6, eff. Aug. 28, 1995.

SUBCHAPTER E. SUITS BROUGHT IN JUSTICE COURT

§ 15.081. Application

This subchapter applies only to suits brought in a justice court.

Acts 1985, 69th Leg., ch. 959, § 1, eff. Sept. 1, 1985.

§ 15.082. Venue: General Rule

Except as otherwise provided by this subchapter or by any other law, a suit in justice court shall be brought in the county and precinct in which one or more defendants reside.

Acts 1985, 69th Leg., ch. 959, § 1, eff. Sept. 1, 1985.

§ 15.0821. Administrative Rules for Transfer

The justices of the peace in each county shall, by majority vote, adopt local rules of administration regarding the transfer of a pending case from one precinct to a different precinct.

Added by Acts 2011, 82nd Leg., 1st C.S., ch. 3 (H.B. 79), § 5.04, eff. Jan. 1, 2012.

§ 15.083. Residence of a Single Man

A single man's residence is where he boards.

Acts 1985, 69th Leg., ch. 959, § 1, eff. Sept. 1, 1985.

§ 15.084. Forcible Entry and Detainer

A suit for forcible entry and detainer shall be brought in the precinct in which all or part of the premises is located.

Acts 1985, 69th Leg., ch. 959, § 1, eff. Sept. 1, 1985.

§ 15.085. Executor; Administrator; Guardian

A suit against an executor, an administrator, or a guardian shall be brought in the county in which the administration or guardianship is pending and in the precinct in which the county seat is located.

Acts 1985, 69th Leg., ch. 959, § 1, eff. Sept. 1, 1985.

§ 15.086. Counties

A suit against a county shall be brought in the precinct in which the county seat of that county is located.

Acts 1985, 69th Leg., ch. 959, § 1, eff. Sept. 1, 1985.

§ 15.087. Option: Suit in Defendant's County of Residence

A suit to which a permissive venue section of this subchapter applies may be brought and maintained either in the county provided for by that section or in the county in which the defendant resides.

Acts 1985, 69th Leg., ch. 959, § 1, eff. Sept. 1, 1985.

§ 15.088. Nonresident; Residence Unknown

A suit against a nonresident of this state or against a person whose residence is unknown may be brought in the county and precinct in which the plaintiff resides.

Acts 1985, 69th Leg., ch. 959, § 1, eff. Sept. 1, 1985.

§ 15.089. Transient Person

A suit against a transient person may be brought in any county and precinct in which the transient person is found.

Acts 1985, 69th Leg., ch. 959, § 1, eff. Sept. 1, 1985.

§ 15.090. Personal Property

A suit to recover personal property may be brought in the county and precinct in which the property is located.

Acts 1985, 69th Leg., ch. 959, § 1, eff. Sept. 1, 1985.

§ 15.091. Rents

A suit to recover rents may be brought in the county and precinct in which all or part of the rented premises is located.

Acts 1985, 69th Leg., ch. 959, § 1, eff. Sept. 1, 1985.

§ 15.092. Contract

(a) Except as otherwise provided by this section, a suit on a written contract that promises performance at a particular place may be brought in the county and precinct in which the contract was to be performed.

(b) A suit on an oral or written contract for labor actually performed may be brought in the county and precinct in which the labor was performed.

(c) A suit by a creditor on a contract for goods, services, or loans intended primarily for personal, family, household, or agricultural use may be brought only in the county and precinct in which the contract was signed or in which the defendant resides.

(d) A contract described by Subsection (c) may not waive the venue provided by that subsection.

Acts 1985, 69th Leg., ch. 959, § 1, eff. Sept. 1, 1985.

§ 15.093. Torts

A tort suit for damages may be brought in the county and precinct in which the injury was inflicted.

Acts 1985, 69th Leg., ch. 959, § 1, eff. Sept. 1, 1985.

§ 15.094. Corporation; Association; Joint-Stock Company

A suit against a private corporation, association, or joint-stock company may be brought in the county and precinct in which:

(1) all or part of the cause of action arose;

(2) the corporation, association, or company has an agency or representative; or

(3) the principal office of the corporation, association, or company is located.

Acts 1985, 69th Leg., ch. 959, § 1, eff. Sept. 1, 1985.

§ 15.095. Railroad Companies; Carriers

A suit against a railroad company, a canal company, or the owners of a line of transportation vehicles for injury to a person or property on the railroad, canal, or line of vehicles or for liability as a carrier may be brought in a precinct through which that railroad, canal, or line of vehicles passes or in a precinct in which the route of that railroad, canal, or vehicle begins or ends.

Acts 1985, 69th Leg., ch. 959, § 1, eff. Sept. 1, 1985.

§ 15.096. Steamboat or Other Vessel

A suit against the owner of a steamboat or other vessel may be brought in the county or precinct in which:

(1) the steamboat or vessel may be found;

(2) the cause of action arose; or

(3) the liability accrued or was contracted.

Acts 1985, 69th Leg., ch. 959, § 1, eff. Sept. 1, 1985.

§ 15.097. Insurance Companies

(a) A suit against a fire, marine, or inland marine insurance company may be brought in the county and precinct in which all or part of the insured property was located.

(b) A suit against an accident and life insurance company or association may be brought in the county and precinct in which one or more of the insured persons resided when the injury or death occurred.

Acts 1985, 69th Leg., ch. 959, § 1, eff. Sept. 1, 1985.

§ 15.098. Pleading Requirements

If a suit is brought in a county or precinct in which the defendant does not reside, the citation or pleading must affirmatively show that the suit comes within an exception provided for by this subchapter.

Acts 1985, 69th Leg., ch. 959, § 1, eff. Sept. 1, 1985.

§ 15.099. More Than One Justice

If there is more than one justice of the peace in a precinct or in an incorporated city or town, suit may be brought before any justice of the peace in that precinct or incorporated city or town.

Acts 1985, 69th Leg., ch. 959, § 1, eff. Sept. 1, 1985.

§ 15.100. Disqualified Justice

If the justice in the proper precinct is not qualified to try the suit, suit may be brought before the nearest qualified justice in the county.

Acts 1985, 69th Leg., ch. 959, § 1, eff. Sept. 1, 1985.

CHAPTER 16. LIMITATIONS

SUBCHAPTER A. LIMITATIONS OF PERSONAL ACTIONS

SUBCHAPTER B. LIMITATIONS OF REAL PROPERTY ACTIONS

SUBCHAPTER C. RESIDUAL LIMITATIONS PERIOD

SUBCHAPTER D. MISCELLANEOUS PROVISIONS

SUBCHAPTER A. LIMITATIONS OF PERSONAL ACTIONS

§ 16.001. Effect of Disability

(a) For the purposes of this subchapter, a person is under a legal disability if the person is:

(1) younger than 18 years of age, regardless of whether the person is married; or

(2) of unsound mind.

(b) If a person entitled to bring a personal action is under a legal disability when the cause of action accrues, the time of the disability is not included in a limitations period.

(c) A person may not tack one legal disability to another to extend a limitations period.

(d) A disability that arises after a limitations period starts does not suspend the running of the period.

Acts 1985, 69th Leg., ch. 959, § 1, eff. Sept. 1, 1985. Amended by Acts 1987, 70th Leg., ch. 1049, § 56, eff. Sept. 1, 1987.

§ 16.002. One-Year Limitations Period

(a) A person must bring suit for malicious prosecution, libel, slander, or breach of promise of marriage not later than one year after the day the cause of action accrues.

(b) A person must bring suit to set aside a sale of property seized under Subchapter E, Chapter 33, Tax

Code,[1] not later than one year after the date the property is sold.

Acts 1985, 69th Leg., ch. 959, § 1, eff. Sept. 1, 1985. Amended by Acts 1995, 74th Leg., ch. 1017, § 3, eff. Aug. 28, 1995.

[1] V.T.C.A., Tax Code § 33.91 et seq.

§ 16.003. Two-Year Limitations Period

(a) Except as provided by Sections 16.010, 16.0031, and 16.0045, a person must bring suit for trespass for injury to the estate or to the property of another, conversion of personal property, taking or detaining the personal property of another, personal injury, forcible entry and detainer, and forcible detainer not later than two years after the day the cause of action accrues.

(b) A person must bring suit not later than two years after the day the cause of action accrues in an action for injury resulting in death. The cause of action accrues on the death of the injured person.

Acts 1985, 69th Leg., ch. 959, § 1, eff. Sept. 1, 1985. Amended by Acts 1995, 74th Leg., ch. 739, § 2, eff. June 15, 1995; Acts 1997, 75th Leg., ch. 26, § 2, eff. May 1, 1997; Acts 2005, 79th Leg., ch. 97, § 3, eff. Sept. 1, 2005.

§ 16.0031. Asbestos-Related or Silica-Related Injuries

(a) In an action for personal injury or death resulting from an asbestos-related injury, as defined by Section 90.001, the cause of action accrues for purposes of Section 16.003 on the earlier of the following dates:

(1) the date of the exposed person's death; or

(2) the date that the claimant serves on a defendant a report complying with Section 90.003 or 90.010(f).

(b) In an action for personal injury or death resulting from a silica-related injury, as defined by Section 90.001, the cause of action accrues for purposes of Section 16.003 on the earlier of the following dates:

(1) the date of the exposed person's death; or

(2) the date that the claimant serves on a defendant a report complying with Section 90.004 or 90.010(f).

Added by Acts 2005, 79th Leg., ch. 97, § 4, eff. Sept. 1, 2005.

§ 16.004. Four-Year Limitations Period

(a) A person must bring suit on the following actions not later than four years after the day the cause of action accrues:

(1) specific performance of a contract for the conveyance of real property;

(2) penalty or damages on the penal clause of a bond to convey real property;

(3) debt;

(4) fraud; or

(5) breach of fiduciary duty.

(b) A person must bring suit on the bond of an executor, administrator, or guardian not later than four years after the day of the death, resignation, removal, or discharge of the executor, administrator, or guardian.

(c) A person must bring suit against his partner for a settlement of partnership accounts, and must bring an action on an open or stated account, or on a mutual and current account concerning the trade of merchandise between merchants or their agents or factors, not later than four years after the day that the cause of action accrues. For purposes of this subsection, the cause of action accrues on the day that the dealings in which the parties were interested together cease.

Acts 1985, 69th Leg., ch. 959, § 1, eff. Sept. 1, 1985. Amended by Acts 1999, 76th Leg., ch. 950, § 1, eff. Aug. 30, 1999.

§ 16.0045. Limitations Period for Claims Arising from Certain Offenses

(a) A person must bring suit for personal injury not later than 30 years after the day the cause of action accrues if the injury arises as a result of conduct that violates:

(1) Section 22.011(a)(2), Penal Code (sexual assault of a child);

(2) Section 22.021(a)(1)(B), Penal Code (aggravated sexual assault of a child);

(3) Section 21.02, Penal Code (continuous sexual abuse of young child or disabled individual);

(4) Section 20A.02(a)(7)(A), (B), (C), (D), or (H) or Section 20A.02(a)(8), Penal Code, involving an activity described by Section 20A.02(a)(7)(A), (B), (C), (D), or (H) or sexual conduct with a child trafficked in the manner described by Section 20A.02(a)(7), Penal Code (certain sexual trafficking of a child);

(5) Section 43.05(a)(2), Penal Code (compelling prostitution by a child); or

(6) Section 21.11, Penal Code (indecency with a child).

(b) A person must bring suit for personal injury not later than five years after the day the cause of action accrues if the injury arises as a result of conduct that violates:

(1) Section 22.011(a)(1), Penal Code (sexual assault);

(2) Section 22.021(a)(1)(A), Penal Code (aggravated sexual assault);

(3) Section 20A.02, Penal Code (trafficking of persons), other than conduct described by Subsection (a)(4); or

(4) Section 43.05(a)(1), Penal Code (compelling prostitution).

(c) In an action for injury resulting in death arising as a result of conduct described by Subsection (a) or (b), the cause of action accrues on the death of the injured person.

(d) A limitations period under this section is tolled for a suit on the filing of a petition by any person in an appropriate court alleging that the identity of the defendant in the suit is unknown and designating the unknown defendant as "John or Jane Doe." The person filing the petition shall proceed with due diligence to discover the identity of the defendant and amend the petition by substituting the real name of the defendant for "John or Jane Doe" not later than the 30th day after the date that the defendant is identified to the plaintiff. The limitations period begins running again on the date that the petition is amended.

Added by Acts 1995, 74th Leg., ch. 739, § 1, eff. June 15, 1995. Amended by Acts 2007, 80th Leg., ch. 593, § 3.01, eff. Sept. 1, 2007; Acts 2011, 82nd Leg., ch. 1 (S.B. 24), § 3.01, eff. Sept. 1, 2011; Acts 2015, 84th Leg., ch. 918 (H.B. 189), § 1, eff. Sept. 1, 2015; Acts 2019, 86th Leg., ch. 1306 (H.B. 3809), § 1, eff. Sept. 1, 2019; Acts 2021, 87th Leg., ch. 221 (H.B. 375), § 2.01, eff. Sept. 1, 2021.

Section 2 of Acts 2019, 86th Leg., ch. 1306 (H.B. 3809) provides:

"The change in law made by this Act applies to a cause of action that accrues on or after the effective date [Sept., 1, 2019] of this Act or a cause of action that accrued before the effective date of this Act, if the limitations period applicable to the cause of action immediately before the effective date of this Act has not expired before the effective date of this Act."

Section 3.01 of Acts 2021, 87th Leg., ch. 221 (H.B. 375) provides:

"The change in law made by this Act applies only to an offense committed on or after the effective date [Sept. 1, 2021] of this Act. An offense committed before the effective date of this Act is governed by the law in effect on the date the offense was committed, and the former law is continued in effect for that purpose. For purposes of this section, an offense was committed before the effective date of this Act if any element of the offense occurred before that date."

§ 16.005. Action for Closing Street or Road

(a) A person must bring suit for any relief from the following acts not later than two years after the day the cause of action accrues:

(1) the passage by a governing body of an incorporated city or town of an ordinance closing and abandoning, or attempting to close and abandon, all or any part of a public street or alley in the city or town, other than a state highway; or

(2) the adoption by a commissioners court of an order closing and abandoning, or attempting to close and abandon, all or any part of a public road or thoroughfare in the county, other than a state highway.

(b) The cause of action accrues when the order or ordinance is passed or adopted.

(c) If suit is not brought within the period provided by this section, the person in possession of the real property receives complete title to the property by limitations and the right of the city or county to revoke or rescind the order or ordinance is barred.

Acts 1985, 69th Leg., ch. 959, § 1, eff. Sept. 1, 1985.

§ 16.006. Carriers of Property

(a) A carrier of property for compensation or hire must bring suit for the recovery of charges not later than three years after the day on which the cause of action accrues.

(b) Except as provided by Subsections (c) and (d), a person must bring suit for overcharges against a carrier of property for compensation or hire not later than three years after the cause of action accrues.

(c) If the person has presented a written claim for the overcharges within the three-year period, the limitations period is extended for six months from the date written notice is given by the carrier to the claimant of disallowance of the claim in whole or in part, as specified in the carrier's notice.

(d) If on or before the expiration of the three-year period, the carrier brings an action under Subsection (a) to recover charges relating to the service or, without beginning an action, collects charges relating to that service, the limitations period is extended for 90 days from the day on which the action is begun or the charges are collected.

(e) A cause of action regarding a shipment of property accrues on the delivery or tender of the property by the carrier.

(f) In this section, "overcharge" means a charge for transportation services in excess of the lawfully applicable amount.

Acts 1985, 69th Leg., ch. 959, § 1, eff. Sept. 1, 1985.

§ 16.007. Return of Execution

A person must bring suit against a sheriff or other officer or the surety of the sheriff or officer for failure to return an execution issued in the person's favor, not later than five years after the date on which the execution was returnable.

Acts 1985, 69th Leg., ch. 959, § 1, eff. Sept. 1, 1985.

§ 16.008. Architects, Engineers, Interior Designers, and Landscape Architects Furnishing Design, Planning, or Inspection of Construction of Improvements

(a) Except as provided by Subsection (a–1), a person must bring suit for damages for a claim listed in Subsection (b) against a registered or licensed architect, engineer, interior designer, or landscape architect in this state, who designs, plans, or inspects the construction of an improvement to real property or equipment attached to real property, not later than 10 years after the substantial completion of the improvement or the beginning of operation of the equipment in an action arising out of a defective or unsafe condition of the real property, the improvement, or the equipment.

(a–1) A governmental entity must bring suit for damages for a claim listed in Subsection (b) against a registered or licensed architect, engineer, interior designer, or landscape architect in this state, who designs, plans, or inspects the construction of an improvement to real property or equipment attached to real property, not later than eight years after the substantial completion of the improvement or the beginning of operation of the equipment in an action arising out of a defective or unsafe condition of the real property, the improvement, or the equipment. This subsection does not apply to a claim arising out of:

(1) a contract entered into by the Texas Department of Transportation;

(2) a project that receives money from the state highway fund or a federal fund designated for highway and mass transit spending; or

(3) a civil works project, as that term is defined under Section 2269.351, Government Code.

(b) This section applies to suit for:

(1) injury, damage, or loss to real or personal property;

(2) personal injury;

(3) wrongful death;

(4) contribution; or

(5) indemnity.

(c) If the claimant presents a written claim for damages, contribution, or indemnity to the architect, engineer, interior designer, or landscape architect within the applicable limitations period, the period is extended for:

(1) two years from the date the claim is presented, for a claim to which Subsection (a) applies; or

(2) one year from the date the claim is presented, for a claim to which Subsection (a–1) applies.

Acts 1985, 69th Leg., ch. 959, § 1, eff. Sept. 1, 1985. Amended by Acts 1997, 75th Leg., ch. 860, § 1, eff. Sept. 1, 1997; Acts 2021, 87th Leg., ch. 484 (H.B. 3069), § 1, eff. June 14, 2021.

Section 3 of Acts 2021, 87th Leg., ch. 484 (H.B. 3069) provides:

"(a) Except as provided by this section, Section 16.008, Civil Practice and Remedies Code, as amended by this Act, applies to a cause of action arising out of a design, plan, or inspection of the construction of an improvement to real property or equipment attached to real property that commences on or after the effective date [June 14, 2021] of this Act. Section 16.008, Civil Practice and Remedies Code, as amended by this Act, does not apply to a cause of action arising out of a design, plan, or inspection that commences on or after the effective date of this Act under a contract entered into before that date.

"(b) A cause of action arising out of a design, plan, or inspection of the construction of an improvement to real property or equipment attached to real property that commenced before the effective date of this Act or arising out of a design, plan, or inspection of the construction of an improvement to real property or equipment attached to real property that commences on or after the effective date of this Act under a contract entered into before that date is governed by the law applicable to the cause of action immediately before the effective date of this Act, and that law is continued in effect for that purpose."

§ 16.009. Persons Furnishing Construction or Repair of Improvements

(a) Except as provided by Subsection (a–1), a claimant must bring suit for damages for a claim listed in Subsection (b) against a person who constructs or repairs an improvement to real property not later than 10 years after the substantial completion of the improvement in an action arising out of a defective or unsafe condition of the real property or a deficiency in the construction or repair of the improvement.

(a–1) A governmental entity must bring suit for damages for a claim listed in Subsection (b) against a person who constructs or repairs an improvement to real property not later than eight years after the substantial completion of the improvement in an action arising out of a defective or unsafe condition of the real property or a deficiency in the construction or repair of the improvement. This subsection does not apply to a claim arising out of:

(1) a contract entered into by the Texas Department of Transportation;

(2) a project that receives money from the state highway fund or a federal fund designated for highway and mass transit spending; or

(3) a civil works project, as that term is defined under Section 2269.351, Government Code.

(b) This section applies to suit for:

(1) injury, damage, or loss to real or personal property;

(2) personal injury;

(3) wrongful death;

(4) contribution; or

(5) indemnity.

(c) If the claimant presents a written claim for damages, contribution, or indemnity to the person performing or furnishing the construction or repair work during the applicable limitations period, the period is extended for:

(1) two years from the date the claim is presented, for a claim to which Subsection (a) applies; or

(2) one year from the date the claim is presented, for a claim to which Subsection (a–1) applies.

(d) If the damage, injury, or death occurs during the last year of the applicable limitations period, the claimant may bring suit not later than two years after the day the cause of action accrues.

(e) This section does not bar an action:

(1) on a written warranty, guaranty, or other contract that expressly provides for a longer effective period;

(2) against a person in actual possession or control of the real property at the time that the damage, injury, or death occurs; or

(3) based on wilful misconduct or fraudulent concealment in connection with the performance of the construction or repair.

(f) This section does not extend or affect a period prescribed for bringing an action under any other law of this state.

Acts 1985, 69th Leg., ch. 959, § 1, eff. Sept. 1, 1985. Amended by Acts 2021, 87th Leg., ch. 484 (H.B. 3069), § 2, eff. June 14, 2021.

Section 4 of Acts 2021, 87th Leg., ch. 484 (H.B. 3069) provides:

"(a) Except as provided by this section, Section 16.009, Civil Practice and Remedies Code, as amended by this Act, applies to a cause of action arising out of construction or repair of an improvement to real property that commences on or after the effective date [June 14, 2021] of this Act. Section 16.009, Civil Practice and Remedies Code, as amended by this Act, does not apply to a cause of action arising out of construction or repair of an improvement to real property that commences on or after the effective date of this Act under a contract entered into before that date.

"(b) A cause of action arising out of construction or repair of an improvement to real property that commenced before the effective date of this Act or arising out of construction or repair of an improvement to real property that commences on or after the effective date of this Act under a contract entered into before that date is governed by the law applicable to the cause of action immediately before the effective date of this Act, and that law is continued in effect for that purpose."

§ 16.010. Misappropriation of Trade Secrets

(a) A person must bring suit for misappropriation of trade secrets not later than three years after the misappropriation is discovered or by the exercise of reasonable diligence should have been discovered.

(b) A misappropriation of trade secrets that continues over time is a single cause of action and the limitations period described by Subsection (a) begins running without regard to whether the misappropriation is a single or continuing act.

Added by Acts 1997, 75th Leg., ch. 26, § 1, eff. May 1, 1997.

§ 16.011. Surveyors

(a) A person must bring suit for damages arising from an injury or loss caused by an error in a survey conducted by a registered public surveyor or a licensed state land surveyor:

(1) not later than 10 years after the date the survey is completed if the survey is completed on or after September 1, 1989; or

(2) not later than September 1, 1991, or 10 years after the date the survey was completed, whichever is later, if the survey was completed before September 1, 1989.

(b) If the claimant presents a written claim for damages to the surveyor during the 10–year limitations period, the period is extended for two years from the date the claim is presented.

(c) This section is a statute of repose and is independent of any other limitations period.

Added by Acts 1989, 71st Leg., ch. 1233, § 1, eff. Sept. 1, 1989. Amended by Acts 2001, 77th Leg., ch. 1173, § 1, eff. Sept. 1, 2001.

§ 16.012. Products Liability

(a) In this section:

(1) "Claimant," "seller," and "manufacturer" have the meanings assigned by Section 82.001.

(2) "Products liability action" means any action against a manufacturer or seller for recovery of damages or other relief for harm allegedly caused

by a defective product, whether the action is based in strict tort liability, strict products liability, negligence, misrepresentation, breach of express or implied warranty, or any other theory or combination of theories, and whether the relief sought is recovery of damages or any other legal or equitable relief, including a suit for:

(A) injury or damage to or loss of real or personal property;

(B) personal injury;

(C) wrongful death;

(D) economic loss; or

(E) declaratory, injunctive, or other equitable relief.

(b) Except as provided by Subsections (c), (d), and (d–1), a claimant must commence a products liability action against a manufacturer or seller of a product before the end of 15 years after the date of the sale of the product by the defendant.

(c) If a manufacturer or seller expressly warrants in writing that the product has a useful safe life of longer than 15 years, a claimant must commence a products liability action against that manufacturer or seller of the product before the end of the number of years warranted after the date of the sale of the product by that seller.

(d) This section does not apply to a products liability action seeking damages for personal injury or wrongful death in which the claimant alleges:

(1) the claimant was exposed to the product that is the subject of the action before the end of 15 years after the date the product was first sold;

(2) the claimant's exposure to the product caused the claimant's disease that is the basis of the action; and

(3) the symptoms of the claimant's disease did not, before the end of 15 years after the date of the first sale of the product by the defendant, manifest themselves to a degree and for a duration that would put a reasonable person on notice that the person suffered some injury.

(d–1) This section does not reduce a limitations period for a cause of action described by Subsection (d) that accrues before the end of the limitations period under this section.

(e) This section does not extend the limitations period within which a products liability action involving the product may be commenced under any other law.

(f) This section applies only to the sale and not to the lease of a product.

(g) This section does not apply to any claim to which the General Aviation Revitalization Act of 1994 (Pub. L. No. 103–298, 108 Stat. 1552 (1994), reprinted in note, 49 U.S.C. Section 40101) or its exceptions are applicable.

Added by Acts 1993, 73rd Leg., ch. 5, § 2, eff. Sept. 1, 1993. Amended by Acts 2003, 78th Leg., ch. 204, § 5.01, eff. Sept. 1, 2003.

§ 16.013. Real Estate Appraisers and Appraisal Firms

(a) In this section:

(1) "Appraisal" has the meaning assigned by Section 1103.003, Occupations Code.

(2) "Appraisal review" has the meaning assigned by Section 1104.003, Occupations Code.

(3) "Real estate appraisal firm" means an entity engaging a real estate appraiser as an owner, member, shareholder, partner, employee, or independent contractor to perform an appraisal or appraisal review.

(4) "Real estate appraiser" means an individual licensed or certified under Chapter 1103, Occupations Code.

(b) Except for an action for fraud or breach of contract, a person must bring suit for damages or other relief arising from an appraisal or appraisal review conducted by a real estate appraiser or appraisal firm not later than the earlier of:

(1) two years after the day the person knew or should have known the facts on which the action is based; or

(2) five years after the day the appraisal or appraisal review was completed.

Added by Acts 2021, 87th Leg., ch. 328 (H.B. 1939), § 1, eff. Sept. 1, 2021.

Section 2 of Acts 2021, 87th Leg., ch. 328 (H.B. 1939) provides:

"Section 16.013, Civil Practice and Remedies Code, as added by this Act, applies only to a cause of action that accrues on or after the effective date [Sept. 1, 2021] of this Act."

SUBCHAPTER B. LIMITATIONS OF REAL PROPERTY ACTIONS

§ 16.021. Definitions

In this subchapter:

(1) "Adverse possession" means an actual and visible appropriation of real property, commenced and continued under a claim of right that is incon-

sistent with and is hostile to the claim of another person.

(2) "Color of title" means a consecutive chain of transfers to the person in possession that:

(A) is not regular because of a muniment that is not properly recorded or is only in writing or because of a similar defect that does not want of intrinsic fairness or honesty; or

(B) is based on a certificate of headright, land warrant, or land scrip.

(3) "Peaceable possession" means possession of real property that is continuous and is not interrupted by an adverse suit to recover the property.

(4) "Title" means a regular chain of transfers of real property from or under the sovereignty of the soil.

Acts 1985, 69th Leg., ch. 959, § 1, eff. Sept. 1, 1985.

§ 16.022. Effect of Disability

(a) For the purposes of this subchapter, a person is under a legal disability if the person is:

(1) younger than 18 years of age, regardless of whether the person is married;

(2) of unsound mind; or

(3) serving in the United States Armed Forces during time of war.

(b) If a person entitled to sue for the recovery of real property or entitled to make a defense based on the title to real property is under a legal disability at the time title to the property vests or adverse possession commences, the time of the disability is not included in a limitations period.

(c) Except as provided by Sections 16.027 and 16.028, after the termination of the legal disability, a person has the same time to present a claim that is allowed to others under this chapter.

Acts 1985, 69th Leg., ch. 959, § 1, eff. Sept. 1, 1985. Amended by Acts 1987, 70th Leg., ch. 1049, § 57, eff. Sept. 1, 1987.

§ 16.023. Tacking of Successive Interests

To satisfy a limitations period, peaceable and adverse possession does not need to continue in the same person, but there must be privity of estate between each holder and his successor.

Acts 1985, 69th Leg., ch. 959, § 1, eff. Sept. 1, 1985.

§ 16.024. Adverse Possession: Three-Year Limitations Period

A person must bring suit to recover real property held by another in peaceable and adverse possession under title or color of title not later than three years after the day the cause of action accrues.

Acts 1985, 69th Leg., ch. 959, § 1, eff. Sept. 1, 1985.

§ 16.025. Adverse Possession: Five-Year Limitations Period

(a) A person must bring suit not later than five years after the day the cause of action accrues to recover real property held in peaceable and adverse possession by another who:

(1) cultivates, uses, or enjoys the property;

(2) pays applicable taxes on the property; and

(3) claims the property under a duly registered deed.

(b) This section does not apply to a claim based on a quitclaim deed, a forged deed, or a deed executed under a forged power of attorney.

Acts 1985, 69th Leg., ch. 959, § 1, eff. Sept. 1, 1985. Amended by Acts 2021, 87th Leg., ch. 94 (S.B. 885), § 1, eff. Sept. 1, 2021.

Section 3 of Acts 2021, 87th Leg., ch. 94 (S.B. 885) provides:

"The change in law made by this Act applies only to a quitclaim deed recorded on or after the effective date [Sept. 1, 2021] of this Act. A quitclaim deed recorded before that date is governed by the law in effect immediately before the effective date of this Act, and that law is continued in effect for that purpose."

§ 16.026. Adverse Possession: 10-Year Limitations Period

(a) A person must bring suit not later than 10 years after the day the cause of action accrues to recover real property held in peaceable and adverse possession by another who cultivates, uses, or enjoys the property.

(b) Without a title instrument, peaceable and adverse possession is limited in this section to 160 acres, including improvements, unless the number of acres actually enclosed exceeds 160. If the number of enclosed acres exceeds 160 acres, peaceable and adverse possession extends to the real property actually enclosed.

(c) Peaceable possession of real property held under a duly registered deed or other memorandum of title that fixes the boundaries of the possessor's claim extends to the boundaries specified in the instrument.

Acts 1985, 69th Leg., ch. 959, § 1, eff. Sept. 1, 1985. Amended by Acts 1989, 71st Leg., ch. 764, § 1, eff. Sept. 1, 1989.

§ 16.0265. Adverse Possession by Cotenant Heir: 15–Year Combined Limitations Period

(a) In this section, "cotenant heir" means one of two or more persons who simultaneously acquire identical, undivided ownership interests in, and rights to possession of, the same real property by operation of the applicable intestate succession laws of this state or a successor in interest of one of those persons.

(b) One or more cotenant heirs of real property may acquire the interests of other cotenant heirs in the property by adverse possession under this section if, for a continuous, uninterrupted 10–year period immediately preceding the filing of the affidavits required by Subsection (c):

(1) the possessing cotenant heir or heirs:

(A) hold the property in peaceable and exclusive possession;

(B) cultivate, use, or enjoy the property; and

(C) pay all property taxes on the property not later than two years after the date the taxes become due; and

(2) no other cotenant heir has:

(A) contributed to the property's taxes or maintenance;

(B) challenged a possessing cotenant heir's exclusive possession of the property;

(C) asserted any other claim against a possessing cotenant heir in connection with the property, such as the right to rental payments from a possessing cotenant heir;

(D) acted to preserve the cotenant heir's interest in the property by filing notice of the cotenant heir's claimed interest in the deed records of the county in which the property is located; or

(E) entered into a written agreement with the possessing cotenant heir under which the possessing cotenant heir is allowed to possess the property but the other cotenant heir does not forfeit that heir's ownership interest.

(c) To make a claim of adverse possession against a cotenant heir under this section, the cotenant heir or heirs claiming adverse possession must:

(1) file in the deed records of the county in which the real property is located an affidavit of heirship in the form prescribed by Section 203.002, Estates Code, and an affidavit of adverse possession that complies with the requirements of Subsection (d);

(2) publish notice of the claim in a newspaper of general circulation in the county in which the property is located for the four consecutive weeks immediately following the date the affidavits required by Subdivision (1) are filed; and

(3) provide written notice of the claim to the last known addresses of all other cotenant heirs by certified mail, return receipt requested.

(d) The affidavits required by Subsection (c) may be filed separately or combined into a single instrument. The affidavit of adverse possession must include:

(1) a legal description of the property that is the subject of the adverse possession;

(2) an attestation that each affiant is a cotenant heir of the property who has been in peaceable and exclusive possession of the property for a continuous, uninterrupted period during the 10 years preceding the filing of the affidavit;

(3) an attestation of cultivation, use, or enjoyment of the property by each affiant during the 10 years preceding the filing of the affidavit;

(4) evidence of payment by the affiant or affiants of all property taxes on the property as provided by Subsection (b) during the 10 years preceding the filing of the affidavit; and

(5) an attestation that there has been no action described by Subsection (b)(2) by another cotenant heir during the 10 years preceding the filing of the affidavit.

(e) A cotenant heir must file a controverting affidavit or bring suit to recover the cotenant heir's interest in real property adversely possessed by another cotenant heir under this section not later than the fifth anniversary of the date a right of adverse possession is asserted by the filing of the affidavits required by Subsection (c).

(f) If a controverting affidavit or judgment is not filed before the fifth anniversary of the date the affidavits required by Subsection (c) are filed and no notice described by Subsection (b)(2)(D) was filed in the 10–year period preceding the filing of the affidavits under Subsection (c), title vests in the adversely possessing cotenant heir or heirs in the manner provided by Section 16.030, precluding all claims by other cotenant heirs.

(g) A bona fide lender for value without notice accepting a voluntary lien against the real property to secure the adversely possessing cotenant heir's indebtedness or a bona fide purchaser for value without notice may conclusively rely on the affidavits required by Subsection (c) if:

(1) the affidavits have been filed of record for the period prescribed by Subsection (e); and

(2) a controverting affidavit or judgment has not been filed during that period.

(h) Without a title instrument, peaceable and adverse possession is limited in this section to 160 acres, including improvements, unless the number of acres actually enclosed exceeds 160 acres. If the number of enclosed acres exceeds 160 acres, peaceable and adverse possession extends to the real property actually enclosed.

(i) Peaceable possession of real property held under a duly registered deed or other memorandum of title that fixes the boundaries of the possessor's claim extends to the boundaries specified in the instrument.

Added by Acts 2017, 85th Leg., ch. 742 (S.B. 1249), § 1, eff. Sept. 1, 2017.

§ 16.027. Adverse Possession: 25-Year Limitations Period Notwithstanding Disability

A person, regardless of whether the person is or has been under a legal disability, must bring suit not later than 25 years after the day the cause of action accrues to recover real property held in peaceable and adverse possession by another who cultivates, uses, or enjoys the property.

Acts 1985, 69th Leg., ch. 959, § 1, eff. Sept. 1, 1985.

§ 16.028. Adverse Possession with Recorded Instrument: 25-Year Limitations Period

(a) A person, regardless of whether the person is or has been under a legal disability, may not maintain an action for the recovery of real property held for 25 years before the commencement of the action in peaceable and adverse possession by another who holds the property in good faith and under a deed or other instrument purporting to convey the property that is recorded in the deed records of the county where any part of the real property is located.

(b) Adverse possession of any part of the real property held under a recorded deed or other recorded instrument that purports to convey the property extends to and includes all of the property described in the instrument, even though the instrument is void on its face or in fact.

(c) A person who holds real property and claims title under this section has a good and marketable title to the property regardless of a disability arising at any time in the adverse claimant or a person claiming under the adverse claimant.

Acts 1985, 69th Leg., ch. 959, § 1, eff. Sept. 1, 1985.

§ 16.029. Evidence of Title to Land by Limitations

(a) In a suit involving title to real property that is not claimed by this state, it is prima facie evidence that the title to the property has passed from the person holding apparent record title to an opposing party if it is shown that:

(1) for one or more years during the 25 years preceding the filing of the suit the person holding apparent record title to the property did not exercise dominion over or pay taxes on the property; and

(2) during that period the opposing parties and those whose estate they own have openly exercised dominion over and have asserted a claim to the land and have paid taxes on it annually before becoming delinquent for as long as 25 years.

(b) This section does not affect a statute of limitations, a right to prove title by circumstantial evidence under the case law of this state, or a suit between a trustee and a beneficiary of the trust.

Acts 1985, 69th Leg., ch. 959, § 1, eff. Sept. 1, 1985.

§ 16.030. Title Through Adverse Possession

(a) If an action for the recovery of real property is barred under this chapter, the person who holds the property in peaceable and adverse possession has full title, precluding all claims.

(b) A person may not acquire through adverse possession any right or title to real property dedicated to public use.

Acts 1985, 69th Leg., ch. 959, § 1, eff. Sept. 1, 1985.

§ 16.031. Enclosed Land

(a) A tract of land that is owned by one person and that is entirely surrounded by land owned, claimed, or fenced by another is not considered enclosed by a fence that encloses any part of the surrounding land.

(b) Possession of the interior tract by the owner or claimant of the surrounding land is not peaceable and adverse possession as described by Section 16.026 unless:

(1) the interior tract is separated from the surrounding land by a fence; or

(2) at least one-tenth of the interior tract is cultivated and used for agricultural purposes or is used for manufacturing purposes.

Acts 1985, 69th Leg., ch. 959, § 1, eff. Sept. 1, 1985.

§ 16.032. Adjacent Land

Possession of land that belongs to another by a person owning or claiming 5,000 or more fenced acres that adjoin the land is not peaceable and adverse as described by Section 16.026 unless:

(1) the land is separated from the adjacent enclosed tract by a substantial fence;

(2) at least one-tenth of the land is cultivated and used for agricultural purposes or used for manufacturing purposes; or

(3) there is actual possession of the land.

Acts 1985, 69th Leg., ch. 959, § 1, eff. Sept. 1, 1985.

§ 16.033. Technical Defects in Instrument

(a) A person with a right of action for the recovery of real property or an interest in real property conveyed by an instrument with one of the following defects must bring suit not later than two years after the day the instrument was filed for record with the county clerk of the county where the real property is located:

(1) lack of the signature of a proper corporate officer, partner, or company officer, manager, or member;

(2) lack of a corporate seal;

(3) failure of the record to show the corporate seal used;

(4) failure of the record to show authority of the board of directors or stockholders of a corporation, partners of a partnership, or officers, managers, or members of a company;

(5) execution and delivery of the instrument by a corporation, partnership, or other company that had been dissolved, whose charter had expired, or whose franchise had been canceled, withdrawn, or forfeited;

(6) acknowledgment of the instrument in an individual, rather than a representative or official, capacity;

(7) execution of the instrument by a trustee without record of the authority of the trustee or proof of the facts recited in the instrument;

(8) failure of the record or instrument to show an acknowledgment or jurat that complies with applicable law; or

(9) wording of the stated consideration that may or might create an implied lien in favor of the grantor.

(b) This section does not apply to a forged instrument.

(c) For the purposes of this section, an instrument affecting real property containing a ministerial defect, omission, or informality in the certificate of acknowledgment that has been filed for record for longer than two years in the office of the county recorder of the county in which the property is located is considered to have been lawfully recorded and to be notice of the existence of the instrument on and after the date the instrument is filed.

Acts 1985, 69th Leg., ch. 959, § 1, eff. Sept. 1, 1985. Amended by Acts 1993, 73rd Leg., ch. 291, § 1, eff. Sept. 1, 1993; Acts 2007, 80th Leg., ch. 819, § 1, eff. June 15, 2007.

§ 16.034. Attorney's Fees

(a) In a suit for the possession of real property between a person claiming under record title to the property and one claiming by adverse possession, if the prevailing party recovers possession of the property from a person unlawfully in actual possession, the court:

(1) shall award costs and reasonable attorney's fees to the prevailing party if the court finds that the person unlawfully in actual possession made a claim of adverse possession that was groundless and made in bad faith; and

(2) may award costs and reasonable attorney's fees to the prevailing party in the absence of a finding described by Subdivision (1).

(b) To recover attorney's fees, the person seeking possession must give the person unlawfully in possession a written demand for that person to vacate the premises. The demand must be given by registered or certified mail at least 10 days before filing the claim for recovery of possession.

(c) The demand must state that if the person unlawfully in possession does not vacate the premises within 10 days and a claim is filed by the person seeking possession, the court may enter a judgment against the person unlawfully in possession for costs and attorney's fees in an amount determined by the court to be reasonable.

Acts 1985, 69th Leg., ch. 959, § 1, eff. Sept. 1, 1985. Amended by Acts 2009, 81st Leg., ch. 901, § 1, eff. Sept. 1, 2009.

§ 16.035. Lien on Real Property

(a) A person must bring suit for the recovery of real property under a real property lien or the foreclosure of a real property lien not later than four years after the day the cause of action accrues.

(b) A sale of real property under a power of sale in a mortgage or deed of trust that creates a real property lien must be made not later than four years after the day the cause of action accrues.

(c) The running of the statute of limitations is not suspended against a bona fide purchaser for value, a lienholder, or a lessee who has no notice or knowledge of the suspension of the limitations period and who acquires an interest in the property when a cause of action on an outstanding real property lien has accrued for more than four years, except as provided by:

(1) Section 16.062, providing for suspension in the event of death; or

(2) Section 16.036, providing for recorded extensions of real property liens.

(d) On the expiration of the four-year limitations period, the real property lien and a power of sale to enforce the real property lien become void.

(e) If a series of notes or obligations or a note or obligation payable in installments is secured by a real property lien, the four-year limitations period does not begin to run until the maturity date of the last note, obligation, or installment.

(f) The limitations period under this section is not affected by Section 3.118, Business & Commerce Code.

(g) In this section, "real property lien" means:

(1) a superior title retained by a vendor in a deed of conveyance or a purchase money note; or

(2) a vendor's lien, a mortgage, a deed of trust, a voluntary mechanic's lien, or a voluntary materialman's lien on real estate, securing a note or other written obligation.

Acts 1985, 69th Leg., ch. 959, § 1, eff. Sept. 1, 1985. Amended by Acts 1997, 75th Leg., ch. 219, § 1, eff. May 23, 1997.

§ 16.036. Extension of Real Property Lien

(a) The party or parties primarily liable for a debt or obligation secured by a real property lien, as that term is defined in Section 16.035, may suspend the running of the four-year limitations period for real property liens through a written extension agreement as provided by this section.

(b) The limitations period is suspended and the lien remains in effect for four years after the extended maturity date of the debt or obligation if the extension agreement is:

(1) signed and acknowledged as provided by law for a deed conveying real property; and

(2) filed for record in the county clerk's office of the county where the real property is located.

(c) The parties may continue to extend the lien by entering, acknowledging, and recording additional extension agreements.

(d) The maturity date stated in the original instrument or in the date of the recorded renewal and extension is conclusive evidence of the maturity date of the debt or obligation.

(e) The limitations period under this section is not affected by Section 3.118, Business & Commerce Code.

Acts 1985, 69th Leg., ch. 959, § 1, eff. Sept. 1, 1985. Amended by Acts 1997, 75th Leg., ch. 219, § 2, eff. May 23, 1997.

§ 16.037. Effect of Extension of Real Property Lien on Third Parties

An extension agreement is void as to a bona fide purchaser for value, a lienholder, or a lessee who deals with real property affected by a real property lien without actual notice of the agreement and before the agreement is acknowledged, filed, and recorded.

Acts 1985, 69th Leg., ch. 959, § 1, eff. Sept. 1, 1985. Amended by Acts 1997, 75th Leg., ch. 219, § 3, eff. May 23, 1997.

§ 16.038. Rescission or Waiver of Accelerated Maturity Date

(a) If the maturity date of a series of notes or obligations or a note or obligation payable in installments is accelerated, and the accelerated maturity date is rescinded or waived in accordance with this section before the limitations period expires, the acceleration is deemed rescinded and waived and the note, obligation, or series of notes or obligations shall be governed by Section 16.035 as if no acceleration had occurred.

(b) Rescission or waiver of acceleration is effective if made by a written notice of a rescission or waiver served as provided in Subsection (c) by the lienholder, the servicer of the debt, or an attorney representing the lienholder on each debtor who, according to the records of the lienholder or the servicer of the debt, is obligated to pay the debt.

(c) Service of a notice under Subsection (b) must be by first class or certified mail and is complete when the notice is deposited in the United States mail, postage prepaid and addressed to the debtor at the debtor's last known address. The affidavit of a person knowledgeable of the facts to the effect that service was completed is prima facie evidence of service.

(d) A notice served under this section does not affect a lienholder's right to accelerate the maturity date of the debt in the future nor does it waive past defaults.

(e) This section does not create an exclusive method for waiver and rescission of acceleration or affect the accrual of a cause of action and the running of the related limitations period under Section 16.035(e) on any subsequent maturity date, accelerated or otherwise, of the note or obligation or series of notes or obligations.

Added by Acts 2015, 84th Leg., ch. 759 (H.B. 2067), § 1, eff. June 17, 2015.

SUBCHAPTER C. RESIDUAL LIMITATIONS PERIOD

§ 16.051. Residual Limitations Period

Every action for which there is no express limitations period, except an action for the recovery of real property, must be brought not later than four years after the day the cause of action accrues.

Acts 1985, 69th Leg., ch. 959, § 1, eff. Sept. 1, 1985.

SUBCHAPTER D. MISCELLANEOUS PROVISIONS

§ 16.061. Rights Not Barred

(a) A right of action of this state or a political subdivision of the state, including a county, an incorporated city or town, a navigation district, a municipal utility district, a port authority, an entity acting under Chapter 54, Transportation Code, a school district, or an entity created under Section 52, Article III, or Section 59, Article XVI, Texas Constitution, is not barred by any of the following sections: 16.001–16.004, 16.006, 16.007, 16.021–16.028, 16.030–16.032, 16.035–16.037, 16.051, 16.062, 16.063, 16.065–16.067, 16.070, 16.071, 31.006, or 71.021.

(b) In this section:

(1) "Navigation district" means a navigation district organized under Section 52, Article III, or Section 59, Article XVI, Texas Constitution.

(2) "Port authority" has the meaning assigned by Section 60.402, Water Code.

(3) "Municipal utility district" means a municipal utility district created under Section 52, Article III, or Section 59, Article XVI, Texas Constitution.

Acts 1985, 69th Leg., ch. 959, § 1, eff. Sept. 1, 1985. Amended by Acts 1989, 71st Leg., ch. 2, § 4.02, eff. Aug. 28, 1989; Acts 1993, 73rd Leg., ch. 782, § 1, eff. Aug. 30, 1993; Acts 1997, 75th Leg., ch. 1070, § 47, eff. Sept. 1, 1997; Acts 2001, 77th Leg., ch. 1420, § 8.204, eff. Sept. 1, 2001.

§ 16.062. Effect of Death

(a) The death of a person against whom or in whose favor there may be a cause of action suspends the running of an applicable statute of limitations for 12 months after the death.

(b) If an executor or administrator of a decedent's estate qualifies before the expiration of the period provided by this section, the statute of limitations begins to run at the time of the qualification.

Acts 1985, 69th Leg., ch. 959, § 1, eff. Sept. 1, 1985.

§ 16.063. Temporary Absence From State

The absence from this state of a person against whom a cause of action may be maintained suspends the running of the applicable statute of limitations for the period of the person's absence.

Acts 1985, 69th Leg., ch. 959, § 1, eff. Sept. 1, 1985.

§ 16.064. Effect of Lack of Jurisdiction

(a) The period between the date of filing an action in a trial court and the date of a second filing of the same action in a different court suspends the running of the applicable statute of limitations for the period if:

(1) because of lack of jurisdiction in the trial court where the action was first filed, the action is dismissed or the judgment is set aside or annulled in a direct proceeding; and

(2) not later than the 60th day after the date the dismissal or other disposition becomes final, the action is commenced in a court of proper jurisdiction.

(b) This section does not apply if the adverse party has shown in abatement that the first filing was made with intentional disregard of proper jurisdiction.

Acts 1985, 69th Leg., ch. 959, § 1, eff. Sept. 1, 1985.

§ 16.065. Acknowledgment of Claim

An acknowledgment of the justness of a claim that appears to be barred by limitations is not admissible in evidence to defeat the law of limitations if made after the time that the claim is due unless the acknowledgment is in writing and is signed by the party to be charged.

Acts 1985, 69th Leg., ch. 959, § 1, eff. Sept. 1, 1985.

§ 16.066. Action on Foreign Judgment

(a) An action on a foreign judgment is barred in this state if the action is barred under the laws of the jurisdiction where rendered.

(b) An action against a person who has resided in this state for 10 years prior to the action may not be brought on a foreign judgment rendered more than 10 years before the commencement of the action in this state.

(c) In this section "foreign judgment" means a judgment or decree rendered in another state or a foreign country.

Acts 1985, 69th Leg., ch. 959, § 1, eff. Sept. 1, 1985.

§ 16.067. Claim Incurred Prior to Arrival in This State

(a) A person may not bring an action to recover a claim against a person who has moved to this state if the claim is barred by the law of limitations of the state or country from which the person came.

(b) A person may not bring an action to recover money from a person who has moved to this state and who was released from its payment by the bankruptcy or insolvency laws of the state or country from which the person came.

(c) A demand that is against a person who has moved to this state and was incurred prior to his arrival in this state is not barred by the law of limitations until the person has lived in this state for 12 months. This subsection does not affect the application of Subsections (a) and (b).

Acts 1985, 69th Leg., ch. 959, § 1, eff. Sept. 1, 1985.

§ 16.068. Amended and Supplemental Pleadings

025' If a filed pleading relates to a cause of action, cross action, counterclaim, or defense that is not subject to a plea of limitation when the pleading is filed, a subsequent amendment or supplement to the pleading that changes the facts or grounds of liability or defense is not subject to a plea of limitation unless the amendment or supplement is wholly based on a new, distinct, or different transaction or occurrence.

Acts 1985, 69th Leg., ch. 959, § 1, eff. Sept. 1, 1985.

§ 16.069. Counterclaim or Cross Claim

(a) If a counterclaim or cross claim arises out of the same transaction or occurrence that is the basis of an action, a party to the action may file the counterclaim or cross claim even though as a separate action it would be barred by limitation on the date the party's answer is required.

(b) The counterclaim or cross claim must be filed not later than the 30th day after the date on which the party's answer is required.

Acts 1985, 69th Leg., ch. 959, § 1, eff. Sept. 1, 1985.

§ 16.070. Contractual Limitations Period

(a) Except as provided by Subsection (b), a person may not enter a stipulation, contract, or agreement that purports to limit the time in which to bring suit on the stipulation, contract, or agreement to a period shorter than two years. A stipulation, contract, or agreement that establishes a limitations period that is shorter than two years is void in this state.

(b) This section does not apply to a stipulation, contract, or agreement relating to the sale or purchase of a business entity if a party to the stipulation, contract, or agreement pays or receives or is obligated to pay or entitled to receive consideration under the stipulation, contract, or agreement having an aggregate value of not less than $500,000.

Acts 1985, 69th Leg., ch. 959, § 1, eff. Sept. 1, 1985. Amended by Acts 1991, 72nd Leg., ch. 840, § 2, eff. Aug. 26, 1991.

§ 16.071. Notice Requirements

(a) A contract stipulation that requires a claimant to give notice of a claim for damages as a condition precedent to the right to sue on the contract is not valid unless the stipulation is reasonable. A stipulation that requires notification within less than 90 days is void.

(b) If notice is required, the claimant may notify any convenient agent of the company that requires the notice.

(c) A contract stipulation between the operator of a railroad, street railway, or interurban railroad and an employee or servant of the operator is void if it requires as a condition precedent to liability:

TX: just need SOME overlap for (w/ OG petition) relation back to apply (not "wholly based").

(1) the employee or servant to notify the system of a claim for damages for personal injury caused by negligence; or

(2) the spouse, parent, or child of a deceased employee or servant to notify the system of a claim of death caused by negligence.

(d) This section applies to a contract between a federal prime contractor and a subcontractor, except that the notice period stipulated in the subcontract may be for a period not less than the period stipulated in the prime contract, minus seven days.

(e) In a suit covered by this section or Section 16.070, it is presumed that any required notice has been given unless lack of notice is specifically pleaded under oath.

(f) This section does not apply to a contract relating to the sale or purchase of a business entity if a party to the contract pays or receives or is obligated to pay or receive consideration under the contract having an aggregate value of not less than $500,000.

Acts 1985, 69th Leg., ch. 959, § 1, eff. Sept. 1, 1985. Amended by Acts 1991, 72nd Leg., ch. 840, § 3, eff. Aug. 26, 1991.

§ 16.072. Saturday, Sunday, or Holiday

If the last day of a limitations period under any statute of limitations falls on a Saturday, Sunday, or holiday, the period for filing suit is extended to include the next day that the county offices are open for business.

Acts 1985, 69th Leg., ch. 959, § 1, eff. Sept. 1, 1985.

CHAPTER 17. PARTIES; CITATION; LONG-ARM JURISDICTION

SUBCHAPTER A. PARTIES TO SUIT

SUBCHAPTER B. CITATION GENERALLY

SUBCHAPTER C. LONG-ARM JURISDICTION IN SUIT ON BUSINESS TRANSACTION OR TORT

SUBCHAPTER D. LONG-ARM JURISDICTION OVER NONRESIDENT MOTOR VEHICLE OPERATOR

SUBCHAPTER E. CITATION OF NONRESIDENTS—MISCELLANEOUS PROVISIONS

SUBCHAPTER A. PARTIES TO SUIT

§ 17.001. Suit on Contract with Several Obligors or Parties Conditionally Liable

(a) Except as provided by this section, the acceptor of a bill of exchange or a principal obligor on a contract may be sued alone or jointly with another liable party, but a judgment may not be rendered against a party not primarily liable unless judgment is also rendered against the principal obligor.

(b) The assignor, endorser, guarantor, or surety on a contract or the drawer of an accepted bill may be sued without suing the maker, acceptor, or other principal obligor, or a suit against the principal obligor may be discontinued, if the principal obligor:

(1) is a nonresident or resides in a place where he cannot be reached by the ordinary process of law;

(2) resides in a place that is unknown and cannot be ascertained by the use of reasonable diligence;

(3) is dead; or

(4) is actually or notoriously insolvent.

Acts 1985, 69th Leg., ch. 959, § 1, eff. Sept. 1, 1985.

§ 17.002. Suit Against Estate for Land Title

In a suit against the estate of a decedent involving the title to real property, the executor or administrator, if any, and the heirs must be made parties defendant.

Acts 1985, 69th Leg., ch. 959, § 1, eff. Sept. 1, 1985.

§ 17.003. Suit Against Nonresident or Transient Property Owner

For the purpose of establishing title to property, settling a lien or encumbrance on property, or determining an estate, interest, lien, or encumbrance, a person who claims an interest in the property may sue another person who claims an adverse interest or a lien or encumbrance but resides outside this state, resides in an unknown place, or is a transient. The plaintiff is not required to have actual possession of the property.

Acts 1985, 69th Leg., ch. 959, § 1, eff. Sept. 1, 1985.

§ 17.004. Suit Against Unknown Heirs or Unknown Stockholders of Defunct Corporation

A person with a claim against property that has accrued to or been granted to the unknown heirs of a deceased individual or the unknown stockholders of a defunct corporation may sue the heirs or stockholders or their heirs or representatives. The action must describe the defendants as the heirs of the named deceased individual or the unknown stockholders of the named corporation.

Acts 1985, 69th Leg., ch. 959, § 1, eff. Sept. 1, 1985.

§ 17.005. Suit Against Unknown Landowner

(a) A person may sue the unknown owner or claimant of an interest in land if:

(1) the person bringing suit claims ownership of an interest in the land or has a claim or cause of action related to the land against the unknown owner or claimant; and

(2) the unknown owner or claimant:

(A) takes or holds the beneficial interest under a conveyance, lease, or written contract that conveyed an interest in the land to a trustee without disclosing the name of the owner of the beneficial interest; or

(B) takes or holds the interest of a dissolved association, joint-stock company, partnership, or other organization under an instrument that did not disclose his name, and the organization had acquired the interest under a conveyance, lease, or written contract that conveyed the interest to the organization in its name without disclosing the names of the members, shareholders, partners, or other persons owning an interest in the organization.

(b) A person may not sue the unknown stockholders of a corporation under this section, but if the plaintiff did not know that the organization was incorporated and the corporate character of the organization was not disclosed in the instrument under which title was acquired, the court retains jurisdiction over the unknown owners even if the organization was in fact incorporated.

Acts 1985, 69th Leg., ch. 959, § 1, eff. Sept. 1, 1985.

SUBCHAPTER B. CITATION GENERALLY

§ 17.021. Service on Certain Noncorporate Business Agents

(a) In an action against an individual, partnership, or unincorporated association that arises in a county in which the individual, partnership, or association has an office, place of business, or agency for transacting business in this state, citation or other civil process may be served on an agent or clerk employed in the office, place of business, or agency if:

(1) the action grows out of or is connected with the business transacted in this state; and

(2) the individual, partnership, or association:

(A) is not a resident of the county;

(B) is not a resident of this state; or

(C) is a resident of the county but has not been found for service of process.

(b) To serve process on an agent or clerk under Subsection (a)(2)(C), the officer making the return of unexecuted process must certify that after diligent search and inquiry the individual, partnership, or association cannot be found and served. The process in the suit may be served on the agent or clerk in any succeeding term of court.

(c) Service of process on an agent or clerk under this section has the effect of personal service on the principal individual, partnership, or unincorporated association and subjects the principal's nonexempt property to the jurisdiction and judgment of the court.

(d) If service is made under this section, a default judgment may not be rendered in the action before the 21st day after the date of service.

(e) Service of process under this section is in addition to other methods of service.

(f) This section does not affect venue.

Acts 1985, 69th Leg., ch. 959, § 1, eff. Sept. 1, 1985.

§ 17.022. Service on Partnership

Citation served on one member of a partnership authorizes a judgment against the partnership and the partner actually served.

Acts 1985, 69th Leg., ch. 959, § 1, eff. Sept. 1, 1985.

§ 17.023. Service on Joint-Stock Association

(a) In an action against a joint-stock association, citation may be served by:

(1) serving the president, vice-president, secretary, cashier, assistant cashier, or treasurer of the association;

(2) serving the local agent of the association in the county in which the suit is brought; or

(3) leaving a copy of the citation at the principal office of the association during office hours.

(b) If no officer on whom citation may be served resides in the county in which suit is brought and the association has no agent in that county, citation may be served on any agent representing the association in this state.

Acts 1985, 69th Leg., ch. 959, § 1, eff. Sept. 1, 1985. Amended by Acts 1987, 70th Leg., ch. 288, § 1, eff. Aug. 31, 1987.

§ 17.024. Service on Political Subdivision

(a) In a suit against a county, citation must be served on the county judge.

(b) In a suit against an incorporated city, town, or village, citation may be served on the mayor, clerk, secretary, or treasurer.

(c) In a suit against a school district, citation may be served on the president of the school board or on the superintendent.

Acts 1985, 69th Leg., ch. 959, § 1, eff. Sept. 1, 1985.

§ 17.025. Assessment of Postage Cost for Mail Service

(a) If a public official is required or permitted by law to serve legal process by mail, including process in a suit for delinquent taxes, the official may:

(1) collect advance payment for the actual cost of the postage required to serve or deliver the process; or

(2) assess the expense of postage as costs.

(b) Charges under this section are in addition to other charges allowed by law for services performed by the official serving the process.

Acts 1985, 69th Leg., ch. 959, § 1, eff. Sept. 1, 1985.

§ 17.026. Service on Secretary of State

(a) In an action in which citation may be served on the secretary of state, service may be made by certified mail, return receipt requested, by the clerk of the court in which the case is pending or by the party or the representative of the party.

(b) The method of service of citation provided by this section is in addition to any other method authorized by statute or the Texas Rules of Civil Procedure for service on the secretary of state.

Added by Acts 1987, 70th Leg., ch. 954, § 1, eff. Sept. 1, 1987.

§ 17.027. Preparation and Service

(a) The plaintiff or his attorney may prepare the appropriate citation for the defendant.

(b) The citation must be in the form prescribed by the Texas Rules of Civil Procedure.

(c) The citation shall be served in the manner prescribed by law.

(d) The plaintiff or his attorney shall comply with the applicable Texas Rules of Civil Procedure governing preparation and issuance of citation.

(e) Repealed by Acts 1997, 75th Leg., ch. 976, § 5, eff. Sept. 1, 1997.

Added by Acts 1987, 70th Leg., ch. 663, § 1, eff. Sept. 1, 1987. Amended by Acts 1997, 75th Leg., ch. 976, § 5, eff. Sept. 1, 1997.

§ 17.028. Service on Financial Institutions

(a) In this section, "financial institution" has the meaning assigned by Section 201.101, Finance Code.

(b) Except as provided by Subsection (c), citation may be served on a financial institution by:

(1) serving the registered agent of the financial institution; or

(2) if the financial institution does not have a registered agent, serving the president or a branch manager at any office located in this state.

(c) Citation may be served on a credit union by:

(1) serving the registered agent of the credit union; or

(2) if the credit union does not have a registered agent, serving the president or vice president.

(d) If citation has not been properly served as provided by this section, a financial institution may maintain an action to set aside the default judgment or any sanctions entered against the financial institution.

(e) A citation served on a credit union that is located in a place of worship may not be served during a worship service.

(f) Service on and delivery to a financial institution of claims against a customer of the financial institution are governed by Section 59.008, Finance Code.

Added by Acts 2007, 80th Leg., ch. 244, § 1, eff. Sept. 1, 2007. Amended by Acts 2013, 83rd Leg., ch. 5 (S.B. 422), § 1, eff. May 2, 2013.

§ 17.029. Service on Inmate of Texas Department of Criminal Justice

(a) In this section, "inmate" means a person confined in a facility operated by or under contract with the Texas Department of Criminal Justice.

(b) In a civil action against an inmate, citation or other civil process may be served on the inmate by serving a person designated under Subsection (c) as an agent for service of civil process.

(c) The warden of each facility operated by or under contract with the Texas Department of Criminal Justice shall designate an employee at the facility to serve as an agent for service of civil process on inmates confined in the facility.

(d) An employee designated under Subsection (c) as an agent for service of civil process shall promptly deliver any civil process served on the employee to the appropriate inmate.

Added by Acts 2011, 82nd Leg., ch. 267 (H.B. 1381), § 1, eff. Sept. 1, 2011.

§ 17.030. Return of Service

(a) The supreme court shall adopt rules of civil procedure requiring a person who serves process to complete a return of service.

(b) The rules:

(1) must provide that the return of service:

(A) is not required to be endorsed or attached to the original process issued; and

(B) may be electronically filed; and

(2) may require that the following information be included in the return of service:

(A) the cause number and case name;

(B) the court in which the case has been filed;

(C) the date and time process was received for service;

(D) the person or entity served;

(E) the address served;

(F) the date of service;

(G) the manner of delivery of service;

(H) a description of process served;

(I) the name of the person serving process; and

(J) if the process server is certified as a process server by the supreme court, the process server's identification number.

(c) A person certified by the supreme court as a process server or a person authorized outside of Texas to serve process shall sign the return of service under penalty of perjury. The return of service is not required to be verified.

(d) A person who knowingly or intentionally falsifies a return of service may be prosecuted for tampering with a governmental record as provided by Chapter 37, Penal Code.

Added by Acts 2011, 82nd Leg., ch. 245 (H.B. 962), § 1, eff. Jan. 1, 2012.

§ 17.031. Expedited Foreclosure Proceedings

For a power of sale exercised by the filing of an application for an expedited court order allowing the foreclosure of a contract lien under the Texas Rules of Civil Procedure 736, service of citation shall be completed in accordance with Rule 736 or 106, Texas Rules of Civil Procedure, or in any other manner provided for petitions under the Texas Rules of Civil Procedure.

Added by Acts 2013, 83rd Leg., ch. 1044 (H.B. 2978), § 1, eff. June 14, 2013.

§ 17.032. Citation by Publication

(a) Notwithstanding any statute or rule requiring a person to publish citation or notice on the public information Internet website maintained as required by Section 72.034, Government Code, and in a newspaper of general circulation, the person may publish the citation or notice only on the public information Internet website if:

(1) the person files a statement of inability to afford payment of court costs under the Texas Rules of Civil Procedure;

(2) the total cost of the required publication exceeds the greater of $200 each week or the amount set by the supreme court under Subsection (b); or

(3) the county in which the publication of the citation or notice is required does not have any newspaper published, printed, or generally circulated in the county.

(b) The supreme court shall adjust for inflation the maximum amount of publication costs established in Subsection (a)(2).

Added by Acts 2019, 86th Leg., ch. 606 (S.B. 891), § 10.03, eff. June 1, 2020.

Section 15.05 of Acts 2019, 86th Leg., ch. 606 (S.B. 891) provides:

"The Office of Court Administration of the Texas Judicial System is required to implement a provision of this Act only if the legislature appropriates money specifically for that purpose. If the legislature does not appropriate money specifically for that purpose, the office may, but is not required to, implement a provision of this Act using other appropriations available for that purpose."

§ 17.033. Substituted Service Through Social Media Presence

(a) If substituted service of citation is authorized under the Texas Rules of Civil Procedure, the court, in accordance with the rules adopted by the supreme court under Subsection (b), may prescribe as a method of service an electronic communication sent to the defendant through a social media presence.

(b) The supreme court shall adopt rules to provide for the substituted service of citation by an electronic communication sent to a defendant through a social media presence.

Added by Acts 2019, 86th Leg., ch. 606 (S.B. 891), § 10.04(a), eff. June 1, 2020.

Section 10.04(c) of Acts 2019, 86th Leg., ch. 606 (S.B. 891) provides:

"Section 17.033, Civil Practice and Remedies Code, as added by this section, applies only to an action commenced on or after the effective date [June 1, 2020] of the rules adopted by the Supreme Court of Texas under that section."

Section 15.05 of Acts 2019, 86th Leg., ch. 606 (S.B. 891) provides:

"The Office of Court Administration of the Texas Judicial System is required to implement a provision of this Act only if the legislature appropriates money specifically for that purpose. If the legislature does not appropriate money specifically for that purpose, the office may, but is not required to, implement a provision of this Act using other appropriations available for that purpose."

SUBCHAPTER C. LONG-ARM JURISDICTION IN SUIT ON BUSINESS TRANSACTION OR TORT

§ 17.041. Definition

In this subchapter, "nonresident" includes:

(1) an individual who is not a resident of this state; and

(2) a foreign corporation, joint-stock company, association, or partnership.

Acts 1985, 69th Leg., ch. 959, § 1, eff. Sept. 1, 1985.

§ 17.042. Acts Constituting Business in This State

In addition to other acts that may constitute doing business, a nonresident does business in this state if the nonresident:

(1) contracts by mail or otherwise with a Texas resident and either party is to perform the contract in whole or in part in this state;

(2) commits a tort in whole or in part in this state; or

(3) recruits Texas residents, directly or through an intermediary located in this state, for employment inside or outside this state.

Acts 1985, 69th Leg., ch. 959, § 1, eff. Sept. 1, 1985.

§ 17.043. Service on Person in Charge of Business

In an action arising from a nonresident's business in this state, process may be served on the person in charge, at the time of service, of any business in which the nonresident is engaged in this state if the nonresident is not required by statute to designate or maintain a resident agent for service of process.

Acts 1985, 69th Leg., ch. 959, § 1, eff. Sept. 1, 1985.

§ 17.044. Substituted Service on Secretary of State

(a) The secretary of state is an agent for service of process or complaint on a nonresident who:

(1) is required by statute to designate or maintain a resident agent or engages in business in this state, but has not designated or maintained a resident agent for service of process;

(2) has one or more resident agents for service of process, but two unsuccessful attempts have been made on different business days to serve each agent; or

(3) is not required to designate an agent for service in this state, but becomes a nonresident after a cause of action arises in this state but before the cause is matured by suit in a court of competent jurisdiction.

(b) The secretary of state is an agent for service of process on a nonresident who engages in business in this state, but does not maintain a regular place of business in this state or a designated agent for service of process, in any proceeding that arises out of the business done in this state and to which the nonresident is a party.

(c) After the death of a nonresident for whom the secretary of state is an agent for service of process under this section, the secretary of state is an agent for service of process on a nonresident administrator, executor, or personal representative of the nonresident. If an administrator, executor, or personal representative for the estate of the deceased nonresident is not appointed, the secretary of state is an agent for service of process on an heir, as determined by the law of the foreign jurisdiction, of the deceased nonresident.

(d) If a nonresident for whom the secretary of state is an agent for service of process under this section is judged incompetent by a court of competent jurisdiction, the secretary of state is an agent for service of process on a guardian or personal representative of the nonresident.

Acts 1985, 69th Leg., ch. 959, § 1, eff. Sept. 1, 1985. Amended by Acts 1987, 70th Leg., ch. 158, § 1, eff. May 25, 1987.

§ 17.045. Notice to Nonresident

(a) If the secretary of state is served with duplicate copies of process for a nonresident, the documents shall contain a statement of the name and address of the nonresident's home or home office and the secretary of state shall immediately mail a copy of the process to the nonresident at the address provided.

(b) If the secretary of state is served with process under Section 17.044(a)(3), he shall immediately mail a copy of the process to the nonresident (if an individual), to the person in charge of the nonresident's business, or to a corporate officer (if the nonresident is a corporation).

(c) If the person in charge of a nonresident's business is served with process under Section 17.043, a copy of the process and notice of the service must be immediately mailed to the nonresident or the nonresident's principal place of business.

(d) The process or notice must be sent by registered mail or by certified mail, return receipt requested.

(e) If the secretary of state is served with duplicate copies of process as an agent for a person who is a nonresident administrator, executor, heir, guardian, or personal representative of a nonresident, the secretary shall require a statement of the person's name and address and shall immediately mail a copy of the process to the person.

Acts 1985, 69th Leg., ch. 959, § 1, eff. Sept. 1, 1985. Amended by Acts 1987, 70th Leg., ch. 158, § 2, eff. May 25, 1987; Acts 2001, 77th Leg., ch. 275, § 1, eff. Sept. 1, 2001.

SUBCHAPTER D. LONG-ARM JURISDICTION OVER NONRESIDENT MOTOR VEHICLE OPERATOR

§ 17.061. Definitions

In this subchapter:

(1) "Agent" includes a servant, employee, heir, legal representative, executor, administrator, or guardian.

(2) "Chairman" means the chairman of the Texas Transportation Commission.

(3) "Motor vehicle" includes a motorcycle.

Acts 1985, 69th Leg., ch. 959, § 1, eff. Sept. 1, 1985. Amended by Acts 1995, 74th Leg., ch. 165, § 22(23), eff. Sept. 1, 1995.

§ 17.062. Substituted Service on Chairman of Texas Transportation Commission

(a) The chairman of the Texas Transportation Commission is an agent for service of process on a person who is a nonresident or an agent of a nonresident in any suit against the person or agent that grows out of a collision or accident in which the person or his agent is involved while operating a motor vehicle in this state.

(b) Process may be served on the chairman in accordance with this section for a nonresident who was a resident at the time the cause of action accrued but has subsequently moved from the state.

Acts 1985, 69th Leg., ch. 959, § 1, eff. Sept. 1, 1985. Amended by Acts 1995, 74th Leg., ch. 165, § 22(24), eff. Sept. 1, 1995.

§ 17.063. Method of Service; Notice to Nonresident

(a) A certified copy of the process must be served on the chairman not later than the 20th day prior to the date of return stated in the process.

(b) Immediately after being served, the chairman by properly addressed letter shall mail to the nonresident or agent:

(1) a copy of the process; and

(2) notice that the process has been served on the chairman.

(c) The notice and copy of the process must be sent to the nonresident or agent by registered mail, or by certified mail, return receipt requested, with the postage prepaid.

(d) After the chairman deposits the copy of the process in the mail, it is presumed that the process was transmitted by the chairman and received by the nonresident or agent. The presumption may be rebutted.

Acts 1985, 69th Leg., ch. 959, § 1, eff. Sept. 1, 1985.

§ 17.064. Same Effect as Personal Service

Service on the chairman has the same effect as personal service on the nonresident.

Acts 1985, 69th Leg., ch. 959, § 1, eff. Sept. 1, 1985.

§ 17.065. Failed Substituted Service

(a) If the notice of service on the chairman cannot be effected by registered or certified mail or if the nonresident or agent refuses to accept delivery of the notice, the plaintiff may have the defendant personally served with a certified copy of the process and a notice stating that the chairman has been served and the date on which he was served.

(b) The return of service under this section must:

(1) state when it was served;

(2) state on whom it was served; and

(3) be signed under penalty of perjury by the party making the service.

(c) The process and notice may be served by any disinterested person competent to make an oath that the process and notice were served.

Acts 1985, 69th Leg., ch. 959, § 1, eff. Sept. 1, 1985. Amended by Acts 2011, 82nd Leg., ch. 245 (H.B. 962), § 2, eff. Jan. 1, 2012.

§ 17.066. Return

An officer who serves process on the chairman under this subchapter shall state on his return the day and hour of service and any other facts required generally for returns of service of citation.

Acts 1985, 69th Leg., ch. 959, § 1, eff. Sept. 1, 1985.

§ 17.067. Default Judgment

If process is served on the chairman under this subchapter, a court may not grant default judgment against the defendant before the 21st day after the day on which the chairman was served.

Acts 1985, 69th Leg., ch. 959, § 1, eff. Sept. 1, 1985.

§ 17.068. Continuance or Postponement

A court may continue or postpone an action in which process is served under this subchapter as necessary to afford the defendant reasonable opportunity to defend.

Acts 1985, 69th Leg., ch. 959, § 1, eff. Sept. 1, 1985.

§ 17.069. Chairman's Certificate

(a) On request of any party and payment of a $25 fee, the chairman shall certify the occurrence or performance of any duty, act, omission, transaction, or happening contemplated or required by this subchapter, including the wording of any registered letter received.

(b) The chairman may make the certification to the court that issued the process or to another court in which an action is pending against the nonresident or agent.

(c) The chairman's certificate and the certified wording of a registered letter are prima facie evidence of the statements contained in the certificate or letter.

Acts 1985, 69th Leg., ch. 959, § 1, eff. Sept. 1, 1985.

SUBCHAPTER E. CITATION OF NONRESIDENTS—MISCELLANEOUS PROVISIONS

§ 17.091. Substituted Service in Delinquent Tax Cases

(a) In a suit to collect delinquent property taxes by the state or a political subdivision of the state in which a defendant in the suit is a nonresident, the secretary of state is an agent for service of process on that defendant if the defendant owns, has, or claims an interest in or a lien against property in this state that is the subject of the suit. This section applies regardless of whether the defendant has resided in this state.

(b) Duplicate copies of the process issued by the clerk of the court in which the suit is pending must be served on the secretary of state not later than the 20th day before the date of return stated in the process. The process must include the name and address of the nonresident's home or home office. The address may be a post office box.

(c) Immediately after being served, the secretary of state shall mail a copy of the process to the nonresident at the address provided under Subsection (b) by certified mail, return receipt requested, with the postage prepaid. The secretary of state shall certify to the court that issued the process that the secretary of state has complied with this section.

(d) Service under this section is in addition to procedures provided by Rule 117a of the Texas Rules of Civil Procedure and has the same effect as personal service.

(e) Service of process on the secretary of state under this section must be accompanied by the fee provided by Section 405.031(a), Government Code, for the maintenance by the secretary of state of a record of the service of process.

(f) In this section, "nonresident" includes:

(1) an individual who is not a resident of this state; and

(2) a foreign corporation, foreign unincorporated association, foreign general partnership, foreign limited partnership, foreign limited liability company, foreign professional association, foreign business trust, foreign cooperative, or foreign real estate investment trust that is not required to appoint a registered agent for service of process in this state under the provisions of the Business Organizations Code.

Acts 1985, 69th Leg., ch. 959, § 1, eff. Sept. 1, 1985. Amended by Acts 1989, 71st Leg., ch. 384, § 14, eff. Sept. 1, 1989; Acts 1991, 72nd Leg., 2nd C.S., ch. 6, § 60, eff. Sept. 1, 1991; Acts 1995, 74th Leg., ch. 579, § 1, eff. Jan. 1, 1996; Acts 1997, 75th Leg., ch. 948, § 5, eff. Sept. 1, 1997; Acts 2001, 77th Leg., ch. 1430, § 34, eff. Sept. 1, 2001; Acts 2005, 79th Leg., ch. 1126, § 28, eff. Sept. 1, 2005; Acts 2009, 81st Leg., ch. 182, § 1, eff. Sept. 1, 2009; Acts 2011, 82nd Leg., ch. 7 (S.B. 582), § 2, eff. Sept. 1, 2011.

§ 17.092. Service on Nonresident Utility Supplier

A nonresident individual or partnership that supplies gas, water, electricity, or other public utility service to a city, town, or village in this state may be served citation by serving the local agent, representative, superintendent, or person in charge of the nonresident's business.

Acts 1985, 69th Leg., ch. 959, § 1, eff. Sept. 1, 1985.

§ 17.093. Service on Foreign Railway

In addition to other methods of service provided by law, process may be served on a foreign railway by serving:

(1) a train conductor who:

(A) handles trains for two or more railway corporations, at least one of which is the foreign corporation and at least one of which is a domestic corporation; and

(B) handles trains for the railway corporations over tracks that cross the state's boundary and on tracks of a domestic corporation within this state; or

(2) an agent who:

(A) has an office in this state; and

(B) sells tickets or makes contracts for the transportation of passengers or property over all or part of the line of the foreign railway.

Acts 1985, 69th Leg., ch. 959, § 1, eff. Sept. 1, 1985.

CHAPTER 18. EVIDENCE

SUBCHAPTER A. DOCUMENTARY EVIDENCE

§ 18.001. Affidavit Concerning Cost and Necessity of Services

(a) This section applies to civil actions only, but not to an action on a sworn account.

(b) Unless a controverting affidavit is served as provided by this section, an affidavit that the amount a person charged for a service was reasonable at the time and place that the service was provided and that the service was necessary is sufficient evidence to support a finding of fact by judge or jury that the amount charged was reasonable or that the service was necessary. The affidavit is not evidence of and does not support a finding of the causation element of the cause of action that is the basis for the civil action.

(c) The affidavit must:

(1) be taken before an officer with authority to administer oaths;

(2) be made by:

(A) the person who provided the service; or

(B) the person in charge of records showing the service provided and charge made; and

(3) include an itemized statement of the service and charge.

(d) The party offering the affidavit in evidence or the party's attorney must serve a copy of the affidavit on each other party to the case by the earlier of:

(1) 90 days after the date the defendant files an answer;

(2) the date the offering party must designate any expert witness under a court order; or

(3) the date the offering party must designate any expert witness as required by the Texas Rules of Civil Procedure.

(d–1) Notwithstanding Subsection (d), if services are provided for the first time by a provider after the date the defendant files an answer, the party offering the affidavit in evidence or the party's attorney must serve a copy of the affidavit for services provided by that provider on each other party to the case by the earlier of:

(1) the date the offering party must designate any expert witness under a court order; or

(2) the date the offering party must designate any expert witness as required by the Texas Rules of Civil Procedure.

(d–2) The party offering the affidavit in evidence or the party's attorney must file notice with the clerk of the court when serving the affidavit that the party or the attorney served a copy of the affidavit in accordance with this section. Except as provided by the Texas Rules of Evidence, the affidavit is not required to be filed with the clerk of the court before the trial commences.

(e) A party intending to controvert a claim reflected by the affidavit must serve a copy of the counteraffidavit on each other party or the party's attorney of record by the earlier of:

(1) 120 days after the date the defendant files its answer;

(2) the date the party offering the counteraffidavit must designate expert witnesses under a court order; or

(3) the date the party offering the counteraffidavit must designate any expert witness as required by the Texas Rules of Civil Procedure.

(e–1) Notwithstanding Subsection (e), if the party offering the affidavit in evidence serves a copy of the affidavit under Subsection (d–1), the party offering the counteraffidavit in evidence or the party's attorney must serve a copy of the counteraffidavit on each other party to the case by the later of:

(1) 30 days after service of the affidavit on the party offering the counteraffidavit in evidence;

(2) the date the party offering the counteraffidavit must designate any expert witness under a court order; or

(3) the date the party offering the counteraffidavit in evidence must designate any expert witness as required by the Texas Rules of Civil Procedure.

(f) The counteraffidavit must give reasonable notice of the basis on which the party serving it intends at trial to controvert the claim reflected by the initial affidavit and must be taken before a person authorized to administer oaths. The counteraffidavit must be made by a person who is qualified, by knowledge, skill, experience, training, education, or other expertise, to testify in contravention of all or part of any of the matters contained in the initial affidavit. The counteraffidavit may not be used to controvert the causation element of the cause of action that is the basis for the civil action.

(g) The party offering the counteraffidavit in evidence or the party's attorney must file written notice with the clerk of the court when serving the counteraffidavit that the party or attorney served a copy of the counteraffidavit in accordance with this section.

(h) If continuing services are provided after a relevant deadline under this section:

(1) a party may supplement an affidavit served by the party under Subsection (d) or (d–1) on or before the 60th day before the date the trial commences; and

(2) a party that served a counteraffidavit under Subsection (e) or (e–1) may supplement the counteraffidavit on or before the 30th day before the date the trial commences.

(i) Notwithstanding Subsections (d), (d–1), (d–2), (e), (e–1), (g), and (h), a deadline under this section may be altered by all parties to an action by agreement or with leave of the court.

Acts 1985, 69th Leg., ch. 959, § 1, eff. Sept. 1, 1985. Amended by Acts 1987, 70th Leg., ch. 167, § 3.04(a), eff. Sept. 1, 1987; Acts 2007, 80th Leg., ch. 978, § 1, eff. Sept. 1, 2007; Acts 2013, 83rd Leg., ch. 560 (S.B. 679), § 1, eff. Sept. 1, 2013; Acts 2019, 86th Leg., ch. 779 (H.B. 1693), § 1, eff. Sept. 1, 2019.

Section 2 of Acts 2019, 86th Leg., ch. 779 (H.B. 1693) provides:

"The change in law made by this Act applies only to an action commenced on or after the effective date [Sept. 1, 2019] of this Act. An action commenced before the effective date of this Act is governed by the law applicable to the action immediately before the effective date of this Act, and that law is continued in effect for that purpose."

§ 18.002. Form of Affidavit

(a) An affidavit concerning cost and necessity of services by the person who provided the service is sufficient if it follows the following form:

No.______________

John Doe) IN THE __________
(Name of Plaintiff)) COURT IN AND FOR
v.) __________ COUNTY,
John Roe) TEXAS
(Name of Defendant))

AFFIDAVIT

Before me, the undersigned authority, personally appeared ________(NAME OF AFFIANT)________, who, being by me duly sworn, deposed as follows:

My name is ________(NAME OF AFFIANT)________. I am of sound mind and capable of making this affidavit.

On ________(DATE)________, I provided a service to ________(NAME OF PERSON WHO RECEIVED SERVICE)________. An itemized statement of the service and the charge for the service is attached to this affidavit and is a part of this affidavit.

The service I provided was necessary and the amount that I charged for the service was reasonable at the time and place that the service was provided.

____
Affiant

SWORN TO AND SUBSCRIBED before me on the ______ day of ______, 19___.

My commission expires:

____

____
Notary Public, State of Texas
Notary's printed name:

____

(b) An affidavit concerning cost and necessity of services by the person who is in charge of records showing the service provided and the charge made is sufficient if it follows the following form:

No.______________

John Doe) IN THE __________
(Name of Plaintiff)) COURT IN AND FOR
v.) __________ COUNTY,
John Roe) TEXAS
(Name of Defendant))

AFFIDAVIT

Before me, the undersigned authority, personally appeared ________(NAME OF AFFIANT)________, who, being by me duly sworn, deposed as follows:

My name is ________(NAME OF AFFIANT)________. I am of sound mind and capable of making this affidavit.

I am the person in charge of records of ________(PERSON WHO PROVIDED THE SERVICE)________. Attached to this affidavit are records that provide an itemized statement of the service and the charge for the service that ________(PERSON WHO PROVIDED THE SERVICE)________ provided to ________(PERSON WHO RECEIVED THE SERVICE)________ on ________(DATE)________. The attached records are a part of this affidavit.

The attached records are kept by me in the regular course of business. The information contained in the records was transmitted to me in the regular course of business by ________(PERSON WHO PROVIDED THE SERVICE)________ or an employee or representative of ________(PERSON WHO PROVIDED THE SERVICE)________ who had personal knowledge of the information. The records were made at or near the time or reasonably soon after the time that the service was provided. The records are the original or an exact duplicate of the original.

The service provided was necessary and the amount charged for the service was reasonable at the time and place that the service was provided.

____
Affiant

SWORN TO AND SUBSCRIBED before me on the ________ day of ________, 19__.

My commission expires:

____

____

Notary Public, State of Texas

Notary's printed name:

____

(b–1) Notwithstanding Subsection (b), an affidavit concerning proof of medical expenses is sufficient if it substantially complies with the following form:

Affidavit of Records Custodian of

____

STATE OF TEXAS §
§
COUNTY OF ____ §

Before me, the undersigned authority, personally appeared ________, who, being by me duly sworn, deposed as follows:

My name is ____________. I am of sound mind and capable of making this affidavit, and personally acquainted with the facts herein stated.

I am a custodian of records for ________. Attached to this affidavit are records that provide an itemized statement of the service and the charge for the service that ________ provided to ________ on ____. The attached records are a part of this affidavit.

The attached records are kept by ________ in the regular course of business, and it was the regular course of business of ________ for an employee or representative of ________, with knowledge of the service provided, to make the record or to transmit information to be included in the record. The records were made in the regular course of business at or near the time or reasonably soon after the time the service was provided. The records are the original or a duplicate of the original.

The services provided were necessary and the amount charged for the services was reasonable at the time and place that the services were provided.

The total amount paid for the services was $____ and the amount currently unpaid but which ________ has a right to be paid after any adjustments or credits is $____.

____

Affiant

SWORN TO AND SUBSCRIBED before me on the ________ day of ____, ____.

____

Notary Public, State of Texas

Notary's printed name:________

My commission expires:________

(b–2) If a medical bill or other itemized statement attached to an affidavit under Subsection (b–1) reflects a charge that is not recoverable, the reference to that charge is not admissible.

(c) The form of an affidavit provided by this section is not exclusive and an affidavit that substantially complies with Section 18.001 is sufficient.

Added by Acts 1993, 73rd Leg., ch. 248, § 1, eff. Aug. 30, 1993. Amended by Acts 2013, 83rd Leg., ch. 560 (S.B. 679), § 2, eff. Sept. 1, 2013.

SUBCHAPTER B. PRESUMPTIONS

§ 18.031. Foreign Interest Rate

Unless the interest rate of another state or country is alleged and proved, the rate is presumed to be the same as that established by law in this state and interest at that rate may be recovered without allegation or proof.

Acts 1985, 69th Leg., ch. 959, § 1, eff. Sept. 1, 1985.

§ 18.032. Traffic Control Device Presumed to be Lawful

(a) In a civil case, proof of the existence of a traffic control device on or alongside a public thoroughfare by a party is prima facie proof of all facts necessary to prove the proper and lawful installation of the device at that place, including proof of competent authority and an ordinance by a municipality or order by the commissioners court of a county.

(b) Proof of the existence of a one-way street sign is prima facie proof that the public thoroughfare on or alongside which the sign is placed was designated by proper and competent authority to be a one-way thoroughfare allowing traffic to go only in the direction indicated by the sign.

(c) In this section, "traffic control device" includes a control light, stop sign, and one-way street sign.

(d) Any party may rebut the prima facie proof established under this section.

Added by Acts 1995, 74th Leg., ch. 165, § 2, eff. Sept. 1, 1995.

§ 18.033. State Land Records

(a) In a dispute between the State of Texas and an upland owner of property fronting on the Gulf of Mexico and the arms of the Gulf of Mexico within the boundaries of the State of Texas, the maps, surveys, and property descriptions filed in the General Land Office in connection with any conveyance by the state or any predecessor government by patent, deed, lease, or other authorized forms of grant shall be presumed to accurately depict the boundary between adjacent upland owners and the state-owned submerged lands.

(b) This presumption applies only to those surveys conducted by a surveyor duly appointed, elected, or licensed, and qualified.

(c) This presumption may be overcome only on a showing of clear and convincing evidence that the boundary as described and depicted in the archives of the General Land Office is erroneous.

Added by Acts 2003, 78th Leg., ch. 148, § 1, eff. Sept. 1, 2003.

SUBCHAPTER C. ADMISSIBILITY

§ 18.061. Communications of Sympathy

(a) A court in a civil action may not admit a communication that:

(1) expresses sympathy or a general sense of benevolence relating to the pain, suffering, or death of an individual involved in an accident;

(2) is made to the individual or a person related to the individual within the second degree by consanguinity or affinity, as determined under Subchapter B, Chapter 573, Government Code;[1] and

(3) is offered to prove liability of the communicator in relation to the individual.

(b) In this section, "communication" means:

(1) a statement;

(2) a writing; or

(3) a gesture that conveys a sense of compassion or commiseration emanating from humane impulses.

(c) Notwithstanding the provisions of Subsections (a) and (b), a communication, including an excited utterance as defined by Rule 803(2) of the Texas Rules of Evidence, which also includes a statement or statements concerning negligence or culpable conduct pertaining to an accident or event, is admissible to prove liability of the communicator.

Added by Acts 1999, 76th Leg., ch. 673, § 1, eff. Sept. 1, 1999.

[1] V.T.C.A., Government Code § 573.021 et seq.

§ 18.062. Certain Information Relating to Identity Theft

(a) Except as provided by Subsection (b), a business record is not admissible in a civil action if the business record is provided to law enforcement personnel in connection with an investigation of an alleged violation of Section 32.51, Penal Code (fraudulent use or possession of identifying information).

(b) A business record described by Subsection (a) is admissible if the party offering the record has obtained the record from a source other than law enforcement personnel.

Added by Acts 2005, 79th Leg., ch. 1059, § 1, eff. June 18, 2005.

SUBCHAPTER D. CERTAIN LOSSES

§ 18.091. Proof of Certain Losses; Jury Instruction

(a) Notwithstanding any other law, if any claimant seeks recovery for loss of earnings, loss of earning capacity, loss of contributions of a pecuniary value, or loss of inheritance, evidence to prove the loss must be presented in the form of a net loss after reduction for income tax payments or unpaid tax liability pursuant to any federal income tax law.

(b) If any claimant seeks recovery for loss of earnings, loss of earning capacity, loss of contributions of a pecuniary value, or loss of inheritance, the court shall instruct the jury as to whether any recovery for compensatory damages sought by the claimant is subject to federal or state income taxes.

Added by Acts 2003, 78th Leg., ch. 204, § 13.09, eff. Sept. 1, 2003.

CHAPTER 19. LOST RECORDS

Section

§ 19.001. Application of Chapter

This chapter applies to:

(1) a deed, bond, bill of sale, mortgage, deed of trust, power of attorney, or conveyance that is required or permitted by law to be acknowledged or recorded and that has been acknowledged or recorded; or

(2) a judgment, order, or decree of a court of record of this state.

Acts 1985, 69th Leg., ch. 959, § 1, eff. Sept. 1, 1985.

§ 19.002. Parol Proof

A person may supply a lost, destroyed, or removed record by parol proof of the record's contents as provided by this chapter.

Acts 1985, 69th Leg., ch. 959, § 1, eff. Sept. 1, 1985.

§ 19.003. Application for Relief

(a) To supply a record that has been lost, destroyed, or removed:

(1) a person interested in an instrument or in a judgment, order, or decree of the district court may file an application with the district clerk of the county in which the record was lost or destroyed or from which the record was removed; or

(2) a person interested in a judgment, order, or decree of a county court may file an application with the clerk of the court to which the record belonged.

(b) The application must be in writing and must set forth the facts that entitle the applicant to relief.

Acts 1985, 69th Leg., ch. 959, § 1, eff. Sept. 1, 1985.

§ 19.004. Citation

(a) If an application is filed to supply a record, the clerk shall issue a citation to the following, as applicable, or to the person's heirs or legal representatives:

(1) each grantor of property, in the case of a record of a deed;

(2) an interested party, in the case of an instrument other than a deed; or

(3) a party adversely interested to the applicant at the time of the rendition, in the case of a judgment, order, or decree.

(b) The citation must direct the person to whom it is issued to appear at a designated term of the court to contest the applicant's right to record a substitute.

(c) Process must be served in the manner provided by law for civil cases.

Acts 1985, 69th Leg., ch. 959, § 1, eff. Sept. 1, 1985.

§ 19.005. Order

(a) On hearing an application to supply a record, if the court is satisfied from the evidence of the previous existence and content of the record and of its loss, destruction, or removal, the court shall enter on its minutes an order containing its findings and a description of the record and its contents.

(b) A certified copy of the order may be recorded in the proper county.

Acts 1985, 69th Leg., ch. 959, § 1, eff. Sept. 1, 1985.

§ 19.006. Effect of Order

The order supplying the record:

(1) stands in the place of the original record;

(2) has the same effect as the original record;

(3) if recorded, may be used as evidence in a court of the state as though it were the original record; and

(4) carries the same rights as the original record, including:

(A) preserving liens from the date of the original record; and

(B) giving parties the right to issue execution under the order as under the original record.

Acts 1985, 69th Leg., ch. 959, § 1, eff. Sept. 1, 1985.

§ 19.007. Method Not Exclusive

The method provided by this chapter for supplying a record is in addition to other methods provided by law.

Acts 1985, 69th Leg., ch. 959, § 1, eff. Sept. 1, 1985.

§ 19.008. Rerecordation of Original Document

Rerecordation of the original document within four years after the date a record of an instrument, judgment, order, or decree was lost, destroyed, or removed is effective from the time of the original recordation.

Acts 1985, 69th Leg., ch. 959, § 1, eff. Sept. 1, 1985.

§ 19.009. Certified Copy

If the loss, destruction, or removal of an original county record is established, a certified copy of the record from the records of that county or from the records of the county from which that county was created may be recorded in the county.

Acts 1985, 69th Leg., ch. 959, § 1, eff. Sept. 1, 1985.

CHAPTER 20. DEPOSITIONS

Section

§ 20.001. Persons Who May Take a Deposition

(a) A deposition on written questions of a witness who is alleged to reside or to be in this state may be taken by:

(1) a clerk of a district court;

(2) a judge or clerk of a county court; or

(3) a notary public of this state.

(b) A deposition of a witness who is alleged to reside or to be outside this state, but inside the United States, may be taken in another state by:

(1) a clerk of a court of record having a seal;

(2) a commissioner of deeds appointed under the laws of this state; or

(3) any notary public.

(c) A deposition of a witness who is alleged to reside or to be outside the United States may be taken by:

(1) a minister, commissioner, or charge d'affaires of the United States who is a resident of and is accredited in the country where the deposition is taken;

(2) a consul general, consul, vice-consul, commercial agent, vice-commercial agent, deputy consul, or consular agent of the United States who is a resident of the country where the deposition is taken; or

(3) any notary public.

(d) A deposition of a witness who is alleged to be a member of the United States Armed Forces or of a United States Armed Forces Auxiliary or who is alleged to be a civilian employed by or accompanying the armed forces or an auxiliary outside the United States may be taken by a commissioned officer in the United States Armed Forces or United States Armed Forces Auxiliary or by a commissioned officer in the United States Armed Forces Reserve or an auxiliary of it. If a deposition appears on its face to have been taken as provided by this subsection and the deposition or any part of it is offered in evidence, it is presumed, absent pleading and proof to the contrary, that the person taking the deposition as a commissioned officer was a commissioned officer on the date that the deposition was taken, and that the deponent was a member of the authorized group of military personnel or civilians.

Acts 1985, 69th Leg., ch. 959, § 1, eff. Sept. 1, 1985. Amended by Acts 1993, 73rd Leg., ch. 1037, § 4, eff. Sept. 1, 1993.

§ 20.002. Testimony Required by Foreign Jurisdiction

If a court of record in any other state or foreign jurisdiction issues a mandate, writ, or commission that requires a witness's testimony in this state, either to written questions or by oral deposition, the witness may be compelled to appear and testify in the same manner and by the same process used for taking testimony in a proceeding pending in this state.

Acts 1985, 69th Leg., ch. 959, § 1, eff. Sept. 1, 1985.

CHAPTER 21. INTERPRETERS

SUBCHAPTER A. INTERPRETERS FOR THE DEAF

Section

SUBCHAPTER B. SPANISH LANGUAGE INTERPRETERS IN CERTAIN BORDER COUNTIES

SUBCHAPTER C. INTERPRETERS FOR COUNTY COURTS AT LAW

SUBCHAPTER D. INTERPRETER FEE

SUBCHAPTER A. INTERPRETERS FOR THE DEAF

§ 21.001. Definition

In this subchapter, "deaf person" means an individual who has a hearing impairment, regardless of whether the person also has a speech impairment, that inhibits the person's comprehension of proceedings or communication with others.

Acts 1985, 69th Leg., ch. 959, § 1, eff. Sept. 1, 1985.

§ 21.002. Interpreters for Deaf Persons

(a) In a civil case or in a deposition, a deaf person who is a party or witness is entitled to have the proceedings interpreted by a court-appointed interpreter. A deaf person who is a juror in any case is entitled to have the proceedings interpreted by a court-appointed interpreter.

(b) The proceedings must be interpreted in a language, including sign language, that the deaf person can understand.

Acts 1985, 69th Leg., ch. 959, § 1, eff. Sept. 1, 1985. Amended by Acts 1987, 70th Leg., ch. 550, § 2, eff. Sept. 1, 1987.

§ 21.003. Qualifications

The interpreter must hold a current legal certificate issued by the National Registry of Interpreters for the Deaf or a current court interpreter certificate issued by the Board for Evaluation of Interpreters in the Department of Assistive and Rehabilitative Services.

Acts 1985, 69th Leg., ch. 959, § 1, eff. Sept. 1, 1985. Amended by Acts 1987, 70th Leg., ch. 434, § 2, eff. June 17, 1987; Acts 2005, 79th Leg., ch. 614, § 10, eff. Sept. 1, 2006.

§ 21.004. Interpreter's Position in Court

If a court is required to appoint an interpreter under this subchapter, the court may not start proceedings until the appointed interpreter is in court in a position not more than 10 feet from and in full view of the deaf person.

Acts 1985, 69th Leg., ch. 959, § 1, eff. Sept. 1, 1985.

§ 21.005. Oath

(a) The interpreter shall take an oath that the interpreter will:

(1) make a true interpretation to the deaf person of all the case proceedings in a language that the deaf person understands; and

(2) repeat the deaf person's answers to questions to counsel, court, or jury in the English language, using the interpreter's best skill and judgment.

(b) An interpreter appointed for a juror shall also take an oath that the interpreter will not:

(1) participate in any manner in the deliberations of the jury;

(2) communicate with any member of the jury regarding the deliberation of the jury except a literal translation of a juror's remarks made during deliberations; or

(3) disclose any of the deliberations with any person following a verdict.

Acts 1985, 69th Leg., ch. 959, § 1, eff. Sept. 1, 1985. Amended by Acts 1987, 70th Leg., ch. 550, § 3, eff. Sept. 1, 1987.

§ 21.006. Fees and Travel Expenses

(a) The interpreter shall be paid a reasonable fee determined by the court after considering the recommended fees of the Texas Commission for the Deaf and Hard of Hearing.

(b) If the interpreter is required to travel, the interpreter's actual expenses of travel, lodging, and meals relating to the case shall be paid at the same rate provided for state employees.

(c) The interpreter's fee and expenses shall be paid from the general fund of the county in which the case was brought.

Acts 1985, 69th Leg., ch. 959, § 1, eff. Sept. 1, 1985. Amended by Acts 1991, 72nd Leg., ch. 353, § 3, eff. Sept. 1, 1991; Acts 1995, 74th Leg., ch. 835, § 13, eff. Sept. 1, 1995.

§ 21.007. Recording of Testimony

(a) On the court's motion or a party's motion, the court may order a video recording of a deaf witness's testimony and the interpreter's interpretation of that testimony to use in verifying the transcription of the reporter's notes.

(b) If a party requests, the clerk of the court shall include the recording in the appellate record.

Acts 1985, 69th Leg., ch. 959, § 1, eff. Sept. 1, 1985.

§ 21.008. Privilege of Interpreter for the Deaf

If a deaf person communicates through an interpreter to a person under circumstances in which the communication would be privileged and the deaf person could not be required to testify about the communication, the privilege applies to the interpreter as well.

Acts 1985, 69th Leg., ch. 959, § 1, eff. Sept. 1, 1985.

§ 21.009. Jury Deliberations; Verdict

(a) The interpreter appointed for a juror may be present and assist the juror during the jury deliberation.

(b) The presence of the interpreter during jury deliberations does not affect the validity of a verdict.

Added by Acts 1987, 70th Leg., ch. 550, § 4, eff. Sept. 1, 1987.

SUBCHAPTER B. SPANISH LANGUAGE INTERPRETERS IN CERTAIN BORDER COUNTIES

§ 21.021. Application

This subchapter applies to a county that:

(1) is part of two or more judicial districts, that has two or more district courts with regular terms, and that is part of a district in which a county borders on the international boundary of the United States and the Republic of Mexico;

(2) borders on the international boundary of the United States and the Republic of Mexico and that is in a judicial district composed of four counties;

(3) borders on the international boundary of the United States and the Republic of Mexico and that has three or more district courts or judicial districts wholly within the county; or

(4) borders on the Gulf of Mexico and that has four or more district courts or judicial districts of which two or more courts or districts are wholly within the county.

Acts 1985, 69th Leg., ch. 959, § 1, eff. Sept. 1, 1985.

§ 21.022. Appointment

(a) On the request of a district judge who has made a determination of need, the commissioners court of the county shall appoint court interpreters on a full-time or part-time basis as necessary to carry out court functions.

(b) The commissioners court shall appoint the court interpreter designated by the district judge requesting the appointment.

Acts 1985, 69th Leg., ch. 959, § 1, eff. Sept. 1, 1985.

§ 21.023. Interpreter's Qualifications

The court interpreter must be well versed in and competent to speak the Spanish and English languages.

Acts 1985, 69th Leg., ch. 959, § 1, eff. Sept. 1, 1985.

SUBCHAPTER C. INTERPRETERS FOR COUNTY COURTS AT LAW

§ 21.031. Appointment; Termination of Employment; Duties

(a) The judge of a county court at law may appoint an official interpreter for that court and may terminate that interpreter's employment at any time.

(b) The commissioners court shall prescribe the duties of the official interpreter.

Acts 1985, 69th Leg., ch. 959, § 1, eff. Sept. 1, 1985.

§ 21.032. Oath

The official interpreter appointed under this subchapter must take the constitutional oath of office and an oath that the interpreter will faithfully interpret all testimony given in court. An oath covers the interpreter's service in all court cases during the interpreter's term of office.

Acts 1985, 69th Leg., ch. 959, § 1, eff. Sept. 1, 1985.

SUBCHAPTER D. INTERPRETER FEE

§ 21.051. Interpreter Fee

The clerk of the court shall collect an interpreter fee of $3 as a court cost in each civil case in which an interpreter is used. The clerk shall collect the fee in the manner provided for other court costs and shall deposit the fee to the credit of the general fund of the county.

Added by Acts 1987, 70th Leg., ch. 167, § 3.05(a), eff. Sept. 1, 1987.

Repeal

Acts 2021, 87th Leg., ch. 472 (S.B. 41), § 5.01(a)(2) repeals this section effective Jan. 1, 2022.

CHAPTER 22. WITNESSES

SUBCHAPTER A. WITNESSES

SUBCHAPTER A. WITNESSES

§ 22.001. Witness Fees

(a) Except as provided by Section 22.002,[1] a witness is entitled to 10 dollars for each day the witness attends court. This fee includes the entitlement for travel and the witness is not entitled to any reimbursement for mileage traveled.

(b) The party who summons the witness shall pay that witness's fee for one day, as provided by this section, at the time the subpoena is served on the witness.

(c) The witness fee must be taxed in the bill of costs as other costs.

Acts 1985, 69th Leg., ch. 959, § 1, eff. Sept. 1, 1985. Amended by Acts 1993, 73rd Leg., ch. 103, § 1, eff. Jan. 1, 1994; Acts 1993, 73rd Leg., ch. 449, § 16, eff. Sept. 1, 1993.

[1] Section 22.002 was renumbered as V.T.C.A., Civil Practice & Remedies Code § 22.003 by Acts 1995, 74th Leg., ch. 76, § 17.01(2). The introductory paragraph to Acts 1995, 74th Leg., ch. 76, § 17.01 provides in part that "appropriate cross-references are changed in order to eliminate duplicate citations or to relocate misplaced provisions."

§ 22.002. Distance for Subpoenas

A witness who is represented to reside 150 miles or less from a county in which a suit is pending or who may be found within that distance at the time of trial on the suit may be subpoenaed in the suit.

Added by Acts 1993, 73rd Leg., ch. 103, § 1, eff. Jan. 1, 1994.

§ 22.003. Fees for Witnesses Summoned by a State Agency

(a) In this section:

(1) "Commercial lodging establishment" means a motel, hotel, inn, apartment, or similar entity that offers lodging to the public in exchange for compensation.

(2) "Commercial transportation company" means an entity that offers transportation of people or goods to the public in exchange for compensation.

(b) A witness summoned by a state agency is entitled to receive from the agency:

(1) one dollar for each day the witness attends court;

(2) mileage at the rate provided by law for state employees if the witness uses the witness's personally owned or leased motor vehicle to attend court;

(3) reimbursement of the witness's transportation expenses if the witness does not use the witness's personally owned or leased motor vehicle to attend court; and

(4) reimbursement of the witness's meal and lodging expenses while attending court if the court is at least 25 miles from the witness's place of residence.

(c) A state agency may directly pay a commercial transportation company for the transportation expenses and a commercial lodging establishment for the lodging expenses of a witness if this section otherwise requires the agency to reimburse the witness for those expenses.

(d) A state agency may not pay a commercial transportation company or a commercial lodging establishment or reimburse a witness for transportation, meal, or lodging expenses under this section at a rate that exceeds the maximum rates provided by law for state employees.

(e) After receiving the witness's affidavit, the court clerk shall issue a certificate showing the fees incurred under this section.

(f) The witness fees must be taxed in the bill of costs as other costs.

Added by Acts 1993, 73rd Leg., ch. 449, § 17, eff. Sept. 1, 1993. Renumbered from V.T.C.A., Civil Practice & Remedies Code § 22.002 by Acts 1995, 74th Leg., ch. 76, § 17.01(2), eff. Sept. 1, 1995.

§ 22.004. Fee for Production or Certification of Documents

(a) A custodian of a record who receives a request for production or certification of a record under a subpoena, a request for production, or other instrument issued under the authority of a tribunal that compels production or certification of a record is entitled to $1 for production or certification of the record. If more than one record is produced or certified, the custodian of the records is entitled to only one fee under this section.

(b) A custodian of a record who produces or certifies a record under Subsection (a), but who is not required to appear in court, is not entitled to a witness fee under Section 22.001.

(c) The party who requests production or certification of a record shall pay the fee required for the record, as provided by this section, at the time the subpoena, request, or other instrument is served.

(d) The fee required by this section must be taxed in the bill of costs as other costs.

(e) The fee required by this section is in addition to any other fee imposed by law for the production or certification of a record.

Added by Acts 1995, 74th Leg., ch. 452, § 1, eff. June 9, 1995.

SUBCHAPTER B. PRIVILEGES

§ 22.011. Privilege From Arrest

(a) A witness is privileged from arrest while attending, going to, and returning from court.

(b) The privilege provided by this section extends for a period computed by allowing one day of travel for each 150 miles of the distance from the courthouse to the witness's residence.

(c) This section does not apply to an arrest for a felony, treason, or breach of the peace.

Acts 1985, 69th Leg., ch. 959, § 1, eff. Sept. 1, 1985. Amended by Acts 1993, 73rd Leg., ch. 103, § 1, eff. Jan. 1, 1994.

SUBCHAPTER C. JOURNALIST'S QUALIFIED TESTIMONIAL PRIVILEGE IN CIVIL PROCEEDINGS

§ 22.021. Definitions

In this subchapter:

(1) "Communication service provider" means a person or the parent, subsidiary, division, or affiliate of a person who transmits information chosen by a customer by electronic means, including:

(A) a telecommunications carrier, as defined by Section 3, Communications Act of 1934 (47 U.S.C. Section 153);

(B) a provider of information service, as defined by Section 3, Communications Act of 1934 (47 U.S.C. Section 153);

(C) a provider of interactive computer service, as defined by Section 230, Communications Act of 1934 (47 U.S.C. Section 230); and

(D) an information content provider, as defined by Section 230, Communications Act of 1934 (47 U.S.C. Section 230).

(2) "Journalist" means a person, including a parent, subsidiary, division, or affiliate of a person, who for a substantial portion of the person's livelihood or for substantial financial gain, gathers, compiles, prepares, collects, photographs, records, writes, edits, reports, investigates, processes, or publishes news or information that is disseminated by a news medium or communication service provider and includes:

(A) a person who supervises or assists in gathering, preparing, and disseminating the news or information; or

(B) notwithstanding the foregoing, a person who is or was a journalist, scholar, or researcher employed by an institution of higher education at the time the person obtained or prepared the requested information, or a person who at the time the person obtained or prepared the requested information:

(i) is earning a significant portion of the person's livelihood by obtaining or preparing information for dissemination by a news medium or communication service provider; or

(ii) was serving as an agent, assistant, employee, or supervisor of a news medium or communication service provider.

(3) "News medium" means a newspaper, magazine or periodical, book publisher, news agency, wire service, radio or television station or network, cable, satellite, or other transmission system or carrier or channel, or a channel or programming service for a station, network, system, or carrier, or an audio or audiovisual production company or Internet company or provider, or the parent, subsidiary, division, or affiliate of that entity, that disseminates news or information to the public by any means, including:

(A) print;

(B) television;

(C) radio;

(D) photographic;

(E) mechanical;

(F) electronic; and

(G) other means, known or unknown, that are accessible to the public.

(4) "Official proceeding" means any type of administrative, executive, legislative, or judicial proceeding that may be conducted before a public servant, including a proceeding under Rule 202, Texas Rules of Civil Procedure.

(5) "Public servant" means a person elected, selected, appointed, employed, or otherwise designated as one of the following, even if the person has not yet qualified for office or assumed the person's duties:

(A) an officer, employee, or agent of government;

(B) a juror;

(C) an arbitrator, referee, or other person who is authorized by law or private written agreement to hear or determine a cause or controversy;

(D) an attorney or notary public when participating in the performance of a governmental function; or

(E) a person who is performing a governmental function under a claim of right, although the person is not legally qualified to do so.

Added by Acts 2009, 81st Leg., ch. 29, § 1, eff. May 13, 2009.

§ 22.022. Purpose

The purpose of this subchapter is to increase the free flow of information and preserve a free and active press and, at the same time, protect the right of the public to effective law enforcement and the fair administration of justice.

Added by Acts 2009, 81st Leg., ch. 29, § 1, eff. May 13, 2009.

§ 22.023. Privilege

(a) Except as otherwise provided by this subchapter, a judicial, legislative, administrative, or other body with the authority to issue a subpoena or other compulsory process may not compel a journalist to testify regarding or to produce or disclose in an official proceeding:

(1) any confidential or nonconfidential information, document, or item obtained or prepared while acting as a journalist; or

(2) the source of any information, document, or item described by Subdivision (1).

(b) A subpoena or other compulsory process may not compel the parent, subsidiary, division, or affiliate of a communication service provider or news medium to disclose the information, documents, or items or the source of any information, documents, or items that are privileged from disclosure under Subsection (a).

Added by Acts 2009, 81st Leg., ch. 29, § 1, eff. May 13, 2009.

§ 22.024. Limited Disclosure Generally

After notice and an opportunity to be heard, a court may compel a journalist, a journalist's employer, or a person with an independent contract with a journalist to testify regarding or to produce or disclose any information, document, or item or the source of any information, document, or item obtained while acting as a journalist, if the person seeking the information, document, or item or the source of any information, document, or item makes a clear and specific showing that:

(1) all reasonable efforts have been exhausted to obtain the information from alternative sources;

(2) the subpoena is not overbroad, unreasonable, or oppressive and, when appropriate, will be limited to the verification of published information and the surrounding circumstances relating to the accuracy of the published information;

(3) reasonable and timely notice was given of the demand for the information, document, or item;

(4) in this instance, the interest of the party subpoenaing the information outweighs the public interest in gathering and dissemination of news, including the concerns of the journalist;

(5) the subpoena or compulsory process is not being used to obtain peripheral, nonessential, or speculative information; and

(6) the information, document, or item is relevant and material to the proper administration of the official proceeding for which the testimony, production, or disclosure is sought and is essential to the maintenance of a claim or defense of the person seeking the testimony, production, or disclosure.

Added by Acts 2009, 81st Leg., ch. 29, § 1, eff. May 13, 2009.

§ 22.025. Notice

An order to compel testimony, production, or disclosure to which a journalist has asserted a privilege under this subchapter may be issued only after timely notice to the journalist, the journalist's employer, or a person who has an independent contract with the journalist and a hearing. The order must include clear and specific findings as to the showing made by the person seeking the testimony, production, or disclosure and the clear and specific evidence on which the court relied in issuing the court's order.

Added by Acts 2009, 81st Leg., ch. 29, § 1, eff. May 13, 2009.

§ 22.026. Publication of Privileged Information

Publication or dissemination by a news medium or communication service provider of information, documents, or items privileged under this subchapter is not a waiver of the journalist's privilege.

Added by Acts 2009, 81st Leg., ch. 29, § 1, eff. May 13, 2009.

§ 22.027. News Media Recordings

Extrinsic evidence of the authenticity of evidence as a condition precedent to the admissibility of the evidence in a civil proceeding is not required with respect to a recording that purports to be a broadcast by a radio or television station that holds a license issued by the Federal Communications Commission at the time of the recording. The court may take judicial notice of the recording license as provided by Rule 201, Texas Rules of Evidence.

Added by Acts 2009, 81st Leg., ch. 29, § 1, eff. May 13, 2009.

CHAPTER 23. JUROR CONTINUANCE

§ 23.001. Definitions

In this chapter:

(1) "Religious organization" means an organization that meets the standards for qualification as a religious organization under Section 11.20, Tax Code.

(2) "Religious holy day" means a day on which the tenets of a religious organization prohibit its members from participating in secular activities, such as court proceedings.

Added by Acts 1987, 70th Leg., ch. 589, § 5, eff. Aug. 31, 1987; Acts 1987, 70th Leg., ch. 825, § 5, eff. Sept. 1, 1987.

§ 23.002. Recess

(a) If a juror in a civil action is required to appear at a court proceeding on a religious holy day observed by the juror, the court or the court's designee[1] shall recess the civil action until the next day the court is in session after the conclusion of the holy day.

(b) A juror seeking a recess must file with the court before the final selection of the jury an affidavit stating:

(1) the grounds for the recess; and

(2) that the juror holds religious beliefs that prohibit him from taking part in a court proceeding on the day for which the recess is sought.

(c) An affidavit filed under Subsection (b) is proof of the facts stated and need not be corroborated.

Added by Acts 1987, 70th Leg., ch. 589, § 5, eff. Aug. 31, 1987; Acts 1987, 70th Leg., ch. 825, § 5, eff. Sept. 1, 1987.

[1] Version of subsec. (a) added by Acts 1987, 70th Leg., ch. 825, § 5, did not contain the phrase "or the court's designee".

CHAPTER 24. RECORDING OF JURY DELIBERATIONS

§ 24.001. Recording Prohibited

A person may not use any device to produce or make an audio, visual, or audio-visual broadcast, recording, or photograph of a jury while the jury is deliberating.

Added by Acts 2003, 78th Leg., ch. 54, § 2, eff. Sept. 1, 2003.

Chapter 25. [Reserved]

CHAPTER 26. CLASS ACTIONS

SUBCHAPTER A. SUPREME COURT RULES

SUBCHAPTER A. SUPREME COURT RULES

§ 26.001. Adoption of Rules by Supreme Court

(a) The supreme court shall adopt rules to provide for the fair and efficient resolution of class actions.

(b) The supreme court shall adopt rules under this chapter on or before December 31, 2003.

Added by Acts 2003, 78th Leg., ch. 204, § 1.01, eff. Sept. 1, 2003.

§ 26.002. Mandatory Guidelines

Rules adopted under Section 26.001 must comply with the mandatory guidelines established by this chapter.

Added by Acts 2003, 78th Leg., ch. 204, § 1.01, eff. Sept. 1, 2003.

§ 26.003. Attorney's Fees

(a) If an award of attorney's fees is available under applicable substantive law, the rules adopted under this chapter must provide that the trial court shall use the Lodestar method to calculate the amount of attorney's fees to be awarded class counsel. The rules may give the trial court discretion to increase or decrease the fee award calculated by using the Lodestar method by no more than four times based on specified factors.

(b) Rules adopted under this chapter must provide that in a class action, if any portion of the benefits recovered for the class are in the form of coupons or other noncash common benefits, the attorney's fees awarded in the action must be in cash and noncash amounts in the same proportion as the recovery for the class.

Added by Acts 2003, 78th Leg., ch. 204, § 1.01, eff. Sept. 1, 2003.

SUBCHAPTER B. CLASS ACTIONS INVOLVING JURISDICTION OF STATE AGENCY

§ 26.051. State Agency with Exclusive or Primary Jurisdiction

(a) Before hearing or deciding a motion to certify a class action, a trial court must hear and rule on all pending pleas to the jurisdiction asserting that an agency of this state has exclusive or primary jurisdiction of the action or a part of the action, or asserting that a party has failed to exhaust administrative remedies. The court's ruling must be reflected in a written order.

(b) If a plea to the jurisdiction described by Subsection (a) is denied and a class is subsequently certified, a person may, as part of an appeal of the order certifying the class action, obtain appellate review of the order denying the plea to the jurisdiction.

(c) This section does not alter or abrogate a person's right to appeal or pursue an original proceeding in an appellate court in regard to a trial court's order granting or denying a plea to the jurisdiction if the right exists under statutory or common law in effect at the time review is sought.

Added by Acts 2003, 78th Leg., ch. 204, § 1.01, eff. Sept. 1, 2003.

CHAPTER 27. ACTIONS INVOLVING THE EXERCISE OF CERTAIN CONSTITUTIONAL RIGHTS

Section

§ 27.001. Definitions

In this chapter:

(1) "Communication" includes the making or submitting of a statement or document in any form or medium, including oral, visual, written, audiovisual, or electronic.

(2) "Exercise of the right of association" means to join together to collectively express, promote, pursue, or defend common interests relating to a governmental proceeding or a matter of public concern.

(3) "Exercise of the right of free speech" means a communication made in connection with a matter of public concern.

(4) "Exercise of the right to petition" means any of the following:

(A) a communication in or pertaining to:

(i) a judicial proceeding;

(ii) an official proceeding, other than a judicial proceeding, to administer the law;

(iii) an executive or other proceeding before a department of the state or federal government or a subdivision of the state or federal government;

(iv) a legislative proceeding, including a proceeding of a legislative committee;

(v) a proceeding before an entity that requires by rule that public notice be given before proceedings of that entity;

(vi) a proceeding in or before a managing board of an educational or eleemosynary institution supported directly or indirectly from public revenue;

(vii) a proceeding of the governing body of any political subdivision of this state;

(viii) a report of or debate and statements made in a proceeding described by Subparagraph (iii), (iv), (v), (vi), or (vii); or

(ix) a public meeting dealing with a public purpose, including statements and discussions at the meeting or other matters of public concern occurring at the meeting;

(B) a communication in connection with an issue under consideration or review by a legislative, executive, judicial, or other governmental body or in another governmental or official proceeding;

(C) a communication that is reasonably likely to encourage consideration or review of an issue by a legislative, executive, judicial, or other governmental body or in another governmental or official proceeding;

(D) a communication reasonably likely to enlist public participation in an effort to effect consideration of an issue by a legislative, executive, judicial, or other governmental body or in another governmental or official proceeding; and

(E) any other communication that falls within the protection of the right to petition government under the Constitution of the United States or the constitution of this state.

(5) "Governmental proceeding" means a proceeding, other than a judicial proceeding, by an officer, official, or body of this state or a political subdivision of this state, including a board or commission, or by an officer, official, or body of the federal government.

(6) "Legal action" means a lawsuit, cause of action, petition, complaint, cross-claim, or counterclaim or any other judicial pleading or filing that requests legal, declaratory, or equitable relief. The term does not include:

(A) a procedural action taken or motion made in an action that does not amend or add a claim for legal, equitable, or declaratory relief;

(B) alternative dispute resolution proceedings; or

(C) post-judgment enforcement actions.

(7) "Matter of public concern" means a statement or activity regarding:

(A) a public official, public figure, or other person who has drawn substantial public attention due to the person's official acts, fame, notoriety, or celebrity;

(B) a matter of political, social, or other interest to the community; or

(C) a subject of concern to the public.

(8) "Official proceeding" means any type of administrative, executive, legislative, or judicial proceeding that may be conducted before a public servant.

(9) "Public servant" means a person elected, selected, appointed, employed, or otherwise designated as one of the following, even if the person has not yet qualified for office or assumed the person's duties:

(A) an officer, employee, or agent of government;

(B) a juror;

(C) an arbitrator, referee, or other person who is authorized by law or private written agreement to hear or determine a cause or controversy;

(D) an attorney or notary public when participating in the performance of a governmental function; or

(E) a person who is performing a governmental function under a claim of right but is not legally qualified to do so.

Added by Acts 2011, 82nd Leg., ch. 341 (H.B. 2973), § 2, eff. June 17, 2011. Amended by Acts 2019, 86th Leg., ch. 378 (H.B. 2730), § 1, eff. Sept. 1, 2019.

Sections 10 and 11 of Acts 2019, 86th Leg., ch. 378 (H.B. 2730) provide:

"Sec. 10. If any provision of this Act or its application to any person or circumstance is held invalid, the invalidity does not affect other provisions or applications of this Act that can be given effect without the invalid provision or application, and to this end the provisions of this Act are declared to be severable.

"Sec. 11. Chapter 27, Civil Practice and Remedies Code, as amended by this Act, applies only to an action filed on or after the effective date [Sept. 1, 2019] of this Act. An action filed before the effective date of this Act is governed by the law in effect immediately before that date, and that law is continued in effect for that purpose."

§ 27.002. Purpose

The purpose of this chapter is to encourage and safeguard the constitutional rights of persons to petition, speak freely, associate freely, and otherwise participate in government to the maximum extent permitted by law and, at the same time, protect the rights of a person to file meritorious lawsuits for demonstrable injury.

Added by Acts 2011, 82nd Leg., ch. 341 (H.B. 2973), § 2, eff. June 17, 2011.

§ 27.003. Motion to Dismiss

(a) If a legal action is based on or is in response to a party's exercise of the right of free speech, right to petition, or right of association or arises from any act of that party in furtherance of the party's communication or conduct described by Section 27.010(b), that party may file a motion to dismiss the legal action. A party under this section does not include a government entity, agency, or an official or employee acting in an official capacity.

(b) A motion to dismiss a legal action under this section must be filed not later than the 60th day after the date of service of the legal action. The parties, upon mutual agreement, may extend the time to file a motion under this section or the court may extend the time to file a motion under this section on a showing of good cause.

(c) Except as provided by Section 27.006(b), on the filing of a motion under this section, all discovery in the legal action is suspended until the court has ruled on the motion to dismiss.

(d) The moving party shall provide written notice of the date and time of the hearing under Section 27.004 not later than 21 days before the date of the hearing unless otherwise provided by agreement of the parties or an order of the court.

(e) A party responding to the motion to dismiss shall file the response, if any, not later than seven days before the date of the hearing on the motion to dismiss unless otherwise provided by an agreement of the parties or an order of the court.

Added by Acts 2011, 82nd Leg., ch. 341 (H.B. 2973), § 2, eff. June 17, 2011. Amended by Acts 2019, 86th Leg., ch. 378 (H.B. 2730), § 2, eff. Sept. 1, 2019.

Sections 10 and 11 of Acts 2019, 86th Leg., ch. 378 (H.B. 2730) provide:

"Sec. 10. If any provision of this Act or its application to any person or circumstance is held invalid, the invalidity does not affect other provisions or applications of this Act that can be given effect without the invalid provision or application, and to this end the provisions of this Act are declared to be severable.

"Sec. 11. Chapter 27, Civil Practice and Remedies Code, as amended by this Act, applies only to an action filed on or after the effective date [Sept. 1, 2019] of this Act. An action filed before the effective date of this Act is governed by the law in effect immediately before that date, and that law is continued in effect for that purpose."

§ 27.004. Hearing

(a) A hearing on a motion under Section 27.003 must be set not later than the 60th day after the date of service of the motion unless the docket conditions of the court require a later hearing, upon a showing of good cause, or by agreement of the parties, but in no event shall the hearing occur more than 90 days after service of the motion under Section 27.003, except as provided by Subsection (c).

(b) In the event that the court cannot hold a hearing in the time required by Subsection (a), the court may take judicial notice that the court's docket conditions required a hearing at a later date, but in no event shall the hearing occur more than 90 days after service of the motion under Section 27.003, except as provided by Subsection (c).

(c) If the court allows discovery under Section 27.006(b), the court may extend the hearing date to allow discovery under that subsection, but in no event shall the hearing occur more than 120 days after the service of the motion under Section 27.003.

Added by Acts 2011, 82nd Leg., ch. 341 (H.B. 2973), § 2, eff. June 17, 2011. Amended by Acts 2013, 83rd Leg., ch. 1042 (H.B. 2935), § 1, eff. June 14, 2013.

§ 27.005. Ruling

(a) The court must rule on a motion under Section 27.003 not later than the 30th day following the date the hearing on the motion concludes.

(b) Except as provided by Subsection (c), on the motion of a party under Section 27.003, a court shall dismiss a legal action against the moving party if the moving party demonstrates that the legal action is based on or is in response to:

(1) the party's exercise of:

(A) the right of free speech;

(B) the right to petition; or

(C) the right of association; or

(2) the act of a party described by Section 27.010(b).

(c) The court may not dismiss a legal action under this section if the party bringing the legal action establishes by clear and specific evidence a prima facie case for each essential element of the claim in question.

(d) Notwithstanding the provisions of Subsection (c), the court shall dismiss a legal action against the moving party if the moving party establishes an affirmative defense or other grounds on which the moving party is entitled to judgment as a matter of law.

Added by Acts 2011, 82nd Leg., ch. 341 (H.B. 2973), § 2, eff. June 17, 2011. Amended by Acts 2013, 83rd Leg., ch. 1042 (H.B. 2935), § 2, eff. June 14, 2013; Acts 2019, 86th Leg., ch. 378 (H.B. 2730), § 3, eff. Sept. 1, 2019.

Sections 10 and 11 of Acts 2019, 86th Leg., ch. 378 (H.B. 2730) provide:

"Sec. 10. If any provision of this Act or its application to any person or circumstance is held invalid, the invalidity does not affect other provisions or applications of this Act that can be given effect without the invalid provision or application, and to this end the provisions of this Act are declared to be severable.

"Sec. 11. Chapter 27, Civil Practice and Remedies Code, as amended by this Act, applies only to an action filed on or after the effective date [Sept. 1, 2019] of this Act. An action filed before the effective date of this Act is governed by the law in effect immediately before that date, and that law is continued in effect for that purpose."

§ 27.006. Proof

(a) In determining whether a legal action is subject to or should be dismissed under this chapter, the court shall consider the pleadings, evidence a court could consider under Rule 166a, Texas Rules of Civil Procedure, and supporting and opposing affidavits stating the facts on which the liability or defense is based.

(b) On a motion by a party or on the court's own motion and on a showing of good cause, the court may allow specified and limited discovery relevant to the motion.

Added by Acts 2011, 82nd Leg., ch. 341 (H.B. 2973), § 2, eff. June 17, 2011. Amended by Acts 2019, 86th Leg., ch. 378 (H.B. 2730), §§ 4, 5, eff. Sept. 1, 2019.

Sections 10 and 11 of Acts 2019, 86th Leg., ch. 378 (H.B. 2730) provide:

"Sec. 10. If any provision of this Act or its application to any person or circumstance is held invalid, the invalidity does not affect other provisions or applications of this Act that can be given effect without the invalid provision or application, and to this end the provisions of this Act are declared to be severable.

"Sec. 11. Chapter 27, Civil Practice and Remedies Code, as amended by this Act, applies only to an action filed on or after the effective date [Sept. 1, 2019] of this Act. An action filed before the effective date of this Act is governed by the law in effect immediately before that date, and that law is continued in effect for that purpose."

§ 27.007. Additional Findings

(a) If the court awards sanctions under Section 27.009(b), the court shall issue findings regarding whether the legal action was brought to deter or prevent the moving party from exercising constitutional rights and is brought for an improper purpose, including to harass or to cause unnecessary delay or to increase the cost of litigation.

(b) The court must issue findings under Subsection (a) not later than the 30th day after the date a request under that subsection is made.

Added by Acts 2011, 82nd Leg., ch. 341 (H.B. 2973), § 2, eff. June 17, 2011. Amended by Acts 2019, 86th Leg., ch. 378 (H.B. 2730), § 6, eff. Sept. 1, 2019.

Sections 10 and 11 of Acts 2019, 86th Leg., ch. 378 (H.B. 2730) provide:

"Sec. 10. If any provision of this Act or its application to any person or circumstance is held invalid, the invalidity does not affect other provisions or applications of this Act that can be given effect without the invalid provision or application, and to this end the provisions of this Act are declared to be severable.

"Sec. 11. Chapter 27, Civil Practice and Remedies Code, as amended by this Act, applies only to an action filed on or after the effective date [Sept. 1, 2019] of this Act. An action filed before the effective date of this Act is governed by the law in effect immediately before that date, and that law is continued in effect for that purpose."

§ 27.0075. Effect of Ruling

Neither the court's ruling on the motion nor the fact that it made such a ruling shall be admissible in evidence at any later stage of the case, and no burden of proof or degree of proof otherwise applicable shall be affected by the ruling.

Added by Acts 2019, 86th Leg., ch. 378 (H.B. 2730), § 7, eff. Sept. 1, 2019.

Sections 10 and 11 of Acts 2019, 86th Leg., ch. 378 (H.B. 2730) provide:

"Sec. 10. If any provision of this Act or its application to any person or circumstance is held invalid, the invalidity does not affect other provisions or applications of this Act that can be given effect without the invalid provision or application, and to this end the provisions of this Act are declared to be severable.

"Sec. 11. Chapter 27, Civil Practice and Remedies Code, as amended by this Act, applies only to an action filed on or after the effective date [Sept. 1, 2019] of this Act. An action filed before the effective date of this Act is governed by the law in effect immediately before that date, and that law is continued in effect for that purpose."

§ 27.008. Appeal

(a) If a court does not rule on a motion to dismiss under Section 27.003 in the time prescribed by Section 27.005, the motion is considered to have been denied by operation of law and the moving party may appeal.

(b) An appellate court shall expedite an appeal or other writ, whether interlocutory or not, from a trial court order on a motion to dismiss a legal action under Section 27.003 or from a trial court's failure to rule on that motion in the time prescribed by Section 27.005.

(c) Repealed by Acts 2013, 83rd Leg., ch. 1042 (H.B. 2935), § 5.

Added by Acts 2011, 82nd Leg., ch. 341 (H.B. 2973), § 2, eff. June 17, 2011. Amended by Acts 2013, 83rd Leg., ch. 1042 (H.B. 2935), § 5, eff. June 14, 2013.

§ 27.009. Damages and Costs

(a) Except as provided by Subsection (c), if the court orders dismissal of a legal action under this chapter, the court:

(1) shall award to the moving party court costs and reasonable attorney's fees incurred in defending against the legal action; and

(2) may award to the moving party sanctions against the party who brought the legal action as the court determines sufficient to deter the party who brought the legal action from bringing similar actions described in this chapter.

(b) If the court finds that a motion to dismiss filed under this chapter is frivolous or solely intended to delay, the court may award court costs and reasonable attorney's fees to the responding party.

(c) If the court orders dismissal of a compulsory counterclaim under this chapter, the court may award to the moving party reasonable attorney's fees incurred in defending against the counterclaim if the court finds that the counterclaim is frivolous or solely intended for delay.

Added by Acts 2011, 82nd Leg., ch. 341 (H.B. 2973), § 2, eff. June 17, 2011. Amended by Acts 2019, 86th Leg., ch. 378 (H.B. 2730), § 8, eff. Sept. 1, 2019.

Sections 10 and 11 of Acts 2019, 86th Leg., ch. 378 (H.B. 2730) provide:

"Sec. 10. If any provision of this Act or its application to any person or circumstance is held invalid, the invalidity does not affect other provisions or applications of this Act that can be given effect without the invalid provision or application, and to this end the provisions of this Act are declared to be severable.

"Sec. 11. Chapter 27, Civil Practice and Remedies Code, as amended by this Act, applies only to an action filed on or after the effective date [Sept. 1, 2019] of this Act. An action filed before the effective date of this Act is governed by the law in effect immediately before that date, and that law is continued in effect for that purpose."

§ 27.010. Exemptions

(a) This chapter does not apply to:

(1) an enforcement action that is brought in the name of this state or a political subdivision of this state by the attorney general, a district attorney, a criminal district attorney, or a county attorney;

(2) a legal action brought against a person primarily engaged in the business of selling or leasing goods or services, if the statement or conduct arises out of the sale or lease of goods, services, or an insurance product, insurance services, or a commercial transaction in which the intended audience is an actual or potential buyer or customer;

(3) a legal action seeking recovery for bodily injury, wrongful death, or survival or to statements made regarding that legal action;

(4) a legal action brought under the Insurance Code or arising out of an insurance contract;

(5) a legal action arising from an officer-director, employee-employer, or independent contractor relationship that:

(A) seeks recovery for misappropriation of trade secrets or corporate opportunities; or

(B) seeks to enforce a non-disparagement agreement or a covenant not to compete;

(6) a legal action filed under Title 1, 2, 4, or 5, Family Code,[1] or an application for a protective order under Subchapter A, Chapter 7B, Code of Criminal Procedure;

(7) a legal action brought under Chapter 17, Business & Commerce Code, other than an action governed by Section 17.49(a) of that chapter;

(8) a legal action in which a moving party raises a defense pursuant to Section 160.010, Occupations Code, Section 161.033, Health and Safety Code, or the Health Care Quality Improvement Act of 1986 (42 U.S.C. 11101 et seq.);

(9) an eviction suit brought under Chapter 24, Property Code;

(10) a disciplinary action or disciplinary proceeding brought under Chapter 81, Government Code, or the Texas Rules of Disciplinary Procedure;

(11) a legal action brought under Chapter 554, Government Code; or

(12) a legal action based on a common law fraud claim.

(b) Notwithstanding Subsections (a)(2), (7), and (12), this chapter applies to:

(1) a legal action against a person arising from any act of that person, whether public or private, related to the gathering, receiving, posting, or processing of information for communication to the public, whether or not the information is actually communicated to the public, for the creation, dissemination, exhibition, or advertisement or other similar promotion of a dramatic, literary, musical, political, journalistic, or otherwise artistic work, including audio-visual work regardless of the means of distribution, a motion picture, a television or radio program, or an article published in a newspaper, website, magazine, or other platform, no matter the method or extent of distribution; and

(2) a legal action against a person related to the communication, gathering, receiving, posting, or processing of consumer opinions or commentary, evaluations of consumer complaints, or reviews or ratings of businesses.

(c) This chapter applies to a legal action against a victim or alleged victim of family violence or dating violence as defined in Chapter 71, Family Code, or an offense under Chapter 20, 20A, 21, or 22, Penal Code, based on or in response to a public or private communication.

Added by Acts 2011, 82nd Leg., ch. 341 (H.B. 2973), § 2, eff. June 17, 2011. Amended by Acts 2013, 83rd Leg., ch. 1042 (H.B. 2935), § 3, eff. June 14, 2013; Acts 2019, 86th Leg., ch. 378 (H.B. 2730), § 9, eff. Sept. 1, 2019; Acts 2021, 87th Leg., ch. 915 (H.B. 3607), § 3.001, eff. Sept. 1, 2021.

[1] V.T.C.A., Family Code § 1.001 et seq.; § 16.001 et seq.; § 71.001 et seq.; § 101.001 et seq.

Sections 10 and 11 of Acts 2019, 86th Leg., ch. 378 (H.B. 2730) provide:

"Sec. 10. If any provision of this Act or its application to any person or circumstance is held invalid, the invalidity does not affect other provisions or applications of this Act that can be given effect without the invalid provision or application, and to this end the provisions of this Act are declared to be severable.

"Sec. 11. Chapter 27, Civil Practice and Remedies Code, as amended by this Act, applies only to an action filed on or after the effective date [Sept. 1, 2019] of this Act. An action filed before the effective date of this Act is governed by the law in effect immediately before that date, and that law is continued in effect for that purpose."

§ 27.011. Construction

(a) This chapter does not abrogate or lessen any other defense, remedy, immunity, or privilege available under other constitutional, statutory, case, or common law or rule provisions.

(b) This chapter shall be construed liberally to effectuate its purpose and intent fully.

Added by Acts 2011, 82nd Leg., ch. 341 (H.B. 2973), § 2, eff. June 17, 2011.

Chapters 28, 29. [Reserved]

CHAPTER 30. MISCELLANEOUS PROVISIONS

Section

§ 30.001. Instrument to Waive Service or Confess Judgment

In an instrument executed before suit is brought, a person may not accept service and waive process, enter an appearance in open court, or confess a judgment.

Acts 1985, 69th Leg., ch. 959, § 1, eff. Sept. 1, 1985.

§ 30.002. Expiration of Judge's Term; Death of Judge

(a) If a district or county judge's term of office expires before the adjournment of the court term at which a case may be tried or during the period prescribed for filing a statement of facts and a bill of exceptions or findings of fact and conclusions of law, the judge may approve the statement of facts and bill of exceptions or file findings of fact and conclusions of law in the case.

(b) If a district or county judge dies before he approves the statement of facts and bill of exceptions or files findings of fact and conclusions of law in a case pending at his death, they may be approved or filed by the judge's successor as provided by Rule 18, Texas Rules of Civil Procedure.

Acts 1985, 69th Leg., ch. 959, § 1, eff. Sept. 1, 1985.

§ 30.003. Legislative Continuance

(a) This section applies to any criminal or civil suit, including matters of probate, and to any matters ancillary to the suit that require action by or the attendance of an attorney, including appeals but excluding temporary restraining orders.

(b) Except as provided by Subsections (c) and (c–1), at any time within 30 days of a date when the legislature is to be in session, at any time during a legislative session, or when the legislature sits as a constitutional convention, the court on application shall continue a case in which a party applying for the continuance or the attorney for that party is a member or member-elect of the legislature and will be or is attending a legislative session. The court shall continue the case until 30 days after the date on which the legislature adjourns.

(c) Except as provided by Subsection (c–1), if the attorney for a party to the case is a member or member-elect of the legislature who was employed on or after the 30th day before the date on which the suit is set for trial, the continuance is discretionary with the court.

(c–1) If the attorney for a party to any criminal case is a member or member-elect of the legislature who was employed on or after the 15th day before the date on which the suit is set for trial, the continuance is discretionary with the court.

(d) The party seeking the continuance must file with the court an affidavit stating the grounds for the continuance. The affidavit is proof of the necessity for a continuance. The affidavit need not be corroborated.

(e) If the member of the legislature is an attorney for a party, the affidavit must contain a declaration that it is the attorney's intention to participate actively in the preparation or presentation of the case and that the attorney has not taken the case for the purpose of obtaining a continuance under this section.

(f) The continuance provided by Subsection (b) is one of right and may not be charged against the party receiving it on any subsequent application for continuance.

(g) If the attorney for a party seeking a continuance under this section is a member or member-elect of the legislature, the attorney shall file a copy of the application for a continuance with the Texas Ethics Commission. The copy must be sent to the commission not later than the third business day after the date on which the attorney files the application with the court.

Acts 1985, 69th Leg., ch. 959, § 1, eff. Sept. 1, 1985. Amended by Acts 1991, 72nd Leg., ch. 304, § 3.13, eff. Jan. 1, 1992; Acts 2003, 78th Leg., ch. 9, § 1, eff. April 24, 2003; Acts 2003, 78th Leg., ch. 249, § 5.09, eff. Sept. 1, 2003.

§ 30.004. Notice to Attorney General for Certain Suits

(a) This section applies to a civil case in which:

(1) the state is named as a party;

(2) an agency in the executive or legislative department is named as a party; or

(3) a party may be represented by the attorney general as authorized by Chapter 104.

(b) On the filing of any petition in a case subject to this section, a copy of the petition shall be mailed to the attorney general at the attorney general's office in Austin, Texas, by United States Postal Service certified mail, return receipt requested.

(c) Mailing notice as required by Subsection (b) does not satisfy any other jurisdictional requirement relating to service of process on a state officer, board, commission, agency, or institution that is a named party in a court proceeding.

(d) Failure to give notice in a case in which notice is required by Subsection (b) results in any default judgment in the case being set aside without costs.

Added by Acts 1987, 70th Leg., ch. 167, § 3.06(a), eff. Sept. 1, 1987.

§ 30.005. Religious Holy Day

(a) In this section:

(1) "Religious organization" means an organization that meets the standards for qualifying as a religious organization under Section 11.20, Tax Code.

(2) "Religious holy day" means a day on which the tenets of a religious organization prohibit its members from participating in secular activities, such as court proceedings.

(b) If a party or an attorney representing a party in a civil action is required to appear at a court proceeding on a religious holy day observed by the party or attorney, the court shall continue the civil action.

(c) A party or an attorney representing a party seeking a continuance must file with the court an affidavit stating:

(1) the grounds for the continuance; and

(2) that the party or attorney holds religious beliefs that prohibit him from taking part in a court proceeding on the day for which the continuance is sought.

(d) An affidavit filed under Subsection (c) of this section is proof of the facts stated and need not be corroborated.

Added by Acts 1987, 70th Leg., ch. 825, § 2, eff. Sept. 1, 1987. Redesignated from V.T.C.A., Civil Practice & Remedies Code § 30.004 by Acts 1989, 71st Leg., ch. 2, § 16.01(1), eff. Aug. 28, 1989. Amended by Acts 1991, 72nd Leg., ch. 815, § 2, eff. Sept. 1, 1991.

§ 30.006. Certain Law Enforcement Agency Records Not Subject to Discovery

(a) In this section, "law enforcement agency" means a governmental agency that employs a peace officer as defined under Article 2.12, Code of Criminal Procedure.

(b) This section does not apply to an action in which a law enforcement agency is a party.

(c) Except as provided by Subsection (d), a court in a civil action may not order discovery from a nonparty law enforcement agency of information, records, documents, evidentiary materials, and tangible things if:

(1) the information, records, documents, evidentiary materials, or tangible things deal with:

(A) the detection, investigation, or prosecution of crime; or

(B) an investigation by the nonparty law enforcement agency that does not result in conviction or deferred adjudication; and

(2) the release of the information, records, documents, evidentiary materials, or tangible things would interfere with the detection, investigation, or prosecution of criminal acts.

(d) On motion of a party, the court may order discovery from a nonparty law enforcement agency of information, records, documents, evidentiary materials, and tangible things described by Subsection (c) if the court determines, after in camera inspection, that:

(1) the discovery sought is relevant; and

(2) there is a specific need for the discovery.

(e) This section does not apply to:

(1) a report of an accident under Chapter 550, Transportation Code; and

(2) photographs, field measurements, scene drawings, and accident reconstruction done in conjunction with the investigation of the underlying accident.

Added by Acts 2007, 80th Leg., ch. 679, § 1, eff. Sept. 1, 2007.

§ 30.007. Production of Financial Institution Records

Civil discovery of a customer record maintained by a financial institution is governed by Section 59.006, Finance Code.

Added by Acts 1995, 74th Leg., ch. 914, § 3, eff. Sept. 1, 1995. Amended by Acts 1999, 76th Leg., ch. 344, § 7.001, eff. Sept. 1, 1999.

§ 30.008. Demand for Jury Trial in Justice Court; Failure to Appear

(a) A justice court may order a party who demands a jury trial in a justice court and who fails to appear for the trial to pay the costs incurred for impaneling the jury.

(b) The justice court may release a party from the obligation to pay costs under this section for good cause.

(c) An order issued by a justice court under this section may be enforced by contempt as prescribed by Section 21.002(c), Government Code.

Added by Acts 1995, 74th Leg., ch. 122, § 3, eff. Sept. 1, 1995. Redesignated from V.T.C.A., Civil Practice & Remedies Code § 30.007 by Acts 1997, 75th Leg., ch. 165, § 31.01(4), eff. Sept. 1, 1997.

§ 30.009. Mistrial in Justice Court or Municipal Court

If a jury in a trial in a justice court or a municipal court is discharged without having rendered a verdict, the cause may be tried again as soon as practicable.

Added by Acts 1995, 74th Leg., ch. 1005, § 2, eff. Sept. 1, 1995. Redesignated from V.T.C.A., Civil Practice & Remedies Code § 30.007 by Acts 1997, 75th Leg., ch. 165, § 31.01(5), eff. Sept. 1, 1997.

§ 30.010. Personal Identifying Information Privileged from Discovery by Inmate or Committed Person

(a) Personal identifying information pertaining to an individual, including the individual's home address, home telephone number, and social security account number, is privileged from discovery by an individual who is imprisoned or confined in any correctional facility or civilly committed as a sexually violent predator under Chapter 841, Health and Safety Code, if the individual to whom the information pertains is:

(1) an employee of any correctional facility;

(2) an officer or employee of the Texas Civil Commitment Office or a person who contracts with the office to perform a service or an employee of that person; or

(3) related within the first degree by consanguinity or affinity to an individual described by Subdivision (1) or (2).

(b) Personal identifying information that is privileged under this section may be discovered by an individual who is imprisoned or confined in a correctional facility or civilly committed as a sexually violent predator under Chapter 841, Health and Safety Code, only if:

(1) the incarcerated individual or committed person shows good cause to the court for the discovery of the information; and

(2) the court renders an order that authorizes discovery of the information.

(c) In this section, "correctional facility" has the meaning assigned by Section 1.07(a), Penal Code.

(d) Notwithstanding Section 22.004, Government Code, the supreme court may not amend or adopt rules in conflict with this section.

Added by Acts 1995, 74th Leg., ch. 302, § 2, eff. June 5, 1995. Redesignated from V.T.C.A., Civil Practice & Remedies Code § 30.07 by Acts 1997, 75th Leg., ch. 165, § 31.01(6), eff. Sept. 1, 1997. Amended by Acts 2017, 85th Leg., ch. 34 (S.B. 1576), §§ 1, 2, eff. Sept. 1, 2017.

§ 30.011. Electronic Subpoena Application

In addition to any other procedure permitted under state law or by court rule, an application for issuance of a subpoena may be made by electronic means.

Added by Acts 1999, 76th Leg., ch. 614, § 1, eff. June 18, 1999.

§ 30.012. Use of Communication Equipment in Certain Proceedings

(a) With the agreement of the parties, and subject to Subsection (b), a trial judge may order that a hearing of a preliminary matter or witness testimony at trial may be conducted by electronic means, including satellite transmission, closed-circuit television transmission, or any other method of two-way electronic communication that is available to the parties, approved by the court, and capable of visually and audibly recording the proceedings.

(b) Witness testimony at trial may be conducted by electronic means only if the witness is deposed before the commencement of the trial.

(c) A court that allows a transmission made under this section shall consider it accurate and include it in the record of the case, unless the court determines otherwise.

(d) A party to a transmission made under this section that is not in court:

(1) shall provide at the party's own expense any equipment that is compatible with the equipment used in court; and

(2) may record the proceedings at the party's own expense.

(e) A copy of a proceeding videotaped by a court under this section may be obtained from the clerk of the court on payment of a reasonable amount to cover the cost of producing the copy.

(f) Expenses incurred by a court in conducting a proceeding or recording a transmission under this section shall be assessed and collected as court costs.

Added by Acts 2001, 77th Leg., ch. 788, § 1, eff. June 14, 2001.

§ 30.013. Confidential Identity in Actions Involving Sexual Abuse of a Minor

(a) In this section:

(1) "Confidential identity" means:

(A) the use of a pseudonym; and

(B) the absence of any other identifying information, including address, telephone number, and social security number.

(2) "Plaintiff" means:

(A) an individual younger than 18 years of age seeking recovery of damages or other relief; and

(B) the parents or legal guardian of the individual.

(b) This section applies only to a civil action against a defendant in which a plaintiff seeks recovery of damages or other relief based on conduct described as a felony in the following sections of the Penal Code:

(1) Section 22.011 (sexual assault); or

(2) Section 22.021 (aggravated sexual assault).

(c) Except as otherwise provided by this section, in an action to which this section applies, the court shall:

(1) make it known to the plaintiff as early as possible in the proceedings of the action that the plaintiff may use a confidential identity in relation to the action;

(2) allow a plaintiff to use a confidential identity in all petitions, filings, and other documents presented to the court;

(3) use the confidential identity in all of the court's proceedings and records relating to the action, including any appellate proceedings; and

(4) maintain the records relating to the action in a manner that protects the confidentiality of the plaintiff.

(d) In a suit to which this section applies, only the following persons are entitled to know the true identifying information about the plaintiff:

(1) the judge;

(2) a party to the action;

(3) the attorney representing a party to the action; and

(4) a person authorized by a written order of a court specific to that person.

(e) The court shall order that a person entitled to know the true identifying information under Subsection (d) may not divulge that information to anyone without a written order of the court. A court shall hold a person who violates the order in contempt.

(f) Notwithstanding Section 22.004, Government Code, the supreme court may not amend or adopt rules in conflict with this section.

(g) A plaintiff is not required to use a confidential identity as provided by this section.

Added by Acts 2009, 81st Leg., ch. 559, § 1, eff. Sept. 1, 2009.

§ 30.014. Pleadings Must Contain Partial Identification Information

(a) In a civil action, including a probate or guardianship proceeding, filed in a district court, county court, statutory county court, or statutory probate court, each party or the party's attorney shall include in its initial pleading:

(1) the last three numbers of the party's driver's license number, if the party has been issued a driver's license; and

(2) the last three numbers of the party's social security number, if the party has been issued a social security number.

(b) A court may, on its own motion or the motion of a party, order that an initial pleading be amended to contain the information listed under Subsection (a) if the court determines that the pleading does not contain that information. A court may find a party in contempt if the party does not amend the pleading as ordered by the court under this subsection.

Added by Acts 2007, 80th Leg., ch. 143, § 1, eff. Sept. 1, 2007. Amended by Acts 2021, 87th Leg., ch. 521 (S.B. 626), § 1, eff. Sept. 1, 2021; Acts 2021, 87th Leg., ch. 576 (S.B. 615), § 1, eff. Sept. 1, 2021.

Section 72(a) of Acts 2021, 87th Leg., ch. 521 (S.B. 626) provides:

"(a) Except as otherwise provided by this Act, the changes in law made by this Act apply to:

"(1) a guardianship created before, on, or after the effective date [Sept. 1, 2021] of this Act; and

"(2) an application for a guardianship pending on, or filed on or after, the effective date of this Act."

§ 30.015. Provision of Current Address of Party in Civil Action

(a) In a civil action filed in a district court, county court, statutory county court, or statutory probate court, each party or the party's attorney must provide the clerk of the court with written notice of the party's name and current residence or business address.

(b) The notice required by Subsection (a) may not be required from any party or party's attorney if such party has not appeared or answered in the civil action.

(c) The notice required by Subsection (a) must be provided at the time the party files its initial pleading with the court or not later than the seventh day after the date the clerk of the court requests the information.

(d) If the party's address changes during the course of a civil action, the party or the party's attorney must provide the clerk of the court with written notice of the party's new address.

(e) If the party or the party's attorney fails to provide the notice required by Subsection (a), the trial court may assess a fine of not more than $50.

(f) It is a defense to a fine assessed under this section that the party or the party's attorney could not reasonably obtain and provide the information required by Subsection (a).

(g) Repealed by Acts 1999, 76th Leg., ch. 251, § 2, eff. Sept. 1, 1999.

Added by Acts 1997, 75th Leg., ch. 887, § 1, eff. Sept. 1, 1997. Amended by Acts 1999, 76th Leg., ch. 251, §§ 1, 2, eff. Sept. 1, 1999.

§ 30.016. Recusal or Disqualification of Certain Judges

(a) In this section, "tertiary recusal motion" means a third or subsequent motion for recusal or disqualification filed against a district court or statutory county court judge by the same party in a case.

(b) A judge who declines recusal after a tertiary recusal motion is filed shall comply with applicable rules of procedure for recusal and disqualification except that the judge shall continue to:

(1) preside over the case;

(2) sign orders in the case; and

(3) move the case to final disposition as though a tertiary recusal motion had not been filed.

(c) A judge hearing a tertiary recusal motion against another judge who denies the motion shall award reasonable and necessary attorney's fees and costs to the party opposing the motion. The party making the motion and the attorney for the party are jointly and severally liable for the award of fees and costs. The fees and costs must be paid before the 31st day after the date the order denying the tertiary recusal motion is rendered, unless the order is properly superseded.

(d) The denial of a tertiary recusal motion is only reviewable on appeal from final judgment.

(e) If a tertiary recusal motion is finally sustained, the new judge for the case shall vacate all orders signed by the sitting judge during the pendency of the tertiary recusal motion.

Added by Acts 1999, 76th Leg., ch. 608, § 1, eff. Sept. 1, 1999. Amended by Acts 2007, 80th Leg., ch. 1297, § 3, eff. Sept. 1, 2007.

§ 30.017. Claims Against Certain Judges

(a) A claim against a district court, statutory probate court, or statutory county court judge that is added to a case pending in the court to which the judge was elected or appointed:

(1) must be made under oath;

(2) may not be based solely on the rulings in the pending case but must plead specific facts supporting each element of the claim in addition to the rulings in the pending case; and

(3) is automatically severed from the case.

(b) The clerk of the court shall assign the claim a new cause number, and the party making the claim shall pay the filing fees.

(c) The presiding judge of the administrative region or the presiding judge of the statutory probate courts shall assign the severed claim to a different judge. The judge shall dismiss the claim if the claim does not satisfy the requirements of Subsection (a)(1) or (2).

Added by Acts 1999, 76th Leg., ch. 608, § 1, eff. Sept. 1, 1999.

§ 30.018. Court Clerk's Execution Docket

(a) The clerk of a court who is required to enter information into an execution docket under the Texas Rules of Civil Procedure or other law may enter and maintain the information in an electronic format that allows the information to be retrieved on the same basis as information would be retrieved manually using an index or cross-index to the docket that is otherwise required by law.

(b) Notwithstanding Section 22.004, Government Code, the supreme court may not amend or adopt rules in conflict with this section.

Added by Acts 2011, 82nd Leg., ch. 421 (S.B. 886), § 1, eff. Sept. 1, 2011.

§§ 30.019, 30.020. [Reserved]

§ 30.021. Award of Attorney's Fees in Relation to Certain Motions to Dismiss

In a civil proceeding, on a trial court's granting or denial, in whole or in part, of a motion to dismiss filed under the rules adopted by the supreme court under Section 22.004(g), Government Code, the court may award costs and reasonable and necessary attorney's fees to the prevailing party. This section does not apply to actions by or against the state, other governmental entities, or public officials acting in their official capacity or under color of law.

Added by Acts 2011, 82nd Leg., ch. 203 (H.B. 274), § 1.02, eff. Sept. 1, 2011. Amended by Acts 2019, 86th Leg., ch. 885 (H.B. 3300), § 1, eff. Sept. 1, 2019.

Section 2 of Acts 2019, 86th Leg., ch. 885 (H.B. 3300) provides:

"The change in law made by this Act applies only to a civil action commenced on or after the effective date [Sept. 1, 2019] of this Act. A civil action commenced before the effective date of this Act is governed by the law applicable to the action immediately before the effective date of this Act, and that law is continued in effect for that purpose."

§ 30.022. Award of Attorney's Fees in Actions Challenging Abortion Laws

(a) Notwithstanding any other law, any person, including an entity, attorney, or law firm, who seeks declaratory or injunctive relief to prevent this state, a political subdivision, any governmental entity or public official in this state, or any person in this state from enforcing any statute, ordinance, rule, regulation, or any other type of law that regulates or restricts abortion or that limits taxpayer funding for individuals or entities that perform or promote abortions, in any state or federal court, or that represents any litigant seeking such relief in any state or federal court, is jointly and severally liable to pay the costs and attorney's fees of the prevailing party.

(b) For purposes of this section, a party is considered a prevailing party if a state or federal court:

(1) dismisses any claim or cause of action brought against the party that seeks the declaratory or injunctive relief described by Subsection (a), regardless of the reason for the dismissal; or

(2) enters judgment in the party's favor on any such claim or cause of action.

(c) Regardless of whether a prevailing party sought to recover costs or attorney's fees in the underlying action, a prevailing party under this section may bring a civil action to recover costs and attorney's fees against a person, including an entity, attorney, or law firm, that sought declaratory or injunctive relief described by Subsection (a) not later than the third anniversary of the date on which, as applicable:

(1) the dismissal or judgment described by Subsection (b) becomes final on the conclusion of appellate review; or

(2) the time for seeking appellate review expires.

(d) It is not a defense to an action brought under Subsection (c) that:

(1) a prevailing party under this section failed to seek recovery of costs or attorney's fees in the underlying action;

(2) the court in the underlying action declined to recognize or enforce the requirements of this section; or

(3) the court in the underlying action held that any provisions of this section are invalid, unconstitutional, or preempted by federal law, notwithstanding the doctrines of issue or claim preclusion.

Added by Acts 2021, 87th Leg., ch. 62 (S.B. 8), § 4, eff. Sept. 1, 2021.

Sections 1, 2, 10 and 11 of Acts 2021, 87th Leg., ch. 62 (S.B. 8) provide:

"Sec. 1. This Act shall be known as the Texas Heartbeat Act."

"Sec. 2. The legislature finds that the State of Texas never repealed, either expressly or by implication, the state statutes enacted before the ruling in *Roe v. Wade*, 410 U.S. 113 (1973), that prohibit and criminalize abortion unless the mother's life is in danger."

"Sec. 10. Every provision in this Act and every application of the provision in this Act are severable from each other. If any provision or application of any provision in this Act to any person, group of persons, or circumstance is held by a court to be invalid, the invalidity does not affect the other provisions or applications of this Act."

"Sec. 11. The change in law made by this Act applies only to an abortion performed or induced on or after the effective date [Sept. 1, 2021] of this Act."

SUBTITLE C. JUDGMENTS

CHAPTER 31. JUDGMENTS

§ 31.001. Passage of Title

A judgment for the conveyance of real property or the delivery of personal property may pass title to the property without additional action by the party against whom the judgment is rendered.

Acts 1985, 69th Leg., ch. 959, § 1, eff. Sept. 1, 1985.

§ 31.002. Collection of Judgment Through Court Proceeding

(a) A judgment creditor is entitled to aid from a court of appropriate jurisdiction, including a justice court, through injunction or other means in order to reach property to obtain satisfaction on the judgment if the judgment debtor owns property, including present or future rights to property, that is not exempt from attachment, execution, or seizure for the satisfaction of liabilities.

(b) The court may:

(1) order the judgment debtor to turn over nonexempt property that is in the debtor's possession or is subject to the debtor's control, together with all documents or records related to the property, to a designated sheriff or constable for execution;

(2) otherwise apply the property to the satisfaction of the judgment; or

(3) appoint a receiver with the authority to take possession of the nonexempt property, sell it, and pay the proceeds to the judgment creditor to the extent required to satisfy the judgment.

(c) The court may enforce the order by contempt proceedings or by other appropriate means in the event of refusal or disobedience.

(d) The judgment creditor may move for the court's assistance under this section in the same proceeding in which the judgment is rendered or in an independent proceeding.

(e) The judgment creditor is entitled to recover reasonable costs, including attorney's fees.

(f) A court may not enter or enforce an order under this section that requires the turnover of the proceeds of, or the disbursement of, property exempt under any statute, including Section 42.0021, Property Code. This subsection does not apply to the enforcement of a child support obligation or a judgment for past due child support.

(g) With respect to turnover of property held by a financial institution in the name of or on behalf of the judgment debtor as customer of the financial institution, the rights of a receiver appointed under Subsection (b)(3) do not attach until the financial institution receives service of a certified copy of the order of receivership in the manner specified by Section 59.008, Finance Code.

(h) A court may enter or enforce an order under this section that requires the turnover of nonexempt property without identifying in the order the specific property subject to turnover.

Acts 1985, 69th Leg., ch. 959, § 1, eff. Sept. 1, 1985. Amended by Acts 1989, 71st Leg., ch. 1015, § 1, eff. June 15, 1989; Acts 1999, 76th Leg., ch. 344, § 7.002, eff. Sept. 1, 1999; Acts 2005, 79th Leg., ch. 52, § 1, eff. May 17, 2005; Acts 2017, 85th Leg., ch. 996 (H.B. 1066), § 1, eff. June 15, 2017; Acts 2019, 86th Leg., ch. 1221 (S.B. 2364), § 1, eff. Sept. 1, 2019.

Section 2 of Acts 2019, 86th Leg., ch. 1221 (S.B. 2364) provides:

"The change in law made by this Act applies to the collection of any judgment, regardless of whether the judgment was entered before, on, or after the effective date [Sept. 1, 2019] of this Act."

§ 31.0025. Authority of Court to Order Turnover of Wages

(a) Notwithstanding any other law, a court may not, at any time before a judgment debtor is paid wages for personal services performed by the debtor, enter or enforce an order that requires the debtor or any other person to turn over the wages for the satisfaction of the judgment.

(b) This section applies to wages in any form, including paycheck, cash, or property.

(c) This section does not apply to the enforcement of a child support obligation or a judgment for past due child support.

Added by Acts 1991, 72nd Leg., ch. 671, § 1, eff. Aug. 26, 1991.

§ 31.003. Judgment Against Partnership

If a suit is against several partners who are jointly indebted under a contract and citation has been served on at least one but not all of the partners, the court may render judgment against the partnership and against the partners who were actually served, but may not award a personal judgment or execution against any partner who was not served.

Acts 1985, 69th Leg., ch. 959, § 1, eff. Sept. 1, 1985.

§ 31.004. Effect of Adjudication in Lower Trial Court

(a) A judgment or a determination of fact or law in a proceeding in a lower trial court is not res judicata and is not a basis for estoppel by judgment in a proceeding in a district court, except that a judgment rendered in a lower trial court is binding on the parties thereto as to recovery or denial of recovery.

(b) This section does not apply to a judgment in probate, guardianship, mental health, or other matter in which a lower trial court has exclusive subject matter jurisdiction on a basis other than the amount in controversy.

(c) For the purposes of this section, a "lower trial court" is a small claims court, a justice of the peace court, a county court, or a statutory county court.

Acts 1985, 69th Leg., ch. 959, § 1, eff. Sept. 1, 1985. Amended by Acts 1987, 70th Leg., ch. 167, § 3.07(a), eff. Sept. 1, 1987.

§ 31.005. Effect of Adjudication in Small Claims or Justice of the Peace Court

A judgment or a determination of fact or law in a proceeding in small claims court or justice of the peace court is not res judicata and does not constitute a basis for estoppel by judgment in a proceeding in a county court or statutory county court, except that the judgment rendered is binding on the parties thereto as to recovery or denial of recovery.

Acts 1985, 69th Leg., ch. 959, § 1, eff. Sept. 1, 1985.

§ 31.006. Revival of Judgment

A dormant judgment may be revived by scire facias or by an action of debt brought not later than the second anniversary of the date that the judgment becomes dormant.

Acts 1985, 69th Leg., ch. 959, § 1, eff. Sept. 1, 1985. Amended by Acts 1995, 74th Leg., ch. 935, § 1, eff. Sept. 1, 1995.

Section 2 of Acts 1995, 74th Leg., ch. 935 provides:

§ 31.007. Parties Responsible for Accounting of Own Costs

(a) Each party to a suit shall be responsible for accurately recording all costs and fees incurred during the course of a lawsuit, if the judgment is to provide for the adjudication of such costs. If the judgment provides that costs are to be borne by the party by whom such costs were incurred, it shall not be necessary for any of the parties to present a record of court costs to the court in connection with the entry of a judgment.

(b) A judge of any court may include in any order or judgment all costs, including the following:

(1) fees of the clerk and service fees due the county;

(2) fees of the court reporter for the original of stenographic transcripts necessarily obtained for use in the suit;

(3) masters, interpreters, and guardians ad litem appointed pursuant to these rules and state statutes; and

(4) such other costs and fees as may be permitted by these rules and state statutes.

Added by Acts 1987, 70th Leg., ch. 663, § 3, eff. Sept. 1, 1987.

§ 31.008. Payment of Unclaimed Judgment

(a) A judgment debtor may pay to the court that rendered the judgment the amount under the judgment owed to a judgment creditor whose location is unknown to the judgment debtor if the judgment debtor complies with Subsections (b) and (c). The payment must be made without offset or reduction for any claims of the judgment debtor. The judgment debtor shall prepare a recordable release of the judgment. The judge or clerk of the court shall execute the release of the judgment on behalf of the creditor and issue the release to the debtor. The release shall recite the cause number, the court, the parties, the date of judgment, the amount of judgment, the amount paid into the court, and the date of the release.

(b) Before being entitled to pay a judgment to a court under Subsection (a), the judgment debtor shall send a letter notifying the judgment creditor of the judgment, by registered or certified mail, return receipt requested, to:

(1) the judgment creditor's last known address;

(2) the address appearing in the judgment creditor's pleadings or other court record, if different from the creditor's last known address;

(3) the address of the judgment creditor's last attorney, as shown in the creditor's pleadings or other court record; and

(4) the address of the judgment creditor's last attorney, as shown in the records of the State Bar of Texas, if that address is different from the address shown in the creditor's pleadings or other court record.

(c) If the judgment creditor does not respond to a notice under Subsection (b) on or before the 15th day after the date on which the notice was sent, the judgment debtor may file an affidavit with the court stating that the judgment debtor has provided the required notice, that the judgment creditor has not responded to the notice, and that the location of the judgment creditor is not known to the judgment debtor.

(d) The court shall hold the amount paid to it by the judgment debtor under Subsection (a) and interest earned on that amount in trust for the judgment creditor.

(e) The clerk of the court shall deposit the trust funds and any interest earned by the funds in the clerk's trust fund account. The clerk shall pay the funds and any interest earned by the funds to the judgment creditor or to the successors to the rights of the judgment creditor. The clerk may presume that the funds are payable to the judgment creditor unless the clerk is furnished with a written assignment of the judgment.

(f) Funds held in the clerk's trust fund account in accordance with this section are subject to escheat under Chapter 72, Property Code.

(g) If the judgment debtor complies with Subsections (b) and (c) and the judgment creditor refuses to accept payment of the amount under the judgment or accepts payment under the judgment and refuses to execute a release of judgment, the court shall set the matter for hearing on a party's motion or on the court's own motion to determine whether or not a release should be filed. On notice and hearing the court may direct the judgment debtor to prepare and file a recordable release of the judgment with the clerk of the court if the court finds that:

(1) the amount under the judgment has been paid into the registry of the court; or

(2) the judgment creditor has accepted payment under the judgment and refused to execute a release of judgment.

(h) In this section:

(1) "Judgment creditor" means a party in whose favor a judgment has been rendered, whether a plaintiff, counterclaimant, cross-claimant, third party plaintiff, or other judgment creditor.

(2) "Judgment debtor" means a party against whom a judgment is rendered.

Added by Acts 1991, 72nd Leg., ch. 730, § 1, eff. Sept. 1, 1991. Amended by Acts 1993, 73rd Leg., ch. 163, § 1, eff. Aug. 30, 1993; Acts 2001, 77th Leg., ch. 656, § 1, eff. Sept. 1, 2001.

§ 31.009. [Blank]

§ 31.010. Turnover by Financial Institution

(a) A financial institution that receives a request to turn over assets or financial information of a judgment debtor to a judgment creditor or a receiver under a turnover order or receivership under Section 31.002 shall be provided and may rely on:

(1) a certified copy of the order or injunction of the court; or

(2) a certified copy of the order of appointment of a receiver under Section 64.001, including a certified copy of:

(A) any document establishing the qualification of the receiver under Section 64.021;

(B) the sworn affidavit under Section 64.022; and

(C) the bond under Section 64.023.

(b) A financial institution that complies with this section is not liable for compliance with a court order, injunction, or receivership authorized by Section 31.002 to:

(1) the judgment debtor;

(2) a party claiming through the judgment debtor;

(3) a co-depositor with the judgment debtor; or

(4) a co-borrower with the judgment debtor.

(c) A financial institution that complies with this section is entitled to recover reasonable costs, including copying costs, research costs, and, if there is a contest, reasonable attorney's fees.

(d) In this section, "financial institution" means a state or national bank, state or federal savings and loan association, state or federal savings bank, state or federal credit union, foreign bank, foreign bank agency, or trust company.

Added by Acts 1999, 76th Leg., ch. 892, § 1, eff. Sept. 1, 1999.

CHAPTER 32. CONTRIBUTION

Section

§ 32.001. Application

(a) This chapter applies only to tort actions.

(b) This chapter does not apply if a right of contribution, indemnity, or recovery between defendants is provided by other statute or by common law.

Acts 1985, 69th Leg., ch. 959, § 1, eff. Sept. 1, 1985.

§ 32.002. Right of Action

A person against whom a judgment is rendered has, on payment of the judgment, a right of action to recover payment from each codefendant against whom judgment is also rendered.

Acts 1985, 69th Leg., ch. 959, § 1, eff. Sept. 1, 1985.

§ 32.003. Recovery

(a) The person may recover from each codefendant against whom judgment is rendered an amount determined by dividing the number of all liable defendants into the total amount of the judgment.

(b) If a codefendant is insolvent, the person may recover from each solvent codefendant an amount determined by dividing the number of solvent defendants into the total amount of the judgment.

(c) Each defendant in the judgment has a right to recover from the insolvent defendant the amount the defendant has had to pay because of the insolvency.

Acts 1985, 69th Leg., ch. 959, § 1, eff. Sept. 1, 1985.

CHAPTER 33. PROPORTIONATE RESPONSIBILITY

SUBCHAPTER A. PROPORTIONATE RESPONSIBILITY

Section

SUBCHAPTER B. CONTRIBUTION

Section

SUBCHAPTER A. PROPORTIONATE RESPONSIBILITY

§ 33.001. Proportionate Responsibility

In an action to which this chapter applies, a claimant may not recover damages if his percentage of responsibility is greater than 50 percent.

Acts 1985, 69th Leg., ch. 959, § 1, eff. Sept. 1, 1985. Amended by Acts 1987, 70th Leg., 1st C.S., ch. 2, § 2.04, eff. Sept. 2, 1987; Acts 1995, 74th Leg., ch. 136, § 1, eff. Sept. 1, 1995.

§ 33.002. Applicability

(a) This chapter applies to:

(1) any cause of action based on tort in which a defendant, settling person, or responsible third party is found responsible for a percentage of the harm for which relief is sought; or

(2) any action brought under the Deceptive Trade Practices–Consumer Protection Act (Subchapter E, Chapter 17, Business & Commerce Code) [1] in which a defendant, settling person, or responsible third party is found responsible for a percentage of the harm for which relief is sought.

(b) Repealed by Acts 2003, 78th Leg., ch. 204, § 4.10(1).

(c) This chapter does not apply to:

(1) an action to collect workers' compensation benefits under the workers' compensation laws of this state (Subtitle A, Title 5, Labor Code) [2] or actions against an employer for exemplary damages arising out of the death of an employee;

(2) a claim for exemplary damages included in an action to which this chapter otherwise applies; or

(3) a cause of action for damages arising from the manufacture of methamphetamine as described by Chapter 99.

(d) to (h) Repealed by Acts 2003, 78th Leg., ch. 204, § 4.10(1).

Added by Acts 1987, 70th Leg., 1st C.S., ch. 2, § 2.05, eff. Sept. 2, 1987. Amended by Acts 1989, 71st Leg., ch. 380, § 4, eff. Sept. 1, 1989; Acts 1995, 74th Leg., ch. 136, § 1, eff. Sept. 1, 1995; Acts 1995, 74th Leg., ch. 414, § 17, eff. Sept. 1, 1995; Acts 2001, 77th Leg., ch. 643, § 2, eff. Sept. 1, 2001; Acts 2003, 78th Leg., ch. 204, §§ 4.01, 4.10(1), eff. Sept. 1, 2003.

[1] V.T.C.A., Bus. & C. Code § 17.41 et seq.
[2] V.T.C.A., Labor Code § 401.001 et seq.

§ 33.003. Determination of Percentage of Responsibility

(a) The trier of fact, as to each cause of action asserted, shall determine the percentage of responsibility, stated in whole numbers, for the following persons with respect to each person's causing or contributing to cause in any way the harm for which recovery of damages is sought, whether by negligent act or omission, by any defective or unreasonably dangerous product, by other conduct or activity that violates an applicable legal standard, or by any combination of these:

(1) each claimant;

(2) each defendant;

(3) each settling person; and

(4) each responsible third party who has been designated under Section 33.004.

(b) This section does not allow a submission to the jury of a question regarding conduct by any person without sufficient evidence to support the submission.

Added by Acts 1987, 70th Leg., 1st C.S., ch. 2, § 2.06, eff. Sept. 2, 1987. Amended by Acts 1995, 74th Leg., ch. 136, § 1, eff. Sept. 1, 1995; Acts 2003, 78th Leg., ch. 204, § 4.02, eff. Sept. 1, 2003.

§ 33.004. Designation of Responsible Third Party

(a) A defendant may seek to designate a person as a responsible third party by filing a motion for leave to designate that person as a responsible third party. The motion must be filed on or before the 60th day before the trial date unless the court finds good cause to allow the motion to be filed at a later date.

(b) Nothing in this section affects the third-party practice as previously recognized in the rules and statutes of this state with regard to the assertion by a defendant of rights to contribution or indemnity. Nothing in this section affects the filing of cross-claims or counterclaims.

(c) Repealed by Acts 2003, 78th Leg., ch. 204, § 4.10(2).

(d) A defendant may not designate a person as a responsible third party with respect to a claimant's cause of action after the applicable limitations period on the cause of action has expired with respect to the responsible third party if the defendant has failed to comply with its obligations, if any, to timely disclose that the person may be designated as a responsible third party under the Texas Rules of Civil Procedure.

(e) Repealed by Acts 2011, 82nd Leg., ch. 203 (H.B. 274), § 5.02.

(f) A court shall grant leave to designate the named person as a responsible third party unless another party files an objection to the motion for leave on or before the 15th day after the date the motion is served.

(g) If an objection to the motion for leave is timely filed, the court shall grant leave to designate the person as a responsible third party unless the objecting party establishes:

(1) the defendant did not plead sufficient facts concerning the alleged responsibility of the person to satisfy the pleading requirement of the Texas Rules of Civil Procedure; and

(2) after having been granted leave to replead, the defendant failed to plead sufficient facts concerning the alleged responsibility of the person to satisfy the pleading requirements of the Texas Rules of Civil Procedure.

(h) By granting a motion for leave to designate a person as a responsible third party, the person named in the motion is designated as a responsible third party for purposes of this chapter without further action by the court or any party.

(i) The filing or granting of a motion for leave to designate a person as a responsible third party or a finding of fault against the person:

(1) does not by itself impose liability on the person; and

(2) may not be used in any other proceeding, on the basis of res judicata, collateral estoppel, or any other legal theory, to impose liability on the person.

(j) Notwithstanding any other provision of this section, if, not later than 60 days after the filing of the defendant's original answer, the defendant alleges in an answer filed with the court that an unknown person committed a criminal act that was a cause of the loss or injury that is the subject of the lawsuit, the court shall grant a motion for leave to designate the unknown person as a responsible third party if:

(1) the court determines that the defendant has pleaded facts sufficient for the court to determine that there is a reasonable probability that the act of the unknown person was criminal;

(2) the defendant has stated in the answer all identifying characteristics of the unknown person, known at the time of the answer; and

(3) the allegation satisfies the pleading requirements of the Texas Rules of Civil Procedure.

(k) An unknown person designated as a responsible third party under Subsection (j) is denominated as "Jane Doe" or "John Doe" until the person's identity is known.

(*l*) After adequate time for discovery, a party may move to strike the designation of a responsible third party on the ground that there is no evidence that the designated person is responsible for any portion of the claimant's alleged injury or damage. The court shall grant the motion to strike unless a defendant produces sufficient evidence to raise a genuine issue of fact regarding the designated person's responsibility for the claimant's injury or damage.

Added by Acts 1995, 74th Leg., ch. 136, § 1, eff. Sept. 1, 1995. Amended by Acts 2003, 78th Leg., ch. 204, §§ 4.03, 4.04, 4.10(2), eff. Sept. 1, 2003; Acts 2011, 82nd Leg., ch. 203 (H.B. 274), §§ 5.01, 5.02, eff. Sept. 1, 2011.

SUBCHAPTER B. CONTRIBUTION

§ 33.011. Definitions

In this chapter:

(1) "Claimant" means a person seeking recovery of damages, including a plaintiff, counterclaimant, cross-claimant, or third-party plaintiff. In an action in which a party seeks recovery of damages for injury to another person, damage to the property of another person, death of another person, or other harm to another person, "claimant" includes:

(A) the person who was injured, was harmed, or died or whose property was damaged; and

(B) any person who is seeking, has sought, or could seek recovery of damages for the injury, harm, or death of that person or for the damage to the property of that person.

(2) "Defendant" includes any person from whom, at the time of the submission of the case to the trier of fact, a claimant seeks recovery of damages.

(3) "Liable defendant" means a defendant against whom a judgment can be entered for at least a portion of the damages awarded to the claimant.

(4) "Percentage of responsibility" means that percentage, stated in whole numbers, attributed by the trier of fact to each claimant, each defendant, each settling person, or each responsible third party with respect to causing or contributing to cause in any way, whether by negligent act or omission, by any defective or unreasonably dangerous product, by other conduct or activity violative of the applicable legal standard, or by any combination of the foregoing, the personal injury, property damage, death, or other harm for which recovery of damages is sought.

(5) "Settling person" means a person who has, at any time, paid or promised to pay money or anything of monetary value to a claimant in consideration of potential liability with respect to the personal injury, property damage, death, or other harm for which recovery of damages is sought.

(6) "Responsible third party" means any person who is alleged to have caused or contributed to causing in any way the harm for which recovery of damages is sought, whether by negligent act or omission, by any defective or unreasonably dangerous product, by other conduct or activity that violates an applicable legal standard, or by any combination of these. The term "responsible third party" does not include a seller eligible for indemnity under Section 82.002.

(7) Repealed by Acts 2003, 78th Leg., ch. 204, § 4.10(3).

Acts 1985, 69th Leg., ch. 959, § 1, eff. Sept. 1, 1985. Amended by Acts 1987, 70th Leg., 1st C.S., ch. 2, § 2.07, eff. Sept. 2, 1987; Acts 1995, 74th Leg., ch. 136, § 1, eff. Sept. 1, 1995; Acts 2003, 78th Leg., ch. 204, §§ 4.05, 4.10(3), eff. Sept. 1, 2003.

§ 33.012. Amount of Recovery

(a) If the claimant is not barred from recovery under Section 33.001, the court shall reduce the amount of damages to be recovered by the claimant with respect to a cause of action by a percentage equal to the claimant's percentage of responsibility.

(b) If the claimant has settled with one or more persons, the court shall further reduce the amount of damages to be recovered by the claimant with respect to a cause of action by the sum of the dollar amounts of all settlements.

(c) Notwithstanding Subsection (b), if the claimant in a health care liability claim filed under Chapter 74 has settled with one or more persons, the court shall further reduce the amount of damages to be recovered by the claimant with respect to a cause of action by an amount equal to one of the following, as elected by the defendant:

(1) the sum of the dollar amounts of all settlements; or

(2) a percentage equal to each settling person's percentage of responsibility as found by the trier of fact.

(d) An election made under Subsection (c) shall be made by any defendant filing a written election before the issues of the action are submitted to the trier of fact and when made, shall be binding on all defendants. If no defendant makes this election or if conflicting elections are made, all defendants are considered to have elected Subsection (c)(1).

(e) This section shall not apply to benefits paid by or on behalf of an employer to an employee pursuant to workers' compensation insurance coverage, as defined in Section 401.011(44), Labor Code, in effect at the time of the act, event, or occurrence made the basis of claimant's suit.

Acts 1985, 69th Leg., ch. 959, § 1, eff. Sept. 1, 1985. Amended by Acts 1987, 70th Leg., 1st C.S., ch. 2, § 2.08, eff. Sept. 2, 1987; Acts 1995, 74th Leg., ch. 136, § 1, eff. Sept. 1, 1995; Acts 2003, 78th Leg., ch. 204, §§ 4.06, 4.10(4), eff. Sept. 1, 2003; Acts 2005, 79th Leg., ch. 277, § 1, eff. June 9, 2005; Acts 2005, 79th Leg., ch. 728, § 23.001(6), eff. Sept. 1, 2005.

§ 33.013. Amount of Liability

(a) Except as provided in Subsection (b), a liable defendant is liable to a claimant only for the percentage of the damages found by the trier of fact equal to that defendant's percentage of responsibility with respect to the personal injury, property damage, death, or other harm for which the damages are allowed.

(b) Notwithstanding Subsection (a), each liable defendant is, in addition to the defendant's liability under Subsection (a), jointly and severally liable for the damages recoverable by the claimant under Section 33.012 with respect to a cause of action if:

(1) the percentage of responsibility attributed to the defendant with respect to a cause of action is greater than 50 percent; or

(2) the defendant, with the specific intent to do harm to others, acted in concert with another person to engage in the conduct described in the following provisions of the Penal Code and in so doing proximately caused the damages legally recoverable by the claimant:

(A) Section 19.02 (murder);

(B) Section 19.03 (capital murder);

(C) Section 20.04 (aggravated kidnapping);

(D) Section 22.02 (aggravated assault);

(E) Section 22.011 (sexual assault);

(F) Section 22.021 (aggravated sexual assault);

(G) Section 22.04 (injury to a child, elderly individual, or disabled individual);

(H) Section 32.21 (forgery);

(I) Section 32.43 (commercial bribery);

(J) Section 32.45 (misapplication of fiduciary property or property of financial institution);

(K) Section 32.46 (fraudulent securing of document execution);

(L) Section 32.47 (fraudulent destruction, removal, or concealment of writing);

(M) conduct described in Chapter 31 the punishment level for which is a felony of the third degree or higher; or

(N) Section 21.02 (continuous sexual abuse of young child or disabled individual).

(c) Repealed by Acts 2003, 78th Leg., ch. 204, § 4.10(5).

(d) This section does not create a cause of action.

(e) Notwithstanding anything to the contrary stated in the provisions of the Penal Code listed in Subsection (b)(2), that subsection applies only if the claimant proves the defendant acted or failed to act with specific intent to do harm. A defendant acts with specific intent to do harm with respect to the nature of the defendant's conduct and the result of the person's conduct when it is the person's conscious effort or desire to engage in the conduct for the purpose of doing substantial harm to others.

(f) The jury may not be made aware through voir dire, introduction into evidence, instruction, or any other means that the conduct to which Subsection (b)(2) refers is defined by the Penal Code.

Acts 1985, 69th Leg., ch. 959, § 1, eff. Sept. 1, 1985. Amended by Acts 1987, 70th Leg., 1st C.S., ch. 2, § 2.09, eff. Sept. 2, 1987; Acts 1995, 74th Leg., ch. 136, § 1, eff. Sept. 1, 1995; Acts 2003, 78th Leg., ch. 204, §§ 4.07, 4.10(5), eff. Sept. 1, 2003; Acts 2007, 80th Leg., ch. 593, § 3.02, eff. Sept. 1, 2007; Acts 2021, 87th Leg., ch. 221 (H.B. 375), § 2.02, eff. Sept. 1, 2021; Acts 2021, 87th Leg., ch. 837 (S.B. 109), § 4, eff. Sept. 1, 2021.

Section 3.01 of Acts 2021, 87th Leg., ch. 221 (H.B. 375) provides:

"The change in law made by this Act applies only to an offense committed on or after the effective date [Sept. 1, 2021] of this Act. An offense committed before the effective date of this Act is governed by the law in effect on the date the offense was committed, and the former law is continued in effect for that purpose. For purposes of this section, an offense was committed before the effective date of this Act if any element of the offense occurred before that date."

Section 8 of Acts 2021, 87th Leg., ch. 837 (S.B. 109) provides:

"The change in law made by this Act applies only to an offense committed on or after the effective date [Sept. 1, 2021] of this Act. An offense committed before the effective date of this Act is governed by the law in effect on the date the offense was committed, and the former law is continued in effect for that purpose. For purposes of this section, an offense was committed before the effective date of this Act if any element of the offense was committed before that date."

§ 33.014. Repealed by Acts 2003, 78th Leg., ch. 204, § 4.10(6), eff. Sept. 1, 2003

§ 33.015. Contribution

(a) If a defendant who is jointly and severally liable under Section 33.013 pays a percentage of the damages for which the defendant is jointly and severally liable greater than his percentage of responsibility, that defendant has a right of contribution for the overpayment against each other liable defendant to the extent that the other liable defendant has not paid the percentage of the damages found by the trier of fact equal to that other defendant's percentage of responsibility.

(b) As among themselves, each of the defendants who is jointly and severally liable under Section 33.013 is liable for the damages recoverable by the claimant under Section 33.012 in proportion to his respective percentage of responsibility. If a defendant who is jointly and severally liable pays a larger proportion of those damages than is required by his percentage of responsibility, that defendant has a right of contribution for the overpayment against each other defendant with whom he is jointly and severally liable under Section 33.013 to the extent that the other defendant has not paid the proportion of those damages required by that other defendant's percentage of responsibility.

(c) If for any reason a liable defendant does not pay or contribute the portion of the damages required by his percentage of responsibility, the amount of the damages not paid or contributed by that defendant shall be paid or contributed by the remaining defendants who are jointly and severally liable for those damages. The additional amount to be paid or contributed by each of the defendants who is jointly and severally liable for those damages shall be in proportion to his respective percentage of responsibility.

(d) No defendant has a right of contribution against any settling person.

Acts 1985, 69th Leg., ch. 959, § 1, eff. Sept. 1, 1985. Amended by Acts 1987, 70th Leg., 1st C.S., ch. 2, § 2.11, eff. Sept. 2, 1987; Acts 1995, 74th Leg., ch. 136, § 1, eff. Sept. 1, 1995.

§ 33.016. Claim Against Contribution Defendant

(a) In this section, "contribution defendant" means any defendant, counterdefendant, or third-party defendant from whom any party seeks contribution with respect to any portion of damages for which that party may be liable, but from whom the claimant seeks no relief at the time of submission.

(b) Each liable defendant is entitled to contribution from each person who is not a settling person and who is liable to the claimant for a percentage of responsibility but from whom the claimant seeks no relief at the time of submission. A party may assert this contribution right against any such person as a contribution defendant in the claimant's action.

(c) The trier of fact shall determine as a separate issue or finding of fact the percentage of responsibility with respect to each contribution defendant and these findings shall be solely for purposes of this section and Section 33.015 and not as a part of the percentages of responsibility determined under Section 33.003. Only the percentage of responsibility of each defendant and contribution defendant shall be included in this determination.

(d) As among liable defendants, including each defendant who is jointly and severally liable under Section 33.013, each contribution defendant's percentage of responsibility is to be included for all purposes of Section 33.015. The amount to be contributed by each contribution defendant pursuant to Section 33.015 shall be in proportion to his respective percentage of responsibility relative to the sum of percentages of responsibility of all liable defendants and liable contribution defendants.

Acts 1985, 69th Leg., ch. 959, § 1, eff. Sept. 1, 1985. Amended by Acts 1987, 70th Leg., 1st C.S., ch. 2, § 2.11A, eff. Sept. 2, 1987; Acts 1995, 74th Leg., ch. 136, § 1, eff. Sept. 1, 1995.

§ 33.017. Preservation of Existing Rights of Indemnity

Nothing in this chapter shall be construed to affect any rights of indemnity granted by any statute, by contract, or by common law. To the extent of any conflict between this chapter and any right to indemnification granted by statute, contract, or common law, those rights of indemnification shall prevail over the provisions of this chapter.

Added by Acts 1995, 74th Leg., ch. 136, § 1, eff. Sept. 1, 1995. Amended by Acts 2003, 78th Leg., ch. 204, § 4.08, eff. Sept. 1, 2003.

CHAPTER 34. EXECUTION ON JUDGMENTS

SUBCHAPTER A. ISSUANCE AND LEVY OF WRIT

Section

SUBCHAPTER A. ISSUANCE AND LEVY OF WRIT

§ 34.001. No Execution on Dormant Judgment

(a) If a writ of execution is not issued within 10 years after the rendition of a judgment of a court of record or a justice court, the judgment is dormant and execution may not be issued on the judgment unless it is revived.

(b) If a writ of execution is issued within 10 years after rendition of a judgment but a second writ is not issued within 10 years after issuance of the first writ, the judgment becomes dormant. A second writ may be issued at any time within 10 years after issuance of the first writ.

(c) This section does not apply to a judgment for child support under the Family Code.

Acts 1985, 69th Leg., ch. 959, § 1, eff. Sept. 1, 1985. Amended by Acts 2009, 81st Leg., ch. 767, § 31, eff. June 19, 2009.

§ 34.002. Effect of Plaintiff's Death

(a) If a plaintiff dies after judgment, any writ of execution must be issued in the name of the plaintiff's legal representative, if any, and in the name of any other plaintiff. An affidavit of death and a certificate of appointment of the legal representative, given under the hand and seal of the clerk of the appointing court, must be filed with the clerk of the court issuing the writ of execution.

(b) If a plaintiff dies after judgment and his estate is not administered, the writ of execution must be issued in the name of all plaintiffs shown in the judgment. An affidavit showing that administration of the estate is unnecessary must be filed with the clerk of the court that rendered judgment. Money collected under the execution shall be paid into the registry of the court, and the court shall order the money partitioned and paid to the parties entitled to it.

(c) Death of a plaintiff after a writ of execution has been issued does not abate the execution, and the writ shall be levied and returned as if the plaintiff were living.

Acts 1985, 69th Leg., ch. 959, § 1, eff. Sept. 1, 1985.

§ 34.003. Effect of Defendant's Death

The death of the defendant after a writ of execution is issued stays the execution proceedings, but any lien acquired by levy of the writ must be recognized and enforced by the county court in the payment of the debts of the deceased.

Acts 1985, 69th Leg., ch. 959, § 1, eff. Sept. 1, 1985.

§ 34.004. Levy on Property Conveyed to Third Party

Property that the judgment debtor has sold, mortgaged, or conveyed in trust may not be seized in execution if the purchaser, mortgagee, or trustee points out other property of the debtor in the county that is sufficient to satisfy the execution.

Acts 1985, 69th Leg., ch. 959, § 1, eff. Sept. 1, 1985.

§ 34.005. Levy on Property of Surety

(a) If the face of a writ of execution or the endorsement of the clerk shows that one of the persons against whom it is issued is surety for another, the officer must first levy on the principal's property that is subject to execution and is located in the county in which the judgment is rendered.

(b) If property of the principal cannot be found that, in the opinion of the officer, is sufficient to satisfy the execution, the officer shall levy first on the principal's property that can be found and then on as much of the property of the surety as is necessary to satisfy the execution.

Acts 1985, 69th Leg., ch. 959, § 1, eff. Sept. 1, 1985.

SUBCHAPTER B. RECOVERY OF SEIZED PROPERTY

§ 34.021. Recovery of Property Before Sale

A person is entitled to recover his property that has been seized through execution of a writ issued by a court if the judgment on which execution is issued is reversed or set aside and the property has not been sold at execution.

Acts 1985, 69th Leg., ch. 959, § 1, eff. Sept. 1, 1985.

§ 34.022. Recovery of Property Value After Sale

(a) A person is entitled to recover from the judgment creditor the market value of the person's property that has been seized through execution of a writ issued by a court if the judgment on which execution is issued is reversed or set aside but the property has been sold at execution.

(b) The amount of recovery is determined by the market value at the time of sale of the property sold.

Acts 1985, 69th Leg., ch. 959, § 1, eff. Sept. 1, 1985.

SUBCHAPTER C. SALE

§ 34.041. Sale at Place Other than Courthouse Door; Date and Time of Sale

(a) If the public sale of real property is required by court order or other law to be made at a place other than the courthouse door, sales under this chapter shall be made at the place designated by that court order or other law.

(b) The commissioners court of a county may designate an area other than an area at the county courthouse where public sales of real property under this chapter will take place that is in a public place within a reasonable proximity of the county courthouse as determined by the commissioners court and in a location as accessible to the public as the courthouse door. The commissioners court shall record that designation in the real property records of the county. A designation by a commissioners court under this section is not a ground for challenging or invalidating any sale. Except for a sale under Subsection (a), a sale must be held at an area designated under this subsection if the sale is held on or after the 90th day after the date the designation is recorded. The commissioners court may by order authorize a county official or employee to identify separate locations within the designated area for the conduct of sales under this section and for the conduct of sales by peace officers under other laws.

(c) A sale of real property under this subchapter must take place between 10 a.m. and 4 p.m. on the first Tuesday of a month or, if the first Tuesday of a month occurs on January 1 or July 4, between 10 a.m. and 4 p.m. on the first Wednesday of the month. Notwithstanding Section 22.004, Government Code, the supreme court may not amend or adopt rules in conflict with this subsection.

Acts 1985, 69th Leg., ch. 959, § 1, eff. Sept. 1, 1985. Amended by Acts 2013, 83rd Leg., ch. 642 (H.B. 699), § 1, eff. Oct. 1, 2013; Acts 2017, 85th Leg., ch. 133 (H.B. 1128), §§ 1, 2, eff. Sept. 1, 2017.

§ 34.042. Sale of City Lots

If real property taken in execution consists of several lots, tracts, or parcels in a city or town, each lot, tract, or parcel must be offered for sale separately unless not susceptible to separate sale because of the character of improvements.

Acts 1985, 69th Leg., ch. 959, § 1, eff. Sept. 1, 1985.

§ 34.043. Sale of Rural Property

(a) If real property taken in execution is not located in a city or town, the defendant in the writ who holds legal or equitable title to the property may divide the property into lots of not less than 50 acres and designate the order in which those lots shall be sold.

(b) The defendant must present to the executing officer:

(1) a plat of the property as divided and as surveyed by the county surveyor of the county in which the property is located; and

(2) field notes of each numbered lot with a certificate of the county surveyor certifying that the notes are correct.

(c) The defendant must present the plat and field notes to the executing officer before the sale at a time that will not delay the sale as advertised.

(d) When a sufficient number of the lots are sold to satisfy the amount of the execution, the officer shall stop the sale.

(e) The defendant shall pay the expenses of the survey and the sale, and those expenses do not constitute an additional cost in the case.

Acts 1985, 69th Leg., ch. 959, § 1, eff. Sept. 1, 1985.

§ 34.044. Stock Shares Subject to Sale

Shares of stock in a corporation or joint-stock company that are owned by a defendant in execution may be sold on execution.

Acts 1985, 69th Leg., ch. 959, § 1, eff. Sept. 1, 1985.

§ 34.0445. Persons Eligible to Purchase Real Property

(a) An officer conducting a sale of real property under this subchapter may not execute or deliver a deed to the purchaser of the property unless the purchaser exhibits to the officer:

(1) an unexpired written statement issued to the person in the manner prescribed by Section 34.015, Tax Code, showing that the county assessor-collector of the county in which the sale is conducted has determined that:

(A) there are no delinquent ad valorem taxes owed by the person to that county; and

(B) for each school district or municipality having territory in the county there are no known or reported delinquent ad valorem taxes owed by the person to that school district or municipality; or

(2) the written registration statement issued to the person in the manner prescribed by Section 34.011, Tax Code, showing that the person is a registered bidder at the sale at which the property is sold.

(b) An individual may not bid on or purchase the property in the name of any other individual. An officer conducting a sale under this subchapter may not execute a deed in the name of or deliver a deed to any person other than the person who was the successful bidder.

(c) The deed executed by the officer conducting the sale must name the successful bidder as the grantee and recite that the successful bidder exhibited to that officer:

(1) an unexpired written statement issued to the person in the manner prescribed by Section 34.015, Tax Code, showing that the county assessor-collector of the county in which the sale was conducted determined that:

(A) there are no delinquent ad valorem taxes owed by the person to that county; and

(B) for each school district or municipality having territory in the county there are no known or reported delinquent ad valorem taxes owed by the person to that school district or municipality; or

(2) the written registration statement issued to the person in the manner prescribed by Section 34.011, Tax Code, showing that the person is a registered bidder at the sale at which the property is sold.

(d) If a deed contains the recital required by Subsection (c), it is conclusively presumed that this section was complied with.

(e) A person who knowingly violates this section commits an offense. An offense under this subsection is a Class B misdemeanor.

(f) To the extent of a conflict between this section and any other law, this section controls.

(g) This section applies only to a sale of real property under this subchapter that is conducted in:

(1) a county with a population of 250,000 or more; or

(2) a county with a population of less than 250,000 in which the commissioners court by order has adopted the provisions of this section.

Added by Acts 2003, 78th Leg., ch. 1010, § 1, eff. Sept. 1, 2003. Amended by Acts 2005, 79th Leg., ch. 86, § 1, eff. May 17, 2005; Acts 2015, 84th Leg., ch. 1126 (H.B. 3951), § 3, eff. Jan. 1, 2016.

§ 34.045. Conveyance of Title After Sale

(a) When the sale has been made and its terms complied with, the officer shall execute and deliver to the purchaser a conveyance of all the right, title, interest, and claim that the defendant in execution had in the property sold.

(b) If the purchaser complies with the terms of the sale but dies before the conveyance is executed, the officer shall execute the conveyance to the purchaser, and the conveyance has the same effect as if it had been executed in the purchaser's lifetime.

Acts 1985, 69th Leg., ch. 959, § 1, eff. Sept. 1, 1985.

§ 34.046. Purchaser Considered Innocent Purchaser Without Notice

The purchaser of property sold under execution is considered to be an innocent purchaser without notice if the purchaser would have been considered an innocent purchaser without notice had the sale been made voluntarily and in person by the defendant.

Acts 1985, 69th Leg., ch. 959, § 1, eff. Sept. 1, 1985.

§ 34.047. Distribution of Sale Proceeds

(a) An officer shall deliver money collected on execution to the entitled party at the earliest opportunity.

(b) The officer is entitled to retain from the proceeds of a sale of personal property an amount equal to the reasonable expenses incurred by him in making the levy and keeping the property.

(c) If more money is received from the sale of property than is sufficient to satisfy the executions held by the officer, the officer shall immediately pay the surplus to the defendant or the defendant's agent or attorney.

Acts 1985, 69th Leg., ch. 959, § 1, eff. Sept. 1, 1985.

§ 34.048. Purchase by Officer Void

If an officer or his deputy conducting an execution sale directly or indirectly purchases the property, the sale is void.

Acts 1985, 69th Leg., ch. 959, § 1, eff. Sept. 1, 1985.

SUBCHAPTER D. DUTIES AND LIABILITIES OF EXECUTING OFFICER

§ 34.061. Duty Toward Seized Personalty; Liability

(a) The officer shall keep securely all personal property on which he has levied and for which no delivery bond is given.

(b) If an injury or loss to an interested party results from the negligence of the officer, the officer and his sureties are liable for the value of the property lost or damaged.

(c) The injured party has the burden to prove:

(1) that the officer took actual possession of the injured party's property; and

(2) the actual value of any property lost or damaged.

Acts 1985, 69th Leg., ch. 959, § 1, eff. Sept. 1, 1985. Amended by Acts 2007, 80th Leg., ch. 421, § 3, eff. Sept. 1, 2007.

§ 34.062. Duty of Successor Officer

If the officer who receives a writ of execution dies or goes out of office before the writ is returned, his successor or the officer authorized to discharge the duties of the office shall proceed in the same manner as the receiving officer was required to proceed.

Acts 1985, 69th Leg., ch. 959, § 1, eff. Sept. 1, 1985.

§ 34.063. Improper Endorsement of Writ

(a) If an officer receives more than one writ of execution on the same day against the same person and fails to number them as received or if an officer falsely endorses a writ of execution, the officer and the officer's sureties are liable to the plaintiff in execution only for actual damages suffered by the plaintiff because of the failure or false endorsement.

(b) The plaintiff in execution has the burden to prove:

(1) the officer failed to properly number or endorse the writ of execution;

(2) the officer's failure precluded the levy of executable property owned by the judgment debtor;

(3) the executable property owned by the judgment debtor was not exempt from execution or levy; and

(4) the plaintiff in execution suffered actual damages.

Acts 1985, 69th Leg., ch. 959, § 1, eff. Sept. 1, 1985. Amended by Acts 2007, 80th Leg., ch. 421, § 4, eff. Sept. 1, 2007.

§ 34.064. Improper Return of Writ

(a) An officer may file an amended or corrected return after the officer has returned a writ to a court.

(b) Once an officer receives actual notice of an error on a return or of the officer's failure to file a return, the officer shall amend the return or file the return not later than the 30th day after the date of the receipt of notice.

(c) An officer who fails or refuses to amend or file the return may be subject to contempt under Section 7.001(b).

Acts 1985, 69th Leg., ch. 959, § 1, eff. Sept. 1, 1985. Amended by Acts 2007, 80th Leg., ch. 421, § 4, eff. Sept. 1, 2007.

§ 34.065. Failure to Levy or Sell

(a) If an officer fails or refuses to levy on or sell property subject to execution and the levy or sale could have taken place, the officer and the officer's sureties are liable to the party entitled to receive the money collected on execution only for actual damages suffered.

(b) The judgment creditor seeking relief under this section has the burden to prove:

(1) the judgment creditor has a valid judgment against the judgment debtor;

(2) the writ of execution was issued to the judgment creditor;

(3) the writ was delivered to the officer;

(4) the judgment creditor's judgment was unpaid and unsatisfied;

(5) the property to be levied on was subject to execution;

(6) the officer failed or refused to levy under the writ; and

(7) the amount of actual damages suffered.

(c) Property to be levied on is subject to execution for purposes of this section if the judgment creditor proves that the judgment debtor owned the property at issue, the property was accessible to the officer under the law, the property was situated in the officer's county, and the property was not exempt from execution.

(d) Before a court may find that an officer failed or refused to levy under the writ for purposes of this section, the court must find that the judgment creditor specifically informed the officer that the property was owned by the judgment debtor and was subject to execution and that the creditor directed the officer to levy on the property.

(e) In this section, "actual damages" is the amount of money the property would have sold for at a constable or sheriff's auction minus any costs of sale, commissions, and additional expenses of execution.

Acts 1985, 69th Leg., ch. 959, § 1, eff. Sept. 1, 1985. Amended by Acts 2007, 80th Leg., ch. 421, § 4, eff. Sept. 1, 2007.

§ 34.066. Improper Sale

(a) If an officer sells property without giving notice as required by the Texas Rules of Civil Procedure or sells property in a manner other than that prescribed by this chapter and the Texas Rules of Civil Procedure, the officer shall be liable only for actual damages sustained by the injured party.

(b) The injured party has the burden to prove that the sale was improper and any actual damages suffered.

Acts 1985, 69th Leg., ch. 959, § 1, eff. Sept. 1, 1985. Amended by Acts 2007, 80th Leg., ch. 421, § 4, eff. Sept. 1, 2007.

§ 34.067. Failure to Deliver Money Collected

If an officer fails or refuses to deliver money collected under an execution when demanded by the person entitled to receive the money, the officer and the officer's sureties are liable to the person for the amount collected and for damages at a rate of one percent a month on that amount if proven by the injured party.

Acts 1985, 69th Leg., ch. 959, § 1, eff. Sept. 1, 1985. Amended by Acts 2007, 80th Leg., ch. 421, § 4, eff. Sept. 1, 2007.

§ 34.068. Rules Governing Actions Under This Chapter

(a) This section applies to any claim for damages brought under Section 7.001, 34.061, 34.063, 34.065, 34.066, or 34.067 or under Section 86.023, Local Government Code.

(b) Suit shall be brought in the form of a lawsuit filed against the officer in the county in which the officer holds office.

(c) All suits must be filed not later than the first anniversary of the date on which the injury accrues.

(d) An officer or a surety may defend the action by stating and proving any defenses provided by law, including any defense that would mitigate damages.

Added by Acts 2007, 80th Leg., ch. 421, § 5, eff. Sept. 1, 2007.

§ 34.069. Payment of Damages

A county, at the discretion of the commissioners court, may pay any judgment taken against an officer under Section 7.001, 34.061, 34.063, 34.064, 34.065, 34.066, or 34.067 or under Section 86.023, Local Government Code, provided that this section does not apply if the officer is finally convicted under Section 39.02 or 39.03, Penal Code.

Added by Acts 2007, 80th Leg., ch. 421, § 5, eff. Sept. 1, 2007.

§ 34.070. Right of Subrogation

An officer against whom a judgment has been taken under Section 7.001, 7.002, 34.061, 34.063, 34.064, 34.065, 34.066, or 34.067 or under Section 86.023, Local Government Code, or a county that has paid the judgment on behalf of the officer under Section 34.069, has a right of subrogation against the debtor or person against whom the writ was issued.

Added by Acts 2007, 80th Leg., ch. 421, § 5, eff. Sept. 1, 2007.

§ 34.071. Duties of Executing Officer

An officer receiving a writ of execution does not have a duty to:

(1) search for property belonging to the judgment debtor;

(2) determine whether property belongs to a judgment debtor;

(3) determine whether property belonging to the judgment debtor is exempt property that is not subject to levy;

(4) determine the priority of liens asserted against property subject to execution; or

(5) make multiple levies for cash or multiple levies at the same location.

Added by Acts 2007, 80th Leg., ch. 421, § 5, eff. Sept. 1, 2007.

§ 34.072. Timing of Execution and Return

(a) An officer receiving a writ of execution may return the writ after the first levy, or attempted levy, if the judgment creditor cannot designate any more executable property currently owned by the judgment debtor at the time of the first levy or first attempted levy.

(b) Notwithstanding Rule 637, Texas Rules of Civil Procedure, an attempt to levy on property may begin any time during the life of the writ, provided that the officer shall allow enough time for completing the sale of the property.

Added by Acts 2007, 80th Leg., ch. 421, § 5, eff. Sept. 1, 2007.

§ 34.073. Transfer of Writ; No Duty to Levy Outside of County

(a) An officer receiving a writ may transfer the writ to another officer in another precinct, or to another law enforcement agency authorized to perform executions, within the county of the first officer who received the writ.

(b) An officer does not have a duty to levy on or sell property not within the officer's county, unless it is real property that is partially in the officer's county and partially within a contiguous county.

Added by Acts 2007, 80th Leg., ch. 421, § 5, eff. Sept. 1, 2007.

§ 34.074. Officer's Surety

(a) An officer's surety may only be liable for the penal sum of the surety bond minus any amounts already paid out under the bond. In no event may an officer's surety be liable for more than the penal sum of the officer's surety bond.

(b) If the officer and the officer's surety are both defendants in an action brought under this chapter, the surety may deposit in the court's registry the amount unpaid under the surety bond and the court shall determine the proper disposition of this sum or order the return of the deposit to the surety in the court's final judgment.

(c) A surety is not a necessary party to an action brought under this chapter or under Section 7.001. Instead, a prevailing party under these provisions may bring a separate action against a surety failing to pay the amount remaining under the bond on a final judgment. This action must be brought on or before 180 days after the date all appeals are exhausted in the underlying action.

Added by Acts 2007, 80th Leg., ch. 421, § 5, eff. Sept. 1, 2007.

§ 34.075. Wrongful Levy

Whenever a distress warrant, writ of execution, sequestration, attachment, or other like writ is levied upon personal property, and the property, or any part of the property, is claimed by any claimant who is not a party to the writ, the only remedy against a sheriff or constable for wrongful levy on the property is by trial of right of property under Part VI, Section 9, Texas Rules of Civil Procedure.

Added by Acts 2007, 80th Leg., ch. 421, § 5, eff. Sept. 1, 2007.

§ 34.076. Exclusive Remedy

This subchapter is the exclusive remedy for violations of an officer's duties with regard to the execution and return of writs without regard to the source of the duty prescribed by law.

Added by Acts 2007, 80th Leg., ch. 421, § 5, eff. Sept. 1, 2007.

CHAPTER 35. ENFORCEMENT OF JUDGMENTS OF OTHER STATES

Section

§ 35.001. Definition

In this chapter, "foreign judgment" means a judgment, decree, or order of a court of the United States or of any other court that is entitled to full faith and credit in this state.

Acts 1985, 69th Leg., ch. 959, § 1, eff. Sept. 1, 1985.

§ 35.002. Short Title

This chapter may be cited as the Uniform Enforcement of Foreign Judgments Act.

Acts 1985, 69th Leg., ch. 959, § 1, eff. Sept. 1, 1985.

§ 35.003. Filing and Status of Foreign Judgments

(a) A copy of a foreign judgment authenticated in accordance with an act of congress or a statute of this state may be filed in the office of the clerk of any court of competent jurisdiction of this state.

(b) The clerk shall treat the foreign judgment in the same manner as a judgment of the court in which the foreign judgment is filed.

(c) A filed foreign judgment has the same effect and is subject to the same procedures, defenses, and proceedings for reopening, vacating, staying, enforcing, or satisfying a judgment as a judgment of the court in which it is filed.

Acts 1985, 69th Leg., ch. 959, § 1, eff. Sept. 1, 1985.

§ 35.004. Affidavit; Notice of Filing

(a) At the time a foreign judgment is filed, the judgment creditor or the judgment creditor's attorney shall file with the clerk of the court an affidavit showing the name and last known post office address of the judgment debtor and the judgment creditor.

(b) The judgment creditor or the judgment creditor's attorney shall:

(1) promptly mail notice of the filing of the foreign judgment to the judgment debtor at the address provided for the judgment debtor under Subsection (a); and

(2) file proof of mailing of the notice with the clerk of the court.

(c) The notice must include the name and post office address of the judgment creditor and if the judgment creditor has an attorney in this state, the attorney's name and address.

(d) On receipt of proof of mailing under Subsection (b), the clerk of the court shall note the mailing in the docket.

Acts 1985, 69th Leg., ch. 959, § 1, eff. Sept. 1, 1985. Amended by Acts 2011, 82nd Leg., ch. 65 (S.B. 428), § 1, eff. May 17, 2011.

§ 35.005. Repealed by Acts 2011, 82nd Leg., ch. 65 (S.B. 428), § 2, eff. May 17, 2011

§ 35.006. Stay

(a) If the judgment debtor shows the court that an appeal from the foreign judgment is pending or will be taken, that the time for taking an appeal has not expired, or that a stay of execution has been granted, has been requested, or will be requested, and proves that the judgment debtor has furnished or will furnish the security for the satisfaction of the judgment required by the state in which it was rendered, the court shall stay enforcement of the foreign judgment until the appeal is concluded, the time for appeal expires, or the stay of execution expires or is vacated.

(b) If the judgment debtor shows the court a ground on which enforcement of a judgment of the court of this state would be stayed, the court shall stay enforcement of the foreign judgment for an appropriate period and require the same security for suspending enforcement of the judgment that is required in this state in accordance with Section 52.006.

Acts 1985, 69th Leg., ch. 959, § 1, eff. Sept. 1, 1985. Amended by Acts 2003, 78th Leg., ch. 204, § 7.01, eff. Sept. 1, 2003.

§ 35.007. Fees

(a) A person filing a foreign judgment shall pay to the clerk of the court the amount as otherwise provided by law for filing suit in the courts of this state.

(b) Filing fees are due and payable at the time of filing.

(c) Fees for other enforcement proceedings are as provided by law for judgments of the courts of this state.

Acts 1985, 69th Leg., ch. 959, § 1, eff. Sept. 1, 1985.

§ 35.008. Optional Procedure

A judgment creditor retains the right to bring an action to enforce a judgment instead of proceeding under this chapter.

Acts 1985, 69th Leg., ch. 959, § 1, eff. Sept. 1, 1985.

CHAPTER 36. ENFORCEMENT OF JUDGMENTS OF OTHER COUNTRIES [REPEALED]

§§ 36.001 to 36.008. Repealed by Acts 2017, 85th Leg., ch. 390 (S.B. 944), § 2, eff. June 1, 2017

CHAPTER 36A. ENFORCEMENT OF JUDGMENTS OF OTHER COUNTRIES

§ 36A.001. Short Title

This chapter may be cited as the Uniform Foreign–Country Money Judgments Recognition Act.

Added by Acts 2017, 85th Leg., ch. 390 (S.B. 944), § 1, eff. June 1, 2017.

§ 36A.002. Definitions

In this chapter:

(1) "Foreign country" means a government other than:

(A) the United States;

(B) a state, district, commonwealth, territory, or insular possession of the United States; or

(C) any other government with respect to which the decision in this state as to whether to recognize a judgment of that government's court is initially subject to determination under Section 1, Article IV, United States Constitution (the full faith and credit clause).

(2) "Foreign-country judgment" means a judgment of a court of a foreign country.

Added by Acts 2017, 85th Leg., ch. 390 (S.B. 944), § 1, eff. June 1, 2017.

§ 36A.003. Applicability

(a) Except as otherwise provided in Subsection (b), this chapter applies to a foreign-country judgment to the extent that the judgment:

(1) grants or denies recovery of a sum of money; and

(2) under the law of the foreign country in which the judgment is rendered, is final, conclusive, and enforceable.

(b) This chapter does not apply to a foreign-country judgment that grants or denies recovery of a sum of money to the extent that the judgment is:

(1) a judgment for taxes;

(2) a fine or other penalty; or

(3) a judgment for divorce, support, or maintenance, or other judgment rendered in connection with domestic relations.

(c) A party seeking recognition of a foreign-country judgment has the burden of establishing that this chapter applies to the foreign-country judgment.

Added by Acts 2017, 85th Leg., ch. 390 (S.B. 944), § 1, eff. June 1, 2017.

§ 36A.004. Standards for Recognition of Foreign–Country Judgment

(a) Except as otherwise provided in Subsections (b) and (c), a court of this state shall recognize a foreign-country judgment to which this chapter applies.

(b) A court of this state may not recognize a foreign-country judgment if:

(1) the judgment was rendered under a judicial system that does not provide impartial tribunals or procedures compatible with the requirements of due process of law;

(2) the foreign court did not have personal jurisdiction over the defendant; or

(3) the foreign court did not have jurisdiction over the subject matter.

(c) A court of this state is not required to recognize a foreign-country judgment if:

(1) the defendant in the proceeding in the foreign court did not receive notice of the proceeding in sufficient time to enable the defendant to defend;

(2) the judgment was obtained by fraud that deprived the losing party of an adequate opportunity to present the party's case;

(3) the judgment or the cause of action on which the judgment is based is repugnant to the public policy of this state or the United States;

(4) the judgment conflicts with another final and conclusive judgment;

(5) the proceeding in the foreign court was contrary to an agreement between the parties under which the dispute in question was to be determined otherwise than by proceedings in the foreign court;

(6) jurisdiction was based only on personal service and the foreign court was a seriously inconvenient forum for the trial of the action;

(7) the judgment was rendered in circumstances that raise substantial doubt about the integrity of the rendering court with respect to the judgment;

(8) the specific proceeding in the foreign court leading to the judgment was not compatible with the requirements of due process of law; or

(9) it is established that the foreign country in which the judgment was rendered does not recognize judgments rendered in this state that, but for the fact that they are rendered in this state, would constitute foreign-country judgments to which this chapter would apply under Section 36A.003.

(d) A party resisting recognition of a foreign-country judgment has the burden of establishing that a ground for nonrecognition stated in Subsection (b) or (c) exists.

Added by Acts 2017, 85th Leg., ch. 390 (S.B. 944), § 1, eff. June 1, 2017.

§ 36A.005. Personal Jurisdiction

(a) A foreign-country judgment may not be refused recognition for lack of personal jurisdiction if:

(1) the defendant was served with process personally in the foreign country;

(2) the defendant voluntarily appeared in the proceeding, other than for the purpose of protecting property seized or threatened with seizure in the proceeding or of contesting the jurisdiction of the court over the defendant;

(3) the defendant, before commencement of the proceeding, agreed to submit to the jurisdiction of the foreign court with respect to the subject matter involved;

(4) the defendant was domiciled in the foreign country when the proceeding was instituted or was a corporation or other form of business organization whose principal place of business was in, or that was organized under the laws of, the foreign country;

(5) the defendant had a business office in the foreign country and the proceeding in the foreign court involved a cause of action arising out of business done by the defendant through that office in the foreign country; or

(6) the defendant operated a motor vehicle or airplane in the foreign country and the proceeding involved a cause of action arising out of that operation.

(b) The list of bases for personal jurisdiction in Subsection (a) is not exclusive. A court of this state may recognize bases of personal jurisdiction other than those listed in Subsection (a) as sufficient to support a foreign-country judgment.

Added by Acts 2017, 85th Leg., ch. 390 (S.B. 944), § 1, eff. June 1, 2017.

§ 36A.006. Procedure for Recognition of Foreign–Country Judgment

(a) If recognition of a foreign-country judgment is sought as an original matter, the issue of recognition may be raised by filing an action seeking recognition of the foreign-country judgment.

(b) If recognition of a foreign-country judgment is sought in a pending action, the issue of recognition may be raised by counterclaim, cross-claim, or affirmative defense.

Added by Acts 2017, 85th Leg., ch. 390 (S.B. 944), § 1, eff. June 1, 2017.

§ 36A.007. Effect of Recognition of Foreign–Country Judgment

If the court in a proceeding under Section 36A.006 finds that the foreign-country judgment is entitled to recognition under this chapter, then, to the extent that the foreign-country judgment grants or denies recovery of a sum of money, the foreign-country judgment is:

(1) conclusive between the parties to the same extent as the judgment of a sister state entitled to full faith and credit in this state would be conclusive; and

(2) enforceable in the same manner and to the same extent as a judgment rendered in this state.

Added by Acts 2017, 85th Leg., ch. 390 (S.B. 944), § 1, eff. June 1, 2017.

§ 36A.008. Stay of Proceedings Pending Appeal of Foreign–Country Judgment

If a party establishes that an appeal from a foreign-country judgment is pending or will be taken, the court may stay any proceedings with regard to the foreign-country judgment until:

(1) the appeal is concluded;

(2) the time for appeal expires; or

(3) the appellant has had sufficient time to prosecute the appeal and has failed to do so.

Added by Acts 2017, 85th Leg., ch. 390 (S.B. 944), § 1, eff. June 1, 2017.

§ 36A.009. Statute of Limitations

An action to recognize a foreign-country judgment must be brought within the earlier of:

(1) the time during which the foreign-country judgment is effective in the foreign country; or

(2) 15 years from the date that the foreign-country judgment became effective in the foreign country.

Added by Acts 2017, 85th Leg., ch. 390 (S.B. 944), § 1, eff. June 1, 2017.

§ 36A.010. Uniformity of Interpretation

In applying and construing this chapter, consideration must be given to the need to promote uniformity of the law with respect to the subject matter of this chapter among states that enact a law based on the uniform act on which this chapter is based.

Added by Acts 2017, 85th Leg., ch. 390 (S.B. 944), § 1, eff. June 1, 2017.

§ 36A.011. Saving Clause

This chapter does not prevent the recognition under principles of comity or otherwise of a foreign-country judgment not within the scope of this chapter.

Added by Acts 2017, 85th Leg., ch. 390 (S.B. 944), § 1, eff. June 1, 2017.

CHAPTER 37. DECLARATORY JUDGMENTS

Section

§ 37.001. Definition

In this chapter, "person" means an individual, partnership, joint-stock company, unincorporated association or society, or municipal or other corporation of any character.

Acts 1985, 69th Leg., ch. 959, § 1, eff. Sept. 1, 1985.

§ 37.002. Short Title, Construction, Interpretation

(a) This chapter may be cited as the Uniform Declaratory Judgments Act.

(b) This chapter is remedial; its purpose is to settle and to afford relief from uncertainty and insecurity with respect to rights, status, and other legal relations; and it is to be liberally construed and administered.

(c) This chapter shall be so interpreted and construed as to effectuate its general purpose to make uniform the law of those states that enact it and to harmonize, as far as possible, with federal laws and regulations on the subject of declaratory judgments and decrees.

Acts 1985, 69th Leg., ch. 959, § 1, eff. Sept. 1, 1985.

§ 37.003. Power of Courts to Render Judgment; Form and Effect

(a) A court of record within its jurisdiction has power to declare rights, status, and other legal relations whether or not further relief is or could be claimed. An action or proceeding is not open to objection on the ground that a declaratory judgment or decree is prayed for.

(b) The declaration may be either affirmative or negative in form and effect, and the declaration has the force and effect of a final judgment or decree.

(c) The enumerations in Sections 37.004 and 37.005 do not limit or restrict the exercise of the general powers conferred in this section in any proceeding in which declaratory relief is sought and a judgment or decree will terminate the controversy or remove an uncertainty.

Acts 1985, 69th Leg., ch. 959, § 1, eff. Sept. 1, 1985.

§ 37.004. Subject Matter of Relief

(a) A person interested under a deed, will, written contract, or other writings constituting a contract or whose rights, status, or other legal relations are affected by a statute, municipal ordinance, contract, or franchise may have determined any question of construction or validity arising under the instrument, statute, ordinance, contract, or franchise and obtain a declaration of rights, status, or other legal relations thereunder.

(b) A contract may be construed either before or after there has been a breach.

(c) Notwithstanding Section 22.001, Property Code, a person described by Subsection (a) may obtain a determination under this chapter when the sole issue concerning title to real property is the determination of the proper boundary line between adjoining properties.

Acts 1985, 69th Leg., ch. 959, § 1, eff. Sept. 1, 1985. Amended by Acts 2007, 80th Leg., ch. 305, § 1, eff. June 15, 2007.

§ 37.005. Declarations Relating to Trust or Estate

A person interested as or through an executor or administrator, including an independent executor or administrator, a trustee, guardian, other fiduciary, creditor, devisee, legatee, heir, next of kin, or cestui que trust in the administration of a trust or of the estate of a decedent, an infant, mentally incapacitated person, or insolvent may have a declaration of rights or legal relations in respect to the trust or estate:

(1) to ascertain any class of creditors, devisees, legatees, heirs, next of kin, or others;

(2) to direct the executors, administrators, or trustees to do or abstain from doing any particular act in their fiduciary capacity;

(3) to determine any question arising in the administration of the trust or estate, including questions of construction of wills and other writings; or

(4) to determine rights or legal relations of an independent executor or independent administrator regarding fiduciary fees and the settling of accounts.

Acts 1985, 69th Leg., ch. 959, § 1, eff. Sept. 1, 1985. Amended by Acts 1987, 70th Leg., ch. 167, § 3.08(a), eff. Sept. 1, 1987; Acts 1999, 76th Leg., ch. 855, § 10, eff. Sept. 1, 1999.

§ 37.0055. Declarations Relating to Liability for Sales and Use Taxes of Another State

(a) In this section, "state" includes any political subdivision of that state.

(b) A district court has original jurisdiction of a proceeding seeking a declaratory judgment that involves:

(1) a party seeking declaratory relief that is a business that is:

(A) organized under the laws of this state or is otherwise owned by a resident of this state; or

(B) a retailer registered with the comptroller under Section 151.106, Tax Code; and

(2) a responding party that:

(A) is an official of another state; and

(B) asserts a claim that the party seeking declaratory relief is required to collect sales or use taxes for that state based on conduct of the business that occurs in whole or in part within this state.

(c) A business described by Subsection (b)(1) is entitled to declaratory relief on the issue of whether the requirement of another state that the business collect and remit sales or use taxes to that state constitutes an undue burden on interstate commerce under Section 8, Article I, United States Constitution.

(d) In determining whether to grant declaratory relief to a business under this section, a court shall consider:

(1) the factual circumstances of the business's operations that give rise to the demand by the other state; and

(2) the decisions of other courts interpreting Section 8, Article I, United States Constitution.

Added by Acts 2007, 80th Leg., ch. 699, § 1, eff. Sept. 1, 2007.

§ 37.006. Parties

(a) When declaratory relief is sought, all persons who have or claim any interest that would be affected by the declaration must be made parties. A declaration does not prejudice the rights of a person not a party to the proceeding.

(b) In any proceeding that involves the validity of a municipal ordinance or franchise, the municipality must be made a party and is entitled to be heard, and if the statute, ordinance, or franchise is alleged to be unconstitutional, the attorney general of the state must also be served with a copy of the proceeding and is entitled to be heard.

Acts 1985, 69th Leg., ch. 959, § 1, eff. Sept. 1, 1985.

§ 37.007. Jury Trial

If a proceeding under this chapter involves the determination of an issue of fact, the issue may be tried and determined in the same manner as issues of fact are tried and determined in other civil actions in the court in which the proceeding is pending.

Acts 1985, 69th Leg., ch. 959, § 1, eff. Sept. 1, 1985.

§ 37.008. Court Refusal to Render

The court may refuse to render or enter a declaratory judgment or decree if the judgment or decree would not terminate the uncertainty or controversy giving rise to the proceeding.

Acts 1985, 69th Leg., ch. 959, § 1, eff. Sept. 1, 1985.

§ 37.009. Costs

In any proceeding under this chapter, the court may award costs and reasonable and necessary attorney's fees as are equitable and just.

Acts 1985, 69th Leg., ch. 959, § 1, eff. Sept. 1, 1985.

§ 37.010. Review

All orders, judgments, and decrees under this chapter may be reviewed as other orders, judgments, and decrees.

Acts 1985, 69th Leg., ch. 959, § 1, eff. Sept. 1, 1985.

§ 37.011. Supplemental Relief

Further relief based on a declaratory judgment or decree may be granted whenever necessary or proper. The application must be by petition to a court having jurisdiction to grant the relief. If the application is deemed sufficient, the court shall, on reasonable notice, require any adverse party whose rights have been adjudicated by the declaratory judgment or decree to show cause why further relief should not be granted forthwith.

Acts 1985, 69th Leg., ch. 959, § 1, eff. Sept. 1, 1985.

CHAPTER 38. ATTORNEY'S FEES

Section

§ 38.001. Recovery of Attorney's Fees

(a) In this section, "organization" has the meaning assigned by Section 1.002, Business Organizations Code.

(b) A person may recover reasonable attorney's fees from an individual or organization other than a quasi-governmental entity authorized to perform a function by state law, a religious organization, a charitable organization, or a charitable trust, in addition to the amount of a valid claim and costs, if the claim is for:

(1) rendered services;

(2) performed labor;

(3) furnished material;

(4) freight or express overcharges;

(5) lost or damaged freight or express;

(6) killed or injured stock;

(7) a sworn account; or

(8) an oral or written contract.

Acts 1985, 69th Leg., ch. 959, § 1, eff. Sept. 1, 1985. Amended by Acts 2021, 87th Leg., ch. 665 (H.B. 1578), § 1, eff. Sept. 1, 2021.

Section 2 of Acts 2021, 87th Leg., ch. 665 (H.B. 1578) provides:

"The change in law made by this Act applies only to an award of attorney's fees in an action commenced on or after the effective date [Sept. 1, 2021] of this Act. An award of attorney's fees in an action commenced before the effective date of this Act is governed by the law applicable to the award immediately before the effective date of this Act, and that law is continued in effect for that purpose."

§ 38.0015. Recovery of Attorney's Fees as Compensatory Damages

(a) A person may recover reasonable attorney's fees from an individual, corporation, or other entity from which recovery is permitted under Section 38.001 as compensatory damages for breach of a construction contract as defined by Section 130.001.

(b) This section may not be construed to create or imply a private cause of action or independent basis to recover attorney's fees.

Added by Acts 2021, 87th Leg., ch. 1015 (H.B. 2416), § 1, eff. Sept. 1, 2021.

Section 2 of Acts 2021, 87th Leg., ch. 1015 (H.B. 2416) provides:

"The change in law made by this Act applies only to a cause of action that accrues on or after the effective date [Sept. 1, 2021] of this Act."

§ 38.002. Procedure for Recovery of Attorney's Fees

To recover attorney's fees under this chapter:

(1) the claimant must be represented by an attorney;

(2) the claimant must present the claim to the opposing party or to a duly authorized agent of the opposing party; and

(3) payment for the just amount owed must not have been tendered before the expiration of the 30th day after the claim is presented.

Acts 1985, 69th Leg., ch. 959, § 1, eff. Sept. 1, 1985.

§ 38.003. Presumption

It is presumed that the usual and customary attorney's fees for a claim of the type described in Section 38.001 are reasonable. The presumption may be rebutted.

Acts 1985, 69th Leg., ch. 959, § 1, eff. Sept. 1, 1985.

§ 38.004. Judicial Notice

The court may take judicial notice of the usual and customary attorney's fees and of the contents of the case file without receiving further evidence in:

(1) a proceeding before the court; or

(2) a jury case in which the amount of attorney's fees is submitted to the court by agreement.

Acts 1985, 69th Leg., ch. 959, § 1, eff. Sept. 1, 1985.

§ 38.005. Liberal Construction

This chapter shall be liberally construed to promote its underlying purposes.

Acts 1985, 69th Leg., ch. 959, § 1, eff. Sept. 1, 1985.

§ 38.006. Exceptions

This chapter does not apply to a contract issued by an insurer that is subject to the provisions of:

(1) Title 11,[1] Insurance Code;

(2) Chapter 541, Insurance Code;

(3) the Unfair Claim Settlement Practices Act (Subchapter A, Chapter 542, Insurance Code);[2] or

(4) Subchapter B, Chapter 542, Insurance Code.[3]

Acts 1985, 69th Leg., ch. 959, § 1, eff. Sept. 1, 1985. Amended by Acts 2005, 79th Leg., ch. 728, § 11.105, eff. Sept. 1, 2005.

[1] V.T.C.A., Insurance Code, § 2501.001 et seq.

[2] V.T.C.A., Insurance Code § 542.001 et seq.

[3] V.T.C.A., Insurance Code § 542.051 et seq.

CHAPTER 39. DEFAULT JUDGMENTS IN CERTAIN CASES DEFENDED BY ATTORNEY GENERAL

Section

§ 39.001. Notice of Intent to Take Default Judgment

Notice of intent to take a default judgment against the state, a state agency, or a party in a civil case for which Chapter 104 authorizes representation by the attorney general shall be mailed to the attorney general at the attorney general's office in Austin, Texas, by United States Postal Service certified mail, return receipt requested, not later than the 10th day before the entry of the default judgment.

Added by Acts 1987, 70th Leg., ch. 167, § 3.09(a), eff. Sept. 1, 1987.

§ 39.002. Failure to Give Notice

Failure to give notice in a case in which notice is required by Section 30.004(b) or Section 39.001 results in any default judgment in the case being set aside without costs.

Added by Acts 1987, 70th Leg., ch. 167, § 3.09(a), eff. Sept. 1, 1987.

CHAPTER 40. AVAILABILITY OF CERTAIN FUNDS TO PAY DAMAGES

Section

§ 40.001. Endowment of Certain Nonprofit Institutions

(a) This section applies only to damages awarded against:

(1) a nonprofit institution or facility:

(A) licensed under Chapter 242, 246, or 247, Health and Safety Code, or Chapter 42, Human Resources Code; and

(B) that, before the date on which the action in which the damages are awarded is filed, is affiliated with:

(i) a nonprofit religious organization that is exempt from federal income tax under Section 501(c)(3), Internal Revenue Code of 1986, as amended, and that is a nonprofit religious organization described by 34 T.A.C. Section 3.322(b)(3), as that provision existed on January 1, 2003, or a convention or association of those organizations; or

(ii) a local Jewish Federation; or

(2) a program operated by an institution or facility described by Subdivision (1).

(b) A claimant may not collect damages awarded against an institution, facility, or program described by Subsection (a) from an endowment fund, restricted fund, or similar fund or account, or the income derived from the corpus of the fund or account, if:

(1) the fund or account is exempt from federal taxation;

(2) the corpus, income, or a distribution from the fund or account is used to assist in funding care provided by a nursing institution licensed under Chapter 242, Health and Safety Code, and affiliated with an organization described by Subsection (a)(1)(B);

(3) the corpus of the fund or account is derived from donations or grants from third parties or public sources; and

(4) the use of the fund or account is temporarily or permanently restricted:

(A) by the donor or grantor at the time the donation or grant is made by:

(i) the express language, action, or agreement of the donor or grantor; or

(ii) the manner in which the donation or grant was solicited by the donee or grantee; or

(B) by the board governing the fund or account at the time the donation or grant is accepted.

Added by Acts 2003, 78th Leg., ch. 133, § 1, eff. May 27, 2003.

CHAPTER 41. DAMAGES

Chapter 41, previously consisting of V.T.C.A., Civil Practice & Remedies §§ 41.001 to 41.009, was amended by Acts 1995, 74th Leg., ch. 19, § 1, effective September 1, 1995, to consist of V.T.C.A., Civil Practice & Remedies §§ 41.001 to 41.013.

§ 41.001. Definitions

In this chapter:

(1) "Claimant" means a party, including a plaintiff, counterclaimant, cross-claimant, or third-party plaintiff, seeking recovery of damages. In a cause of action in which a party seeks recovery of damages related to injury to another person, damage to the property of another person, death of another person, or other harm to another person, "claimant" includes both that other person and the party seeking recovery of damages.

(2) "Clear and convincing" means the measure or degree of proof that will produce in the mind of the trier of fact a firm belief or conviction as to the truth of the allegations sought to be established.

(3) "Defendant" means a party, including a counterdefendant, cross-defendant, or third-party defendant, from whom a claimant seeks relief.

(4) "Economic damages" means compensatory damages intended to compensate a claimant for actual economic or pecuniary loss; the term does not include exemplary damages or noneconomic damages.

(5) "Exemplary damages" means any damages awarded as a penalty or by way of punishment but not for compensatory purposes. Exemplary damages are neither economic nor noneconomic damages. "Exemplary damages" includes punitive damages.

(6) "Fraud" means fraud other than constructive fraud.

(7) "Malice" means a specific intent by the defendant to cause substantial injury or harm to the claimant.

(7-a) "Net worth" means the total assets of a person minus the total liabilities of the person on a date determined appropriate by the trial court.

(8) "Compensatory damages" means economic and noneconomic damages. The term does not include exemplary damages.

(9) "Future damages" means damages that are incurred after the date of the judgment. Future damages do not include exemplary damages.

(10) "Future loss of earnings" means a pecuniary loss incurred after the date of the judgment, including:

(A) loss of income, wages, or earning capacity; and

(B) loss of inheritance.

(11) "Gross negligence" means an act or omission:

(A) which when viewed objectively from the standpoint of the actor at the time of its occurrence involves an extreme degree of risk, considering the probability and magnitude of the potential harm to others; and

(B) of which the actor has actual, subjective awareness of the risk involved, but nevertheless proceeds with conscious indifference to the rights, safety, or welfare of others.

(12) "Noneconomic damages" means damages awarded for the purpose of compensating a claimant for physical pain and suffering, mental or emotional pain or anguish, loss of consortium, disfigurement, physical impairment, loss of companionship and society, inconvenience, loss of enjoyment of life, injury to reputation, and all other nonpecuniary losses of any kind other than exemplary damages.

(13) "Periodic payments" means the payment of money or its equivalent to the recipient of future damages at defined intervals.

Added by Acts 1987, 70th Leg., 1st C.S., ch. 2, § 2.12, eff. Sept. 2, 1987. Amended by Acts 1995, 74th Leg., ch. 19, § 1, eff. Sept. 1, 1995; Acts 2003, 78th Leg., ch. 204, § 13.02, eff. Sept. 1, 2003; Acts 2015, 84th Leg., ch. 1159 (S.B. 735), § 1, eff. Sept. 1, 2015.

§ 41.002. Applicability

(a) This chapter applies to any action in which a claimant seeks damages relating to a cause of action.

(b) This chapter establishes the maximum damages that may be awarded in an action subject to this chapter, including an action for which damages are awarded under another law of this state. This chapter does not apply to the extent another law establishes a lower maximum amount of damages for a particular claim.

(c) Except as provided by Subsections (b) and (d), in an action to which this chapter applies, the provisions of this chapter prevail over all other law to the extent of any conflict.

(d) Notwithstanding any provision to the contrary, this chapter does not apply to:

(1) Section 15.21, Business & Commerce Code (Texas Free Enterprise and Antitrust Act of 1983);

(2) an action brought under the Deceptive Trade Practices–Consumer Protection Act (Subchapter E, Chapter 17, Business & Commerce Code)[1] except as specifically provided in Section 17.50 of that Act;

(3) an action brought under Chapter 36, Human Resources Code;[2] or

(4) an action brought under Chapter 21, Insurance Code.[3]

Added by Acts 1987, 70th Leg., 1st C.S., ch. 2, § 2.12, eff. Sept. 2, 1987. Amended by Acts 1989, 71st Leg., ch. 380, § 5, eff. Sept. 1, 1989; Acts 1989, 71st Leg., ch. 1129, § 16, eff. Sept. 1, 1989; Acts 1995, 74th Leg., ch. 19, § 1, eff. Sept. 1, 1995; Acts 1995, 74th Leg., ch. 260, § 9, eff. May 30, 1995; Acts 1997, 75th Leg., ch. 165, § 4.01, eff. Sept. 1, 1997; Acts 2003, 78th Leg., ch. 204, § 13.03, eff. Sept. 1, 2003; Acts 2005, 79th Leg., ch. 806, § 18, eff. Sept. 1, 2005.

[1] V.T.C.A., Bus. & Com. Code § 17.41 et seq.

[2] V.T.C.A., Human Resources Code § 36.001 et seq.

[3] V.T.C.A., Insurance Code art. 21.01 et seq.

§ 41.003. Standards for Recovery of Exemplary Damages

(a) Except as provided by Subsection (c), exemplary damages may be awarded only if the claimant proves by clear and convincing evidence that the harm with respect to which the claimant seeks recovery of exemplary damages results from:

(1) fraud;

(2) malice; or

(3) gross negligence.

(b) The claimant must prove by clear and convincing evidence the elements of exemplary damages as provided by this section. This burden of proof may not be shifted to the defendant or satisfied by evidence of ordinary negligence, bad faith, or a deceptive trade practice.

(c) If the claimant relies on a statute establishing a cause of action and authorizing exemplary damages in specified circumstances or in conjunction with a specified culpable mental state, exemplary damages may be awarded only if the claimant proves by clear and convincing evidence that the damages result from the specified circumstances or culpable mental state.

(d) Exemplary damages may be awarded only if the jury was unanimous in regard to finding liability for and the amount of exemplary damages.

(e) In all cases where the issue of exemplary damages is submitted to the jury, the following instruction shall be included in the charge of the court:

"You are instructed that, in order for you to find exemplary damages, your answer to the question regarding the amount of such damages must be unanimous."

Added by Acts 1987, 70th Leg., 1st C.S., ch. 2, § 2.12, eff. Sept. 2, 1987. Amended by Acts 1995, 74th Leg., ch. 19, § 1, eff. Sept. 1, 1995; Acts 2003, 78th Leg., ch. 204, § 13.04, eff. Sept. 1, 2003.

§ 41.004. Factors Precluding Recovery

(a) Except as provided by Subsection (b), exemplary damages may be awarded only if damages other than nominal damages are awarded.

(b) Exemplary damages may not be awarded to a claimant who elects to have his recovery multiplied under another statute.

Added by Acts 1987, 70th Leg., 1st C.S., ch. 2, § 2.12, eff. Sept. 2, 1987. Amended by Acts 1995, 74th Leg., ch. 19, § 1, eff. Sept. 1, 1995; Acts 2003, 78th Leg., ch. 204, § 13.05, eff. Sept. 1, 2003.

§ 41.005. Harm Resulting from Criminal Act

(a) In an action arising from harm resulting from an assault, theft, or other criminal act, a court may not award exemplary damages against a defendant because of the criminal act of another.

(b) The exemption provided by Subsection (a) does not apply if:

(1) the criminal act was committed by an employee of the defendant;

(2) the defendant is criminally responsible as a party to the criminal act under the provisions of Chapter 7, Penal Code;

(3) the criminal act occurred at a location where, at the time of the criminal act, the defendant was maintaining a common nuisance under the provisions of Chapter 125, Civil Practice and Remedies Code, and had not made reasonable attempts to abate the nuisance; or

(4) the criminal act resulted from the defendant's intentional or knowing violation of a statutory duty under Subchapter D, Chapter 92, Property Code,[1] and the criminal act occurred after the statutory deadline for compliance with that duty.

(c) In an action arising out of a criminal act committed by an employee, the employer may be liable for punitive damages but only if:

(1) the principal authorized the doing and the manner of the act;

(2) the agent was unfit and the principal acted with malice in employing or retaining him;

(3) the agent was employed in a managerial capacity and was acting in the scope of employment; or

(4) the employer or a manager of the employer ratified or approved the act.

Added by Acts 1995, 74th Leg., ch. 19, § 1, eff. Sept. 1, 1995.

[1] V.T.C.A., Property Code § 92.151 et seq.

§ 41.006. Award Specific to Defendant

In any action in which there are two or more defendants, an award of exemplary damages must be specific as to a defendant, and each defendant is liable only for the amount of the award made against that defendant.

Added by Acts 1987, 70th Leg., 1st C.S., ch. 2, § 2.12, eff. Sept. 2, 1987. Redesignated from V.T.C.A., Civil Practice & Remedies Code § 41.005 by Acts 1995, 74th Leg., ch. 19, § 1, eff. Sept. 1, 1995.

§ 41.007. Prejudgment Interest

Prejudgment interest may not be assessed or recovered on an award of exemplary damages.

Added by Acts 1987, 70th Leg., 1st C.S., ch. 2, § 2.12, eff. Sept. 2, 1987. Redesignated from V.T.C.A., Civil Practice & Remedies Code § 41.006 by Acts 1995, 74th Leg., ch. 19, § 1, eff. Sept. 1, 1995.

§ 41.008. Limitation on Amount of Recovery

(a) In an action in which a claimant seeks recovery of damages, the trier of fact shall determine the amount of economic damages separately from the amount of other compensatory damages.

(b) Exemplary damages awarded against a defendant may not exceed an amount equal to the greater of:

(1)(A) two times the amount of economic damages; plus

(B) an amount equal to any noneconomic damages found by the jury, not to exceed $750,000; or

(2) $200,000.

(c) This section does not apply to a cause of action against a defendant from whom a plaintiff seeks recovery of exemplary damages based on conduct described as a felony in the following sections of the Penal Code if, except for Sections 49.07 and 49.08, the conduct was committed knowingly or intentionally:

(1) Section 19.02 (murder);

(2) Section 19.03 (capital murder);

(3) Section 20.04 (aggravated kidnapping);

(4) Section 22.02 (aggravated assault);

(5) Section 22.011 (sexual assault);

(6) Section 22.021 (aggravated sexual assault);

(7) Section 22.04 (injury to a child, elderly individual, or disabled individual, but not if the conduct occurred while providing health care as defined by Section 74.001 of this code);

(8) Section 32.21 (forgery);

(9) Section 32.43 (commercial bribery);

(10) Section 32.45 (misapplication of fiduciary property or property of financial institution);

(11) Section 32.46 (fraudulent securing of document execution);

(12) Section 32.47 (fraudulent destruction, removal, or concealment of writing);

(13) Chapter 31 (theft) the punishment level for which is a felony of the third degree or higher;

(14) Section 49.07 (intoxication assault);

(15) Section 49.08 (intoxication manslaughter);

(16) Section 21.02 (continuous sexual abuse of young child or disabled individual); or

(17) Chapter 20A (trafficking of persons).

(d) In this section, "intentionally" and "knowingly" have the same meanings assigned those terms in Sections 6.03(a) and (b), Penal Code.

(e) The provisions of this section may not be made known to a jury by any means, including voir dire, introduction into evidence, argument, or instruction.

(f) This section does not apply to a cause of action for damages arising from the manufacture of methamphetamine as described by Chapter 99.

Added by Acts 1987, 70th Leg., 1st C.S., ch. 2, § 2.12, eff. Sept. 2, 1987. Redesignated from V.T.C.A., Civil Practice & Remedies Code § 41.007 and amended by Acts 1995, 74th Leg., ch. 19, § 1, eff. Sept. 1, 1995. Amended by Acts 2001, 77th Leg., ch. 643, § 3, eff. Sept. 1, 2001; Acts 2003, 78th Leg., ch. 204, § 13.06, eff. Sept. 1, 2003; Acts 2007, 80th Leg., ch. 593, § 3.03, eff. Sept. 1, 2007; Acts 2009, 81st Leg., ch. 309, § 2, eff. June 19, 2009; Acts 2021, 87th Leg., ch. 221 (H.B. 375), § 2.03, eff. Sept. 1, 2021; Acts 2021, 87th Leg., ch. 837 (S.B. 109), § 5, eff. Sept. 1, 2021.

Section 3.01 of Acts 2021, 87th Leg., ch. 221 (H.B. 375) provides:

"The change in law made by this Act applies only to an offense committed on or after the effective date [Sept. 1, 2021] of this Act. An offense committed before the effective date of this Act is governed by the law in effect on the date the offense was committed, and the former law is continued in effect for that purpose. For purposes of this section, an offense was committed before the effective date of this Act if any element of the offense occurred before that date."

Section 8 of Acts 2021, 87th Leg., ch. 837 (S.B. 109) provides:

"The change in law made by this Act applies only to an offense committed on or after the effective date [Sept. 1, 2021] of this Act. An offense committed before the effective date of this Act is governed by the law in effect on the date the offense was committed, and the former law is continued in effect for that purpose. For purposes of this section, an offense was committed before the effective date of this Act if any element of the offense was committed before that date."

§ 41.009. Bifurcated Trial

(a) On motion by a defendant, the court shall provide for a bifurcated trial under this section. A motion under this subsection shall be made prior to voir dire examination of the jury or at a time specified by a pretrial court order issued under Rule 166, Texas Rules of Civil Procedure.

(b) In an action with more than one defendant, the court shall provide for a bifurcated trial on motion of any defendant.

(c) In the first phase of a bifurcated trial, the trier of fact shall determine:

(1) liability for compensatory and exemplary damages; and

(2) the amount of compensatory damages.

(d) If liability for exemplary damages is established during the first phase of a bifurcated trial, the trier of fact shall, in the second phase of the trial, determine the amount of exemplary damages to be awarded, if any.

Added by Acts 1995, 74th Leg., ch. 19, § 1, eff. Sept. 1, 1995.

§ 41.010. Considerations in Making Award

(a) Before making an award of exemplary damages, the trier of fact shall consider the definition and purposes of exemplary damages as provided by Section 41.001.

(b) Subject to Section 41.008, the determination of whether to award exemplary damages and the amount of exemplary damages to be awarded is within the discretion of the trier of fact.

Added by Acts 1995, 74th Leg., ch. 19, § 1, eff. Sept. 1, 1995. Amended by Acts 2003, 78th Leg., ch. 204, § 13.07, eff. Sept. 1, 2003.

§ 41.0105. Evidence Relating to Amount of Economic Damages

In addition to any other limitation under law, recovery of medical or health care expenses incurred is limited to the amount actually paid or incurred by or on behalf of the claimant.

Added by Acts 2003, 78th Leg., ch. 204, § 13.08, eff. Sept. 1, 2003.

§ 41.011. Evidence Relating to Amount of Exemplary Damages

(a) In determining the amount of exemplary damages, the trier of fact shall consider evidence, if any, relating to:

(1) the nature of the wrong;

(2) the character of the conduct involved;

(3) the degree of culpability of the wrongdoer;

(4) the situation and sensibilities of the parties concerned;

(5) the extent to which such conduct offends a public sense of justice and propriety; and

(6) the net worth of the defendant.

(b) Evidence that is relevant only to the amount of exemplary damages that may be awarded is not admissible during the first phase of a bifurcated trial.

Added by Acts 1995, 74th Leg., ch. 19, § 1, eff. Sept. 1, 1995.

§ 41.0115. Discovery of Evidence of Net Worth for Exemplary Damages Claim

(a) On the motion of a party and after notice and a hearing, a trial court may authorize discovery of evidence of a defendant's net worth if the court finds in a written order that the claimant has demonstrated a substantial likelihood of success on the merits of a claim for exemplary damages. Evidence submitted by a party to the court in support of or in opposition to a motion made under this subsection may be in the form of an affidavit or a response to discovery.

(b) If a trial court authorizes discovery under Subsection (a), the court's order may only authorize use of the least burdensome method available to obtain the net worth evidence.

(c) When reviewing an order authorizing or denying discovery of net worth evidence under this section, the reviewing court may consider only the evidence submitted by the parties to the trial court in support of or in opposition to the motion described by Subsection (a).

(d) If a party requests net worth discovery under this section, the court shall presume that the requesting party has had adequate time for the discovery of facts relating to exemplary damages for purposes of allowing the party from whom net worth discovery is sought to move for summary judgment on the requesting party's claim for exemplary damages under Rule 166a(i), Texas Rules of Civil Procedure.

Added by Acts 2015, 84th Leg., ch. 1159 (S.B. 735), § 2, eff. Sept. 1, 2015.

§ 41.012. Jury Instructions

In a trial to a jury, the court shall instruct the jury with regard to Sections 41.001, 41.003, 41.010, and 41.011.

Added by Acts 1995, 74th Leg., ch. 19, § 1, eff. Sept. 1, 1995.

§ 41.013. Judicial Review of Award

(a) Except as provided for in Subsection (b), an appellate court that reviews the evidence with respect to a finding by a trier of fact concerning liability for exemplary damages or with respect to the amount of exemplary damages awarded shall state, in a written opinion, the court's reasons for upholding or disturbing the finding or award. The written opinion shall address the evidence or lack of evidence with specificity, as it relates to the liability for or amount of exemplary damages, in light of the requirements of this chapter.

(b) This section does not apply to the supreme court with respect to its consideration of an application for writ of error.

Added by Acts 1995, 74th Leg., ch. 19, § 1, eff. Sept. 1, 1995.

§ 41.014. Interest on Damages Subject to Medicare Subrogation

(a) Subject to this section, postjudgment interest does not accrue on the unpaid balance of an award of damages to a plaintiff attributable to any portion of the award to which the United States has a subrogation right under 42 U.S.C. Section 1395y(b)(2)(B) before the defendant receives a recovery demand letter issued by the Centers for Medicare and Medicaid Services or a designated contractor under 42 C.F.R. Section 411.22.

(b) Postjudgment interest under this section does not accrue if the defendant pays the unpaid balance before the 31st day after the date the defendant receives the recovery demand letter.

(c) If the defendant appeals the award of damages, this section does not apply.

(d) This section does not prevent the accrual of postjudgment interest on any portion of an award to which the United States does not have a subrogation right under 42 U.S.C. Section 1395y(b)(2)(B).

Added by Acts 2013, 83rd Leg., ch. 870 (H.B. 658), § 1, eff. Sept. 1, 2013.

CHAPTER 42. SETTLEMENT

Section

§ 42.001. Definitions

In this chapter:

(1) "Claim" means a request, including a counterclaim, cross-claim, or third-party claim, to recover monetary damages.

(2) "Claimant" means a person making a claim.

(3) "Defendant" means a person from whom a claimant seeks recovery on a claim, including a counterdefendant, cross-defendant, or third-party defendant.

(4) "Governmental unit" means the state, a unit of state government, or a political subdivision of this state.

(5) "Litigation costs" means money actually spent and obligations actually incurred that are directly related to the action in which a settlement offer is made. The term includes:

(A) court costs;

(B) reasonable deposition costs;

(C) reasonable fees for not more than two testifying expert witnesses; and

(D) reasonable attorney's fees.

(6) "Settlement offer" means an offer to settle or compromise a claim made in compliance with Section 42.003.

Added by Acts 2003, 78th Leg., ch. 204, § 2.01, eff. Sept. 1, 2003. Amended by Acts 2011, 82nd Leg., ch. 203 (H.B. 274), § 4.01, eff. Sept. 1, 2011.

§ 42.002. Applicability and Effect

(a) The settlement procedures provided in this chapter apply only to claims for monetary relief.

(b) This chapter does not apply to:

(1) a class action;

(2) a shareholder's derivative action;

(3) an action by or against a governmental unit;

(4) an action brought under the Family Code;

(5) an action to collect workers' compensation benefits under Subtitle A, Title 5, Labor Code;[1] or

(6) an action filed in a justice of the peace court or a small claims court.

(c) This chapter does not apply until a defendant files a declaration that the settlement procedure allowed by this chapter is available in the action. If there is more than one defendant, the settlement procedure allowed by this chapter is available only in relation to the defendant that filed the declaration and to the parties that make or receive offers of settlement in relation to that defendant.

(d) This chapter does not limit or affect the ability of any person to:

(1) make an offer to settle or compromise a claim that does not comply with Section 42.003; or

(2) offer to settle or compromise a claim in an action to which this chapter does not apply.

(e) An offer to settle or compromise that does not comply with Section 42.003 or an offer to settle or compromise made in an action to which this chapter does not apply does not entitle any party to recover litigation costs under this chapter.

Added by Acts 2003, 78th Leg., ch. 204, § 2.01, eff. Sept. 1, 2003. Amended by Acts 2011, 82nd Leg., ch. 203 (H.B. 274), § 4.02, eff. Sept. 1, 2011.

[1] V.T.C.A., Labor Code § 401.001 et seq.

§ 42.003. Making Settlement Offer

(a) A settlement offer must:

(1) be in writing;

(2) state that it is made under this chapter;

(3) state the terms by which the claims may be settled;

(4) state a deadline by which the settlement offer must be accepted; and

(5) be served on all parties to whom the settlement offer is made.

(b) The parties are not required to file a settlement offer with the court.

Added by Acts 2003, 78th Leg., ch. 204, § 2.01, eff. Sept. 1, 2003. Amended by Acts 2011, 82nd Leg., ch. 203 (H.B. 274), § 4.03, eff. Sept. 1, 2011.

§ 42.004. Awarding Litigation Costs

(a) If a settlement offer is made and rejected and the judgment to be rendered will be significantly less favorable to the rejecting party than was the settlement offer, the offering party shall recover litigation costs from the rejecting party.

(b) A judgment will be significantly less favorable to the rejecting party than is the settlement offer if:

(1) the rejecting party is a claimant and the award will be less than 80 percent of the rejected offer; or

(2) the rejecting party is a defendant and the award will be more than 120 percent of the rejected offer.

(c) The litigation costs that may be recovered by the offering party under this section are limited to those litigation costs incurred by the offering party after the date the rejecting party rejected the settlement offer.

(d) The litigation costs that may be awarded under this chapter to any party may not be greater than the total amount that the claimant recovers or would recover before adding an award of litigation costs under this chapter in favor of the claimant or subtracting as an offset an award of litigation costs under this chapter in favor of the defendant.

(e) If a claimant or defendant is entitled to recover fees and costs under another law, that claimant or defendant may not recover litigation costs in addition to the fees and costs recoverable under the other law.

(f) If a claimant or defendant is entitled to recover fees and costs under another law, the court must not include fees and costs incurred by that claimant or defendant after the date of rejection of the settlement offer when calculating the amount of the judgment to be rendered under Subsection (a).

(g) If litigation costs are to be awarded against a claimant, those litigation costs shall be awarded to the defendant in the judgment as an offset against the claimant's recovery from that defendant.

Added by Acts 2003, 78th Leg., ch. 204, § 2.01, eff. Sept. 1, 2003. Amended by Acts 2011, 82nd Leg., ch. 203 (H.B. 274), § 4.04, eff. Sept. 1, 2011.

§ 42.005. Supreme Court to Make Rules

(a) The supreme court shall promulgate rules implementing this chapter. The rules must be limited to settlement offers made under this chapter. The rules must be in effect on January 1, 2004.

(b) The rules promulgated by the supreme court must provide:

(1) the date by which a defendant or defendants must file the declaration required by Section 42.002(c);

(2) the date before which a party may not make a settlement offer;

(3) the date after which a party may not make a settlement offer; and

(4) procedures for:

(A) making an initial settlement offer;

(B) making successive settlement offers;

(C) withdrawing a settlement offer;

(D) accepting a settlement offer;

(E) rejecting a settlement offer; and

(F) modifying the deadline for making, withdrawing, accepting, or rejecting a settlement offer.

(c) The rules promulgated by the supreme court must address actions in which there are multiple parties and must provide that if the offering party joins another party or designates a responsible third party after making the settlement offer, the party to whom the settlement offer was made may declare the offer void.

(d) The rules promulgated by the supreme court may:

(1) designate other actions to which the settlement procedure of this chapter does not apply; and

(2) address other matters considered necessary by the supreme court to the implementation of this chapter.

Added by Acts 2003, 78th Leg., ch. 204, § 2.01, eff. Sept. 1, 2003.

CHAPTER 43. PRINCIPAL AND SURETY

Section

§ 43.001. Definition

In this chapter, "surety" includes:

(1) an endorser, a guarantor, and a drawer of a draft that has been accepted; and

(2) every other form of suretyship, whether created by express contract or by operation of law.

Added by Acts 2007, 80th Leg., ch. 885, § 2.11, eff. April 1, 2009.

§ 43.002. Suit on Accrued Right of Action

(a) When a right of action accrues on a contract for the payment of money or performance of an act, a surety on the contract may, by written notice, require the obligee to without delay bring a suit on the contract.

(b) A surety who provides notice to an obligee under Subsection (a) is discharged from all liability on the contract if the obligee:

(1) is not under a legal disability; and

(2) does not:

(A) bring a suit on the contract during:

(i) the first term of court after receipt of the notice; or

(ii) the second term of court if good cause is shown for the delay; or

(B) prosecute the suit to judgment and execution.

Added by Acts 2007, 80th Leg., ch. 885, § 2.11, eff. April 1, 2009.

§ 43.003. Priority of Execution

(a) If a judgment granted against two or more defendants finds a suretyship relationship between or among the defendants, the court shall order the sheriff to levy the execution in the following order:

(1) against the principal's property located in the county where the judgment was granted;

(2) if the sheriff cannot find enough of the principal's property in that county to satisfy the execution, against as much of the principal's property as the sheriff finds; and

(3) against as much of the surety's property as is necessary to make up the balance of the amount shown in the writ of execution.

(b) The clerk shall note the order to the sheriff on the writ of execution.

Added by Acts 2007, 80th Leg., ch. 885, § 2.11, eff. April 1, 2009.

§ 43.004. Subrogation Rights of Surety

(a) A judgment is not discharged by a surety's payment of the judgment in whole or part if the payment:

(1) is compelled; or

(2) if made voluntarily, is applied to the judgment because of the suretyship relationship.

(b) A surety who pays on a judgment as described by Subsection (a) is subrogated to all of the judgment creditor's rights under the judgment. A subrogated surety is entitled to execution on the judgment against:

(1) the principal's property for the amount of the surety's payment, plus interest and costs; and

(2) if there is more than one surety, both the principal's property and the property of the cosurety or cosureties for the amount by which the surety's payment exceeds the surety's proportionate share of the judgment, plus interest and costs.

(c) A subrogated surety seeking execution on the judgment under Subsection (b) shall apply for execution to the clerk or court. The execution shall be levied, collected, and returned as in other cases.

Added by Acts 2007, 80th Leg., ch. 885, § 2.11, eff. April 1, 2009.

§ 43.005. Officer Treated as Surety

(a) An officer has the rights of a surety provided by Section 43.004 if the officer is compelled to pay a judgment in whole or part because of the officer's default.

(b) An officer does not have the rights of a surety provided by Section 43.004 if the officer:

(1) does not pay over money collected; or

(2) wastes property that is levied on by the officer or is in the officer's possession.

Added by Acts 2007, 80th Leg., ch. 885, § 2.11, eff. April 1, 2009.

SUBTITLE D. APPEALS

CHAPTER 51. APPEALS

SUBCHAPTER A. APPEALS FROM JUSTICE COURT

SUBCHAPTER A. APPEALS FROM JUSTICE COURT

§ 51.001. Appeal From Justice Court to County or District Court

(a) In a case tried in justice court in which the judgment or amount in controversy exceeds $250, exclusive of costs, or in which the appeal is expressly provided by law, a party to a final judgment may appeal to the county court.

(b) In a county in which the civil jurisdiction of the county court has been transferred to the district court, a party to a final judgment in a case covered by this section may appeal to the district court.

Acts 1985, 69th Leg., ch. 959, § 1, eff. Sept. 1, 1985. Amended by Acts 2007, 80th Leg., ch. 553, § 2, eff. Sept. 1, 2007.

§ 51.002. Certiorari From Justice Court

(a) After final judgment in a case tried in justice court in which the judgment or amount in controversy exceeds $250, exclusive of costs, a person may remove the case from the justice court to the county court by writ of certiorari.

(b) In a county in which the civil jurisdiction of the county court has been transferred from the county court to the district court, a person may remove a case covered by this section from the justice court to the district court by writ of certiorari.

(c) If a writ of certiorari to remove a case is served on a justice of the peace, the justice shall immediately make a certified copy of the entries made on his docket and of the bill of costs, as provided in cases of appeals, and shall immediately send them and the original papers in the case to the clerk of the county or district court, as appropriate.

(d) This section does not apply to a case of forcible entry and detainer.

Acts 1985, 69th Leg., ch. 959, § 1, eff. Sept. 1, 1985. Amended by Acts 2007, 80th Leg., ch. 553, § 3, eff. Sept. 1, 2007.

SUBCHAPTER B. APPEALS FROM COUNTY OR DISTRICT COURT

§ 51.011. Appeal From County or District Court After Certiorari From Justice Court

If a county or district court hears a case on certiorari from a justice court, a person may take an appeal or writ of error from the judgment of the county or district court. The appeal or writ of error is subject to the rules that apply in a case appealed from a justice court.

Acts 1985, 69th Leg., ch. 959, § 1, eff. Sept. 1, 1985.

§ 51.012. Appeal or Writ of Error to Court of Appeals

In a civil case in which the judgment or amount in controversy exceeds $250, exclusive of interest and costs, a person may take an appeal or writ of error to the court of appeals from a final judgment of the district or county court.

Acts 1985, 69th Leg., ch. 959, § 1, eff. Sept. 1, 1985. Amended by Acts 2009, 81st Leg., ch. 1351, § 1, eff. Sept. 1, 2009.

§ 51.013. Time for Taking Writ of Error to Court of Appeals

In a case in which a writ of error to the court of appeals is allowed, the writ of error may be taken at any time within six months after the date the final judgment is rendered.

Acts 1985, 69th Leg., ch. 959, § 1, eff. Sept. 1, 1985.

§ 51.014. Appeal from Interlocutory Order

(a) A person may appeal from an interlocutory order of a district court, county court at law, statutory probate court, or county court that:

(1) appoints a receiver or trustee;

(2) overrules a motion to vacate an order that appoints a receiver or trustee;

(3) certifies or refuses to certify a class in a suit brought under Rule 42 of the Texas Rules of Civil Procedure;

(4) grants or refuses a temporary injunction or grants or overrules a motion to dissolve a temporary injunction as provided by Chapter 65;

(5) denies a motion for summary judgment that is based on an assertion of immunity by an individual who is an officer or employee of the state or a political subdivision of the state;

(6) denies a motion for summary judgment that is based in whole or in part upon a claim against or defense by a member of the electronic or print media, acting in such capacity, or a person whose communication appears in or is published by the electronic or print media, arising under the free speech or free press clause of the First Amendment to the United States Constitution, or Article I, Section 8, of the Texas Constitution, or Chapter 73;

(7) grants or denies the special appearance of a defendant under Rule 120a, Texas Rules of Civil Procedure, except in a suit brought under the Family Code;

(8) grants or denies a plea to the jurisdiction by a governmental unit as that term is defined in Section 101.001;

(9) denies all or part of the relief sought by a motion under Section 74.351(b), except that an appeal may not be taken from an order granting an extension under Section 74.351;

(10) grants relief sought by a motion under Section 74.351(*l*);

(11) denies a motion to dismiss filed under Section 90.007;

(12) denies a motion to dismiss filed under Section 27.003;

(13) denies a motion for summary judgment filed by an electric utility regarding liability in a suit subject to Section 75.0022;

(14) denies a motion filed by a municipality with a population of 500,000 or more in an action filed under Section 54.012(6) or 214.0012, Local Government Code; or

Text of (a)(15), as added by Acts 2021, 87th Leg., ch. 167 (S.B. 232), § 1

(15) makes a preliminary determination on a claim under Section 74.353.

Text of (a)(15), as added by Acts 2021, 87th Leg., ch. 528 (S.B. 6), § 1

(15) overrules an objection filed under Section 148.003(d) or denies all or part of the relief sought by a motion under Section 148.003(f).

Text of (a)(15), as added by Acts 2021, 87th Leg., ch. 813 (H.B. 2086), § 1

(15) grants or denies a motion for summary judgment filed by a contractor based on Section 97.002.

(b) An interlocutory appeal under Subsection (a), other than an appeal under Subsection (a)(4) or in a suit brought under the Family Code, stays the commencement of a trial in the trial court pending resolution of the appeal. An interlocutory appeal under Subsection (a)(3), (5), (8), or (12) also stays all other proceedings in the trial court pending resolution of that appeal.

(c) A denial of a motion for summary judgment, special appearance, or plea to the jurisdiction described by Subsection (a)(5), (7), or (8) is not subject to the automatic stay under Subsection (b) unless the motion, special appearance, or plea to the jurisdiction is filed and requested for submission or hearing before the trial court not later than the later of:

(1) a date set by the trial court in a scheduling order entered under the Texas Rules of Civil Procedure; or

(2) the 180th day after the date the defendant files:

(A) the original answer;

(B) the first other responsive pleading to the plaintiff's petition; or

(C) if the plaintiff files an amended pleading that alleges a new cause of action against the defendant and the defendant is able to raise a defense to the new cause of action under Subsection (a)(5), (7), or (8), the responsive pleading that raises that defense.

(d) On a party's motion or on its own initiative, a trial court in a civil action may, by written order, permit an appeal from an order that is not otherwise appealable if:

(1) the order to be appealed involves a controlling question of law as to which there is a substantial ground for difference of opinion; and

(2) an immediate appeal from the order may materially advance the ultimate termination of the litigation.

(d-1) Subsection (d) does not apply to an action brought under the Family Code.

(e) An appeal under Subsection (d) does not stay proceedings in the trial court unless:

(1) the parties agree to a stay; or

(2) the trial or appellate court orders a stay of the proceedings pending appeal.

(f) An appellate court may accept an appeal permitted by Subsection (d) if the appealing party, not later than the 15th day after the date the trial court signs the order to be appealed, files in the court of appeals having appellate jurisdiction over the action an application for interlocutory appeal explaining why an appeal is warranted under Subsection (d). If the court of appeals accepts the appeal, the appeal is governed by the procedures in the Texas Rules of Appellate Procedure for pursuing an accelerated appeal. The date the court of appeals enters the order accepting the appeal starts the time applicable to filing the notice of appeal.

Acts 1985, 69th Leg., ch. 959, § 1, eff. Sept. 1, 1985. Amended by Acts 1987, 70th Leg., ch. 167, § 3.10, eff. Sept. 1, 1987; Acts 1989, 71st Leg., ch. 915, § 1, eff. June 14, 1989; Acts 1993, 73rd Leg., ch. 855, § 1, eff. Sept. 1, 1993; Acts 1997, 75th Leg., ch. 1296, § 1, eff. June 20, 1997; Acts 2001, 77th Leg., ch. 1389, § 1, eff. Sept. 1, 2001; Acts 2003, 78th Leg., ch. 204, § 1.03, eff. Sept. 1, 2003; Acts 2005, 79th Leg., ch. 97, § 5, eff. Sept. 1, 2005; Acts 2005, 79th Leg., ch. 1051, §§ 1, 2, eff. June 18, 2005; Acts 2011, 82nd Leg., ch. 203 (H.B. 274), § 3.01, eff. Sept. 1, 2011; Acts 2013, 83rd Leg., ch. 44 (H.B. 200), § 1, eff. May 16, 2013; Acts 2013, 83rd Leg., ch. 604 (S.B. 1083), § 1, eff. Sept. 1, 2013; Acts 2013, 83rd Leg., ch. 916 (H.B. 1366), § 1, eff. Sept. 1, 2013; Acts 2013, 83rd Leg., ch. 961 (H.B. 1874), § 1, eff. Sept. 1, 2013; Acts 2013, 83rd Leg., ch. 1042 (H.B. 2935), § 4, eff. June 14, 2013; Acts 2015, 84th Leg., ch. 1236 (S.B. 1296), §§ 3.001, 3.002, eff. Sept. 1, 2015; Acts 2019, 86th Leg., ch. 1273 (H.B. 36), § 1, eff. June 14, 2019; Acts 2021, 87th Leg., ch. 167 (S.B. 232), § 1, eff. Sept. 1, 2021; Acts 2021, 87th Leg., ch. 528 (S.B. 6), § 1, eff. June 14, 2021; Acts 2021, 87th Leg., ch. 813 (H.B. 2086), § 1, eff. June 16, 2021.

Section 4 of Acts 2021, 87th Leg., ch. 167 (S.B. 232) provides:

"The change in law made by this Act applies only to an action commenced on or after the effective date [Sept. 1, 2021] of this Act. An action commenced before the effective date of this Act is governed by the law as it existed immediately before the effective date of this Act, and that law is continued in effect for that purpose."

§ 51.015. Costs of Appeal

In the case of an appeal brought pursuant to Section 51.014(6), if the order appealed from is affirmed, the court of appeals shall order the appellant to pay all costs and reasonable attorney fees of the appeal; otherwise, each party shall be liable for and taxed its own costs of the appeal.

Added by Acts 1993, 73rd Leg., ch. 855, § 1, eff. Sept. 1, 1993.

§ 51.016. Appeal Arising Under Federal Arbitration Act

In a matter subject to the Federal Arbitration Act (9 U.S.C. Section 1 et seq.), a person may take an appeal or writ of error to the court of appeals from the judgment or interlocutory order of a district court, county court at law, or county court under the same circumstances that an appeal from a federal district court's order or decision would be permitted by 9 U.S.C. Section 16.

Added by Acts 2009, 81st Leg., ch. 820, § 1, eff. Sept. 1, 2009.

§ 51.017. Service of Notice on Court Reporter

(a) In addition to requirements for service of notice of appeal imposed by Rule 25.1(e), Texas Rules of Appellate Procedure, notice of appeal, including an interlocutory appeal, must be served on each court reporter responsible for preparing the reporter's record.

(b) Notwithstanding Section 22.004, Government Code, the supreme court may not amend or adopt rules in conflict with this section.

Added by Acts 2019, 86th Leg., ch. 606 (S.B. 891), § 7.02, eff. Sept. 1, 2019.

Section 15.05 of Acts 2019, 86th Leg., ch. 606 (S.B. 891) provides:

"The Office of Court Administration of the Texas Judicial System is required to implement a provision of this Act only if the legislature appropriates money specifically for that purpose. If the legislature does not appropriate money specifically for that purpose, the office may, but is not required to, implement a provision of this Act using other appropriations available for that purpose."

CHAPTER 52. SECURITY FOR JUDGMENTS PENDING APPEAL

§ 52.001. Definition

In this chapter, "security" means a bond or deposit posted, as provided by the Texas Rules of Appellate Procedure, by a judgment debtor to suspend execution of the judgment during appeal of the judgment.

Added by Acts 1989, 71st Leg., ch. 1178, § 1, eff. Sept. 1, 1989.

§§ 52.002 to 52.004. Repealed by Acts 2003, 78th Leg., ch. 204, § 7.03, eff. Sept. 1, 2003

§ 52.005. Conflict with Texas Rules of Appellate Procedure

(a) To the extent that this chapter conflicts with the Texas Rules of Appellate Procedure, this chapter controls.

(b) Notwithstanding Section 22.004, Government Code, the supreme court may not adopt rules in conflict with this chapter.

(c) The Texas Rules of Appellate Procedure apply to any proceeding, cause of action, or claim to which Section 52.002 does not apply.

Added by Acts 1989, 71st Leg., ch. 1178, § 1, eff. Sept. 1, 1989.

§ 52.006. Amount of Security for Money Judgment

(a) Subject to Subsection (b), when a judgment is for money, the amount of security must equal the sum of:

(1) the amount of compensatory damages awarded in the judgment;

(2) interest for the estimated duration of the appeal; and

(3) costs awarded in the judgment.

(b) Notwithstanding any other law or rule of court, when a judgment is for money, the amount of security must not exceed the lesser of:

(1) 50 percent of the judgment debtor's net worth; or

(2) $25 million.

(c) On a showing by the judgment debtor that the judgment debtor is likely to suffer substantial economic harm if required to post security in an amount required under Subsection (a) or (b), the trial court shall lower the amount of the security to an amount that will not cause the judgment debtor substantial economic harm.

(d) An appellate court may review the amount of security as allowed under Rule 24, Texas Rules of Appellate Procedure, except that when a judgment is for money, the appellate court may not modify the amount of security to exceed the amount allowed under this section.

(e) Nothing in this section prevents a trial court from enjoining the judgment debtor from dissipating or transferring assets to avoid satisfaction of the judgment, but the trial court may not make any order that interferes with the judgment debtor's use, transfer, conveyance, or dissipation of assets in the normal course of business.

Added by Acts 2003, 78th Leg., ch. 204, § 7.02, eff. Sept. 1, 2003.

TITLE 3. EXTRAORDINARY REMEDIES

CHAPTER 61. ATTACHMENT

SUBCHAPTER A. AVAILABILITY OF REMEDY

§ 61.001. General Grounds

A writ of original attachment is available to a plaintiff in a suit if:

(1) the defendant is justly indebted to the plaintiff;

(2) the attachment is not sought for the purpose of injuring or harassing the defendant;

(3) the plaintiff will probably lose his debt unless the writ of attachment is issued; and

(4) specific grounds for the writ exist under Section 61.002.

Acts 1985, 69th Leg., ch. 959, § 1, eff. Sept. 1, 1985.

§ 61.002. Specific Grounds

Attachment is available if:

(1) the defendant is not a resident of this state or is a foreign corporation or is acting as such;

(2) the defendant is about to move from this state permanently and has refused to pay or secure the debt due the plaintiff;

(3) the defendant is in hiding so that ordinary process of law cannot be served on him;

(4) the defendant has hidden or is about to hide his property for the purpose of defrauding his creditors;

(5) the defendant is about to remove his property from this state without leaving an amount sufficient to pay his debts;

(6) the defendant is about to remove all or part of his property from the county in which the suit is brought with the intent to defraud his creditors;

(7) the defendant has disposed of or is about to dispose of all or part of his property with the intent to defraud his creditors;

(8) the defendant is about to convert all or part of his property into money for the purpose of placing it beyond the reach of his creditors; or

(9) the defendant owes the plaintiff for property obtained by the defendant under false pretenses.

Acts 1985, 69th Leg., ch. 959, § 1, eff. Sept. 1, 1985.

§ 61.0021. Grounds for Attachment in Suit for Sexual Assault

(a) Notwithstanding any other provision of this code, attachment is available to a plaintiff who:

(1) has general grounds for issuance under Sections 61.001(2) and (3); and

(2) institutes a suit for personal injury arising as a result of conduct that violates:

(A) Section 22.011(a)(2), Penal Code (sexual assault of a child);

(B) Section 22.021(a)(1)(B), Penal Code (aggravated sexual assault of a child);

(C) Section 21.02, Penal Code (continuous sexual abuse of young child or disabled individual); or

(D) Section 21.11, Penal Code (indecency with a child).

(b) A court may issue a writ of attachment in a suit described by Subsection (a) in an amount the court determines to be appropriate to provide for the counseling and medical needs of the plaintiff.

Added by Acts 2009, 81st Leg., ch. 946, § 1, eff. Sept. 1, 2009. Amended by Acts 2021, 87th Leg., ch. 221 (H.B. 375), § 2.04, eff. Sept. 1, 2021.

Section 3.01 of Acts 2021, 87th Leg., ch. 221 (H.B. 375) provides:

"The change in law made by this Act applies only to an offense committed on or after the effective date [Sept. 1, 2021] of this Act. An offense committed before the effective date of this Act is governed by the law in effect on the date the offense was committed, and the former law is continued in effect for that purpose. For purposes of this section, an offense was committed before the effective date of this Act if any element of the offense occurred before that date."

§ 61.003. Pending Suit Required

A writ of attachment may be issued in a proper case at the initiation of a suit or at any time during the progress of a suit, but may not be issued before a suit has been instituted.

Acts 1985, 69th Leg., ch. 959, § 1, eff. Sept. 1, 1985.

§ 61.004. Available for Debt Not Due

A writ of attachment may be issued even though the plaintiff's debt or demand is not due. The proceedings relating to the writ shall be as in other cases, except that final judgment may not be rendered against the defendant until the debt or demand becomes due.

Acts 1985, 69th Leg., ch. 959, § 1, eff. Sept. 1, 1985.

§ 61.005. Certain Torts and Unliquidated Demands

Nothing in this chapter prevents issuance of a writ of attachment in a suit founded in tort or on an unliquidated demand against an individual, partnership, association, or corporation on whom personal service cannot be obtained in this state.

Acts 1985, 69th Leg., ch. 959, § 1, eff. Sept. 1, 1985.

SUBCHAPTER B. ISSUANCE

§ 61.021. Who May Issue

The judge or clerk of a district or county court or a justice of the peace may issue a writ of original attachment returnable to his court.

Acts 1985, 69th Leg., ch. 959, § 1, eff. Sept. 1, 1985.

§ 61.022. Affidavit

(a) Except as provided by Subsection (a-1), to apply for a writ of attachment, a plaintiff or the plaintiff's agent or attorney must file with the court an affidavit that states:

(1) general grounds for issuance under Sections 61.001(1), (2), and (3);

(2) the amount of the demand; and

(3) specific grounds for issuance under Section 61.002.

(a-1) To apply for a writ of attachment under Section 61.0021, a plaintiff or the plaintiff's agent or attorney must file with the court an affidavit that states:

(1) general grounds for issuance under Sections 61.001(2) and (3);

(2) specific grounds for issuance under Section 61.0021(a); and

(3) the amount of the demand based on the estimated cost of counseling and medical needs of the plaintiff.

(b) The affidavit shall be filed with the papers of the case.

Acts 1985, 69th Leg., ch. 959, § 1, eff. Sept. 1, 1985. Amended by Acts 2009, 81st Leg., ch. 946, § 2, eff. Sept. 1, 2009.

§ 61.023. Bond

(a) Before a writ of attachment may be issued, the plaintiff must execute a bond that:

(1) has two or more good and sufficient sureties;

(2) is payable to the defendant;

(3) is in an amount fixed by the judge or justice issuing the writ; and

(4) is conditioned on the plaintiff prosecuting his suit to effect and paying all damages and costs adjudged against him for wrongful attachment.

(b) The plaintiff shall deliver the bond to the officer issuing the writ for that officer's approval. The bond shall be filed with the papers of the case.

Acts 1985, 69th Leg., ch. 959, § 1, eff. Sept. 1, 1985.

SUBCHAPTER C. LEVY

§ 61.041. Subject Property

A writ of attachment may be levied only on property that by law is subject to levy under a writ of execution.

Acts 1985, 69th Leg., ch. 959, § 1, eff. Sept. 1, 1985.

§ 61.042. Attachment of Personalty

The officer attaching personal property shall retain possession until final judgment unless the property is:

(1) replevied;

(2) sold as provided by law; or

(3) claimed by a third party who posts bond and tries his right to the property.

Acts 1985, 69th Leg., ch. 959, § 1, eff. Sept. 1, 1985.

§ 61.043. Attachment of Realty

(a) To attach real property, the officer levying the writ shall immediately file a copy of the writ and the applicable part of the return with the county clerk of each county in which the property is located.

(b) If the writ of attachment is quashed or vacated, the court that issued the writ shall send a certified copy of the order to the county clerk of each county in which the property is located.

Acts 1985, 69th Leg., ch. 959, § 1, eff. Sept. 1, 1985.

§ 61.044. Claim on Attached Personalty by Third Party

A person other than the defendant may claim attached personal property by making an affidavit and giving bond in the manner provided by law for trial of right of property.

Acts 1985, 69th Leg., ch. 959, § 1, eff. Sept. 1, 1985.

§ 61.045. Attachment of Personalty Held by Financial Institution

Service of a writ of attachment on a financial institution relating to personal property held by the financial institution in the name of or on behalf of a customer of the financial institution is governed by Section 59.008, Finance Code.

Added by Acts 1999, 76th Leg., ch. 344, § 7.003, eff. Sept. 1, 1999.

SUBCHAPTER D. LIEN

§ 61.061. Attachment Lien

Unless quashed or vacated, an executed writ of attachment creates a lien from the date of levy on the real property attached, on the personal property held by the attaching officer, and on the proceeds of any attached personal property that may have been sold.

Acts 1985, 69th Leg., ch. 959, § 1, eff. Sept. 1, 1985.

§ 61.062. Judgment and Foreclosure

(a) If the plaintiff recovers in the suit, the attachment lien is foreclosed as in the case of other liens. The court shall direct proceeds from personal property previously sold to be applied to the satisfaction of the judgment and the sale of personal property remaining in the hands of the officer and of the real property levied on to satisfy the judgment.

(b) If the writ of attachment on real property was issued from a county or justice court, the court is not required to enter an order or decree foreclosing the lien, but to preserve the lien the judgment must briefly recite the issuance and levy of the writ. The land may be sold under execution after judgment, and the sale vests in the purchaser all of the estate of the defendant in the land at the time of the levy.

Acts 1985, 69th Leg., ch. 959, § 1, eff. Sept. 1, 1985.

§ 61.063. Judgment on Replevied Property

A judgment against a defendant who has replevied attached personal property shall be against the defendant and his sureties on the replevy bond for the amount of the judgment plus interest and costs or for an amount equal to the value of the replevied property plus interest, according to the terms of the replevy bond.

Acts 1985, 69th Leg., ch. 959, § 1, eff. Sept. 1, 1985.

SUBCHAPTER E. WORKS OF FINE ART

§ 61.081. Exemption When en Route to or in an Exhibition

(a) Subject to the limitations of this section, a court may not issue and a person may not serve any process of attachment, execution, sequestration, replevin, or distress or of any kind of seizure, levy, or sale on a work of fine art while it is:

(1) en route to an exhibition; or

(2) in the possession of the exhibitor or on display as part of the exhibition.

(b) The restriction on the issuance and service of process in Subsection (a) applies only for a period that:

(1) begins on the date that the work of fine art is en route to an exhibition; and

(2) ends on the earlier of the following dates:

(A) six months after the date that the work of fine art is en route to the exhibition; or

(B) the date that the exhibition ends.

(c) Subsection (a) does not apply to a work of fine art if, at any other time, issuance and service of process in relation to the work has been restricted as provided by Subsection (a).

(d) Subsection (a) does not apply if theft of the work of art from its owner is alleged and found proven by the court.

(e) A court shall, in issuing service of process described by Subsection (a), require that the person serving the process give notice to the exhibitor not less than seven days before the date the period under

Subsection (b) ends of the person's intent to serve process.

(f) In this section, "exhibition" means an exhibition:

(1) held under the auspices or supervision of:

(A) an organization exempt from federal income tax under Section 501(a), Internal Revenue Code of 1986, as amended, by being listed as an exempt organization in Section 501(c)(3) of the code; or

(B) a public or private institution of higher education;

(2) held for a cultural, educational, or charitable purpose; and

(3) not held for the profit of the exhibitor.

Added by Acts 1999, 76th Leg., ch. 1043, § 1, eff. Aug. 30, 1999.

§ 61.082. Handling and Transportation

A court may not issue any process of attachment, execution, sequestration, replevin, or distress or of any kind of seizure, levy, or sale on a work of fine art unless the court requires, as part of the order authorizing the process, that the work of fine art is handled and transported in a manner that complies with the accepted standards of the artistic community for works of fine art, including, if appropriate, measures relating to the maintenance of proper environmental conditions, proper maintenance, security, and insurance coverage.

Added by Acts 1999, 76th Leg., ch. 1043, § 1, eff. Aug. 30, 1999.

CHAPTER 62. SEQUESTRATION

SUBCHAPTER A. AVAILABILITY OF REMEDY

SUBCHAPTER B. ISSUANCE

SUBCHAPTER C. DISSOLUTION AND REPLEVY

SUBCHAPTER D. CARE AND MANAGEMENT OF SEQUESTERED PROPERTY

SUBCHAPTER A. AVAILABILITY OF REMEDY

§ 62.001. Grounds

A writ of sequestration is available to a plaintiff in a suit if:

(1) the suit is for title or possession of personal property or fixtures or for foreclosure or enforcement of a mortgage, lien, or security interest on personal property or fixtures and a reasonable conclusion may be drawn that there is immediate danger that the defendant or the party in possession of the property will conceal, dispose of, ill-treat, waste, or destroy the property or remove it from the county during the suit;

(2) the suit is for title or possession of real property or for foreclosure or enforcement of a mortgage or lien on real property and a reasonable conclusion may be drawn that there is immediate danger that the defendant or the party in possession of the property will use his possession to injure or ill-treat the property or waste or convert to his own use the timber, rents, fruits, or revenue of the property;

(3) the suit is for the title or possession of property from which the plaintiff has been ejected by force or violence; or

(4) the suit is to try the title to real property, to remove a cloud from the title of real property, to foreclose a lien on real property, or to partition real property and the plaintiff makes an oath that one or more of the defendants is a nonresident of this state.

Acts 1985, 69th Leg., ch. 959, § 1, eff. Sept. 1, 1985.

§ 62.002. Pending Suit Required

A writ of sequestration may be issued at the initiation of a suit or at any time before final judgment.

Acts 1985, 69th Leg., ch. 959, § 1, eff. Sept. 1, 1985.

§ 62.003. Available for Claim Not Due

A writ of sequestration may be issued for personal property under a mortgage or a lien even though the right of action on the mortgage or lien has not accrued. The proceedings relating to the writ shall be as in other cases, except that final judgment may not be rendered against the defendant until the right of action has accrued.

Acts 1985, 69th Leg., ch. 959, § 1, eff. Sept. 1, 1985.

SUBCHAPTER B. ISSUANCE

§ 62.021. Who May Issue

A district or county court judge or a justice of the peace may issue writs of sequestration returnable to his court.

Acts 1985, 69th Leg., ch. 959, § 1, eff. Sept. 1, 1985.

§ 62.022. Application

The application for a writ of sequestration must be made under oath and must set forth:

(1) the specific facts stating the nature of the plaintiff's claim;

(2) the amount in controversy, if any; and

(3) the facts justifying issuance of the writ.

Acts 1985, 69th Leg., ch. 959, § 1, eff. Sept. 1, 1985.

§ 62.023. Required Statement of Rights

(a) A writ of sequestration must prominently display the following statement on the face of the writ:

YOU HAVE A RIGHT TO REGAIN POSSESSION OF THE PROPERTY BY FILING A REPLEVY BOND. YOU HAVE A RIGHT TO SEEK TO REGAIN POSSESSION OF THE PROPERTY BY FILING WITH THE COURT A MOTION TO DISSOLVE THIS WRIT.

(b) The statement must be printed in 10-point type and in a manner intended to advise a reasonably attentive person of its contents.

Acts 1985, 69th Leg., ch. 959, § 1, eff. Sept. 1, 1985.

SUBCHAPTER C. DISSOLUTION AND REPLEVY

§ 62.041. Motion for Dissolution; Stay

(a) The defendant may seek dissolution of an issued writ of sequestration by filing a written motion with the court.

(b) The right to seek dissolution is cumulative of the right of replevy.

(c) The filing of a motion to dissolve stays proceedings under the writ until the issue is determined.

Acts 1985, 69th Leg., ch. 959, § 1, eff. Sept. 1, 1985.

§ 62.042. Hearing on Motion

Unless the parties agree to an extension, the court shall conduct a hearing on the motion and determine the issue not later than the 10th day after the motion is filed.

Acts 1985, 69th Leg., ch. 959, § 1, eff. Sept. 1, 1985.

§ 62.043. Dissolution

(a) Following the hearing, the writ must be dissolved unless the party who secured its issuance proves the specific facts alleged and the grounds relied on for issuance.

(b) If the writ is dissolved, the action proceeds as if the writ had not been issued.

Acts 1985, 69th Leg., ch. 959, § 1, eff. Sept. 1, 1985.

§ 62.044. Compulsory Counterclaim for Wrongful Sequestration

(a) If a writ is dissolved, any action for damages for wrongful sequestration must be brought as a compulsory counterclaim.

(b) In addition to damages, the party who sought dissolution of the writ may recover reasonable attorney's fees incurred in dissolution of the writ.

Acts 1985, 69th Leg., ch. 959, § 1, eff. Sept. 1, 1985.

§ 62.045. Wrongful Sequestration of Consumer Goods

(a) If a writ that sought to sequester consumer goods is dissolved, the defendant or party in possession of the goods is entitled to reasonable attorney's fees and to damages equal to the greater of:

(1) $100;

(2) the finance charge contracted for; or

(3) actual damages.

(b) Damages may not be awarded for the failure of the plaintiff to prove by a preponderance of the evidence the specific facts alleged if the failure is the result of a bona fide error. For a bona fide error to be available as a defense, the plaintiff must prove the use of reasonable procedures to avoid the error.

(c) In this section, "consumer goods" has the meaning assigned by the Business & Commerce Code.

Acts 1985, 69th Leg., ch. 959, § 1, eff. Sept. 1, 1985. Amended by Acts 1987, 70th Leg., ch. 167, § 3.11, eff. Sept. 1, 1987.

§ 62.046. Liability for Fruit of Replevied Property

(a) In a suit for enforcement of a mortgage or lien on property, a defendant who replevies the property is not required to account for the fruits, hire, revenue, or rent of the property.

(b) This section does not apply to a plaintiff who replevies the property.

Acts 1985, 69th Leg., ch. 959, § 1, eff. Sept. 1, 1985.

SUBCHAPTER D. CARE AND MANAGEMENT OF SEQUESTERED PROPERTY

§ 62.061. Officer's Liability and Duty of Care

(a) An officer who executes a writ of sequestration shall care for and manage in a prudent manner the sequestered property he retains in custody.

(b) If the officer entrusts sequestered property to another person, the officer is responsible for the acts of that person relating to the property.

(c) The officer is liable for injuries to the sequestered property resulting from his neglect or mismanagement or from the neglect or mismanagement of a person to whom he entrusts the property.

Acts 1985, 69th Leg., ch. 959, § 1, eff. Sept. 1, 1985.

§ 62.062. Compensation of Officer

(a) An officer who retains custody of sequestered property is entitled to just compensation and reasonable charges to be determined by the court that issued the writ.

(b) The officer's compensation and charges shall be taxed and collected as a cost of suit.

Acts 1985, 69th Leg., ch. 959, § 1, eff. Sept. 1, 1985.

§ 62.063. Indemnification of Officer for Money Spent

If an officer is required to expend money in the security, management, or care of sequestered property, he may retain possession of the property until the money is repaid by the party seeking to replevy the property or by that party's agent or attorney.

Acts 1985, 69th Leg., ch. 959, § 1, eff. Sept. 1, 1985.

CHAPTER 63. GARNISHMENT

Section

Section

§ 63.001. Grounds

A writ of garnishment is available if:

(1) an original attachment has been issued;

(2) a plaintiff sues for a debt and makes an affidavit stating that:

(A) the debt is just, due, and unpaid;

(B) within the plaintiff's knowledge, the defendant does not possess property in Texas subject to execution sufficient to satisfy the debt; and

(C) the garnishment is not sought to injure the defendant or the garnishee; or

(3) a plaintiff has a valid, subsisting judgment and makes an affidavit stating that, within the plaintiff's knowledge, the defendant does not possess property in Texas subject to execution sufficient to satisfy the judgment.

Acts 1985, 69th Leg., ch. 959, § 1, eff. Sept. 1, 1985.

§ 63.002. Who May Issue

The clerk of a district or county court or a justice of the peace may issue a writ of garnishment returnable to his court.

Acts 1985, 69th Leg., ch. 959, § 1, eff. Sept. 1, 1985.

§ 63.003. Effect of Service

(a) After service of a writ of garnishment, the garnishee may not deliver any effects or pay any debt to the defendant. If the garnishee is a corporation or joint-stock company, the garnishee may not permit or recognize a sale or transfer of shares or an interest alleged to be owned by the defendant.

(b) A payment, delivery, sale, or transfer made in violation of Subsection (a) is void as to the amount of the debt, effects, shares, or interest necessary to satisfy the plaintiff's demand.

Acts 1985, 69th Leg., ch. 959, § 1, eff. Sept. 1, 1985.

§ 63.004. Current Wages Exempt

Except as otherwise provided by state or federal law, current wages for personal service are not subject to garnishment. The garnishee shall be discharged from the garnishment as to any debt to the defendant for current wages.

Acts 1985, 69th Leg., ch. 959, § 1, eff. Sept. 1, 1985. Amended by Acts 1997, 75th Leg., ch. 466, § 1, eff. Sept. 1, 1997.

§ 63.005. Place for Trial

(a) If a garnishee other than a foreign corporation is not a resident of the county in which the original suit is pending or was tried and a party to the suit files an affidavit controverting the garnishee's answer, the issues raised by the answer and controverting affidavit shall be tried in the county in which the garnishee resides. The issues may be tried in a court of that county that has jurisdiction of the amount of the original judgment if the plaintiff files with the court a certified copy of the judgment in the original suit and a certified copy of the proceedings in garnishment, including the plaintiff's application for the writ, the garnishee's answer, and the controverting affidavit.

(b) If a garnishee whose answer is controverted is a foreign corporation, the issues raised by the answer and controverting affidavit shall be tried in the court in which the original suit is pending or was tried.

Acts 1985, 69th Leg., ch. 959, § 1, eff. Sept. 1, 1985.

§ 63.006. Administrative Fee for Certain Costs Incurred by Employers

(a) An employer who is required by state or federal law to deduct from the current wages of an employee an amount garnished under a withholding order may deduct monthly an administrative fee as provided by Subsection (b) from the employee's disposable earnings in addition to the amount required to be withheld under the withholding order. This section does not apply to income withholding under Chapter 158, Family Code.

(b) The administrative fee deducted under Subsection (a) may not exceed the lesser of:

(1) the actual administrative cost incurred by the employer in complying with the withholding order; or

(2) $10.

(c) For the purposes of this section, "withholding order" means:

(1) a withholding order issued under Section 488A, Part F, Subchapter IV, Higher Education Act of 1965 (20 U.S.C. Section 1095a); and

(2) any analogous order issued under a state or federal law that:

(A) requires the garnishment of an employee's current wages; and

(B) does not contain an express provision authorizing or prohibiting the payment of the administrative costs incurred by the employer in complying with the garnishment by the affected employee.

Added by Acts 1997, 75th Leg., ch. 466, § 2, eff. Sept. 1, 1997.

§ 63.007. Garnishment of Funds Held in Inmate Trust Fund

(a) A writ of garnishment may be issued against an inmate trust fund held under the authority of the Texas Department of Criminal Justice under Section 501.014, Government Code, to encumber money that is held for the benefit of an inmate in the fund.

(b) The state's sovereign immunity to suit is waived only to the extent necessary to authorize a garnishment action in accordance with this section.

Added by Acts 1997, 75th Leg., ch. 1409, § 6, eff. Sept. 1, 1997. Renumbered from § 63.006 by Acts 1999, 76th Leg., ch. 62, § 19.01(4), eff. Sept. 1, 1999.

§ 63.008. Financial Institution as Garnishee

Service of a writ of garnishment on a financial institution named as the garnishee in the writ is governed by Section 59.008, Finance Code.

Added by Acts 1999, 76th Leg., ch. 344, § 7.004, eff. Sept. 1, 1999.

CHAPTER 64. RECEIVERSHIP

SUBCHAPTER A. GENERAL PROVISIONS

SUBCHAPTER B. QUALIFICATIONS, OATH, AND BOND

SUBCHAPTER C. POWERS AND DUTIES

SUBCHAPTER D. CLAIMS AND LIABILITIES

SUBCHAPTER E. PROVISIONS RELATING TO RECEIVERSHIP OF CORPORATIONS

SUBCHAPTER F. RECEIVER FOR CERTAIN MINERAL INTERESTS

SUBCHAPTER G. RECEIVER FOR CERTAIN MISSING PERSONS

SUBCHAPTER A. GENERAL PROVISIONS

§ 64.001. Availability of Remedy

(a) A court of competent jurisdiction may appoint a receiver:

(1) in an action by a vendor to vacate a fraudulent purchase of property;

(2) in an action by a creditor to subject any property or fund to his claim;

(3) in an action between partners or others jointly owning or interested in any property or fund;

(4) in an action by a mortgagee for the foreclosure of the mortgage and sale of the mortgaged property;

(5) for a corporation that is insolvent, is in imminent danger of insolvency, has been dissolved, or has forfeited its corporate rights; or

(6) in any other case in which a receiver may be appointed under the rules of equity.

(b) Under Subsection (a)(1), (2), or (3), the receiver may be appointed on the application of the plaintiff in the action or another party. The party must have a probable interest in or right to the property or fund, and the property or fund must be in danger of being lost, removed, or materially injured.

(c) Under Subsection (a)(4), the court may appoint a receiver only if:

(1) it appears that the mortgaged property is in danger of being lost, removed, or materially injured; or

(2) the condition of the mortgage has not been performed and the property is probably insufficient to discharge the mortgage debt.

(d) A court having family law jurisdiction or a probate court located in the county in which a missing person, as defined by Article 63.001, Code of Criminal Procedure, resides or, if the missing person is not a resident of this state, located in the county in which the majority of the property of a missing person's estate is located may, on the court's own motion or on the application of an interested party, appoint a receiver for the missing person if:

(1) it appears that the estate of the missing person is in danger of injury, loss, or waste; and

(2) the estate of the missing person is in need of a representative.

Acts 1985, 69th Leg., ch. 959, § 1, eff. Sept. 1, 1985. Amended by Acts 1997, 75th Leg., ch. 1376, § 4, eff. Sept. 1, 1997; Acts 1999, 76th Leg., ch. 1081, §§ 1, 3, eff. Sept. 1, 1999.

§ 64.002. Persons Not Entitled to Appointment

(a) A court may not appoint a receiver for a corporation, partnership, or individual on the petition of the same corporation, partnership, or individual.

(b) A court may appoint a receiver for a corporation on the petition of one or more stockholders of the corporation.

(c) This section does not prohibit:

(1) appointment of a receiver for a partnership in an action arising between partners; or

(2) appointment of a receiver over all or part of the marital estate in a suit filed under Title 1 or 5, Family Code.[1]

Acts 1985, 69th Leg., ch. 959, § 1, eff. Sept. 1, 1985. Amended by Acts 1987, 70th Leg., ch. 167, § 3.12(a), eff. Sept. 1, 1987; Acts 1997, 75th Leg., ch. 165, § 7.06, eff. Sept. 1, 1997.

[1] V.T.C.A., Family Code § 1.001 et seq. or V.T.C.A., Family Code § 101.001 et seq.

§ 64.003. Foreign Appointment

A court outside this state may not appoint a receiver for:

(1) a person who resides in this state and for whom appointment of a receiver has been applied for in this state; or

(2) property located in this state.

Acts 1985, 69th Leg., ch. 959, § 1, eff. Sept. 1, 1985.

§ 64.004. Application of Equity Rules

Unless inconsistent with this chapter or other general law, the rules of equity govern all matters relating to the appointment, powers, duties, and liabilities of a receiver and to the powers of a court regarding a receiver.

Acts 1985, 69th Leg., ch. 959, § 1, eff. Sept. 1, 1985.

SUBCHAPTER B. QUALIFICATIONS, OATH, AND BOND

§ 64.021. Qualifications; Residence Requirement

(a) To be appointed as a receiver for property that is located entirely or partly in this state, a person must:

(1) be a citizen and qualified voter of this state at the time of appointment; and

(2) not be a party, attorney, or other person interested in the action for appointment of a receiver.

(b) The appointment of a receiver who is disqualified under Subsection (a)(1) is void as to property in this state.

(c) A receiver must maintain actual residence in this state during the receivership.

Acts 1985, 69th Leg., ch. 959, § 1, eff. Sept. 1, 1985.

§ 64.022. Oath

Before a person assumes the duties of a receiver, he must be sworn to perform the duties faithfully.

Acts 1985, 69th Leg., ch. 959, § 1, eff. Sept. 1, 1985.

§ 64.023. Bond

Before a person assumes the duties of a receiver, he must execute a good and sufficient bond that is:

(1) approved by the appointing court;

(2) in an amount fixed by the court; and

(3) conditioned on faithful discharge of his duties as receiver in the named action and obedience to the orders of the court.

Acts 1985, 69th Leg., ch. 959, § 1, eff. Sept. 1, 1985.

SUBCHAPTER C. POWERS AND DUTIES

§ 64.031. General Powers and Duties

Subject to the control of the court, a receiver may:

(1) take charge and keep possession of the property;

(2) receive rents;

(3) collect and compromise demands;

(4) make transfers; and

(5) perform other acts in regard to the property as authorized by the court.

Acts 1985, 69th Leg., ch. 959, § 1, eff. Sept. 1, 1985.

§ 64.032. Inventory

As soon as possible after appointment, a receiver shall return to the appointing court an inventory of all property received.

Acts 1985, 69th Leg., ch. 959, § 1, eff. Sept. 1, 1985.

§ 64.033. Suits by Receiver

A receiver may bring suits in his official capacity without permission of the appointing court.

Acts 1985, 69th Leg., ch. 959, § 1, eff. Sept. 1, 1985.

§ 64.034. Investments, Loans, and Contributions of Funds

(a) Except as provided by Subsection (b), on an order of the court to which all parties consent, a receiver may invest for interest any funds that he holds.

(b) A receiver appointed for a missing person under Section 64.001(d) who has on hand an amount of money belonging to the missing person in excess of the amount needed for current necessities and expenses may, on order of the court, invest, lend, or contribute all or a part of the excess amount in the manner provided by Chapter 1161, Estates Code, for investments, loans, or contributions by guardians. The receiver shall report to the court all transactions involving the excess amount in the manner that reports are required of guardians.

Acts 1985, 69th Leg., ch. 959, § 1, eff. Sept. 1, 1985. Amended by Acts 1999, 76th Leg., ch. 1081, § 4, eff. Sept. 1, 1999; Acts 2017, 85th Leg., ch. 324 (S.B. 1488), § 22.002, eff. Sept. 1, 2017.

§ 64.035. **Deposit of Certain Railroad Funds**

If a receiver operates a railroad that lies wholly within this state, the receiver shall deposit all money that comes into his hands, from operation of the railroad or otherwise, in a place in this state directed by the court. The money shall remain on deposit until properly disbursed. If any portion of the railroad lies in another state, the court shall require the receiver to deposit in this state a share of the funds that is at least proportionate to the value of the property of the company in this state.

Acts 1985, 69th Leg., ch. 959, § 1, eff. Sept. 1, 1985.

§ 64.036. **Receivership Property Held by Financial Institution**

Service or delivery of a notice of receivership, or a demand or instruction by or on behalf of a receiver, relating to receivership property held by a financial institution in the name of or on behalf of a customer of the financial institution is governed by Section 59.008, Finance Code.

Added by Acts 1999, 76th Leg., ch. 344, § 7.005, eff. Sept. 1, 1999.

SUBCHAPTER D. CLAIMS AND LIABILITIES

§ 64.051. **Application of Funds; Preferences**

(a) A receiver shall apply the earnings of property held in receivership to the payment of the following claims in the order listed:

(1) court costs of suit;

(2) wages of employees due by the receiver;

(3) debts owed for materials and supplies purchased by the receiver for the improvement of the property held as receiver;

(4) debts due for improvements made during the receivership to the property held as receiver;

(5) claims and accounts against the receiver on contracts made by the receiver, personal injury claims and claims for stock against the receiver accruing during the receivership, and judgments rendered against the receiver for personal injuries and for stock killed; and

(6) judgments recovered in suits brought before the receiver was appointed.

(b) Claims listed in this section have a preference lien on the earnings of the property held by the receiver.

(c) The court shall ensure that the earnings are paid in the order of preference listed in this section.

Acts 1985, 69th Leg., ch. 959, § 1, eff. Sept. 1, 1985.

§ 64.052. **Suits Against Receiver**

(a) A receiver who holds property in this state may be sued in his official capacity in a court of competent jurisdiction without permission of the appointing court.

(b) A suit against a receiver may be brought where the person whose property is in receivership resides.

(c) In a suit against a receiver, citation may be served on the receiver or on any agent of the receiver who resides in the county in which the suit is brought.

(d) The discharge of a receiver does not abate a suit against the receiver or affect the right of a party to sue the receiver.

Acts 1985, 69th Leg., ch. 959, § 1, eff. Sept. 1, 1985.

§ 64.053. **Payment of Judgment Against Receiver**

The court that appointed a receiver shall order any judgment against the receiver to be paid from funds held by the receiver.

Acts 1985, 69th Leg., ch. 959, § 1, eff. Sept. 1, 1985.

§ 64.054. **Judgment Lien**

A judgment rendered against a receiver in a cause of action arising during the receivership is a lien on all property held by the receiver. The lien is superior to the mortgage lien of a mortgagee who instituted the receivership.

Acts 1985, 69th Leg., ch. 959, § 1, eff. Sept. 1, 1985.

§ 64.055. **Execution on Judgment**

(a) To obtain payment on a judgment against a receiver, the owner of the judgment may apply to the court that appointed the receiver for an order that the receiver pay the judgment. If the receiver possesses money that is subject to payment of the judgment, but the court refuses to order payment, the owner of the judgment may apply to the court that issued the judgment for execution on the judgment.

(b) The owner of the judgment must file with the court that issued the judgment an affidavit reciting that:

(1) he applied to the court that appointed the receiver for an order of payment;

(2) it was shown to the appointing court that the receiver had money subject to payment of the judgment at that time; and

(3) the appointing court refused to order the receiver to pay the judgment.

(c) The court that issued the judgment shall issue execution that may be levied on any property held by the receiver. The property shall be sold as under ordinary execution, and the sale of the property conveys title to the purchaser.

Acts 1985, 69th Leg., ch. 959, § 1, eff. Sept. 1, 1985.

§ 64.056. Liability of Persons Receiving Receivership Property

(a) A person to whom a receiver delivers property held in receivership, including the owner of the property, a person who receives it for the owner, or an assignee of the owner is liable to the extent of the value of the property for the liabilities of the receiver arising during the receivership that are unpaid at the time of the receiver's discharge. The person receiving the property may be made a defendant to a suit against the receiver, and if judgment is rendered against the receiver, the court shall also render judgment against that defendant.

(b) A judgment against a receiver or an unpaid claim that arose during the receivership and has not been sued on at the date the receiver is discharged constitutes a preference lien on the property held by the receiver on the date of discharge. The lien is superior to the mortgage lien of a mortgagee who instituted the receivership. The person who received the property is liable on the judgment or claim to the extent of the value of the property.

Acts 1985, 69th Leg., ch. 959, § 1, eff. Sept. 1, 1985.

SUBCHAPTER E. PROVISIONS RELATING TO RECEIVERSHIP OF CORPORATIONS

§ 64.071. Venue for Appointment

An action to have a receiver appointed for a corporation with property in this state shall be brought in the county in which the principal office of the corporation is located.

Acts 1985, 69th Leg., ch. 959, § 1, eff. Sept. 1, 1985.

§ 64.072. Limited Duration

(a) Except as provided by this section, a court may not administer a corporation in receivership for more than three years after the date the receiver is appointed, and the court shall wind up the affairs of the corporation within that period.

(b) A court may, from time to time, extend the duration of a corporate receivership if:

(1) litigation prevents the court from winding up the affairs of the corporation within three years; or

(2) the receiver is operating the corporation as a going concern.

(c) To extend the duration of a corporate receivership, the court must have received an application for the extension and, following notice to all attorneys of record, must conduct a hearing on the extension. As required by the best interests of all concerned parties, the court may prescribe conditions for the extension and extend it for a term within the limits provided by Subsection (d). The court shall enter into its minutes the proper order extending the receivership.

(d) A court may not extend a corporate receivership for more than five years beyond the original three years, except that the court may extend for any additional period the receivership of a corporation organized under former Article 3.05(A)(2), Texas Miscellaneous Corporation Laws Act (Article 1302–3.05, Vernon's Texas Civil Statutes), Section 2.006, Business Organizations Code, before September 1, 2009, or a railroad corporation organized under the Business Organizations Code or former Title 112, Revised Statutes.

Acts 1985, 69th Leg., ch. 959, § 1, eff. Sept. 1, 1985. Amended by Acts 2011, 82nd Leg., ch. 91 (S.B. 1303), § 5.001, eff. Sept. 1, 2011.

§ 64.0721. Termination of Railroad Receivership

(a) A receiver of a railroad company located wholly within this state that has been in receivership for more than 50 years may apply to the court that appointed the receiver requesting the court to:

(1) terminate the receivership; and

(2) disburse any assets of the railroad company remaining after the payment of the company's debts to one or more nonprofit charitable organizations chosen by the receiver for use in providing services within the county in which the receiver was appointed.

(b) After a receiver makes an application under Subsection (a), the receiver shall publish notice of the proposed termination of the receivership for seven consecutive days in a newspaper of general circulation in the county in which the receivership is located. The notice must state that a person with an interest in the assets of the railroad company may file a claim with the court that appointed the receiver not later than the 90th day after the final day of the publication of the notice.

(c) After the expiration of the period for filing claims provided by Subsection (b) and after the court resolves all claims filed with the court relating to the railroad company, the court shall disburse any remaining assets of the receivership to the nonprofit charitable organizations chosen by the receiver that are acceptable to the court in its discretion.

(d) Any noncash assets of a railroad company that exist when its receivership is terminated under this section escheat to the state.

Added by Acts 1997, 75th Leg., ch. 821, § 1, eff. June 17, 1997.

§ 64.073. Earnings on Improved Property Liable for Debts

(a) A corporation in receivership shall contribute to the payment of any floating debts against it an amount equal to the full value of current earnings spent by the receiver for:

(1) improvements to the corporate property held by the receiver, the purchase of rolling stock or machinery, and other improvements that increase the value of the property; or

(2) the extension of a road or the acquisition of land in connection with a road.

(b) If property of a corporation in receivership is sold under court order in a lien foreclosure, the court shall order the clerk to retain from the sale proceeds an amount equal to the value of improvements made by the receiver to the property sold and shall order that money to be paid to persons with a claim, debt, or judgment against the corporation. The courts shall require an amount of cash sufficient for that purpose to be paid in at the date of sale.

Acts 1985, 69th Leg., ch. 959, § 1, eff. Sept. 1, 1985.

§ 64.074. Claims Preference Against Current Earnings

A judgment or claim existing against a corporation at the time the receiver is appointed or a judgment in an action existing at that time shall be paid out of the earnings of the corporation earned during the receivership in preference to the mortgage of a mortgagee who instituted the receivership. The judgment or claim is a lien on those earnings.

Acts 1985, 69th Leg., ch. 959, § 1, eff. Sept. 1, 1985.

§ 64.075. Forfeiture of Charter for Unqualified Receiver

If a person who is not a citizen and qualified voter of this state is appointed receiver for a domestic corporation that owns property in this state, the corporation forfeits its charter. The attorney general shall immediately bring suit in the nature of quo warranto for forfeiture of the charter.

Acts 1985, 69th Leg., ch. 959, § 1, eff. Sept. 1, 1985.

§ 64.076. Suits Against Railroad Receiver: Venue and Service

An action against the receiver of a railroad company may be brought in any county through or into which the railroad is constructed, and citation may be served on the receiver, the general or division superintendent, or an agent of the receiver who resides in the county in which the suit is brought. If no agent of the receiver resides in the county in which the suit is brought, citation may be served on any agent of the receiver in this state.

Acts 1985, 69th Leg., ch. 959, § 1, eff. Sept. 1, 1985.

SUBCHAPTER F. RECEIVER FOR CERTAIN MINERAL INTERESTS

§ 64.091. Receiver for Mineral Interests Owned by Nonresident or Absentee

(a) The purpose of this section is to encourage the exploration and development of mineral resources.

(b) In the following actions, a district court may appoint a receiver for the mineral interest or leasehold interest under a mineral lease owned by a nonresident or absent defendant:

(1) an action that is brought by a person claiming or owning an undivided mineral interest in land in this state or an undivided leasehold interest under a mineral lease of land in this state and that has one or more defendants who have, claim, or own an undivided mineral interest in the same property; or

(2) an action that is brought by a person claiming or owning an undivided leasehold interest under a mineral lease of land in this state and that has one or more defendants who have, claim, or own an undivided leasehold interest under a mineral lease of the same property.

(b–1) The defendant for whom the receiver is sought must:

(1) be a person whose residence or identity is unknown or a nonresident; and

(2) have not paid taxes on the interest or rendered it for taxes during the five-year period immediately preceding the filing of the action.

(c) The plaintiff in the action must allege by verified petition and prove that he:

(1) has made a diligent but unsuccessful effort to locate the defendant; and

(2) will suffer substantial damage or injury unless the receiver is appointed.

(d) In an action under Subsection (b)(1):

(1) the plaintiff, in the verified petition, must name the last known owner or the last record owner of the interest as defendant;

(2) the plaintiff must serve notice on the defendant by publication as provided by the Texas Rules of Civil Procedure;

(3) the court may appoint as receiver the county judge and his successors or any other resident of the county in which the land is located;

(4) notwithstanding the Texas Rules of Civil Procedure, the applicant is not required to post bond; and

(5) the receiver is not required to post bond.

(e) A receivership created under this subchapter continues as long as the defendant or his heirs, assigns, or personal representatives fail to appear in court in person or by agent or attorney to claim the defendant's interest.

(f) As ordered by the court, the receiver shall immediately:

(1) execute and deliver to a lessee or successive lessees mineral leases on the outstanding undivided mineral interests;

(2) execute and deliver to a lessee or successive lessees an assignment of the outstanding undivided leasehold interest; and

(3) enter into a unitization agreement authorized by the Railroad Commission of Texas.

(g) A lease executed by a receiver under this section may authorize the lessee to pool and unitize land subject to the lease with adjacent land into a unit not to exceed 160 acres for an oil well or 640 acres for a gas well plus 10 percent tolerance or into a unit that substantially conforms to a larger unit prescribed or permitted by governmental rule.

(h) Money consideration paid for the execution of a lease, assignment, or unitization agreement by the receiver must be paid to the clerk of the court in which the case is pending before the receiver executes the instrument. The court shall apply the money to the costs accruing in the case and retain any balance for the use and benefit of the nonresident or person of unknown residence who owns the mineral or leasehold interest. Payments made at a later time under the lease, assignment, or unitization agreement shall be paid into the registry of the court and impounded for the use and benefit of the owner of the mineral or leasehold interest.

(i) This section is cumulative of other laws relating to removal of a cloud from title or appointment of a receiver.

(j) In this section:

(1) "Mineral lease" includes any lease of oil, gas, or other minerals that contains provisions necessary or incident to the orderly exploration, development, and recovery of oil, gas, or other minerals.

(2) "Leasehold interest" includes ownership created under a mineral lease or carved out of a leasehold estate granted under a mineral lease, including production payments, overriding royalty interests, and working interests.

(3) "Lessee" includes an assignee under an assignment of a mineral lease.

(k) To the extent that Subsection (d)(2) conflicts with the Texas Rules of Civil Procedure, Subsection (d)(2) controls. Notwithstanding Section 22.004, Government Code, the supreme court may not amend or adopt rules in conflict with Subsection (d)(2).

Acts 1985, 69th Leg., ch. 959, § 1, eff. Sept. 1, 1985. Amended by Acts 1989, 71st Leg., ch. 492, § 1, eff. June 14, 1989; Acts 1989, 71st Leg., ch. 998, § 1, eff. Sept. 1, 1989; Acts 1991, 72nd Leg., ch. 16, § 3.01, eff. Aug. 26, 1991; Acts 2009, 81st Leg., ch. 87, § 5.002, eff. Sept. 1, 2009; Acts 2009, 81st Leg., ch. 292, § 1, eff. June 19, 2009.

§ 64.092. Receiver for Contingent Interests in Minerals

(a) On the application of a person who has a vested, contingent, or possible interest in land or an estate subject to a contingent future interest, a district court of the county in which all or part of the land is located may appoint a receiver for the land or estate, pending the occurrence of the contingency and the vesting of the future interest, if:

(1) the land or estate is susceptible to drainage of oil, gas, or other minerals;

(2) lease of the land for oil, gas, or mineral development and the safe and proper investment of the proceeds will inure to the benefit and advantage of the persons entitled to the proceeds; or

(3) lease of the land for the production of oil, gas, or other minerals is necessary for the conservation, preservation, or protection of the land or estate or of a present, contingent, or future interest in the land or estate.

(b) As authorized or directed by the court, a receiver appointed under Subsection (a) may:

(1) lease the land for the development of oil, gas, or other minerals at public or private sale and on terms and conditions directed by the court; and

(2) receive, hold, and invest the proceeds of the lease for the benefit of persons who are entitled or may become entitled to those proceeds according to their respective rights and interests.

(c) On the application of a person who has a vested, contingent, or possible interest in land or an estate that is under an oil, gas, or mineral lease and is subject to a contingent future interest, a district court of the county in which all or part of the land is located may appoint a receiver for the contingent future interests, pending the occurrence of the contingency and the vesting of the future interest, if:

(1) the lease fails to provide for pooling or contains pooling provisions that are ineffective as to the contingent future interest covered by the lease; and

(2) the pooling of the contingent future interest:

(A) is necessary to protect correlative rights;

(B) is necessary to prevent the physical or economic waste of oil, gas, or other minerals;

(C) will inure to the benefit and advantage of the persons entitled to the future interest; or

(D) is necessary for the conservation, preservation, or protection of the land or estate or of a present, contingent, or future interest in the land or estate.

(d) The lessee or an assignee of the lessee may apply for appointment of a receiver under Subsection (c). As authorized or directed by the court, the receiver appointed under that subsection may:

(1) amend the lease to authorize pooling for the contingent future interest on terms and conditions and for additional consideration directed by the court; and

(2) receive, hold, and invest the additional consideration for the benefit of the persons who are entitled or may become entitled to that consideration, according to their respective rights and interests.

(e) A court appointing a receiver under this section may confer on the receiver all powers necessary to the exercise of the receiver's authority.

(f) A lease executed or amended by a receiver under this section may authorize the lessee and his assigns to pool all or part of the land subject to the lease with adjacent land into a unit not to exceed 160 acres for an oil well or 640 acres for a gas well plus 10 percent tolerance or into a unit that substantially conforms to a larger unit prescribed or permitted by governmental rule.

(g) In an action for appointment of a receiver under this section, a person who has a vested, contingent, or possible interest in the land must be cited in the manner and for the time provided for in actions concerning title to land. A person not in being must be cited in the manner and for the time provided in actions against unknown owners or claimants of interest in land. In an action brought under Subsection (c), a person is not a necessary party if:

(1) the person's interest in the land subject to the lease is effectively subject to pooling authority under the lease; and

(2) enlargement of the pooling authority as to the person's interest is not sought.

(h) The court appointing a receiver under this section may order that, after payment of court costs, money paid to the receiver be deposited in the registry of the court for the use and benefit of the persons who are entitled or may become entitled to the money, according to their respective rights and interests. If the court then discharges the receiver, it may order that later payments under the lease accruing to the contingent future interest be deposited in the same manner and for the same purpose.

(i) This section does not apply to a mineral lease on land on which drilling began before October 5, 1949. This section does not authorize a lease of mineral interests on land subject to existing homestead rights without the written consent of the owner of the homestead rights given in the manner provided by law for the conveyance of homesteads.

(j) In this section, "contingent future interest" means a legal or equitable interest arising by way of remainder, reversion, possibility of reverter, executory devise, on the occurrence of a condition subsequent, or otherwise.

Acts 1985, 69th Leg., ch. 959, § 1, eff. Sept. 1, 1985.

§ 64.093. Receiver for Royalty Interests Owned by Nonresident or Absentee

(a) A district court may appoint a receiver for the royalty interest owned by a nonresident or absent defendant in an action that:

(1) is brought by a person claiming or owning an undivided mineral interest in land in this state or an undivided leasehold interest under a mineral lease of land in the state; and

(2) has one or more defendants who have, claim, or own an undivided royalty interest in that property.

(b) The defendant for whom the receiver is sought must:

(1) be a person whose residence or identity is unknown or a nonresident; and

(2) not have paid taxes on the interest or rendered it for taxes during the five-year period immediately preceding the filing of the action.

(c) The plaintiff in the action must allege by verified petition and prove that the plaintiff:

(1) has made a diligent but unsuccessful effort to locate the defendant; and

(2) will suffer substantial damage or injury unless the receiver is appointed.

(d) In an action under Subsection (a):

(1) the plaintiff, in the petition, must name the last known owner or the last record owner of the interest as defendant;

(2) the plaintiff must serve notice on the defendant by publication as provided by the Texas Rules of Civil Procedure;

(3) the court may appoint as receiver the county judge or any other resident of the county in which the land is located;

(4) notwithstanding the Texas Rules of Civil Procedure, the applicant is not required to post bond; and

(5) the receiver is not required to post bond.

(e) A receivership created under this section continues as long as the defendant or the defendant's heirs, assigns, or personal representatives fail to appear in court in person or by agent or attorney to claim the defendant's interest.

(f) As ordered by the court, the receiver shall immediately:

(1) ratify a mineral lease executed by a person owning an undivided mineral interest in the property;

(2) ratify a pooling agreement executed by a person owning an undivided mineral interest in the property or an undivided leasehold interest in the property; or

(3) enter into a unitization agreement authorized by the Railroad Commission of Texas.

(g) A lease ratified by a receiver under this section may authorize the lessee to pool and unitize land subject to the lease with adjacent land into a unit not to exceed 160 acres for an oil well or 640 acres for a gas well plus 10 percent tolerance or into a unit that substantially conforms to a larger unit prescribed or permitted by governmental rule. A pooling agreement ratified by a receiver under this section may allow a pooled unit not to exceed 160 acres for an oil well or 640 acres for a gas well plus 10 percent tolerance or into a unit that substantially conforms to a larger unit prescribed or permitted by governmental rule.

(h) The monetary consideration, if any, due for the execution of a ratification, pooling agreement, or unitization agreement by the receiver must be paid to the clerk of the court in which the case is pending before the receiver executes the instrument. It is, however, recognized that, because ratifications, pooling agreements, and unitization agreements are typically entered into in consideration of the future benefits accruing to the grantor thereof, an initial monetary consideration is not typically paid for the execution of such instruments. The court shall apply the money to the costs accruing in the case and retain any balance for the owner of the royalty interest. Payments made at a later time under the lease, pooled unit, or unitization agreement shall be paid into the registry of the court and impounded for the owner of the royalty interest.

(i) This section is cumulative of other laws relating to removal of a cloud from title or appointment of a receiver.

(j) In this section:

(1) "Mineral lease" includes any lease of oil, gas, or other minerals that contains provisions necessary or incident to the orderly exploration, development, and recovery of oil, gas, or other minerals.

(2) "Leasehold interest" includes ownership created under a mineral lease or carved out of a leasehold estate granted under a mineral lease,

including production payments, overriding royalty interests, and working interests.

(3) "Pooling agreement" includes any agreement that pools or unitizes land with adjacent land for production of oil, gas, or other minerals.

(4) "Royalty interest" includes any interest in the lands entitled to share in the production of oil, gas, or other minerals that is not required to execute a mineral lease or any other instrument in order to vest in the mineral interest owner or mineral leasehold interest owner the right and power, as to that interest, to develop oil, gas, or other minerals produced solely from those lands.

(k) To the extent that Subsection (d)(2) conflicts with the Texas Rules of Civil Procedure, Subsection (d)(2) controls. Notwithstanding Section 22.004, Government Code, the supreme court may not amend or adopt rules in conflict with Subsection (d)(2).

Added by Acts 1999, 76th Leg., ch. 1483, § 1, eff. Aug. 30, 1999. Amended by Acts 2009, 81st Leg., ch. 292, § 2, eff. June 19, 2009.

SUBCHAPTER G. RECEIVER FOR CERTAIN MISSING PERSONS

§ 64.101. Notice and Citation for Receivership for Certain Missing Persons

(a) On the filing of an application for the appointment of a receiver for a missing person under Section 64.001(d), the court clerk shall issue a citation that states that the application for receivership was filed and includes:

(1) the name of the missing person; and

(2) the name of the applicant.

(b) The citation must cite all persons interested in the welfare of the missing person to appear at the time and place stated in the notice for purposes of contesting the application. The citation shall be posted.

(c) Except as provided by Section 17.032, the citation shall be published on the public information Internet website maintained as required by Section 72.034, Government Code, as added by Chapter 606 (S.B. 891), Acts of the 86th Legislature, Regular Session, 2019, and in a newspaper of general circulation:

(1) once in the county in which the missing person resides; and

(2) once in each county in which property of the missing person's estate is located.

Added by Acts 1999, 76th Leg., ch. 1081, § 5, eff. Sept. 1, 1999. Amended by Acts 2021, 87th Leg., ch. 934 (H.B. 3774), § 9.01, eff. Sept. 1, 2021.

Section 15.02 of Acts 2021, 87th Leg., ch. 934 (H.B. 3774) provides:

"Not later than May 1, 2022, the Supreme Court of Texas shall adopt rules and promulgate forms under Section 22.0042, Government Code, as added by this article.

Section 18.01 of Acts 2021, 87th Leg., ch. 934 (H.B. 3774) provides:

"A state agency subject to this Act is required to implement a provision of this Act only if the legislature appropriates money specifically for that purpose. If the legislature does not appropriate money specifically for that purpose, the state agency may, but is not required to, implement a provision of this Act using other appropriations available for that purpose."

§ 64.102. Proceeding to Appoint Receiver

(a) The court shall appoint an attorney ad litem to represent the interests of a missing person at a proceeding to appoint a receiver for the missing person under Section 64.001(d). To be eligible for appointment as an attorney ad litem under this subsection, a person must be certified in the same manner and to the same extent as a person who is appointed as an attorney ad litem for a proposed ward under Section 1054.001, Estates Code.

(b) The court may appoint a guardian ad litem for a missing person if the court determines that the appointment would be in the best interest of the missing person. A guardian ad litem appointed under this subsection is an officer of the court. The guardian ad litem shall protect the missing person in a manner that will enable the court to determine the appropriate action to take in relation to the best interest of the missing person.

(c) An attorney ad litem or a guardian ad litem appointed under this section is entitled to reasonable compensation for services in an amount set by the court to be charged as costs in the proceeding.

(d) The cost of a proceeding instituted for the appointment of a receiver for a missing person under Section 64.001(d) shall be paid from the receivership, if a receivership is created. If the court denies an application for appointment of a receiver, the applicant shall pay the costs of the proceeding.

(e) The term of a receivership for a missing person granted under Section 64.001(d) may not exceed six months unless, before the expiration of the term and for good cause shown, the court extends the receivership for another term not to exceed six months.

Added by Acts 1999, 76th Leg., ch. 1081, § 5, eff. Sept. 1, 1999. Amended by Acts 2017, 85th Leg., ch. 324 (S.B. 1488), § 22.003, eff. Sept. 1, 2017.

§ 64.103. Bond

The bond under Section 64.023 required to be executed by a receiver for a missing person appointed under Section 64.001(d) must be set in an amount the court considers necessary to protect the estate of the missing person.

Added by Acts 1999, 76th Leg., ch. 1081, § 5, eff. Sept. 1, 1999.

§ 64.104. Expenditures by Receiver

If, during the receivership for a missing person under Section 64.001(d), the needs of the spouse or dependent children of the missing person require the use of the income or corpus of the estate for education, clothing, or subsistence, the court may, with or without application, by order entered in the minutes of the court, appropriate an amount of the income or corpus sufficient for that purpose. The income or corpus shall be used by the receiver to pay claims for education, clothing, or subsistence that are presented to the court and approved and ordered to be paid.

Added by Acts 1999, 76th Leg., ch. 1081, § 5, eff. Sept. 1, 1999.

§ 64.105. Receiver's Expenses, Account, and Compensation

(a) All necessary expenses incurred by a receiver appointed under Section 64.001(d) for a missing person in administering the property shall be reported to the court at intervals not longer than six months in length, as required by the court, and shall be reported in an annual report filed not later than the 60th day after the end of each calendar year if the court extends the receivership in accordance with Section 64.102(e). The report shall be made to the court by a sworn statement of account, including a report of:

(1) the receiver's acts;

(2) the condition of the property;

(3) the status of the threatened danger to the property; and

(4) the progress made toward abatement of the threatened danger.

(b) If the court is satisfied that the statement is correct and reasonable in all respects, the court shall promptly by order approve the report and authorize the reimbursement of the receiver from the funds under the receiver's control.

(c) For official services rendered, the receiver is entitled to be compensated in the same manner and amount as is provided by Title 3, Estates Code, for similar services rendered by guardians of estates.

Added by Acts 1999, 76th Leg., ch. 1081, § 5, eff. Sept. 1, 1999. Amended by Acts 2017, 85th Leg., ch. 324 (S.B. 1488), § 22.004, eff. Sept. 1, 2017.

§ 64.106. Closing Receivership

When the threatened danger has abated and the estate of a missing person for whom a receiver was appointed under Section 64.001(d) is no longer liable to injury, loss, or waste for the lack of a representative or when the receivership terminates under Section 64.102(e), whichever occurs earlier, the receiver shall:

(1) report to the court; and

(2) file with the clerk a full and final sworn account of:

(A) all property received by the receiver;

(B) all sums paid out;

(C) all acts performed by the receiver with respect to the property; and

(D) all property remaining in the receiver's control.

Added by Acts 1999, 76th Leg., ch. 1081, § 5, eff. Sept. 1, 1999.

§ 64.107. Action of Court

(a) If, on hearing the report and account required under Section 64.106, the court is satisfied that the danger of injury, loss, or waste has abated and that the report and account are correct, the court shall render an order finding that the danger has abated and that the report and account are correct and shall direct the receiver to deliver the property to the person from whom the receiver took possession as receiver, to the missing person, or to another person the court finds to be entitled to possession of the estate. The person to whom the property is delivered shall execute and file with the clerk an appropriate receipt for the property delivered.

(b) The order of the court shall discharge the receiver and the receiver's sureties.

(c) If the court is not satisfied that the danger has abated, or is not satisfied with the report and account, the court shall render an order continuing the receivership in effect until the court is satisfied that the danger has abated and that the report and account are correct, subject to the limitation prescribed by Section 64.102(e) for the extension of a receivership.

Added by Acts 1999, 76th Leg., ch. 1081, § 5, eff. Sept. 1, 1999.

§ 64.108. Recordation of Proceedings

All orders, bonds, reports, accounts, and notices in the receivership proceedings under this subchapter shall be recorded in the minutes of the court.

Added by Acts 1999, 76th Leg., ch. 1081, § 5, eff. Sept. 1, 1999.

CHAPTER 65. INJUNCTION

SUBCHAPTER A. GENERAL PROVISIONS

SUBCHAPTER A. GENERAL PROVISIONS

§ 65.001. Application of Equity Principles

The principles governing courts of equity govern injunction proceedings if not in conflict with this chapter or other law.

Acts 1985, 69th Leg., ch. 959, § 1, eff. Sept. 1, 1985.

§ 65.002. Restraining Order or Injunction Affecting Customer of Financial Institution

Service or delivery of a restraining order or injunction affecting property held by a financial institution in the name of or on behalf of a customer of the financial institution is governed by Section 59.008, Finance Code.

Added by Acts 1999, 76th Leg., ch. 344, § 7.006, eff. Sept. 1, 1999.

SUBCHAPTER B. AVAILABILITY OF REMEDY

§ 65.011. Grounds Generally

A writ of injunction may be granted if:

(1) the applicant is entitled to the relief demanded and all or part of the relief requires the restraint of some act prejudicial to the applicant;

(2) a party performs or is about to perform or is procuring or allowing the performance of an act relating to the subject of pending litigation, in violation of the rights of the applicant, and the act would tend to render the judgment in that litigation ineffectual;

(3) the applicant is entitled to a writ of injunction under the principles of equity and the statutes of this state relating to injunctions;

(4) a cloud would be placed on the title of real property being sold under an execution against a party having no interest in the real property subject to execution at the time of sale, irrespective of any remedy at law; or

(5) irreparable injury to real or personal property is threatened, irrespective of any remedy at law.

Acts 1985, 69th Leg., ch. 959, § 1, eff. Sept. 1, 1985. Amended by Acts 1987, 70th Leg., ch. 167, § 3.17, eff. Sept. 1, 1987.

§ 65.012. Operation of Well or Mine

(a) A court may issue an injunction or temporary restraining order prohibiting subsurface drilling or mining operations only if an adjacent landowner filing an application claims that a wrongful act caused injury to his surface or improvements or loss of or injury to his minerals and if the party against whom the injunction is sought is unable to respond in damages for the resulting injuries.

(b) To secure the payment of any injuries that may be sustained by the complainant as a result of subsurface drilling or mining operations, the party against whom an injunction is sought under this section shall enter into a good and sufficient bond in an amount fixed by the court hearing the application.

(c) The court may appoint a trustee or receiver instead of requiring a bond if the court considers it necessary to protect the interests involved in litigation concerning an injunction under this section. The trustee or receiver has the powers prescribed by the court and shall take charge of and hold the minerals produced from the drilling or mining operation or the proceeds from the disposition of those minerals, subject to the final disposition of the litigation.

Acts 1985, 69th Leg., ch. 959, § 1, eff. Sept. 1, 1985.

§ 65.013. Stay of Judgment or Proceeding

An injunction may not be granted to stay a judgment or proceeding at law except to stay as much of the recovery or cause of action as the complainant in his petition shows himself equitably entitled to be relieved against and as much as will cover the costs.

Acts 1985, 69th Leg., ch. 959, § 1, eff. Sept. 1, 1985.

§ 65.014. Limitations on Stay of Execution of Judgment

(a) Except as provided by Subsection (b), an injunction to stay execution of a valid judgment may not be granted more than one year after the date on which the judgment was rendered unless:

(1) the application for the injunction has been delayed because of fraud or false promises of the plaintiff in the judgment practiced or made at the time of or after rendition of the judgment; or

(2) an equitable matter or defense arises after the rendition of the judgment.

(b) If the applicant for an injunction to stay execution of a judgment was absent from the state when the judgment was rendered and was unable to apply for the writ within one year after the date of rendition, the injunction may be granted at any time within two years after that date.

Acts 1985, 69th Leg., ch. 959, § 1, eff. Sept. 1, 1985.

§ 65.015. Closing of Streets

An injunction may not be granted to stay or prevent the governing body of an incorporated city from vacating, abandoning, or closing a street or alley except on the suit of a person:

(1) who is the owner or lessee of real property abutting the part of the street or alley vacated, abandoned, or closed; and

(2) whose damages have neither been ascertained and paid in a condemnation suit by the city nor released.

Acts 1985, 69th Leg., ch. 959, § 1, eff. Sept. 1, 1985.

§ 65.016. Violation of Revenue Law

At the instance of the county or district attorney or the attorney general, a court by injunction may prevent, prohibit, or restrain the violation of any revenue law of this state.

Added by Acts 1989, 71st Leg., ch. 2, § 4.03(a), eff. Aug. 28, 1989.

§ 65.017. Cigarette Seller, Distributor, or Manufacturer

In addition to any other remedy provided by law, a person may bring an action in good faith for appropriate injunctive relief if the person sells, distributes, or manufactures cigarettes and sustains a direct economic or commercial injury as a result of a violation of:

(1) Section 48.015, Penal Code; or

(2) Section 154.0415, Tax Code.

Added by Acts 2007, 80th Leg., ch. 885, § 2.12, eff. April 1, 2009.

SUBCHAPTER C. JURISDICTION OF PROCEEDINGS; VENUE

§ 65.021. Jurisdiction of Proceeding

(a) The judge of a district or county court in term or vacation shall hear and determine applications for writs of injunction.

(b) This section does not limit injunction jurisdiction granted by law to other courts.

Acts 1985, 69th Leg., ch. 959, § 1, eff. Sept. 1, 1985.

§ 65.022. Return of Writ; Hearing by Nonresident Judge

(a) Except as provided by this section, a writ of injunction is returnable only to the court granting the writ.

(b) A district judge may grant a writ returnable to a court other than his own if the resident judge refuses to act or cannot hear and act on the application because of his absence, sickness, inability, inaccessibility, or disqualification. Those facts must be fully set out in the application or in an affidavit accompanying the application. A judge who refuses to act shall note that refusal and the reasons for refusal on the writ. A district judge may not grant the writ if the application has been acted on by another district judge.

(c) A district judge may grant a writ returnable to a court other than his own to stay execution or restrain foreclosure, sale under a deed of trust, trespass, removal of property, or an act injurious to or impairing riparian or easement rights if satisfactory proof is made to the nonresident judge that it is impracticable for the applicant to reach the resident judge and procure the action of the resident judge in time to put into effect the purposes of the application.

(d) A district judge may grant a writ returnable to a court other than his own if the resident judge cannot be reached by the ordinary and available means of travel and communication in sufficient time to put into effect the purpose of the writ sought. In seeking a writ under this subsection, the applicant or attorney for the applicant shall attach to the application an affidavit that fully states the facts of the inaccessibility and the efforts made to reach and communicate with the resident judge. The judge to whom application is made shall refuse to hear the application unless he determines that the applicant made fair and reasonable efforts to reach and communicate with the resident judge. The injunction may be dissolved on a showing that the applicant did not first make reasonable efforts to procure a hearing on the application before the resident judge.

Acts 1985, 69th Leg., ch. 959, § 1, eff. Sept. 1, 1985.

§ 65.023. Place for Trial

(a) Except as provided by Subsection (b), a writ of injunction against a party who is a resident of this state shall be tried in a district or county court in the county in which the party is domiciled. If the writ is granted against more than one party, it may be tried in the proper court of the county in which either party is domiciled.

(b) A writ of injunction granted to stay proceedings in a suit or execution on a judgment must be tried in the court in which the suit is pending or the judgment was rendered.

Acts 1985, 69th Leg., ch. 959, § 1, eff. Sept. 1, 1985.

SUBCHAPTER D. INJUNCTION OBTAINED FOR PURPOSES OF DELAYING COLLECTION OF MONEY

§ 65.031. Dissolution; Award of Damages

If on final hearing a court dissolves in whole or in part an injunction enjoining the collection of money and the injunction was obtained only for delay, the court may assess damages in an amount equal to 10 percent of the amount released by dissolution of the injunction, exclusive of costs.

Acts 1985, 69th Leg., ch. 959, § 1, eff. Sept. 1, 1985.

SUBCHAPTER E. APPLICANT'S BOND FOR TEMPORARY RESTRAINING ORDER OR TEMPORARY INJUNCTION

§ 65.041. Bond not Required for Issuance of Temporary Restraining Order for Certain Indigent Applicants

A court may not require an applicant for a temporary restraining order to execute a bond to the adverse party before the order may issue if:

(1) the applicant submits an affidavit that meets the requirements of Section 65.043 to the court; and

(2) the court finds that the order is intended to restrain the adverse party from foreclosing on the applicant's residential homestead.

Added by Acts 1989, 71st Leg., ch. 391, § 1, eff. Aug. 28, 1989.

§ 65.042. Bond not Required for Issuance of Temporary Injunction for Certain Indigent Applicants

(a) A court may not require an applicant for a temporary injunction to execute a bond to the adverse party before the injunction may issue if:

(1) the applicant submits an affidavit that meets the requirements of Section 65.043 to the court; and

(2) the court finds that the injunction is intended to enjoin the adverse party from foreclosing on the applicant's residential homestead.

(b) If the affidavit submitted under Subsection (a)(1) is contested under Section 65.044, the court may not issue a temporary injunction unless the court finds that the applicant is financially unable to execute the bond.

Added by Acts 1989, 71st Leg., ch. 391, § 1, eff. Aug. 28, 1989.

§ 65.043. Affidavit

(a) The affidavit must contain complete information relating to each and every person liable for the indebtedness secured by or with an ownership interest in the residential homestead concerning the following matters:

(1) identity;

(2) income, including income from employment, dividends, interest, and any other source other than from a government entitlement;

(3) spouse's income, if known to the applicant;

(4) description and estimated value of real and personal property, other than the applicant's homestead;

(5) cash and checking account;

(6) debts and monthly expenses;

(7) dependents; and

(8) any transfer to any person of money or other property with a value in excess of $1,000 made within one year of the affidavit without fair consideration.

(b) The affidavit must state: "I am not financially able to post a bond to cover any judgment against me in this case. All financial information that I provided to the lender was true and complete and contained no false statements or material omissions at the time it was provided to the lender. Upon oath and under penalty of perjury, the statements made in this affidavit are true."

(c) In the event the applicant is married, both spouses must execute the affidavit.

(d) The affidavit must be verified.

Added by Acts 1989, 71st Leg., ch. 391, § 1, eff. Aug. 28, 1989.

§ 65.044. Contest of Affidavit

(a) A party may not contest an affidavit filed by an applicant for a temporary restraining order as provided by Section 65.041.

(b) A party may contest an affidavit filed by an applicant for a temporary injunction as provided by Section 65.042:

(1) after service of a temporary restraining order in the case; or

(2) if a temporary restraining order was not applied for or issued, after service of notice of the hearing on the application for the temporary injunction.

(c) A party contests an affidavit by filing a written motion and giving notice to all parties of the motion in accordance with Rule 21a of the Texas Rules of Civil Procedure.

(d) The court shall hear the contest at the hearing on the application for a temporary injunction and determine whether the applicant is financially able to execute a bond against the adverse party as required by the Texas Rules of Civil Procedure. In making its determination, the court may not consider:

(1) any income from a government entitlement that the applicant receives; or

(2) the value of the applicant's residential homestead.

(e) The court may order the applicant to post and file with the clerk a bond as required by the Texas Rules of Civil Procedure only if the court determines that the applicant is financially able to execute the bond.

(f) An attorney who represents an applicant and who provides legal services without charge to the applicant and without a contractual agreement for payment contingent on any event may file an affidavit with the court describing the financial nature of the representation.

Added by Acts 1989, 71st Leg., ch. 391, § 1, eff. Aug. 28, 1989.

§ 65.045. Conflict With Texas Rules of Civil Procedure

(a) To the extent that this subchapter conflicts with the Texas Rules of Civil Procedure, this subchapter controls.

(b) Notwithstanding Section 22.004, Government Code, the supreme court may not amend or adopt rules in conflict with this subchapter.

(c) The district courts and statutory county courts in a county may not adopt local rules in conflict with this subchapter.

Added by Acts 1989, 71st Leg., ch. 391, § 1, eff. Aug. 28, 1989.

CHAPTER 66. QUO WARRANTO

Section

§ 66.001. Grounds

An action in the nature of quo warranto is available if:

(1) a person usurps, intrudes into, or unlawfully holds or executes a franchise or an office, including

an office in a corporation created by the authority of this state;

(2) a public officer does an act or allows an act that by law causes a forfeiture of his office;

(3) an association of persons acts as a corporation without being legally incorporated;

(4) a corporation does or omits an act that requires a surrender or causes a forfeiture of its rights and privileges as a corporation;

(5) a corporation exercises power not granted by law;

(6) a railroad company charges an extortionate rate for transportation of freight or passengers; or

(7) a railroad company unlawfully refuses to move over its lines the cars of another railroad company.

Acts 1985, 69th Leg., ch. 959, § 1, eff. Sept. 1, 1985.

§ 66.002. Initiation of Suit

(a) If grounds for the remedy exist, the attorney general or the county or district attorney of the proper county may petition the district court of the proper county or a district judge if the court is in vacation for leave to file an information in the nature of quo warranto.

(b) The petition must state that the information is sought in the name of the State of Texas.

(c) The attorney general or county or district attorney may file the petition on his own motion or at the request of an individual relator.

(d) If there is probable ground for the proceeding, the judge shall grant leave to file the information, order the information to be filed, and order process to be issued.

Acts 1985, 69th Leg., ch. 959, § 1, eff. Sept. 1, 1985.

§ 66.003. Judgment

If the person against whom the information is filed is found guilty as charged, the court:

(1) shall enter judgment removing the person from the office or franchise;

(2) shall enter judgment for the costs of prosecution in favor of the relator; and

(3) may fine the person for usurping, intruding into, or unlawfully holding and executing the office or franchise.

Acts 1985, 69th Leg., ch. 959, § 1, eff. Sept. 1, 1985.

TITLE 4. LIABILITY IN TORT

CHAPTER 71. WRONGFUL DEATH; SURVIVAL; INJURIES OCCURRING OUT OF STATE

SUBCHAPTER A. WRONGFUL DEATH

SUBCHAPTER A. WRONGFUL DEATH

§ 71.001. Definitions

In this subchapter:

(1) "Corporation" means a municipal, private, public, or quasi-public corporation other than a county or a common or independent school district.

(2) "Person" means an individual, association of individuals, joint-stock company, or corporation or a trustee or receiver of an individual, association of individuals, joint-stock company, or corporation.

(3) "Death" includes, for an individual who is an unborn child, the failure to be born alive.

(4) "Individual" includes an unborn child at every stage of gestation from fertilization until birth.

Acts 1985, 69th Leg., ch. 959, § 1, eff. Sept. 1, 1985. Amended by Acts 2003, 78th Leg., ch. 822, § 1.01, eff. Sept. 1, 2003.

§ 71.002. Cause of Action

(a) An action for actual damages arising from an injury that causes an individual's death may be brought if liability exists under this section.

(b) A person is liable for damages arising from an injury that causes an individual's death if the injury was caused by the person's or his agent's or servant's wrongful act, neglect, carelessness, unskillfulness, or default.

(c) A person is liable for damages arising from an injury that causes an individual's death if:

(1) the person is a proprietor, owner, charterer, or hirer of an industrial or public utility plant or of a railroad, street railway, steamboat, stagecoach, or other vehicle for the transportation of goods or passengers; and

(2) the injury was caused by the person's or his agent's or servant's wrongful act, neglect, carelessness, unskillfulness, or default.

(d) A person is liable for damages arising from an injury that causes an individual's death if:

(1) the person is a receiver, trustee, or other person in charge of or in control of a railroad, street railway, steamboat, stagecoach, or other vehicle for the transportation of goods or passengers, of an industrial or public utility plant, or of other machinery; and

(2) the injury was caused by:

(A) the person's wrongful act, neglect, carelessness, unskillfulness, or default;

(B) the person's servant's or agent's wrongful act, neglect, carelessness, unfitness, unskillfulness, or default; or

(C) a bad or unsafe condition of the railroad, street railway, or other machinery under the person's control or operation.

(e) A person is liable for damages arising from an injury that causes an individual's death if:

(1) the person is a receiver, trustee, or other person in charge of or in control of a railroad, street railway, steamboat, stagecoach, or other vehicle for the transportation of goods or passengers, of an industrial or public utility plant, or of other machinery; and

(2) the action could have been brought against the owner of the railroad, street railway, or other machinery if he had been acting as operator.

Acts 1985, 69th Leg., ch. 959, § 1, eff. Sept. 1, 1985.

§ 71.003. Application; Certain Conduct Excepted

(a) This subchapter applies only if the individual injured would have been entitled to bring an action for the injury if the individual had lived or had been born alive.

(b) This subchapter applies whether the injury occurs inside or outside this state.

(c) This subchapter does not apply to a claim for the death of an individual who is an unborn child that is brought against:

(1) the mother of the unborn child;

(2) a physician or other licensed health care provider, if the death is the intended result of a lawful medical procedure performed by the physician or health care provider with the requisite consent;

(3) a person who dispenses or administers a drug in accordance with law, if the death is the result of the dispensation or administration of the drug; or

(4) a physician or other health care provider licensed in this state, if the death directly or indirectly is caused by, associated with, arises out of, or relates to a lawful medical or health care practice or procedure of the physician or the health care provider.

Acts 1985, 69th Leg., ch. 959, § 1, eff. Sept. 1, 1985. Amended by Acts 2003, 78th Leg., ch. 822, § 1.02, eff. Sept. 1, 2003.

§ 71.004. Benefitting From and Bringing Action

(a) An action to recover damages as provided by this subchapter is for the exclusive benefit of the surviving spouse, children, and parents of the deceased.

(b) The surviving spouse, children, and parents of the deceased may bring the action or one or more of those individuals may bring the action for the benefit of all.

(c) If none of the individuals entitled to bring an action have begun the action within three calendar months after the death of the injured individual, his executor or administrator shall bring and prosecute the action unless requested not to by all those individuals.

Acts 1985, 69th Leg., ch. 959, § 1, eff. Sept. 1, 1985.

§ 71.005. Evidence Relating to Marital Status

In an action under this subchapter, evidence of the actual ceremonial remarriage of the surviving spouse is admissible, if it is true, but the defense is prohibited from directly or indirectly mentioning or alluding to a common-law marriage, an extramarital relationship, or the marital prospects of the surviving spouse.

Acts 1985, 69th Leg., ch. 959, § 1, eff. Sept. 1, 1985.

§ 71.0055. Evidence of Pregnancy

In an action under this subchapter for the death of an individual who is an unborn child, the plaintiff shall provide medical or other evidence that the mother of the individual was pregnant at the time of the individual's death.

Added by Acts 2003, 78th Leg., ch. 822, § 1.03, eff. Sept. 1, 2003.

§ 71.006. Effect of Felonious Act

An action under this subchapter is not precluded because the death is caused by a felonious act or because there may be a criminal proceeding in relation to the felony.

Acts 1985, 69th Leg., ch. 959, § 1, eff. Sept. 1, 1985.

§ 71.007. Ineffective Agreement

An agreement between the owner of a railroad, street railway, steamboat, stagecoach, or other vehicle for the transportation of goods or passengers, of an industrial or public utility plant, or of other machinery and an individual, corporation, trustee, receiver, lessee, joint-stock association, or other entity in control of or operating the vehicle, plant, or other machinery does not release the owner or the entity controlling or operating the vehicle, plant, or other machinery from liability provided by this subchapter.

Acts 1985, 69th Leg., ch. 959, § 1, eff. Sept. 1, 1985.

§ 71.008. Death of Defendant

(a) If a defendant dies while an action under this subchapter is pending or if the individual against whom the action may have been instituted dies before the action is begun, the executor or administrator of the estate may be made a defendant, and the action may be prosecuted as though the defendant or individual were alive.

(b) A judgment in favor of the plaintiff shall be paid in due course of administration.

Acts 1985, 69th Leg., ch. 959, § 1, eff. Sept. 1, 1985.

§ 71.009. Exemplary Damages

When the death is caused by the wilful act or omission or gross negligence of the defendant, exemplary as well as actual damages may be recovered.

Acts 1985, 69th Leg., ch. 959, § 1, eff. Sept. 1, 1985.

§ 71.010. Award and Apportionment of Damages

(a) The jury may award damages in an amount proportionate to the injury resulting from the death.

(b) The damages awarded shall be divided, in shares as found by the jury in its verdict, among the individuals who are entitled to recover and who are alive at that time.

Acts 1985, 69th Leg., ch. 959, § 1, eff. Sept. 1, 1985.

§ 71.011. Damages Not Subject to Debts

Damages recovered in an action under this subchapter are not subject to the debts of the deceased.

Acts 1985, 69th Leg., ch. 959, § 1, eff. Sept. 1, 1985.

§ 71.012. Qualification of Foreign Personal Representative

If the executor or administrator of the estate of a nonresident individual is the plaintiff in an action under this subchapter, the foreign personal representative of the estate who has complied with the requirements of Chapter 503, Estates Code, for the probate of a foreign will is not required to apply for ancillary letters testamentary under Section 501.006, Estates Code, to bring and prosecute the action.

Added by Acts 1999, 76th Leg., ch. 382, § 1, eff. May 29, 1999. Amended by Acts 2017, 85th Leg., ch. 324 (S.B. 1488), § 22.005, eff. Sept. 1, 2017; Acts 2019, 86th Leg., ch. 846 (H.B. 2780), § 1, eff. Sept. 1, 2019.

SUBCHAPTER B. SURVIVAL

§ 71.021. Survival of Cause of Action

(a) A cause of action for personal injury to the health, reputation, or person of an injured person does not abate because of the death of the injured person or because of the death of a person liable for the injury.

(b) A personal injury action survives to and in favor of the heirs, legal representatives, and estate of the injured person. The action survives against the liable person and the person's legal representatives.

(c) The suit may be instituted and prosecuted as if the liable person were alive.

Acts 1985, 69th Leg., ch. 959, § 1, eff. Sept. 1, 1985.

§ 71.022. Qualification of Foreign Personal Representative

If the executor or administrator of the estate of a nonresident individual is the plaintiff in an action under this subchapter, the foreign personal representative of the estate who has complied with the requirements of Chapter 503, Estates Code, for the probate of a foreign will is not required to apply for ancillary letters testamentary under Section 501.006, Estates Code, to bring and prosecute the action.

Added by Acts 1999, 76th Leg., ch. 382, § 2, eff. May 29, 1999. Amended by Acts 2017, 85th Leg., ch. 324 (S.B. 1488), § 22.006, eff. Sept. 1, 2017; Acts 2019, 86th Leg., ch. 846 (H.B. 2780), § 1, eff. Sept. 1, 2019.

SUBCHAPTER C. DEATH OR INJURY CAUSED BY ACT OR OMISSION OUT OF STATE

§ 71.031. Act or Omission Out of State

(a) An action for damages for the death or personal injury of a citizen of this state, of the United States, or of a foreign country may be enforced in the courts of this state, although the wrongful act, neglect, or default causing the death or injury takes place in a foreign state or country, if:

(1) a law of the foreign state or country or of this state gives a right to maintain an action for damages for the death or injury;

(2) the action is begun in this state within the time provided by the laws of this state for beginning the action;

(3) for a resident of a foreign state or country, the action is begun in this state within the time provided by the laws of the foreign state or country in which the wrongful act, neglect, or default took place; and

(4) in the case of a citizen of a foreign country, the country has equal treaty rights with the United States on behalf of its citizens.

(b) Except as provided by Subsection (a), all matters pertaining to procedure in the prosecution or maintenance of the action in the courts of this state are governed by the law of this state.

(c) The court shall apply the rules of substantive law that are appropriate under the facts of the case.

Acts 1985, 69th Leg., ch. 959, § 1, eff. Sept. 1, 1985. Amended by Acts 1997, 75th Leg., ch. 424, § 3, eff. May 29, 1997.

SUBCHAPTER D. FORUM NON CONVENIENS

§ 71.051. Forum Non Conveniens

(a) Repealed by Acts 2003, 78th Leg., ch. 204, § 3.09.

(b) If a court of this state, on written motion of a party, finds that in the interest of justice and for the convenience of the parties a claim or action to which this section applies would be more properly heard in a forum outside this state, the court shall decline to exercise jurisdiction under the doctrine of forum non conveniens and shall stay or dismiss the claim or action. In determining whether to grant a motion to stay or dismiss an action under the doctrine of forum non conveniens, the court shall consider whether:

(1) an alternate forum exists in which the claim or action may be tried;

(2) the alternate forum provides an adequate remedy;

(3) maintenance of the claim or action in the courts of this state would work a substantial injustice to the moving party;

(4) the alternate forum, as a result of the submission of the parties or otherwise, can exercise jurisdiction over all the defendants properly joined to the plaintiff's claim;

(5) the balance of the private interests of the parties and the public interest of the state predominate in favor of the claim or action being brought in an alternate forum, which shall include consideration of the extent to which an injury or death resulted from acts or omissions that occurred in this state; and

(6) the stay or dismissal would not result in unreasonable duplication or proliferation of litigation.

(c) The court may set terms and conditions for staying or dismissing a claim or action under this section as the interests of justice may require, giving due regard to the rights of the parties to the claim or action. If a moving party violates a term or condition of a stay or dismissal, the court shall withdraw the order staying or dismissing the claim or action and proceed as if the order had never been issued. Notwithstanding any other law, the court shall have continuing jurisdiction for purposes of this subsection.

(d) A request for stay or dismissal under this section is timely if it is filed not later than 180 days after the time required for filing a motion to transfer venue of the claim or action. The court may rule on a motion filed under this section only after a hearing with notice to all parties not less than 21 days before the date specified for the hearing. The court shall afford all of the parties ample opportunity to obtain discovery of information relevant to the motion prior to a hearing on a motion under this section. The moving party shall have the responsibility to request and obtain a hearing on such motion at a reasonable time prior to commencement of the trial, and in no case shall the hearing be held less than 30 days prior to trial.

(e) The court may not stay or dismiss a plaintiff's claim under Subsection (b) if the plaintiff is a legal resident of this state or a derivative claimant of a legal resident of this state. The determination of whether a claim may be stayed or dismissed under Subsection (b) shall be made with respect to each plaintiff without regard to whether the claim of any other plaintiff may be stayed or dismissed under Subsection (b) and without regard to a plaintiff's country of citizenship or national origin. If an action involves both plaintiffs who are legal residents of this state and plaintiffs who are not, the court shall consider the factors provided by Subsection (b) and determine whether to deny the motion or to stay or dismiss the claim of any plaintiff who is not a legal resident of this state.

(f) A court that grants a motion to stay or dismiss an action under the doctrine of forum non conveniens shall set forth specific findings of fact and conclusions of law.

(g) Any time limit established by this section may be extended by the court at the request of any party for good cause shown.

(h) For purposes of Subsection (e):

(1) "Derivative claimant" means a person whose damages were caused by personal injury to or the wrongful death of another.

(2) "Plaintiff" means a party seeking recovery of damages for personal injury or wrongful death. The term does not include:

(A) a counterclaimant, cross-claimant, or third-party plaintiff or a person who is assigned a cause of action for personal injury; or

(B) a representative, administrator, guardian, or next friend who is not otherwise a derivative claimant of a legal resident of this state.

(i) This section applies to actions for personal injury or wrongful death. This section shall govern the courts of this state in determining issues under the doctrine of forum non conveniens in the actions to which it applies, notwithstanding Section 71.031(a) or any other law.

Added by Acts 1993, 73rd Leg., ch. 4, § 1, eff. Aug. 30, 1993. Amended by Acts 1995, 74th Leg., ch. 567, § 1, eff. Sept. 1, 1995; Acts 1997, 75th Leg., ch. 424, § 1, eff. May 29, 1997; Acts 2003, 78th Leg., ch. 204, §§ 3.04, 3.09, eff. Sept. 1, 2003; Acts 2005, 79th Leg., ch. 248, § 1, eff. Sept. 1, 2005; Acts 2015, 84th Leg., ch. 537 (H.B. 1692), § 1, eff. June 16, 2015.

§ 71.052. Repealed by Acts 2003, 78th Leg., ch. 204, § 3.09, eff. Sept. 1, 2003

CHAPTER 72. LIABILITY OF MOTOR VEHICLE OWNER OR OPERATOR

SUBCHAPTER A. LIABILITY TO GUEST

SUBCHAPTER B. ACTIONS REGARDING COMMERCIAL MOTOR VEHICLES

SUBCHAPTER A. LIABILITY TO GUEST

§ 72.001. Limited Liability

A person who is related to the owner or operator of a motor vehicle within the second degree by consanguinity or affinity, as determined under Chapter 573, Government Code, and who is being transported in the motor vehicle over a public highway of this state as a guest without payment for the transportation has a cause of action against the owner or operator of the motor vehicle for injury, death, or loss in an accident only if the accident was intentional on the part of the owner or operator or was caused by his heedlessness or reckless disregard of the rights of others.

Acts 1985, 69th Leg., ch. 959, § 1, eff. Sept. 1, 1985. Amended by Acts 1991, 72nd Leg., ch. 561, § 7, eff. Aug. 26, 1991; Acts 1995, 74th Leg., ch. 76, § 5.95(27), eff. Sept. 1, 1995.

The source law for this section, Vernon's Ann.Civ.St. art 6701b, was declared unconstitutional by Whitworth v. Bynum, 699 S.W.2d 194 (Tex. 1985).

Section 6 of Acts 2021, 87th Leg., ch. 785 (H.B. 19) provides:

"The changes in law made by this Act apply only to an action commenced on or after the effective date [Sept. 1, 2021] of this Act. An action commenced before the effective date of this Act is governed by the law applicable to the action immediately before the effective date of this Act, and that law is continued in effect for that purpose."

§ 72.002. Limitation Not Applicable

There is no limitation under this subchapter on the liability of an owner or operator who is not related to the guest within the second degree by consanguinity or affinity.

Acts 1985, 69th Leg., ch. 959, § 1, eff. Sept. 1, 1985. Amended by Acts 2021, 87th Leg., ch. 785 (H.B. 19), § 3, eff. Sept. 1, 2021.

Section 6 of Acts 2021, 87th Leg., ch. 785 (H.B. 19) provides:

"The changes in law made by this Act apply only to an action commenced on or after the effective date [Sept. 1, 2021] of this Act. An action commenced before the effective date of this Act is governed by the law applicable to the action immediately before the effective date of this Act, and that law is continued in effect for that purpose."

§ 72.003. Effect on Other Liability

(a) This subchapter does not affect judicially developed or developing rules under which a person is or is not totally or partially immune from tort liability by virtue of family relationship.

(b) This subchapter does not relieve the owner or operator of a motor vehicle being demonstrated to a prospective purchaser or relieve a public carrier of responsibility for injuries sustained by a passenger being transported.

Acts 1985, 69th Leg., ch. 959, § 1, eff. Sept. 1, 1985. Amended by Acts 2021, 87th Leg., ch. 785 (H.B. 19), § 3, eff. Sept. 1, 2021.

Section 6 of Acts 2021, 87th Leg., ch. 785 (H.B. 19) provides:

"The changes in law made by this Act apply only to an action commenced on or after the effective date [Sept. 1, 2021] of this Act. An action commenced before the effective date of this Act is governed by the law applicable to the action immediately before the effective date of this Act, and that law is continued in effect for that purpose."

§ 72.004. Offset for Medical Expenses Paid

(a) The owner or operator or his liability insurance carrier is entitled to an offset against any award made to the guest on a liability claim in an amount equal to the amount paid by the owner, operator, or insurance carrier for medical expenses of the guest.

(b) This section does not authorize a direct action against a liability insurance carrier.

Acts 1985, 69th Leg., ch. 959, § 1, eff. Sept. 1, 1985.

Section 6 of Acts 2021, 87th Leg., ch. 785 (H.B. 19) provides:

"The changes in law made by this Act apply only to an action commenced on or after the effective date [Sept. 1, 2021] of this Act. An action commenced before the effective date of this Act is governed by the law applicable to the action immediately before the effective date of this Act, and that law is continued in effect for that purpose."

SUBCHAPTER B. ACTIONS REGARDING COMMERCIAL MOTOR VEHICLES

§ 72.051. Definitions

In this subchapter:

(1) "Accident" means an event in which operating a commercial motor vehicle causes bodily injury or death.

(2) "Civil action" means an action in which:

(A) a claimant seeks recovery of damages for bodily injury or death caused in an accident; and

(B) a defendant:

(i) operated a commercial motor vehicle involved in the accident; or

(ii) owned, leased, or otherwise held or exercised legal control over a commercial motor vehicle or operator of a commercial motor vehicle involved in the accident.

(3) "Claimant" means a person, including a decedent's estate, seeking or who has sought recovery of damages in a civil action. The term includes a plaintiff, counterclaimant, cross-claimant, third-party plaintiff, and an intervenor. The term does not include a passenger in a commercial motor vehicle unless the person is an employee of the owner, lessor, lessee, or operator of the vehicle.

(4) "Commercial motor vehicle" means a motor vehicle being used for commercial purposes in interstate or intrastate commerce to transport property or passengers, deliver or transport goods, or provide services. The term does not include a motor vehicle being used at the time of the accident for personal, family, or household purposes.

(5) "Compensatory damages" has the meaning assigned by Section 41.001.

(6) "Employee" means a person who works for another person for compensation. The term includes a person deemed an employee under state or federal law and any other agent or person for whom an employer may be liable under respondeat superior.

(7) "Exemplary damages" has the meaning assigned by Section 41.001.

(8) "Motor vehicle" means a self-propelled device in which a person or property can be transported on a public highway. The term includes a trailer when in use with a self-propelled device described by this subdivision. The term does not include a device used exclusively upon stationary rails or tracks.

(9) "Operated," "operating," and "operation," when used with respect to a commercial motor vehicle, means to cause the vehicle to move or function in any respect, including driving, stopping, or parking the vehicle or otherwise putting the vehicle into use or operation. These terms include a commercial motor vehicle that has become disabled.

(10) "Video" means an electronic representation of a sequence of images, with or without accompanying audio, depicting either stationary or moving scenes, regardless of the manner in which the sequence of images is captured, recorded, or stored.

Added by Acts 2021, 87th Leg., ch. 785 (H.B. 19), § 4, eff. Sept. 1, 2021.

Section 6 of Acts 2021, 87th Leg., ch. 785 (H.B. 19) provides:

"The changes in law made by this Act apply only to an action commenced on or after the effective date [Sept. 1, 2021] of this Act. An action commenced before the effective date of this Act is governed by the law applicable to the action immediately before the effective date of this Act, and that law is continued in effect for that purpose."

§ 72.052. Bifurcated Trial in Certain Commercial Motor Vehicle Accident Actions

(a) In a civil action under this subchapter, on motion by a defendant, the court shall provide for a bifurcated trial under this section.

(b) A motion under this section shall be made on or before the later of:

(1) the 120th day after the date the defendant bringing the motion files the defendant's original answer; or

(2) the 30th day after the date a claimant files a pleading adding a claim or cause of action against the defendant bringing the motion.

(c) The trier of fact shall determine liability for and the amount of compensatory damages in the first phase of a bifurcated trial under this section.

(d) The trier of fact shall determine liability for and the amount of exemplary damages in the second phase of a bifurcated trial under this section.

(e) For purposes of this section, a finding by the trier of fact in the first phase of a bifurcated trial that an employee defendant was negligent in operating an employer defendant's commercial motor vehicle may serve as a basis for the claimant to proceed in the second phase of the trial on a claim against the employer defendant, such as negligent entrustment, that requires a finding by the trier of fact that the employee was negligent in operating the vehicle as a prerequisite to the employer defendant being found negligent in relation to the employee defendant's operation of the vehicle. This subsection does not apply to a claimant who has pursued a claim described by this subsection in the first phase of a trial that is bifurcated under this section.

Added by Acts 2021, 87th Leg., ch. 785 (H.B. 19), § 4, eff. Sept. 1, 2021.

Section 6 of Acts 2021, 87th Leg., ch. 785 (H.B. 19) provides:

"The changes in law made by this Act apply only to an action commenced on or after the effective date [Sept. 1, 2021] of this Act. An action commenced before the effective date of this Act is governed by the law applicable to the action immediately before the effective date of this Act, and that law is continued in effect for that purpose."

§ 72.053. Failure to Comply With Regulations or Standards

(a) In this section, "regulation or standard" includes a statute, regulation, rule, or order regulating equipment or conduct adopted or promulgated by the federal government, a state government, a local government, or a governmental agency or authority.

(b) In a civil action under this subchapter, evidence of a defendant's failure to comply with a regulation or standard is admissible in the first phase of a trial bifurcated under Section 72.052 only if, in addition to complying with other requirements of law:

(1) the evidence tends to prove that failure to comply with the regulation or standard was a proximate cause of the bodily injury or death for which damages are sought in the action; and

(2) the regulation or standard is specific and governs, or is an element of a duty of care applicable to, the defendant, the defendant's employee, or the defendant's property or equipment when any of those is at issue in the action.

(c) Nothing in this section prevents a claimant from pursuing a claim for exemplary damages under Chapter 41 relating to the defendant's failure to comply with other applicable regulations or standards, or from presenting evidence on that claim in the second phase of a bifurcated trial.

Added by Acts 2021, 87th Leg., ch. 785 (H.B. 19), § 4, eff. Sept. 1, 2021.

Section 6 of Acts 2021, 87th Leg., ch. 785 (H.B. 19) provides:

"The changes in law made by this Act apply only to an action commenced on or after the effective date [Sept. 1, 2021] of this Act. An action commenced before the effective date of this Act is governed by the law applicable to the action immediately before the effective date of this Act, and that law is continued in effect for that purpose."

§ 72.054. Liability for Employee Negligence in Operating Commercial Motor Vehicle

(a) Except as provided by Subsection (d), in a civil action under this subchapter, an employer defendant's liability for damages caused by the ordinary negligence of a person operating the defendant's commercial motor vehicle shall be based only on respondeat superior if the defendant stipulates, within the time provided by Section 72.052 for filing a motion to bifurcate, that, at the time of the accident, the person operating the vehicle was:

(1) the defendant's employee; and

(2) acting within the scope of employment.

(b) Except as provided by Subsection (c), if an employer defendant stipulates in accordance with Subsection (a) and the trial is bifurcated under Section 72.052, a claimant may not, in the first phase of the trial, present evidence on an ordinary negligence claim against the employer defendant, such as negligent entrustment, that requires a finding by the trier of fact that the employer defendant's employee was negligent in operating a vehicle as a prerequisite to the employer defendant being found negligent in relation to the employee defendant's operation of the vehicle. This subsection does not prevent a claimant from presenting evidence allowed by Section 72.053(b).

(c) In a civil action under this subchapter in which an employer defendant is regulated by the Motor Carrier Safety Improvement Act of 1999 (Pub. L. No. 106–159) or Chapter 644, Transportation Code, a party may present any of the following evidence in the first phase of a trial that is bifurcated under Section 72.052 if applicable to a defendant in the action:

(1) whether the employee who was operating the employer defendant's commercial motor vehicle at the time of the accident that is the subject of the civil action:

(A) was licensed to drive the vehicle at the time of the accident;

(B) was disqualified from driving the vehicle under 49 C.F.R. Section 383.51, 383.52, or 391.15 at the time of the accident;

(C) was subject to an out-of-service order, as defined by 49 C.F.R. Section 390.5, at the time of the accident;

(D) was driving the vehicle in violation of a license restriction imposed under 49 C.F.R. Section 383.95 or Section 522.043, Transportation Code, at the time of the accident;

(E) had received a certificate of driver's road test from the employer defendant as required by 49 C.F.R. Section 391.31 or had an equivalent certificate or license as provided by 49 C.F.R. Section 391.33;

(F) had been medically certified as physically qualified to operate the vehicle under 49 C.F.R. Section 391.41;

(G) was operating the vehicle when prohibited from doing so under 49 C.F.R. Section 382.201, 382.205, 382.207, 382.215, 395.3, or 395.5 or 37 T.A.C. Section 4.12, as applicable, on the day of the accident;

(H) was texting or using a handheld mobile telephone while driving the vehicle in violation of 49 C.F.R. Section 392.80 or 392.82 at the time of the accident;

(I) provided the employer defendant with an application for employment as required by 49 C.F.R. Section 391.21(a) if the accident occurred on or before the first anniversary of the date the employee began employment with the employer defendant; and

(J) refused to submit to a controlled substance test as required by 49 C.F.R. Section 382.303, 382.305, 382.307, 382.309, or 382.311 during the two years preceding the date of the accident; and

(2) whether the employer defendant:

(A) allowed the employee to operate the employer's commercial motor vehicle on the day of the accident in violation of 49 C.F.R. Section 382.201, 382.205, 382.207, 382.215, 382.701(d), 395.3, or 395.5 or 37 T.A.C. Section 4.12, as applicable;

(B) had complied with 49 C.F.R. Section 382.301 in regard to controlled-substance testing of the employee driver if:

(i) the employee driver was impaired because of the use of a controlled substance at the time of the accident; and

(ii) the accident occurred on or before the 180th day after the date the employee driver began employment with the employer defendant;

(C) had made the investigations and inquiries as provided by 49 C.F.R. Section 391.23(a) in regard to the employee driver if the accident occurred on or before the first anniversary of the date the employee driver began employment with the employer defendant; and

(D) was subject to an out-of-service order, as defined by 49 C.F.R. Section 390.5, at the time of the accident.

(d) If a civil action is bifurcated under Section 72.052, evidence admissible under Subsection (c) is:

(1) admissible in the first phase of the trial only to prove ordinary negligent entrustment by the employer defendant to the employee who was driving the employer defendant's commercial motor vehicle at the time of the accident that is the subject of the action; and

(2) the only evidence that may be presented by the claimant in the first phase of the trial on the negligent entrustment claim.

(e) The provisions of Subsection (c) may not be construed to create a new rule or regulation or subject a person to a rule or regulation not applicable to the person without regard to this section.

(f) Nothing in this section prevents a claimant from pursuing:

(1) an ordinary negligence claim against an employer defendant for a claim, such as negligent maintenance, that does not require a finding of negligence by an employee as a prerequisite to an employer defendant being found negligent for its conduct or omission, or from presenting evidence on that claim in the first phase of a bifurcated trial; or

(2) a claim for exemplary damages under Chapter 41 for an employer defendant's conduct or omissions in relation to the accident that is the subject of the action, or from presenting evidence on that claim in the second phase of a bifurcated trial.

Added by Acts 2021, 87th Leg., ch. 785 (H.B. 19), § 4, eff. Sept. 1, 2021.

Section 6 of Acts 2021, 87th Leg., ch. 785 (H.B. 19) provides:

"The changes in law made by this Act apply only to an action commenced on or after the effective date [Sept. 1, 2021] of this Act. An action commenced before the effective date of this Act is governed by the law applicable to the action immediately before the effective date of this Act, and that law is continued in effect for that purpose."

§ 72.055. Admissibility of Visual Depictions of Accident

(a) In a civil action under this subchapter, a court may not require expert testimony for admission into evidence of a photograph or video of a vehicle or object involved in an accident that is the subject of the action except as necessary to authenticate the photograph or video.

(b) If properly authenticated under the Texas Rules of Evidence, a photograph or video of a vehicle or object involved in an accident that is the subject of a civil action under this subchapter is presumed admissible, even if the photograph or video tends to support or refute an assertion regarding the severity of damages or injury to an object or person involved in the accident.

Added by Acts 2021, 87th Leg., ch. 785 (H.B. 19), § 4, eff. Sept. 1, 2021.

Section 6 of Acts 2021, 87th Leg., ch. 785 (H.B. 19) provides:

"The changes in law made by this Act apply only to an action commenced on or after the effective date [Sept. 1, 2021] of this Act. An action commenced before the effective date of this Act is governed by the law applicable to the action immediately before the effective date of this Act, and that law is continued in effect for that purpose."

CHAPTER 73. LIBEL

SUBCHAPTER A. GENERAL PROVISIONS

SUBCHAPTER B. CORRECTION, CLARIFICATION, OR RETRACTION BY PUBLISHER

SUBCHAPTER A. GENERAL PROVISIONS

§ 73.001. Elements of Libel

A libel is a defamation expressed in written or other graphic form that tends to blacken the memory of the dead or that tends to injure a living person's reputation and thereby expose the person to public hatred, contempt or ridicule, or financial injury or to impeach any person's honesty, integrity, virtue, or reputation or to publish the natural defects of anyone and thereby expose the person to public hatred, ridicule, or financial injury.

Acts 1985, 69th Leg., ch. 959, § 1, eff. Sept. 1, 1985.

§ 73.002. Privileged Matters

(a) The publication by a newspaper or other periodical of a matter covered by this section is privileged and is not a ground for a libel action. This privilege does not extend to the republication of a matter if it is proved that the matter was republished with actual malice after it had ceased to be of public concern.

(b) This section applies to:

(1) a fair, true, and impartial account of:

(A) a judicial proceeding, unless the court has prohibited publication of a matter because in its judgment the interests of justice demand that the matter not be published;

(B) an official proceeding, other than a judicial proceeding, to administer the law;

(C) an executive or legislative proceeding (including a proceeding of a legislative committee), a proceeding in or before a managing board of an educational or eleemosynary institution supported from the public revenue, of the governing body of a city or town, of a county commissioners court, and of a public school board or a report of or debate and statements made in any of those proceedings; or

(D) the proceedings of a public meeting dealing with a public purpose, including statements and discussion at the meeting or other matters of public concern occurring at the meeting; and

(2) reasonable and fair comment on or criticism of an official act of a public official or other matter of public concern published for general information.

Acts 1985, 69th Leg., ch. 959, § 1, eff. Sept. 1, 1985.

§ 73.003. Mitigating Factors

(a) To determine the extent and source of actual damages and to mitigate exemplary damages, the defendant in a libel action may give evidence of the following matters if they have been specially pleaded:

(1) all material facts and circumstances surrounding the claim for damages and defenses to the claim;

(2) all facts and circumstances under which the libelous publication was made; and

(3) any public apology, correction, or retraction of the libelous matter made and published by the defendant.

(b) To mitigate exemplary damages, the defendant in a libel action may give evidence of the intention with which the libelous publication was made if the matter has been specially pleaded.

Acts 1985, 69th Leg., ch. 959, § 1, eff. Sept. 1, 1985.

§ 73.004. Liability of Broadcaster

(a) A broadcaster is not liable in damages for a defamatory statement published or uttered in or as a part of a radio or television broadcast by one other than the broadcaster unless the complaining party proves that the broadcaster failed to exercise due care to prevent the publication or utterance of the statement in the broadcast.

(b) In this section, "broadcaster" means an owner, licensee, or operator of a radio or television station or network of stations and the agents and employees of the owner, licensee, or operator.

Acts 1985, 69th Leg., ch. 959, § 1, eff. Sept. 1, 1985.

§ 73.005. Truth a Defense

(a) The truth of the statement in the publication on which an action for libel is based is a defense to the action.

(b) In an action brought against a newspaper or other periodical or broadcaster, the defense described by Subsection (a) applies to an accurate reporting of allegations made by a third party regarding a matter of public concern.

(c) This section does not abrogate or lessen any other remedy, right, cause of action, defense, immunity, or privilege available under the Constitution of the United States or this state or as provided by any statute, case, or common law or rule.

Acts 1985, 69th Leg., ch. 959, § 1, eff. Sept. 1, 1985. Amended by Acts 2015, 84th Leg., ch. 191 (S.B. 627), § 1, eff. May 28, 2015.

§ 73.006. Other Defenses

This chapter does not affect the existence of common law, statutory law, or other defenses to libel.

Acts 1985, 69th Leg., ch. 959, § 1, eff. Sept. 1, 1985.

SUBCHAPTER B. CORRECTION, CLARIFICATION, OR RETRACTION BY PUBLISHER

§ 73.051. Short Title

This subchapter may be cited as the Defamation Mitigation Act. This subchapter shall be liberally construed.

Added by Acts 2013, 83rd Leg., ch. 950 (H.B. 1759), § 2, eff. June 14, 2013.

§ 73.052. Purpose

The purpose of this subchapter is to provide a method for a person who has been defamed by a publication or broadcast to mitigate any perceived damage or injury.

Added by Acts 2013, 83rd Leg., ch. 950 (H.B. 1759), § 2, eff. June 14, 2013.

§ 73.053. Definition

In this subchapter, "person" means an individual, corporation, business trust, estate, trust, partnership, association, joint venture, or other legal or commercial entity. The term does not include a government or governmental subdivision, agency, or instrumentality.

Added by Acts 2013, 83rd Leg., ch. 950 (H.B. 1759), § 2, eff. June 14, 2013.

§ 73.054. Applicability

(a) This subchapter applies to a claim for relief, however characterized, from damages arising out of harm to personal reputation caused by the false content of a publication.

(b) This subchapter applies to all publications, including writings, broadcasts, oral communications, electronic transmissions, or other forms of transmitting information.

Added by Acts 2013, 83rd Leg., ch. 950 (H.B. 1759), § 2, eff. June 14, 2013.

§ 73.055. Request for Correction, Clarification, or Retraction

(a) A person may maintain an action for defamation only if:

(1) the person has made a timely and sufficient request for a correction, clarification, or retraction from the defendant; or

(2) the defendant has made a correction, clarification, or retraction.

(b) A request for a correction, clarification, or retraction is timely if made during the period of limitation for commencement of an action for defamation.

(c) If not later than the 90th day after receiving knowledge of the publication, the person does not request a correction, clarification, or retraction, the person may not recover exemplary damages.

(d) A request for a correction, clarification, or retraction is sufficient if it:

(1) is served on the publisher;

(2) is made in writing, reasonably identifies the person making the request, and is signed by the individual claiming to have been defamed or by the person's authorized attorney or agent;

(3) states with particularity the statement alleged to be false and defamatory and, to the extent known, the time and place of publication;

(4) alleges the defamatory meaning of the statement; and

(5) specifies the circumstances causing a defamatory meaning of the statement if it arises from something other than the express language of the publication.

(e) A period of limitation for commencement of an action under this section is tolled during the period allowed by Sections 73.056 and 73.057.

Added by Acts 2013, 83rd Leg., ch. 950 (H.B. 1759), § 2, eff. June 14, 2013.

§ 73.056. Disclosure of Evidence of Falsity

(a) A person who has been requested to make a correction, clarification, or retraction may ask the person making the request to provide reasonably available information regarding the falsity of the allegedly defamatory statement not later than the 30th day after the date the person receives the request. Any information requested under this section must be provided by the person seeking the correction, clarification, or retraction not later than the 30th day after the date the person receives the request.

(b) If a correction, clarification, or retraction is not made, a person who, without good cause, fails to disclose the information requested under Subsection (a) may not recover exemplary damages, unless the publication was made with actual malice.

Added by Acts 2013, 83rd Leg., ch. 950 (H.B. 1759), § 2, eff. June 14, 2013.

§ 73.057. Timely and Sufficient Correction, Clarification, or Retraction

(a) A correction, clarification, or retraction is timely if it is made not later than the 30th day after receipt of:

(1) the request for the correction, clarification, or retraction; or

(2) the information requested under Section 73.056(a).

(b) A correction, clarification, or retraction is sufficient if it is published in the same manner and medium as the original publication or, if that is not possible, with a prominence and in a manner and medium reasonably likely to reach substantially the same audience as the publication complained of and:

(1) is publication of an acknowledgment that the statement specified as false and defamatory is erroneous;

(2) is an allegation that the defamatory meaning arises from other than the express language of the publication and the publisher disclaims an intent to communicate that meaning or to assert its truth;

(3) is a statement attributed to another person whom the publisher identifies and the publisher disclaims an intent to assert the truth of the statement; or

(4) is publication of the requestor's statement of the facts, as set forth in a request for correction, clarification, or retraction, or a fair summary of the statement, exclusive of any portion that is defamatory of another, obscene, or otherwise improper for publication.

(c) If a request for correction, clarification, or retraction has specified two or more statements as false and defamatory, the correction, clarification, or retraction may deal with the statements individually in any manner provided by Subsection (b).

(d) Except as provided by Subsection (e), a correction, clarification, or retraction is published with a prominence and in a manner and medium reasonably likely to reach substantially the same audience as the publication complained of if:

(1) it is published in a later issue, edition, or broadcast of the original publication;

(2) publication is in the next practicable issue, edition, or broadcast of the original publication because the publication will not be published within the time limits established for a timely correction, clarification, or retraction; or

(3) the original publication no longer exists and if the correction, clarification, or retraction is published in the newspaper with the largest general circulation in the region in which the original publication was distributed.

(e) If the original publication was on the Internet, a correction, clarification, or retraction is published with a prominence and in a manner and medium reasonably likely to reach substantially the same audience as the publication complained of if the publisher appends to the original publication the correction, clarification, or retraction.

Added by Acts 2013, 83rd Leg., ch. 950 (H.B. 1759), § 2, eff. June 14, 2013.

§ 73.058. Challenges to Correction, Clarification, or Retraction or to Request for Correction, Clarification, or Retraction

(a) If a defendant in an action under this subchapter intends to rely on a timely and sufficient correction, clarification, or retraction, the defendant's intention to do so, and the correction, clarification, or retraction relied on, must be stated in a notice served on the plaintiff on the later of:

(1) the 60th day after service of the citation; or

(2) the 10th day after the date the correction, clarification, or retraction is made.

(b) A correction, clarification, or retraction is timely and sufficient unless the plaintiff challenges the timeliness or sufficiency not later than the 20th day after the date notice under Subsection (a) is served. If a plaintiff challenges the timeliness or sufficiency, the plaintiff must state the challenge in a motion to declare the correction, clarification, or retraction untimely or insufficient served not later than the 30th day after the date notice under Subsection (a) is served on the plaintiff or the 30th day after the date the correction, clarification, or retraction is made, whichever is later.

(c) If a defendant intends to challenge the sufficiency or timeliness of a request for a correction, clarification, or retraction, the defendant must state the challenge in a motion to declare the request insufficient or untimely served not later than the 60th day after the date of service of the citation.

(d) Unless there is a reasonable dispute regarding the actual contents of the request for correction, clarification, or retraction, the sufficiency and timeliness of a request for correction, clarification, or retraction is a question of law. At the earliest appropriate time before trial, the court shall rule, as a matter of law, whether the request for correction, clarification, or retraction meets the requirements of this subchapter.

Added by Acts 2013, 83rd Leg., ch. 950 (H.B. 1759), § 2, eff. June 14, 2013.

§ 73.059. Effect of Correction, Clarification, or Retraction

If a correction, clarification, or retraction is made in accordance with this subchapter, regardless of whether the person claiming harm made a request, a person may not recover exemplary damages unless the publication was made with actual malice.

Added by Acts 2013, 83rd Leg., ch. 950 (H.B. 1759), § 2, eff. June 14, 2013.

§ 73.060. Scope of Protection

A timely and sufficient correction, clarification, or retraction made by a person responsible for a publication constitutes a correction, clarification, or retraction made by all persons responsible for that publication but does not extend to an entity that republished the information.

Added by Acts 2013, 83rd Leg., ch. 950 (H.B. 1759), § 2, eff. June 14, 2013.

§ 73.061. Admissibility of Evidence of Correction, Clarification, or Retraction

(a) A request for a correction, clarification, or retraction, the contents of the request, and the acceptance or refusal of the request are not admissible evidence at a trial.

(b) The fact that a correction, clarification, or retraction was made and the contents of the correction, clarification, or retraction are not admissible in evidence at trial except in mitigation of damages under Section 73.003(a)(3). If a correction, clarification, or retraction is received into evidence, the request for the correction, clarification, or retraction may also be received into evidence.

(c) The fact that an offer of a correction, clarification, or retraction was made and the contents of the offer, and the fact that the correction, clarification, or retraction was refused, are not admissible in evidence at trial.

Added by Acts 2013, 83rd Leg., ch. 950 (H.B. 1759), § 2, eff. June 14, 2013.

§ 73.062. Abatement

(a) A person against whom a suit is pending who does not receive a written request for a correction, clarification, or retraction, as required by Section 73.055, may file a plea in abatement not later than the 30th day after the date the person files an original answer in the court in which the suit is pending.

(b) A suit is automatically abated, in its entirety, without the order of the court, beginning on the 11th day after the date a plea in abatement is filed under Subsection (a) if the plea in abatement:

(1) is verified and alleges that the person against whom the suit is pending did not receive the written request as required by Section 73.055; and

(2) is not controverted in an affidavit filed by the person bringing the claim before the 11th day after the date on which the plea in abatement is filed.

(c) An abatement under Subsection (b) continues until the 60th day after the date that the written request is served or a later date agreed to by the parties. If a controverting affidavit is filed under Subsection (b)(2), a hearing on the plea in abatement will take place as soon as practical considering the court's docket.

(d) All statutory and judicial deadlines under the Texas Rules of Civil Procedure relating to a suit abated under Subsection (b), other than those provided in this section, will be stayed during the pendency of the abatement period under this section.

Added by Acts 2013, 83rd Leg., ch. 950 (H.B. 1759), § 2, eff. June 14, 2013.

CHAPTER 74. MEDICAL LIABILITY

SUBCHAPTER A. GENERAL PROVISIONS

SUBCHAPTER B. NOTICE AND PLEADINGS

SUBCHAPTER C. INFORMED CONSENT

SUBCHAPTER D. EMERGENCY CARE

SUBCHAPTER E. RES IPSA LOQUITUR

SUBCHAPTER F. STATUTE OF LIMITATIONS

SUBCHAPTER G. LIABILITY LIMITS

SUBCHAPTER H. PROCEDURAL PROVISIONS

SUBCHAPTER I. EXPERT WITNESSES

SUBCHAPTER J. ARBITRATION AGREEMENTS

SUBCHAPTER K. PAYMENT FOR FUTURE LOSSES

Acts 2003, 78th Leg., ch. 204, § 10.01 amended Chapter 74 effective September 1, 2003. The former Chapter 74, Good Samaritan Law: Liability for Emergency Care, consisting of V.T.C.A., Civil Practice & Remedies Code §§ 74.001 and 74.002, was revised as Chapter 74, Medical Liability, consisting of V.T.C.A., Civil Practice & Remedies Code §§ 74.001 to 74.507.

SUBCHAPTER A. GENERAL PROVISIONS

§ 74.001. Definitions

(a) In this chapter:

(1) "Affiliate" means a person who, directly or indirectly, through one or more intermediaries, controls, is controlled by, or is under common control with a specified person, including any direct or indirect parent or subsidiary.

(2) "Claimant" means a person, including a decedent's estate, seeking or who has sought recovery of damages in a health care liability claim. All persons claiming to have sustained damages as the result of the bodily injury or death of a single person are considered a single claimant.

(3) "Control" means the possession, directly or indirectly, of the power to direct or cause the direction of the management and policies of the person, whether through ownership of equity or securities, by contract, or otherwise.

(4) "Court" means any federal or state court.

(5) "Disclosure panel" means the Texas Medical Disclosure Panel.

(6) "Economic damages" has the meaning assigned by Section 41.001.

(7) "Emergency medical care" means bona fide emergency services provided after the sudden onset of a medical or traumatic condition manifesting itself by acute symptoms of sufficient severity, including severe pain, such that the absence of immediate medical attention could reasonably be expected to result in placing the patient's health in serious jeopardy, serious impairment to bodily functions, or serious dysfunction of any bodily organ or part. The term does not include medical care or treatment that occurs after the patient is stabilized and is capable of receiving medical treatment as a nonemergency patient or that is unrelated to the original medical emergency.

(8) "Emergency medical services provider" means a licensed public or private provider to which Chapter 773, Health and Safety Code, applies.

(9) "Gross negligence" has the meaning assigned by Section 41.001.

(10) "Health care" means any act or treatment performed or furnished, or that should have been performed or furnished, by any health care provider for, to, or on behalf of a patient during the patient's medical care, treatment, or confinement.

(11) "Health care institution" includes:

(A) an ambulatory surgical center;

(B) an assisted living facility licensed under Chapter 247, Health and Safety Code;

(C) an emergency medical services provider;

(D) a health services district created under Chapter 287, Health and Safety Code;

(E) a home and community support services agency;

(F) a hospice;

(G) a hospital;

(H) a hospital system;

(I) an intermediate care facility for the mentally retarded or a home and community-based services waiver program for persons with mental retardation adopted in accordance with Section 1915(c) of the federal Social Security Act (42 U.S.C. Section 1396n), as amended;

(J) a nursing home; or

(K) an end stage renal disease facility licensed under Section 251.011, Health and Safety Code.

(12)(A) "Health care provider" means any person, partnership, professional association, corporation, facility, or institution duly licensed, certified, registered, or chartered by the State of Texas to provide health care, including:

(i) a registered nurse;

(ii) a dentist;

(iii) a podiatrist;

(iv) a pharmacist;

(v) a chiropractor;

(vi) an optometrist;

(vii) a health care institution; or

(viii) a health care collaborative certified under Chapter 848, Insurance Code.

(B) The term includes:

(i) an officer, director, shareholder, member, partner, manager, owner, or affiliate of a health care provider or physician; and

(ii) an employee, independent contractor, or agent of a health care provider or physician acting in the course and scope of the employment or contractual relationship.

(13) "Health care liability claim" means a cause of action against a health care provider or physician for treatment, lack of treatment, or other claimed departure from accepted standards of medical care, or health care, or safety or professional or administrative services directly related to health care, which proximately results in injury to or death of a claimant, whether the claimant's claim or cause of action sounds in tort or contract. The term does not include a cause of action described by Section 406.033(a) or 408.001(b), Labor Code, against an employer by an employee or the employee's surviving spouse or heir.

(14) "Home and community support services agency" means a licensed public or provider agency to which Chapter 142, Health and Safety Code, applies.

(15) "Hospice" means a hospice facility or activity to which Chapter 142, Health and Safety Code, applies.

(16) "Hospital" means a licensed public or private institution as defined in Chapter 241, Health and Safety Code, or licensed under Chapter 577, Health and Safety Code.

(17) "Hospital system" means a system of hospitals located in this state that are under the common governance or control of a corporate parent.

(18) "Intermediate care facility for the mentally retarded" means a licensed public or private institution to which Chapter 252, Health and Safety Code, applies.

(19) "Medical care" means any act defined as practicing medicine under Section 151.002, Occupations Code, performed or furnished, or which should have been performed, by one licensed to practice medicine in this state for, to, or on behalf of a patient during the patient's care, treatment, or confinement.

(20) "Noneconomic damages" has the meaning assigned by Section 41.001.

(21) "Nursing home" means a licensed public or private institution to which Chapter 242, Health and Safety Code, applies.

(22) "Pharmacist" means one licensed under Chapter 551, Occupations Code, who, for the purposes of this chapter, performs those activities limited to the dispensing of prescription medicines which result in health care liability claims and does not include any other cause of action that may exist at common law against them, including but not limited to causes of action for the sale of mishandled or defective products.

(23) "Physician" means:

(A) an individual licensed to practice medicine in this state;

(B) a professional association organized under the Texas Professional Association Act (Article 1528f, Vernon's Texas Civil Statutes) by an individual physician or group of physicians;

(C) a partnership or limited liability partnership formed by a group of physicians;

(D) a nonprofit health corporation certified under Section 162.001, Occupations Code; or

(E) a company formed by a group of physicians under the Texas Limited Liability Company Act (Article 1528n, Vernon's Texas Civil Statutes).

(24) "Professional or administrative services" means those duties or services that a physician or health care provider is required to provide as a condition of maintaining the physician's or health care provider's license, accreditation status, or certification to participate in state or federal health care programs.

(25) "Representative" means the spouse, parent, guardian, trustee, authorized attorney, or other authorized legal agent of the patient or claimant.

(b) Any legal term or word of art used in this chapter, not otherwise defined in this chapter, shall have such meaning as is consistent with the common law.

Added by Acts 2003, 78th Leg., ch. 204, § 10.01, eff. Sept. 1, 2003. Amended by Acts 2011, 82nd Leg., 1st C.S., ch. 7 (S.B. 7), § 4.02, eff. Sept. 28, 2011; Acts 2015, 84th Leg., ch. 728 (H.B. 1403), § 1, eff. Sept. 1, 2015.

§ 74.002. Conflict with Other Law and Rules of Civil Procedure

(a) In the event of a conflict between this chapter and another law, including a rule of procedure or evidence or court rule, this chapter controls to the extent of the conflict.

(b) Notwithstanding Subsection (a), in the event of a conflict between this chapter and Section 101.023, 102.003, or 108.002, those sections of this code control to the extent of the conflict.

(c) The district courts and statutory county courts in a county may not adopt local rules in conflict with this chapter.

Added by Acts 2003, 78th Leg., ch. 204, § 10.01, eff. Sept. 1, 2003.

§ 74.003. Sovereign Immunity Not Waived

This chapter does not waive sovereign immunity from suit or from liability.

Added by Acts 2003, 78th Leg., ch. 204, § 10.01, eff. Sept. 1, 2003.

§ 74.004. Exception from Certain Laws

(a) Notwithstanding any other law, Sections 17.41–17.63, Business & Commerce Code, do not apply to physicians or health care providers with respect to claims for damages for personal injury or death resulting, or alleged to have resulted, from negligence on the part of any physician or health care provider.

(b) This section does not apply to pharmacists.

Added by Acts 2003, 78th Leg., ch. 204, § 10.01, eff. Sept. 1, 2003.

SUBCHAPTER B. NOTICE AND PLEADINGS

§ 74.051. Notice

(a) Any person or his authorized agent asserting a health care liability claim shall give written notice of such claim by certified mail, return receipt requested, to each physician or health care provider against whom such claim is being made at least 60 days before the filing of a suit in any court of this state based upon a health care liability claim. The notice must be accompanied by the authorization form for release of protected health information as required under Section 74.052.

(b) In such pleadings as are subsequently filed in any court, each party shall state that it has fully complied with the provisions of this section and Section 74.052 and shall provide such evidence thereof as the judge of the court may require to determine if the provisions of this chapter have been met.

(c) Notice given as provided in this chapter shall toll the applicable statute of limitations to and including a period of 75 days following the giving of the notice, and this tolling shall apply to all parties and potential parties.

(d) All parties shall be entitled to obtain complete and unaltered copies of the patient's medical records from any other party within 45 days from the date of receipt of a written request for such records; provided, however, that the receipt of a medical authorization in the form required by Section 74.052 executed by the claimant herein shall be considered compliance by the claimant with this subsection.

(e) For the purposes of this section, and notwithstanding Chapter 159, Occupations Code, or any other law, a request for the medical records of a deceased person or a person who is incompetent shall be deemed to be valid if accompanied by an authorization in the form required by Section 74.052 signed by a parent, spouse, or adult child of the deceased or incompetent person.

Added by Acts 2003, 78th Leg., ch. 204, § 10.01, eff. Sept. 1, 2003.

§ 74.052. Authorization Form for Release of Protected Health Information

(a) Notice of a health care claim under Section 74.051 must be accompanied by a medical authorization in the form specified by this section. Failure to provide this authorization along with the notice of health care claim shall abate all further proceedings against the physician or health care provider receiving the notice until 60 days following receipt by the physician or health care provider of the required authorization.

(b) If the authorization required by this section is modified or revoked, the physician or health care provider to whom the authorization has been given shall have the option to abate all further proceedings until 60 days following receipt of a replacement authorization that must comply with the form specified by this section.

(c) The medical authorization required by this section shall be in the following form and shall be construed in accordance with the "Standards for Privacy of Individually Identifiable Health Information" (45 C.F.R. Parts 160 and 164).

AUTHORIZATION FORM FOR RELEASE OF PROTECTED HEALTH INFORMATION

Patient Name:____________________
Patient Date of Birth:____________________
Patient Address:____________________
________ Street ________ City, State, ZIP
Patient Telephone:____________________
Patient E-mail:____________________

NOTICE TO PHYSICIAN OR HEALTH CARE PROVIDER: THIS AUTHORIZATION FORM HAS BEEN AUTHORIZED BY THE TEXAS LEGISLATURE PURSUANT TO SECTION 74.052, CIVIL PRACTICE AND REMEDIES CODE. YOU ARE REQUIRED TO PROVIDE THE MEDICAL AND BILLING RECORDS AS REQUESTED IN THIS AUTHORIZATION.

A. I, ________ (name of patient or authorized representative), hereby authorize ________ (name of physician or other health care provider to whom the notice of health care claim is directed) to obtain and disclose (within the parameters set out below) the protected health information and associated billing records described below for the following specific purposes (check all that apply):

[ ] To facilitate the investigation and evaluation of the health care claim described in the accompanying Notice of Health Care Claim.

[ ] Defense of any litigation arising out of the claim made the basis of the accompanying Notice of Health Care Claim.

[ ] Other—Specify:____________

B. The health information to be obtained, used, or disclosed extends to and includes the verbal as well as written and electronic and is specifically described as follows:

1. The health information and billing records in the custody of the physicians or health care providers who have examined, evaluated, or treated ________ (patient) in connection with the injuries alleged to have been sustained in connection with

the claim asserted in the accompanying Notice of Health Care Claim.

Names and current addresses of treating physicians or health care providers:

1.__________________
2.__________________
3.__________________
4.__________________
5.__________________
6.__________________
7.__________________
8.__________________

This authorization extends to an additional physician or health care provider that may in the future evaluate, examine, or treat __________ (patient) for injuries alleged in connection with the claim made the basis of the attached Notice of Health Care Claim only if the claimant gives notice to the recipient of the attached Notice of Health Care Claim of that additional physician or health care provider;

2. The health information and billing records in the custody of the following physicians or health care providers who have examined, evaluated, or treated __________ (patient) during a period commencing five years prior to the incident made the basis of the accompanying Notice of Health Care Claim.

Names and current addresses of treating physicians or health care providers, if applicable:

1.__________________
2.__________________
3.__________________
4.__________________
5.__________________
6.__________________
7.__________________
8.__________________

C. Exclusions

1. Providers excluded from authorization.

The following constitutes a list of physicians or health care providers possessing health care information concerning __________ (patient) to whom this authorization does not apply because I contend that such health care information is not relevant to the damages being claimed or to the physical, mental, or emotional condition of __________ (patient) arising out of the claim made the basis of the accompanying Notice of Health Care Claim. List the names of each physician or health care provider to whom this authorization does not extend and the inclusive dates of examination, evaluation, or treatment to be withheld from disclosure, or state "none":

1.__________________
2.__________________
3.__________________
4.__________________
5.__________________
6.__________________
7.__________________
8.__________________

2. By initialing below, the patient or patient's personal or legal representative excludes the following information from this authorization:

________ HIV/AIDS test results and/or treatment

________ Drug/alcohol/substance abuse treatment

________ Mental health records (mental health records do not include psychotherapy notes)

________ Genetic information (including genetic test results)

D. The persons or class of persons to whom the patient's health information and billing records will be disclosed or who will make use of said information are:

1. Any and all physicians or health care providers providing care or treatment to __________ (patient);

2. Any liability insurance entity providing liability insurance coverage or defense to any physician or health care provider to whom Notice of Health Care Claim has been given with regard to the care and treatment of __________ (patient);

3. Any consulting or testifying experts employed by or on behalf of __________ (name of physician or health care provider to whom Notice of Health Care Claim has been given) with regard to the matter set out in the Notice of Health Care Claim accompanying this authorization;

4. Any attorneys (including secretarial, clerical, experts, or paralegal staff) employed by or on behalf of __________ (name of physician or health care provider to whom Notice of Health Care Claim has been given) with regard to the matter set out in the Notice of Health Care Claim accompanying this authorization;

5. Any trier of the law or facts relating to any suit filed seeking damages arising out of the medical care or treatment of __________ (patient).

E. This authorization shall expire upon resolution of the claim asserted or at the conclusion of any litigation instituted in connection with the subject matter of the Notice of Health Care Claim accompanying this authorization, whichever occurs sooner.

F. I understand that, without exception, I have the right to revoke this authorization at any time by giving notice in writing to the person or persons named in Section B above of my intent to revoke this authorization. I understand that prior actions taken in reliance on this authorization by a person that had permission to access my protected health information will not be affected. I further understand the consequence of any such revocation as set out in Section 74.052, Civil Practice and Remedies Code.

G. I understand that the signing of this authorization is not a condition for continued treatment, payment, enrollment, or eligibility for health plan benefits.

H. I understand that information used or disclosed pursuant to this authorization may be subject to redisclosure by the recipient and may no longer be protected by federal HIPAA privacy regulations.

Name of Patient

____

Signature of Patient/Personal or Legal Representative

____

Description of Personal or Legal Representative's Authority

____

Date

____

Added by Acts 2003, 78th Leg., ch. 204, § 10.01, eff. Sept. 1, 2003. Amended by Acts 2017, 85th Leg., ch. 506 (H.B. 2891), § 1, eff. June 9, 2017; Acts 2019, 86th Leg., ch. 115 (S.B. 1565), § 1, eff. Sept. 1, 2019.

§ 74.053. Pleadings Not to State Damage Amount; Special Exception; Exclusion from Section

Pleadings in a suit based on a health care liability claim shall not specify an amount of money claimed as damages. The defendant may file a special exception to the pleadings on the ground the suit is not within the court's jurisdiction, in which event the plaintiff shall inform the court and defendant in writing of the total dollar amount claimed. This section does not prevent a party from mentioning the total dollar amount claimed in examining prospective jurors on voir dire or in argument to the court or jury.

Added by Acts 2003, 78th Leg., ch. 204, § 10.01, eff. Sept. 1, 2003.

SUBCHAPTER C. INFORMED CONSENT

§ 74.101. Theory of Recovery

In a suit against a physician or health care provider involving a health care liability claim that is based on the failure of the physician or health care provider to disclose or adequately disclose the risks and hazards involved in the medical care or surgical procedure rendered by the physician or health care provider, the only theory on which recovery may be obtained is that of negligence in failing to disclose the risks or hazards that could have influenced a reasonable person in making a decision to give or withhold consent.

Added by Acts 2003, 78th Leg., ch. 204, § 10.01, eff. Sept. 1, 2003.

§ 74.102. Texas Medical Disclosure Panel

(a) The Texas Medical Disclosure Panel is created to determine which risks and hazards related to medical care and surgical procedures must be disclosed by health care providers or physicians to their patients or persons authorized to consent for their patients and to establish the general form and substance of such disclosure.

(b) The disclosure panel established herein is administratively attached to the Texas Department of Health. The Texas Department of Health, at the request of the disclosure panel, shall provide administrative assistance to the panel; and the Texas Department of Health and the disclosure panel shall coordinate administrative responsibilities in order to avoid unnecessary duplication of facilities and services. The Texas Department of Health, at the request of the panel, shall submit the panel's budget request to the legislature. The panel shall be subject, except where inconsistent, to the rules and procedures of the Texas Department of Health; however, the duties and responsibilities of the panel as set forth in this chapter shall be exercised solely by the disclosure panel, and the board or Texas Department of Health shall have no authority or responsibility with respect to same.

(c) The disclosure panel is composed of nine members, with three members licensed to practice law in this state and six members licensed to practice medicine in this state. Members of the disclosure panel shall be selected by the commissioner of health.

(d) At the expiration of the term of each member of the disclosure panel so appointed, the commissioner shall select a successor, and such successor shall serve for a term of six years, or until his successor is selected. Any member who is absent for three consecutive meetings without the consent of a majority of the disclosure panel present at each such meeting may be removed by the commissioner at the request of the disclosure panel submitted in writing and signed by the chairman. Upon the death, resignation, or removal of any member, the commissioner shall fill the vacancy by selection for the unexpired portion of the term.

(e) Members of the disclosure panel are not entitled to compensation for their services, but each panelist is entitled to reimbursement of any necessary expense incurred in the performance of his duties on the panel, including necessary travel expenses.

(f) Meetings of the panel shall be held at the call of the chairman or on petition of at least three members of the panel. Notwithstanding Chapter 551, Government Code, or any other law, if any member of the panel is physically present at a meeting, any number of the other members of the panel may attend the meeting by use of telephone conference call, videoconferencing, or other similar telecommunication method for purposes of establishing a quorum or voting or for any other meeting purpose allowing a panel member to fully participate in any panel meeting. This subsection applies without regard to the subject matter discussed or considered by the panel at the meeting. A meeting held by telephone conference call, videoconferencing, or other similar telecommunication method:

(1) is subject to the notice requirements applicable to other meetings of the panel;

(2) may not be held unless the notice of the meeting specifies the location of the meeting at which a member of the panel will be physically present;

(3) must be open to the public and audible to the public at the location specified in the notice under Subdivision (2); and

(4) must provide two-way audio communication between all panel members attending the meeting during the entire meeting, and, if the two-way audio communication link with any member attending the meeting is disrupted at any time, the meeting may not continue until the two-way audio communication link is reestablished.

(g) At the first meeting of the panel each year after its members assume their positions, the panelists shall select one of the panel members to serve as chairman and one of the panel members to serve as vice chairman, and each such officer shall serve for a term of one year. The chairman shall preside at meetings of the panel, and in his absence, the vice chairman shall preside.

(h) Employees of the Texas Department of Health shall serve as the staff for the panel.

Added by Acts 2003, 78th Leg., ch. 204, § 10.01, eff. Sept. 1, 2003. Amended by Acts 2005, 79th Leg., ch. 1287, § 1, eff. June 18, 2005.

§ 74.103. Duties of Disclosure Panel

(a) To the extent feasible, the panel shall identify and make a thorough examination of all medical treatments and surgical procedures in which physicians and health care providers may be involved in order to determine which of those treatments and procedures do and do not require disclosure of the risks and hazards to the patient or person authorized to consent for the patient.

(b) The panel shall prepare separate lists of those medical treatments and surgical procedures that do and do not require disclosure and, for those treatments and procedures that do require disclosure, shall establish the degree of disclosure required and the form in which the disclosure will be made. Each provision of a disclosure form prepared under this subsection must be made available in English and Spanish.

(c) Lists prepared under Subsection (b) together with written explanations of the degree and form of disclosure shall be published in the Texas Register.

(d) At least annually, or at such other period the panel may determine from time to time, the panel will identify and examine any new medical treatments and surgical procedures that have been developed since its last determinations, shall assign them to the proper list, and shall establish the degree of disclosure required and the form in which the disclosure will be made. The panel will also examine such treatments and procedures for the purpose of revising lists previously published. These determinations shall be published in the Texas Register.

Added by Acts 2003, 78th Leg., ch. 204, § 10.01, eff. Sept. 1, 2003. Amended by Acts 2005, 79th Leg., ch. 307, § 1, eff. Sept. 1, 2005.

§ 74.104. Duty of Physician or Health Care Provider

Before a patient or a person authorized to consent for a patient gives consent to any medical care or surgical procedure that appears on the disclosure panel's list requiring disclosure, the physician or health care provider shall disclose to the patient or person authorized to consent for the patient the risks and hazards involved in that kind of care or procedure. A physician or health care provider shall be considered to have complied with the requirements of this section if disclosure is made as provided in Section 74.105.

Added by Acts 2003, 78th Leg., ch. 204, § 10.01, eff. Sept. 1, 2003.

§ 74.105. Manner of Disclosure

Consent to medical care that appears on the disclosure panel's list requiring disclosure shall be considered effective under this chapter if it is given in writing, signed by the patient or a person authorized to give the consent and by a competent witness, and if the written consent specifically states the risks and hazards that are involved in the medical care or surgical procedure in the form and to the degree required by the disclosure panel under Section 74.103.

Added by Acts 2003, 78th Leg., ch. 204, § 10.01, eff. Sept. 1, 2003.

§ 74.106. Effect of Disclosure

(a) In a suit against a physician or health care provider involving a health care liability claim that is based on the negligent failure of the physician or health care provider to disclose or adequately disclose the risks and hazards involved in the medical care or surgical procedure rendered by the physician or health care provider:

(1) both disclosure made as provided in Section 74.104 and failure to disclose based on inclusion of any medical care or surgical procedure on the panel's list for which disclosure is not required shall be admissible in evidence and shall create a rebuttable presumption that the requirements of Sections 74.104 and 74.105 have been complied with and this presumption shall be included in the charge to the jury; and

(2) failure to disclose the risks and hazards involved in any medical care or surgical procedure required to be disclosed under Sections 74.104 and 74.105 shall be admissible in evidence and shall create a rebuttable presumption of a negligent failure to conform to the duty of disclosure set forth in Sections 74.104 and 74.105, and this presumption shall be included in the charge to the jury; but failure to disclose may be found not to be negligent if there was an emergency or if for some other reason it was not medically feasible to make a disclosure of the kind that would otherwise have been negligence.

(b) If medical care or surgical procedure is rendered with respect to which the disclosure panel has made no determination either way regarding a duty of disclosure, the physician or health care provider is under the duty otherwise imposed by law.

Added by Acts 2003, 78th Leg., ch. 204, § 10.01, eff. Sept. 1, 2003.

§ 74.107. Informed Consent for Hysterectomies

(a) The disclosure panel shall develop and prepare written materials to inform a patient or person authorized to consent for a patient of the risks and hazards of a hysterectomy.

(b) The materials shall be available in English, Spanish, and any other language the panel considers appropriate. The information must be presented in a manner understandable to a layperson.

(c) The materials must include:

(1) a notice that a decision made at any time to refuse to undergo a hysterectomy will not result in the withdrawal or withholding of any benefits provided by programs or projects receiving federal funds or otherwise affect the patient's right to future care or treatment;

(2) the name of the person providing and explaining the materials;

(3) a statement that the patient or person authorized to consent for the patient understands that the hysterectomy is permanent and nonreversible and that the patient will not be able to become pregnant or bear children if she undergoes a hysterectomy;

(4) a statement that the patient has the right to seek a consultation from a second physician;

(5) a statement that the patient or person authorized to consent for the patient has been informed that a hysterectomy is a removal of the uterus through an incision in the lower abdomen or vagina and that additional surgery may be necessary to remove or repair other organs, including an ovary, tube, appendix, bladder, rectum, or vagina;

(6) a description of the risks and hazards involved in the performance of the procedure; and

(7) a written statement to be signed by the patient or person authorized to consent for the patient indicating that the materials have been provided and explained to the patient or person authorized to consent for the patient and that the patient or

person authorized to consent for the patient understands the nature and consequences of a hysterectomy.

(d) The physician or health care provider shall obtain informed consent under this section and Section 74.104 from the patient or person authorized to consent for the patient before performing a hysterectomy unless the hysterectomy is performed in a life-threatening situation in which the physician determines obtaining informed consent is not reasonably possible. If obtaining informed consent is not reasonably possible, the physician or health care provider shall include in the patient's medical records a written statement signed by the physician certifying the nature of the emergency.

(e) The disclosure panel may not prescribe materials under this section without first consulting with the Texas State Board of Medical Examiners.

Added by Acts 2003, 78th Leg., ch. 204, § 10.01, eff. Sept. 1, 2003.

SUBCHAPTER D. EMERGENCY CARE

§ 74.151. Liability for Emergency Care

(a) A person who in good faith administers emergency care is not liable in civil damages for an act performed during the emergency unless the act is wilfully or wantonly negligent, including a person who:

(1) administers emergency care using an automated external defibrillator; or

(2) administers emergency care as a volunteer who is a first responder as the term is defined under Section 421.095, Government Code.

(b) This section does not apply to care administered:

(1) for or in expectation of remuneration, provided that being legally entitled to receive remuneration for the emergency care rendered shall not determine whether or not the care was administered for or in anticipation of remuneration; or

(2) by a person who was at the scene of the emergency because he or a person he represents as an agent was soliciting business or seeking to perform a service for remuneration.

(c), (d) Deleted by Acts 2003, 78th Leg., ch. 204, § 10.01.

(e) Except as provided by this subsection, this section does not apply to a person whose negligent act or omission was a producing cause of the emergency for which care is being administered. This subsection does not apply to liability of a school district or district school officer or employee arising from an act or omission under a program or practice or procedure developed under Subchapter G, Chapter 38, Education Code, other than liability arising from wilful or intentional misconduct.

Acts 1985, 69th Leg., ch. 959, § 1, eff. Sept. 1, 1985. Amended by Acts 1993, 73rd Leg., ch. 960, § 1, eff. Aug. 30, 1993; Acts 1999, 76th Leg., ch. 679, § 2, eff. Sept. 1, 1999. Renumbered from V.T.C.A., Civil Practice & Remedies Code § 74.001 and amended by Acts 2003, 78th Leg., ch. 204, § 10.01, eff. Sept. 1, 2003. Amended by Acts 2007, 80th Leg., ch. 705, § 1, eff. June 15, 2007; Acts 2013, 83rd Leg., ch. 1321 (S.B. 460), § 1, eff. Sept. 1, 2013; Acts 2019, 86th Leg., ch. 352 (H.B. 18), § 3.01, eff. Dec. 1, 2019.

Section 4.03 of Acts 2019, 86th Leg., ch. 352 (H.B. 18) provides:

"Any change in law made by this Act that imposes a new duty or requirement on a school district or an open-enrollment charter school applies beginning with the 2020–2021 school year."

§ 74.152. Unlicensed Medical Personnel

Persons not licensed or certified in the healing arts who in good faith administer emergency care as emergency medical service personnel are not liable in civil damages for an act performed in administering the care unless the act is wilfully or wantonly negligent. This section applies without regard to whether the care is provided for or in expectation of remuneration.

Acts 1985, 69th Leg., ch. 959, § 1, eff. Sept. 1, 1985. Renumbered from V.T.C.A., Civil Practice & Remedies Code § 74.002 and amended by Acts 2003, 78th Leg., ch. 204, § 10.01, eff. Sept. 1, 2003.

§ 74.153. Standard of Proof in Cases Involving Emergency Medical Care

(a) Except as provided by Subsection (b), in a suit involving a health care liability claim against a physician or health care provider for injury to or death of a patient arising out of the provision of emergency medical care in a hospital emergency department, in an obstetrical unit, or in a surgical suite immediately following the evaluation or treatment of a patient in a hospital emergency department, the claimant bringing the suit may prove that the treatment or lack of treatment by the physician or health care provider departed from accepted standards of medical care or health care only if the claimant shows by a preponderance of the evidence that the physician or health care provider, with willful and wanton negligence, deviated from the degree of care and skill that is reasonably expected of an ordinarily prudent physician or health care provider in the same or similar circumstances.

(b) Subsection (a) does not apply to:

(1) medical care or treatment:

(A) provided after the patient is:

(i) stabilized; and

(ii) receiving medical care or treatment as a non-emergency patient; or

(B) that is unrelated to a medical emergency; or

(2) a physician or health care provider whose negligent act or omission proximately causes a stable patient to require emergency medical care.

Added by Acts 2003, 78th Leg., ch. 204, § 10.01, eff. Sept. 1, 2003. Amended by Acts 2019, 86th Leg., ch. 1364 (H.B. 2362), § 1, eff. Sept. 1, 2019.

Section 2 of Acts 2019, 86th Leg., ch. 1364 (H.B. 2362) provides:

"Section 74.153, Civil Practice and Remedies Code, as amended by this Act, applies only to an action commenced on or after the effective date [Sept. 1, 2019] of this Act. An action commenced before the effective date of this Act is governed by the law applicable to the action immediately before the effective date of this Act, and that law is continued in effect for that purpose."

§ 74.154. Jury Instructions in Cases Involving Emergency Medical Care

(a) In an action for damages that involves a claim of negligence arising from the provision of emergency medical care in a hospital emergency department or obstetrical unit or in a surgical suite immediately following the evaluation or treatment of a patient in a hospital emergency department, the court shall instruct the jury to consider, together with all other relevant matters:

(1) whether the person providing care did or did not have the patient's medical history or was able or unable to obtain a full medical history, including the knowledge of preexisting medical conditions, allergies, and medications;

(2) the presence or lack of a preexisting physician-patient relationship or health care provider-patient relationship;

(3) the circumstances constituting the emergency; and

(4) the circumstances surrounding the delivery of the emergency medical care.

(b) The provisions of Subsection (a) do not apply to medical care or treatment:

(1) that occurs after the patient is stabilized and is capable of receiving medical treatment as a non-emergency patient;

(2) that is unrelated to the original medical emergency; or

(3) that is related to an emergency caused in whole or in part by the negligence of the defendant.

Added by Acts 2003, 78th Leg., ch. 204, § 10.01, eff. Sept. 1, 2003.

§ 74.155. Liability of Physicians, Health Care Providers, and First Responders During Pandemic

(a) In this section:

(1) "Disaster declaration" means a declaration of a state of disaster or emergency by the president of the United States applicable to the entire state, a declaration of a state of disaster by the governor under Chapter 418, Government Code, for the entire state, and any amendment, modification, or extension of the declaration.

(2) "First responder" has the meaning assigned by Section 421.095, Government Code.

(3) "Pandemic disease" means an infectious disease that spreads to a significant portion of the population of the United States and that poses a substantial risk of a significant number of human fatalities, illnesses, or permanent long-term disabilities.

(b) Except in a case of reckless conduct or intentional, wilful, or wanton misconduct, a physician, health care provider, or first responder is not liable for an injury, including economic and noneconomic damages, or death arising from care, treatment, or failure to provide care or treatment relating to or impacted by a pandemic disease or a disaster declaration related to a pandemic disease if the physician, health care provider, or first responder proves by a preponderance of the evidence that:

(1) a pandemic disease or disaster declaration related to a pandemic disease was a producing cause of the care, treatment, or failure to provide care or treatment that allegedly caused the injury or death; or

(2) the individual who suffered injury or death was diagnosed or reasonably suspected to be infected with a pandemic disease at the time of the care, treatment, or failure to provide care or treatment.

(c) A physician, health care provider, or first responder may not use the showing under Subsection (b)(2) as a defense to liability under Subsection (b) for negligent care, treatment, or failure to provide care or treatment if a claimant proves by a preponderance of the evidence that the respective diagnosis, treatment, or reasonable suspicion of infection with a pandemic disease at the time of the care, treatment, or failure to provide care or treatment was not a producing cause of the individual's injury or death.

(d) Care, treatment, or failure to provide care or treatment relating to or impacted by a pandemic disease or a disaster declaration related to a pandemic disease under Subsection (b) includes:

(1) screening, assessing, diagnosing, or treating an individual who is infected or suspected of being infected with a pandemic disease;

(2) prescribing, administering, or dispensing a drug or medicine for off-label or investigational use to treat an individual who is infected or suspected of being infected with a pandemic disease;

(3) diagnosing or treating an individual who is infected or suspected of being infected with a pandemic disease outside the normal area of the physician's or provider's specialty, if any;

(4) delaying or canceling nonurgent or elective medical, surgical, or dental procedures;

(5) delaying, canceling, or not accepting in-person appointments for office or clinical visits, diagnostic tests, scheduled treatment, physical or occupational therapy, or any other diagnosis or treatment of an illness or condition not related to a pandemic disease;

(6) using medical devices, equipment, or supplies outside of their normal use, including using or modifying such devices, equipment, or supplies for an unapproved use, to treat an individual who is infected or suspected of being infected with a pandemic disease;

(7) conducting tests on or providing treatment to an individual who is infected or suspected of being infected with a pandemic disease outside the premises of a health care facility;

(8) acts or omissions caused by a lack of personnel or staffing, facilities, medical devices, supplies, or other resources attributable to a pandemic disease that renders a physician, health care provider, or first responder unable to provide the same level or manner of care to any individual that otherwise would have been acquired in the absence of the disease; and

(9) acts or omissions arising from the use or nonuse of personal protective equipment.

(e) This section does not alter the scope of practice of a physician, health care provider, or first responder under the laws of this state.

(f) A defense under this section is in addition to any other defense, immunity, or limitation of liability provided by law. This section does not constitute a waiver of sovereign immunity of this state or governmental immunity of a political subdivision.

(g) A physician, health care provider, or first responder who intends to raise a defense under Subsection (b) must provide to a claimant specific facts that support an assertion under Subsection (b)(1) or (2) not later than the later of:

(1) the 60th day after the date the claimant serves an expert report on the physician, health care provider, or first responder under Section 74.351; or

(2) the 120th day after the date the physician, health care provider, or first responder files an original answer in the suit.

(h) This section applies only to a claim arising from care, treatment, or failure to provide care or treatment that occurred during a period beginning on the date that the president of the United States or the governor makes a disaster declaration related to a pandemic disease and ending on the date the declaration terminates.

(i) This section does not create a civil cause of action.

Added by Acts 2021, 87th Leg., ch. 528 (S.B. 6), § 2, eff. June 14, 2021.

Sections 4 and 5 of Acts 2021, 87th Leg., ch. 528 (S.B. 6) provide:

"Sec. 4. (a) For purposes of Section 74.155, Civil Practice and Remedies Code, as added by this Act, the legislature finds that:

"(1) the widespread effect of Coronavirus Disease 2019 ("COVID–19") in this state has resulted in a state of disaster as declared by the governor under Section 418.014, Government Code;

"(2) the frequency and severity of such cases in this state have severely taxed the physicians and health care providers, including health care institutions, stressed the state's health care system, and created shortages of medical staff, therapeutics, hospital beds, testing equipment, and safety supplies;

"(3) physicians and health care providers often have inadequate facilities to respond to the disaster;

"(4) physicians and health care providers often have inadequate test kits and monitoring devices to properly assess all those presenting themselves for care or treatment;

"(5) because of the number and severity of cases, many physicians and health care providers in this state have been forced to prioritize care and treatment;

"(6) many physicians and health care providers have placed themselves, their loved ones, and their livelihoods at risk by trying to respond to the disaster;

"(7) at the current time, there is no certainty as far as how long this crisis will last;

"(8) a pandemic, including the COVID–19 pandemic, requires an enormous response from governments working in coordination with physicians and health care providers in the community;

"(9) protecting physicians and health care providers from unnecessary liability supports their efforts during a pandemic, including the COVID–19 pandemic; and

"(10) there is a strong public interest to be served by this Act.

"(b) Because of the conditions stated in Subsection (a) of this section, the purpose of Section 74.155, Civil Practice and Remedies Code, as added by this Act, is to improve and modify the system by which health care liability claims are determined in order to:

"(1) promote the public health, safety, and welfare of all citizens and ensure access to care and treatment during a pandemic by broadly protecting physicians and health care providers, including health care institutions, in this state from liability that may relate to the care or treatment of individuals associated with a pandemic, including COVID-19;

"(2) provide for prompt and swift medical and health care responses to the citizens of this state suffering from COVID-19;

"(3) recognize that many physicians and health care providers responding to these situations may not have the full benefits of the medical devices and facilities they would in non-disaster situations;

"(4) encourage physicians and health care providers from other states to respond, if necessary, to the COVID-19 disaster in this state as declared by the president of the United States and by the governor; and

"(5) ensure that the focus and resources of physicians and health care providers in responding to the COVID-19 disaster are being addressed.

"(c) For purposes of Section 74.155 and Chapter 148, Civil Practice and Remedies Code, as added by this Act, the legislature finds that while some settled expectations regarding claims to which this Act applies may be impaired by this Act, the Act serves a compelling public interest in establishing certain procedures and standards for addressing potential claims against individuals and entities faced with an unprecedented public health emergency that has had severe and adverse impacts on both the health and safety of individuals and the ordinary functioning of governmental entities, the judicial system, the health care delivery system, educational and religious institutions, businesses, nonprofit entities, and others whose daily lives have been upended by the emergency.

"Sec. 5. (a) Section 74.155 and Chapter 148, Civil Practice and Remedies Code, as added by this Act, apply only to an action commenced on or after March 13, 2020, for which a judgment has not become final before the effective date of this Act. An action commenced before March 13, 2020, or an action for which a judgment has become final before the effective date of this Act is governed by the law applicable to the action immediately before the effective date of this Act, and that law is continued in effect for that purpose.

"(b) In an action commenced before the effective date of this Act and to which Section 74.155, Civil Practice and Remedies Code, as added by this Act, applies, a physician, health care provider, or first responder who intends to raise a defense under Subsection (b) of that section must provide to the claimant specific facts required under Subsection (g) of that section not later than the later of:

"(1) the 60th day after the effective date of this Act;

"(2) the 120th day after the date the physician, health care provider, or first responder files an original answer in the suit; or

"(3) the 60th day after the date the claimant serves an expert report on the physician, health care provider, or first responder under Section 74.351, Civil Practice and Remedies Code."

SUBCHAPTER E. RES IPSA LOQUITUR

§ 74.201. Application of Res Ipsa Loquitur

The common law doctrine of res ipsa loquitur shall only apply to health care liability claims against health care providers or physicians in those cases to which it has been applied by the appellate courts of this state as of August 29, 1977.

Added by Acts 2003, 78th Leg., ch. 204, § 10.01, eff. Sept. 1, 2003.

SUBCHAPTER F. STATUTE OF LIMITATIONS

§ 74.251. Statute of Limitations on Health Care Liability Claims

(a) Notwithstanding any other law and subject to Subsection (b), no health care liability claim may be commenced unless the action is filed within two years from the occurrence of the breach or tort or from the date the medical or health care treatment that is the subject of the claim or the hospitalization for which the claim is made is completed; provided that, minors under the age of 12 years shall have until their 14th birthday in which to file, or have filed on their behalf, the claim. Except as herein provided this section applies to all persons regardless of minority or other legal disability.

(b) A claimant must bring a health care liability claim not later than 10 years after the date of the act or omission that gives rise to the claim. This subsection is intended as a statute of repose so that all claims must be brought within 10 years or they are time barred.

Added by Acts 2003, 78th Leg., ch. 204, § 10.01, eff. Sept. 1, 2003.

For validity of this section, see Adams v. Gottwald, D.D.S., P.C., 179 S.W.3d 101 (Tex. App.—San Antonio 2005, pet. denied).

SUBCHAPTER G. LIABILITY LIMITS

§ 74.301. Limitation on Noneconomic Damages

(a) In an action on a health care liability claim where final judgment is rendered against a physician or health care provider other than a health care institution, the limit of civil liability for noneconomic damages of the physician or health care provider other than a health care institution, inclusive of all persons and entities for which vicarious liability theories may apply, shall be limited to an amount not to exceed $250,000 for each claimant, regardless of the number of defendant physicians or health care providers other than a health care institution against whom the claim is asserted or the number of separate causes of action on which the claim is based.

(b) In an action on a health care liability claim where final judgment is rendered against a single health care institution, the limit of civil liability for noneconomic damages inclusive of all persons and entities for which vicarious liability theories may apply, shall be limited to an amount not to exceed $250,000 for each claimant.

(c) In an action on a health care liability claim where final judgment is rendered against more than one health care institution, the limit of civil liability for noneconomic damages for each health care institution, inclusive of all persons and entities for which vicarious liability theories may apply, shall be limited to an amount not to exceed $250,000 for each claimant and the limit of civil liability for noneconomic damages for all health care institutions, inclusive of all persons and entities for which vicarious liability theories may apply, shall be limited to an amount not to exceed $500,000 for each claimant.

Added by Acts 2003, 78th Leg., ch. 204, § 10.01, eff. Sept. 1, 2003.

§ 74.302. Alternative Limitation on Noneconomic Damages

(a) In the event that Section 74.301 is stricken from this subchapter or is otherwise to any extent invalidated by a method other than through legislative means, the following, subject to the provisions of this section, shall become effective:

(1) In an action on a health care liability claim where final judgment is rendered against a physician or health care provider other than a health care institution, the limit of civil liability for noneconomic damages of the physician or health care provider other than a health care institution, inclusive of all persons and entities for which vicarious liability theories may apply, shall be limited to an amount not to exceed $250,000 for each claimant, regardless of the number of defendant physicians or health care providers other than a health care institution against whom the claim is asserted or the number of separate causes of action on which the claim is based.

(2) In an action on a health care liability claim where final judgment is rendered against a single health care institution, the limit of civil liability for noneconomic damages inclusive of all persons and entities for which vicarious liability theories may apply, shall be limited to an amount not to exceed $250,000 for each claimant.

(3) In an action on a health care liability claim where final judgment is rendered against more than one health care institution, the limit of civil liability for noneconomic damages for each health care institution, inclusive of all persons and entities for which vicarious liability theories may apply, shall be limited to an amount not to exceed $250,000 for each claimant and the limit of civil liability for noneconomic damages for all health care institutions, inclusive of all persons and entities for which vicarious liability theories may apply, shall be limited to an amount not to exceed $500,000 for each claimant.

(b) Effective before September 1, 2005, Subsection (a) of this section applies to any physician or health care provider that provides evidence of financial responsibility in the following amounts in effect for any act or omission to which this subchapter applies:

(1) at least $100,000 for each health care liability claim and at least $300,000 in aggregate for all health care liability claims occurring in an insurance policy year, calendar year, or fiscal year for a physician participating in an approved residency program;

(2) at least $200,000 for each health care liability claim and at least $600,000 in aggregate for all health care liability claims occurring in an insurance policy year, calendar year, or fiscal year for a physician or health care provider, other than a hospital; and

(3) at least $500,000 for each health care liability claim and at least $1.5 million in aggregate for all health care liability claims occurring in an insurance policy year, calendar year, or fiscal year for a hospital.

(c) Effective September 1, 2005, Subsection (a) of this section applies to any physician or health care provider that provides evidence of financial responsibility in the following amounts in effect for any act or omission to which this subchapter applies:

(1) at least $100,000 for each health care liability claim and at least $300,000 in aggregate for all health care liability claims occurring in an insurance policy year, calendar year, or fiscal year for a physician participating in an approved residency program;

(2) at least $300,000 for each health care liability claim and at least $900,000 in aggregate for all health care liability claims occurring in an insurance policy year, calendar year, or fiscal year for a physician or health care provider, other than a hospital; and

(3) at least $750,000 for each health care liability claim and at least $2.25 million in aggregate for all health care liability claims occurring in an insurance policy year, calendar year, or fiscal year for a hospital.

(d) Effective September 1, 2007, Subsection (a) of this section applies to any physician or health care provider that provides evidence of financial responsibility in the following amounts in effect for any act or omission to which this subchapter applies:

(1) at least $100,000 for each health care liability claim and at least $300,000 in aggregate for all health care liability claims occurring in an insurance policy year, calendar year, or fiscal year for a physician participating in an approved residency program;

(2) at least $500,000 for each health care liability claim and at least $1 million in aggregate for all health care liability claims occurring in an insurance policy year, calendar year, or fiscal year for a physician or health care provider, other than a hospital; and

(3) at least $1 million for each health care liability claim and at least $3 million in aggregate for all health care liability claims occurring in an insurance policy year, calendar year, or fiscal year for a hospital.

(e) Evidence of financial responsibility may be established at the time of judgment by providing proof of:

(1) the purchase of a contract of insurance or other plan of insurance authorized by this state or federal law or regulation;

(2) the purchase of coverage from a trust organized and operating under Article 21.49-4, Insurance Code;

(3) the purchase of coverage or another plan of insurance provided by or through a risk retention group or purchasing group authorized under applicable laws of this state or under the Product Liability Risk Retention Act of 1981 (15 U.S.C. Section 3901 et seq.), as amended, or the Liability Risk Retention Act of 1986 (15 U.S.C. Section 3901 et seq.), as amended, or any other contract or arrangement for transferring and distributing risk relating to legal liability for damages, including cost or defense, legal costs, fees, and other claims expenses; or

(4) the maintenance of financial reserves in or an irrevocable letter of credit from a federally insured financial institution that has its main office or a branch office in this state.

Added by Acts 2003, 78th Leg., ch. 204, § 10.01, eff. Sept. 1, 2003.

§ 74.303. Limitation on Damages

(a) In a wrongful death or survival action on a health care liability claim where final judgment is rendered against a physician or health care provider, the limit of civil liability for all damages, including exemplary damages, shall be limited to an amount not to exceed $500,000 for each claimant, regardless of the number of defendant physicians or health care providers against whom the claim is asserted or the number of separate causes of action on which the claim is based.

(b) When there is an increase or decrease in the consumer price index with respect to the amount of that index on August 29, 1977, the liability limit prescribed in Subsection (a) shall be increased or decreased, as applicable, by a sum equal to the amount of such limit multiplied by the percentage increase or decrease in the consumer price index, as published by the Bureau of Labor Statistics of the United States Department of Labor, that measures the average changes in prices of goods and services purchased by urban wage earners and clerical workers' families and single workers living alone (CPI-W: Seasonally Adjusted U.S. City Average—All Items), between August 29, 1977, and the time at which damages subject to such limits are awarded by final judgment or settlement.

(c) Subsection (a) does not apply to the amount of damages awarded on a health care liability claim for the expenses of necessary medical, hospital, and custodial care received before judgment or required in the future for treatment of the injury.

(d) The liability of any insurer under the common law theory of recovery commonly known in Texas as the "Stowers Doctrine" shall not exceed the liability of the insured.

(e) In any action on a health care liability claim that is tried by a jury in any court in this state, the following shall be included in the court's written instructions to the jurors:

(1) "Do not consider, discuss, nor speculate whether or not liability, if any, on the part of any party is or is not subject to any limit under applicable law."

(2) "A finding of negligence may not be based solely on evidence of a bad result to the claimant in question, but a bad result may be considered by you, along with other evidence, in determining the issue of negligence. You are the sole judges of the weight, if any, to be given to this kind of evidence."

Added by Acts 2003, 78th Leg., ch. 204, § 10.01, eff. Sept. 1, 2003.

SUBCHAPTER H. PROCEDURAL PROVISIONS

§ 74.351. Expert Report

(a) In a health care liability claim, a claimant shall, not later than the 120th day after the date each defendant's original answer is filed or a later date required under Section 74.353, serve on that party or the party's attorney one or more expert reports, with a curriculum vitae of each expert listed in the report for each physician or health care provider against whom a liability claim is asserted. The date for serving the report may be extended by written agreement of the affected parties. Each defendant physician or health care provider whose conduct is implicated in a report must file and serve any objection to the sufficiency of the report not later than the later of the 21st day after the date the report is served or the 21st day after the date the defendant's answer is filed, failing which all objections are waived.

(b) If, as to a defendant physician or health care provider, an expert report has not been served within the period specified by Subsection (a), the court, on the motion of the affected physician or health care provider, shall, subject to Subsection (c), enter an order that:

(1) awards to the affected physician or health care provider reasonable attorney's fees and costs of court incurred by the physician or health care provider; and

(2) dismisses the claim with respect to the physician or health care provider, with prejudice to the refiling of the claim.

(c) If an expert report has not been served within the period specified by Subsection (a) because elements of the report are found deficient, the court may grant one 30-day extension to the claimant in order to cure the deficiency. If the claimant does not receive notice of the court's ruling granting the extension until after the applicable deadline has passed, then the 30-day extension shall run from the date the plaintiff first received the notice.

(d) to (h) [Subsections (d)-(h) reserved]

(i) Notwithstanding any other provision of this section, a claimant may satisfy any requirement of this section for serving an expert report by serving reports of separate experts regarding different physicians or health care providers or regarding different issues arising from the conduct of a physician or health care provider, such as issues of liability and causation. Nothing in this section shall be construed to mean that a single expert must address all liability and causation issues with respect to all physicians or health care providers or with respect to both liability and causation issues for a physician or health care provider.

(j) Nothing in this section shall be construed to require the serving of an expert report regarding any issue other than an issue relating to liability or causation.

(k) Subject to Subsection (t), an expert report served under this section:

(1) is not admissible in evidence by any party;

(2) shall not be used in a deposition, trial, or other proceeding; and

(3) shall not be referred to by any party during the course of the action for any purpose.

(*l*) A court shall grant a motion challenging the adequacy of an expert report only if it appears to the court, after hearing, that the report does not represent an objective good faith effort to comply with the definition of an expert report in Subsection (r)(6).

(m) to (q) [Subsections (m)-(q) reserved]

(r) In this section:

(1) "Affected parties" means the claimant and the physician or health care provider who are directly affected by an act or agreement required or permitted by this section and does not include other parties to an action who are not directly affected by that particular act or agreement.

(2) "Claim" means a health care liability claim.

(3) [reserved]

(4) "Defendant" means a physician or health care provider against whom a health care liability claim is asserted. The term includes a third-party defendant, cross-defendant, or counterdefendant.

(5) "Expert" means:

(A) with respect to a person giving opinion testimony regarding whether a physician departed from accepted standards of medical care, an expert qualified to testify under the requirements of Section 74.401;

(B) with respect to a person giving opinion testimony regarding whether a health care provider departed from accepted standards of health care, an expert qualified to testify under the requirements of Section 74.402;

(C) with respect to a person giving opinion testimony about the causal relationship between the injury, harm, or damages claimed and the alleged departure from the applicable standard of care in any health care liability claim, a physician who is otherwise qualified to render opinions on such causal relationship under the Texas Rules of Evidence;

(D) with respect to a person giving opinion testimony about the causal relationship between the injury, harm, or damages claimed and the alleged departure from the applicable standard of care for a dentist, a dentist or physician who is otherwise qualified to render opinions on such causal relationship under the Texas Rules of Evidence; or

(E) with respect to a person giving opinion testimony about the causal relationship between the injury, harm, or damages claimed and the alleged departure from the applicable standard of care for a podiatrist, a podiatrist or physician who is otherwise qualified to render opinions on such causal relationship under the Texas Rules of Evidence.

(6) "Expert report" means a written report by an expert that provides a fair summary of the expert's opinions as of the date of the report regarding applicable standards of care, the manner in which the care rendered by the physician or health care provider failed to meet the standards, and the causal relationship between that failure and the injury, harm, or damages claimed.

(s) Until a claimant has served the expert report and curriculum vitae as required by Subsection (a), all discovery in a health care liability claim is stayed except for the acquisition by the claimant of information, including medical or hospital records or other documents or tangible things, related to the patient's health care through:

(1) written discovery as defined in Rule 192.7, Texas Rules of Civil Procedure;

(2) depositions on written questions under Rule 200, Texas Rules of Civil Procedure; and

(3) discovery from nonparties under Rule 205, Texas Rules of Civil Procedure.

(t) If an expert report is used by the claimant in the course of the action for any purpose other than to meet the service requirement of Subsection (a), the restrictions imposed by Subsection (k) on use of the expert report by any party are waived.

(u) Notwithstanding any other provision of this section, after a claim is filed all claimants, collectively, may take not more than two depositions before the expert report is served as required by Subsection (a).

Added by Acts 2003, 78th Leg., ch. 204, § 10.01, eff. Sept. 1, 2003. Amended by Acts 2005, 79th Leg., ch. 635, § 1, eff. Sept. 1, 2005; Acts 2013, 83rd Leg., ch. 870 (H.B. 658), § 2, eff. Sept. 1, 2013; Acts 2021, 87th Leg., ch. 167 (S.B. 232), § 2, eff. Sept. 1, 2021.

Section 4 of Acts 2021, 87th Leg., ch. 167 (S.B. 232) provides:

"The change in law made by this Act applies only to an action commenced on or after the effective date [Sept. 1, 2021] of this Act. An action commenced before the effective date of this Act is governed by the law as it existed immediately before the effective date of this Act, and that law is continued in effect for that purpose."

§ 74.351. Expert Report

§ 74.352. Discovery Procedures

(a) In every health care liability claim the plaintiff shall within 45 days after the date of filing of the original petition serve on the defendant's attorney or, if no attorney has appeared for the defendant, on the defendant full and complete answers to the appropriate standard set of interrogatories and full and complete responses to the appropriate standard set of requests for production of documents and things promulgated by the Health Care Liability Discovery Panel.

(b) Every physician or health care provider who is a defendant in a health care liability claim shall within 45 days after the date on which an answer to the petition was due serve on the plaintiff's attorney or, if the plaintiff is not represented by an attorney, on the plaintiff full and complete answers to the appropriate standard set of interrogatories and complete responses to the standard set of requests for production of documents and things promulgated by the Health Care Liability Discovery Panel.

(c) Except on motion and for good cause shown, no objection may be asserted regarding any standard interrogatory or request for production of documents and things, but no response shall be required where a particular interrogatory or request is clearly inapplicable under the circumstances of the case.

(d) Failure to file full and complete answers and responses to standard interrogatories and requests for production of documents and things in accordance with Subsections (a) and (b) or the making of a groundless objection under Subsection (c) shall be grounds for sanctions by the court in accordance with the Texas Rules of Civil Procedure on motion of any party.

(e) The time limits imposed under Subsections (a) and (b) may be extended by the court on the motion of a responding party for good cause shown and shall be extended if agreed in writing between the responding party and all opposing parties. In no event shall an extension be for a period of more than an additional 30 days.

(f) If a party is added by an amended pleading, intervention, or otherwise, the new party shall file full and complete answers to the appropriate standard set of interrogatories and full and complete responses to the standard set of requests for production of documents and things no later than 45 days after the date of filing of the pleading by which the party first appeared in the action.

(g) If information or documents required to provide full and complete answers and responses as required by this section are not in the possession of the responding party or attorney when the answers or responses are filed, the party shall supplement the answers and responses in accordance with the Texas Rules of Civil Procedure.

(h) Nothing in this section shall preclude any party from taking additional non-duplicative discovery of any other party. The standard sets of interrogatories provided for in this section shall not constitute, as to each plaintiff and each physician or health care provider who is a defendant, the first of the two sets of interrogatories permitted under the Texas Rules of Civil Procedure.

Added by Acts 2003, 78th Leg., ch. 204, § 10.01, eff. Sept. 1, 2003.

§ 74.353. Preliminary Determination for Expert Report Requirement

(a) On motion of a claimant filed not later than 30 days after the date each defendant's original answer is filed, a court may issue a preliminary determination regarding whether a claim made by the claimant is a health care liability claim for the purposes of Section 74.351.

(b) If a court determines under Subsection (a) or (c) that a claim is a health care liability claim for purposes of Section 74.351, the claimant shall serve an expert report as required by Section 74.351 not later than the later of:

(1) 120 days after the date each defendant's original answer is filed;

(2) 60 days after the date the court issues the preliminary determination under Subsection (a) or (c); or

(3) a date agreed to in writing by the affected parties.

(c) If a court does not issue a preliminary determination under Subsection (a) before the 91st day after the date that a claimant files a motion under that subsection, the court shall issue a preliminary determination that the claim is a health care liability claim for the purposes of Section 74.351.

(d) A preliminary determination under this section is subject to interlocutory appeal by either the claimant or defendant.

(e) If on interlocutory appeal an appellate court reverses a trial court's preliminary determination that a claim is not a health care liability claim, the claimant shall serve an expert report as required by Section 74.351 not later than 120 days after the date that the appellate court issues an opinion reversing the preliminary determination.

(f) A preliminary determination under this section applies only to the issue of whether a claimant is required to serve an expert report under Section 74.351.

Added by Acts 2021, 87th Leg., ch. 167 (S.B. 232), § 3, eff. Sept. 1, 2021.

Section 4 of Acts 2021, 87th Leg., ch. 167 (S.B. 232) provides:

"The change in law made by this Act applies only to an action commenced on or after the effective date [Sept. 1, 2021] of this Act. An action commenced before the effective date of this Act is governed by the law as it existed immediately before the effective date of this Act, and that law is continued in effect for that purpose."

SUBCHAPTER I. EXPERT WITNESSES

§ 74.401. Qualifications of Expert Witness in Suit Against Physician

(a) In a suit involving a health care liability claim against a physician for injury to or death of a patient, a person may qualify as an expert witness on the issue of whether the physician departed from accepted standards of medical care only if the person is a physician who:

(1) is practicing medicine at the time such testimony is given or was practicing medicine at the time the claim arose;

(2) has knowledge of accepted standards of medical care for the diagnosis, care, or treatment of the illness, injury, or condition involved in the claim; and

(3) is qualified on the basis of training or experience to offer an expert opinion regarding those accepted standards of medical care.

(b) For the purpose of this section, "practicing medicine" or "medical practice" includes, but is not limited to, training residents or students at an accredited school of medicine or osteopathy or serving as a consulting physician to other physicians who provide direct patient care, upon the request of such other physicians.

(c) In determining whether a witness is qualified on the basis of training or experience, the court shall consider whether, at the time the claim arose or at the time the testimony is given, the witness:

(1) is board certified or has other substantial training or experience in an area of medical practice relevant to the claim; and

(2) is actively practicing medicine in rendering medical care services relevant to the claim.

(d) The court shall apply the criteria specified in Subsections (a), (b), and (c) in determining whether an expert is qualified to offer expert testimony on the issue of whether the physician departed from accepted standards of medical care, but may depart from those criteria if, under the circumstances, the court determines that there is a good reason to admit the expert's testimony. The court shall state on the record the reason for admitting the testimony if the court departs from the criteria.

(e) A pretrial objection to the qualifications of a witness under this section must be made not later than the later of the 21st day after the date the objecting party receives a copy of the witness's curriculum vitae or the 21st day after the date of the witness's deposition. If circumstances arise after the date on which the objection must be made that could not have been reasonably anticipated by a party before that date and that the party believes in good faith provide a basis for an objection to a witness's qualifications, and if an objection was not made previously, this subsection does not prevent the party from making an objection as soon as practicable under the circumstances. The court shall conduct a hearing to determine whether the witness is qualified as soon as practicable after the filing of an objection and, if possible, before trial. If the objecting party is unable to object in time for the hearing to be conducted before the trial, the hearing shall be conducted outside the presence of the jury. This subsection does not prevent a party from examining or cross-examining a witness at trial about the witness's qualifications.

(f) This section does not prevent a physician who is a defendant from qualifying as an expert.

(g) In this subchapter, "physician" means a person who is:

(1) licensed to practice medicine in one or more states in the United States; or

(2) a graduate of a medical school accredited by the Liaison Committee on Medical Education or the American Osteopathic Association only if testifying as a defendant and that testimony relates to that defendant's standard of care, the alleged departure from that standard of care, or the causal relationship between the alleged departure from that standard of care and the injury, harm, or damages claimed.

Added by Acts 2003, 78th Leg., ch. 204, § 10.01, eff. Sept. 1, 2003.

§ 74.402. Qualifications of Expert Witness in Suit Against Health Care Provider

(a) For purposes of this section, "practicing health care" includes:

(1) training health care providers in the same field as the defendant health care provider at an accredited educational institution; or

(2) serving as a consulting health care provider and being licensed, certified, or registered in the same field as the defendant health care provider.

(b) In a suit involving a health care liability claim against a health care provider, a person may qualify as an expert witness on the issue of whether the health care provider departed from accepted standards of care only if the person:

(1) is practicing health care in a field of practice that involves the same type of care or treatment as that delivered by the defendant health care provider, if the defendant health care provider is an individual, at the time the testimony is given or was practicing that type of health care at the time the claim arose;

(2) has knowledge of accepted standards of care for health care providers for the diagnosis, care, or treatment of the illness, injury, or condition involved in the claim; and

(3) is qualified on the basis of training or experience to offer an expert opinion regarding those accepted standards of health care.

(c) In determining whether a witness is qualified on the basis of training or experience, the court shall consider whether, at the time the claim arose or at the time the testimony is given, the witness:

(1) is certified by a licensing agency of one or more states of the United States or a national professional certifying agency, or has other substantial training or experience, in the area of health care relevant to the claim; and

(2) is actively practicing health care in rendering health care services relevant to the claim.

(d) The court shall apply the criteria specified in Subsections (a), (b), and (c) in determining whether an expert is qualified to offer expert testimony on the issue of whether the defendant health care provider departed from accepted standards of health care but may depart from those criteria if, under the circumstances, the court determines that there is good reason to admit the expert's testimony. The court shall state on the record the reason for admitting the testimony if the court departs from the criteria.

(e) This section does not prevent a health care provider who is a defendant, or an employee of the defendant health care provider, from qualifying as an expert.

(f) A pretrial objection to the qualifications of a witness under this section must be made not later than the later of the 21st day after the date the objecting party receives a copy of the witness's curriculum vitae or the 21st day after the date of the witness's deposition. If circumstances arise after the date on which the objection must be made that could not have been reasonably anticipated by a party before that date and that the party believes in good faith provide a basis for an objection to a witness's qualifications, and if an objection was not made previously, this subsection does not prevent the party from making an objection as soon as practicable under the circumstances. The court shall conduct a hearing to determine whether the witness is qualified as soon as practicable after the filing of an objection and, if possible, before trial. If the objecting party is unable to object in time for the hearing to be conducted before the trial, the hearing shall be conducted outside the presence of the jury. This subsection does not prevent a party from examining or cross-examining a witness at trial about the witness's qualifications.

Added by Acts 2003, 78th Leg., ch. 204, § 10.01, eff. Sept. 1, 2003.

§ 74.403. Qualifications of Expert Witness on Causation in Health Care Liability Claim

(a) Except as provided by Subsections (b) and (c), in a suit involving a health care liability claim against a physician or health care provider, a person may qualify as an expert witness on the issue of the causal relationship between the alleged departure from accepted standards of care and the injury, harm, or damages claimed only if the person is a physician and is otherwise qualified to render opinions on that causal relationship under the Texas Rules of Evidence.

(b) In a suit involving a health care liability claim against a dentist, a person may qualify as an expert witness on the issue of the causal relationship between the alleged departure from accepted standards of care and the injury, harm, or damages claimed if the person is a dentist or physician and is otherwise qualified to render opinions on that causal relationship under the Texas Rules of Evidence.

(c) In a suit involving a health care liability claim against a podiatrist, a person may qualify as an expert witness on the issue of the causal relationship between the alleged departure from accepted standards of care and the injury, harm, or damages claimed if the person is a podiatrist or physician and is otherwise qualified to render opinions on that causal relationship under the Texas Rules of Evidence.

(d) A pretrial objection to the qualifications of a witness under this section must be made not later than the later of the 21st day after the date the objecting party receives a copy of the witness's curriculum vitae or the 21st day after the date of the witness's deposition. If circumstances arise after the date on which the objection must be made that could not have been reasonably anticipated by a party before that date and that the party believes in good faith provide a basis for an objection to a witness's qualifications, and if an objection was not made previously, this subsection does not prevent the party from making an objection as soon as practicable under the circumstances. The court shall conduct a hearing to determine whether the witness is qualified as soon as practicable after the filing of an objection and, if possible, before trial. If the objecting party is unable to object in time for the hearing to be conducted before the trial, the hearing shall be conducted outside the presence of the jury. This subsection does not prevent a party from examining or cross-examining a witness at trial about the witness's qualifications.

Added by Acts 2003, 78th Leg., ch. 204, § 10.01, eff. Sept. 1, 2003.

SUBCHAPTER J. ARBITRATION AGREEMENTS

§ 74.451. Arbitration Agreements

(a) No physician, professional association of physicians, or other health care provider shall request or require a patient or prospective patient to execute an agreement to arbitrate a health care liability claim unless the form of agreement delivered to the patient contains a written notice in 10-point boldface type clearly and conspicuously stating:

UNDER TEXAS LAW, THIS AGREEMENT IS INVALID AND OF NO LEGAL EFFECT UNLESS IT

IS ALSO SIGNED BY AN ATTORNEY OF YOUR OWN CHOOSING. THIS AGREEMENT CONTAINS A WAIVER OF IMPORTANT LEGAL RIGHTS, INCLUDING YOUR RIGHT TO A JURY. YOU SHOULD NOT SIGN THIS AGREEMENT WITHOUT FIRST CONSULTING WITH AN ATTORNEY.

(b) A violation of this section by a physician or professional association of physicians constitutes a violation of Subtitle B, Title 3, Occupations Code,[1] and shall be subject to the enforcement provisions and sanctions contained in that subtitle.

(c) A violation of this section by a health care provider other than a physician shall constitute a false, misleading, or deceptive act or practice in the conduct of trade or commerce within the meaning of Section 17.46 of the Deceptive Trade Practices–Consumer Protection Act (Subchapter E, Chapter 17, Business & Commerce Code[2]), and shall be subject to an enforcement action by the consumer protection division under that act and subject to the penalties and remedies contained in Section 17.47, Business & Commerce Code, notwithstanding Section 74.004 or any other law.

(d) Notwithstanding any other provision of this section, a person who is found to be in violation of this section for the first time shall be subject only to injunctive relief or other appropriate order requiring the person to cease and desist from such violation, and not to any other penalty or sanction.

Added by Acts 2003, 78th Leg., ch. 204, § 10.01, eff. Sept. 1, 2003.

[1] V.T.C.A., Occupations Code § 151.001 et seq.
[2] V.T.C.A., Bus. & C. § 17.41 et seq.

For validity of this section, see Fredericksburg Care Company, L.P. v. Perez, Tex. 2015, 461 S.W.3d 513.

SUBCHAPTER K. PAYMENT FOR FUTURE LOSSES

§ 74.501. Definitions

In this subchapter:

(1) "Future damages" means damages that are incurred after the date of judgment for:

(A) medical, health care, or custodial care services;

(B) physical pain and mental anguish, disfigurement, or physical impairment;

(C) loss of consortium, companionship, or society; or

(D) loss of earnings.

(2) "Future loss of earnings" means the following losses incurred after the date of the judgment:

(A) loss of income, wages, or earning capacity and other pecuniary losses; and

(B) loss of inheritance.

(3) "Periodic payments" means the payment of money or its equivalent to the recipient of future damages at defined intervals.

Added by Acts 2003, 78th Leg., ch. 204, § 10.01, eff. Sept. 1, 2003.

§ 74.502. Scope of Subchapter

This subchapter applies only to an action on a health care liability claim against a physician or health care provider in which the present value of the award of future damages, as determined by the court, equals or exceeds $100,000.

Added by Acts 2003, 78th Leg., ch. 204, § 10.01, eff. Sept. 1, 2003.

§ 74.503. Court Order for Periodic Payments

(a) At the request of a defendant physician or health care provider or claimant, the court shall order that medical, health care, or custodial services awarded in a health care liability claim be paid in whole or in part in periodic payments rather than by a lump-sum payment.

(b) At the request of a defendant physician or health care provider or claimant, the court may order that future damages other than medical, health care, or custodial services awarded in a health care liability claim be paid in whole or in part in periodic payments rather than by a lump sum payment.

(c) The court shall make a specific finding of the dollar amount of periodic payments that will compensate the claimant for the future damages.

(d) The court shall specify in its judgment ordering the payment of future damages by periodic payments the:

(1) recipient of the payments;

(2) dollar amount of the payments;

(3) interval between payments; and

(4) number of payments or the period of time over which payments must be made.

Added by Acts 2003, 78th Leg., ch. 204, § 10.01, eff. Sept. 1, 2003.

§ 74.504. Release

The entry of an order for the payment of future damages by periodic payments constitutes a release of the health care liability claim filed by the claimant.

Added by Acts 2003, 78th Leg., ch. 204, § 10.01, eff. Sept. 1, 2003.

§ 74.505. Financial Responsibility

(a) As a condition to authorizing periodic payments of future damages, the court shall require a defendant who is not adequately insured to provide evidence of financial responsibility in an amount adequate to assure full payment of damages awarded by the judgment.

(b) The judgment must provide for payments to be funded by:

(1) an annuity contract issued by a company licensed to do business as an insurance company, including an assignment within the meaning of Section 130, Internal Revenue Code of 1986, as amended;

(2) an obligation of the United States;

(3) applicable and collectible liability insurance from one or more qualified insurers; or

(4) any other satisfactory form of funding approved by the court.

(c) On termination of periodic payments of future damages, the court shall order the return of the security, or as much as remains, to the defendant.

Added by Acts 2003, 78th Leg., ch. 204, § 10.01, eff. Sept. 1, 2003.

§ 74.506. Death of Recipient

(a) On the death of the recipient, money damages awarded for loss of future earnings continue to be paid to the estate of the recipient of the award without reduction.

(b) Periodic payments, other than future loss of earnings, terminate on the death of the recipient.

(c) If the recipient of periodic payments dies before all payments required by the judgment are paid, the court may modify the judgment to award and apportion the unpaid damages for future loss of earnings in an appropriate manner.

(d) Following the satisfaction or termination of any obligations specified in the judgment for periodic payments, any obligation of the defendant physician or health care provider to make further payments ends and any security given reverts to the defendant.

Added by Acts 2003, 78th Leg., ch. 204, § 10.01, eff. Sept. 1, 2003.

§ 74.507. Award of Attorney's Fees

For purposes of computing the award of attorney's fees when the claimant is awarded a recovery that will be paid in periodic payments, the court shall:

(1) place a total value on the payments based on the claimant's projected life expectancy; and

(2) reduce the amount in Subdivision (1) to present value.

Added by Acts 2003, 78th Leg., ch. 204, § 10.01, eff. Sept. 1, 2003.

CHAPTER 74A. LIMITATION OF LIABILITY RELATING TO HEALTH INFORMATION EXCHANGES

§ 74A.001. Definitions

In this chapter:

(1) "Gross negligence" has the meaning assigned by Section 41.001.

(2) "Health care provider" means any individual, partnership, professional association, corporation, facility, or institution duly licensed, certified, registered, or chartered by this state to provide health care or medical care, including a physician. The term includes:

(A) an officer, director, shareholder, member, partner, manager, owner, or affiliate of a physician or other health care provider; and

(B) an employee, independent contractor, or agent of a physician or other health care provider acting in the course and scope of the employment or contractual relationship.

(3) "Health information exchange" has the meaning assigned by Section 182.151, Health and Safety Code. The term includes:

(A) an officer, director, shareholder, member, partner, manager, owner, or affiliate of the health information exchange; and

(B) an employee, independent contractor, or agent of the health information exchange acting in the course and scope of the employment or contractual relationship.

(4) "Malice" has the meaning assigned by Section 41.001.

(5) "Physician" means:

(A) an individual licensed to practice medicine in this state under Subtitle B, Title 3, Occupations Code;

(B) a professional association organized by an individual physician or a group of physicians;

(C) a partnership or limited liability partnership formed by a group of physicians;

(D) a limited liability company formed by a group of physicians;

(E) a nonprofit health corporation certified by the Texas Medical Board under Chapter 162, Occupations Code; or

(F) a single legal entity authorized to practice medicine in this state owned by a group of physicians.

Added by Acts 2015, 84th Leg., ch. 1085 (H.B. 2641), § 1, eff. Sept. 1, 2015.

§ 74A.002. Limitation on Liability of Health Care Providers Relating to Health Information Exchanges

(a) Unless the health care provider acts with malice or gross negligence, a health care provider who provides patient information to a health information exchange is not liable for any damages, penalties, or other relief related to the obtainment, use, or disclosure of that information in violation of federal or state privacy laws by a health information exchange, another health care provider, or any other person.

(b) Nothing in this section may be construed to create a cause of action or to create a standard of care, obligation, or duty that forms the basis for a cause of action.

Added by Acts 2015, 84th Leg., ch. 1085 (H.B. 2641), § 1, eff. Sept. 1, 2015.

§ 74A.003. Applicability of Other Law

The protections, immunities, and limitations of liability provided by this chapter are in addition to any other protections, immunities, and limitations of liability provided by other law.

Added by Acts 2015, 84th Leg., ch. 1085 (H.B. 2641), § 1, eff. Sept. 1, 2015.

CHAPTER 75. LIMITATION OF LANDOWNERS' LIABILITY

§ 75.001. Definitions

In this chapter:

(1) "Agricultural land" means land that is located in this state and that is suitable for:

(A) use in production of plants and fruits grown for human or animal consumption, or plants grown for the production of fibers, floriculture, viticulture, horticulture, or planting seed;

(B) forestry and the growing of trees for the purpose of rendering those trees into lumber, fiber, or other items used for industrial, commercial, or personal consumption; or

(C) domestic or native farm or ranch animals kept for use or profit.

(2) "Premises" includes land, roads, water, watercourse, private ways, and buildings, structures, machinery, and equipment attached to or located on the land, road, water, watercourse, or private way.

(3) "Recreation" means an activity such as:

(A) hunting;

(B) fishing;

(C) swimming;

(D) boating;

(E) camping;

(F) picnicking;

(G) hiking;

(H) pleasure driving, including off-road motorcycling and off-road automobile driving and the use of off-highway vehicles;

(I) nature study, including bird-watching;

(J) cave exploration;

(K) waterskiing and other water sports;

(L) any other activity associated with enjoying nature or the outdoors;

(M) bicycling and mountain biking;

(N) disc golf;

(O) on-leash and off-leash walking of dogs;

(P) radio control flying and related activities; or

(Q) rock climbing.

(4) "Governmental unit" has the meaning assigned by Section 101.001.

Acts 1985, 69th Leg., ch. 959, § 1, eff. Sept. 1, 1985. Amended by Acts 1989, 71st Leg., ch. 62, § 1, eff. Sept. 1, 1989; Acts 1989, 71st Leg., ch. 736, § 1, eff. Sept. 1, 1989; Acts 1995, 74th Leg., ch. 520, § 1, eff. Aug. 28, 1995; Acts 1997, 75th Leg., ch. 56, § 1, eff. Sept. 1, 1997; Acts 2005, 79th Leg., ch. 116, § 1, eff. Sept. 1, 2005; Acts 2005, 79th Leg., ch. 932, § 1, eff. Sept. 1, 2005; Acts 2007, 80th Leg., ch. 659, § 1, eff. June 15, 2007; Acts 2015, 84th Leg., ch. 1071 (H.B. 2303), § 1, eff. June 19, 2015; Acts 2019, 86th Leg., ch. 740 (H.B. 687), § 1, eff. June 10, 2019; Acts 2019, 86th Leg., ch. 959 (S.B. 230), § 1, eff. June 14, 2019; Acts 2019, 86th Leg., ch. 1233 (H.B. 1548), § 2, eff. June 14, 2019.

Section 2 of Acts 2019, 86th Leg., ch. 740 (H.B. 687) provides:

"The change in law made by this Act applies only to a cause of action that accrues on or after the effective date [June 10, 2019] of this Act. A cause of action that accrued before the effective date of this Act is governed by the law applicable to the cause of action immediately before the effective date of this Act, and that law is continued in effect for that purpose."

Section 2 of Acts 2019, 86th Leg., ch. 959 (S.B. 230) provides:

"The change in law made by this Act applies only to a cause of action that accrues on or after the effective date [June 14, 2019] of this Act. A cause of action that accrued before the effective date of this Act is governed by the law applicable to the cause of action immediately before the effective date of this Act, and that law is continued in effect for that purpose."

§ 75.002. Liability Limited

(a) An owner, lessee, or occupant of agricultural land:

(1) does not owe a duty of care to a trespasser on the land; and

(2) is not liable for any injury to a trespasser on the land, except for wilful or wanton acts or gross negligence by the owner, lessee, or other occupant of agricultural land.

(b) If an owner, lessee, or occupant of agricultural land gives permission to another or invites another to enter the premises for recreation, the owner, lessee, or occupant, by giving the permission, does not:

(1) assure that the premises are safe for that purpose;

(2) owe to the person to whom permission is granted or to whom the invitation is extended a greater degree of care than is owed to a trespasser on the premises; or

(3) assume responsibility or incur liability for any injury to any individual or property caused by any act of the person to whom permission is granted or to whom the invitation is extended.

(c) If an owner, lessee, or occupant of real property other than agricultural land gives permission to another to enter the premises for recreation, the owner, lessee, or occupant, by giving the permission, does not:

(1) assure that the premises are safe for that purpose;

(2) owe to the person to whom permission is granted a greater degree of care than is owed to a trespasser on the premises; or

(3) assume responsibility or incur liability for any injury to any individual or property caused by any act of the person to whom permission is granted.

(d) Subsections (a), (b), and (c) shall not limit the liability of an owner, lessee, or occupant of real property who has been grossly negligent or has acted with malicious intent or in bad faith.

(e) In this section, "recreation" means, in addition to its meaning under Section 75.001, the following activities only if the activities take place on premises owned, operated, or maintained by a governmental unit for the purposes of those activities:

(1) hockey and in-line hockey;

(2) skating, in-line skating, roller-skating, skateboarding, and roller-blading;

(3) soap box derby use; and

(4) paintball use.

(f) Notwithstanding Subsections (b) and (c), if a person enters premises owned, operated, or maintained by a governmental unit and engages in recreation on those premises, the governmental unit does not owe to the person a greater degree of care than is owed to a trespasser on the premises.

(g) Any premises a governmental unit owns, operates, or maintains and on which the recreational activities described in Subsections (e)(1)–(4) are conducted shall post and maintain a clearly readable sign in a clearly visible location on or near the premises. The sign shall contain the following warning language:

WARNING

TEXAS LAW (CHAPTER 75, CIVIL PRACTICE AND REMEDIES CODE) LIMITS THE LIABILITY OF A GOVERNMENTAL UNIT FOR DAMAGES ARISING DIRECTLY FROM HOCKEY, IN-LINE HOCKEY, SKATING, IN-LINE SKATING, ROLLER-SKATING,

SKATEBOARDING, ROLLER-BLADING, PAINTBALL USE, OR SOAP BOX DERBY USE ON PREMISES THAT THE GOVERNMENTAL UNIT OWNS, OPERATES, OR MAINTAINS FOR THAT PURPOSE.

(h) An owner, lessee, or occupant of real property in this state is liable for trespass as a result of migration or transport of any air contaminant, as defined in Section 382.003(2), Health and Safety Code, other than odor, only upon a showing of actual and substantial damages by a plaintiff in a civil action.

(i) Subsections (b) and (c) do not affect any liability of an owner, lessee, or occupant of real property for an injury occurring outside the boundaries of the real property caused by an activity described by Section 75.001(3)(P) that originates within the boundaries of the real property.

Acts 1985, 69th Leg., ch. 959, § 1, eff. Sept. 1, 1985. Amended by Acts 1989, 71st Leg., ch. 62, § 2, eff. Sept. 1, 1989; Acts 1997, 75th Leg., ch. 56, § 2, eff. Sept. 1, 1997; Acts 1999, 76th Leg., ch. 734, § 1, eff. Sept. 1, 1999; Acts 2003, 78th Leg., ch. 204, § 21.01, eff. Sept. 1, 2003; Acts 2003, 78th Leg., ch. 739, § 1, eff. Sept. 1, 2003; Acts 2005, 79th Leg., ch. 116, § 2, eff. Sept. 1, 2005; Acts 2005, 79th Leg., ch. 932, § 2, eff. Sept. 1, 2005; Acts 2007, 80th Leg., ch. 227, § 1, eff. May 25, 2007; Acts 2007, 80th Leg., ch. 659, § 2, eff. June 15, 2007.

§ 75.0021. Repealed by Acts 2017, 85th Leg., ch. 815 (H.B. 931), § 2, eff. Sept. 1, 2017

§ 75.0022. Limited Liability of Certain Electric Utilities

(a) In this section:

(1) "Electric utility" has the meaning assigned by Section 31.002, Utilities Code.

(2) "Person" includes an individual, as defined by Section 71.001.

(3) "Premises" includes the land owned, occupied, or leased by an electric utility, or covered by an easement owned by an electric utility, with respect to which public access and use is allowed in a written agreement with a political subdivision under Subsection (c).

(4) "Serious bodily injury" means an injury that creates a substantial risk of death or that causes serious permanent disfigurement or protracted loss or impairment of the function of a body part or organ.

(b) Repealed by Acts 2017, 85th Leg., ch. 815 (H.B. 931), § 2.

(c) An electric utility, as the owner, easement holder, occupant, or lessee of land, may enter into a written agreement with a political subdivision to allow public access to and use of the premises of the electric utility for recreation, exercise, relaxation, travel, or pleasure.

(d) The electric utility, by entering into an agreement under this section or at any time during the term of the agreement, does not:

(1) assure that the premises are safe for recreation, exercise, relaxation, travel, or pleasure;

(2) owe to a person entering the premises for recreation, exercise, relaxation, travel, or pleasure, or accompanying another person entering the premises for recreation, exercise, relaxation, travel, or pleasure, a greater degree of care than is owed to a trespasser on the premises; or

(3) except as provided by Subsection (e), assume responsibility or incur any liability for:

(A) damages arising from or related to bodily or other personal injury to or death of any person who enters the premises for recreation, exercise, relaxation, travel, or pleasure or accompanies another person entering the premises for recreation, exercise, relaxation, travel, or pleasure;

(B) property damage sustained by any person who enters the premises for recreation, exercise, relaxation, travel, or pleasure or accompanies another person entering the premises for recreation, exercise, relaxation, travel, or pleasure; or

(C) an act of a third party that occurs on the premises, regardless of whether the act is intentional.

(e) Subsection (d) does not limit the liability of an electric utility for serious bodily injury or death of a person proximately caused by the electric utility's wilful or wanton acts or gross negligence with respect to a dangerous condition existing on the premises.

(f) The limitation on liability provided by this section applies only to a cause of action brought by a person who enters the premises for recreation, exercise, relaxation, travel, or pleasure or accompanies another person entering the premises for recreation, exercise, relaxation, travel, or pleasure.

(g) The doctrine of attractive nuisance does not apply to a claim that is subject to this section.

(h) A written agreement entered into under this section may require the political subdivision to provide or pay for insurance coverage for any defense costs or other litigation costs incurred by the electric utility for damage claims under this section.

Added by Acts 2013, 83rd Leg., ch. 44 (H.B. 200), § 3, eff. May 16, 2013. Amended by Acts 2017, 85th Leg., ch. 815 (H.B. 931), § 2, eff. Sept. 1, 2017.

§ 75.0025. Limited Liability of Persons Allowing Certain Uses of Land

(a) In this section, "community garden" means the premises used for recreational gardening by a group of people residing in a neighborhood or community for the purpose of providing fresh produce for the benefit of the residents of the neighborhood or community.

(b) An owner, lessee, or occupant of land that gives permission to another person to enter and use the land as a community garden does not by giving that permission:

(1) ensure that the premises are safe; or

(2) assume responsibility or incur any liability for:

(A) damages arising from or related to any bodily or other personal injury to or death of any person who enters the premises for a purpose related to a community garden;

(B) property damage sustained by any person who enters the premises for a purpose related to a community garden; or

(C) an act of a third party that occurs on the premises.

(c) The doctrine of attractive nuisance does not apply to a claim that is subject to this section.

(d) This section does not limit the liability of an owner, lessee, or occupant of land for an injury caused by wilful or wanton acts or gross negligence by the owner, lessee, or occupant.

(e) An owner, lessee, or occupant of land that allows the use of the premises as a community garden shall post and maintain a clearly readable sign in a clearly visible location on or near the premises. The sign must contain the following warning language:

Added by Acts 2015, 84th Leg., ch. 679 (H.B. 262), § 1, eff. Sept. 1, 2015.

§ 75.003. Application and Effect of Chapter

(a) This chapter does not relieve any owner, lessee, or occupant of real property of any liability that would otherwise exist for deliberate, wilful, or malicious injury to a person or to property.

(b) This chapter does not affect the doctrine of attractive nuisance, except:

(1) as provided by Section 75.0022(g) or 75.0025(c); and

(2) the doctrine of attractive nuisance may not be the basis for liability of an owner, lessee, or occupant of agricultural land for any injury to a trespasser over the age of 16 years.

(c) Except for a governmental unit, this chapter applies only to an owner, lessee, or occupant of real property who:

(1) does not charge for entry to the premises;

(2) charges for entry to the premises, but whose total charges collected in the previous calendar year for all recreational use of the entire premises of the owner, lessee, or occupant are not more than 20 times the total amount of ad valorem taxes imposed on the premises for the previous calendar year; or

(3) has liability insurance coverage in effect on an act or omission described by Section 75.004(a) and in the amounts equal to or greater than those provided by that section.

(d) This chapter does not create any liability.

(e) Except as otherwise provided, this chapter applies to a governmental unit.

(f) This chapter does not waive sovereign immunity.

(g) To the extent that this chapter limits the liability of a governmental unit under circumstances in which the governmental unit would be liable under Chapter 101, this chapter controls.

(h) In the case of agricultural land, an owner, lessee, or occupant of real property who does not charge for entry to the premises because the individuals entering the premises for recreation are invited social guests satisfies the requirement of Subsection (c)(1).

Acts 1985, 69th Leg., ch. 959, § 1, eff. Sept. 1, 1985. Amended by Acts 1987, 70th Leg., ch. 832, § 5, eff. Sept. 1, 1987; Acts 1989, 71st Leg., ch. 62, § 3, eff. Sept. 1, 1989; Acts 1995, 74th Leg., ch. 520, § 2, eff. Aug. 28, 1995; Acts 1997, 75th Leg., ch. 56, § 3, eff. Sept. 1, 1997; Acts 2003, 78th Leg., ch. 429, § 1, eff. Sept. 1, 2003; Acts 2013, 83rd Leg., ch. 44 (H.B. 200), § 4, eff. May 16, 2013; Acts 2015, 84th Leg., ch. 679 (H.B. 262), § 2, eff. Sept. 1, 2015.

§ 75.004. Limitation on Monetary Damages for Private Landowners

(a) Subject to Subsection (b), the liability of an owner, lessee, or occupant of agricultural land used for recreational purposes for an act or omission by the owner, lessee, or occupant relating to the premises that results in damages to a person who has entered the premises is limited to a maximum amount of $500,000 for each person and $1 million for each single occurrence of bodily injury or death and $100,000 for each single occurrence for injury to or destruction of property. In the case of agricultural land, the total liability of an owner, lessee, or occupant for a single occurrence is limited to $1 million, and the liability also is subject to the limits for each single occurrence of bodily injury or death and each single occurrence for injury to or destruction of property stated in this subsection.

(b) This section applies only to an owner, lessee, or occupant of agricultural land used for recreational purposes who has liability insurance coverage in effect on an act or omission described by Subsection (a) and in the amounts equal to or greater than those provided by Subsection (a). The coverage may be provided under a contract of insurance or other plan of insurance authorized by statute. The limit of liability insurance coverage applicable with respect to agricultural land may be a combined single limit in the amount of $1 million for each single occurrence.

(c) This section does not affect the liability of an insurer or insurance plan in an action under Chapter 541, Insurance Code, or an action for bad faith conduct, breach of fiduciary duty, or negligent failure to settle a claim.

(d) This section does not apply to a governmental unit.

Added by Acts 1995, 74th Leg., ch. 520, § 3, eff. Aug. 28, 1995. Amended by Acts 1997, 75th Leg., ch. 56, § 4, eff. Sept. 1, 1997; Acts 2005, 79th Leg., ch. 728, § 11.106, eff. Sept. 1, 2005.

§ 75.005. [Blank]

§ 75.006. Liability Limited for Actions of Firefighter, Federal Law Enforcement Officer, or Peace Officer

(a) In this section:

(1) "Federal law enforcement officer" means a law enforcement officer as defined by 5 U.S.C. Section 8331(20).

(2) "Firefighter" means a member of a fire department who performs a function listed in Section 419.021(3)(C), Government Code.

(3) "Livestock" has the meaning assigned by Section 1.003, Agriculture Code.

(4) "Peace officer" has the meaning assigned by Section 1.07, Penal Code, or other state or federal law.

(b) A landowner is not liable for damages arising from an incident or accident caused by livestock of the landowner due to an act or omission of a firefighter or a peace officer who has entered the landowner's property with or without the permission of the landowner, regardless of whether the damage occurs on the landowner's property.

(c) An owner, lessee, or occupant of agricultural land is not liable for any damage or injury to any person or property that arises from the actions of a peace officer or federal law enforcement officer when the officer enters or causes another person to enter the agricultural land with or without the permission of the owner, lessee, or occupant, regardless of whether the damage or injury occurs on the agricultural land.

(d) The owner, lessee, or occupant of agricultural land is not liable for any damage or injury to any person or property that arises from the actions of an individual who, because of the actions of a peace officer or federal law enforcement officer, enters or causes another person to enter the agricultural land without the permission of the owner, lessee, or occupant.

(e) This section does not limit the liability of an owner, lessee, or occupant of agricultural land for any damage or injury that arises from a wilful or wanton act or gross negligence by the owner, lessee, or occupant.

Added by Acts 2009, 81st Leg., ch. 786, § 1, eff. Sept. 1, 2009. Amended by Acts 2011, 82nd Leg., ch. 101 (S.B. 1160), §§ 1, 2, eff. May 20, 2011.

§ 75.007. Trespassers

(a) In this section, "trespasser" means a person who enters the land of another without any legal right, express or implied.

(b) An owner, lessee, or occupant of land does not owe a duty of care to a trespasser on the land and is not liable for any injury to a trespasser on the land, except that an owner, lessee, or occupant owes a duty to refrain from injuring a trespasser wilfully, wantonly, or through gross negligence.

(c) Notwithstanding Subsection (b), an owner, lessee, or occupant of land may be liable for injury to a child caused by a highly dangerous artificial condition on the land if:

(1) the place where the artificial condition exists is one upon which the owner, lessee, or occupant knew or reasonably should have known that children were likely to trespass;

(2) the artificial condition is one that the owner, lessee, or occupant knew or reasonably should have

known existed, and that the owner, lessee, or occupant realized or should have realized involved an unreasonable risk of death or serious bodily harm to such children;

(3) the injured child, because of the child's youth, did not discover the condition or realize the risk involved in intermeddling with the condition or coming within the area made dangerous by the condition;

(4) the utility to the owner, lessee, or occupant of maintaining the artificial condition and the burden of eliminating the danger were slight as compared with the risk to the child involved; and

(5) the owner, lessee, or occupant failed to exercise reasonable care to eliminate the danger or otherwise protect the child.

(d) An owner, lessee, or occupant of land whose actions are justified under Subchapter C or D, Chapter 9, Penal Code, is not liable to a trespasser for damages arising from those actions.

(e) This section does not affect Section 75.001, 75.002, 75.003, or 75.004 or create or increase the liability of any person.

Added by Acts 2011, 82nd Leg., ch. 101 (S.B. 1160), § 3, eff. May 20, 2011. Amended by Acts 2017, 85th Leg., ch. 815 (H.B. 931), § 1, eff. Sept. 1, 2017.

CHAPTER 75A. LIMITED LIABILITY FOR AGRITOURISM ACTIVITIES

Section

§ 75A.001. Definitions

In this chapter:

(1) "Agricultural land" means land that is located in this state and that is suitable for:

(A) use in production of plants and fruits grown for human or animal consumption, or plants grown for the production of fibers, floriculture, viticulture, horticulture, or planting seed; or

(B) domestic or native farm or ranch animals kept for use or profit.

(2) "Agritourism activity" means an activity on agricultural land for recreational or educational purposes of participants, without regard to compensation.

(3) "Agritourism entity" means a person engaged in the business of providing an agritourism activity, without regard to compensation, including a person who displays exotic animals to the public on agricultural land.

(4) "Agritourism participant" means an individual, other than an employee of an agritourism entity, who engages in an agritourism activity.

(5) "Agritourism participant injury" means an injury sustained by an agritourism participant, including bodily injury, emotional distress, death, property damage, or any other loss arising from the person's participation in an agritourism activity.

(6) "Premises" has the meaning assigned by Section 75.001.

(7) "Recreation" has the meaning assigned by Section 75.001.

Added by Acts 2015, 84th Leg., ch. 1152 (S.B. 610), § 1, eff. June 19, 2015.

§ 75A.002. Limited Liability

(a) Except as provided by Subsection (b), an agritourism entity is not liable to any person for an agritourism participant injury or damages arising out of the agritourism participant injury if:

(1) at the time of the agritourism activity from which the injury arises, the warning prescribed by Section 75A.003 was posted in accordance with that section; or

(2) the agritourism entity obtained in accordance with Section 75A.004 a written agreement and warning statement from the agritourism participant with respect to the agritourism activity from which the injury arises.

(b) This section does not limit liability for an injury:

(1) proximately caused by:

(A) the agritourism entity's negligence evidencing a disregard for the safety of the agritourism participant;

(B) one of the following dangers, of which the agritourism entity had actual knowledge or reasonably should have known:

(i) a dangerous condition on the land, facilities, or equipment used in the activity; or

(ii) the dangerous propensity, that is not disclosed to the agritourism participant, of a particular animal used in the activity; or

(C) the agritourism entity's failure to train or improper training of an employee of the agritourism entity actively involved in an agritourism activity; or

(2) intentionally caused by the agritourism entity.

(c) A limitation on liability provided by this section to an agritourism entity is in addition to other limitations of liability.

Added by Acts 2015, 84th Leg., ch. 1152 (S.B. 610), § 1, eff. June 19, 2015.

§ 75A.003. Posted Warning

For the purposes of limitation of liability under Section 75A.002(a)(1), an agritourism entity must post and maintain a sign in a clearly visible location on or near any premises on which an agritourism activity is conducted. The sign must contain the following language:

WARNING

UNDER TEXAS LAW (CHAPTER 75A, CIVIL PRACTICE AND REMEDIES CODE), AN AGRITOURISM ENTITY IS NOT LIABLE FOR ANY INJURY TO OR DEATH OF AN AGRITOURISM PARTICIPANT RESULTING FROM AN AGRITOURISM ACTIVITY.

Added by Acts 2015, 84th Leg., ch. 1152 (S.B. 610), § 1, eff. June 19, 2015.

§ 75A.004. Signed Agreement and Warning

For the purposes of limitation of liability under Section 75A.002(a)(2), a written agreement and warning statement is considered effective and enforceable if it:

(1) is signed before the agritourism participant participates in an agritourism activity;

(2) is signed by the agritourism participant or, if the agritourism participant is a minor, the agritourism participant's parent, managing conservator, or guardian;

(3) is in a document separate from any other agreement between the agritourism participant and the agritourism entity other than a different warning, consent, or assumption of risk statement;

(4) is printed in not less than 10–point bold type; and

(5) contains the following language:

AGREEMENT AND WARNING

I UNDERSTAND AND ACKNOWLEDGE THAT AN AGRITOURISM ENTITY IS NOT LIABLE FOR ANY INJURY TO OR DEATH OF AN AGRITOURISM PARTICIPANT RESULTING FROM AGRITOURISM ACTIVITIES. I UNDERSTAND THAT I HAVE ACCEPTED ALL RISK OF INJURY, DEATH, PROPERTY DAMAGE, AND OTHER LOSS THAT MAY RESULT FROM AGRITOURISM ACTIVITIES.

Added by Acts 2015, 84th Leg., ch. 1152 (S.B. 610), § 1, eff. June 19, 2015.

CHAPTER 76. FOOD DONORS

§ 76.001. Definitions

In this chapter:

(1) "Donate" means to give without requiring anything of monetary value from the recipient.

(2) "Intentional misconduct" means conduct that the actor knows is harmful to the health or well-being of another person.

(3) "Nonprofit organization" means an incorporated or unincorporated organization that has been established and is operating for religious, charitable, or educational purposes and that does not distribute any of its income to its members, directors, or officers.

(4) "Person" means an individual, corporation, partnership, organization, association, or governmental entity.

(5) "Gleaner" means a person who harvests for free distribution to the needy an agricultural crop that has been donated by the owner.

Acts 1985, 69th Leg., ch. 959, § 1, eff. Sept. 1, 1985. Amended by Acts 1989, 71st Leg., ch. 301, § 1, eff. June 14, 1989; Acts 1989, 71st Leg., ch. 1093, § 1, eff. June 16, 1989.

§ 76.002. Short Title

This chapter may be cited as the Good Faith Donor Act.

Acts 1985, 69th Leg., ch. 959, § 1, eff. Sept. 1, 1985.

§ 76.003. Apparently Wholesome Food

For the purposes of this chapter, food is apparently wholesome if the food meets all quality standards of local, county, state, and federal agricultural and health laws and rules, even though the food is not readily marketable due to appearance, age, freshness, grade, size, surplus, or other condition. Canned goods that are leaking, swollen, dented on a seam, or no longer airtight are not apparently wholesome food.

Acts 1985, 69th Leg., ch. 959, § 1, eff. Sept. 1, 1985.

§ 76.004. Liability for Damages from Donated Food

(a) A person or gleaner is not subject to civil or criminal liability arising from the condition of apparently wholesome food that the person or gleaner donates to a church, a not-for-profit organization or a nonprofit organization for distribution to the needy, if the food is apparently wholesome at the time of donation. This subsection does not apply to an injury or death that results from an act or omission of the donor constituting gross negligence, recklessness, or intentional misconduct.

(b) A person who is allowing his or her fields to be gleaned by volunteers for distribution to the needy is not subject to civil or criminal liability that arises due to the injury of a gleaner, unless an injury or death results from an act or omission of the person constituting gross negligence, recklessness, or intentional misconduct.

(c) A nonprofit organization is not subject to civil or criminal liability arising from the condition of apparently wholesome food that it distributes to the needy at no charge in substantial compliance with applicable local, county, state, and federal laws and rules regarding the storage and handling of food for distribution to the public, if the food is apparently wholesome at the time of distribution. This subsection does not apply to an injury or death that results from an act or omission of the organization constituting gross negligence, recklessness, or intentional misconduct.

(d) This chapter does not create any liability.

Acts 1985, 69th Leg., ch. 959, § 1, eff. Sept. 1, 1985. Amended by Acts 1989, 71st Leg., ch. 1093, § 2, eff. June 16, 1989; Acts 2015, 84th Leg., ch. 517 (H.B. 1050), § 1, eff. June 16, 2015.

CHAPTER 77. TRANSPLANTS AND TRANSFUSIONS

Section

§ 77.001. Definition

In this chapter, "human body part" means any tissue, organ, blood, or components thereof from a human.

Acts 1985, 69th Leg., ch. 959, § 1, eff. Sept. 1, 1985.

§ 77.002. Policy

It is important to the health and welfare of the people of this state that scientific knowledge, skills, and materials be available for the procedures of transplantation, injection, transfusion, or other transfer of human body parts. The imposition of strict liability on persons and organizations engaged in these scientific procedures inhibits the exercise of sound medical judgment and restricts the availability of the knowledge, skills, and materials. It is therefore the public policy of this state to promote the health and welfare of the people by limiting the legal liability arising from those scientific procedures to instances of negligence.

Acts 1985, 69th Leg., ch. 959, § 1, eff. Sept. 1, 1985.

§ 77.003. Limitation of Liability

(a) A person who donates, obtains, prepares, transplants, injects, transfuses, or transfers a human body part from a living or dead human to another human or a person who assists or participates in that activity is not liable as a result of that activity except for negligence, gross negligence, or an intentional tort.

(b) The Deceptive Trade Practices-Consumer Protection Act (Subchapter E, Chapter 17, Business & Commerce Code [1]) does not apply with respect to claims for damages for personal injury or death resulting or alleged to have resulted from negligence on the part of the person described in Subsection (a) of this section in connection with an activity designated in said subsection.

(c) The implied warranties of merchantability and fitness do not apply to the furnishing of human body parts by blood banks, tissue banks, or other similar organizations. For purposes of this chapter, those human body parts are not considered commodities subject to sale or barter.

Acts 1985, 69th Leg., ch. 959, § 1, eff. Sept. 1, 1985. Amended by Acts 1987, 70th Leg., ch. 1093, § 6, eff. Aug. 31, 1987.

[1] V.T.C.A., Business & Commerce Code § 17.41 et seq.

§ 77.004. Blood Bank: Compensation of Seller

(a) This section applies only to a blood bank licensed either by the Division of Biological Standards of the National Institute of Health or by the American Association of Blood Banks.

(b) A blood bank may not pay cash for blood. A blood bank may not pay a blood seller by check unless the check is sent by United States mail to the seller after the 15th day following the day the blood is taken from the seller.

(c) If a blood bank violates Subsection (b) and the blood contains harmful substances, the blood bank is not entitled to the immunity established by this chapter. The blood bank has the burden of establishing that the blood was not purchased in violation of Subsection (b).

Acts 1985, 69th Leg., ch. 959, § 1, eff. Sept. 1, 1985.

CHAPTER 78. CERTAIN FIRE FIGHTERS AND FIRE-FIGHTING ENTITIES

Acts 1997, 75th Leg., ch. 899, § 1 amended Chapter 78 effective September 1, 1997. The former Chapter 78, Volunteer Fire Fighters, consisting only of V.T.C.A., Civil Practice & Remedies Code § 78.001, was amended as Chapter 78, Certain Fire Fighters and Fire-Fighting Entities, consisting of V.T.C.A., Civil Practice & Remedies Code §§ 78.001 to 78.054.

SUBCHAPTER A. VOLUNTEER FIRE FIGHTERS AND FIRE DEPARTMENTS

§ 78.001. Liability

A volunteer fire fighter or a volunteer fire department is not liable for damage to property resulting from the fire fighter's or the department's reasonable and necessary action in fighting or extinguishing a fire on the property.

Acts 1985, 69th Leg., ch. 959, § 1, eff. Sept. 1, 1985. Amended by Acts 1997, 75th Leg., ch. 899, § 1, eff. Sept. 1, 1997.

SUBCHAPTER B. MARINE FIRE-FIGHTING SERVICES

§ 78.051. Definitions

In this subchapter:

(1) "Fire emergency" means an emergency response involving fire protection or prevention, rescue, emergency medical, or hazardous material response services.

(2) "Fire fighter" means an employee of a nonprofit fire department.

(3) "Governmental unit" has the meaning assigned by Chapter 101.

(4) "Nonprofit fire department" means a nonprofit organization that is:

(A) exempt from federal income tax under Section 501(a) of the Internal Revenue Code of 1986 (26 U.S.C. Section 501(a)) by being listed as an exempt organization in Section 501(c)(4) of that code;

(B) composed of member owners; and

(C) organized to offer and provide:

(i) fire protection, prevention, and inspection services; and

(ii) emergency response services, including rescue, emergency medical, and hazardous material response services.

Added by Acts 1997, 75th Leg., ch. 899, § 1, eff. Sept. 1, 1997.

§ 78.052. Applicability of Subchapter: Marine Fire Emergency

This subchapter applies only to damages for personal injury, death, or property damage arising from an error or omission of:

(1) a nonprofit fire department providing services to respond to marine fire emergencies under contract to a governmental unit, if the error or omission occurs in responding to a marine fire emergency:

(A) on the navigable waters of this state;

(B) in any place into which a vessel enters or from which a vessel departs the waterway leading to that place from the Gulf of Mexico or the Gulf Intracoastal Waterway;

(C) on property owned or under the control of the governmental unit; or

(D) at the request of the governmental unit in the interest of public safety; or

(2) a fire fighter providing services described by Subdivision (1).

Added by Acts 1997, 75th Leg., ch. 899, § 1, eff. Sept. 1, 1997.

§ 78.053. Liability

(a) A nonprofit fire department is liable for damages described by Section 78.052 only to the extent that the governmental unit with which the nonprofit fire department is contracting would be liable under Chapter 101.

(b) Section 101.106 applies to a claimant in a suit against a fire fighter as if the fire fighter were an employee of a governmental unit and the nonprofit fire department were a governmental unit.

Added by Acts 1997, 75th Leg., ch. 899, § 1, eff. Sept. 1, 1997.

§ 78.054. Individual Immunities

A fire fighter is liable for damages described by Section 78.052 only to the extent an analogous employee of the governmental unit with which the nonprofit fire department is contracting would be liable and is entitled to the common law immunities applicable to the employee of the governmental unit.

Added by Acts 1997, 75th Leg., ch. 899, § 1, eff. Sept. 1, 1997.

SUBCHAPTER C. FIRE–FIGHTING SERVICES

§ 78.101. Definitions

In this subchapter:

(1) "Emergency response" means a response involving fire protection or prevention, rescue, emergency medical, or hazardous material response services.

(2) "Volunteer fire department" means a nonprofit organization that is:

(A) operated by its members;

(B) exempt from the state sales tax under Section 151.310, Tax Code, or the state franchise tax under Section 171.083, Tax Code; and

(C) organized to provide an emergency response.

(3) "Volunteer fire fighter" means a member of a volunteer fire department.

Added by Acts 2003, 78th Leg., ch. 204, § 19.02, eff. Sept. 1, 2003.

§ 78.102. Applicability of Subchapter: Emergency Response

This subchapter applies only to damages for personal injury, death, or property damage, other than property damage to which Subchapter A applies, arising from an error or omission of:

(1) a volunteer fire department while involved in or providing an emergency response; or

(2) a volunteer fire fighter while involved in or providing an emergency response as a member of a volunteer fire department.

Added by Acts 2003, 78th Leg., ch. 204, § 19.02, eff. Sept. 1, 2003.

§ 78.103. Liability of Volunteer Fire Department

A volunteer fire department is:

(1) liable for damages described by Section 78.102 only to the extent that a county providing the same or similar services would be liable under Chapter 101; and

(2) entitled to the exclusions, exceptions, and defenses applicable to a county under Chapter 101 and other statutory or common law.

Added by Acts 2003, 78th Leg., ch. 204, § 19.02, eff. Sept. 1, 2003.

§ 78.104. Liability of Volunteer Fire Fighter

A volunteer fire fighter is:

(1) liable for damages described by Section 78.102 only to the extent that an employee providing the same or similar services for a county would be liable; and

(2) entitled to the exclusions, exceptions, immunities, and defenses applicable to an employee of a county under Chapter 101 and other statutory or common law.

Added by Acts 2003, 78th Leg., ch. 204, § 19.02, eff. Sept. 1, 2003.

SUBCHAPTER D. LIABILITY FOR TRAINING EXERCISES

§ 78.151. Liability for Training Exercises

A person is not liable for damages resulting from the person's execution of a training exercise intended to prepare the person to respond to a fire or emergency to which this chapter applies to the same extent that the person would not be liable under this chapter for damages resulting from the person's actions in responding to a fire or emergency.

Added by Acts 2015, 84th Leg., ch. 1039 (H.B. 1666), § 1, eff. Sept. 1, 2015.

CHAPTER 78A. LIABILITY OF FIRST RESPONDERS FOR ROADSIDE ASSISTANCE

§ 78A.001. Definitions

In this chapter:

(1) "First responder" means a law enforcement, fire protection, or emergency medical services employee or volunteer, including:

(A) a peace officer as defined by Article 2.12, Code of Criminal Procedure;

(B) fire protection personnel as defined by Section 419.021, Government Code;

(C) a volunteer firefighter who is:

(i) certified by the Texas Commission on Fire Protection or by the State Firefighters' and Fire Marshals' Association of Texas; or

(ii) a member of an organized volunteer firefighting unit that renders fire-fighting services without remuneration and conducts a minimum of two drills each month, each two hours long; and

(D) an individual certified as emergency medical services personnel by the Department of State Health Services.

(2) "Roadside assistance" means assistance to the owner, operator, or passenger of a motor vehicle with an incident related to the operation of the motor vehicle, including jump-starting or replacing a motor vehicle battery, lockout assistance, replacing a flat tire, and roadside vehicle breakdown assistance.

Added by Acts 2017, 85th Leg., ch. 1150 (H.B. 590), § 1, eff. Sept. 1, 2017.

§ 78A.002. Liability of First Responder

A first responder who in good faith provides roadside assistance is not liable in civil damages for damage to the motor vehicle affected by the incident for which the roadside assistance is provided that is caused by an act or omission that occurs during the performance of the act of roadside assistance unless the act or omission constitutes gross negligence, recklessness, or intentional misconduct.

Added by Acts 2017, 85th Leg., ch. 1150 (H.B. 590), § 1, eff. Sept. 1, 2017.

CHAPTER 79. LIABILITY OF PERSONS ASSISTING IN HAZARDOUS OR DANGEROUS SITUATIONS

§ 79.001. Definitions

In this chapter:

(1) "Hazardous material" means:

(A) a substance classified as a hazardous material under state or federal law or under a rule adopted pursuant to state or federal law; or

(B) a chemical, petroleum product, gas, or other substance that, if discharged or released, is likely to create an imminent danger to individuals, property, or the environment.

(2) "Person" means an individual, association, corporation, or other private legal entity.

Acts 1985, 69th Leg., ch. 959, § 1, eff. Sept. 1, 1985.

§ 79.002. Hazardous Materials

(a) Except in a case of reckless conduct or intentional, wilful, or wanton misconduct, a person is immune from civil liability for an act or omission that occurs in giving care, assistance, or advice with respect to the management of an incident that:

(1) has already occurred;

(2) is related to the storage or transportation of a hazardous material; and

(3) endangers or threatens to endanger individuals, property, or the environment as a result of the spillage, seepage, or other release of a hazardous material or as a result of fire or explosion involving a hazardous material.

(b) This section does not apply to a person giving care, assistance, or advice for or in expectation of compensation from or on behalf of the recipient of the care, assistance, or advice in excess of reimbursement for expenses incurred.

Acts 1985, 69th Leg., ch. 959, § 1, eff. Sept. 1, 1985. Amended by Acts 2003, 78th Leg., ch. 58, § 3, eff. Sept. 1, 2003.

§ 79.003. Disaster Assistance

(a) Except in a case of reckless conduct or intentional, wilful, or wanton misconduct, a person is immune from civil liability for an act or omission that occurs in giving care, assistance, or advice with respect to the management of an incident:

(1) that is a man-made or natural disaster that endangers or threatens to endanger individuals, property, or the environment, including a major disaster declared by the president of the United States or a disaster declared under Section 418.014, Government Code; and

(2) in which the care, assistance, or advice is provided at the request of:

(A) an authorized representative of a local, state, or federal agency, including a fire department, a police department, an emergency management agency, and a disaster response agency; or

(B) a charitable organization, as that term is defined by Section 84.003, that provides services to mitigate the effects of a disaster described by Subdivision (1).

(b) Subsection (a) does not apply to a person giving care, assistance, or advice for or in expectation of compensation from or on behalf of the recipient of the care, assistance, or advice in excess of reimbursement for expenses incurred.

(c) Notwithstanding Chapter 101 or any other law, an entity and the authorized representative of the entity are not liable under the laws of this state for the act or omission of a person providing care, assistance, or advice on request under Subsection (a)(2)(A).

(d) Notwithstanding Chapter 84 or any other law, a charitable organization is not liable under the laws of this state for the act or omission of a person providing care, assistance, or advice on request under Subsection (a)(2)(B).

(e) The immunities provided by this section are in addition to any other immunity or limitations of liability provided by law, including Subchapter D, Chapter 74, this chapter, or Chapter 78 or 78A of this code or Section 418.006, Government Code.

Added by Acts 2003, 78th Leg., ch. 58, § 1, eff. Sept. 1, 2003. Amended by Acts 2019, 86th Leg., ch. 385 (H.B. 3365), § 1, eff. June 2, 2019.

Section 2 of Acts 2019, 86th Leg., ch. 385 (H.B. 3365) provides:

"Section 79.003, Civil Practice and Remedies Code, as amended by this Act, applies only to a cause of action that accrues on or after the effective date [June 2, 2019] of this Act."

§ 79.0031. Liability of Volunteer Health Care Provider or Health Care Institution

(a) In this section:

(1) "Health care institution" has the meaning assigned by Section 74.001.

(2) "Volunteer health care provider" has the meaning assigned by Section 84.003. The term includes an individual who is not affiliated with a charitable organization.

(b) Except in the case of reckless conduct or intentional, wilful, or wanton misconduct, a volunteer health care provider is immune from civil liability for an act or omission that occurs in giving care, assistance, or advice if the care, assistance, or advice is provided:

(1) in relation to an incident that is a man-made or natural disaster that endangers or threatens to endanger individuals, property, or the environment; and

(2) within the scope of the provider's practice under the laws of this state.

(c) A health care institution is immune from civil liability for an act or omission by a volunteer health care provider providing care, assistance, or advice at the institution's facility or under the institution's direction if:

(1) the provider is immune from civil liability under Subsection (b); and

(2) the institution does not have an expectation of compensation from or on behalf of the recipient of the care, assistance, or advice in excess of reimbursement for expenses incurred by the institution in connection with the provision of the care, assistance, or advice.

(d) The immunity provided by this section is in addition to any other immunity or limitations of liability provided by law.

Added by Acts 2019, 86th Leg., ch. 74 (S.B. 752), § 1, eff. Sept. 1, 2019.

Section 2 of Acts 2019, 86th Leg., ch. 74 (S.B. 752) provides:

"Section 79.0031, Civil Practice and Remedies Code, as added by this Act, does not apply to a cause of action that accrued before the effective date [Sept. 1, 2019] of this Act."

§ 79.004. Liability for Training Exercises

Except in a case of reckless conduct or intentional, wilful, or wanton misconduct, a person who is immune from civil liability for an act or omission that occurs in giving care, assistance, or advice with respect to the management of an incident to which this chapter applies is immune from civil liability for an act or omission that occurs during the execution of a training exercise intended to prepare the person to give that care, assistance, or advice.

Added by Acts 2015, 84th Leg., ch. 1039 (H.B. 1666), § 2, eff. Sept. 1, 2015.

CHAPTER 80. TRESPASS: OUTDOOR SIGN

Section

§ 80.001. Definition

In this chapter, "sign" means an outdoor structure, sign, display, light device, figure, painting, drawing, message, plaque, poster, billboard, or any other thing that is designed, intended, or used to advertise or inform.

Added by Acts 1989, 71st Leg., ch. 2, § 4.04(a), eff. Aug. 28, 1989.

§ 80.002. Trespass

A trespass occurs when an individual:

(1) erects or places a sign on premises without the permission of the owner of the premises; or

(2) after the expiration or termination of an agreement with the owner of the premises for the erection, placement, or maintenance of a sign on the premises and before the expiration of the period described by Section 80.003(b)(2), fails to remove or abandons a sign or fails to obtain from the owner of the premises permission for the continued use or maintenance of the sign on the premises.

Added by Acts 1989, 71st Leg., ch. 2, § 4.04(a), eff. Aug. 28, 1989. Amended by Acts 1999, 76th Leg., ch. 440, § 1, eff. Sept. 1, 1999.

§ 80.003. Damages

(a) The owner of the premises is entitled to recover damages equal to the amount of payments received by or accruing to the owner of the sign from the rental, sale, lease, or other use of the sign during the period after the expiration of the 30th day after the date on which the written notice required by Subsection (b)(1) is received and before the date on which the sign is removed or permission for the continued use or maintenance of the sign is obtained.

(b) The owner of the premises may not recover damages for trespass under this section unless:

(1) the owner of the premises sends, by certified mail, return receipt requested, to the owner of the sign written demand for removal of the sign, stating in detail the act constituting the trespass and the location where the sign has been erected, placed, or maintained; and

(2) the owner of the sign fails to remove the sign or obtain permission from the owner of the premises for the continued use or maintenance of the sign before the 30th day after the date on which the notice described by Subdivision (1) was received.

Added by Acts 1989, 71st Leg., ch. 2, § 4.04(a), eff. Aug. 28, 1989. Amended by Acts 1999, 76th Leg., ch. 440, § 1, eff. Sept. 1, 1999.

CHAPTER 81. SEXUAL EXPLOITATION BY MENTAL HEALTH SERVICES PROVIDER

Section

§ 81.001. Definitions

In this chapter:

(1) "Mental health services" means assessment, diagnosis, treatment, or counseling in a professional relationship to assist an individual or group in:

(A) alleviating mental or emotional illness, symptoms, conditions, or disorders, including alcohol or drug addiction;

(B) understanding conscious or subconscious motivations;

(C) resolving emotional, attitudinal, or relationship conflicts; or

(D) modifying feelings, attitudes, or behaviors that interfere with effective emotional, social, or intellectual functioning.

(2) "Mental health services provider" means an individual, licensed or unlicensed, who performs or purports to perform mental health services, including a:

(A) licensed social worker as defined by Section 505.002, Occupations Code;

(B) chemical dependency counselor as defined by Section 504.001, Occupations Code;

(C) licensed professional counselor as defined by Section 503.002, Occupations Code;

(D) licensed marriage and family therapist as defined by Section 502.002, Occupations Code;

(E) member of the clergy;

(F) physician who is practicing medicine as defined by Section 151.002, Occupations Code;

(G) psychologist offering psychological services as defined by Section 501.003, Occupations Code; or

(H) special officer for mental health assignment certified under Section 1701.404, Occupations Code.

(3) "Patient" means an individual who seeks or obtains mental health services. The term includes a person who has contact with a special officer for mental health assignment because of circumstances relating to the person's mental health.

(4) "Sexual contact" means:

(A) "deviate sexual intercourse" as defined by Section 21.01, Penal Code;

(B) "sexual contact" as defined by Section 21.01, Penal Code;

(C) "sexual intercourse" as defined by Section 21.01, Penal Code; or

(D) requests by the mental health services provider for conduct described by Paragraph (A), (B), or (C). "Sexual contact" does not include conduct described by Paragraph (A) or (B) that is a part of a professionally recognized medical treatment of a patient.

(5) "Sexual exploitation" means a pattern, practice, or scheme of conduct, which may include sexual contact, that can reasonably be construed as being for the purposes of sexual arousal or gratification or sexual abuse of any person. The term does not include obtaining information about a patient's sexual history within standard accepted practice while treating a sexual or marital dysfunction.

(6) "Therapeutic deception" means a representation by a mental health services provider that sexual contact with, or sexual exploitation by, the mental health services provider is consistent with, or a part of, a patient's or former patient's treatment.

(7) "Mental health services," as defined by this section, provided by a member of the clergy does not include religious, moral, and spiritual counseling, teaching, and instruction.

Added by Acts 1993, 73rd Leg., ch. 573, § 2.01, eff. Sept. 1, 1993. Amended by Acts 1999, 76th Leg., ch. 1102, § 1, eff. Sept. 1, 1999; Acts 2001, 77th Leg., ch. 1420, § 14.731, eff. Sept. 1, 2001.

§ 81.002. Sexual Exploitation Cause of Action

A mental health services provider is liable to a patient or former patient of the mental health services provider for damages for sexual exploitation if the patient or former patient suffers, directly or indirectly, a physical, mental, or emotional injury caused by, resulting from, or arising out of:

(1) sexual contact between the patient or former patient and the mental health services provider;

(2) sexual exploitation of the patient or former patient by the mental health services provider; or

(3) therapeutic deception of the patient or former patient by the mental health services provider.

Added by Acts 1993, 73rd Leg., ch. 573, § 2.01, eff. Sept. 1, 1993.

§ 81.003. Liability of Employer

(a) An employer of a mental health services provider is liable to a patient or former patient of the mental health services provider for damages if the patient or former patient is injured as described by Section 81.002 and the employer:

(1) fails to make inquiries of an employer or former employer, whose name and address have been disclosed to the employer and who employed the mental health services provider as a mental health services provider within the five years before the date of disclosure, concerning the possible occurrence of sexual exploitation by the mental health services provider of patients or former patients of the mental health services provider; or

(2) knows or has reason to know that the mental health services provider engaged in sexual exploitation of a patient or former patient and the employer failed to:

(A) report the suspected sexual exploitation as required by Section 81.006; or

(B) take necessary action to prevent or stop the sexual exploitation by the mental health services provider.

(b) An employer or former employer of a mental health services provider is liable to a patient or former patient of the mental health services provider for damages if the patient or former patient is injured as described by Section 81.002 and the employer or former employer:

(1) knows of the occurrence of sexual exploitation by the mental health services provider of a patient or former patient;

(2) receives a specific request by an employer or prospective employer of the mental health services provider, engaged in the business of providing mental health services, concerning the possible existence or nature of sexual exploitation by the mental health services provider; and

(3) fails to disclose the occurrence of the sexual exploitation.

(c) An employer or former employer is liable under this section only to the extent that the failure to take the action described by Subsection (a) or (b) was a proximate and actual cause of damages sustained.

(d) If a mental health professional who sexually exploits a patient or former patient is a member of the clergy and the sexual exploitation occurs when the professional is acting as a member of the clergy, liability if any under this section is limited to the church, congregation, or parish in which the member of the clergy carried out the clergy member's pastoral duties:

(1) at the time the sexual exploitation occurs, if the liability is based on a violation of Subsection (a); or

(2) at the time of the previous occurrence of sexual exploitation, if the liability is based on a violation of Subsection (b).

(e) Nothing in Subsection (d) shall prevent the extension of liability under this section beyond the local church, congregation, or parish where the current or previous sexual exploitation occurred, as appropriate under Subsection (d), if the patient proves that officers or employees of the religious denomination in question at the regional, state, or national level:

(1) knew or should have known of the occurrences of sexual exploitation by the mental health services provider;

(2) received reports of such occurrences and failed to take necessary action to prevent or stop such sexual exploitation by the mental health services provider and that such failure was a proximate and actual cause of the damages; or

(3) knew or should have known of the mental health professional's propensity to engage in sexual exploitation.

Added by Acts 1993, 73rd Leg., ch. 573, § 2.01, eff. Sept. 1, 1993. Amended by Acts 2011, 82nd Leg., ch. 1199 (S.B. 43), § 1, eff. June 17, 2011.

§ 81.004. Damages

(a) A plaintiff who prevails in a suit under this section may recover actual damages, including damages for mental anguish even if an injury other than mental anguish is not shown.

(b) In addition to an award under Subsection (a), a plaintiff who prevails in a suit under this section may recover exemplary damages and reasonable attorney fees.

Added by Acts 1993, 73rd Leg., ch. 573, § 2.01, eff. Sept. 1, 1993.

§ 81.005. Defenses

(a) It is not a defense to an action brought under Section 81.002 or 81.003 that the sexual exploitation of the patient or former patient occurred:

(1) with the consent of the patient or former patient;

(2) outside the therapy or treatment sessions of the patient or former patient; or

(3) off the premises regularly used by the mental health services provider for the therapy or treatment sessions of the patient or former patient.

(b) It is a defense to an action brought under Section 81.002 or 81.003 by a former patient that the person was not emotionally dependent on the mental health services provider when the sexual exploitation began and the mental health services provider terminated mental health services with the patient more than two years before the date the sexual exploitation began.

(c) A person is considered not emotionally dependent for purposes of this chapter if the nature of the patient's or former patient's emotional condition and the nature of the treatment provided by the mental health services provider are not such that the mental health services provider knows or has reason to believe that the patient or former patient is unable to withhold consent to the sexual exploitation.

Added by Acts 1993, 73rd Leg., ch. 573, § 2.01, eff. Sept. 1, 1993.

§ 81.006. Duty to Report

(a) If a mental health services provider or the employer of a mental health services provider has reasonable cause to suspect that a patient has been the victim of sexual exploitation by a mental health services provider during the course of treatment, or if a patient alleges sexual exploitation by a mental health services provider during the course of treatment, the mental health services provider or the employer shall report the alleged conduct not later than the 30th day after the date the person became aware of the conduct or the allegations to:

(1) the prosecuting attorney in the county in which the alleged sexual exploitation occurred; and

(2) any state licensing board that has responsibility for the mental health services provider's licensing.

(b) Before making a report under this section, the reporter shall inform the alleged victim of the reporter's duty to report and shall determine if the alleged victim wants to remain anonymous.

(c) A report under this section need contain only the information needed to:

(1) identify the reporter;

(2) identify the alleged victim, unless the alleged victim has requested anonymity; and

(3) express suspicion that sexual exploitation has occurred.

(d) Information in a report is privileged information and is for the exclusive use of the prosecuting attorney or state licensing board that receives the information. A person who receives privileged information may not disclose the information except to the extent that disclosure is consistent with the authorized purposes for which the person first obtained the information. The identity of an alleged victim of sexual exploitation by a mental health services provider may not be disclosed by the reporter, or by a person who has received or has access to a report or record, unless the alleged victim has consented to the disclosure in writing.

(e) A person who intentionally violates Subsection (a) or (d) is subject to disciplinary action by that person's appropriate licensing board and also commits an offense. An offense under this subsection is a Class C misdemeanor.

Added by Acts 1993, 73rd Leg., ch. 573, § 2.01, eff. Sept. 1, 1993.

§ 81.007. Limited Immunity From Liability

(a) A person who, in good faith, makes a report required by Section 81.006 is immune from civil or criminal liability resulting from the filing of that report.

(b) Reporting under this chapter is presumed to be done in good faith.

(c) The immunity provided by this section does not apply to liability resulting from sexual exploitation by a mental health services provider of a patient or former patient.

Added by Acts 1993, 73rd Leg., ch. 573, § 2.01, eff. Sept. 1, 1993.

§ 81.008. Admission of Evidence

(a) In an action for sexual exploitation, evidence of the plaintiff's sexual history and reputation is not admissible unless:

(1) the plaintiff claims damage to sexual functioning; or

(2)(A) the defendant requests a hearing before trial and makes an offer of proof of the relevancy of the history or reputation; and

(B) the court finds that the history or reputation is relevant and that the probative value of the evidence outweighs its prejudicial effect.

(b) The court may allow the admission only of specific information or examples of the plaintiff's conduct that are determined by the court to be relevant. The court's order shall detail the information or conduct that is admissible and no other such evidence may be introduced.

Added by Acts 1993, 73rd Leg., ch. 573, § 2.01, eff. Sept. 1, 1993.

§ 81.009. Limitations

(a) Except as otherwise provided by this section, an action under this chapter must be filed before the third anniversary of the date the patient or former patient understood or should have understood the conduct for which liability is established under Section 81.002 or 81.003.

(b) If a patient or former patient entitled to file an action under this chapter is unable to bring the action because of the effects of the sexual exploitation, continued emotional dependence on the mental health services provider, or threats, instructions, or statements by the mental health services provider, the deadline for filing an action under this chapter is tolled during that period, except that the deadline may not be tolled for more than 15 years.

(c) This section does not apply to a patient or former patient who is a "child" or a "minor" as defined by Section 101.003, Family Code, until that patient or former patient has reached the age of 18. If the action is brought by a parent, guardian, or other person having custody of the child or minor, it must be brought within the period set forth in this section.

Added by Acts 1993, 73rd Leg., ch. 573, § 2.01, eff. Sept. 1, 1993. Amended by Acts 1997, 75th Leg., ch. 165, § 7.07, eff. Sept. 1, 1997.

§ 81.010. Injunctive Relief Against Governmental Units

(a) In this section, "governmental unit" has the meaning assigned by Section 101.001(3)(B).

(b) Subject to Subsection (c), a patient, a former patient, or another person acting on behalf of a patient or former patient may bring an action under this section against a governmental unit that is an employer of a mental health services provider, including a special officer for mental health assignment, who commits any conduct described by Section 81.002(1), (2), or (3) in relation to the patient or former patient. In an action brought under this subsection, the patient or former patient may obtain:

(1) an order requiring the governmental unit to discharge the mental health services provider who committed the conduct;

(2) court costs; and

(3) reasonable attorney's fees, as determined by the court.

(c) A patient, former patient, or person acting on behalf of a patient or former patient may not bring an action under Subsection (b) unless, 60 days before the date that action is to be filed, the person notifies the governmental unit in writing of its intention to bring an action under this section. The notice must reasonably describe the facts giving rise to the claim. If, before the 60th day after the date the notice is provided under this section, the governmental unit discharges the mental health services provider who committed the conduct with respect to which the claim is filed, the person may not bring suit under Subsection (b).

(d) Governmental immunity to suit is waived and abolished only to the extent of the liability created by Subsection (b).

Added by Acts 1999, 76th Leg., ch. 1102, § 2, eff. Sept. 1, 1999.

CHAPTER 82. PRODUCTS LIABILITY

Section

§ 82.001. Definitions

In this chapter:

(1) "Claimant" means a party seeking relief, including a plaintiff, counterclaimant, or cross-claimant.

(2) "Products liability action" means any action against a manufacturer or seller for recovery of damages arising out of personal injury, death, or property damage allegedly caused by a defective product whether the action is based in strict tort liability, strict products liability, negligence, misrepresentation, breach of express or implied warranty, or any other theory or combination of theories.

(3) "Seller" means a person who is engaged in the business of distributing or otherwise placing, for any commercial purpose, in the stream of commerce for use or consumption a product or any component part thereof.

(4) "Manufacturer" means a person who is a designer, formulator, constructor, rebuilder, fabricator, producer, compounder, processor, or assembler of any product or any component part thereof and who places the product or any component part thereof in the stream of commerce.

Added by Acts 1993, 73rd Leg., ch. 5, § 1, eff. Sept. 1, 1993.

For validity of this section, see Johnson v. Novartis Pharm. Corporation, 845 F. App'x 305 (5th Cir. 2021).

§ 82.002. Manufacturer's Duty to Indemnify

(a) A manufacturer shall indemnify and hold harmless a seller against loss arising out of a products liability action, except for any loss caused by the seller's negligence, intentional misconduct, or other act or omission, such as negligently modifying or altering the product, for which the seller is independently liable.

(b) For purposes of this section, "loss" includes court costs and other reasonable expenses, reasonable attorney fees, and any reasonable damages.

(c) Damages awarded by the trier of fact shall, on final judgment, be deemed reasonable for purposes of this section.

(d) For purposes of this section, a wholesale distributor or retail seller who completely or partially assembles a product in accordance with the manufacturer's instructions shall be considered a seller.

(e) The duty to indemnify under this section:

(1) applies without regard to the manner in which the action is concluded; and

(2) is in addition to any duty to indemnify established by law, contract, or otherwise.

(f) A seller eligible for indemnification under this section shall give reasonable notice to the manufacturer of a product claimed in a petition or complaint to be defective, unless the manufacturer has been served as a party or otherwise has actual notice of the action.

(g) A seller is entitled to recover from the manufacturer court costs and other reasonable expenses, reasonable attorney fees, and any reasonable damages incurred by the seller to enforce the seller's right to indemnification under this section.

Added by Acts 1993, 73rd Leg., ch. 5, § 1, eff. Sept. 1, 1993.

§ 82.003. Liability of Nonmanufacturing Sellers

(a) A seller that did not manufacture a product is not liable for harm caused to the claimant by that product unless the claimant proves:

(1) that the seller participated in the design of the product;

(2) that the seller altered or modified the product and the claimant's harm resulted from that alteration or modification;

(3) that the seller installed the product, or had the product installed, on another product and the claimant's harm resulted from the product's installation onto the assembled product;

(4) that:

(A) the seller exercised substantial control over the content of a warning or instruction that accompanied the product;

(B) the warning or instruction was inadequate; and

(C) the claimant's harm resulted from the inadequacy of the warning or instruction;

(5) that:

(A) the seller made an express factual representation about an aspect of the product;

(B) the representation was incorrect;

(C) the claimant relied on the representation in obtaining or using the product; and

(D) if the aspect of the product had been as represented, the claimant would not have been harmed by the product or would not have suffered the same degree of harm;

(6) that:

(A) the seller actually knew of a defect to the product at the time the seller supplied the product; and

(B) the claimant's harm resulted from the defect; or

(7) that the manufacturer of the product is:

(A) insolvent; or

(B) not subject to the jurisdiction of the court.

(b) This section does not apply to a manufacturer or seller whose liability in a products liability action is governed by Chapter 2301, Occupations Code. In the event of a conflict, Chapter 2301, Occupations Code, prevails over this section.

(c) If after service on a nonresident manufacturer through the secretary of state in the manner prescribed by Subchapter C[1], Chapter 17, the manufacturer fails to answer or otherwise make an appearance in the time required by law, it is conclusively presumed for the purposes of Subsection (a)(7)(B) that the manufacturer is not subject to the jurisdiction of the court unless the seller is able to secure personal jurisdiction over the manufacturer in the action.

Added by Acts 2003, 78th Leg., ch. 204, § 5.02, eff. Sept. 1, 2003. Amended by Acts 2009, 81st Leg., ch. 1351, § 2(a), eff. Sept. 1, 2009.

[1] V.T.C.A., Civil Practice and Remedies Code § 17.041 et seq.

§ 82.004. Inherently Unsafe Products

(a) In a products liability action, a manufacturer or seller shall not be liable if:

(1) the product is inherently unsafe and the product is known to be unsafe by the ordinary consumer who consumes the product with the ordinary knowledge common to the community; and

(2) the product is a common consumer product intended for personal consumption, such as:

(A) sugar, castor oil, alcohol, tobacco, and butter, as identified in Comment i to Section 402A of the Restatement (Second) of Torts; or

(B) an oyster.

(b) For purposes of this section, the term "products liability action" does not include an action based on manufacturing defect or breach of an express warranty.

Added by Acts 1993, 73rd Leg., ch. 5, § 1, eff. Sept. 1, 1993. Amended by Acts 2007, 80th Leg., ch. 1146, § 1, eff. Sept. 1, 2007.

§ 82.005. Design Defects

(a) In a products liability action in which a claimant alleges a design defect, the burden is on the claimant to prove by a preponderance of the evidence that:

(1) there was a safer alternative design; and

(2) the defect was a producing cause of the personal injury, property damage, or death for which the claimant seeks recovery.

(b) In this section, "safer alternative design" means a product design other than the one actually used that in reasonable probability:

(1) would have prevented or significantly reduced the risk of the claimant's personal injury, property damage, or death without substantially impairing the product's utility; and

(2) was economically and technologically feasible at the time the product left the control of the manufacturer or seller by the application of existing or reasonably achievable scientific knowledge.

(c) This section does not supersede or modify any statute, regulation, or other law of this state or of the United States that relates to liability for, or to relief in the form of, abatement of nuisance, civil penalties, cleanup costs, cost recovery, an injunction, or restitution that arises from contamination or pollution of the environment.

(d) This section does not apply to:

(1) a cause of action based on a toxic or environmental tort as defined by Sections 33.013(c)(2) and (3); or

(2) a drug or device, as those terms are defined in the federal Food, Drug, and Cosmetic Act (21 U.S.C. Section 321).

(e) This section is not declarative, by implication or otherwise, of the common law with respect to any product and shall not be construed to restrict the courts of this state in developing the common law with respect to any product which is not subject to this section.

Added by Acts 1993, 73rd Leg., ch. 5, § 1, eff. Sept. 1, 1993.

§ 82.006. Firearms and Ammunition

(a) In a products liability action brought against a manufacturer or seller of a firearm or ammunition that alleges a design defect in the firearm or ammunition, the burden is on the claimant to prove, in addition to any other elements that the claimant must prove, that:

(1) the actual design of the firearm or ammunition was defective, causing the firearm or ammunition not to function in a manner reasonably expected by an ordinary consumer of firearms or ammunition; and

(2) the defective design was a producing cause of the personal injury, property damage, or death.

(b) The claimant may not prove the existence of the defective design by a comparison or weighing of the benefits of the firearm or ammunition against the risk of personal injury, property damage, or death posed by its potential to cause such injury, damage, or death when discharged.

Added by Acts 1993, 73rd Leg., ch. 5, § 1, eff. Sept. 1, 1993.

§ 82.007. Medicines

(a) In a products liability action alleging that an injury was caused by a failure to provide adequate warnings or information with regard to a pharmaceutical product, there is a rebuttable presumption that the defendant or defendants, including a health care provider, manufacturer, distributor, and prescriber, are not liable with respect to the allegations involving failure to provide adequate warnings or information if:

(1) the warnings or information that accompanied the product in its distribution were those approved by the United States Food and Drug Administration for a product approved under the Federal Food, Drug, and Cosmetic Act (21 U.S.C. Section 301 et seq.), as amended, or Section 351, Public Health Service Act (42 U.S.C. Section 262), as amended; or

(2) the warnings provided were those stated in monographs developed by the United States Food and Drug Administration for pharmaceutical products that may be distributed without an approved new drug application.

(b) The claimant may rebut the presumption in Subsection (a) as to each defendant by establishing that:

(1) the defendant, before or after pre-market approval or licensing of the product, withheld from or misrepresented to the United States Food and Drug Administration required information that was mate-

rial and relevant to the performance of the product and was causally related to the claimant's injury;

(2) the pharmaceutical product was sold or prescribed in the United States by the defendant after the effective date of an order of the United States Food and Drug Administration to remove the product from the market or to withdraw its approval of the product;

(3)(A) the defendant recommended, promoted, or advertised the pharmaceutical product for an indication not approved by the United States Food and Drug Administration;

(B) the product was used as recommended, promoted, or advertised; and

(C) the claimant's injury was causally related to the recommended, promoted, or advertised use of the product;

(4)(A) the defendant prescribed the pharmaceutical product for an indication not approved by the United States Food and Drug Administration;

(B) the product was used as prescribed; and

(C) the claimant's injury was causally related to the prescribed use of the product; or

(5) the defendant, before or after pre-market approval or licensing of the product, engaged in conduct that would constitute a violation of 18 U.S.C. Section 201 and that conduct caused the warnings or instructions approved for the product by the United States Food and Drug Administration to be inadequate.

Added by Acts 2003, 78th Leg., ch. 204, § 5.02, eff. Sept. 1, 2003.

For validity of this section, see Atkinson v. Luitpold Pharmaceuticals, Inc., 2020 WL 4518022 (U.S. District Court, E.D. Pennsylvania, 2020).

§ 82.008. Compliance with Government Standards

(a) In a products liability action brought against a product manufacturer or seller, there is a rebuttable presumption that the product manufacturer or seller is not liable for any injury to a claimant caused by some aspect of the formulation, labeling, or design of a product if the product manufacturer or seller establishes that the product's formula, labeling, or design complied with mandatory safety standards or regulations adopted and promulgated by the federal government, or an agency of the federal government, that were applicable to the product at the time of manufacture and that governed the product risk that allegedly caused harm.

(b) The claimant may rebut the presumption in Subsection (a) by establishing that:

(1) the mandatory federal safety standards or regulations applicable to the product were inadequate to protect the public from unreasonable risks of injury or damage; or

(2) the manufacturer, before or after marketing the product, withheld or misrepresented information or material relevant to the federal government's or agency's determination of adequacy of the safety standards or regulations at issue in the action.

(c) In a products liability action brought against a product manufacturer or seller, there is a rebuttable presumption that the product manufacturer or seller is not liable for any injury to a claimant allegedly caused by some aspect of the formulation, labeling, or design of a product if the product manufacturer or seller establishes that the product was subject to pre-market licensing or approval by the federal government, or an agency of the federal government, that the manufacturer complied with all of the government's or agency's procedures and requirements with respect to pre-market licensing or approval, and that after full consideration of the product's risks and benefits the product was approved or licensed for sale by the government or agency. The claimant may rebut this presumption by establishing that:

(1) the standards or procedures used in the particular pre-market approval or licensing process were inadequate to protect the public from unreasonable risks of injury or damage; or

(2) the manufacturer, before or after pre-market approval or licensing of the product, withheld from or misrepresented to the government or agency information that was material and relevant to the performance of the product and was causally related to the claimant's injury.

(d) This section does not extend to manufacturing flaws or defects even though the product manufacturer has complied with all quality control and manufacturing practices mandated by the federal government or an agency of the federal government.

(e) This section does not extend to products covered by Section 82.007.

Added by Acts 2003, 78th Leg., ch. 204, § 5.02, eff. Sept. 1, 2003.

CHAPTER 83. USE OF FORCE OR DEADLY FORCE

Another Chapter 83, Liability for Stalking, consisting of §§ 83.001 to 83.006, and added by Acts 1995, 74th Leg., ch. 662, § 1, was renumbered as Chapter 85, consisting of V.T.C.A., Civil Practice & Remedies Code §§ 85.001 to 85.006, by Acts 1997, 75th Leg., ch. 165, § 31.01(7).

§ 83.001. Civil Immunity

A defendant who uses force or deadly force that is justified under Chapter 9, Penal Code, is immune from civil liability for personal injury or death that results from the defendant's use of force or deadly force, as applicable.

Added by Acts 1995, 74th Leg., ch. 235, § 2, eff. Sept. 1, 1995. Amended by Acts 2007, 80th Leg., ch. 1, § 4, eff. Sept. 1, 2007.

§§ 83.002 to 83.006. Renumbered as V.T.C.A., Civil Practice & Remedies Code §§ 85.002 to 85.006 by Acts 1997, 75th Leg., ch. 165, § 31.01(7), eff. Sept. 1, 1997

CHAPTER 84. CHARITABLE IMMUNITY AND LIABILITY

§ 84.001. Name of Act

This Act may be cited as the Charitable Immunity and Liability Act of 1987.

Added by Acts 1987, 70th Leg., ch. 370, § 1, eff. Sept. 1, 1987.

§ 84.002. Findings and Purposes

The Legislature of the State of Texas finds that:

(1) robust, active, bona fide, and well-supported charitable organizations are needed within Texas to perform essential and needed services;

(2) the willingness of volunteers to offer their services to these organizations is deterred by the perception of personal liability arising out of the services rendered to these organizations;

(3) because of these concerns over personal liability, volunteers are withdrawing from services in all capacities;

(4) these same organizations have a further problem in obtaining and affording liability insurance for the organization and its employees and volunteers;

(5) these problems combine to diminish the services being provided to Texas and local communities because of higher costs and fewer programs;

(6) the citizens of this state have an overriding interest in the continued and increased delivery of these services that must be balanced with other policy considerations; and

(7) because of the above conditions and policy considerations, it is the purpose of this Act to reduce the liability exposure and insurance costs of these organizations and their employees and volunteers in order to encourage volunteer services and maximize the resources devoted to delivering these services.

Added by Acts 1987, 70th Leg., ch. 370, § 1, eff. Sept. 1, 1987.

§ 84.003. Definitions

In this chapter:

(1) "Charitable organization" means:

(A) any organization exempt from federal income tax under Section 501(a) of the Internal Revenue Code of 1986 [1] by being listed as an exempt organization in Section 501(c)(3) or 501(c)(4) of the code, [2] if it is a corporation, foundation, community chest, church, or fund organized and operated exclusively for charitable, religious, prevention of cruelty to children or animals, youth sports and youth recreational, neighborhood crime prevention or patrol, fire protection or prevention, emergency medical or hazardous material response services, or educational purposes, including private primary or secondary schools if accredited by a member association of the Texas Private School Accreditation Commission but excluding fraternities, sororities, and secret societies, or is organized and operated exclusively for the promotion of social welfare by being primarily engaged in promoting the common good and general welfare of the people in a community;

(B) any bona fide charitable, religious, prevention of cruelty to children or animals, youth sports and youth recreational, neighborhood crime prevention or patrol, or educational organization, excluding fraternities, sororities, and secret societies, or other organization organized and operated exclusively for the promotion of social welfare by being primarily engaged in promoting the common good and general welfare of the people in a community, and that:

(i) is organized and operated exclusively for one or more of the above purposes;

(ii) does not engage in activities which in themselves are not in furtherance of the purpose or purposes;

(iii) does not directly or indirectly participate or intervene in any political campaign on behalf of or in opposition to any candidate for public office;

(iv) dedicates its assets to achieving the stated purpose or purposes of the organization;

(v) does not allow any part of its net assets on dissolution of the organization to inure to the benefit of any group, shareholder, or individual; and

(vi) normally receives more than one-third of its support in any year from private or public gifts, grants, contributions, or membership fees;

(C) a homeowners association as defined by Section 528(c) of the Internal Revenue Code of 1986 [3] or which is exempt from federal income tax under Section 501(a) of the Internal Revenue Code of 1986 by being listed as an exempt organization in Section 501(c)(4) of the code;

(D) a volunteer center, as that term is defined by Section 411.126, Government Code;

(E) a local chamber of commerce that:

(i) is exempt from federal income tax under Section 501(a) of the Internal Revenue Code of 1986 by being listed as an exempt organization in Section 501(c)(6) of the code; [4]

(ii) does not directly or indirectly participate or intervene in any political campaign on behalf of or in opposition to any candidate for public office; and

(iii) does not directly or indirectly contribute to a political action committee that makes expenditures to any candidates for public office; or

(F) any organization exempt from federal income tax under Section 501(a) of the Internal Revenue Code of 1986 by being listed as an exempt organization in Section 501(c)(3) or 501(c)(5) of the code, if it is an organization or corporation organized and operated exclusively for wildfire mitigation, range management, or prescribed burning purposes.

(2) "Volunteer" means a person rendering services for or on behalf of a charitable organization who does not receive compensation in excess of reimbursement for expenses incurred. The term includes a person serving as a director, officer, trustee, or direct service volunteer, including a volunteer health care provider.

(3) "Employee" means any person, including an officer or director, who is in the paid service of a charitable organization, but does not include an independent contractor.

(4) Repealed by Acts 2003, 78th Leg., ch. 204, § 18.03(1).

(5) "Volunteer health care provider" means an individual who voluntarily provides health care services without compensation or expectation of compensation and who is:

(A) an individual who is licensed to practice medicine under Subtitle B, Title 3, Occupations Code [5];

(B) a retired physician who is eligible to provide health care services, including a retired physician who is licensed but exempt from paying the required annual registration fee under Section 156.002, Occupations Code;

(C) a physician assistant licensed under Chapter 204, Occupations Code, or a retired physician assistant who is eligible to provide health care services under the law of this state;

(D) a registered nurse, including an advanced nurse practitioner, or vocational nurse, licensed under Chapter 301, Occupations Code, or a retired vocational nurse or registered nurse, including a retired advanced nurse practitioner, who is eligible to provide health care services under the law of this state;

(E) a pharmacist licensed under Subtitle J, Title 3, Occupations Code, [6] or a retired pharmacist who is eligible to provide health care services under the law of this state;

(F) a podiatrist licensed under Chapter 202, Occupations Code, or a retired podiatrist who is eligible to provide health care services under the law of this state;

(G) a dentist licensed under Subtitle D, Title 3, Occupations Code, [7] or a retired dentist who is eligible to provide health care services under the law of this state;

(H) a dental hygienist licensed under Subtitle D, Title 3, Occupations Code, or a retired dental hygienist who is eligible to provide health care services under the law of this state;

(I) an optometrist or therapeutic optometrist licensed under Chapter 351, Occupations Code, or a retired optometrist or therapeutic optometrist who is eligible to provide health care services under the law of this state;

(J) a physical therapist or physical therapist assistant licensed under Chapter 453, Occupations Code, or a retired physical therapist or physical therapist assistant who is eligible to provide health care services under the law of this state;

(K) an occupational therapist or occupational therapy assistant licensed under Chapter 454, Occupations Code, or a retired occupational therapist or occupational therapy assistant who is eligible to provide health care services under the law of this state;

(L) an audiologist, assistant in audiology, speech-language pathologist, or assistant in speech-language pathology licensed under Chapter 401, Occupations Code, or a retired audiologist, assistant in audiology, speech-language pathologist, or assistant in speech-language pathology who is eligible to provide health care services under the laws of this state; or

(M) a social worker licensed under Chapter 505, Occupations Code, or a retired social worker who is eligible to engage in the practice of social work under the law of this state.

(6) "Hospital system" means a system of hospitals and other health care providers located in this state that are under the common governance or control of a corporate parent.

(7) "Person responsible for the patient" means:

(A) the patient's parent, managing conservator, or guardian;

(B) the patient's grandparent;

(C) the patient's adult brother or sister;

(D) another adult who has actual care, control, and possession of the patient and has written authorization to consent for the patient from the parent, managing conservator, or guardian of the patient;

(E) an educational institution in which the patient is enrolled that has written authorization to consent for the patient from the parent, managing conservator, or guardian of the patient; or

(F) any other person with legal responsibility for the care of the patient.

Added by Acts 1987, 70th Leg., ch. 370, § 1, eff. Sept. 1, 1987. Amended by Acts 1989, 71st Leg., ch. 634, § 1, eff. Sept. 1, 1989; Acts 1997, 75th Leg., ch. 403, § 1, eff. Sept. 1, 1997; Acts 1999, 76th Leg., ch. 400, § 1, eff. Sept. 1, 1999; Acts 2001, 77th Leg., ch. 77, § 1, eff. May 14, 2001; Acts 2001, 77th Leg., ch. 538, § 1, eff. Sept. 1, 2001; Acts 2001, 77th Leg., ch. 1420, § 14.732, eff. Sept. 1, 2001; Acts 2003, 78th Leg., ch. 93, § 1, eff. Sept. 1, 2003; Acts 2003, 78th Leg., ch. 204, §§ 10.02, 10.03, 10.04, 18.03(1) eff. Sept. 1, 2003; Acts 2003, 78th Leg., ch. 553, § 2.001, eff. Feb. 1, 2004; Acts 2003, 78th Leg., ch. 895, § 1, eff. Sept. 1, 2003; Acts 2007, 80th Leg., ch. 239, § 1, eff. Sept. 1, 2007; Acts 2009, 81st Leg., ch. 791, § 1, eff. Sept. 1, 2009; Acts 2011, 82nd Leg., ch. 39 (S.B. 1846), § 1, eff. May 9, 2011; Acts 2015, 84th Leg., ch. 14 (S.B. 378), § 1, eff. Sept. 1, 2015; Acts 2015, 84th Leg., ch. 169 (H.B. 2119), § 1, eff. Sept. 1, 2015.

[1] 26 U.S.C.A. § 501(a).

[2] 26 U.S.C.A. §§ 501(c)(3), 501(c)(4).

[3] 26 U.S.C.A. § 528(c).

[4] 26 U.S.C.A. § 501(c)(6).

[5] V.T.C.A., Occupations Code § 151.001 et seq.

[6] V.T.C.A., Occupations Code § 551.001 et seq.

[7] V.T.C.A., Occupations Code § 251.001 et seq.

§ 84.004. Volunteer Liability

(a) Except as provided by Subsection (d) and Section 84.007, a volunteer of a charitable organization is immune from civil liability for any act or omission resulting in death, damage, or injury if the volunteer was acting in the course and scope of the volunteer's duties or functions, including as an officer, director, or trustee within the organization.

(b) Repealed by Acts 2003, 78th Leg., ch. 204, § 18.03(2).

(c) Except as provided by Subsection (d) and Section 84.007, a volunteer health care provider who is serving as a direct service volunteer of a charitable organization is immune from civil liability for any act or omission resulting in death, damage, or injury to a patient if:

(1) the volunteer commits the act or omission in the course of providing health care services to the patient;

(2) the services provided are within the scope of the license of the volunteer; and

(3) before the volunteer provides health care services, the patient or, if the patient is a minor or is otherwise legally incompetent, the person responsible for the patient signs a written statement that acknowledges:

(A) that the volunteer is providing care that is not administered for or in expectation of compensation; and

(B) the limitations on the recovery of damages from the volunteer in exchange for receiving the health care services.

(d) A volunteer of a charitable organization is liable to a person for death, damage, or injury to the person or his property proximately caused by any act or omission arising from the operation or use of any motor-driven equipment, including an airplane, to the extent insurance coverage is required by Chapter 601, Transportation Code, and to the extent of any existing insurance coverage applicable to the act or omission.

(e) The provisions of this section apply only to the liability of volunteers and do not apply to the liability of the organization for acts or omissions of volunteers.

(f) Subsection (c) applies even if:

(1) the patient is incapacitated due to illness or injury and cannot sign the acknowledgment statement required by that subsection; or

(2) the patient is a minor or is otherwise legally incompetent and the person responsible for the patient is not reasonably available to sign the acknowledgment statement required by that subsection.

Added by Acts 1987, 70th Leg., ch. 370, § 1, eff. Sept. 1, 1987. Amended by Acts 1997, 75th Leg., ch. 165, § 30.179, eff. Sept. 1, 1997; Acts 1999, 76th Leg., ch. 400, § 2, eff. Sept. 1, 1999; Acts 2003, 78th Leg., ch. 204, §§ 10.05, 18.01, 18.03(2), eff. Sept. 1, 2003.

§ 84.005. Employee Liability

Except as provided in Section 84.007 of this Act, in any civil action brought against an employee of a nonhospital charitable organization for damages based on an act or omission by the person in the course and scope of the person's employment, the liability of the employee is limited to money damages in a maximum amount of $500,000 for each person and $1,000,000 for each single occurrence of bodily injury or death and $100,000 for each single occurrence for injury to or destruction of property.

Added by Acts 1987, 70th Leg., ch. 370, § 1, eff. Sept. 1, 1987.

§ 84.006. Organization Liability

Except as provided in Section 84.007 of this Act, in any civil action brought against a nonhospital charitable organization for damages based on an act or omission by the organization or its employees or volunteers, the liability of the organization is limited to money damages in a maximum amount of $500,000 for each person and $1,000,000 for each single occurrence of bodily injury or death and $100,000 for each single occurrence for injury to or destruction of property.

Added by Acts 1987, 70th Leg., ch. 370, § 1, eff. Sept. 1, 1987.

§ 84.0061. Organizational Liability for Transportation Services Provided to Certain Welfare Recipients

(a) In this section, "religious charitable organization" means a charitable organization that is also a "religious organization" as the term is defined by Section 464.051, Health and Safety Code.

(b) Subject to Subsection (e), a religious charitable organization that owns or leases a motor vehicle is not liable for damages arising from the negligent use of the vehicle by a person to whom the organization has entrusted the vehicle to provide transportation services during the provision of those services described by Subsection (c) to a person who:

(1) is a recipient of:

(A) financial assistance under Chapter 31, Human Resources Code; or

(B) nutritional assistance under Chapter 33, Human Resources Code; and

(2) is participating in or applying to participate in:

(A) a work or employment activity under Chapter 31, Human Resources Code; or

(B) the food stamp employment and training program.

(c) Transportation services include transportation to and from the location of the:

(1) work, employment, or any training activity or program; or

(2) provider of any child-care services necessary for a person described by Subsection (b)(1) to participate in the work, employment, or training activity or program.

(d) Except as expressly provided in Subsection (b), this section does not limit, or in any way affect or diminish, other legal duties or causes of action arising from the use of a motor vehicle, including the condition of the vehicle itself and causes of action arising under Chapter 41.

(e) This section does not apply to any claim arising from injury, death, or property damage in which the operator of the vehicle was intoxicated, as the term is defined in Section 49.01, Penal Code.

Added by Acts 2001, 77th Leg., ch. 991, § 1, eff. June 15, 2001.

§ 84.0065. Organization Liability of Hospitals

(a) Except as provided by Section 84.007, in any civil action brought against a hospital or hospital system, or its employees, officers, directors, or volunteers, for damages based on an act or omission by the hospital or hospital system, or its employees, officers, directors, or volunteers, the liability of the hospital or hospital system is limited to money damages in a maximum amount of $500,000 for any act or omission resulting in death, damage, or injury to a patient if the patient or, if the patient is a minor or is otherwise legally incompetent, the person responsible for the patient signs a written statement that acknowledges:

(1) that the hospital is providing care that is not administered for or in expectation of compensation; and

(2) the limitations on the recovery of damages from the hospital in exchange for receiving the health care services.

(b) Subsection (a) applies even if:

(1) the patient is incapacitated due to illness or injury and cannot sign the acknowledgment statement required by that subsection; or

(2) the patient is a minor or is otherwise legally incompetent and the person responsible for the patient is not reasonably available to sign the acknowledgment statement required by that subsection.

Added by Acts 2003, 78th Leg., ch. 204, § 10.06, eff. Sept. 1, 2003.

§ 84.0066. Liability for Disclosing Sexual Misconduct

(a) A charitable organization, or an employee, volunteer, or independent contractor of a charitable organization, acting in good faith, is immune from civil liability for any act to disclose to an individual's current or prospective employer information reasonably believed to be true about an allegation that an individual who was employed by or served as a volunteer or independent contractor for the charitable organization or its associated charitable organizations:

(1) engaged in sexual misconduct;

(2) sexually abused another individual;

(3) sexually harassed another individual; or

(4) committed an offense under any of the following provisions of the Penal Code:

(A) Section 20A.02(a)(3), (4), (7), or (8) (sex trafficking of persons);

(B) Section 20A.03 (continuous trafficking of persons), if based partly or wholly on conduct that constitutes an offense under Section 20A.02(a)(3), (4), (7), or (8);

(C) Section 22.011 (sexual assault) or 22.021 (aggravated sexual assault); or

(D) Chapter 21 (sexual offenses) or 43 (public indecency).

(b) Immunity from civil liability under Subsection (a) applies in relation to an allegation described by that subsection that was required to have been reported as abuse under Chapter 261, Family Code, only if the allegation has been, at the time of the act to disclose, previously reported to an appropriate agency under Section 261.103, Family Code.

(c) An individual is not immune under this section from civil or criminal liability for:

(1) disclosing the individual's own conduct that constitutes:

(A) sexual misconduct;

(B) sexual abuse of another individual;

(C) sexual harassment of another individual; or

(D) an offense under any of the following provisions of the Penal Code:

(i) Section 20A.02(a)(3), (4), (7), or (8) (sex trafficking of persons);

(ii) Section 20A.03 (continuous trafficking of persons), if based partly or wholly on conduct that constitutes an offense under Section 20A.02(a)(3), (4), (7), or (8);

(iii) Section 22.011 (sexual assault) or 22.021 (aggravated sexual assault); or

(iv) Chapter 21 (sexual offenses) or 43 (public indecency); or

(2) acting in bad faith or with a malicious purpose in making a disclosure described by Subsection (a).

Added by Acts 2019, 86th Leg., ch. 925 (H.B. 4345), § 1, eff. June 10, 2019.

Section 2 of Acts 2019, 86th Leg., ch. 925 (H.B. 4345) provides:

"Section 84.0066, Civil Practice and Remedies Code, as added by this Act, does not apply to a cause of action that accrued before the effective date [June 10, 2019] of this Act. A cause of action that accrued before the effective date of this Act is governed by the law applicable to the cause of action immediately before that date, and the former law is continued in effect for that purpose."

§ 84.007. Applicability

(a) This chapter does not apply to an act or omission that is intentional, wilfully negligent, or done with conscious indifference or reckless disregard for the safety of others.

(b) This chapter does not limit or modify the duties or liabilities of a member of the board of directors or an officer to the organization or its members and shareholders.

(c) This chapter does not limit the liability of an organization or its employees or volunteers if the organization was formed substantially to limit its liability under this chapter.

(d) This chapter does not apply to organizations formed to dispose, remove, or store hazardous waste, industrial solid waste, radioactive waste, municipal solid waste, garbage, or sludge as those terms are defined under applicable state and federal law. This subsection shall be liberally construed to effectuate its purpose.

(e) Sections 84.005 and 84.006 of this chapter do not apply to a health care provider as defined in Section 74.001, unless the provider is a federally funded migrant or community health center under the Public Health Service Act (42 U.S.C.A. Sections 254b and 254c) or is a nonprofit health maintenance organization created and operated by a community center under Section 534.101, Health and Safety Code, or unless the provider usually provides discounted services at or below costs based on the ability of the beneficiary to pay. Acceptance of Medicare or Medicaid payments will not disqualify a health care provider under this section. In no event shall Sections 84.005 and 84.006 of this chapter apply to a general hospital or special hospital as defined in Chapter 241, Health and Safety Code, or a facility or institution licensed under Subtitle C, Title 7, Health and Safety Code,[1] or Chapter 242, Health and Safety Code, or to any health maintenance organization created and operating under Chapter 843, Insurance Code, except for a nonprofit health maintenance organization created under Section 534.101, Health and Safety Code.

(f) This chapter does not apply to a governmental unit or employee of a governmental unit as defined in the Texas Tort Claims Act (Subchapter A, Chapter 101, Civil Practice and Remedies Code).[2]

(g) Sections 84.005 and 84.006 of this Act do not apply to any charitable organization that does not have liability insurance coverage in effect on any act or omission to which this chapter applies. The coverage shall apply to the acts or omissions of the organization and its employees and volunteers and be in the amount of at least $500,000 for each person and $1,000,000 for each single occurrence for death or bodily injury and $100,000 for each single occurrence for injury to or destruction of property. The coverage may be provided under a contract for insurance, a plan providing for self-insured retention that the charitable organization has fully paid or establishes to a court that it is capable of fully and immediately paying, a Lloyd's plan, an indemnity policy to which all requirements for payment have been or will be met, or other plan of insurance authorized by statute and may be satisfied by the purchase of a $1,000,000 bodily injury and property damage combined single limit policy. For the purposes of this chapter, coverage amounts are inclusive of a self-insured retention, a Lloyd's plan, or an indemnity policy to which all requirements for payment have been or will be met. Nothing in this chapter shall limit liability of any insurer or insurance plan in an action under Chapter 541, Insurance Code, or in an action for bad faith conduct, breach of fiduciary duty, or negligent failure to settle a claim.

(h) This chapter does not apply to:

(1) a statewide trade association that represents local chambers of commerce; or

(2) a cosponsor of an event or activity with a local chamber of commerce unless the cosponsor is a charitable organization under this chapter.

Added by Acts 1987, 70th Leg., ch. 370, § 1, eff. Sept. 1, 1987. Amended by Acts 1991, 72nd Leg., ch. 14, § 284(14), (20), eff. Sept. 1, 1991; Acts 1991, 72nd Leg., ch. 76, § 6, eff. Sept. 1, 1991; Acts 1997, 75th Leg., ch. 835, § 3, eff. Sept. 1, 1997; Acts 1997, 75th Leg., ch. 1297, § 1, eff. Sept. 1, 1997; Acts 2003, 78th Leg., ch. 93, § 2, eff. Sept. 1, 2003; Acts 2003, 78th Leg., ch. 204, § 18.02, eff. Sept. 1, 2003; Acts 2003, 78th Leg., ch. 1276, § 10A.507, eff. Sept. 1, 2003; Acts 2005, 79th Leg., ch. 133, § 1, eff. Sept. 1, 2005; Acts 2011, 82nd Leg., ch. 39 (S.B. 1846), § 2, eff. May 9, 2011.

[1] V.T.C.A., Health and Safety Code § 571.001 et seq.

[2] V.T.C.A., Civil Practice and Remedies Code § 101.001 et seq.

§ 84.008. Severability

If any clause or provision of this chapter or its application to any person or organization is held unconstitutional, such invalidity does not affect other clauses, provisions, or applications of this chapter that can be given effect without the invalid clause or provision and shall not affect or nullify the remainder of the Act or any other clause or provision, but the effect shall be confined to the clause or provision held to be invalid or unconstitutional and to this end the Act is declared to be severable.

Added by Acts 1987, 70th Leg., ch. 370, § 1, eff. Sept. 1, 1987.

CHAPTER 85. LIABILITY FOR STALKING

Section

Chapter 83, Liability for Stalking, consisting of V.T.C.A., Civil Practice & Remedies Code §§ 83.001 to 83.006, was added by Acts 1995, 74th Leg., ch. 662, § 1. Acts 1997, 75th Leg., ch. 165, § 31.01(7) renumbered this chapter as Chapter 85, consisting of V.T.C.A., Civil Practice & Remedies Code §§ 85.001 to 85.006, effective September 1, 1997.

§ 85.001. Definitions

In this chapter:

(1) "Claimant" means a party seeking to recover damages under this chapter, including a plaintiff, counterclaimant, cross-claimant, or third-party plaintiff. In an action in which a party seeks recovery of damages under this chapter on behalf of another person, "claimant" includes both that other person and the party seeking recovery of damages.

(2) "Defendant" includes any party from whom a claimant seeks recovery of damages under this chapter.

(3) "Family" has the meaning assigned by Section 71.003, Family Code.

(4) "Harassing behavior" means conduct by the defendant directed specifically toward the claimant, including following the claimant, that is reasonably likely to harass, annoy, alarm, abuse, torment, or embarrass the claimant.

Added by Acts 1995, 74th Leg., ch. 662, § 1, eff. June 14, 1995. Renumbered from V.T.C.A., Civil Practice and Remedies Code § 83.001 by Acts 1997, 75th Leg., ch. 165, § 31.01(7), eff. Sept. 1, 1997. Amended by Acts 2003, 78th Leg., ch. 1276, § 7.002(b), eff. Sept. 1, 2003.

§ 85.002. Liability

A defendant is liable, as provided by this chapter, to a claimant for damages arising from stalking of the claimant by the defendant.

Added by Acts 1995, 74th Leg., ch. 662, § 1, eff. June 14, 1995. Renumbered from V.T.C.A., Civil Practice and Remedies Code § 83.002 by Acts 1997, 75th Leg., ch. 165, § 31.01(7), eff. Sept. 1, 1997.

§ 85.003. Proof

(a) A claimant proves stalking against a defendant by showing:

(1) on more than one occasion the defendant engaged in harassing behavior;

(2) as a result of the harassing behavior, the claimant reasonably feared for the claimant's safety or the safety of a member of the claimant's family; and

(3) the defendant violated a restraining order prohibiting harassing behavior or:

(A) the defendant, while engaged in harassing behavior, by acts or words threatened to inflict bodily injury on the claimant or to commit an offense against the claimant, a member of the claimant's family, or the claimant's property;

(B) the defendant had the apparent ability to carry out the threat;

(C) the defendant's apparent ability to carry out the threat caused the claimant to reasonably fear for the claimant's safety or the safety of a family member;

(D) the claimant at least once clearly demanded that the defendant stop the defendant's harassing behavior;

(E) after the demand to stop by the claimant, the defendant continued the harassing behavior; and

(F) the harassing behavior has been reported to the police as a stalking offense.

(b) The claimant must, as part of the proof of the behavior described by Subsection (a)(1), submit evidence other than evidence based on the claimant's own perceptions and beliefs.

Added by Acts 1995, 74th Leg., ch. 662, § 1, eff. June 14, 1995. Renumbered from V.T.C.A., Civil Practice and Remedies Code § 83.003 by Acts 1997, 75th Leg., ch. 165, § 31.01(7), eff. Sept. 1, 1997.

§ 85.004. Damages

A claimant who prevails in a suit under this chapter may recover actual damages and, subject to Chapter 41, exemplary damages.

Added by Acts 1995, 74th Leg., ch. 662, § 1, eff. June 14, 1995. Renumbered from V.T.C.A., Civil Practice and Remedies Code § 83.004 by Acts 1997, 75th Leg., ch. 165, § 31.01(7), eff. Sept. 1, 1997.

§ 85.005. Defense

It is a defense to an action brought under this chapter that the defendant was engaged in conduct that consisted of activity in support of constitutionally or statutorily protected rights.

Added by Acts 1995, 74th Leg., ch. 662, § 1, eff. June 14, 1995. Renumbered from V.T.C.A., Civil Practice and Remedies Code § 83.005 by Acts 1997, 75th Leg., ch. 165, § 31.01(7), eff. Sept. 1, 1997.

§ 85.006. Cause of Action Cumulative

The cause of action created by this chapter is cumulative of any other remedy provided by common law or statute.

Added by Acts 1995, 74th Leg., ch. 662, § 1, eff. June 14, 1995. Renumbered from V.T.C.A., Civil Practice & Remedies Code § 83.006 by Acts 1997, 75th Leg., ch. 165, § 31.01(7), eff. Sept. 1, 1997.

CHAPTER 86. LIABILITY FOR CERTAIN INJURIES TO CONVICTED PERSONS

Chapter 87, Liability for Certain Injuries to Convicted Persons, consisting of §§ 87.001 to 87.007, was added by Acts 1995, 74th Leg., ch. 604, § 1. Acts 1997, 75th Leg., ch. 165, § 31.01(8) renumbered this chapter as Chapter 86, consisting of V.T.C.A., Civil Practice & Remedies Code §§ 86.001 to 86.007, effective September 1, 1997.

§ 86.001. Definition

In this chapter, "claimant" means a party, including a plaintiff, counterclaimant, cross-claimant, or third-party claimant, seeking recovery of damages.

Added by Acts 1995, 74th Leg., ch. 604, § 1, eff. Aug. 28, 1995. Renumbered from V.T.C.A., Civil Practice & Remedies Code § 87.001 by Acts 1997, 75th Leg., ch. 165, § 31.01(8), eff. Sept. 1, 1997.

§ 86.002. Recovery of Damages for Injury to Convicted Person Prohibited

(a) A claimant who has been convicted of a felony or misdemeanor may not recover damages for an injury sustained during the commission of the felony or misdemeanor if the injury would not have been sustained but for the commission of the felony or misdemeanor.

(b) Subsection (a) does not bar the claimant from recovering damages if the claimant shows that:

(1) the damages arose from an act entirely separate from any act intended to result in the:

(A) prevention of the commission of a felony or misdemeanor by the claimant; or

(B) apprehension of the claimant during or immediately after the commission of the felony or misdemeanor; and

(2) the damages did not arise from a premises defect or other circumstance that the claimant was exposed to as a result of the commission of the felony or misdemeanor.

Added by Acts 1995, 74th Leg., ch. 604, § 1, eff. Aug. 28, 1995. Renumbered from V.T.C.A., Civil Practice and Remedies Code § 87.002 by Acts 1997, 75th Leg., ch. 165, § 31.01(8), eff. Sept. 1, 1997.

§ 86.003. Derivative Claims

Section 86.002 applies to a claim for damages made by a claimant other than a convicted person if:

(1) the claimant's right to recovery results from an injury to a convicted person, including a claim for the wrongful death of the convicted person or a claim for loss of consortium with or loss of the companionship of the convicted person; and

(2) the convicted person's right to recovery would be barred under Section 86.002.

Added by Acts 1995, 74th Leg., ch. 604, § 1, eff. Aug. 28, 1995. Renumbered from V.T.C.A., Civil Practice and Remedies Code § 87.003 by Acts 1997, 75th Leg., ch. 165, § 31.01(8), eff. Sept. 1, 1997.

§ 86.004. Claimant Liable for Court Costs and Fees and Attorney's Fees

A claimant who is barred from recovery under this chapter is liable to the person against whom the claim is brought for court costs and fees and reasonable attorney's fees incurred in defending against the claim.

Added by Acts 1995, 74th Leg., ch. 604, § 1, eff. Aug. 28, 1995. Renumbered from V.T.C.A., Civil Practice and Remedies Code § 87.004 by Acts 1997, 75th Leg., ch. 165, § 31.01(8), eff. Sept. 1, 1997.

§ 86.005. Certain Traffic Law Violations Excluded

This chapter does not apply to a claim arising from an offense defined by Subtitle C, Title 7, Transportation Code.[1]

Added by Acts 1995, 74th Leg., ch. 604, § 1, eff. Aug. 28, 1995. Renumbered from V.T.C.A., Civil Practice and Remedies Code § 87.005 and amended by Acts 1997, 75th Leg., ch. 165, §§ 30.180, 31.01(8), eff. Sept. 1, 1997.

[1] V.T.C.A., Transportation Code § 541.001 et seq.

§ 86.006. Convicted Person

For purposes of this chapter, a person is considered convicted in a case if:

(1) sentence is imposed; or

(2) the person receives a fine, probation, or deferred adjudication.

Added by Acts 1995, 74th Leg., ch. 604, § 1, eff. Aug. 28, 1995. Renumbered from V.T.C.A., Civil Practice and Remedies Code § 87.006 by Acts 1997, 75th Leg., ch. 165, § 31.01(8), eff. Sept. 1, 1997.

§ 86.007. Applicability

This chapter does not apply to:

(1) a claim for an injury sustained during the commission of an offense under Section 30.05, Penal Code, other than a trespass in a habitation or shelter, brought by a person who has not been convicted of another crime that occurred in conjunction with the trespass; or

(2) a claim in which the conduct of the owner of the premises is grossly negligent or intentional, other than conduct justified under Subchapter C, Chapter 9, Penal Code.[1]

Added by Acts 1995, 74th Leg., ch. 604, § 1, eff. Aug. 28, 1995. Renumbered from V.T.C.A., Civil Practice and Remedies Code § 87.007 by Acts 1997, 75th Leg., ch. 165, § 31.01(8), eff. Sept. 1, 1997.

[1] V.T.C.A., Penal Code § 9.31 et seq.

CHAPTER 87. LIABILITY ARISING FROM FARM ANIMALS

Another Chapter 87, Liability for Certain Injuries to Convicted Persons, consisting of §§ 87.001 to 87.007, and added by Acts 1995, 74th Leg., ch. 604, § 1, was renumbered as Chapter 86, consisting of V.T.C.A., Civil Practice & Remedies Code §§ 86.001 to 86.007, by Acts 1997, 75th Leg., ch. 165, § 31.01(8).

§ 87.001. Definitions

In this chapter:

(1) "Engages in a farm animal activity" means riding, handling, training, driving, loading, unloading, feeding, vaccinating, exercising, weaning, transporting, producing, herding, corralling, branding, or dehorning of, assisting in or providing health management activities for, assisting in the medical treatment of, being a passenger on, or assisting a participant or sponsor with a farm animal. The term includes management of a show involving farm animals and engagement in routine or customary activities on a farm to handle and manage farm animals. The term does not include being a spectator at a farm animal activity unless the spectator is in an unauthorized area and in immediate proximity to the farm animal activity.

(2) "Equine animal" means a horse, pony, mule, donkey, or hinny.

(2–a) "Farm" means any real estate, land area, facility, or ranch used wholly or partly for raising, cultivating, propagating, fattening, grazing, or any other farming, livestock, agricultural, apicultural, or aquacultural operation.

(2–b) "Farm animal" means:

(A) an equine animal;

(B) a bovine animal;

(C) a sheep or goat;

(D) a pig or hog;

(E) a ratite, including an ostrich, rhea, or emu;

(F) a chicken or other fowl; or

(G) a honeybee kept in a managed colony.

(3) "Farm animal activity" means:

(A) a farm animal show, fair, competition, performance, rodeo, event, or parade that involves any farm animal;

(B) training or teaching activities involving a farm animal;

(C) owning, raising, boarding, or pasturing a farm animal, including daily care;

(D) riding, inspecting, evaluating, handling, transporting, loading, or unloading a farm animal belonging to another, without regard to whether the owner receives monetary consideration or other thing of value for the use of the farm animal or permits a prospective purchaser of the farm animal to ride, inspect, evaluate, handle, load, or unload the farm animal;

(E) informal farm animal activity, including a ride, trip, or hunt that is sponsored by a farm animal activity sponsor or a farm owner or lessee;

(F) placing or replacing horseshoes on an equine animal;

(G) examining or administering medical treatment to a farm animal by a veterinarian;

(H) assisting in or providing animal health management activities, including vaccination;

(I) assisting in or conducting customary tasks on a farm concerning farm animals;

(J) transporting or moving a farm animal; or

(K) without regard to whether the participants are compensated, rodeos and single event competitions, including team roping, calf roping, and single steer roping.

(4) "Farm animal activity sponsor" means:

(A) a person or group who sponsors, owns, organizes, or provides the facilities for a farm animal activity, including facilities for a pony club, 4–H club, hunt club, riding club, therapeutic riding program, or high school or college class, program, or activity, without regard to whether the person operates for profit; or

(B) an owner or operator of, instructor at, or promoter for facilities, including a stable, clubhouse, pony ride string, fair, or arena at which a farm animal activity is held.

(5) "Farm animal professional" means a person engaged for compensation:

(A) to instruct a participant or rent to a participant a farm animal for the purpose of riding, driving, or being a passenger on the farm animal;

(B) to rent equipment or tack to a participant;

(C) to examine or administer medical treatment to a farm animal as a veterinarian or to provide nonmedical care or treatment to a farm animal, including vaccination;

(D) to provide veterinarian or farrier services;

(E) to assist in or provide animal health management activities, including vaccination;

(F) to provide other care, feeding, and husbandry of farm animals;

(G) to assist in or conduct customary tasks on a farm concerning farm animals; or

(H) to transport or move a farm animal.

(6) "Livestock animal" means:

(A) an animal raised for human consumption; or

(B) a farm animal.

(6–a) "Livestock producer" means a person who owns, handles, breeds, raises, buys, sells, or feeds livestock animals.

(7) "Livestock show" means a nonprofit event at which more than two species or breeds of livestock animals are gathered for exhibition or competition.

(8) "Livestock show sponsor" means a recognized group or association that organizes and sanctions a livestock show, including a political subdivision or nonprofit organization that is exempt from federal income tax under Section 501(a), Internal Revenue Code of 1986, as amended, by being listed as an exempt organization in Section 501(c)(3) of that code.

(9) "Participant" means:

(A) with respect to a farm animal activity, a person who engages in the activity, without regard to whether the person:

(i) is an amateur or professional;

(ii) pays for the activity or participates in the activity for free; or

(iii) is an independent contractor or employee; and

(B) with respect to a livestock show, a person who registers for and is allowed by a livestock show sponsor to compete in a livestock show by showing an animal on a competitive basis, or a person who assists that person.

Added by Acts 1995, 74th Leg., ch. 549, § 1, eff. Sept. 1, 1995. Amended by Acts 2001, 77th Leg., ch. 1108, § 2, eff. Sept. 1, 2001; Acts 2011, 82nd Leg., ch. 896 (S.B. 479), § 2, eff. June 17, 2011; Acts 2021, 87th Leg., ch. 219 (H.B. 365), § 2, eff. Sept. 1, 2021.

Section 6 of Acts 2021, 87th Leg., ch. 219 (H.B. 365) provides:

"The change in law made by this Act applies only to a cause of action that accrues on or after the effective date [Sept. 1, 2021] of this Act. A cause of action that accrued before the effective date of this Act is governed by the law as it existed immediately before the effective date of this Act, and that law is continued in effect for that purpose."

§ 87.002. Applicability of Chapter

This chapter does not apply to an activity regulated by the Texas Racing Commission.

Added by Acts 1995, 74th Leg., ch. 549, § 1, eff. Sept. 1, 1995.

§ 87.0021. Certain Labor Laws Not Affected

Nothing in this chapter affects the applicability of Chapter 406, Labor Code, or an employer's ability to refuse to subscribe to the workers' compensation system.

Added by Acts 2021, 87th Leg., ch. 219 (H.B. 365), § 3, eff. Sept. 1, 2021.

Section 6 of Acts 2021, 87th Leg., ch. 219 (H.B. 365) provides:

"The change in law made by this Act applies only to a cause of action that accrues on or after the effective date [Sept. 1, 2021] of this Act. A cause of action that accrued before the effective date of this Act is governed by the law as it existed immediately before the effective date of this Act, and that law is continued in effect for that purpose."

§ 87.003. Limitation on Liability

Except as provided by Section 87.004, all persons, including a farm animal activity sponsor, farm animal professional, farm owner or lessee, livestock producer, livestock show participant, or livestock show sponsor, are not liable for property damage or damages arising from the personal injury or death of a participant in a farm animal activity or livestock show if the property damage, injury, or death results from the dangers or conditions that are an inherent risk of a farm animal, a farm animal activity, the showing of an animal on a competitive basis in a livestock show, or the raising or handling of livestock on a farm, including:

(1) the propensity of a farm animal or livestock animal to behave in ways that may result in personal injury or death to a person on the animal, handling the animal, or otherwise around the animal;

(2) the unpredictability of a farm animal's or livestock animal's reaction to sound, a sudden movement, or an unfamiliar object, person, or other animal;

(3) with respect to farm animal activities involving equine animals, certain land conditions and hazards, including surface and subsurface conditions;

(4) a collision with another animal or an object; or

(5) the potential of a participant to act in a negligent manner that may contribute to injury to the participant or another, including failing to maintain control over a farm animal or livestock animal or not acting within the participant's ability.

Added by Acts 1995, 74th Leg., ch. 549, § 1, eff. Sept. 1, 1995. Amended by Acts 2001, 77th Leg., ch. 1108, § 3, eff. Sept. 1, 2001; Acts 2011, 82nd Leg., ch. 896 (S.B. 479), § 3, eff. June 17, 2011; Acts 2021, 87th Leg., ch. 219 (H.B. 365), § 4, eff. Sept. 1, 2021.

Section 6 of Acts 2021, 87th Leg., ch. 219 (H.B. 365) provides:

"The change in law made by this Act applies only to a cause of action that accrues on or after the effective date [Sept. 1, 2021] of this Act. A cause of action that accrued before the effective date of this Act is governed by the law as it existed immediately before the effective date of this Act, and that law is continued in effect for that purpose."

§ 87.004. Exceptions to Limitation on Liability

A person, including a farm animal activity sponsor, farm animal professional, farm owner or lessee, livestock show participant, or livestock show sponsor, may be liable for property damage or damages arising from the personal injury or death caused by a participant in a farm animal activity or livestock show if:

(1) the injury or death was caused by faulty equipment or tack used in the farm animal activity or livestock show, the person provided the equipment or tack, and the person knew or should have known that the equipment or tack was faulty;

(2) the person provided the farm animal or livestock animal and the person did not make a reasonable and prudent effort to determine the ability of the participant to engage safely in the farm animal activity, including a work activity, or livestock show and determine the ability of the participant to safely manage the farm animal or livestock animal, taking into account the participant's representations of ability;

(3) the injury or death was caused by a dangerous latent condition of land for which warning signs, written notices, or verbal warnings were not conspicuously posted or provided to the participant, and the land was owned, leased, or otherwise under the control of the person at the time of the injury or death and the person knew of the dangerous latent condition;

(4) the person committed an act or omission with wilful or wanton disregard for the safety of the participant and that act or omission caused the injury;

(5) the person intentionally caused the property damage, injury, or death; or

(6) with respect to a livestock show, the injury or death occurred as a result of an activity connected with the livestock show and the person invited or otherwise allowed the injured or deceased person to participate in the activity and the injured or deceased person was not a participant as defined by Section 87.001(9)(B).

Added by Acts 1995, 74th Leg., ch. 549, § 1, eff. Sept. 1, 1995. Amended by Acts 2001, 77th Leg., ch. 1108, § 4, eff. Sept. 1, 2001; Acts 2011, 82nd Leg., ch. 896 (S.B. 479), § 4, eff. June 17, 2011; Acts 2021, 87th Leg., ch. 219 (H.B. 365), § 4, eff. Sept. 1, 2021.

Section 6 of Acts 2021, 87th Leg., ch. 219 (H.B. 365) provides:

"The change in law made by this Act applies only to a cause of action that accrues on or after the effective date [Sept. 1, 2021] of this Act. A cause of action that accrued before the effective date of this Act is governed by the law as it existed immediately before the effective date of this Act, and that law is continued in effect for that purpose."

§ 87.005. Warning Notice

(a) A farm animal professional or a farm owner or lessee shall post and maintain a sign that contains the warning contained in Subsection (c) if the professional, owner, or lessee manages or controls a farm, stable, corral, or arena where the professional, owner, or lessee conducts a farm animal activity. The professional, owner, or lessee must post the sign in a clearly visible location on or near the stable, corral, or arena.

(b) A farm animal professional or a farm owner or lessee shall include the warning contained in Subsection (c) in every written contract that the professional, owner, or lessee enters into with a participant, including an employee or independent contractor, for professional services, instruction, or the rental of equipment or tack or a farm animal. The warning must be included without regard to whether the contract involves farm animal activities on or off the location or site of the business of the farm animal professional or farm owner or lessee. The warning must be clearly readable.

(c) The warning posted by a farm animal professional or a farm owner or lessee under this section must be as follows:

WARNING

UNDER TEXAS LAW (CHAPTER 87, CIVIL PRACTICE AND REMEDIES CODE), A FARM ANIMAL PROFESSIONAL OR FARM OWNER OR LESSEE IS NOT LIABLE FOR AN INJURY TO OR THE DEATH OF A PARTICIPANT IN FARM ANIMAL ACTIVITIES, INCLUDING AN EMPLOYEE OR INDEPENDENT CONTRACTOR, RESULTING FROM THE INHERENT RISKS OF FARM ANIMAL ACTIVITIES.

(d) A livestock show sponsor shall post and maintain a sign that contains the warning prescribed by Subsection (f) if the livestock show sponsor manages or controls a stable, barn, corral, or arena at which the livestock show sponsor conducts a livestock show. The livestock show sponsor must post the sign in a clearly visible location near the stable, barn, corral, or arena.

(e) A livestock show sponsor shall include the warning prescribed by Subsection (f) in every written contract that the sponsor enters into with a livestock show participant. The warning must be clearly readable.

(f) The warning posted by a livestock show sponsor under this section must be as follows:

WARNING

UNDER TEXAS LAW (CHAPTER 87, CIVIL PRACTICE AND REMEDIES CODE), A LIVESTOCK SHOW SPONSOR IS NOT LIABLE FOR AN INJURY TO OR THE DEATH OF A PARTICIPANT IN A LIVESTOCK SHOW RESULTING FROM THE INHERENT RISKS OF LIVESTOCK SHOW ACTIVITIES.

Added by Acts 1995, 74th Leg., ch. 549, § 1, eff. Sept. 1, 1995. Amended by Acts 2001, 77th Leg., ch. 1108, § 5, eff. Sept. 1, 2001; Acts 2011, 82nd Leg., ch. 896 (S.B. 479), § 5, eff. June 17, 2011; Acts 2021, 87th Leg., ch. 219 (H.B. 365), § 5, eff. Sept. 1, 2021.

Section 6 of Acts 2021, 87th Leg., ch. 219 (H.B. 365) provides:

"The change in law made by this Act applies only to a cause of action that accrues on or after the effective date [Sept. 1, 2021] of this Act. A cause of action that accrued before the effective date of this Act is governed by the law as it existed immediately before the effective date of this Act, and that law is continued in effect for that purpose."

§§ 87.006, 87.007. Renumbered as V.T.C.A., Civil Practice & Remedies Code §§ 86.006, 86.007 by Acts 1997, 75th Leg., ch. 165, § 31.01(8), eff. Sept. 1, 1997

CHAPTER 88. HEALTH CARE LIABILITY

Section

Another Chapter 88, Donation of Medical Devices, consisting of §§ 88.001 to 88.003 and added by Acts 1997, 75th Leg., ch. 662, § 1, was renumbered as Chapter 89, consisting of V.T.C.A., Civil Practice & Remedies Code §§ 89.001 to 89.003, by Acts 1999, 76th Leg., ch. 62, § 19.01(5).

§ 88.001. Definitions

In this chapter:

(1) "Appropriate and medically necessary" means the standard for health care services as determined by physicians and health care providers in accordance with the prevailing practices and standards of the medical profession and community.

(2) "Enrollee" means an individual who is enrolled in a health care plan, including covered dependents.

(3) "Health care plan" means any plan whereby any person undertakes to provide, arrange for, pay

for, or reimburse any part of the cost of any health care services.

(4) "Health care provider" means a person or entity as defined in Section 74.001.

(5) "Health care treatment decision" means a determination made when medical services are actually provided by the health care plan and a decision which affects the quality of the diagnosis, care, or treatment provided to the plan's insureds or enrollees.

(6) "Health insurance carrier" means an authorized insurance company that issues policies of accident and health insurance under Chapter 1201, Insurance Code.

(7) "Health maintenance organization" means an organization licensed under Chapter 843, Insurance Code.

(8) "Managed care entity" means any entity which delivers, administers, or assumes risk for health care services with systems or techniques to control or influence the quality, accessibility, utilization, or costs and prices of such services to a defined enrollee population, but does not include an employer purchasing coverage or acting on behalf of its employees or the employees of one or more subsidiaries or affiliated corporations of the employer or a pharmacy licensed by the State Board of Pharmacy.

(9) "Physician" means:

(A) an individual licensed to practice medicine in this state;

(B) a professional association organized under the Texas Professional Association Act (Article 1528f, Vernon's Texas Civil Statutes) or a nonprofit health corporation certified under Section 5.01, Medical Practice Act (Article 4495b, Vernon's Texas Civil Statutes); or

(C) another person wholly owned by physicians.

(10) "Ordinary care" means, in the case of a health insurance carrier, health maintenance organization, or managed care entity, that degree of care that a health insurance carrier, health maintenance organization, or managed care entity of ordinary prudence would use under the same or similar circumstances. In the case of a person who is an employee, agent, ostensible agent, or representative of a health insurance carrier, health maintenance organization, or managed care entity, "ordinary care" means that degree of care that a person of ordinary prudence in the same profession, specialty, or area of practice as such person would use in the same or similar circumstances.

Added by Acts 1997, 75th Leg., ch. 163, § 1, eff. Sept. 1, 1997. Amended by Acts 2003, 78th Leg., ch. 1276, § 10A.508, eff. Sept. 1, 2003; Acts 2005, 79th Leg., ch. 134, § 1, eff. Sept. 1, 2005; Acts 2005, 79th Leg., ch. 728, § 11.107, eff. Sept. 1, 2005.

§ 88.0015. Inapplicability to ERISA-Regulated Employee Benefit Plan

This chapter does not apply to an employee benefit plan regulated under the Employee Retirement Income Security Act of 1974 (29 U.S.C. Section 1001 et seq.).

Added by Acts 2005, 79th Leg., ch. 306, § 1, eff. June 17, 2005.

§ 88.002. Application

(a) A health insurance carrier, health maintenance organization, or other managed care entity for a health care plan has the duty to exercise ordinary care when making health care treatment decisions and is liable for damages for harm to an insured or enrollee proximately caused by its failure to exercise such ordinary care.

(b) A health insurance carrier, health maintenance organization, or other managed care entity for a health care plan is also liable for damages for harm to an insured or enrollee proximately caused by the health care treatment decisions made by its:

(1) employees;

(2) agents;

(3) ostensible agents; or

(4) representatives who are acting on its behalf and over whom it has the right to exercise influence or control or has actually exercised influence or control which result in the failure to exercise ordinary care.

(c) It shall be a defense to any action asserted against a health insurance carrier, health maintenance organization, or other managed care entity for a health care plan that:

(1) neither the health insurance carrier, health maintenance organization, or other managed care entity, nor any employee, agent, ostensible agent, or representative for whose conduct such health insurance carrier, health maintenance organization, or other managed care entity is liable under Subsection (b), controlled, influenced, or participated in the health care treatment decision; and

(2) the health insurance carrier, health maintenance organization, or other managed care entity did not deny or delay payment for any treatment prescribed or recommended by a provider to the insured or enrollee.

(d) The standards in Subsections (a) and (b) create no obligation on the part of the health insurance carrier, health maintenance organization, or other managed care entity to provide to an insured or enrollee treatment which is not covered by the health care plan of the entity.

(e) This chapter does not create any liability on the part of an employer, an employer group purchasing organization, or a pharmacy licensed by the State Board of Pharmacy that purchases coverage or assumes risk on behalf of its employees.

(f) A health insurance carrier, health maintenance organization, or managed care entity may not remove a physician or health care provider from its plan or refuse to renew the physician or health care provider with its plan for advocating on behalf of an enrollee for appropriate and medically necessary health care for the enrollee.

(g) A health insurance carrier, health maintenance organization, or other managed care entity may not enter into a contract with a physician, hospital, or other health care provider or pharmaceutical company which includes an indemnification or hold harmless clause for the acts or conduct of the health insurance carrier, health maintenance organization, or other managed care entity. Any such indemnification or hold harmless clause in an existing contract is hereby declared void.

(h) Nothing in any law of this state prohibiting a health insurance carrier, health maintenance organization, or other managed care entity from practicing medicine or being licensed to practice medicine may be asserted as a defense by such health insurance carrier, health maintenance organization, or other managed care entity in an action brought against it pursuant to this section or any other law.

(i) In an action against a health insurance carrier, health maintenance organization, or managed care entity, a finding that a physician or other health care provider is an employee, agent, ostensible agent, or representative of such health insurance carrier, health maintenance organization, or managed care entity shall not be based solely on proof that such person's name appears in a listing of approved physicians or health care providers made available to insureds or enrollees under a health care plan.

(j) This chapter does not apply to workers' compensation insurance coverage as defined in Section 401.011, Labor Code.

(k) An enrollee who files an action under this chapter shall comply with the requirements of Section 74.351 as it relates to expert reports.

Added by Acts 1997, 75th Leg., ch. 163, § 1, eff. Sept. 1, 1997. Amended by Acts 2005, 79th Leg., ch. 134, § 2, eff. Sept. 1, 2005.

§ 88.003. Limitations on Cause of Action

(a) A person may not maintain a cause of action under this chapter against a health insurance carrier, health maintenance organization, or other managed care entity that is required to comply with or otherwise complies with the utilization review requirements of Article 21.58A, Insurance Code, or Chapter 843, Insurance Code, unless the affected insured or enrollee or the insured's or enrollee's representative:

(1) has exhausted the appeals and review applicable under the utilization review requirements; or

(2) before instituting the action:

(A) gives written notice of the claim as provided by Subsection (b); and

(B) agrees to submit the claim to a review by an independent review organization under Article 21.58A, Insurance Code, as required by Subsections (c) and (d).

(b) The notice required by Subsection (a)(2)(A) must be delivered or mailed to the health insurance carrier, health maintenance organization, or managed care entity against whom the action is made not later than the 30th day before the date the claim is filed.

(c) The insured or enrollee or the insured's or enrollee's representative must submit the claim to a review by an independent review organization if the health insurance carrier, health maintenance organization, or managed care entity against whom the claim is made requests the review not later than the 14th day after the date notice under Subsection (a)(2)(A) is received by the health insurance carrier, health maintenance organization, or managed care entity. If the health insurance carrier, health maintenance organization, or managed care entity does not request the review within the period specified by this subsection, the insured or enrollee or the insured's or enrollee's representative is not required to submit the claim to independent review before maintaining the action.

(d) A review conducted under Subsection (c) as requested by a health insurance carrier, health maintenance organization, or managed care entity must be performed in accordance with Article 21.58C, Insurance Code. The health insurance carrier, health maintenance organization, or managed care entity requesting the review must agree to comply with Subdivisions (2), (3), and (4), Section 6A, Article 21.58A, Insurance Code.

(e) Subject to Subsection (f), if the enrollee has not complied with Subsection (a), an action under this section shall not be dismissed by the court, but the court may, in its discretion, order the parties to submit to an independent review or mediation or other nonbinding alternative dispute resolution and may abate the action for a period of not to exceed 30 days for such purposes. Such orders of the court shall be the sole remedy available to a party complaining of an enrollee's failure to comply with Subsection (a).

(f) The enrollee is not required to comply with Subsection (c) and no abatement or other order pursuant to Subsection (e) for failure to comply shall be imposed if the enrollee has filed a pleading alleging in substance that:

(1) harm to the enrollee has already occurred because of the conduct of the health insurance carrier, health maintenance organization, or managed care entity or because of an act or omission of an employee, agent, ostensible agent, or representative of such carrier, organization, or entity for whose conduct it is liable under Section 88.002(b); and

(2) the review would not be beneficial to the enrollee, unless the court, upon motion by a defendant carrier, organization, or entity finds after hearing that such pleading was not made in good faith, in which case the court may enter an order pursuant to Subsection (e).

(g) If the insured or enrollee or the insured's or enrollee's representative seeks to exhaust the appeals and review or provides notice, as required by Subsection (a), before the statute of limitations applicable to a claim against a managed care entity has expired, the limitations period is tolled until the later of:

(1) the 30th day after the date the insured or enrollee or the insured's or enrollee's representative has exhausted the process for appeals and review applicable under the utilization review requirements; or

(2) the 40th day after the date the insured or enrollee or the insured's or enrollee's representative gives notice under Subsection (a)(2)(A).

(h) This section does not prohibit an insured or enrollee from pursuing other appropriate remedies, including injunctive relief, a declaratory judgment, or relief available under law, if the requirement of exhausting the process for appeal and review places the insured's or enrollee's health in serious jeopardy.

Added by Acts 1997, 75th Leg., ch. 163, § 1, eff. Sept. 1, 1997. Amended by Acts 1999, 76th Leg., ch. 1327, § 1, eff. Sept. 1, 1999; Acts 2003, 78th Leg., ch. 1276, § 10A.509, eff. Sept. 1, 2003.

CHAPTER 89. DONATION OF MEDICAL DEVICES

Chapter 88, Donation of Medical Devices, consisting of §§ 88.001 to 88.003, was added by Acts 1997, 75th Leg., ch. 662, § 1. Acts 1999, 76th Leg., ch. 62, § 19.01(5) renumbered this chapter as Chapter 89, consisting of V.T.C.A., Civil Practice & Remedies Code §§ 89.001 to 89.003, effective September 1, 1999.

§ 89.001. Definitions

In this chapter:

(1) "Device" means braces, artificial appliances, durable medical equipment, and other medical supplies. The term does not include a medical device that is injected, implanted, or otherwise placed in the human body.

(2) "Donate" means to give without requiring anything of monetary value from the recipient.

(3) "Nonprofit health care organization" means:

(A) an organization that is exempt from federal income tax under Section 501(a) of the Internal Revenue Code of 1986 (26 U.S.C. Section 501) by being listed as an exempt organization in Section 501(c)(3) or 501(c)(4) of that code and that is organized and operated for the purpose of providing free or reduced cost health care; or

(B) a bona fide charitable organization that is organized and operated for the purpose of providing free or reduced cost health care, that dedicates its assets to charitable purposes, and that does not provide net earnings to, or operate in a manner that inures to the benefit of, an officer, employee, or shareholder of the organization.

Added by Acts 1997, 75th Leg., ch. 662, § 1, eff. Sept. 1, 1997. Renumbered from V.T.C.A., Civil Practice & Remedies Code § 88.001 by Acts 1999, 76th Leg., ch. 62, § 19.01(5), eff. Sept. 1, 1999.

§ 89.002. Liability for Damages from Donated Device

A person authorized to possess a device is not liable for personal injury, property damage, or death resulting from the nature, age, packaging, or condition of a device that the person donates in good faith to an entity that is authorized to possess the device and that is a nonprofit health care organization for use in providing free or reduced cost health care.

Added by Acts 1997, 75th Leg., ch. 662, § 1, eff. Sept. 1, 1997. Renumbered from V.T.C.A., Civil Practice & Remedies Code § 88.002 by Acts 1999, 76th Leg., ch. 62, § 19.01(5), eff. Sept. 1, 1999.

§ 89.003. Exceptions

(a) This chapter does not apply to a person who donates a device:

(1) knowing that use of the device would be harmful to the health or well-being of another person;

(2) with actual conscious indifference to the health or well-being of another person; or

(3) in violation of state or federal law.

(b) This chapter does not apply to a nonprofit health care organization unless the organization has liability insurance in effect that satisfies the requirements of Section 84.007(g).

Added by Acts 1997, 75th Leg., ch. 662, § 1, eff. Sept. 1, 1997. Renumbered from V.T.C.A., Civil Practice & Remedies Code § 88.003 by Acts 1999, 76th Leg., ch. 62, § 19.01(5), eff. Sept. 1, 1999.

CHAPTER 90. CLAIMS INVOLVING ASBESTOS AND SILICA

SUBCHAPTER A. GENERAL PROVISIONS

Section

Section

SUBCHAPTER B. ASBESTOS OR SILICA TRUST CLAIMS

SUBCHAPTER A. GENERAL PROVISIONS

§ 90.001. Definitions

In this chapter:

(1) "Asbestos" means chrysotile, amosite, crocidolite, tremolite asbestos, anthophyllite asbestos, actinolite asbestos, and any of these minerals that have been chemically treated or altered.

(2) "Asbestos-related injury" means personal injury or death allegedly caused, in whole or in part, by inhalation or ingestion of asbestos.

(3) "Asbestosis" means bilateral diffuse interstitial fibrosis of the lungs caused by inhalation of asbestos fibers.

(4) "Certified B-reader" means a person who has successfully completed the x-ray interpretation course sponsored by the National Institute for Occupational Safety and Health (NIOSH) and passed the B-reader certification examination for x-ray interpretation and whose NIOSH certification is current at the time of any readings required by this chapter.

(5) "Chest x-ray" means chest films that are taken in accordance with all applicable state and federal regulatory standards and in the posterior-anterior view.

(6) "Claimant" means an exposed person and any person who is seeking recovery of damages for or arising from the injury or death of an exposed person.

(7) "Defendant" means a person against whom a claim arising from an asbestos-related injury or a silica-related injury is made.

(8) "Exposed person" means a person who is alleged to have suffered an asbestos-related injury or a silica-related injury.

(9) "FEV1" means forced expiratory volume in the first second, which is the maximal volume of air expelled in one second during performance of simple spirometric tests.

(10) "FVC" means forced vital capacity, which is the maximal volume of air expired with maximum effort from a position of full inspiration.

(11) "ILO system of classification" means the radiological rating system of the International Labor Office in "Guidelines for the Use of ILO International Classification of Radiographs of Pneumoconioses" (2000), as amended.

(12) "MDL pretrial court" means the district court to which related cases are transferred for consolidated or coordinated pretrial proceedings under Rule 13, Texas Rules of Judicial Administration.

(13) "MDL rules" means the rules adopted by the supreme court under Subchapter H, Chapter 74, Government Code.[1]

(14) "Mesothelioma" means a rare form of cancer allegedly caused in some instances by exposure to asbestos in which the cancer invades cells in the membrane lining:

(A) the lungs and chest cavity (the pleural region);

(B) the abdominal cavity (the peritoneal region); or

(C) the heart (the pericardial region).

(15) "Nonmalignant asbestos-related injury" means an asbestos-related injury other than mesothelioma or other cancer.

(16) "Nonmalignant silica-related injury" means a silica-related injury other than cancer.

(17) "Physician board certified in internal medicine" means a physician who is certified by the American Board of Internal Medicine or the American Osteopathic Board of Internal Medicine.

(18) "Physician board certified in occupational medicine" means a physician who is certified in the subspecialty of occupational medicine by the American Board of Preventive Medicine or the American Osteopathic Board of Preventive Medicine.

(19) "Physician board certified in oncology" means a physician who is certified in the subspecialty of medical oncology by the American Board of Internal Medicine or the American Osteopathic Board of Internal Medicine.

(20) "Physician board certified in pathology" means a physician who holds primary certification in anatomic pathology or clinical pathology from the American Board of Pathology or the American Osteopathic Board of Internal Medicine and whose professional practice:

(A) is principally in the field of pathology; and

(B) involves regular evaluation of pathology materials obtained from surgical or postmortem specimens.

(21) "Physician board certified in pulmonary medicine" means a physician who is certified in the subspecialty of pulmonary medicine by the American Board of Internal Medicine or the American Osteopathic Board of Internal Medicine.

(22) "Plethysmography" means the test for determining lung volume, also known as "body plethysmography;" in which the subject of the test is enclosed in a chamber that is equipped to measure pressure, flow, or volume change.

(23) "Pulmonary function testing" means spirometry, lung volume, and diffusion capacity testing performed in accordance with Section 90.002 using equipment, methods of calibration, and techniques that meet:

(A) the criteria incorporated in the American Medical Association Guides to the Evaluation of Permanent Impairment and reported in 20 C.F.R. Part 404, Subpart P, Appendix 1, Part (A), Sections 3.00(E) and (F)(2003); and

(B) the interpretative standards in the Official Statement of the American Thoracic Society entitled "Lung Function Testing: Selection of Reference Values and Interpretative Strategies," as published in 144 American Review of Respiratory Disease 1202–1218 (1991).

(24) "Report" means a report required by Section 90.003, 90.004, or 90.010(f)(1).

(25) "Respirable," with respect to silica, means particles that are less than 10 microns in diameter.

(26) "Serve" means to serve notice on a party in compliance with Rule 21a, Texas Rules of Civil Procedure.

(27) "Silica" means a respirable form of crystalline silicon dioxide, including alpha quartz, cristobalite, and tridymite.

(28) "Silica-related injury" means personal injury or death allegedly caused, in whole or in part, by inhalation of silica.

(29) "Silicosis" means interstitial fibrosis of the lungs caused by inhalation of silica, including:

(A) acute silicosis, which may occur after exposure to very high levels of silica within a period of months to five years after the initial exposure;

(B) accelerated silicosis; and

(C) chronic silicosis.

Added by Acts 2005, 79th Leg., ch. 97, § 2, eff. Sept. 1, 2005.

[1] V.T.C.A., Government Code § 74.161 et seq.

§ 90.002. Pulmonary Function Testing

Pulmonary function testing required by this chapter must be interpreted by a physician:

(1) who is licensed in this state or another state of the United States;

(2) who is board certified in pulmonary medicine, internal medicine, or occupational medicine; and

(3) whose license and certification were not on inactive status at the time the testing was interpreted.

Added by Acts 2005, 79th Leg., ch. 97, § 2, eff. Sept. 1, 2005.

§ 90.003. Reports Required for Claims Involving Asbestos-Related Injury

(a) A claimant asserting an asbestos-related injury must serve on each defendant the following information:

(1) a report by a physician who is board certified in pulmonary medicine, occupational medicine, internal medicine, oncology, or pathology and whose license and certification were not on inactive status at the time the report was made stating that:

(A) the exposed person has been diagnosed with malignant mesothelioma or other malignant asbestos-related cancer; and

(B) to a reasonable degree of medical probability, exposure to asbestos was a cause of the diagnosed mesothelioma or other cancer in the exposed person; or

(2) a report by a physician who is board certified in pulmonary medicine, internal medicine, or occupational medicine and whose license and certification were not on inactive status at the time the report was made that:

(A) verifies that the physician or a medical professional employed by and under the direct supervision and control of the physician:

(i) performed a physical examination of the exposed person, or if the exposed person is deceased, reviewed available records relating to the exposed person's medical condition;

(ii) took a detailed occupational and exposure history from the exposed person or, if the exposed person is deceased, from a person knowledgeable about the alleged exposure or exposures that form the basis of the action; and

(iii) took a detailed medical and smoking history that includes a thorough review of the exposed person's past and present medical problems and their most probable cause;

(B) sets out the details of the exposed person's occupational, exposure, medical, and smoking history and verifies that at least 10 years have elapsed between the exposed person's first exposure to asbestos and the date of diagnosis;

(C) verifies that the exposed person has:

(i) a quality 1 or 2 chest x-ray that has been read by a certified B-reader according to the ILO system of classification as showing:

(a) bilateral small irregular opacities (s, t, or u) with a profusion grading of 1/1 or higher, for an action filed on or after May 1, 2005;

(b) bilateral small irregular opacities (s, t, or u) with a profusion grading of 1/0 or higher, for an action filed before May 1, 2005; or

(c) bilateral diffuse pleural thickening graded b2 or higher including blunting of the costophrenic angle; or

(ii) pathological asbestosis graded 1(B) or higher under the criteria published in "Asbestos-Associated Diseases," 106 Archives of Pathology and Laboratory Medicine 11, Appendix 3 (October 8, 1982);

(D) verifies that the exposed person has asbestos-related pulmonary impairment as demonstrated by pulmonary function testing showing:

(i) forced vital capacity below the lower limit of normal or below 80 percent of predicted and FEV1/FVC ratio (using actual values) at or above the lower limit of normal or at or above 65 percent; or

(ii) total lung capacity, by plethysmography or timed gas dilution, below the lower limit of normal or below 80 percent of predicted;

(E) verifies that the physician has concluded that the exposed person's medical findings and impairment were not more probably the result of causes other than asbestos exposure revealed by the exposed person's occupational, exposure, medical, and smoking history; and

(F) is accompanied by copies of all ILO classifications, pulmonary function tests, including printouts of all data, flow volume loops, and other information demonstrating compliance with the equipment, quality, interpretation, and reporting standards set out in this chapter, lung volume tests, diagnostic imaging of the chest, pathology reports, or other testing reviewed by the physician in reaching the physician's conclusions.

(b) The detailed occupational and exposure history required by Subsection (a)(2)(A)(ii) must describe:

(1) the exposed person's principal employments and state whether the exposed person was exposed to airborne contaminants, including asbestos fibers and other dusts that can cause pulmonary impairment; and

(2) the nature, duration, and frequency of the exposed person's exposure to airborne contaminants, including asbestos fibers and other dusts that can cause pulmonary impairment.

(c) If a claimant's pulmonary function test results do not meet the requirements of Subsection (a)(2)(D)(i) or (ii), the claimant may serve on each defendant a report by a physician who is board certified in pulmonary medicine, internal medicine, or occupational medicine and whose license and certification were not on inactive status at the time the report was made that:

(1) verifies that the physician has a physician-patient relationship with the exposed person;

(2) verifies that the exposed person has a quality 1 or 2 chest x-ray that has been read by a certified B-reader according to the ILO system of classification as showing bilateral small irregular opacities (s, t, or u) with a profusion grading of 2/1 or higher;

(3) verifies that the exposed person has restrictive impairment from asbestosis and includes the specific pulmonary function test findings on which the physician relies to establish that the exposed person has restrictive impairment;

(4) verifies that the physician has concluded that the exposed person's medical findings and impairment were not more probably the result of causes other than asbestos exposure revealed by the exposed person's occupational, exposure, medical, and smoking history; and

(5) is accompanied by copies of all ILO classifications, pulmonary function tests, including printouts of all data, flow volume loops, and other information demonstrating compliance with the equipment, quality, interpretation, and reporting standards set out in this chapter, lung volume tests, diagnostic imaging of the chest, pathology reports, or other testing reviewed by the physician in reaching the physician's conclusions.

(d) If a claimant's radiologic findings do not meet the requirements of Subsection (a)(2)(C)(i), the claimant may serve on each defendant a report by a physician who is board certified in pulmonary medicine, internal medicine, or occupational medicine and whose license and certification were not on inactive status at the time the report was made that:

(1) verifies that the physician has a physician-patient relationship with the exposed person;

(2) verifies that the exposed person has asbestos-related pulmonary impairment as demonstrated by pulmonary function testing showing:

(A) either:

(i) forced vital capacity below the lower limit of normal or below 80 percent of predicted and total lung capacity, by plethysmography, below the lower limit of normal or below 80 percent of predicted; or

(ii) forced vital capacity below the lower limit of normal or below 80 percent of predicted and FEV1/FVC ratio (using actual values) at or above the lower limit of normal or at or above 65 percent; and

(B) diffusing capacity of carbon monoxide below the lower limit of normal or below 80 percent of predicted;

(3) verifies that the exposed person has a computed tomography scan or high-resolution computed tomography scan showing either bilateral pleural disease or bilateral parenchymal disease consistent with asbestos exposure;

(4) verifies that the physician has concluded that the exposed person's medical findings and impairment were not more probably the result of causes other than asbestos exposure as revealed by the exposed person's occupational, exposure, medical, and smoking history; and

(5) is accompanied by copies of all computed tomography scans, ILO classifications, pulmonary function tests, including printouts of all data, flow volume loops, and other information demonstrating compliance with the equipment, quality, interpretation, and reporting standards set out in this chapter, lung volume tests, diagnostic imaging of the chest, pathology reports, or other testing reviewed by the physician in reaching the physician's conclusions.

Added by Acts 2005, 79th Leg., ch. 97, § 2, eff. Sept. 1, 2005.

§ 90.004. Reports Required for Claims Involving Silica-Related Injury

(a) A claimant asserting a silica-related injury must serve on each defendant a report by a physician who is board certified in pulmonary medicine, internal medicine, oncology, pathology, or, with respect to a claim for silicosis, occupational medicine and whose license and certification were not on inactive status at the time the report was made that:

(1) verifies that the physician or a medical professional employed by and under the direct supervision and control of the physician:

(A) performed a physical examination of the exposed person, or if the exposed person is deceased, reviewed available records relating to the exposed person's medical condition;

(B) took a detailed occupational and exposure history from the exposed person or, if the exposed person is deceased, from a person knowledgeable about the alleged exposure or exposures that form the basis of the action; and

(C) took a detailed medical and smoking history that includes a thorough review of the exposed person's past and present medical problems and their most probable cause;

(2) sets out the details of the exposed person's occupational, exposure, medical, and smoking history;

(3) verifies that the exposed person has one or more of the following:

(A) a quality 1 or 2 chest x-ray that has been read by a certified B-reader according to the ILO system of classification as showing:

(i) bilateral predominantly nodular opacities (p, q, or r) occurring primarily in the upper lung fields, with a profusion grading of 1/1 or higher, for an action filed on or after May 1, 2005; or

(ii) bilateral predominantly nodular opacities (p, q, or r) occurring primarily in the upper lung fields, with a profusion grading of 1/0 or higher, for an action filed before May 1, 2005;

(B) pathological demonstration of classic silicotic nodules exceeding one centimeter in diameter as published in "Diseases Associated with Exposure to Silica and Nonfibrous Silicate Minerals," 112 Archives of Pathology and Laboratory Medicine 7 (July 1988);

(C) progressive massive fibrosis radiologically established by large opacities greater than one centimeter in diameter; or

(D) acute silicosis; and

(4) is accompanied by copies of all ILO classifications, pulmonary function tests, including printouts of all data, flow volume loops, and other information demonstrating compliance with the equipment, quality, interpretation, and reporting standards set out in this chapter, lung volume tests, diagnostic imaging of the chest, pathology reports, or other testing reviewed by the physician in reaching the physician's conclusions.

(b) If the claimant is asserting a claim for silicosis, the report required by Subsection (a) must also verify that:

(1) there has been a sufficient latency period for the applicable type of silicosis;

(2) the exposed person has at least Class 2 or higher impairment due to silicosis, according to the American Medical Association Guides to the Evaluation of Permanent Impairment and reported in 20 C.F.R. Part 404, Subpart P, Appendix 1, Part (A), Sections 3.00(E) and (F)(2003); and

(3) the physician has concluded that the exposed person's medical findings and impairment were not more probably the result of causes other than silica exposure revealed by the exposed person's occupational, exposure, medical, and smoking history.

(c) If the claimant is asserting a claim for silica-related lung cancer, the report required by Subsection (a) must also:

(1) include a diagnosis that the exposed person has primary lung cancer and that inhalation of silica was a substantial contributing factor to that cancer; and

(2) verify that at least 15 years have elapsed from the date of the exposed person's first exposure to silica until the date of diagnosis of the exposed person's primary lung cancer.

(d) If the claimant is asserting a claim for any disease other than silicosis and lung cancer alleged to be related to exposure to silica, the report required by Subsection (a) must also verify that the physician has diagnosed the exposed person with a disease other than silicosis or silica-related lung cancer and has concluded that the exposed person's disease is not more probably the result of causes other than silica exposure.

(e) The detailed occupational and exposure history required by Subsection (a)(1)(B) must describe:

(1) the exposed person's principal employments and state whether the exposed person was exposed

to airborne contaminants, including silica and other dusts that can cause pulmonary impairment; and

(2) the nature, duration, and frequency of the exposed person's exposure to airborne contaminants, including silica and other dusts that can cause pulmonary impairment.

Added by Acts 2005, 79th Leg., ch. 97, § 2, eff. Sept. 1, 2005.

§ 90.005. Prohibited Basis for Diagnosis

(a) For purposes of this chapter, a physician may not, as the basis for a diagnosis, rely on the reports or opinions of any doctor, clinic, laboratory, or testing company that performed an examination, test, or screening of the exposed person's medical condition that was conducted in violation of any law, regulation, licensing requirement, or medical code of practice of the state in which the examination, test, or screening was conducted.

(b) If a physician relies on any information in violation of Subsection (a), the physician's opinion or report does not comply with the requirements of this chapter.

Added by Acts 2005, 79th Leg., ch. 97, § 2, eff. Sept. 1, 2005.

§ 90.006. Serving Reports

(a) In an action filed on or after the date this chapter becomes law, a report prescribed by Section 90.003 or 90.004 must be served on each defendant not later than the 30th day after the date that defendant answers or otherwise enters an appearance in the action.

(b) In an action pending on the date this chapter becomes law and in which the trial, or any new trial or retrial following motion, appeal, or otherwise, commences on or before the 90th day after the date this chapter becomes law, a claimant is not required to serve a report on any defendant unless a mistrial, new trial, or retrial is subsequently granted or ordered.

(c) In an action pending on the date this chapter becomes law and in which the trial, or any new trial or retrial following motion, appeal, or otherwise, commences after the 90th day after the date this chapter becomes law, a report must be served on each defendant on or before the earlier of the following dates:

(1) the 60th day before trial commences; or

(2) the 180th day after the date this chapter becomes law.

Added by Acts 2005, 79th Leg., ch. 97, § 2, eff. Sept. 1, 2005.

§ 90.007. Motion to Dismiss in Action Filed on or After September 1, 2005

(a) In an action filed on or after September 1, 2005, if a claimant fails to timely serve a report on a defendant, or serves on the defendant a report that does not comply with the requirements of Section 90.003 or 90.004, the defendant may file a motion to dismiss the claimant's asbestos-related claims or silica-related claims. The motion must be filed on or before the 30th day after the date the report is served on the defendant. If a claimant fails to serve a report on the defendant, the motion must be filed on or before the 30th day after the date the report was required to be served on the defendant under Section 90.006. If the basis of the motion is that the claimant has served on the defendant a report that does not comply with Section 90.003 or 90.004, the motion must include the reasons why the report does not comply with that section.

(b) A claimant may file a response to a motion to dismiss on or before the 15th day after the date the motion to dismiss is served. A report required by Section 90.003 or 90.004 may be filed, amended, or supplemented within the time required for responding to a motion to dismiss. The service of an amended or supplemental report does not require the filing of an additional motion to dismiss if the reasons stated in the original motion to dismiss are sufficient to require dismissal under this chapter.

(c) Except as provided by Section 90.010(d) or (e), if the court is of the opinion that a motion to dismiss is meritorious, the court shall, by written order, grant the motion and dismiss all of the claimant's asbestos-related claims or silica-related claims, as appropriate, against the defendant. A dismissal under this section is without prejudice to the claimant's right, if any, to assert claims for an asbestos-related injury or a silica-related injury in a subsequent action.

(d) On the filing of a motion to dismiss under this section, all further proceedings in the action are stayed until the motion is heard and determined by the court.

(e) On the motion of a party showing good cause, the court may shorten or extend the time limits provided in this section for filing or serving motions, responses, or reports.

Added by Acts 2005, 79th Leg., ch. 97, § 2, eff. Sept. 1, 2005. Amended by Acts 2013, 83rd Leg., ch. 146 (H.B. 1325), §§ 1, 2, eff. Sept. 1, 2013.

§ 90.008. Voluntary Dismissal

Before serving a report required by Section 90.003 or 90.004, a claimant seeking damages arising from an asbestos-related injury or silica-related injury may voluntarily dismiss the claimant's action. If a claimant files a voluntary dismissal under this section, the claimant's voluntary dismissal is without prejudice to the claimant's right to file a subsequent action seeking damages arising from an asbestos-related injury or a silica-related injury.

Added by Acts 2005, 79th Leg., ch. 97, § 2, eff. Sept. 1, 2005.

§ 90.009. Joinder of Claimants

Unless all parties agree otherwise, claims relating to more than one exposed person may not be joined for a single trial.

Added by Acts 2005, 79th Leg., ch. 97, § 2, eff. Sept. 1, 2005.

§ 90.010. Multidistrict Litigation Proceedings

(a) The MDL rules apply to any action pending on the date this chapter becomes law in which the claimant alleges personal injury or death from exposure to asbestos or silica unless:

(1) the action was filed before September 1, 2003, and trial has commenced or is set to commence on or before the 90th day after the date this chapter becomes law, except that the MDL rules shall apply to the action if the trial does not commence on or before the 90th day after the date this chapter becomes law;

(2) the action was filed before September 1, 2003, and the claimant serves a report that complies with Section 90.003 or 90.004 on or before the 90th day after the date this chapter becomes law; or

(3) the action was filed before September 1, 2003, and the exposed person has been diagnosed with malignant mesothelioma, other malignant asbestos-related cancer, or malignant silica-related cancer.

(b) If the claimant fails to serve a report complying with Section 90.003 or 90.004 on or before the 90th day after the date this chapter becomes law under Subsection (a)(2), the defendant may file a notice of transfer to the MDL pretrial court. If the MDL pretrial court determines that the claimant served a report that complies with Section 90.003 or 90.004 on or before the 90th day after the date this chapter becomes law, the MDL pretrial court shall remand the action to the court in which the action was filed. If the MDL pretrial court determines that the report was not served on or before the 90th day after the date this chapter becomes law or that the report served does not comply with Section 90.003 or 90.004, the MDL pretrial court shall retain jurisdiction over the action pursuant to the MDL rules.

(c) In an action transferred to an MDL pretrial court in which the exposed person is living and has been diagnosed with malignant mesothelioma, other malignant asbestos-related cancer, malignant silica-related cancer, or acute silicosis, the MDL pretrial court shall expedite the action in a manner calculated to provide the exposed person with a trial or other disposition in the shortest period that is fair to all parties and consistent with the principles of due process. The MDL pretrial court should, as far as reasonably possible, ensure that such action is brought to trial or final disposition within six months from the date the action is transferred to the MDL pretrial court, provided that all discovery and case management requirements of the MDL pretrial court have been satisfied.

(d) In an action that was pending on August 31, 2005, that was transferred to and remains pending in an MDL pretrial court, the MDL pretrial court shall not remand such action for trial unless:

(1) the claimant serves a report complying with Section 90.003 or 90.004; or

(2)(A) the claimant does not serve a report that complies with Section 90.003 or 90.004;

(B) the claimant serves a report complying with Subsection (f)(1); and

(C) the court, on motion and hearing, makes the findings required by Subsection (f)(2).

(d–1) Beginning on September 1, 2014, the MDL pretrial court shall dismiss each action for an asbestos-related injury or a silica-related injury that was pending on August 31, 2005, unless a report was served on or after September 1, 2013, that complies with Section 90.003, Section 90.004, or Subsection (f). The MDL pretrial court shall provide for the dismissal of such actions in a case management order entered for that purpose. All actions for a silica-related injury shall be dismissed on or before August 31, 2015. All actions for an asbestos-related injury shall be dismissed on or before December 31, 2015.

(e) In an action filed on or after the date this chapter becomes law that is transferred to an MDL pretrial court and in which the claimant does not serve on a defendant a report that complies with Section 90.003 or 90.004, the MDL pretrial court shall, on motion by a defendant, dismiss the action under Section 90.007 unless:

(1) the claimant serves a report that complies with Subsection (f)(1); and

(2) the court, on motion and hearing, makes the findings required by Subsection (f)(2).

(f) In an action in which the claimant seeks remand for trial under Subsection (d)(2) or denial of a motion to dismiss under Subsection (e):

(1) the claimant shall serve on each defendant a report that:

(A) complies with the requirements of Sections 90.003(a)(2)(A), (B), (E), and (F) and 90.003(b) or Sections 90.004(a)(1), (2), and (4) and 90.004(e); and

(B) verifies that:

(i) the physician making the report has a physician-patient relationship with the exposed person;

(ii) pulmonary function testing has been performed on the exposed person and the physician making the report has interpreted the pulmonary function testing;

(iii) the physician making the report has concluded, to a reasonable degree of medical probability, that the exposed person has radiographic, pathologic, or computed tomography evidence establishing bilateral pleural disease or bilateral parenchymal disease caused by exposure to asbestos or silica; and

(iv) the physician has concluded that the exposed person has asbestos-related or silica-related physical impairment comparable to the impairment the exposed person would have had if the exposed person met the criteria set forth in Section 90.003 or 90.004; and

(2) the MDL pretrial court shall determine whether:

(A) the report and medical opinions offered by the claimant are reliable and credible;

(B) due to unique or extraordinary physical or medical characteristics of the exposed person, the medical criteria set forth in Sections 90.003 and 90.004 do not adequately assess the exposed person's physical impairment caused by exposure to asbestos or silica; and

(C) the claimant has produced sufficient credible evidence for a finder of fact to reasonably find that the exposed person is physically impaired as the result of exposure to asbestos or silica to a degree comparable to the impairment the exposed person would have had if the exposed person met the criteria set forth in Section 90.003 or 90.004.

(g) A court's determination under Subsection (f) shall be made after conducting an evidentiary hearing at which the claimant and any defendant to the action may offer supporting or controverting evidence. The parties shall be permitted a reasonable opportunity to conduct discovery before the evidentiary hearing.

(h) The court shall state its findings under Subsection (f)(2) in writing and shall address in its findings:

(1) the unique or extraordinary physical or medical characteristics of the exposed person that justify the application of this section; and

(2) the reasons the criteria set forth in Sections 90.003 and 90.004 do not adequately assess the exposed person's physical impairment caused by exposure to asbestos or silica.

(i) Any findings made by a court under Subsection (f) are not admissible for any purpose at a trial on the merits.

(j) Subsections (d)(2) and (e)–(i) apply only in exceptional and limited circumstances in which the exposed person does not satisfy the medical criteria of Section 90.003 or 90.004 but can demonstrate meaningful asbestos-related or silica-related physical impairment that satisfies the requirements of Subsection (f). Subsections (d)(2) and (e)–(i) have limited application and shall not be used to negate the requirements of this chapter.

(k) On or before September 1, 2010, each MDL pretrial court having jurisdiction over cases to which this chapter applies shall deliver a report to the governor, lieutenant governor, and the speaker of the house of representatives stating:

(1) the number of cases on the court's multidistrict litigation docket as of August 1, 2010;

(2) the number of cases on the court's multidistrict litigation docket as of August 1, 2010, that do not meet the criteria of Section 90.003 or 90.004, to the extent known;

(3) the court's evaluation of the effectiveness of the medical criteria established by Sections 90.003 and 90.004;

(4) the court's recommendation, if any, as to how medical criteria should be applied to the cases on the court's multidistrict litigation docket as of August 1, 2010; and

(5) any other information regarding the administration of cases in the MDL pretrial courts that the court deems appropriate.

(*l*) A dismissal under Subsection (d–1) is without prejudice to the claimant's right to file a subsequent action seeking damages arising from an asbestos-related injury or a silica-related injury.

(m) This chapter and Section 16.0031 apply to a subsequent action for an asbestos-related injury or a silica-related injury filed by a claimant whose action was dismissed under Subsection (d–1) or by a claimant in an action described by Subsection (d) who voluntarily dismissed the action under Section 90.008.

(n) If a claimant subsequently refiles an action for an asbestos-related injury or a silica-related injury that was dismissed under Subsection (d–1), the refiled action is treated for purposes of determining the applicable law as if that claimant's action had never been dismissed but, instead, had remained pending until the claimant served a report that complied with Section 90.003, Section 90.004, or Subsection (f).

(*o*) A claimant whose action was dismissed under Subsection (d–1) may serve the petition and citation for any subsequently filed action for an asbestos-related or silica-related injury by certified mail, return receipt requested, or other method approved by the MDL pretrial court that is likely to accomplish service in a cost-effective manner, on a person who was a defendant in the dismissed action.

Added by Acts 2005, 79th Leg., ch. 97, § 2, eff. Sept. 1, 2005. Amended by Acts 2013, 83rd Leg., ch. 146 (H.B. 1325), § 3, eff. Sept. 1, 2013; Acts 2015, 84th Leg., ch. 532 (H.B. 1492), § 2, eff. Sept. 1, 2015.

§ 90.011. Bankruptcy

Nothing in this chapter is intended to affect the rights of any party in a bankruptcy proceeding or affect the ability of any person to satisfy the claim criteria for compensable claims or demands under a trust established pursuant to a plan of reorganization under Chapter 11 of the United States Bankruptcy Code (11 U.S.C. Section 1101 et seq.).

Added by Acts 2005, 79th Leg., ch. 97, § 2, eff. Sept. 1, 2005.

§ 90.012. Supreme Court Rulemaking

The supreme court may promulgate amendments to the Texas Rules of Civil Procedure regarding the joinder of claimants in asbestos-related actions or silica-related actions if the rules are consistent with Section 90.009.

Added by Acts 2005, 79th Leg., ch. 97, § 2, eff. Sept. 1, 2005.

SUBCHAPTER B. ASBESTOS OR SILICA TRUST CLAIMS

§ 90.051. Definitions

In this subchapter:

(1) "Asbestos or silica trust" means a claims facility, a claims agent, a qualified settlement fund, or any other entity that:

(A) is created under 11 U.S.C. Section 524(g) or another applicable law for the benefit of creditors of a bankrupt person;

(B) is formed for the purpose of compensating claimants for asbestos- or silica-related injuries; and

(C) is in existence on the date trial in an action asserting an asbestos- or silica-related injury is set to commence.

(2) "Trust claim" means any filing with or claim against an asbestos or silica trust seeking recovery of compensation or damages for or arising from the asbestos- or silica-related injury of an exposed person.

(3) "Trust claim material" means documentation filed as part of or in connection with a trust claim, including:

(A) documentation that a claimant submits or provides to an asbestos or silica trust for the purpose of demonstrating asbestos or silica exposure, the existence of an asbestos- or silica-related injury, or the validity of a trust claim; and

(B) claim forms and other materials that an asbestos or silica trust requires a claimant to submit.

Added by Acts 2015, 84th Leg., ch. 532 (H.B. 1492), § 3, eff. Sept. 1, 2015.

§ 90.052. Requirement to Make Trust Claims

(a) Except as provided by Subsection (d), a claimant who has filed an action to recover damages for or arising from an asbestos- or silica-related injury shall make a trust claim against each asbestos or silica trust the claimant believes may owe compensation or damages to the claimant for the injury that is the basis of the claimant's action.

(b) A claimant must make each trust claim required under this section not later than:

(1) the 150th day before the date trial in the action is set to commence; or

(2) a date provided by court order if trial is set to commence on or before January 31, 2016.

(c) A claimant may file a motion seeking relief from the obligation to make a trust claim otherwise required by this section if the claimant believes that the fees and expenses, including attorney's fees, for filing the trust claim exceed the claimant's reasonably anticipated recovery from the trust.

(d) If a claimant files a motion under Subsection (c), the court shall determine whether the claimant's fees and expenses, including attorney's fees, for making the trust claim exceed the claimant's reasonably anticipated recovery from the trust. If the court determines that the claimant's fees and expenses exceed the claimant's reasonably anticipated recovery, the claimant is not required to make the trust claim but shall provide the court with a verified statement of the exposed person's exposure history to asbestos or silica that is covered by the trust.

Added by Acts 2015, 84th Leg., ch. 532 (H.B. 1492), § 3, eff. Sept. 1, 2015.

§ 90.053. Notice of Trust Claim; Production of Trust Claim Material

(a) A claimant in an action to recover damages for or arising from an asbestos- or silica-related injury shall serve on each party notice of, and trust claim material relating to, each trust claim made by or on behalf of the exposed person. The notice must:

(1) identify each trust claim made by or on behalf of the exposed person;

(2) state the amount of any trust claim payment made to compensate for the exposed person's injury; and

(3) state the date each trust claim was made and whether a request for individual or enhanced review or for a deferral, delay, suspension, or tolling of the claim has been submitted to the trust.

(b) The claimant shall serve the notice and trust claim materials required by Subsection (a) not later than:

(1) the 120th day before the date trial in the action is set to commence; or

(2) a date provided by court order if the court entered an order under Section 90.052(b).

(c) The notice and trust claim materials required to be served under Subsection (a) are in addition to any notice or materials required to be served or produced under other law, rule, order, or applicable agreement.

(d) If a claimant makes a trust claim after the date provided by Section 90.052(b) but before the date that trial in the action commences, the claimant shall serve the notice of, and trust claim material relating to, the trust claim as required by Subsection (a) reasonably promptly after making the trust claim, but not later than the earlier of:

(1) the date that trial commences; or

(2) the 15th day after the date the additional trust claim is made.

(e) If a claimant discovers that the notice or trust claim materials provided by the claimant under this section were incomplete or incorrect at the time the notice or trust claim materials were served or that the notice or trust claim materials as served are no longer complete and correct, the claimant shall supplement the notice and the production of trust claim materials. The claimant shall serve the supplemental notice or trust claim materials reasonably promptly after the claimant discovers the necessity for the supplementation, but not later than the 15th day after the date the claimant discovers the necessity for the supplementation.

(f) A claimant shall serve notice of, and trust claim material relating to, a trust claim regardless of whether the claim is for an injury resulting in cancer or an injury not resulting in cancer.

Added by Acts 2015, 84th Leg., ch. 532 (H.B. 1492), § 3, eff. Sept. 1, 2015.

§ 90.054. Failure to Make Trust Claim or Provide Notice and Trust Claim Material

(a) An MDL pretrial court may not remand an action to a trial court and a trial court may not commence trial in the action unless the claimant has:

(1) made each trust claim as required by this subchapter; and

(2) served the notice of, and trust claim material relating to, those trust claims in accordance with Section 90.053.

(b) If a claimant received compensation from an asbestos or silica trust for an injury that also gave rise to a judgment against a defendant for the same injury and the claimant failed to serve the relevant notice and trust claim material as required by Section 90.053, the trial court, on a defendant's or judgment debtor's motion and after reasonable notice to the parties, may impose an appropriate sanction, including setting aside the judgment and ordering a new trial.

(c) This section may not be construed to require payment of a trust claim by an asbestos or silica trust before the MDL pretrial court remands the action for trial or before a judgment is rendered in the action.

Added by Acts 2015, 84th Leg., ch. 532 (H.B. 1492), § 3, eff. Sept. 1, 2015.

§ 90.055. Motion to Stay

(a) A defendant may file a motion requesting a stay of the proceedings under Section 90.057 on or before the later of:

(1) the 60th day before the date trial in the action is set to commence;

(2) the 15th day after the date the defendant first obtains asbestos- or silica-exposure information that could support an additional asbestos or silica trust claim by the claimant; or

(3) a date provided by court order if the court entered an order under Section 90.052(b).

(b) The motion described by Subsection (a) must include:

(1) a list of asbestos or silica trusts not disclosed by the claimant against which the defendant in good faith believes the claimant may make a successful trust claim; and

(2) information supporting the additional trust claim described by Subdivision (1), including information that may be used to meet the trust claim requirements of an asbestos or silica trust described by Subdivision (1).

Added by Acts 2015, 84th Leg., ch. 532 (H.B. 1492), § 3, eff. Sept. 1, 2015.

§ 90.056. Response to Motion to Stay

(a) Not later than the 14th day after the date the defendant files a motion to stay under Section 90.055 or the date provided by court order under Section 90.052(b), the claimant may file a response:

(1) stating and providing proof that the claimant has made a trust claim identified in the defendant's motion and served the notice of, and trust claim material relating to, the claim as prescribed by Section 90.053; or

(2) requesting a determination by the court that the fees and expenses, including attorney's fees, for filing a trust claim identified in the motion exceed the claimant's reasonably anticipated recovery from the trust.

(b) If the claimant files a response making a request under Subsection (a)(2), the court shall determine whether the claimant's fees and expenses, including attorney's fees, for making the relevant trust claim exceed the claimant's reasonably anticipated recovery from the trust. If the court determines that the claimant's fees and expenses exceed the claimant's reasonably anticipated recovery, the claimant is not required to make the trust claim but shall provide the court with a verified statement of the exposed person's exposure history to asbestos or silica that is covered by the trust.

Added by Acts 2015, 84th Leg., ch. 532 (H.B. 1492), § 3, eff. Sept. 1, 2015.

§ 90.057. Stay of Proceedings

(a) The court shall grant a motion to stay under Section 90.055 if the court determines the motion was timely filed and the claimant is likely to receive compensation from a trust identified by the motion. The stay shall continue until the claimant provides proof that the claimant has made the claim and served notice of, and trust claim material relating to, the claim as prescribed by Section 90.053.

(b) The court may not stay the proceedings if, with respect to each trust claim identified in the motion:

(1) the court determines that the claimant has satisfied the requirements of Section 90.053(a); or

(2) the court makes a determination described by Section 90.052(d) or 90.056(b).

Added by Acts 2015, 84th Leg., ch. 532 (H.B. 1492), § 3, eff. Sept. 1, 2015.

§ 90.058. Evidence of Trust Claims

(a) Trust claim material is presumed to be authentic, relevant, and discoverable in an action to which this subchapter applies.

(b) Notwithstanding an agreement, including a confidentiality agreement, trust claim material is presumed to not be privileged in an action to which this subchapter applies.

(c) This section may not be construed to affect the application of Section 33.003 to an action governed by this chapter.

Added by Acts 2015, 84th Leg., ch. 532 (H.B. 1492), § 3, eff. Sept. 1, 2015.

CHAPTER 91. LIABILITY OF VOLUNTEER HEALTH CARE PRACTITIONERS

Section

§ 91.001. Definitions

In this chapter:

(1) "Health care practitioner" means a person who is licensed:

(A) to practice medicine under Subtitle B, Title 3, Occupations Code;[1]

(B) as a physician assistant under Chapter 204, Occupations Code;

(C) as an advanced nurse practitioner under Chapter 301, Occupations Code; or

(D) as a chiropractor under Chapter 201, Occupations Code.

(2) "School" means any private or public school offering academic instruction in any grade level from kindergarten through grade 12.

Added by Acts 2003, 78th Leg., ch. 749, § 1, eff. Sept. 1, 2003.

[1] V.T.C.A., Occupations Code § 151.001 et seq.

§ 91.002. Health Care Practitioner Liability

Subject to Section 91.003, a health care practitioner who, without compensation or expectation of compensation, conducts a physical examination or medical screening of a patient for the purpose of determining the physical health and fitness of the patient to participate in a school-sponsored extracurricular or sporting activity is immune from civil liability for any act or omission resulting in the death of or injury to the patient if:

(1) the health care practitioner was acting in good faith and in the course and scope of the health care practitioner's duties;

(2) the health care practitioner commits the act or omission in the course of conducting the physical examination or medical screening of the patient;

(3) the services provided to the patient are within the scope of the license of the health care practitioner; and

(4) before the health care practitioner conducts the physical examination or medical screening, the patient or, if the patient is a minor or is otherwise legally incompetent, the patient's parent, managing conservator, legal guardian, or other person with legal responsibility for the care of the patient signs a written statement that acknowledges:

(A) that the health care practitioner is conducting a physical examination or medical screening that is not administered for or in expectation of compensation; and

(B) the limitations on the recovery of damages from the health care practitioner in connection with the physical examination or medical screening being performed.

Added by Acts 2003, 78th Leg., ch. 749, § 1, eff. Sept. 1, 2003. Amended by Acts 2011, 82nd Leg., ch. 1099 (S.B. 1545), § 1, eff. Sept. 1, 2011.

§ 91.003. Insurance Required

(a) Section 91.002 applies only to a health care practitioner who has liability insurance coverage in effect to cover any act or omission to which this chapter applies. The health care practitioner's liability coverage must cover the acts or omissions of the health care practitioner and must be in the amount of at least $100,000 per person and $300,000 for each single occurrence of death or bodily injury and $100,000 for each single occurrence for injury to or destruction of property.

(b) The coverage may be provided under a contract of insurance or other plan of insurance and may be satisfied by the purchase of a $300,000 bodily injury and property damage combined single-limit policy.

Added by Acts 2003, 78th Leg., ch. 749, § 1, eff. Sept. 1, 2003.

§ 91.004. Applicability

(a) This chapter does not apply to an act or omission that is intentional, wilfully or wantonly negligent, or done with conscious indifference or reckless disregard for the safety of others.

(b) This chapter does not:

(1) limit the liability of a school district to its students, teachers, or staff; or

(2) affect a school district's liability limits or immunities under Chapter 101.

(c) This chapter does not apply to a governmental unit or employee of a governmental unit as defined by Section 101.001.

(d) This chapter does not limit the liability of an insurer or insurance plan in an action under Chapter 21, Insurance Code, or in an action for bad faith conduct, breach of fiduciary duty, or negligent failure to settle a claim.

Added by Acts 2003, 78th Leg., ch. 749, § 1, eff. Sept. 1, 2003.

CHAPTER 91A. LIABILITY OF VOLUNTEER AUDIOLOGISTS AND SPEECH-LANGUAGE PATHOLOGISTS

Section

§ 91A.001. Definitions

In this chapter:

(1) "Audiologist" means an individual licensed to practice audiology by the Texas Department of Licensing and Regulation.

(2) "Speech-language pathologist" means an individual licensed to practice speech-language pathology by the Texas Department of Licensing and Regulation.

Added by Acts 2009, 81st Leg., ch. 658, § 1, eff. Sept. 1, 2009. Amended by Acts 2017, 85th Leg., ch. 324 (S.B. 1488), § 4.001, eff. Sept. 1, 2017.

§ 91A.002. Immunity from Liability

An audiologist or speech-language pathologist who, without compensation or expectation of compensation, conducts a speech, language, or hearing evaluation or screening is immune from civil liability for any act or omission resulting in the death or injury to the patient if:

(1) the audiologist or speech-language pathologist was acting in good faith and in the course and scope of the audiologist's or speech-language pathologist's duties;

(2) the audiologist or speech-language pathologist commits the act or omission in the course of conducting the speech, language, or hearing examination or screening; and

(3) the services provided to the patient are within the scope of the license of the audiologist or speech-language pathologist.

Added by Acts 2009, 81st Leg., ch. 658, § 1, eff. Sept. 1, 2009.

§ 91A.003. Applicability

This chapter does not apply to an act or omission that is intentional, wilfully or wantonly negligent, or done with conscious indifference or reckless disregard for the safety of others.

Added by Acts 2009, 81st Leg., ch. 658, § 1, eff. Sept. 1, 2009.

CHAPTER 91B. LIABILITY OF VOLUNTEER VETERINARY PRACTITIONERS

Section

§ 91B.001 Definitions

In this chapter, "certified veterinary assistant," "licensed veterinary technician," and "veterinarian" have the meanings assigned by Section 801.002, Occupations Code.

Added by Acts 2021, 87th Leg., ch. 827 (H.B. 2850), § 1, eff. Sept. 1, 2021.

Section 3 of Acts 2021, 87th Leg., ch. 827 (H.B. 2850) provides:

"'Chapter 91B, Civil Practice and Remedies Code, as added by this Act, does not apply to a cause of action that accrued before the effective date [Sept. 1, 2021] of this Act. A cause of action that accrued before the effective date of this Act is govornod by the law applicable to the cause of action immediately before the effective date of this Act, and that law is continued in effect for that purpose."

§ 91B.002. Immunity from Liability

(a) Except as provided by Section 91B.003, a certified veterinary assistant, licensed veterinary technician, or veterinarian who in good faith and as a volunteer provides veterinary care or treatment to an injured animal is immune from civil liability for an act or omission that occurs in providing that care or treatment if the care or treatment is provided:

(1) in response to an incident that is a man-made or natural disaster that injures, endangers, or threatens to endanger the animal;

(2) at the request of the owner of the animal or an authorized representative of a local, state, or federal agency, including a fire department, a police department, an emergency management agency, or a disaster response agency; and

(3) within the scope of practice authorized and level of supervision required under Chapter 801, Occupations Code.

(b) This section does not apply to a certified veterinary assistant, licensed veterinary technician, or veterinarian giving veterinary care or treatment for or in expectation of compensation from or on behalf of the owner of the animal in excess of reimbursement for expenses incurred.

Added by Acts 2021, 87th Leg., ch. 827 (H.B. 2850), § 1, eff. Sept. 1, 2021.

Section 3 of Acts 2021, 87th Leg., ch. 827 (H.B. 2850) provides:

"Chapter 91B, Civil Practice and Remedies Code, as added by this Act, does not apply to a cause of action that accrued before the effective date [Sept. 1, 2021] of this Act. A cause of action that accrued before the effective date of this Act is governed by the law applicable to the cause of action immediately before the effective date of this Act, and that law is continued in effect for that purpose."

§ 91B.003. Applicability

This chapter does not apply to an act or omission that is grossly negligent or intentional misconduct.

Added by Acts 2021, 87th Leg., ch. 827 (H.B. 2850), § 1, eff. Sept. 1, 2021.

Section 3 of Acts 2021, 87th Leg., ch. 827 (H.B. 2850) provides:

"Chapter 91B, Civil Practice and Remedies Code, as added by this Act, does not apply to a cause of action that accrued before the effective date [Sept. 1, 2021] of this Act. A cause of action that accrued before the effective date of this Act is governed by the law applicable to the cause of action immediately before the effective date of this Act, and that law is continued in effect for that purpose."

CHAPTER 92. LIMITATION OF LIABILITY FOR PERSON ASSISTING CERTAIN ANIMALS

§ 92.001. Definitions

In this chapter:

(1) "Animal control agency" means a municipal or county animal control office, or a state, county, or municipal law enforcement agency, that collects, impounds, or keeps stray, homeless, abandoned, or unwanted animals.

(2) "Livestock animal" means an equine animal or an animal raised primarily for use as food for human consumption or to produce fiber for human use and includes horses, cattle, sheep, swine, goats, and poultry.

(3) "Nonlivestock animal" means a service animal or an animal maintained as a pet in the home or on the property of the animal's owner and includes captured wildlife or an exotic animal maintained as a pet. The term does not include a livestock animal.

(4) "Running at large" means not under the control of the owner or handler while:

(A) on the premises of another without the consent of the owner of the premises or any other person authorized to give consent; or

(B) on a highway, a public road or street, or any other place open to the public generally.

(5) "Service animal" has the meaning assigned by the Americans with Disabilities Act of 1990 (42 U.S.C. Section 12101 et seq.).

Added by Acts 2011, 82nd Leg., ch. 530 (H.B. 2471), § 1, eff. Sept. 1, 2011.

§ 92.002. Limitation of Liability

(a) In this section, "emergency" includes:

(1) a natural disaster, including an earthquake, fire, flood, or storm;

(2) a hazardous chemical or substance incident; and

(3) a vehicular collision with an animal or other transportation accident in which an animal is injured or is otherwise in need of assistance to protect the animal's health or life.

(b) A person who in good faith and without compensation renders or obtains medical care or treatment for a nonlivestock animal that is injured or in distress because of an emergency, abandoned, running at large, or stray is not liable for civil damages for an injury to the animal resulting from an act or omission in rendering or obtaining the medical care or treatment, unless the person commits gross negligence, if:

(1) the person first takes reasonable steps to locate the animal's owner by:

(A) attempting to contact the animal's owner using the contact information located on the animal's identification tag, collar, or chip, if any, or taking other reasonable action to contact the owner; or

(B) notifying an animal control agency with authority over the area where the person resides, or an animal control agency with authority over the area where the person took custody of the animal if that area lies outside of the municipality or county where the person resides, that the animal is in the person's custody and providing the animal control agency with the person's contact information; or

(2) a veterinarian determines that the animal:

(A) needs immediate medical treatment to alleviate pain or save the animal's life; or

(B) exhibits visible signs of recent abuse as described by Section 42.092(b), Penal Code.

Added by Acts 2011, 82nd Leg., ch. 530 (H.B. 2471), § 1, eff. Sept. 1, 2011.

§ 92.003. Limitation of Liability for Animal Control Agencies and Certain Employees

An animal control agency or an employee of an animal control agency acting within the scope of the person's employment that in good faith takes into custody and cares for a nonlivestock animal that is abandoned, running at large, or stray is not liable for civil damages for an injury to the animal arising from an act or omission in caring for the animal, except in a case of gross negligence, if the animal control agency obtains custody of the animal from a person not affiliated with the animal control agency and that person certifies in writing that the person has taken reasonable steps to locate the owner as provided by Section 92.002.

Added by Acts 2011, 82nd Leg., ch. 530 (H.B. 2471), § 1, eff. Sept. 1, 2011.

§ 92.004. Effect on Other Law

(a) This chapter does not limit the application of or supersede Section 822.013, Health and Safety Code, or Section 801.358, Occupations Code.

(b) This chapter does not create any civil liability or waive any defense, immunity, or jurisdictional bar available under state law.

Added by Acts 2011, 82nd Leg., ch. 530 (H.B. 2471), § 1, eff. Sept. 1, 2011.

CHAPTER 92A. LIMITATION OF LIABILITY FOR REMOVING CERTAIN INDIVIDUALS FROM MOTOR VEHICLE

Section

§ 92A.001. Definitions

In this chapter:

(1) "Motor vehicle" means a vehicle that is self-propelled or a trailer or semitrailer designed for use with a self-propelled vehicle.

(2) "Vulnerable individual" means:

(A) a child younger than seven years of age; or

(B) an individual who by reason of age or physical or mental disease, defect, or injury is substantially unable to protect the individual's self from harm.

Added by Acts 2017, 85th Leg., ch. 694 (H.B. 478), § 1, eff. Sept. 1, 2017.

§ 92A.002. Limitation of Liability

A person who, by force or otherwise, enters a motor vehicle for the purpose of removing a vulnerable individual from the vehicle is immune from civil liability for damages resulting from that entry or removal if the person:

(1) determines that:

(A) the motor vehicle is locked; or

(B) there is no reasonable method for the individual to exit the motor vehicle without assistance;

(2) has a good faith and reasonable belief, based on known circumstances, that entry into the motor vehicle is necessary to avoid imminent harm to the individual;

(3) before entering the motor vehicle, ensures that law enforcement is notified or 911 is called if the person is not a law enforcement officer or other first responder;

(4) uses no more force to enter the motor vehicle and remove the individual than is necessary; and

(5) remains with the individual in a safe location that is in reasonable proximity to the motor vehicle until a law enforcement officer or other first responder arrives.

Added by Acts 2017, 85th Leg., ch. 694 (H.B. 478), § 1, eff. Sept. 1, 2017.

§ 92A.003. Effect on Other Laws

This chapter does not affect limitation under Section 74.151 or 74.152 of a person's liability for good faith administration of emergency care.

Added by Acts 2017, 85th Leg., ch. 694 (H.B. 478), § 1, eff. Sept. 1, 2017.

CHAPTER 93. ASSUMPTION OF THE RISK AND CERTAIN OTHER AFFIRMATIVE DEFENSES

Section

§ 93.001. Assumption of the Risk: Affirmative Defense

(a) It is an affirmative defense to a civil action for damages for personal injury or death that the plaintiff, at the time the cause of action arose, was:

(1) committing a felony, for which the plaintiff has been finally convicted, that was the sole cause of the damages sustained by the plaintiff; or

(2) committing or attempting to commit suicide, and the plaintiff's conduct in committing or attempting to commit suicide was the sole cause of the damages sustained; provided, however, if the suicide or attempted suicide was caused in whole or in

part by a failure on the part of any defendant to comply with an applicable legal standard, then such suicide or attempted suicide shall not be a defense.

(b) This section does not apply in any action brought by an employee, or the surviving beneficiaries of an employee, under the Workers' Compensation Law of Texas, or in an action against an insurer based on a contract of insurance, a statute, or common law.

(c) In an action to which this section applies, this section shall prevail over any other law.

Added by Acts 1987, 70th Leg., ch. 824, § 1, eff. Sept. 1, 1987. Amended by Acts 1997, 75th Leg., ch. 437, § 1, eff. Sept. 1, 1997.

§ 93.002. Dry Fire Hydrants: Affirmative Defense

(a) It is an affirmative defense to a civil action for damages brought against a defendant who is an owner, lessee, or occupant of real property who permits a fire-fighting agency to connect a dry fire hydrant to a source of water on the property or to install a dry fire hydrant on the property that the damages arise from:

(1) the condition or use of the dry fire hydrant;

(2) the installation or maintenance of the dry fire hydrant; or

(3) the failure of the water source to contain an adequate supply of water during a fire.

(b) This section does not apply to:

(1) an action for damages arising from an act or omission of the owner, lessee, or occupant of real property that is intentional, wilfully or wantonly negligent, or done with conscious indifference or reckless disregard for the safety of others; or

(2) an action for damages arising from a condition of the real property on which the dry fire hydrant is located.

(c) In this section:

(1) "Dry fire hydrant" means a fire hydrant that is connected to a stock tank, pond, or other similar source of water from which water is pumped in case of fire.

(2) "Fire-fighting agency" means any entity that provides fire-fighting services, including:

(A) a volunteer fire department; and

(B) a political subdivision of this state authorized to provide fire-fighting services.

Added by Acts 1997, 75th Leg., ch. 437, § 1, eff. Sept. 1, 1997.

CHAPTER 94. LIABILITY OF SPORTS OFFICIALS AND ORGANIZATIONS

Section

§ 94.001. Definitions

In this chapter:

(1) "Athletic competition" means any competitive group or solo sporting activity and includes:

(A) football, baseball, soccer, basketball, hockey, swimming, track, wrestling, bike or foot races, triathlon, equestrian competitions, golf, marksmanship competitions, darts, billiards, Frisbee golf, fishing tournaments, car racing, and any similar activity that involves any aspect of physical competition, coordination, endurance, or stamina; and

(B) a rodeo, livestock show, or related event or competition.

(2) "Sponsoring organization" means the individual, club, association, or entity that undertakes to organize, underwrite, sanction, or promote:

(A) an interscholastic, intercollegiate, or other organized amateur athletic competition; or

(B) any rodeo, livestock show, or related event or competition.

(3) "Sports official" means a person who officiates, judges, or in any manner enforces contest rules in any official capacity with respect to:

(A) an interscholastic, intercollegiate, or other organized amateur athletic competition and includes a referee, umpire, linesman, side judge, track or field marshal, timekeeper, or scorekeeper or any other person involved in supervising competitive play; or

(B) any rodeo, livestock show, or related event or competition.

Added by Acts 2015, 84th Leg., ch. 348 (H.B. 1040), § 1, eff. June 9, 2015.

§ 94.002. Liability of Sports Official

(a) A sports official who is engaged in an athletic competition is not liable for civil damages, including personal injury, wrongful death, property damage, or other loss related to any act, error, or omission that results from a risk inherent in the nature of the competitive activity in which the claimant chose to participate unless the act, error, or omission constitutes:

(1) gross negligence; or

(2) wanton, wilful, or intentional misconduct.

(b) Whether a risk is inherent in the nature of a competitive activity is dependent upon:

(1) the nature of the sport in question;

(2) the conduct that is generally accepted in the sport; and

(3) whether the harm occurred during the pursuit of the purposes of the competition.

(c) A mere violation of the rules of play of an athletic competition or failing to call a penalty, missing a call, or failing to enforce competition rules cannot in itself form the basis for liability under this chapter.

Added by Acts 2015, 84th Leg., ch. 348 (H.B. 1040), § 1, eff. June 9, 2015.

§ 94.003. Liability of Sponsoring Organization

A sponsoring organization cannot be held liable for an act, error, or omission of a sports official absent any new, independent, and separate act, error, or omission of the sponsoring organization that gave rise to the harm.

Added by Acts 2015, 84th Leg., ch. 348 (H.B. 1040), § 1, eff. June 9, 2015.

CHAPTER 95. PROPERTY OWNER'S LIABILITY FOR ACTS OF INDEPENDENT CONTRACTORS AND AMOUNT OF RECOVERY

Section

§ 95.001. Definitions

In this chapter:

(1) "Claim" means a claim for damages caused by negligence, including a counterclaim, cross-claim, or third party claim.

(2) "Claimant" means a party making a claim subject to this chapter.

(3) "Property owner" means a person or entity that owns real property primarily used for commercial or business purposes.

Added by Acts 1995, 74th Leg., ch. 136, § 2, eff. Sept. 1, 1996.

§ 95.002. Applicability

This chapter applies only to a claim:

(1) against a property owner, contractor, or subcontractor for personal injury, death, or property damage to an owner, a contractor, or a subcontractor or an employee of a contractor or subcontractor; and

(2) that arises from the condition or use of an improvement to real property where the contractor or subcontractor constructs, repairs, renovates, or modifies the improvement.

Added by Acts 1995, 74th Leg., ch. 136, § 2, eff. Sept. 1, 1996.

§ 95.003. Liability for Acts of Independent Contractors

A property owner is not liable for personal injury, death, or property damage to a contractor, subcontractor, or an employee of a contractor or subcontractor who constructs, repairs, renovates, or modifies an improvement to real property, including personal injury, death, or property damage arising from the failure to provide a safe workplace unless:

(1) the property owner exercises or retains some control over the manner in which the work is performed, other than the right to order the work to start or stop or to inspect progress or receive reports; and

(2) the property owner had actual knowledge of the danger or condition resulting in the personal injury, death, or property damage and failed to adequately warn.

Added by Acts 1995, 74th Leg., ch. 136, § 2, eff. Sept. 1, 1996.

§ 95.004. Evidence Admissible

In the trial of a case against a contractor, subcontractor, or property owner for personal injury, property damage, or death to a contractor, a subcontractor, or an employee of a contractor or subcontractor that arises from the condition or use of an improvement to real property where the contractor or subcontractor constructs, repairs, renovates, or modifies the improvement, the trial judge, outside the presence of the jury, shall receive evidence of workers' compensation benefits paid and shall deduct the amount of the benefits from the damages awarded by the trier of fact. The deduction for workers' compensation benefits does not apply unless the workers' compensation carrier's subrogation rights have been waived.

Added by Acts 1995, 74th Leg., ch. 136, § 2, eff. Sept. 1, 1996.

CHAPTER 95A. ACTIONS INVOLVING THE CARRYING OF HANDGUNS ON CERTAIN PROPERTY

Section

§ 95A.0001. Evidence of Failure to Forbid Handguns

The fact that a card, sign, or other document described by Section 30.06(c)(3) or 30.07(c)(3), Penal Code, is not posted on the property of a business or any other evidence that a person failed to exercise the person's option to forbid the carrying of a handgun by a license holder on the property:

(1) is not admissible as evidence in a trial on the merits in an action:

(A) against a person, including a business or other entity, who owns, controls, or manages the property; and

(B) in which the cause of action arises from an injury sustained on the property; and

(2) does not support a cause of action described by Subdivision (1) against a person described by that subdivision.

Added by Acts 2019, 86th Leg., ch. 974 (S.B. 772), § 1, eff. Sept. 1, 2019.

Section 2 of Acts 2019, 86th Leg., ch. 974 (S.B. 772) provides:

"Chapter 95A, Civil Practice and Remedies Code, as added by this Act, does not apply to a cause of action that accrued before the effective date [Sept. 1, 2019] of this Act."

CHAPTER 96. FALSE DISPARAGEMENT OF PERISHABLE FOOD PRODUCTS

Section

§ 96.001. Definition

In this chapter, "perishable food product" means a food product of agriculture or aquaculture that is sold or distributed in a form that will perish or decay beyond marketability within a limited period of time.

Added by Acts 1995, 74th Leg., ch. 80, § 1, eff. Sept. 1, 1995.

§ 96.002. Liability

(a) A person is liable as provided by Subsection (b) if:

(1) the person disseminates in any manner information relating to a perishable food product to the public;

(2) the person knows the information is false; and

(3) the information states or implies that the perishable food product is not safe for consumption by the public.

(b) A person who is liable under Subsection (a) is liable to the producer of the perishable food product for damages and any other appropriate relief arising from the person's dissemination of the information.

Added by Acts 1995, 74th Leg., ch. 80, § 1, eff. Sept. 1, 1995.

§ 96.003. Proof

In determining if information is false, the trier of fact shall consider whether the information was based on reasonable and reliable scientific inquiry, facts, or data.

Added by Acts 1995, 74th Leg., ch. 80, § 1, eff. Sept. 1, 1995.

§ 96.004. Certain Marketing or Labeling Excluded

A person is not liable under this chapter for marketing or labeling any agricultural product in a manner that indicates that the product:

(1) was grown or produced by using or not using a chemical or drug;

(2) was organically grown; or

(3) was grown without the use of any synthetic additive.

Added by Acts 1995, 74th Leg., ch. 80, § 1, eff. Sept. 1, 1995.

CHAPTER 97. LIABILITY OF PERSONS PROVIDING SERVICES FOR A GOVERNMENTAL UNIT

Section

§ 97.001. Liability of Correctional Facilities and Officers Barred for Certain Acts of Inmates

A correctional facility or an officer or employee of a correctional facility is not liable for damages arising from an act committed by a person confined in the correctional facility that is in violation of Section 38.111, Penal Code. This section does not apply if the officer or employee of the correctional facility knowingly assists or participates in the conduct prohibited by Section 38.111, Penal Code.

Added by Acts 2001, 77th Leg., ch. 1337, § 2, eff. Sept. 1, 2001. Amended by Acts 2003, 78th Leg., ch. 584, § 3, eff. Sept. 1, 2003.

§ 97.002. Limit on Liability of Certain Highway, Road, and Street Contractors

A contractor who constructs or repairs a highway, road, or street for the Texas Department of Transportation is not liable to a claimant for personal injury, property damage, or death arising from the performance of the construction or repair if, at the time of the personal injury, property damage, or death, the contractor is in compliance with contract documents material to the condition or defect that was the proximate cause of the personal injury, property damage, or death.

Added by Acts 2003, 78th Leg., ch. 584, § 1, eff. Sept. 1, 2003.

CHAPTER 98. LIABILITY FOR TRAFFICKING OF PERSONS

§ 98.001. Definition

In this chapter, "trafficking of persons" means conduct that constitutes an offense under Chapter 20A, Penal Code.

Added by Acts 2009, 81st Leg., ch. 309, § 1, eff. June 19, 2009.

§ 98.002. Liability

(a) A defendant who engages in the trafficking of persons or who intentionally or knowingly benefits from participating in a venture that traffics another person is liable to the person trafficked, as provided by this chapter, for damages arising from the trafficking of that person by the defendant or venture.

(b) It is not a defense to liability under this chapter that a defendant has been acquitted or has not been prosecuted or convicted under Chapter 20A, Penal Code, or has been convicted of a different offense or of a different type or class of offense, for the conduct that is alleged to give rise to liability under this chapter.

Added by Acts 2009, 81st Leg., ch. 309, § 1, eff. June 19, 2009.

§ 98.0025. Shareholder and Member Liability

(a) This section applies to a legal entity governed by Title 2, 3, or 7, Business Organizations Code.[1]

(b) Notwithstanding any provision of the Business Organizations Code, if a legal entity described by Subsection (a) is liable under Section 98.002, a shareholder or member of that entity is jointly and severally liable with the entity to the person trafficked for damages arising from the trafficking of that person if the person demonstrates that the shareholder or member caused the entity to be used for the purpose of trafficking that person and did traffic that person for the direct personal benefit of the shareholder or member.

Added by Acts 2015, 84th Leg., ch. 283 (H.B. 968), § 1, eff. June 1, 2015.

[1] V.T.C.A., Business Organization Code §§ 20.001 et seq., 101.001 et seq., 301.001 et seq.

§ 98.003. Damages

(a) A claimant who prevails in a suit under this chapter shall be awarded:

(1) actual damages, including damages for mental anguish even if an injury other than mental anguish is not shown;

(2) court costs; and

(3) reasonable attorney's fees.

(b) In addition to an award under Subsection (a), a claimant who prevails in a suit under this chapter may recover exemplary damages.

Added by Acts 2009, 81st Leg., ch. 309, § 1, eff. June 19, 2009.

§ 98.004. Cause of Action Cumulative

The cause of action created by this chapter is cumulative of any other remedy provided by common law or statute.

Added by Acts 2009, 81st Leg., ch. 309, § 1, eff. June 19, 2009.

§ 98.005. Joint and Several Liability

A person who engages in the trafficking of persons or who intentionally or knowingly benefits from participating in a venture that traffics another person and is found liable under this chapter or other law for any amount of damages arising from the trafficking is jointly liable with any other defendant for the entire amount of damages arising from the trafficking.

Added by Acts 2009, 81st Leg., ch. 309, § 1, eff. June 19, 2009.

§ 98.006. Liberal Construction and Application

This chapter shall be liberally construed and applied to promote its underlying purpose to protect persons from human trafficking and provide adequate remedies to victims of human trafficking.

Added by Acts 2009, 81st Leg., ch. 309, § 1, eff. June 19, 2009.

§ 98.007. Confidential Identity in Certain Actions

(a) In this section, "confidential identity" means:

(1) the use of a pseudonym; and

(2) the absence of any other identifying information, including address, telephone number, and social security number.

(b) Except as otherwise provided by this section, in an action under this chapter, the court shall:

(1) make it known to the claimant as early as possible in the proceedings of the action that the claimant may use a confidential identity in relation to the action;

(2) allow a claimant to use a confidential identity in all petitions, filings, and other documents presented to the court;

(3) use the confidential identity in all of the court's proceedings and records relating to the action, including any appellate proceedings; and

(4) maintain the records relating to the action in a manner that protects the confidentiality of the claimant.

(c) In an action under this chapter, only the following persons are entitled to know the true identifying information about the claimant:

(1) the judge;

(2) a party to the action;

(3) the attorney representing a party to the action; and

(4) a person authorized by a written order of a court specific to that person.

(d) The court shall order that a person entitled to know the true identifying information under Subsection (c) may not divulge that information to anyone without a written order of the court. A court shall hold a person who violates the order in contempt.

(e) Notwithstanding Section 22.004, Government Code, the supreme court may not amend or adopt rules in conflict with this section.

(f) A claimant is not required to use a confidential identity as provided by this section.

Added by Acts 2021, 87th Leg., ch. 807 (H.B. 1540), § 4, eff. Sept. 1, 2021.

Section 63(b) of Acts 2021, 87th Leg., ch. 807 (H.B. 1540) provides:

"Section 98.007, Civil Practice and Remedies Code, as added by this Act, applies only to an action filed on or after the effective date [Sept. 1, 2021] of this Act."

Section 63(d) of Acts 2021, 87th Leg., ch. 807 (H.B. 1540) provides:

"Except as otherwise provided by this section, the changes in law made by this Act apply only to an offense committed on or after the effective date of this Act. An offense committed before the effective date of this Act is governed by the law in effect on the date the offense was committed, and the former law is continued in effect for that purpose. For purposes of this section, an offense was committed before the effective date of this Act if any element of the offense occurred before that date."

CHAPTER 98A. LIABILITY FOR COMPELLED PROSTITUTION AND CERTAIN PROMOTION OF PROSTITUTION

Section

§ 98A.001. Definitions

In this chapter:

(1) "Advertisement" means any communication that promotes a commercial product or service, including a communication on an Internet website operated for a commercial purpose.

(1-a) "Aggravated online promotion of prostitution" means conduct that constitutes an offense under Section 43.041, Penal Code.

(2) "Aggravated promotion of prostitution" means conduct that constitutes an offense under Section 43.04, Penal Code.

(3) "Compelled prostitution" means prostitution resulting from compelling prostitution.

(4) "Compelling prostitution" means conduct that constitutes an offense under Section 43.05, Penal Code.

(4–a) "Online promotion of prostitution" means conduct that constitutes an offense under Section 43.031, Penal Code.

(5) "Promotion of prostitution" means conduct that constitutes an offense under Section 43.03, Penal Code.

(6) "Prostitution" means conduct that constitutes an offense under Section 43.02, Penal Code.

(7) "Victim of compelled prostitution" and "victim" mean a person who commits prostitution as a result of another person's compelling prostitution.

Added by Acts 2013, 83rd Leg., ch. 187 (S.B. 94), § 1, eff. Sept. 1, 2013. Amended by Acts 2019, 86th Leg., ch. 413 (S.B. 20), § 3.03, eff. Sept. 1, 2019.

§ 98A.002. Liability

(a) A defendant is liable to a victim of compelled prostitution, as provided by this chapter, for damages arising from the compelled prostitution if the defendant:

(1) engages in compelling prostitution with respect to the victim;

(2) knowingly or intentionally engages in promotion of prostitution, online promotion of prostitution, aggravated promotion of prostitution, or aggravated online promotion of prostitution that results in compelling prostitution with respect to the victim; or

(3) purchases an advertisement that the defendant knows or reasonably should know constitutes promotion of prostitution or aggravated promotion of prostitution, and the publication of the advertisement results in compelling prostitution with respect to the victim.

(b) It is not a defense to liability under this chapter that:

(1) the defendant:

(A) is related to the victim by affinity or consanguinity, has been in a consensual sexual relationship with the victim, or has resided with the victim in a household; or

(B) has paid or otherwise compensated the victim for prostitution; or

(2) the victim:

(A) voluntarily engaged in prostitution before or after the compelled prostitution occurred; or

(B) did not attempt to escape, flee, or otherwise terminate contact with the defendant at the time the compelled prostitution allegedly occurred.

Added by Acts 2013, 83rd Leg., ch. 187 (S.B. 94), § 1, eff. Sept. 1, 2013. Amended by Acts 2019, 86th Leg., ch. 413 (S.B. 20), § 3.04, eff. Sept. 1, 2019.

§ 98A.003. Damages

(a) A claimant who prevails in a suit under this chapter shall be awarded:

(1) actual damages, including damages for mental anguish even if an injury other than mental anguish is not shown;

(2) court costs; and

(3) reasonable attorney's fees.

(b) In addition to an award under Subsection (a), a claimant who prevails in a suit under this chapter may recover exemplary damages.

Added by Acts 2013, 83rd Leg., ch. 187 (S.B. 94), § 1, eff. Sept. 1, 2013.

§ 98A.004. Cause of Action Cumulative

The cause of action created by this chapter is cumulative of any other remedy provided by common law or statute, except that a person may not recover damages in a suit under this chapter in which the cause of action is based on a transaction or occurrence that is the basis for a suit under Chapter 98.

Added by Acts 2013, 83rd Leg., ch. 187 (S.B. 94), § 1, eff. Sept. 1, 2013.

§ 98A.005. Joint and Several Liability

A person who engages in conduct described by Section 98A.002 and is found liable under this chapter or other law for any amount of damages arising from that conduct is jointly and severally liable with any other defendant for the entire amount of damages arising from that conduct.

Added by Acts 2013, 83rd Leg., ch. 187 (S.B. 94), § 1, eff. Sept. 1, 2013.

§ 98A.006. Liberal Construction and Application

This chapter shall be liberally construed and applied to promote its underlying purpose to protect persons from compelled prostitution and provide adequate remedies to victims of compelled prostitution.

Added by Acts 2013, 83rd Leg., ch. 187 (S.B. 94), § 1, eff. Sept. 1, 2013.

CHAPTER 98B. UNLAWFUL DISCLOSURE OR PROMOTION OF INTIMATE VISUAL MATERIAL

§ 98B.001. Definitions

In this chapter:

(1) "Intimate parts," "promote," "sexual conduct," and "visual material" have the meanings assigned by Section 21.16, Penal Code.

(2) "Intimate visual material" means visual material that depicts a person:

(A) with the person's intimate parts exposed; or

(B) engaged in sexual conduct.

Added by Acts 2015, 84th Leg., ch. 852 (S.B. 1135), § 2, eff. Sept. 1, 2015.

§ 98B.002. Liability for Unlawful Disclosure or Promotion of Certain Intimate Visual Material

(a) A defendant is liable, as provided by this chapter, to a person depicted in intimate visual material for damages arising from the disclosure of the material if:

(1) the defendant discloses the intimate visual material without the effective consent of the depicted person and with the intent to harm that person;

(2) at the time of the disclosure, the defendant knows or has reason to believe that the intimate visual material was obtained by the defendant or created under circumstances in which the depicted person had a reasonable expectation that the material would remain private;

(3) the disclosure of the intimate visual material causes harm to the depicted person; and

(4) the disclosure of the intimate visual material reveals the identity of the depicted person in any manner, including through:

(A) any accompanying or subsequent information or material related to the intimate visual material; or

(B) information or material provided by a third party in response to the disclosure of the intimate visual material.

(b) A defendant is liable, as provided by this chapter, to a person depicted in intimate visual material for damages arising from the promotion of the material if, knowing the character and content of the material, the defendant promotes intimate visual material described by Subsection (a) on an Internet website or other forum for publication that is owned or operated by the defendant.

Added by Acts 2015, 84th Leg., ch. 852 (S.B. 1135), § 2, eff. Sept. 1, 2015. Amended by Acts 2019, 86th Leg., ch. 1354 (H.B. 98), § 1, eff. Sept. 1, 2019.

Section 3(a) of Acts 2019, 86th Leg., ch. 1354 (H.B. 98) provides:

"Section 98B.002, Civil Practice and Remedies Code, as amended by this Act, applies only to a cause of action that accrues on or after the effective date [Sept. 1, 2019] of this Act. A cause of action that accrues before the effective date of this Act is governed by the law applicable to the cause of action immediately before the effective date of this Act, and that law is continued in effect for that purpose."

§ 98B.003. Damages

(a) A claimant who prevails in a suit under this chapter shall be awarded:

(1) actual damages, including damages for mental anguish;

(2) court costs; and

(3) reasonable attorney's fees.

(b) In addition to an award under Subsection (a), a claimant who prevails in a suit under this chapter may recover exemplary damages.

Added by Acts 2015, 84th Leg., ch. 852 (S.B. 1135), § 2, eff. Sept. 1, 2015.

§ 98B.004. Injunctive Relief

(a) A court in which a suit is brought under this chapter, on the motion of a party, may issue a temporary restraining order or a temporary or permanent injunction to restrain and prevent the disclosure or promotion of intimate visual material with respect to the person depicted in the material.

(b) A court that issues a temporary restraining order or a temporary or permanent injunction under Subsection (a) may award to the party who brought the motion damages in the amount of:

(1) $1,000 for each violation of the court's order or injunction, if the disclosure or promotion of intimate visual material is wilful or intentional; or

(2) $500 for each violation of the court's order or injunction, if the disclosure or promotion of intimate visual material is not wilful or intentional.

Added by Acts 2015, 84th Leg., ch. 852 (S.B. 1135), § 2, eff. Sept. 1, 2015.

§ 98B.005. Cause of Action Cumulative

The cause of action created by this chapter is cumulative of any other remedy provided by common law or statute.

Added by Acts 2015, 84th Leg., ch. 852 (S.B. 1135), § 2, eff. Sept. 1, 2015.

§ 98B.006. Jurisdiction

A court has personal jurisdiction over a defendant in a suit brought under this chapter if:

(1) the defendant resides in this state;

(2) the claimant who is depicted in the intimate visual material resides in this state;

(3) the intimate visual material is stored on a server that is located in this state; or

(4) the intimate visual material is available for view in this state.

Added by Acts 2015, 84th Leg., ch. 852 (S.B. 1135), § 2, eff. Sept. 1, 2015.

§ 98B.007. Liberal Construction and Application; Certain Conduct Excepted

(a) This chapter shall be liberally construed and applied to promote its underlying purpose to protect persons from, and provide adequate remedies to victims of, the disclosure or promotion of intimate visual material.

(b) This chapter does not apply to a claim brought against an interactive computer service, as defined by 47 U.S.C. Section 230, for a disclosure or promotion consisting of intimate visual material provided by another person.

Added by Acts 2015, 84th Leg., ch. 852 (S.B. 1135), § 2, eff. Sept. 1, 2015.

CHAPTER 99. LIABILITY FOR MANUFACTURE OF METHAMPHETAMINE

§ 99.001. Applicability

This chapter applies only to a person who manufactures methamphetamine in violation of Section 481.112, Health and Safety Code, without regard to whether the person is convicted of the offense.

Added by Acts 2001, 77th Leg., ch. 643, § 1, eff. Sept. 1, 2001.

§ 99.002. Strict Liability for Damages Arising from Manufacture

A person who manufactures methamphetamine is strictly liable for damages for personal injury, death, or property damage arising from the manufacture.

Added by Acts 2001, 77th Leg., ch. 643, § 1, eff. Sept. 1, 2001.

§ 99.003. Strict Liability and Minimum Damages for Exposure

A person who manufactures methamphetamine is strictly liable for any exposure by an individual to the manufacturing process, including exposure to the methamphetamine itself or any of the byproducts or waste products incident to the manufacture, for the greater of:

(1) actual damages for personal injury, death, or property damage as a result of the exposure; or

(2) $20,000 for each incident of exposure.

Added by Acts 2001, 77th Leg., ch. 643, § 1, eff. Sept. 1, 2001. Amended by Acts 2005, 79th Leg., ch. 282, § 1, eff. Aug. 1, 2005.

§ 99.004. Joint and Several Liability

A person who manufactures methamphetamine and is found liable under this chapter or other law for any amount of damages arising from the manufacture is jointly liable with any other defendant for the entire amount of damages arising from the manufacture.

Added by Acts 2001, 77th Leg., ch. 643, § 1, eff. Sept. 1, 2001.

§ 99.005. Chapter 33 Does Not Apply

Chapter 33 does not apply in an action for damages arising from the manufacture of methamphetamine.

Added by Acts 2001, 77th Leg., ch. 643, § 1, eff. Sept. 1, 2001.

§ 99.006. No Limitation on Exemplary Damages

Section 41.008(b) does not apply in an action for damages arising from the manufacture of methamphetamine.

Added by Acts 2001, 77th Leg., ch. 643, § 1, eff. Sept. 1, 2001.

CHAPTER 100. USE OF FORCE IN DEFENSE OF COMMERCIAL NUCLEAR POWER PLANTS

Section

§ 100.001. Affirmative Defense

It is an affirmative defense to a civil action for damages for personal injury or death brought against a person performing duties under Article 2.122(f), Code of Criminal Procedure, the person's employer, or the owner of a commercial nuclear power plant where the person was working, that at the time the cause of action arose the person was justified in using force under Chapter 9, Penal Code.

Added by Acts 2003, 78th Leg., ch. 1237, § 4, eff. June 20, 2003.

CHAPTER 100A. LIMITED LIABILITY FOR SPACE FLIGHT ACTIVITIES

Section

§ 100A.001. Definitions

In this chapter:

(1) "Launch" means a placement or attempted placement of a launch vehicle and spacecraft, if any, in a suborbital trajectory, earth orbit, or outer space, including activities involved in the preparation of a launch vehicle or spacecraft for launch.

(1–a) "Launch vehicle" means any vehicle and its stages or components designed to operate in or place spacecraft, if any, in a suborbital trajectory, in earth orbit, or in outer space.

(2) "Reentry" means a return or attempt to return of a launch vehicle, reentry vehicle, or spacecraft from a suborbital trajectory, from earth orbit, or from outer space to earth, including activities involved in the recovery of a launch vehicle, reentry vehicle, or spacecraft.

(2–a) "Reentry vehicle" means any vehicle, including its stages or components, or spacecraft designed to return from earth orbit or outer space to earth, or a reusable launch vehicle designed to return from earth orbit or outer space to earth, substantially intact.

(2–b) "Spacecraft" has the meaning assigned by Section 507.001, Local Government Code.

(3) "Space flight activities" means activities and training in any phase of preparing for and undertaking space flight, including:

(A) the research, development, testing, or manufacture of a launch vehicle, reentry vehicle, or spacecraft;

(B) the preparation of a launch vehicle, reentry vehicle, payload, spacecraft, crew, or space flight participant for launch, space flight, and reentry;

(C) the conduct of the launch;

(D) conduct occurring between the launch and reentry;

(E) the preparation of a launch vehicle, reentry vehicle, payload, spacecraft, crew, or space flight participant for reentry;

(F) the conduct of reentry and descent;

(G) the conduct of the landing; and

(H) the conduct of postlanding recovery of a launch vehicle, reentry vehicle, payload, spacecraft, crew, or space flight participant.

(4) "Space flight entity" means a person who conducts space flight activities and who, to the extent required by federal law, has obtained the appropriate Federal Aviation Administration license or other authorization, including safety approval and a payload determination. The term includes:

(A) a manufacturer or supplier of components, services, spacecraft, launch vehicles, or reentry vehicles used by the entity and reviewed by the Federal Aviation Administration as part of issuing the license or other authorization;

(B) an employee, officer, director, owner, stockholder, member, manager, advisor, or partner of the entity, manufacturer, or supplier;

(C) an owner or lessor of real property on which space flight activities are conducted, including a municipality, county, political subdivision, or spaceport development corporation under Section 507.001, Local Government Code, in this state with a contractual relationship with a space flight entity; and

(D) a municipality, county, economic development organization, or other political subdivision in the territory or extraterritorial jurisdiction of which space flight activities are conducted.

(5) "Space flight participant" means an individual, who is not crew, carried aboard a spacecraft, launch vehicle, or reentry vehicle.

(6) "Space flight participant injury" means an injury sustained by a space flight participant, including bodily injury, emotional distress, death, disability, property damage, or any other loss arising from the individual's participation in space flight activities.

(7) "Crew" means a human being who performs activities relating to the launch, reentry, or other operation of or in a spacecraft, launch vehicle, or reentry vehicle.

Added by Acts 2011, 82nd Leg., ch. 3 (S.B. 115), § 1, eff. April 21, 2011. Amended by Acts 2013, 83rd Leg., ch. 953 (H.B. 1791), § 1, eff. Sept. 1, 2013.

§ 100A.002. Limited Liability

(a) Except as provided by this section, a space flight entity is not liable to any person for damages resulting from nuisance arising from testing, launching, reentering, or landing or subject to any claim for nuisance arising from testing, launching, reentering, or landing.

(b) Except as provided by this section, a space flight entity is not liable to any person for a space flight participant injury or damages arising out of space flight activities if the space flight participant has signed the agreement required by Section 100A.003 and given written consent as required by 51 U.S.C. Section 50905. This subsection does not limit liability for a space flight participant injury:

(1) proximately caused by the space flight entity's gross negligence evidencing wilful or wanton disregard for the safety of the space flight participant; or

(2) intentionally caused by the space flight entity.

(c) This section precludes injunctive relief with respect to space flight activities.

(d) This section does not:

(1) limit liability for breach of a contract for use of real property by a space flight entity; or

(2) preclude an action by a federal or state governmental entity to enforce a valid statute or regulation.

Added by Acts 2011, 82nd Leg., ch. 3 (S.B. 115), § 1, eff. April 21, 2011. Amended by Acts 2013, 83rd Leg., ch. 953 (H.B. 1791), § 2, eff. Sept. 1, 2013.

§ 100A.003. Warning Required

(a) A space flight participant must sign an agreement and warning statement before participating in any space flight activity. The agreement must include the following language and any other language required by federal law:

AGREEMENT AND WARNING

I UNDERSTAND AND ACKNOWLEDGE THAT A SPACE FLIGHT ENTITY IS NOT LIABLE FOR ANY INJURY TO OR DEATH OF A SPACE FLIGHT PARTICIPANT RESULTING FROM SPACE FLIGHT ACTIVITIES. I UNDERSTAND THAT I HAVE ACCEPTED ALL RISK OF INJURY, DEATH, PROPERTY DAMAGE, AND OTHER LOSS THAT MAY RESULT FROM SPACE FLIGHT ACTIVITIES.

(b) An agreement under Subsection (a) is considered effective and enforceable if it is:

(1) in writing;

(2) in a document separate from any other agreement between the space flight participant and the space flight entity other than a different warning, consent, or assumption of risk statement;

(3) printed in not less than 10-point bold type;

(4) signed by the space flight participant on behalf of the space flight participant and any heirs, executors, administrators, representatives, attorneys, successors, and assignees of the space flight participant; and

(5) signed by a competent witness.

Added by Acts 2011, 82nd Leg., ch. 3 (S.B. 115), § 1, eff. April 21, 2011. Amended by Acts 2013, 83rd Leg., ch. 953 (H.B. 1791), § 3, eff. Sept. 1, 2013.

§ 100A.004. Agreement Effective and Enforceable

(a) Except as provided by Subsection (b), an agreement between a space flight entity and a space flight participant limiting or otherwise affecting liability arising out of space flight activity is effective and enforceable and is not unconscionable or against public policy.

(b) An agreement described by this section may not limit liability for an injury:

(1) proximately caused by the space flight entity's gross negligence evidencing wilful or wanton disregard for the safety of the space flight participant; or

(2) intentionally caused by a space flight entity.

Added by Acts 2011, 82nd Leg., ch. 3 (S.B. 115), § 1, eff. April 21, 2011.

TITLE 5. GOVERNMENTAL LIABILITY

CHAPTER 101. TORT CLAIMS

SUBCHAPTER A. GENERAL PROVISIONS

SUBCHAPTER A. GENERAL PROVISIONS

§ 101.001. Definitions

In this chapter:

(1) "Emergency service organization" means:

(A) a volunteer fire department, rescue squad, or an emergency medical services provider that is:

(i) operated by its members; and

(ii) exempt from state taxes by being listed as an exempt organization under Section 151.310 or 171.083, Tax Code; or

(B) a local emergency management or homeland security organization that is:

(i) formed and operated as a state resource in accordance with the statewide homeland security strategy developed by the governor under Section 421.002, Government Code; and

(ii) responsive to the Texas Division of Emergency Management in carrying out an all-hazards emergency management program under Section 418.112, Government Code.

(2) "Employee" means a person, including an officer or agent, who is in the paid service of a governmental unit by competent authority, but does not include an independent contractor, an agent or employee of an independent contractor, or a person who performs tasks the details of which the governmental unit does not have the legal right to control.

(3) "Governmental unit" means:

(A) this state and all the several agencies of government that collectively constitute the government of this state, including other agencies bearing different designations, and all departments, bureaus, boards, commissions, offices, agencies, councils, and courts;

(B) a political subdivision of this state, including any city, county, school district, junior college district, levee improvement district, drainage district, irrigation district, water improvement district, water control and improvement district, water control and preservation district, freshwater supply district, navigation district, conservation and reclamation district, soil conservation district, communication district, public health district, and river authority;

(C) an emergency service organization; and

(D) any other institution, agency, or organ of government the status and authority of which are derived from the Constitution of Texas or from laws passed by the legislature under the constitution.

(4) "Motor-driven equipment" does not include:

(A) equipment used in connection with the operation of floodgates or water release equipment by river authorities created under the laws of this state; or

(B) medical equipment, such as iron lungs, located in hospitals.

(5) "Scope of employment" means the performance for a governmental unit of the duties of an employee's office or employment and includes being in or about the performance of a task lawfully assigned to an employee by competent authority.

(6) "State government" means an agency, board, commission, department, or office, other than a district or authority created under Article XVI, Section 59, of the Texas Constitution, that:

(A) was created by the constitution or a statute of this state; and

(B) has statewide jurisdiction.

Acts 1985, 69th Leg., ch. 959, § 1, eff. Sept. 1, 1985. Amended by Acts 1987, 70th Leg., ch. 693, § 1, eff. June 19, 1987; Acts 1991, 72nd Leg., ch. 476, § 1, eff. Aug. 26, 1991; Acts 1995, 74th Leg., ch. 827, § 1, eff. Aug. 28, 1995; Acts 1997, 75th Leg., ch. 968, § 1, eff. Sept. 1, 1997; Acts 2011, 82nd Leg., ch. 1101 (S.B. 1560), § 1, eff. June 17, 2011.

§ 101.002. Short Title

This chapter may be cited as the Texas Tort Claims Act.

Acts 1985, 69th Leg., ch. 959, § 1, eff. Sept. 1, 1985.

§ 101.003. Remedies Additional

The remedies authorized by this chapter are in addition to any other legal remedies.

Acts 1985, 69th Leg., ch. 959, § 1, eff. Sept. 1, 1985.

§ 101.004. Status of Medical Residents and Fellows

For purposes of this chapter, a resident or fellow in a graduate medical training program for physicians that is sponsored by a governmental unit, including a medical and dental unit as defined by Section 61.003, Education Code, is considered to be an employee of a governmental unit regardless of the method or source of payment of the resident or fellow.

Added by Acts 2019, 86th Leg., ch. 648 (S.B. 1755), § 1, eff. June 10, 2019.

SUBCHAPTER B. TORT LIABILITY OF GOVERNMENTAL UNITS

§ 101.021. Governmental Liability

A governmental unit in the state is liable for:

(1) property damage, personal injury, and death proximately caused by the wrongful act or omission or the negligence of an employee acting within his scope of employment if:

(A) the property damage, personal injury, or death arises from the operation or use of a motor-driven vehicle or motor-driven equipment; and

(B) the employee would be personally liable to the claimant according to Texas law; and

(2) personal injury and death so caused by a condition or use of tangible personal or real property if the governmental unit would, were it a private person, be liable to the claimant according to Texas law.

Acts 1985, 69th Leg., ch. 959, § 1, eff. Sept. 1, 1985.

§ 101.0211. No Liability for Joint Enterprise

(a) The common law doctrine of vicarious liability because of participation in a joint enterprise does not impose liability for a claim brought under this chapter on:

(1) a water district created pursuant to either Sections 52(b)(1) and (2), Article III, or Section 59, Article XVI, Texas Constitution, regardless of how created; or

(2) a municipality with respect to the use of a municipal airport for space flight activities as defined by Section 100A.001 unless the municipality would otherwise be liable under Section 101.021.

(b) This section does not affect a limitation on liability or damages provided by this chapter, including a limitation under Section 101.023.

Added by Acts 2001, 77th Leg., ch. 1423, § 35, eff. June 17, 2001. Amended by Acts 2013, 83rd Leg., ch. 50 (H.B. 278), § 2, eff. Sept. 1, 2013.

§ 101.0215. Liability of a Municipality

(a) A municipality is liable under this chapter for damages arising from its governmental functions, which are those functions that are enjoined on a municipality by law and are given it by the state as part of the state's sovereignty, to be exercised by the municipality in the interest of the general public, including but not limited to:

(1) police and fire protection and control;

(2) health and sanitation services;

(3) street construction and design;

(4) bridge construction and maintenance and street maintenance;

(5) cemeteries and cemetery care;

(6) garbage and solid waste removal, collection, and disposal;

(7) establishment and maintenance of jails;

(8) hospitals;

(9) sanitary and storm sewers;

(10) airports, including when used for space flight activities as defined by Section 100A.001;

(11) waterworks;

(12) repair garages;

(13) parks and zoos;

(14) museums;

(15) libraries and library maintenance;

(16) civic, convention centers, or coliseums;

(17) community, neighborhood, or senior citizen centers;

(18) operation of emergency ambulance service;

(19) dams and reservoirs;

(20) warning signals;

(21) regulation of traffic;

(22) transportation systems;

(23) recreational facilities, including but not limited to swimming pools, beaches, and marinas;

(24) vehicle and motor driven equipment maintenance;

(25) parking facilities;

(26) tax collection;

(27) firework displays;

(28) building codes and inspection;

(29) zoning, planning, and plat approval;

(30) engineering functions;

(31) maintenance of traffic signals, signs, and hazards;

(32) water and sewer service;

(33) animal control;

(34) community development or urban renewal activities undertaken by municipalities and authorized under Chapters 373 and 374, Local Government Code;

(35) latchkey programs conducted exclusively on a school campus under an interlocal agreement with the school district in which the school campus is located; and

(36) enforcement of land use restrictions under Subchapter E, Chapter 212, Local Government Code. [1]

(b) This chapter does not apply to the liability of a municipality for damages arising from its proprietary functions, which are those functions that a municipality may, in its discretion, perform in the interest of the inhabitants of the municipality, including but not limited to:

(1) the operation and maintenance of a public utility;

(2) amusements owned and operated by the municipality; and

(3) any activity that is abnormally dangerous or ultrahazardous.

(c) The proprietary functions of a municipality do not include those governmental activities listed under Subsection (a).

Added by Acts 1987, 70th Leg., 1st C.S., ch. 2, § 3.02, eff. Sept. 2, 1987. Amended by Acts 1997, 75th Leg., ch. 152, § 1, eff. Sept. 1, 1997; Acts 1999, 76th Leg., ch. 1170, § 2, eff. June 18, 1999; Acts 2001, 77th Leg., ch. 1399, § 1, eff. June 16, 2001; Acts 2013, 83rd Leg., ch. 50 (H.B. 278), § 1, eff. Sept. 1, 2013.

[1] V.T.C.A., Local Government Code § 212.131 et seq.

§ 101.022. Duty Owed: Premise and Special Defects

(a) Except as provided in Subsection (c), if a claim arises from a premise defect, the governmental unit owes to the claimant only the duty that a private person owes to a licensee on private property, unless the claimant pays for the use of the premises.

(b) The limitation of duty in this section does not apply to the duty to warn of special defects such as excavations or obstructions on highways, roads, or streets or to the duty to warn of the absence, condition, or malfunction of traffic signs, signals, or warning devices as is required by Section 101.060.

(c) If a claim arises from a premise defect on a toll highway, road, or street, the governmental unit owes to the claimant only the duty that a private person owes to a licensee on private property.

Acts 1985, 69th Leg., ch. 959, § 1, eff. Sept. 1, 1985. Amended by Acts 2005, 79th Leg., ch. 281, § 2.88, eff. June 14, 2005.

§ 101.023. Limitation on Amount of Liability

(a) Liability of the state government under this chapter is limited to money damages in a maximum amount of $250,000 for each person and $500,000 for each single occurrence for bodily injury or death and

$100,000 for each single occurrence for injury to or destruction of property.

(b) Except as provided by Subsection (c), liability of a unit of local government under this chapter is limited to money damages in a maximum amount of $100,000 for each person and $300,000 for each single occurrence for bodily injury or death and $100,000 for each single occurrence for injury to or destruction of property.

(c) Liability of a municipality under this chapter is limited to money damages in a maximum amount of $250,000 for each person and $500,000 for each single occurrence for bodily injury or death and $100,000 for each single occurrence for injury to or destruction of property.

(d) Except as provided by Section 78.001, liability of an emergency service organization under this chapter is limited to money damages in a maximum amount of $100,000 for each person and $300,000 for each single occurrence for bodily injury or death and $100,000 for each single occurrence for injury to or destruction of property.

Acts 1985, 69th Leg., ch. 959, § 1, eff. Sept. 1, 1985. Amended by Acts 1987, 70th Leg., 1st C.S., ch. 2, § 3.03, eff. Sept. 2, 1987; Acts 1995, 74th Leg., ch. 827, § 2, eff. Aug. 28, 1995; Acts 1997, 75th Leg., ch. 968, § 2, eff. Sept. 1, 1997.

§ 101.024. Exemplary Damages

This chapter does not authorize exemplary damages.

Acts 1985, 69th Leg., ch. 959, § 1, eff. Sept. 1, 1985.

§ 101.025. Waiver of Governmental Immunity; Permission to Sue

(a) Sovereign immunity to suit is waived and abolished to the extent of liability created by this chapter.

(b) A person having a claim under this chapter may sue a governmental unit for damages allowed by this chapter.

Acts 1985, 69th Leg., ch. 959, § 1, eff. Sept. 1, 1985.

§ 101.026. Individual's Immunity Preserved

To the extent an employee has individual immunity from a tort claim for damages, it is not affected by this chapter.

Acts 1985, 69th Leg., ch. 959, § 1, eff. Sept. 1, 1985.

§ 101.027. Liability Insurance

(a) Each governmental unit other than a unit of state government may purchase insurance policies protecting the unit and the unit's employees against claims under this chapter. A unit of state government may purchase such a policy only to the extent that the unit is authorized or required to do so under other law.

(b) The policies may relinquish to the insurer the right to investigate, defend, compromise, and settle any claim under this chapter to which the insurance coverage extends.

(c) This state or a political subdivision of the state may not require an employee to purchase liability insurance as a condition of employment if the state or the political subdivision is insured by a liability insurance policy.

Acts 1985, 69th Leg., ch. 959, § 1, eff. Sept. 1, 1985. Amended by Acts 1999, 76th Leg., ch. 1499, § 1.01, eff. Sept. 1, 1999.

§ 101.028. Workers' Compensation Insurance

A governmental unit that has workers' compensation insurance or that accepts the workers' compensation laws of this state is entitled to the privileges and immunities granted by the workers' compensation laws of this state to private individuals and corporations.

Acts 1985, 69th Leg., ch. 959, § 1, eff. Sept. 1, 1985.

§ 101.029. Liability for Certain Conduct of State Prison Inmates

(a) The Department of Criminal Justice is liable for property damage, personal injury, and death proximately caused by the wrongful act or omission or the negligence of an inmate or state jail defendant housed in a facility operated by the department if:

(1) the property damage, personal injury, or death arises from the operation or use of a motor-driven vehicle or motor-driven equipment;

(2) the inmate or defendant would be personally liable to the claimant for the property damage, personal injury, or death according to Texas law were the inmate or defendant a private person acting in similar circumstances; and

(3) the act, omission, or negligence was committed by the inmate or defendant acting in the course and scope of a task or activity that:

(A) the inmate or defendant performed at the request of an employee of the department; and

(B) the inmate or defendant performed under the control or supervision of the department.

(b) A claimant may not name the inmate or state jail defendant whose act or omission gave rise to the claim as a codefendant in an action brought under this section.

(c) A judgment in an action or a settlement of a claim against the Department of Criminal Justice under this section bars any action involving the same subject matter by the claimant against the inmate or state jail defendant whose act or omission gave rise to the claim. A judgment in an action or a settlement of a claim against an inmate or state jail defendant bars any action involving the same subject matter by the claimant against the Department of Criminal Justice under this section.

(d) This section does not apply to property damage, personal injury, or death sustained by an inmate or state jail defendant.

Added by Acts 1995, 74th Leg., ch. 321, § 1.108, eff. Sept. 1, 1995. Amended by Acts 1999, 76th Leg., ch. 313, § 1, eff. Sept. 1, 1999.

SUBCHAPTER C. EXCLUSIONS AND EXCEPTIONS

§ 101.051. School and Junior College Districts Partially Excluded

Except as to motor vehicles, this chapter does not apply to a school district or to a junior college district.

Acts 1985, 69th Leg., ch. 959, § 1, eff. Sept. 1, 1985.

§ 101.052. Legislative

This chapter does not apply to a claim based on an act or omission of the legislature or a member of the legislature acting in his official capacity or to the legislative functions of a governmental unit.

Acts 1985, 69th Leg., ch. 959, § 1, eff. Sept. 1, 1985.

§ 101.053. Judicial

(a) This chapter does not apply to a claim based on an act or omission of a court of this state or any member of a court of this state acting in his official capacity or to a judicial function of a governmental unit. "Official capacity" means all duties of office and includes administrative decisions or actions.

(b) This chapter does not apply to a claim based on an act or omission of an employee in the execution of a lawful order of any court.

Acts 1985, 69th Leg., ch. 959, § 1, eff. Sept. 1, 1985. Amended by Acts 1987, 70th Leg., 1st C.S., ch. 2, § 3.04, eff. Sept. 2, 1987.

§ 101.054. State Military Personnel

This chapter does not apply to a claim arising from the activities of the state military forces when on active duty under the lawful orders of competent authority.

Acts 1985, 69th Leg., ch. 959, § 1, eff. Sept. 1, 1985.

§ 101.055. Certain Governmental Functions

This chapter does not apply to a claim arising:

(1) in connection with the assessment or collection of taxes by a governmental unit;

(2) from the action of an employee while responding to an emergency call or reacting to an emergency situation if the action is in compliance with the laws and ordinances applicable to emergency action, or in the absence of such a law or ordinance, if the action is not taken with conscious indifference or reckless disregard for the safety of others; or

(3) from the failure to provide or the method of providing police or fire protection.

Acts 1985, 69th Leg., ch. 959, § 1, eff. Sept. 1, 1985. Amended by Acts 1987, 70th Leg., 1st C.S., ch. 2, § 3.05, eff. Sept. 2, 1987; Acts 1995, 74th Leg., ch. 139, § 1, eff. Sept. 1, 1995.

§ 101.056. Discretionary Powers

This chapter does not apply to a claim based on:

(1) the failure of a governmental unit to perform an act that the unit is not required by law to perform; or

(2) a governmental unit's decision not to perform an act or on its failure to make a decision on the performance or nonperformance of an act if the law leaves the performance or nonperformance of the act to the discretion of the governmental unit.

Acts 1985, 69th Leg., ch. 959, § 1, eff. Sept. 1, 1985.

§ 101.057. Civil Disobedience and Certain Intentional Torts

This chapter does not apply to a claim:

(1) based on an injury or death connected with any act or omission arising out of civil disobedience, riot, insurrection, or rebellion; or

(2) arising out of assault, battery, false imprisonment, or any other intentional tort, including a tort involving disciplinary action by school authorities.

Acts 1985, 69th Leg., ch. 959, § 1, eff. Sept. 1, 1985.

§ 101.058. Landowner's Liability

To the extent that Chapter 75 limits the liability of a governmental unit under circumstances in which the governmental unit would be liable under this chapter, Chapter 75 controls.

Added by Acts 1995, 74th Leg., ch. 520, § 4, eff. Aug. 28, 1995.

§ 101.059. Attractive Nuisances

This chapter does not apply to a claim based on the theory of attractive nuisance.

Acts 1985, 69th Leg., ch. 959, § 1, eff. Sept. 1, 1985.

§ 101.060. Traffic and Road Control Devices

(a) This chapter does not apply to a claim arising from:

(1) the failure of a governmental unit initially to place a traffic or road sign, signal, or warning device if the failure is a result of discretionary action of the governmental unit;

(2) the absence, condition, or malfunction of a traffic or road sign, signal, or warning device unless the absence, condition, or malfunction is not corrected by the responsible governmental unit within a reasonable time after notice; or

(3) the removal or destruction of a traffic or road sign, signal, or warning device by a third person unless the governmental unit fails to correct the removal or destruction within a reasonable time after actual notice.

(b) The signs, signals, and warning devices referred to in this section are those used in connection with hazards normally connected with the use of the roadway.

(c) This section does not apply to the duty to warn of special defects such as excavations or roadway obstructions.

Acts 1985, 69th Leg., ch. 959, § 1, eff. Sept. 1, 1985.

§ 101.061. Tort Committed Before January 1, 1970

This chapter does not apply to a claim based on an act or omission that occurred before January 1, 1970.

Acts 1985, 69th Leg., ch. 959, § 1, eff. Sept. 1, 1985.

§ 101.062. 9–1–1 Emergency Service

(a) In this section, "9–1–1 service" and "public agency" have the meanings assigned those terms by Section 771.001, Health and Safety Code.

(b) This chapter applies to a claim against a public agency that arises from an action of an employee of the public agency or a volunteer under direction of the public agency and that involves providing 9–1–1 service or responding to a 9–1–1 emergency call only if the action violates a statute or ordinance applicable to the action.

Added by Acts 1987, 70th Leg., ch. 236, § 2, eff. Aug. 31, 1987. Amended by Acts 1991, 72nd Leg., ch. 14, § 284(3), eff. Sept. 1, 1991.

§ 101.063. Members of Public Health District

A governmental unit that is a member of a public health district is not liable under this chapter for any conduct of the district's personnel or for any condition or use of the district's property.

Added by Acts 1991, 72nd Leg., ch. 476, § 2, eff. Aug. 26, 1991.

§ 101.064. Land Acquired Under Foreclosure of Lien or by Conveyance in Satisfaction of Certain Tax Debt

(a) This chapter does not apply to a claim:

(1) against a political subdivision of this state that acquires land:

(A) as a result of the foreclosure of a lien held by the political subdivision, including land that was bid off to the political subdivision under Section 34.01, Tax Code; or

(B) under Section 31.061, Tax Code;

(2) that arises after the date the land was acquired and before the date the land is sold, conveyed, or exchanged by the political subdivision; and

(3) that arises from:

(A) the condition of the land;

(B) a premises defect on the land; or

(C) an action committed by any person, other than an agent or employee of the political subdivision, on the land.

(b) In this section, "land" includes any building or improvement located on land acquired by a political subdivision.

Added by Acts 1995, 74th Leg., ch. 139, § 5, eff. Sept. 1, 1995; Acts 1995, 74th Leg., ch. 442, § 1, eff. Sept. 1, 1995. Amended by Acts 1997, 75th Leg., ch. 712, § 2, eff. June 17, 1997; Acts 2015, 84th Leg., ch. 240 (S.B. 450), § 1, eff. Sept. 1, 2015.

§ 101.065. Negligence of Off–Duty Law Enforcement Officers

This chapter does not apply to the wrongful act or omission or the negligence of an officer commissioned by the Department of Public Safety if the officer was not on active duty at the time the act, omission, or negligence occurred. This section applies without regard to whether the officer was wearing a uniform purchased under Section 411.0078, Government Code, at the time the act, omission, or negligence occurred.

Added by Acts 1995, 74th Leg., ch. 738, § 2, eff. Sept. 1, 1995. Redesignated from V.T.C.A., Civil Practice and Remedies Code § 101.058 by Acts 1997, 75th Leg., ch. 165, § 31.01(9), eff. Sept. 1, 1997.

§ 101.066. Computer Date Failure

This chapter does not apply to a claim for property damage caused by a computer date failure as described by Section 147.003.

Added by Acts 1999, 76th Leg., ch. 128, § 3, eff. May 19, 1999.

§ 101.067. Graffiti Removal

This chapter does not apply to a claim for property damage caused by the removal of graffiti under Section 250.006, Local Government Code.

Added by Acts 2009, 81st Leg., ch. 1130, § 27, eff. Sept. 1, 2009.

SUBCHAPTER D. PROCEDURES

§ 101.101. Notice

(a) A governmental unit is entitled to receive notice of a claim against it under this chapter not later than six months after the day that the incident giving rise to the claim occurred. The notice must reasonably describe:

(1) the damage or injury claimed;

(2) the time and place of the incident; and

(3) the incident.

(b) A city's charter and ordinance provisions requiring notice within a charter period permitted by law are ratified and approved.

(c) The notice requirements provided or ratified and approved by Subsections (a) and (b) do not apply if the governmental unit has actual notice that death has occurred, that the claimant has received some injury, or that the claimant's property has been damaged.

Acts 1985, 69th Leg., ch. 959, § 1, eff. Sept. 1, 1985.

§ 101.102. Commencement of Suit

(a) A suit under this chapter shall be brought in state court in the county in which the cause of action or a part of the cause of action arises.

(b) The pleadings of the suit must name as defendant the governmental unit against which liability is to be established.

(c) In a suit against the state, citation must be served on the secretary of state. In other suits, citation must be served as in other civil cases unless no method of service is provided by law, in which case service may be on the administrative head of the governmental unit being sued. If the administrative head of the governmental unit is not available, the court in which the suit is pending may authorize service in any manner that affords the governmental unit a fair opportunity to answer and defend the suit.

Acts 1985, 69th Leg., ch. 959, § 1, eff. Sept. 1, 1985. Amended by Acts 1987, 70th Leg., 1st C.S., ch. 2, § 3.06, eff. Sept. 2, 1987.

§ 101.103. Legal Representation

(a) The attorney general shall defend each action brought under this chapter against a governmental unit that has authority and jurisdiction coextensive with the geographical limits of this state. The attorney general may be fully assisted by counsel provided by an insurance carrier.

(b) A governmental unit having an area of jurisdiction smaller than the entire state shall employ its own counsel according to the organic act under which the unit operates, unless the governmental unit has relinquished to an insurance carrier the right to defend against the claim.

Acts 1985, 69th Leg., ch. 959, § 1, eff. Sept. 1, 1985.

§ 101.104. Evidence of Insurance Coverage

(a) Neither the existence nor the amount of insurance held by a governmental unit is admissible in the trial of a suit under this chapter.

(b) Neither the existence nor the amount of the insurance is subject to discovery.

Acts 1985, 69th Leg., ch. 959, § 1, eff. Sept. 1, 1985.

§ 101.105. Settlement

(a) A cause of action under this chapter may be settled and compromised by the governmental unit if, in a case involving the state the governor determines, or if, in other cases the governing body of the governmental unit determines, that the compromise is in the best interests of the governmental unit.

(b) Approval is not required if the governmental unit has acquired insurance under this chapter.

Acts 1985, 69th Leg., ch. 959, § 1, eff. Sept. 1, 1985.

§ 101.106. Election of Remedies

(a) The filing of a suit under this chapter against a governmental unit constitutes an irrevocable election by the plaintiff and immediately and forever bars any suit or recovery by the plaintiff against any individual employee of the governmental unit regarding the same subject matter.

(b) The filing of a suit against any employee of a governmental unit constitutes an irrevocable election by the plaintiff and immediately and forever bars any suit or recovery by the plaintiff against the governmental unit regarding the same subject matter unless the governmental unit consents.

(c) The settlement of a claim arising under this chapter shall immediately and forever bar the claimant from any suit against or recovery from any employee of the same governmental unit regarding the same subject matter.

(d) A judgment against an employee of a governmental unit shall immediately and forever bar the party obtaining the judgment from any suit against or recovery from the governmental unit.

(e) If a suit is filed under this chapter against both a governmental unit and any of its employees, the employees shall immediately be dismissed on the filing of a motion by the governmental unit.

(f) If a suit is filed against an employee of a governmental unit based on conduct within the general scope of that employee's employment and if it could have been brought under this chapter against the governmental unit, the suit is considered to be against the employee in the employee's official capacity only. On the employee's motion, the suit against the employee shall be dismissed unless the plaintiff files amended pleadings dismissing the employee and naming the governmental unit as defendant on or before the 30th day after the date the motion is filed.

Acts 1985, 69th Leg., ch. 959, § 1, eff. Sept. 1, 1985. Amended by Acts 2003, 78th Leg., ch. 204, § 11.05, eff. Sept. 1, 2003.

§ 101.107. Payment and Collection of Judgment

(a) A judgment in a suit under this chapter may be enforced only in the same manner and to the same extent as other judgments against the governmental unit are enforceable as provided by law, unless the governmental unit has liability or indemnity insurance protection, in which case the holder of the judgment may collect the judgment, to the extent of the insurer's liability, as provided in the insurance or indemnity contract or policy or as otherwise provided by law.

(b) A judgment or a portion of a judgment that is not payable by an insurer need not be paid by a governmental unit until the first fiscal year following the fiscal year in which the judgment becomes final.

(c) If in a fiscal year the aggregate amount of judgments under this chapter against a governmental unit that become final, excluding the amount payable by an insurer, exceeds one percent of the unit's budgeted tax funds for the fiscal year, excluding general obligation debt service requirements, the governmental unit may pay the judgments in equal annual installments for a period of not more than five years. If payments are extended under this subsection, the governmental unit shall pay interest on the unpaid balance at the rate provided by law.

Acts 1985, 69th Leg., ch. 959, § 1, eff. Sept. 1, 1985.

§ 101.108. Ad Valorem Taxes for Payment of Judgment

(a) A governmental unit not fully covered by liability insurance may levy an ad valorem tax for the payment of any final judgment under this chapter.

(b) If necessary to pay the amount of a judgment, the ad valorem tax rate may exceed any legal tax rate limit applicable to the governmental unit except a limit imposed by the constitution.

Acts 1985, 69th Leg., ch. 959, § 1, eff. Sept. 1, 1985.

§ 101.109. Payment of Claims Against Certain Universities

A claim under this chapter against a state-supported senior college or university is payable only by a direct legislative appropriation made to satisfy claims unless insurance has been acquired as provided by this chapter. If insurance has been acquired, the claimant is entitled to payment to the extent of the coverage as in other cases.

Acts 1985, 69th Leg., ch. 959, § 1, eff. Sept. 1, 1985.

CHAPTER 102. TORT CLAIMS PAYMENTS BY LOCAL GOVERNMENTS

Section

§ 102.001. Definitions

In this chapter:

(1) "Employee" includes an officer, volunteer, or employee, a former officer, volunteer, or employee, and the estate of an officer, volunteer, or employee or former officer, volunteer, or employee of a local government. The term includes a member of a governing board. The term does not include a county extension agent.

(2) "Local government" means a county, city, town, special purpose district, including a soil and water conservation district, and any other political subdivision of the state.

Acts 1985, 69th Leg., ch. 959, § 1, eff. Sept. 1, 1985. Amended by Acts 1987, 70th Leg., 1st C.S., ch. 2, § 3.07, eff. Sept. 2, 1987; Acts 1999, 76th Leg., ch. 1115, § 1, eff. June 18, 1999; Acts 2007, 80th Leg., ch. 996, § 1, eff. June 15, 2007.

§ 102.002. Payment of Certain Tort Claims

(a) A local government may pay actual damages awarded against an employee of the local government if the damages:

(1) result from an act or omission of the employee in the course and scope of his employment for the local government; and

(2) arise from a cause of action for negligence.

(b) The local government may also pay the court costs and attorney's fees awarded against an employee for whom the local government may pay damages under this section.

(c) Except as provided by Subsection (e), a local government may not pay damages awarded against an employee that:

(1) arise from a cause of action for official misconduct; or

(2) arise from a cause of action involving a wilful or wrongful act or omission or an act or omission constituting gross negligence.

(d) A local government may not pay damages awarded against an employee to the extent the damages are recoverable under an insurance contract or a self-insurance plan authorized by statute.

(e) A local government that does not give a bond under Section 1105.101(b), Estates Code, shall pay damages awarded against an employee of the local government arising from a cause of action described by Subsection (c) if the liability results from the employee's appointment as guardian of the person or estate of a ward under the Estates Code and the action or omission for which the employee was found liable was in the course and scope of the person's employment with the local government.

Acts 1985, 69th Leg., ch. 959, § 1, eff. Sept. 1, 1985. Amended by Acts 1997, 75th Leg., ch. 924, § 3, eff. Sept. 1, 1997; Acts 2017, 85th Leg., ch. 324 (S.B. 1488), § 22.007, eff. Sept. 1, 2017.

§ 102.003. Maximum Payments

Payments under this chapter by a local government may not exceed:

(1) $100,000 to any one person or $300,000 for any single occurrence in the case of personal injury or death; or

(2) $10,000 for a single occurrence of property damage, unless the local government is liable in the local government's capacity as guardian under the Estates Code and does not give a bond under Section 1105.101(b), Estates Code, in which event payments may not exceed the amount of the actual property damages.

Acts 1985, 69th Leg., ch. 959, § 1, eff. Sept. 1, 1985. Amended by Acts 1997, 75th Leg., ch. 924, § 4, eff. Sept. 1, 1997; Acts 2017, 85th Leg., ch. 324 (S.B. 1488), § 22.008, eff. Sept. 1, 2017.

§ 102.004. Defense Counsel

(a) A local government may provide legal counsel to represent a defendant for whom the local government may pay damages under this chapter. The counsel provided by the local government may be the local government's regularly employed counsel, unless there is a potential conflict of interest between the local government and the defendant, in which case the local government may employ other legal counsel to defend the suit.

(b) Legal counsel provided under this section may settle the portion of a suit that may result in the payment of damages by the local government under this chapter.

Acts 1985, 69th Leg., ch. 959, § 1, eff. Sept. 1, 1985.

§ 102.005. Security for Court Costs Not Required

In a case defended under this chapter, neither the defendant nor a local government is required to advance security for costs or to give bond on appeal or writ of error.

Acts 1985, 69th Leg., ch. 959, § 1, eff. Sept. 1, 1985.

§ 102.006. Other Laws Not Affected

This chapter does not affect:

(1) Chapter 101 of this code (the Texas Tort Claims Act); or

(2) a defense, immunity, or jurisdictional bar available to a local government or an employee.

Acts 1985, 69th Leg., ch. 959, § 1, eff. Sept. 1, 1985.

CHAPTER 103. COMPENSATION TO PERSONS WRONGFULLY IMPRISONED

SUBCHAPTER A. ELIGIBILITY; NOTICE OF ELIGIBILITY

Acts 2001, 77th Leg., ch. 1488, § 1, amended Chapter 103, formerly consisting of §§ 103.001 to 103.007, to consist of §§ 103.001 to 103.154.

DISPOSITION TABLE

Showing where the subject matter of provisions contained in former Chapter 103, Compensation to Persons Wrongfully Imprisoned, may be found in Chapter 103, Subchapter C, Filing Suit, as amended by Acts 2001, 77th Leg., ch. 1488, § 1.

Former Section	Amended Section
103.001	103.101
103.002	103.101
103.003	103.102
103.004	103.103
103.005	103.104
103.006	103.105
103.007	—

SUBCHAPTER A. ELIGIBILITY; NOTICE OF ELIGIBILITY

§ 103.001. Claimants Entitled to Compensation and Health Benefits Coverage

(a) A person is entitled to compensation if:

(1) the person has served in whole or in part a sentence in prison under the laws of this state; and

(2) the person:

(A) has received a full pardon on the basis of innocence for the crime for which the person was sentenced;

(B) has been granted relief in accordance with a writ of habeas corpus that is based on a court finding or determination that the person is actually innocent of the crime for which the person was sentenced; or

(C) has been granted relief in accordance with a writ of habeas corpus and:

(i) the state district court in which the charge against the person was pending has entered an order dismissing the charge; and

(ii) the district court's dismissal order is based on a motion to dismiss in which the state's attorney states that no credible evidence exists that inculpates the defendant and, either in the motion or in an affidavit, the state's attorney states that the state's attorney believes that the defendant is actually innocent of the crime for which the person was sentenced.

(b) A person is not entitled to compensation under Subsection (a) for any part of a sentence in prison during which the person was also serving a concurrent sentence for another crime to which Subsection (a) does not apply.

(c) If a deceased person would be entitled to compensation under Subsection (a)(2) if living, including a person who received a posthumous pardon, the person's heirs, legal representatives, and estate are entitled to lump-sum compensation under Section 103.052.

(d) Subject to this section, a person entitled to compensation under Subsection (a) is also eligible to obtain group health benefit plan coverage through the Texas Department of Criminal Justice as if the person were an employee of the department. This subsection does not entitle the person's spouse or other dependent or family member to group health benefit plan coverage. Coverage may be obtained under this subsection for a period of time equal to the total period the claimant served for the crime for which the claimant was wrongfully imprisoned, including any period during which the claimant was released on parole or to mandatory supervision or required to register under Chapter 62, Code of Criminal Procedure. A person who elects to obtain coverage under this subsection shall pay a monthly contribution equal to the total amount of the monthly contributions for that coverage for an employee of the department.

(e) Notwithstanding Section 103.053(c), annuity payments may be reduced by an amount necessary to make the payments required by Subsection (d), and that amount shall be transferred to an appropriate account as provided by the comptroller by rule to fund that coverage.

Acts 1985, 69th Leg., ch. 959, § 1, eff. Sept. 1, 1985. Amended by Acts 2001, 77th Leg., ch. 1488, § 1, eff. June 15, 2001; Acts 2009, 81st Leg., ch. 180, § 2, eff. Sept. 1, 2009; Acts 2011, 82nd Leg., ch. 698 (H.B. 417), § 2, eff. June 17, 2011; Acts 2011, 82nd Leg., ch. 1107 (S.B. 1686), §§ 1, 2, eff. Sept. 1, 2011.

§ 103.002. Notice to Wrongfully Imprisoned Person

(a) In this section:

(1) "Department" means the Texas Department of Criminal Justice.

(2) "Penal institution" has the meaning assigned by Article 62.001, Code of Criminal Procedure.

(3) "Wrongfully imprisoned person" has the meaning assigned by Section 501.091, Government Code, as added by Chapter 1389 (S.B. 1847), Acts of the 81st Legislature, Regular Session, 2009.

(b) The department shall provide to each wrongfully imprisoned person information, both orally and in writing, that includes:

(1) guidance on how to obtain compensation under this chapter; and

(2) a list of and contact information for nonprofit advocacy groups, identified by the department, that assist wrongfully imprisoned persons in filing claims for compensation under this chapter.

(c) The department must provide the information required under Subsection (b):

(1) at the time of the release of the wrongfully imprisoned person from a penal institution; or

(2) as soon as practicable after the department has reason to believe that the person is entitled to compensation under Section 103.001(a).

Added by Acts 2011, 82nd Leg., ch. 698 (H.B. 417), § 3, eff. June 17, 2011.

§ 103.003. Limitation on Time to File

A person seeking compensation under this chapter must file an application with the comptroller for compensation under Subchapter B[1] not later than the third anniversary of the date:

(1) the person on whose imprisonment the claim is based received a pardon as provided by Section 103.001(a)(2)(A);

(2) the person's application for a writ of habeas corpus was granted as provided by Section 103.001(a)(2)(B); or

(3) an order of dismissal described by Section 103.001(a)(2)(C) was signed.

Added by Acts 2001, 77th Leg., ch. 1488, § 1, eff. June 15, 2001. Amended by Acts 2009, 81st Leg., ch. 180, § 3, eff. Sept. 1, 2009; Acts 2011, 82nd Leg., ch. 698 (H.B. 417), § 4, eff. June 17, 2011.

[1] V.T.C.A., Civil Practice & Remedies Code § 103.051 et seq.

§§ 103.004 to 103.006. Redesignated as V.T.C.A., Civil Practice & Remedies Code §§ 103.103 to 103.105 and amended by Acts 2001, 77th Leg., ch. 1488, § 1, eff. June 15, 2001

§ 103.007. Deleted by Acts 2001, 77th Leg., ch. 1488, § 1, eff. June 15, 2001

SUBCHAPTER B. ADMINISTRATIVE PROCEEDING

§ 103.051. Application Procedure

(a) To apply for compensation under this subchapter, the claimant must file with the comptroller's judiciary section:

(1) an application for compensation provided for that purpose by the comptroller;

(2) a verified copy of the pardon, court order, motion to dismiss, and affidavit, as applicable, justifying the application for compensation;

(3) a statement provided by the Texas Department of Criminal Justice and any county or municipality that incarcerated the person on whose imprisonment the claim is based in connection with the relevant sentence verifying the length of incarceration;

(4) if applicable, a statement from the Department of Public Safety verifying registration as a sex offender and length of registration;

(5) if applicable, a statement from the Texas Department of Criminal Justice verifying the length of time spent on parole; and

(6) if the claimant is applying for compensation under Section 103.052(a)(2), a certified copy of each child support order under which child support payments became due during the time the claimant served in prison and copies of the official child support payment records described by Section 234.009, Family Code, for that period.

(b) The comptroller shall determine:

(1) the eligibility of the claimant; and

(2) the amount of compensation owed to an eligible claimant.

(b–1) In determining the eligibility of a claimant, the comptroller shall consider only the verified copies of documents filed under Subsection (a)(2). If the filed documents do not clearly indicate on their face that the person is entitled to compensation under Section 103.001(a)(2), the comptroller shall deny the claim. The comptroller's duty to determine the eligibility of a claimant under this section is purely ministerial.

(c) The comptroller must make a determination of eligibility and the amount owed as required by Subsection (b) not later than the 45th day after the date the application is received.

(d) If the comptroller denies the claim, the comptroller must state the reason for the denial. Not later than the 30th day after the date the denial is received, the claimant must submit an application to cure any problem identified. Not later than the 45th day after the date an application is received under this subsection, the comptroller shall determine the claimant's eligibility and the amount owed.

(e) If the comptroller denies a claim after the claimant submits an application under Subsection (d), the claimant may bring an action for mandamus relief.

(f) To apply for coverage through the Texas Department of Criminal Justice under Section 103.001(d), the claimant must file with the department:

(1) an application for coverage provided for that purpose by the department; and

(2) a statement by the comptroller that the comptroller has determined the claimant to be eligible for compensation under this subchapter.

Added by Acts 2001, 77th Leg., ch. 1488, § 1, eff. June 15, 2001. Amended by Acts 2003, 78th Leg., ch. 1310, § 1, eff. June 20, 2003; Acts 2007, 80th Leg., ch. 1190, § 1, eff. Sept. 1, 2007; Acts 2007, 80th Leg., ch. 1388, § 2, eff. Sept. 1, 2007; Acts 2009, 81st Leg., ch. 87, § 5.003, eff. Sept. 1, 2009; Acts 2009, 81st Leg., ch. 180, § 4, eff. Sept. 1, 2009; Acts 2011, 82nd Leg., ch. 698 (H.B. 417), § 5, eff. June 17, 2011; Acts 2011, 82nd Leg., ch. 1107 (S.B. 1686), § 3, eff. Sept. 1, 2011.

§ 103.052. Lump–Sum Compensation

(a) A person who meets the requirements of Section 103.001 is entitled to compensation in an amount equal to:

(1) $80,000 multiplied by the number of years served in prison, expressed as a fraction to reflect partial years; and

(2) compensation for child support payments owed by the person on whose imprisonment the claim is based that became due and interest on child support arrearages that accrued during the time served in prison but were not paid.

(b) A person who, after serving a sentence in a Texas prison for which the person is entitled to compensation under Subsection (a)(1), was released on parole or required to register as a sex offender under Chapter 62, Code of Criminal Procedure, is entitled to compensation in an amount equal to $25,000 multiplied by the number of years served either on parole or as a registered sex offender, expressed as a fraction to reflect partial years.

(c) The amount of compensation under Subsection (a)(2) to which a person is entitled shall be paid on the person's behalf in a lump-sum payment to the state disbursement unit, as defined by Section 101.0302, Family Code, for distribution to the obligee under the child support order.

Added by Acts 2001, 77th Leg., ch. 1488, § 1, eff. June 15, 2001. Amended by Acts 2007, 80th Leg., ch. 1190, § 2, eff. Sept. 1, 2007; Acts 2009, 81st Leg., ch. 180, § 5, eff. Sept. 1, 2009.

§ 103.053. Annuity Compensation Generally; Standard Annuity Payments

(a) A person entitled to compensation under Section 103.001(a) is entitled to standard annuity payments under this section unless the person elects to receive alternative annuity payments under Section 103.0535.

(a–1) Standard annuity payments are based on a present value sum equal to the amount to which the person is entitled under Sections 103.052(a)(1) and (b).

(b) Standard annuity payments are payable in equal monthly installments for the life of the claimant.

(c) Annuity payments under this chapter must be based on a five percent per annum interest rate and other actuarial factors within the discretion of the comptroller. Annuity payments under this chapter may not be accelerated, deferred, increased, or decreased. A person entitled to annuity payments under this chapter, including a claimant's spouse or designated beneficiary entitled to payments under Section 103.0535, may not sell, mortgage or otherwise encumber, or anticipate the payments, wholly or partly, by assignment or otherwise.

Added by Acts 2009, 81st Leg., ch. 180, § 6, eff. Sept. 1, 2009. Amended by Acts 2015, 84th Leg., ch. 689 (H.B. 638), § 1, eff. Sept. 1, 2015.

§ 103.0535. Alternative Annuity Compensation

(a) A person entitled to compensation under Section 103.001(a) may elect to receive reduced alternative annuity payments under this section instead of standard annuity payments.

(b) Alternative annuity payments are payable throughout the life of the claimant and are actuarially reduced from the standard annuity payments to their actuarial equivalent under the option selected under Subsection (c).

(c) A claimant may select one of the following options, which provide that:

(1) after the claimant's death, the alternative annuity payments are payable to and throughout the life of the claimant's spouse;

(2) after the claimant's death, three-fourths of the initial alternative annuity payment amount is payable to and throughout the life of the claimant's spouse;

(3) after the claimant's death, one-half of the initial alternative annuity payment amount is payable to and throughout the life of the claimant's spouse;

(4) if the claimant dies before 180 monthly alternative annuity payments have been made, the remainder of the 180 payments are payable to the claimant's spouse or designated beneficiary; or

(5) if the claimant dies before 120 monthly alternative annuity payments have been made, the remainder of the 120 payments are payable to the claimant's spouse or designated beneficiary.

(d) An election under this section must be made not later than the 45th day after the date:

(1) on which the claimant files with the comptroller the application required by Section 103.051; or

(2) on which the claimant experiences one of the following life-changing events:

(A) marriage or divorce of the claimant;

(B) the addition of a dependent of the claimant; or

(C) the death of a dependent, spouse, or beneficiary of the claimant.

(d–1) An election under Subsection (d) must be made on a form prescribed by the comptroller that:

(1) identifies the claimant's spouse or designated beneficiary according to Section 103.0536; and

(2) specifies the option selected under Subsection (c).

(e) A claimant who elects to receive alternative annuity payments under this section that are payable to the claimant and the claimant's spouse and survives the claimant's spouse is entitled to an increase in the amount of the claimant's monthly annuity payments so that the claimant's monthly payments equal the monthly payments the claimant would have received had the claimant not elected to receive the alternative annuity payments. The claimant is entitled to the increased payments beginning the month after the month in which the claimant's spouse dies and ending on the date of the claimant's death.

Added by Acts 2015, 84th Leg., ch. 689 (H.B. 638), § 2, eff. Sept. 1, 2015. Amended by Acts 2019, 86th Leg., ch. 621 (S.B. 1151), § 1, eff. June 10, 2019.

Section 3 of Acts 2019, 86th Leg., ch. 621 (S.B. 1151) provides:

"(a) Notwithstanding Section 103.0535(d), Civil Practice and Remedies Code, as amended by this Act, a person entitled to compensation under Section 103.001(a), Civil Practice and Remedies Code, who started receiving annuity payments before the effective date [June 10, 2019] of this Act may elect to receive any remaining payments as alternative annuity payments under Section 103.0535, Civil Practice and Remedies Code, as amended by this Act, by filing the form described by Section 103.0535(d–1), Civil Practice and Remedies Code, as added by this Act, with the comptroller after December 31, 2019, and before March 1, 2020. The value of alternative annuity payments elected under this subsection must be actuarially equivalent to the remaining value of the annuity payments the person would receive absent the election. This subsection does not affect the ability of a person described by this subsection to make an election under Section 103.0535(d), Civil Practice and Remedies Code, as amended by this Act, following a life-changing event described by that subsection.

"(b) Not later than December 1, 2019, the comptroller shall provide notice to all persons entitled to compensation under Section 103.001(a), Civil Practice and Remedies Code, of:

"(1) the opportunity described by Subsection (a) of this section to elect to receive alternative annuity payments under Section 103.0535, Civil Practice and Remedies Code, as amended by this Act; and

"(2) the opportunity to elect to receive alternative annuity payments after a life-changing event under Section 103.0535(d), Civil Practice and Remedies Code, as amended by this Act.

"(c) The comptroller shall provide the notice required by Subsection (b) of this section by:

"(1) certified mail to a person's last known address; and

"(2) phone call to the phone number that the comptroller has on file for the person."

§ 103.0536. Designated Beneficiary

(a) A claimant who selects a designated beneficiary to receive the remainder of the alternative annuity payments payable under Section 103.0535(c)(4) or (5) may designate:

(1) one designated beneficiary to receive the remainder of the annuity payments;

(2) two or more designated beneficiaries to receive the remainder of the annuity payments in equal amounts; or

(3) a primary designated beneficiary to receive the remainder of the annuity payments and an additional beneficiary.

(b) If a designated beneficiary designated under Subsection (a)(2) dies before the remainder of the annuity payments are paid, the comptroller shall recalculate the payments so that the remaining designated beneficiaries receive the remainder of the annuity payments in equal amounts.

(c) An additional beneficiary designated under Subsection (a)(3) takes the place of the primary beneficiary if the primary beneficiary dies before the remainder of the annuity payments are paid. A claimant may select not more than four additional beneficiaries and shall determine the order in which the additional beneficiaries are to succeed the primary beneficiary. The remainder of the annuity payments under this subsection are paid to one beneficiary at a time until the beneficiary dies or the remaining annuity payments are paid. If each additional beneficiary dies before the remainder of the annuity payments are paid, the remainder of the annuity payments are payable to the claimant's estate.

(d) A designated beneficiary under this section must be a dependent of the claimant. For purposes of this subsection, "dependent" includes a claimant's spouse, minor child, and any other person for whom the claimant is legally obligated to provide support, including alimony.

Added by Acts 2015, 84th Leg., ch. 689 (H.B. 638), § 2, eff. Sept. 1, 2015.

§ 103.054. Payment of Certain Tuition and Fees

If requested by the claimant before the seventh anniversary of the relevant date described by Section 103.003, tuition for up to 120 credit hours, including tuition charged under Section 54.0513, Education Code, or any other law granting an educational institution discretion to set the tuition rate, and any mandatory fees associated with attendance at the institution, charged by a career center or public institution of higher education shall be paid on behalf of the claimant.

Added by Acts 2009, 81st Leg., ch. 180, § 6, eff. Sept. 1, 2009. Amended by Acts 2011, 82nd Leg., ch. 698 (H.B. 417), § 6, eff. June 17, 2011.

SUBCHAPTER C. FEES

A former Subchapter C, Filing Suit, consisting of §§ 103.101 to 103.105, was repealed by Acts 2009, 81st Leg., ch. 180, § 12(2), eff. Sept. 1, 2009.

§ 103.101. Fees Limited; Prerequisites to Fee Agreement

(a) A person, including an attorney, may not charge or collect a fee for preparing, filing, or curing a claimant's application under Section 103.051 unless the fee is based on a reasonable hourly rate.

(b) An attorney may enter into a fee agreement with a claimant for services related to an application under Section 103.051 only after the attorney has disclosed in writing to the claimant the hourly rate that will be charged for the services.

(c) An attorney may not collect a fee for preparing, filing, or curing a claimant's application under Section 103.051 before a final determination is made by the comptroller that the claimant is eligible or ineligible for compensation under this chapter.

Added by Acts 2011, 82nd Leg., ch. 698 (H.B. 417), § 7, eff. June 17, 2011.

§ 103.102. Submission of Fee Report

(a) Together with an application for compensation under this chapter or not later than the 14th day after the date the application or cured application is filed, a person seeking payment for preparing, filing, or curing the application must file a fee report with the comptroller's judiciary section.

(b) A fee report under this section must include:

(1) the total dollar amount sought for fees;

(2) the number of hours the person worked preparing, filing, or curing the application; and

(3) the name of the applicant.

(c) A fee report under this section is public information subject to Chapter 552, Government Code.

Added by Acts 2011, 82nd Leg., ch. 698 (H.B. 417), § 7, eff. June 17, 2011.

§§ 103.101 to 103.105. Repealed by Acts 2009, 81st Leg., ch. 180, § 12(2), eff. Sept. 1, 2009

SUBCHAPTER D. PAYMENTS AND LIMITATIONS

§ 103.151. Administrative Payment of Compensation

(a) The comptroller shall make the compensation due a claimant under Section 103.052 and the lump-sum payment, if any, to be paid to the state disbursement unit, as defined by Section 101.0302, Family Code, under Subchapter B,[1] to the extent that funds are available and appropriated for that purpose, not later than the 30th day after the date the comptroller grants the application. A claim for lump-sum compensation payable under Section 103.052(a) or (b) shall survive the death of the claimant in favor of the heirs, legal representatives, and estate of the claimant.

(b) The comptroller shall begin making annuity payments under Section 103.053(a) or 103.0535 on the first anniversary of the date of payment of the compensation due under Section 103.052.

(c) If appropriated funds are insufficient to pay the amount due a claimant and the amount to be paid to the state disbursement unit, as defined by Section 101.0302, Family Code, money shall be paid under the procedure described by Section 103.152.

Added by Acts 2001, 77th Leg., ch. 1488, § 1, eff. June 15, 2001. Amended by Acts 2007, 80th Leg., ch. 1190, § 5, eff. Sept. 1, 2007; Acts 2009, 81st Leg., ch. 180, § 7, eff. Sept. 1, 2009; Acts 2015, 84th Leg., ch. 689 (H.B. 638), § 3, eff. Sept. 1, 2015.

[1] V.T.C.A., Civil Practice & Remedies Code § 103.051 et seq.

§ 103.152. Payment of Compensation

(a) Not later than November 1 of each even-numbered year, the comptroller shall provide a list of claimants entitled to payment under Subchapter B[1] and the amounts due for each claimant to the governor, the lieutenant governor, and the chair of the appropriate committee in each house of the legislature so that the legislature may appropriate the amount needed to pay the amount owed to each claimant and the amount to be paid to the state disbursement unit, as defined by Section 101.0302, Family Code, on the claimant's behalf.

(b) Not later than September 1 of the year in which an appropriation under this chapter has been made by the legislature, the comptroller shall pay the required amount to each claimant and the state disbursement unit, as defined by Section 101.0302, Family Code.

(c) Repealed by Acts 2009, 81st Leg., ch. 180, § 12(3).

Added by Acts 2001, 77th Leg., ch. 1488, § 1, eff. June 15, 2001. Amended by Acts 2007, 80th Leg., ch. 1190, § 6, eff. Sept. 1, 2007; Acts 2009, 81st Leg., ch. 180, §§ 8, 12(3), eff. Sept. 1, 2009.

[1] V.T.C.A., Civil Practice & Remedies Code § 103.051 et seq.

§ 103.153. Employees Not Liable After Payment of Compensation

(a) In this section, "employee" and "governmental unit" have the meanings assigned by Section 101.001.

(b) A person who receives compensation under this chapter may not bring any action involving the same subject matter, including an action involving the person's arrest, conviction, or length of confinement, against any governmental unit or an employee of any governmental unit.

Added by Acts 2001, 77th Leg., ch. 1488, § 1, eff. June 15, 2001.

§ 103.154. Termination of Payments

(a) Except as provided by Subsection (c), compensation payments under this chapter terminate if, after the date the claimant becomes eligible for compensation under Section 103.001, the claimant is convicted of a crime punishable as a felony. Annuity payments to a claimant's spouse or designated beneficiary under this chapter terminate if, after the date the spouse or designated beneficiary begins receiving annuity payments, the spouse or designated beneficiary is convicted of a crime punishable as a felony. Payments terminate under this subsection on the date of the felony conviction. If annuity payments to a designated beneficiary are terminated under this subsection, the remainder of the annuity payments are payable under Section 103.0536 as if the beneficiary died on the date of termination.

(b) Except as provided by Sections 103.0535 and 103.0536:

(1) annuity payments to a person under this chapter terminate on the date of the person's death; and

(2) payments scheduled to be paid after that date are credited to the state and may not be paid to any other person, including the person's surviving spouse, heirs, devisees, or beneficiaries under the person's will, or to the person's estate.

(c) This section does not apply to compensation for child support payments and interest on child support arrearages to be paid on a person's behalf under this chapter to the state disbursement unit, as defined by Section 101.0302, Family Code.

Added by Acts 2001, 77th Leg., ch. 1488, § 1, eff. June 15, 2001. Amended by Acts 2007, 80th Leg., ch. 1190, § 7, eff. Sept. 1, 2007; Acts 2009, 81st Leg., ch. 180, § 9, eff. Sept. 1, 2009; Acts 2015, 84th Leg., ch. 689 (H.B. 638), § 4, eff. Sept. 1, 2015.

CHAPTER 104. STATE LIABILITY FOR CONDUCT OF PUBLIC SERVANTS

§ 104.001. State Liability; Persons Covered

In a cause of action based on conduct described in Section 104.002, the state shall indemnify the following persons, without regard to whether the persons performed their services for compensation, for actual damages, court costs, and attorney's fees adjudged against:

(1) an employee, a member of the governing board, or any other officer of a state agency, institution, or department;

(2) a former employee, former member of the governing board, or any other former officer of a state agency, institution, or department who was an employee or officer when the act or omission on which the damages are based occurred;

(3) a physician or psychiatrist licensed in this state who was performing services under a contract with any state agency, institution, or department or a racing official performing services under a contract with the Texas Racing Commission when the act or omission on which the damages are based occurred;

(3–a) a phlebotomist licensed in this state who was performing services under a contract with the Texas Department of Criminal Justice when the act or omission on which the damages are based occurred;

(4) a chaplain or spiritual advisor who was performing services under contract with the Texas Department of Criminal Justice or the Texas Juvenile Justice Department when the act or omission on which the damages are based occurred;

(5) a person serving on the governing board of a foundation, corporation, or association at the request and on behalf of an institution of higher education, as that term is defined by Section 61.003(8), Education Code, not including a public junior college;

(6) a state contractor who signed a waste manifest as required by a state contract; or

(7) the estate of a person listed in this section.

Acts 1985, 69th Leg., ch. 959, § 1, eff. Sept. 1, 1985. Amended by Acts 1987, 70th Leg., ch. 1099, § 47, eff. Sept. 1, 1987; Acts 1987, 70th Leg., 1st C.S., ch. 2, § 3.08, eff. Sept. 2, 1987; Acts 1987, 70th Leg., 2nd C.S., ch. 29, § 1, eff. Oct. 20, 1987; Acts 1991, 72nd Leg., ch. 386, § 72, eff. Aug. 26, 1991; Acts 1995, 74th Leg., ch. 139, § 2, eff. Sept. 1, 1995; Acts 1995, 74th Leg., ch. 883, § 5, eff. Aug. 28, 1995; Acts 2001, 77th Leg., ch. 1082, § 1, eff. June 15, 2001; Acts 2007, 80th Leg., ch. 292, § 1, eff. June 15, 2007; Acts 2015, 84th Leg., ch. 734 (H.B. 1549), § 1, eff. Sept. 1, 2015.

§ 104.002. State Liability; Conduct Covered

(a) Except as provided by Subsection (b), the state is liable for indemnification under this chapter only if the damages are based on an act or omission by the person in the course and scope of the person's office, employment, or contractual performance for or service on behalf of the agency, institution, or department and if:

(1) the damages arise out of a cause of action for negligence, except a wilful or wrongful act or an act of gross negligence; or

(2) the damages arise out of a cause of action for deprivation of a right, privilege, or immunity secured by the constitution or laws of this state or the United States, except when the court in its judgment or the jury in its verdict finds that the person acted in bad faith, with conscious indifference or reckless disregard; or

(3) indemnification is in the interest of the state as determined by the attorney general or his designee.

(b) The state is liable for indemnification under this chapter if:

(1) the person is liable for the damages solely because the person signed an industrial solid waste or hazardous waste manifest or other record required by Section 361.036, Health and Safety Code;

(2) the person signed the manifest or record in the course and scope of the person's office, employment, or contractual performance or service on behalf of the agency, institution, or department; and

(3) the person or company who signed the manifest did not increase or aggravate circumstances of contamination by grossly negligent acts or wilful misconduct.

Acts 1985, 69th Leg., ch. 959, § 1, eff. Sept. 1, 1985. Amended by Acts 1987, 70th Leg., 1st C.S., ch. 2, § 3.09, eff. Sept. 2, 1987; Acts 1991, 72nd Leg., ch. 702, § 1, eff. Aug. 26, 1991; Acts 1995, 74th Leg., ch. 883, § 6, eff. Aug. 28, 1995.

§ 104.003. Limits on Amount of Recoverable Damages

(a) Except as provided by Subsection (c) or a specific appropriation, state liability for indemnification under this chapter may not exceed:

(1) $100,000 to a single person indemnified and, if more than one person is indemnified, $300,000 for a single occurrence in the case of personal injury, death, or deprivation of a right, privilege, or immunity; and

(2) $10,000 for each single occurrence of damage to property.

(b) The state is not liable under this chapter to the extent that damages are recoverable under and are in excess of the deductible limits of:

(1) a contract of insurance; or

(2) a plan of self-insurance authorized by statute.

(c) The limits on state liability provided by Subsection (a) do not apply if the state liability is based on Section 104.002(b).

(d) For the purposes of this section, a claim arises out of a single occurrence, if the claim arises from a common nucleus of operative facts, regardless of the number of claimants or the number of separate acts or omissions.

Acts 1985, 69th Leg., ch. 959, § 1, eff. Sept. 1, 1985. Amended by Acts 1987, 70th Leg., ch. 1049, § 59, eff. Sept. 1, 1987; Acts 1987, 70th Leg., 1st C.S., ch. 2, § 3.10, eff. Sept. 2, 1987; Acts 1989, 71st Leg., ch. 785, § 3.09, eff. Sept. 1, 1989; Acts 1991, 72nd Leg., ch. 702, § 2, eff. Aug. 26, 1991; Acts 1995, 74th Leg., ch. 139, § 3, eff. Sept. 1, 1995; Acts 1997, 75th Leg., ch. 468, § 2, eff. May 30, 1997; Acts 2003, 78th Leg., ch. 531, § 1, eff. June 20, 2003.

§ 104.0035. State Liability; Criminal Prosecution

(a) The state shall indemnify a person for reasonable attorney's fees incurred in defense of a criminal prosecution against the person if:

(1) the person is covered by Section 104.001;

(2) the attorney general determines that the conduct for which the person is criminally prosecuted could give rise to a civil cause of action covered by Section 104.002;

(3) the person is found not guilty after a trial or appeal or the complaint, information, or indictment is dismissed without a plea of guilty or nolo contendere being entered; and

(4) the attorney general determines that the complaint, information, or indictment presented against the person was dismissed because:

(A) the presentment was made on mistake, false information, or other similar basis, indicating absence of probable cause to believe, at the time of the dismissal, the person committed the offense; or

(B) the complaint, information, or indictment was void.

(b) State liability for indemnification under this section may not exceed $10,000 for the prosecution of a criminal offense or the prosecution of two or more offenses prosecuted in a single criminal action.

(c) This section does not apply to a person who is criminally prosecuted for operating a motor vehicle while intoxicated under Section 49.04, Penal Code, for intoxication assault committed while operating a motor vehicle under Section 49.07, Penal Code, or for intoxication manslaughter under Section 49.08, Penal Code.

(d) An initial determination of the liability of the state for indemnification and the reasonableness of attorney's fees under this section shall be made by the attorney general upon application by any person other than:

(1) an employee or former employee of the attorney general's office; or

(2) the attorney general or a former attorney general.

(e) If the attorney general determines under Subsection (d) that the state is liable for indemnification, the attorney general shall indemnify the person for reasonable attorney's fees as provided by this section from funds appropriated for that purpose. If the attorney general determines that the state is not liable for indemnification, the person may appeal to a district court in Travis County. A person who is not entitled to an initial determination under Subsection (d) may bring an action in a district court in Travis County.

(f) The district court in Travis County has jurisdiction to hear a suit under this section and may issue an order directing the attorney general's office to indemnify the person for reasonable attorney's fees as provided by this section. The judgment of the district court is final and is not subject to appeal.

Added by Acts 1987, 70th Leg., 2nd C.S., ch. 29, § 2, eff. Oct. 20, 1987. Amended by Acts 1995, 74th Leg., ch. 76, § 14.02, eff. Sept. 1, 1995.

§ 104.004. Defense by Attorney General

(a) The attorney general shall defend a public servant or estate listed in Section 104.001 in a cause of action covered by this chapter.

(b) The attorney general may settle or compromise the portion of a lawsuit that may result in state liability under this chapter.

(c) It is not a conflict of interest for the attorney general to defend a person under this chapter and also to prosecute a legal action against that person as required or authorized by law if different assistant attorneys general are assigned the responsibility for each action.

Acts 1985, 69th Leg., ch. 959, § 1, eff. Sept. 1, 1985. Amended by Acts 1987, 70th Leg., 1st C.S., ch. 2, § 3.11, eff. Sept. 2, 1987.

§ 104.005. Service of Process or Timely Notice to Attorney General Required

Except as provided by Section 104.0035, the state is not liable for the defense of an action covered by this chapter or for damages, court costs, or attorney's fees unless:

(1) the attorney general has been served in the case and the state has been given an opportunity to defend the suit; or

(2) the person against whom the action is brought delivers to the attorney general all process served on the person not later than the 10th day after the date of service.

Acts 1985, 69th Leg., ch. 959, § 1, eff. Sept. 1, 1985. Amended by Acts 1987, 70th Leg., 2nd C.S., ch. 29, § 3, eff. Oct. 20, 1987.

§ 104.006. Security or Bond

In a cause of action defended by the attorney general under this chapter, the attorney general or the individual or estate represented may not be required to advance security for cost or to give bond on appeal or on review by writ of error.

Acts 1985, 69th Leg., ch. 959, § 1, eff. Sept. 1, 1985.

§ 104.007. Funds for Defense

(a) Only funds appropriated from the General Revenue Fund to the attorney general may be used to conduct the defense of an action that the attorney general is required to defend under this chapter.

(b) Conducting the defense of an action covered by this chapter includes investigating, taking depositions, making discovery, preparing for trial, preparing exhibits or other evidence, and participating in actual trial.

Acts 1985, 69th Leg., ch. 959, § 1, eff. Sept. 1, 1985.

§ 104.008. No Waiver of Defenses

This chapter does not waive a defense, immunity, or jurisdictional bar available to the state or its officers, employees, or contractors.

Acts 1985, 69th Leg., ch. 959, § 1, eff. Sept. 1, 1985.

§ 104.009. Directors' and Officers' Liability Insurance

(a) A state agency, institution, or department may purchase a directors' and officers' liability insurance policy applicable to damages for conduct described under Section 104.002 and other conduct customarily covered under directors' and officers' liability insurance policies for the benefit of:

(1) a director or officer of the agency, institution, or department;

(2) a member of a governing board, commission, or council of the agency, institution, or department; or

(3) a member of the executive staff of the agency, institution, or department.

(b) An insurance policy purchased under this section must have a deductible applicable to the liability of the state agency, institution, or department in an amount equal to the amount of the limits of liability established under Section 104.003. The deductible applicable to an individual's liability may be set at a lower amount.

(c) The purchase of an insurance policy under this section does not waive a defense, immunity, or jurisdictional bar available to the state agency, institution, or department purchasing the insurance or to the insured.

Added by Acts 1997, 75th Leg., ch. 468, § 1, eff. May 30, 1997.

CHAPTER 105. FRIVOLOUS CLAIM OR REGULATORY ACTION BY STATE AGENCY

Section

§ 105.001. Definitions

In this chapter:

(1) "Fees and other expenses" means:

(A) the reasonable expenses of witnesses incurred in preparing to testify or in attending or testifying;

(B) a reasonable fee for the professional services of an expert witness; and

(C) the reasonable costs of a study, analysis, engineering report, test, or other project the court finds to be necessary for the preparation of the party's case.

(2) "Party" means an individual, partnership, corporation, association, or public or private organization other than a state agency.

(3) "State agency" means a board, commission, department, office, or other agency that:

(A) is in the executive branch of state government;

(B) was created by the constitution or a statute of this state; and

(C) has statewide jurisdiction.

Acts 1985, 69th Leg., ch. 959, § 1, eff. Sept. 1, 1985.

§ 105.002. Recovery of Fees, Expenses, and Attorney's Fees for Frivolous Claim

A party to a civil suit in a court of this state brought by or against a state agency in which the agency asserts a cause of action against the party, either originally or as a counterclaim or cross claim, is entitled to recover, in addition to all other costs allowed by law or rule, a total amount not to exceed $1 million for fees, expenses, and reasonable attorney's fees incurred by the party in defending the agency's action if:

(1) the court finds that the action is frivolous; and

(2) the action is dismissed or judgment is awarded to the party.

Acts 1985, 69th Leg., ch. 959, § 1, eff. Sept. 1, 1985. Amended by Acts 2019, 86th Leg., ch. 504 (S.B. 27), § 2, eff. Sept. 1, 2019.

Section 7 of Acts 2019, 86th Leg., ch. 504 (S.B. 27) provides:

"The change in law made by this Act applies only to a claim filed or regulatory action taken on or after the effective date [Sept. 1, 2019] of this Act. A claim filed or regulatory action taken before the effective date of this Act is governed by the law applicable to the claim or regulatory action immediately before the effective date of this Act, and that law is continued in effect for that purpose."

§ 105.003. Motion of Frivolous Claim

(a) To recover under Section 105.002, the party must file a written motion alleging that the agency's claim is frivolous. The motion may be filed at any time after the filing of the pleadings in which the agency's cause of action is alleged.

(b) The motion must set forth the facts that justify the party's claim.

(c) The motion must state that if the action is dismissed or judgment is awarded to the party, the party intends to submit a motion to the court to recover fees, expenses, and reasonable attorney's fees.

Acts 1985, 69th Leg., ch. 959, § 1, eff. Sept. 1, 1985. Amended by Acts 2019, 86th Leg., ch. 504 (S.B. 27), § 3, eff. Sept. 1, 2019.

Section 7 of Acts 2019, 86th Leg., ch. 504 (S.B. 27) provides:

"The change in law made by this Act applies only to a claim filed or regulatory action taken on or after the effective date [Sept. 1, 2019] of this Act. A claim filed or regulatory action taken before the effective date of this Act is governed by the law applicable to the claim or regulatory action immediately before the effective date of this Act, and that law is continued in effect for that purpose."

§ 105.004. Payment of Costs

The agency shall pay the fees and expenses from funds appropriated for operation of the agency, funds appropriated for the payment of fees and expenses under this chapter, or other funds available for that purpose.

Acts 1985, 69th Leg., ch. 959, § 1, eff. Sept. 1, 1985.

§ 105.005. Recovery of Attorney's Fees and Costs in Frivolous Regulatory Action

The court reviewing a decision in a contested case under Chapter 2001, Government Code, may award a person, in addition to all other costs allowed by law or rule, an amount not to exceed $1 million for reasonable attorney's fees and costs incurred in defending against a frivolous regulatory action during the contested case and judicial review of the decision in the contested case if:

(1) the person prevails on review; and

(2) there is a final determination that the regulatory action is frivolous.

Added by Acts 2019, 86th Leg., ch. 504 (S.B. 27), § 4, eff. Sept. 1, 2019.

Section 7 of Acts 2019, 86th Leg., ch. 504 (S.B. 27) provides:

"The change in law made by this Act applies only to a claim filed or regulatory action taken on or after the effective date [Sept. 1, 2019] of this Act. A claim filed or regulatory action taken before the effective date of this Act is governed by the law applicable to the claim or regulatory action immediately before the effective date of this Act, and that law is continued in effect for that purpose."

CHAPTER 106. DISCRIMINATION BECAUSE OF RACE, RELIGION, COLOR, SEX, OR NATIONAL ORIGIN

Section

§ 106.001. Prohibited Acts

(a) An officer or employee of the state or of a political subdivision of the state who is acting or purporting to act in an official capacity may not, because of a person's race, religion, color, sex, or national origin:

(1) refuse to issue to the person a license, permit, or certificate;

(2) revoke or suspend the person's license, permit, or certificate;

(3) refuse to permit the person to use facilities open to the public and owned, operated, or managed by or on behalf of the state or a political subdivision of the state;

(4) refuse to permit the person to participate in a program owned, operated, or managed by or on behalf of the state or a political subdivision of the state;

(5) refuse to grant a benefit to the person;

(6) impose an unreasonable burden on the person; or

(7) refuse to award a contract to the person.

(b) This section does not apply to a public school official who is acting under a plan reasonably designed to end discriminatory school practices.

(c) This section does not prohibit the adoption of a program designed to increase the participation of businesses owned and controlled by women, minorities, or disadvantaged persons in public contract awards.

Acts 1985, 69th Leg., ch. 959, § 1, eff. Sept. 1, 1985. Amended by Acts 1987, 70th Leg., ch. 1058, § 1, eff. Aug. 31, 1987; Acts 1991, 72nd Leg., ch. 597, § 56, eff. Sept. 1, 1991; Acts 1991, 72nd Leg., ch. 665, § 1, eff. June 16, 1991; Acts 1999, 76th Leg., ch. 1499, § 1.02, eff. Sept. 1, 1999.

§ 106.002. Remedies

(a) If a person has violated or there are reasonable grounds to believe a person is about to violate Section 106.001, the person aggrieved by the violation or threatened violation may sue for preventive relief, including a permanent or temporary injunction, a restraining order, or any other order.

(b) In an action under this section, unless the state is the prevailing party, the court may award the prevailing party reasonable attorney's fees as a part of the costs. The state's liability for costs is the same as that of a private person.

Acts 1985, 69th Leg., ch. 959, § 1, eff. Sept. 1, 1985.

§ 106.003. Penalties

(a) A person commits an offense if the person knowingly violates Section 106.001.

(b) An offense under this section is a misdemeanor punishable by:

(1) a fine of not more than $1,000;

(2) confinement in the county jail for not more than one year; or

(3) both the fine and confinement.

Acts 1985, 69th Leg., ch. 959, § 1, eff. Sept. 1, 1985.

§ 106.004. Inapplicability to Certain Claims

This chapter does not authorize a claim for preventive relief against the Texas Department of Criminal Justice, an employee of the department, or any other agency, agent, employee, or officer of this state if:

(1) the claim is brought by a person housed in a facility operated by or under contract with the department; and

(2) the claim accrued while the person was housed in the facility.

Added by Acts 1995, 74th Leg., ch. 378, § 4, eff. June 8, 1995.

CHAPTER 107. PERMISSION TO SUE THE STATE

Another Chapter 107, Limitation of Liability for Public Servants, consisting of §§ 107.001 to 107.003, was added by Acts 1987, 70th Leg., 1st C.S., ch. 2, § 3.12. The chapter was redesignated as Chapter 108, consisting of V.T.C.A., Civil Practice & Remedies Code §§ 108.001 to 108.003, by Acts 1989, 71st Leg., ch. 2, § 16.01(3).

§ 107.001. Grants of Permission Covered

This chapter applies to resolutions granting permission to sue the state or any of the agencies of government that collectively constitute the government of this state, including agencies, departments, bureaus, boards, commissions, offices, councils, courts, and institutions of higher education as defined by Section 61.003, Education Code.

Added by Acts 1987, 70th Leg., ch. 524, § 1, eff. Aug. 31, 1987. Amended by Acts 2005, 79th Leg., ch. 728, § 3.001, eff. Sept. 1, 2005.

§ 107.002. Effect of Grant of Permission

(a) A resolution that grants a person permission to sue the state has the following effect and the permission is granted subject to the following conditions:

(1) the claimant may sue for any relief to which the claimant is entitled as a result of the described claim;

(2) the suit must be filed before the second anniversary of the effective date of the resolution;

(3) service of citation and other required process must be made on the attorney general and on a person named in the resolution as a representative of the affected state agency;

(4) the suit must be tried as other civil suits;

(5) neither the state, nor any of its employees, agents, departments, agencies, or political subdivisions, admits to liability for, or to the truth of, any allegation asserted by the claimant;

(6) the alleged cause of action must be proved under the law of this state as in other civil suits;

(7) the state does not waive any defense, of law or fact, available to the state or to any of its employees or agents;

(8) the state reserves every defense, except the defense of immunity from suit without legislative permission;

(9) the state's ability to plead res judicata to any issue is not affected;

(10) the state does not grant permission to recover exemplary or punitive damages;

(11) the state's sovereign immunity under the Eleventh Amendment to the United States Constitution is not waived; and

(12) the state does not grant permission to be sued in any federal court.

(b) A resolution granting permission to sue does not waive to any extent immunity from liability.

Added by Acts 1987, 70th Leg., ch. 524, § 1, eff. Aug. 31, 1987.

§ 107.003. Method Exclusive

(a) A resolution may grant permission to sue the state only in accordance with this chapter.

(b) A resolution may not alter the effect of the permission as described by Section 107.002, except that a resolution may further limit the relief to which the claimant may be entitled.

Added by Acts 1987, 70th Leg., ch. 524, § 1, eff. Aug. 31, 1987.

§ 107.004. Additional Conditions

A resolution may specifically provide additional conditions to which a grant of permission to sue is subject.

Added by Acts 1987, 70th Leg., ch. 524, § 1, eff. Aug. 31, 1987.

§ 107.005. Effect on Other Laws

This chapter does not affect a waiver of immunity from suit contained in other law.

Added by Acts 1987, 70th Leg., ch. 524, § 1, eff. Aug. 31, 1987.

CHAPTER 108. LIMITATION OF LIABILITY FOR PUBLIC SERVANTS

Chapter 107, Limitation of Liability for Public Servants, consisting of V.T.C.A., Civil Practice & Remedies Code §§ 107.001 to 107.003, was added by Acts 1987, 70th Leg., 1st C.S., ch. 2, § 3.12. Acts 1989, 71st Leg., ch. 2, § 16.01(3) redesignated this chapter as Chapter 108, consisting of V.T.C.A., Civil Practice & Remedies Code §§ 108.001 to 108.003, effective August 28, 1989.

§ 108.001. Definitions

In this chapter:

(1) "Public servant" means a person who is:

(A) a public official elected or appointed to serve a governmental unit and acting in that capacity when the act or omission on which the damages were based occurred; or

(B) covered by Section 104.001 or Section 102.001.

(2) "Public servant" does not include an independent contractor, an agent or employee of an independent contractor, or another person who performs a contract for a unit of government.

(3) "Public servant" includes a licensed physician who provides emergency or postemergency stabilization services to patients in a hospital owned or operated by a unit of local government.

Added by Acts 1987, 70th Leg., 1st C.S., ch. 2, § 3.12, eff. Sept. 2, 1987. Redesignated from V.T.C.A., Civil Practice & Remedies Code § 107.001 by Acts 1989, 71st Leg., ch. 2, § 16.01(3), eff. Aug. 28, 1989. Amended by Acts 1995, 74th Leg., ch. 139, § 4, eff. Sept. 1, 1995; Acts 2003, 78th Leg., ch. 204, § 11.06, eff. Sept. 1, 2003.

§ 108.002. Limitation of Liability

(a) Except in an action arising under the constitution or laws of the United States, a public servant is not personally liable for damages in excess of $100,000 arising from personal injury, death, or deprivation of a right, privilege, or immunity if:

(1) the damages are the result of an act or omission by the public servant in the course and scope of the public servant's office, employment, or contractual performance for or service on behalf of a state agency, institution, department, or local government; and

(2) for the amount not in excess of $100,000, the public servant is covered:

(A) by the state's obligation to indemnify under Chapter 104;

(B) by a local government's authorization to indemnify under Chapter 102;

(C) by liability or errors and omissions insurance; or

(D) by liability or errors and omissions coverage under an interlocal agreement.

(b) Except in an action arising under the constitution or laws of the United States, a public servant is not liable for damages in excess of $100,000 for property damage if:

(1) the damages are the result of an act or omission by the public servant in the course and scope of the public servant's office, employment, or contractual performance for or service on behalf of a state agency, institution, department, or local government; and

(2) for the amount not in excess of $100,000, the public servant is covered:

(A) by the state's obligation to indemnify under Chapter 104;

(B) by a local government's authorization to indemnify under Chapter 102;

(C) by liability or errors and omissions insurance; or

(D) by liability or errors and omissions coverage under an interlocal agreement.

(c) Repealed by Acts 2003, 78th Leg., ch. 204, § 11.07; Acts 2003, 78th Leg., ch. 289, § 5.

Added by Acts 1987, 70th Leg., 1st C.S., ch. 2, § 3.12, eff. Sept. 2, 1987. Redesignated from V.T.C.A., Civil Practice & Remedies Code § 107.002 by Acts 1989, 71st Leg., ch. 2, § 16.01(3), eff. Aug. 28, 1989. Amended by Acts 1995, 74th Leg., ch. 139, § 4, eff. Sept. 1, 1995; Acts 2003, 78th Leg., ch. 204, §§ 11.01, 11.07, eff. Sept. 1, 2003; Acts 2003, 78th Leg., ch. 289, §§ 1, 5, eff. Sept. 1, 2003.

§ 108.003. State Liability Not Affected

(a) This chapter does not affect the liability for indemnification of the state under Chapter 104 or of a local government under Chapter 102.

(b) This chapter does not impose liability or waive immunity for a public servant who has common law, statutory, or other immunity.

Added by Acts 1987, 70th Leg., 1st C.S., ch. 2, § 3.12, eff. Sept. 2, 1987. Redesignated from V.T.C.A., Civil Practice & Remedies Code § 107.003 by Acts 1989, 71st Leg., ch. 2, § 16.01(3), eff. Aug. 28, 1989. Amended by Acts 1995, 74th Leg., ch. 139, § 4, eff. Sept. 1, 1995.

§ 108.004. Computer Date Failure

Except in an action arising under the constitution or laws of the United States, a public servant is not personally liable for property damages caused by a computer date failure as described by Section 147.003.

Added by Acts 1999, 76th Leg., ch. 128, § 4, eff. May 19, 1999.

CHAPTER 109. APPROPRIATIONS FOR PAYMENT OF CLAIMS AGAINST STATE AGENCIES

Section

§ 109.001. Definition

In this chapter, "state agency" means any entity that constitutes the state government for purposes of Section 101.001.

Added by Acts 1993, 73rd Leg., ch. 1005, § 1, eff. Sept. 1, 1993.

§ 109.0015. Repealed by Acts 2005, 79th Leg., ch. 741, § 10(a), eff. June 17, 2005

§ 109.002. Applicability; Appropriations and Payments for Certain Claims

(a) This chapter applies to appropriations and payments made in relation to:

(1) a claim for which the state government is liable under Chapter 101 that results from the conduct of a state agency; and

(2) indemnification of an employee, member of a governing board, or other officer of a state agency under Chapter 104.

(b) Except as provided by Section 109.007, the legislature may not make an appropriation to pay a claim for which the state government is liable under Chapter 101 and that results from the conduct of a state agency except in accordance with Section 109.003.

(c) Except as provided by Section 109.007, the legislature may not make an appropriation to indemnify an employee, member of a governing board, or other officer of a state agency under Chapter 104 except in accordance with Section 109.003.

Added by Acts 1993, 73rd Leg., ch. 1005, § 1, eff. Sept. 1, 1993. Amended by Acts 2001, 77th Leg., ch. 1414, § 1, eff. Sept. 1, 2001.

§ 109.003. Source of Appropriation

An appropriation subject to this chapter shall be made from otherwise unappropriated amounts in a special fund or account that may be appropriated to the affected state agency and that may be used for that purpose, to the extent those amounts are available. To the extent those amounts are not available, the appropriation may be made from the general revenue fund.

Added by Acts 1993, 73rd Leg., ch. 1005, § 1, eff. Sept. 1, 1993.

§ 109.004. Payment of Claim by Agency

(a) This section does not apply to the payment of a claim if the legislature has specifically:

(1) identified the claim; and

(2) appropriated money to pay the claim.

(b) Subject to Subsections (c) and (d), a state agency may pay a claim subject to this chapter only from money appropriated to that agency in the General Appropriations Act.

(c) The amount paid under this section by a state agency for a single claim may not exceed a limitation imposed by the General Appropriations Act on the amount that may be paid by the agency on a single claim.

(d) The total of all amounts paid by a state agency from money appropriated to the agency for any fiscal year under this section may not exceed a limitation imposed by the General Appropriations Act on the amount that may be paid under this section by a state agency for that fiscal year.

Added by Acts 1993, 73rd Leg., ch. 1005, § 1, eff. Sept. 1, 1993. Amended by Acts 2001, 77th Leg., ch. 1414, § 2, eff. Sept. 1, 2001.

§ 109.005. Reports

(a) The comptroller shall notify an affected state agency of:

(1) each claim subject to this chapter paid by the comptroller under this chapter for that state agency;

(2) the amount of the claim;

(3) the amount of the claim paid from a special fund or account; and

(4) the subject matter of the claim.

(b) Each agency shall summarize the information reported to it by the comptroller under Subsection (a) and report that information as part of the agency's annual report to the budget division of the governor's office and to the Legislative Budget Board as required by the General Appropriations Act.

Added by Acts 1993, 73rd Leg., ch. 1005, § 1, eff. Sept. 1, 1993. Amended by Acts 2001, 77th Leg., ch. 1414, § 3, eff. Sept. 1, 2001.

§ 109.006. Appropriation for Claim Not Limited

This chapter does not limit the amount the legislature may appropriate to pay claims subject to this chapter.

Added by Acts 1993, 73rd Leg., ch. 1005, § 1, eff. Sept. 1, 1993.

§ 109.007. Exceptions

This chapter does not apply to an appropriation:

(1) to pay or indemnify a person for a negligent act or omission in the diagnosis, care, or treatment of a health care or mental health care patient, without regard to whether the claim is based on tort or contract principles;

(2) to pay a claim based on the conduct of a state medical school or of a hospital affiliated with an institution of higher education of this state;

(3) to pay a claim based on the conduct of an institution of higher education; or

(4) to pay a claim based on the conduct of a state law enforcement agency, including the Texas Department of Public Safety, or of a state corrections agency, including the Texas Department of Criminal Justice and the Board of Pardons and Paroles.

Added by Acts 1993, 73rd Leg., ch. 1005, § 1, eff. Sept. 1, 1993.

CHAPTER 110. RELIGIOUS FREEDOM

Section

A former Chapter 110, State Liability for Indemnification of Certain Health Care Professionals, consisting of §§ 110.001 to 110.007, expired September 1, 1997, pursuant to former § 110.007.

§ 110.001. Definitions

(a) In this chapter:

(1) "Free exercise of religion" means an act or refusal to act that is substantially motivated by sincere religious belief. In determining whether an act or refusal to act is substantially motivated by sincere religious belief under this chapter, it is not necessary to determine that the act or refusal to act is motivated by a central part or central requirement of the person's sincere religious belief.

(2) "Government agency" means:

(A) this state or a municipality or other political subdivision of this state; and

(B) any agency of this state or a municipality or other political subdivision of this state, including a department, bureau, board, commission, office, agency, council, or public institution of higher education.

(3) "Place of worship" means a building or grounds where religious activities are conducted.

(4) "Public official" means any elected or appointed officer, employee, or agent of this state or any political subdivision, board, commission, bureau, or other public body established by law.

(b) In determining whether an interest is a compelling governmental interest under Section 110.003, a court shall give weight to the interpretation of compelling interest in federal case law relating to the free exercise of religion clause of the First Amendment of the United States Constitution.

Added by Acts 1999, 76th Leg., ch. 399, § 1, eff. Aug. 30, 1999. Amended by Acts 2021, 87th Leg., ch. 799 (H.B. 1239), § 1, eff. June 16, 2021.

Section 5 of Acts 2021, 87th Leg., ch. 799 (H.B. 1239) provides:

"Chapter 110, Civil Practice and Remedies Code, as amended by this Act, applies only to a claim or defense that accrues on or after the effective date [June 16, 2021] of this Act. A claim or defense that accrued before the effective date of this Act is governed by the law in effect immediately before the effective date of this Act, and that law is continued in effect for that purpose."

§ 110.002. Application

(a) This chapter applies to any ordinance, rule, order, decision, practice, or other exercise of governmental authority.

(b) This chapter applies to an act of a government agency, in the exercise of governmental authority, granting or refusing to grant a government benefit to an individual.

(c) This chapter applies to each law of this state unless the law is expressly made exempt from the application of this chapter by reference to this chapter.

(d) For purposes of a state of disaster declared under Chapter 418, Government Code:

(1) this chapter is not considered a regulatory statute; and

(2) a provision of this chapter may not be suspended.

Added by Acts 1999, 76th Leg., ch. 399, § 1, eff. Aug. 30, 1999. Amended by Acts 2021, 87th Leg., ch. 799 (H.B. 1239), § 2, eff. June 16, 2021.

Section 5 of Acts 2021, 87th Leg., ch. 799 (H.B. 1239) provides:

"Chapter 110, Civil Practice and Remedies Code, as amended by this Act, applies only to a claim or defense that accrues on or after the effective date [June 16, 2021] of this Act. A claim or defense that accrued before the effective date of this Act is governed by the law in effect immediately before the effective date of this Act, and that law is continued in effect for that purpose."

§ 110.003. Religious Freedom Protected

(a) Subject to Subsection (b), a government agency may not substantially burden a person's free exercise of religion.

(b) Subsection (a) does not apply if the government agency demonstrates that the application of the burden to the person:

(1) is in furtherance of a compelling governmental interest; and

(2) is the least restrictive means of furthering that interest.

(c) A government agency that makes the demonstration required by Subsection (b) is not required to separately prove that the remedy and penalty provisions of the law, ordinance, rule, order, decision, practice, or other exercise of governmental authority that imposes the substantial burden are the least restrictive means to ensure compliance or to punish the failure to comply.

Added by Acts 1999, 76th Leg., ch. 399, § 1, eff. Aug. 30, 1999.

§ 110.0031. Prohibition on Orders Closing Places of Worship

A government agency or public official may not issue an order that closes or has the effect of closing places of worship in this state or in a geographic area of this state.

Added by Acts 2021, 87th Leg., ch. 799 (H.B. 1239), § 3, eff. June 16, 2021.

Section 5 of Acts 2021, 87th Leg., ch. 799 (H.B. 1239) provides:

"Chapter 110, Civil Practice and Remedies Code, as amended by this Act, applies only to a claim or defense that accrues on or after the effective date [June 16, 2021] of this Act. A claim or defense that accrued before the effective date of this Act is governed by the law in effect immediately before the effective date of this Act, and that law is continued in effect for that purpose."

§ 110.004. Defense

A person whose free exercise of religion has been substantially burdened in violation of Section 110.003 or 110.0031 may assert that violation as a defense in a judicial or administrative proceeding without regard to whether the proceeding is brought in the name of the state or by any other person.

Added by Acts 1999, 76th Leg., ch. 399, § 1, eff. Aug. 30, 1999. Amended by Acts 2021, 87th Leg., ch. 799 (H.B. 1239), § 4, eff. June 16, 2021.

Section 5 of Acts 2021, 87th Leg., ch. 799 (H.B. 1239) provides:

"Chapter 110, Civil Practice and Remedies Code, as amended by this Act, applies only to a claim or defense that accrues on or after the effective date [June 16, 2021] of this Act. A claim or defense that accrued before the effective date of this Act is governed by the law in effect immediately before the effective date of this Act, and that law is continued in effect for that purpose."

§ 110.005. Remedies

(a) Any person, other than a government agency, who successfully asserts a claim or defense under this chapter is entitled to recover:

(1) declaratory relief under Chapter 37;

(2) injunctive relief to prevent the threatened violation or continued violation;

(3) compensatory damages for pecuniary and nonpecuniary losses; and

(4) reasonable attorney's fees, court costs, and other reasonable expenses incurred in bringing the action.

(b) Compensatory damages awarded under Subsection (a)(3) may not exceed $10,000 for each entire, distinct controversy, without regard to the number of members or other persons within a religious group who claim injury as a result of the government agency's exercise of governmental authority. A claimant is not entitled to recover exemplary damages under this chapter.

(c) An action under this section must be brought in district court.

(d) A person may not bring an action for damages or declaratory or injunctive relief against an individual, other than an action brought against an individual acting in the individual's official capacity as an officer of a government agency.

(e) This chapter does not affect the application of Section 498.0045 or 501.008, Government Code, or Chapter 14 of this code.

Added by Acts 1999, 76th Leg., ch. 399, § 1, eff. Aug. 30, 1999.

§ 110.006. Notice; Right to Accommodate

(a) A person may not bring an action to assert a claim under this chapter unless, 60 days before bringing the action, the person gives written notice to the government agency by certified mail, return receipt requested:

(1) that the person's free exercise of religion is substantially burdened by an exercise of the government agency's governmental authority;

(2) of the particular act or refusal to act that is burdened; and

(3) of the manner in which the exercise of governmental authority burdens the act or refusal to act.

(b) Notwithstanding Subsection (a), a claimant may, within the 60-day period established by Subsection (a), bring an action for declaratory or injunctive relief and associated attorney's fees, court costs, and other reasonable expenses, if:

(1) the exercise of governmental authority that threatens to substantially burden the person's free exercise of religion is imminent; and

(2) the person was not informed and did not otherwise have knowledge of the exercise of the governmental authority in time to reasonably provide the notice.

(c) A government agency that receives a notice under Subsection (a) may remedy the substantial burden on the person's free exercise of religion.

(d) A remedy implemented by a government agency under this section:

(1) may be designed to reasonably remove the substantial burden on the person's free exercise of religion;

(2) need not be implemented in a manner that results in an exercise of governmental authority that is the least restrictive means of furthering the governmental interest, notwithstanding any other provision of this chapter; and

(3) must be narrowly tailored to remove the particular burden for which the remedy is implemented.

(e) A person with respect to whom a substantial burden on the person's free exercise of religion has been cured by a remedy implemented under this section may not bring an action under Section 110.005.

(f) A person who complies with an inmate grievance system as required under Section 501.008, Government Code, is not required to provide a separate written notice under Subsection (a). In conjunction with the inmate grievance system, the government agency may remedy a substantial burden on the person's free exercise of religion in the manner described by, and subject to, Subsections (c), (d), and (e).

(g) In dealing with a claim that a person's free exercise of religion has been substantially burdened in violation of this chapter, an inmate grievance system, including an inmate grievance system required under Section 501.008, Government Code, must provide to the person making the claim a statement of the government agency's rationale for imposing the burden, if any exists, in connection with any adverse determination made in connection with the claim.

Added by Acts 1999, 76th Leg., ch. 399, § 1, eff. Aug. 30, 1999.

§ 110.007. One-Year Limitations Period

(a) A person must bring an action to assert a claim for damages under this chapter not later than one year after the date the person knew or should have known of the substantial burden on the person's free exercise of religion.

(b) Mailing notice under Section 110.006 tolls the limitations period established under this section until the 75th day after the date on which the notice was mailed.

Added by Acts 1999, 76th Leg., ch. 399, § 1, eff. Aug. 30, 1999.

§ 110.008. Sovereign Immunity Waived

(a) Subject to Section 110.006, sovereign immunity to suit and from liability is waived and abolished to the extent of liability created by Section 110.005, and a claimant may sue a government agency for damages allowed by that section.

(b) Notwithstanding Subsection (a), this chapter does not waive or abolish sovereign immunity to suit and from liability under the Eleventh Amendment to the United States Constitution.

Added by Acts 1999, 76th Leg., ch. 399, § 1, eff. Aug. 30, 1999.

§ 110.009. Effect on Rights

(a) This chapter does not authorize a government agency to burden a person's free exercise of religion.

(b) The protection of religious freedom afforded by this chapter is in addition to the protections provided under federal law and the constitutions of this state and the United States. This chapter may not be construed to affect or interpret Section 4, 5, 6, or 7, Article I, Texas Constitution.

Added by Acts 1999, 76th Leg., ch. 399, § 1, eff. Aug. 30, 1999.

§ 110.010. Application to Certain Cases

Notwithstanding any other provision of this chapter, a municipality has no less authority to adopt or apply laws and regulations concerning zoning, land use planning, traffic management, urban nuisance, or historic preservation than the authority of the municipality that existed under the law as interpreted by the federal courts before April 17, 1990. This chapter does not affect the authority of a municipality to adopt or apply laws and regulations as that authority has been interpreted by any court in cases that do not involve the free exercise of religion.

Added by Acts 1999, 76th Leg., ch. 399, § 1, eff. Aug. 30, 1999.

§ 110.011. Civil Rights

(a) Except as provided in Subsection (b), this chapter does not establish or eliminate a defense to a civil action or criminal prosecution under a federal or state civil rights law.

(b) This chapter is fully applicable to claims regarding the employment, education, or volunteering of those who perform duties, such as spreading or teaching faith, performing devotional services, or internal governance, for a religious organization. For the purposes of this subsection, an organization is a religious organization if:

(1) the organization's primary purpose and function are religious, it is a religious school organized primarily for religious and educational purposes, or it is a religious charity organized primarily for religious and charitable purposes; and

(2) it does not engage in activities that would disqualify it from tax exempt status under Section 501(c)(3), Internal Revenue Code of 1986, as it existed on August 30, 1999.

Added by Acts 1999, 76th Leg., ch. 399, § 1, eff. Aug. 30, 1999.

§ 110.012. Grant to Religious Organization Not Affected

Notwithstanding Section 110.002(b), this chapter does not affect the grant or denial of an appropriation or other grant of money or benefits to a religious organization, nor does it affect the grant or denial of a tax exemption to a religious organization.

Added by Acts 1999, 76th Leg., ch. 399, § 1, eff. Aug. 30, 1999.

CHAPTER 111. LIMITATION ON SETTLEMENT OF CLAIM OR ACTION AGAINST THE STATE

Section

§ 111.001. Purpose; Applicability

(a) The purposes of this chapter include providing a means for the legislature to determine the extent to which this state waives its sovereign immunity with regard to a settlement of a claim or action against the state that requires an expenditure of state funds.

(b) This chapter applies to any settlement described by Section 111.003(a) of a claim or action against this state seeking any relief under any theory of recovery, including a mandamus action against a state officer or official, that is brought or may be brought in or before any court, administrative agency, or other tribunal.

(c) For purposes of this chapter, a reference to this state includes any agency, institution, or other entity of state government.

(d) This chapter does not apply to a refund of a tax, fee, or any related penalty or interest.

Added by Acts 2007, 80th Leg., ch. 1004, § 1, eff. June 15, 2007.

§ 111.002. Definition

In this chapter, "settlement" includes a consent decree, an agreed judgment, or any other settlement or compromise of a claim or action.

Added by Acts 2007, 80th Leg., ch. 1004, § 1, eff. June 15, 2007.

§ 111.003. Limitation on Settlement Without Legislative Consent or Approval

(a) The attorney general or other attorney representing this state may not enter into a settlement of a claim or action against this state without the consent or approval of the legislature in accordance with this chapter if the settlement:

(1) requires this state to pay total monetary damages in an amount that exceeds $10,000,000 in a state fiscal biennium; or

(2) commits this state to a course of action that in reasonable probability will entail a continuing increased expenditure of state funds over subsequent state fiscal bienniums.

(b) A settlement described by Subsection (a) entered into without the prior consent or approval of the legislature is void unless the settlement is expressly conditioned on obtaining subsequent approval by the legislature in accordance with this chapter.

Added by Acts 2007, 80th Leg., ch. 1004, § 1, eff. June 15, 2007. Amended by Acts 2011, 82nd Leg., ch. 424 (S.B. 899), § 1, eff. Sept. 1, 2011.

§ 111.004. Form of Consent or Approval

(a) The legislature may consent to or approve a settlement described by Section 111.003(a) only by a resolution adopted by both houses of the legislature.

(b) Legislative consent under this chapter may but is not required to be expressed in the form of a resolution granting permission to sue the state that limits the relief to which a claimant may be entitled or provides additional conditions to which a grant of permission to sue is subject.

Added by Acts 2007, 80th Leg., ch. 1004, § 1, eff. June 15, 2007.

§ 111.005. Appropriations

(a) An appropriation of state funds to pay or comply with a settlement does not constitute consent to or approval of the settlement for purposes of this chapter.

(b) A resolution consenting to or approving a settlement under this chapter does not and may not require the legislature to appropriate a particular amount for a particular purpose.

Added by Acts 2007, 80th Leg., ch. 1004, § 1, eff. June 15, 2007.

§ 111.006. Report by Attorney General

Not later than September 1 of each even-numbered year, the attorney general shall send to the lieutenant governor, the speaker of the house of representatives, and each member of the Senate Finance Committee and the House Appropriations Committee a report describing each claim or action pending as of September 1 of that year that has been or that in the opinion of the attorney general may be settled in a manner that will require prior consent or subsequent approval by the legislature under this chapter.

Added by Acts 2007, 80th Leg., ch. 1004, § 1, eff. June 15, 2007.

CHAPTER 112. LIMITATION OF LIABILITY FOR GOVERNMENTAL UNITS

§ 112.001. Certain Actions of First Responders and Volunteer Emergency Services Personnel

(a) In this section:

(1) "First responder" and "volunteer emergency services personnel" have the meanings assigned by Section 46.01, Penal Code.

(2) "Governmental unit" has the meaning assigned by Section 101.001.

(b) A governmental unit is not liable in a civil action arising from the discharge of a handgun by an individual who is a first responder or volunteer emergency services personnel and licensed to carry the handgun under Subchapter H, Chapter 411, Government Code.[1]

(c) The discharge of a handgun by an individual who is a first responder or volunteer emergency services personnel and licensed to carry the handgun under Subchapter H, Chapter 411, Government Code, is outside the course and scope of the individual's duties as a first responder or volunteer emergency services personnel, as applicable.

(d) This section may not be construed to waive the immunity from suit or liability of a governmental unit under Chapter 101 or any other law.

Added by Acts 2017, 85th Leg., ch. 1143 (H.B. 435), § 1, eff. Sept. 1, 2017. Amended by Acts 2021, 87th Leg., ch. 1026 (H.B. 1069), §§ 1, 2, eff. Sept. 1, 2021.

[1] V.T.C.A. Government Code § 411.171 et seq.

Section 11 of Acts 2021, 87th Leg., ch. 1026 (H.B. 1069) provides:

"Section 112.001, Civil Practice and Remedies Code, as amended by this Act, applies only to a cause of action that accrues on or after September 1, 2021. A cause of action that accrues before September 1, 2021, is governed by the law in effect immediately before that date, and the former law is continued in effect for that purpose."

CHAPTER 113. WATER SUPPLY CONTRACT CLAIM AGAINST LOCAL DISTRICT OR AUTHORITY

§ 113.001. Definitions

In this chapter:

(1) "Adjudicating a claim" means the bringing of a civil suit and prosecution to final judgment in court and includes the bringing of an authorized arbitration proceeding and prosecution to final resolution in accordance with any mandatory procedures established in the contract that is the subject of the dispute under Section 113.002.

(2) "Local district or authority" means a special-purpose district or authority, including a levee improvement district, drainage district, irrigation district, water improvement district, water control and improvement district, water control and preservation district, fresh water supply district, navigation district, special utility district, and river authority, and any conservation and reclamation district.

Added by Acts 2013, 83rd Leg., ch. 1138 (H.B. 3511), § 1, eff. June 14, 2013; Acts 2013, 83rd Leg., ch. 1340 (S.B. 958), § 1, eff. June 14, 2013.

§ 113.002. Waiver of Immunity to Suit for Claim Regarding Water Supply Contract

A local district or authority that enters into a written contract stating the essential terms under which the local district or authority is to provide water to a purchaser for use in connection with the generation of electricity waives sovereign immunity to suit for the purpose of adjudicating a claim that the local district or authority breached the contract by not providing water, or access to water, according to the contract's terms.

Added by Acts 2013, 83rd Leg., ch. 1138 (H.B. 3511), § 1, eff. June 14, 2013; Acts 2013, 83rd Leg., ch. 1340 (S.B. 958), § 1, eff. June 14, 2013.

§ 113.003. Remedies

(a) Except as provided by Subsection (b), remedies awarded in a proceeding adjudicating a claim under this chapter may include any remedy available for breach of contract that is not inconsistent with the terms of the contract, including the cost of cover and specific performance.

(b) Remedies awarded in a proceeding adjudicating a claim under this chapter may not include consequential or exemplary damages.

Added by Acts 2013, 83rd Leg., ch. 1138 (H.B. 3511), § 1, eff. June 14, 2013; Acts 2013, 83rd Leg., ch. 1340 (S.B. 958), § 1, eff. June 14, 2013.

§ 113.004. No Waiver of Other Defenses

This chapter does not waive a defense or a limitation on damages available to a party to a contract other than sovereign immunity to suit.

Added by Acts 2013, 83rd Leg., ch. 1138 (H.B. 3511), § 1, eff. June 14, 2013; Acts 2013, 83rd Leg., ch. 1340 (S.B. 958), § 1, eff. June 14, 2013.

§ 113.005. No Waiver of Immunity to Suit in Federal Court

This chapter does not waive sovereign immunity to suit in federal court.

Added by Acts 2013, 83rd Leg., ch. 1138 (H.B. 3511), § 1, eff. June 14, 2013; Acts 2013, 83rd Leg., ch. 1340 (S.B. 958), § 1, eff. June 14, 2013.

§ 113.006. No Waiver of Immunity to Suit for Tort Liability

This chapter does not waive sovereign immunity to suit for a cause of action for a negligent or intentional tort.

Added by Acts 2013, 83rd Leg., ch. 1138 (H.B. 3511), § 1, eff. June 14, 2013; Acts 2013, 83rd Leg., ch. 1340 (S.B. 958), § 1, eff. June 14, 2013.

§ 113.007. No New or Additional Water Rights

This chapter does not grant any user of water any new or additional rights to water or any new or additional priority to water rights. This chapter does not confer any rights inconsistent with the terms of the contract that is the subject of a dispute under Section 113.002.

Added by Acts 2013, 83rd Leg., ch. 1138 (H.B. 3511), § 1, eff. June 14, 2013; Acts 2013, 83rd Leg., ch. 1340 (S.B. 958), § 1, eff. June 14, 2013.

§ 113.008. Authority of Regulatory Agencies; Compliance with Regulatory Order

(a) This chapter does not limit the authority of the Texas Commission on Environmental Quality or any other state regulatory agency.

(b) Compliance with an order of the Texas Commission on Environmental Quality, or any other state regulatory agency that expressly curtails water delivery to a specific electric generating facility is not considered a breach of contract for the purposes of this chapter.

Added by Acts 2013, 83rd Leg., ch. 1138 (H.B. 3511), § 1, eff. June 14, 2013; Acts 2013, 83rd Leg., ch. 1340 (S.B. 958), § 1, eff. June 14, 2013.

§ 113.009. No Third–Party Beneficiaries

(a) This chapter waives sovereign immunity only for the benefit of:

(1) a party to the contract that is the subject of a dispute under Section 113.002; or

(2) the assignee of a party to the contract, if assignment of an interest in the contract is permitted by the terms of the contract.

(b) Except for an assignment described by Subsection (a)(2), a party authorized by this chapter to sue for a cause of action of breach of contract may not transfer or assign that cause of action to any person.

Added by Acts 2013, 83rd Leg., ch. 1138 (H.B. 3511), § 1, eff. June 14, 2013; Acts 2013, 83rd Leg., ch. 1340 (S.B. 958), § 1, eff. June 14, 2013.

CHAPTER 114. ADJUDICATION OF CLAIMS ARISING UNDER WRITTEN CONTRACTS WITH STATE AGENCIES

§ 114.001. Definitions

In this chapter:

(1) "Adjudication" of a claim means the bringing of a civil suit and prosecution to final judgment in county or state court.

(2) "Contract subject to this chapter" means a written contract stating the essential terms of the agreement for providing goods or services to the state agency that is properly executed on behalf of the state agency. The term does not include a contract that is subject to Section 201.112, Transportation Code.

(3) "State agency" means an agency, department, commission, bureau, board, office, council, court, or other entity that is in any branch of state government and that is created by the constitution or a statute of this state, including a university system or a system of higher education. The term does not include a county, municipality, court of a county or municipality, special purpose district, or other political subdivision of this state.

Added by Acts 2013, 83rd Leg., ch. 1260 (H.B. 586), § 1, eff. Sept. 1, 2013.

§ 114.002. Applicability

This chapter applies only to a claim for breach of a written contract for engineering, architectural, or construction services or for materials related to engineering, architectural, or construction services brought by a party to the written contract, in which the amount in controversy is not less than $250,000, excluding penalties, costs, expenses, prejudgment interest, and attorney's fees.

Added by Acts 2013, 83rd Leg., ch. 1260 (H.B. 586), § 1, eff. Sept. 1, 2013.

§ 114.003. Waiver of Immunity to Suit for Certain Claims

A state agency that is authorized by statute or the constitution to enter into a contract and that enters into a contract subject to this chapter waives sovereign immunity to suit for the purpose of adjudicating a claim for breach of an express provision of the contract, subject to the terms and conditions of this chapter.

Added by Acts 2013, 83rd Leg., ch. 1260 (H.B. 586), § 1, eff. Sept. 1, 2013.

§ 114.004. Limitations on Adjudication Awards

(a) The total amount of money awarded in an adjudication brought against a state agency for breach of an express provision of a contract subject to this chapter is limited to the following:

(1) the balance due and owed by the state agency under the contract as it may have been amended, including any amount owed as compensation for the increased cost to perform the work as a direct result of owner-caused delays or acceleration if the contract expressly provides for that compensation;

(2) the amount owed for written change orders;

(3) reasonable and necessary attorney's fees based on an hourly rate that are equitable and just if the contract expressly provides that recovery of attorney's fees is available to all parties to the contract; and

(4) interest at the rate specified by the contract or, if a rate is not specified, the rate for post-judgment interest under Section 304.003(c), Finance Code, but not to exceed 10 percent.

(b) Damages awarded in an adjudication brought against a state agency arising under a contract subject to this chapter may not include:

(1) consequential damages;

(2) exemplary damages; or

(3) damages for unabsorbed home office overhead.

Added by Acts 2013, 83rd Leg., ch. 1260 (H.B. 586), § 1, eff. Sept. 1, 2013.

§ 114.005. Contractual Adjudication Procedures Enforceable

Adjudication procedures, including requirements for serving notices or engaging in alternative dispute resolution proceedings before bringing a suit or an arbitration proceeding, that are stated in the contract subject to this chapter or that are established by the state agency and expressly incorporated into the contract are enforceable, except to the extent those procedures conflict with the terms of this chapter.

Added by Acts 2013, 83rd Leg., ch. 1260 (H.B. 586), § 1, eff. Sept. 1, 2013.

§ 114.006. No Waiver of Other Defenses

This chapter does not waive a defense or a limitation on damages available to a party to a contract, other than a bar against suit based on sovereign immunity.

Added by Acts 2013, 83rd Leg., ch. 1260 (H.B. 586), § 1, eff. Sept. 1, 2013.

§ 114.007. No Waiver of Immunity to Suit in Federal Court

This chapter does not waive sovereign immunity to suit in federal court.

Added by Acts 2013, 83rd Leg., ch. 1260 (H.B. 586), § 1, eff. Sept. 1, 2013.

§ 114.008. No Waiver of Immunity to Suit for Tort Liability

This chapter does not waive sovereign immunity to a claim arising from a cause of action for negligence, fraud, tortious interference with a contract, or any other tort.

Added by Acts 2013, 83rd Leg., ch. 1260 (H.B. 586), § 1, eff. Sept. 1, 2013.

§ 114.009. Employment Contracts Exempt

This chapter does not apply to an employment contract between a state agency and an employee of that agency.

Added by Acts 2013, 83rd Leg., ch. 1260 (H.B. 586), § 1, eff. Sept. 1, 2013.

§ 114.010. Venue

A suit under this chapter may be brought in a district court in:

(1) a county in which the events or omissions giving rise to the claim occurred; or

(2) a county in which the principal office of the state agency is located.

Added by Acts 2013, 83rd Leg., ch. 1260 (H.B. 586), § 1, eff. Sept. 1, 2013.

§ 114.011. Limitation on Remedies

Satisfaction and payment of any judgment under this chapter may not be paid from funds appropriated to the state agency from general revenue unless the funds are specifically appropriated for that purpose. Property of the state or any agency, department, or office of the state is not subject to seizure, attachment, garnishment, or any other creditors' remedy to satisfy a judgment taken under this chapter.

Added by Acts 2013, 83rd Leg., ch. 1260 (H.B. 586), § 1, eff. Sept. 1, 2013.

§ 114.012. Exclusive Remedy

A claim to which this chapter applies may not be brought under Chapter 2260, Government Code, against the state or a unit of state government as defined by Section 2260.001, Government Code.

Added by Acts 2013, 83rd Leg., ch. 1260 (H.B. 586), § 1, eff. Sept. 1, 2013.

§ 114.013. Report

Before January 1 of each even-numbered year, each state agency shall report to the governor, the comptroller, and each house of the legislature the cost of defense to the state agency and the office of the attorney general in an adjudication brought against the agency under a contract subject to this chapter. Included in the report shall be the amount claimed in any adjudication pending on the date of the report.

Added by Acts 2013, 83rd Leg., ch. 1260 (H.B. 586), § 1, eff. Sept. 1, 2013.

CHAPTER 115. [RESERVED]

CHAPTER 116. SETTLEMENT OF CLAIM OR ACTION AGAINST GOVERNMENTAL UNIT

Section

§ 116.001. Definition

In this chapter, "governmental unit" has the meaning assigned by Section 101.001.

Added by Acts 2017, 85th Leg., ch. 688 (H.B. 53), § 1, eff. Sept. 1, 2017.

§ 116.002. Certain Settlement Terms Prohibited

(a) A governmental unit may not enter into a settlement of a claim or action against the governmental unit in which:

(1) the amount of the settlement is equal to or greater than $30,000;

(2) the money that would be used to pay the settlement is:

(A) derived from taxes collected by a governmental unit;

(B) received from the state; or

(C) insurance proceeds received from an insurance policy for which the premium was paid with taxes collected by a governmental unit or money received from the state; and

(3) a condition of the settlement requires a party seeking affirmative relief against the governmental unit to agree not to disclose any fact, allegation, evidence, or other matter to any other person, including a journalist or other member of the media.

(b) A settlement agreement provision entered into in violation of Subsection (a) is void and unenforceable.

Added by Acts 2017, 85th Leg., ch. 688 (H.B. 53), § 1, eff. Sept. 1, 2017.

§ 116.003. Effect of Chapter

This chapter does not affect information that is privileged or confidential under other law.

Added by Acts 2017, 85th Leg., ch. 688 (H.B. 53), § 1, eff. Sept. 1, 2017.

TITLE 6. MISCELLANEOUS PROVISIONS

CHAPTER 121. ACKNOWLEDGMENTS AND PROOFS OF WRITTEN INSTRUMENTS

Section

§ 121.001. Officers Who May Take Acknowledgments or Proofs

(a) An acknowledgment or proof of a written instrument may be taken in this state by:

(1) a clerk of a district court;

(2) a judge or clerk of a county court;

(3) a notary public;

(4) a county tax assessor-collector or an employee of the county tax assessor-collector if the instrument is required or authorized to be filed in the office of the county tax assessor-collector; or

(5) an employee of a personal bond office if the acknowledgment or proof of a written instrument is required or authorized by Article 17.04, Code of Criminal Procedure.

(b) An acknowledgment or proof of a written instrument may be taken outside this state, but inside the United States or its territories, by:

(1) a clerk of a court of record having a seal;

(2) a commissioner of deeds appointed under the laws of this state; or

(3) a notary public.

(c) An acknowledgment or proof of a written instrument may be taken outside the United States or its territories by:

(1) a minister, commissioner, or charge d'affaires of the United States who is a resident of and is accredited in the country where the acknowledgment or proof is taken;

(2) a consul-general, consul, vice-consul, commercial agent, vice-commercial agent, deputy consul, or consular agent of the United States who is a resident of the country where the acknowledgment or proof is taken; or

(3) a notary public or any other official authorized to administer oaths in the jurisdiction where the acknowledgment or proof is taken.

(d) A commissioned officer of the United States Armed Forces or of a United States Armed Forces Auxiliary may take an acknowledgment or proof of a written instrument of a member of the armed forces, a member of an armed forces auxiliary, or a member's spouse. If an acknowledgment or a proof is taken under this subsection, it is presumed, absent pleading and proof to the contrary, that the commissioned officer who signed was a commissioned officer on the date that the officer signed, and that the acknowledging person was a member of the authorized group of military personnel or spouses. The failure of the commissioned officer to attach an official seal to the certificate of acknowledgment or proof of an instrument does not invalidate the acknowledgment or proof.

Acts 1985, 69th Leg., ch. 959, § 1, eff. Sept. 1, 1985. Amended by Acts 1987, 70th Leg., ch. 891, § 1, eff. Sept. 1, 1987; Acts 1995, 74th Leg., ch. 165, § 18, eff. Sept. 1, 1995; Acts 2001, 77th Leg., ch. 986, § 2, eff. June 15, 2001.

§ 121.002. Corporate Acknowledgments

(a) An employee of a corporation is not disqualified because of his employment from taking an acknowledgment or proof of a written instrument in which the corporation has an interest.

(b) An officer who is a shareholder in a corporation is not disqualified from taking an acknowledgment or proof of an instrument in which the corporation has an interest unless:

(1) the corporation has 1,000 or fewer shareholders; and

(2) the officer owns more than one-tenth of one percent of the issued and outstanding stock.

Acts 1985, 69th Leg., ch. 959, § 1, eff. Sept. 1, 1985.

§ 121.003. Authority of Officers

In a proceeding to prove a written instrument, an officer authorized by this chapter to take an acknowledgment or a proof of a written instrument is also authorized to:

(1) administer oaths;

(2) employ and swear interpreters; and

(3) issue subpoenas.

Acts 1985, 69th Leg., ch. 959, § 1, eff. Sept. 1, 1985.

§ 121.004. Method of Acknowledgment

(a) To acknowledge a written instrument for recording, the grantor or person who executed the instrument must appear before an officer and must state that he executed the instrument for the purposes and consideration expressed in it.

(b) The officer shall:

(1) make a certificate of the acknowledgment;

(2) sign the certificate; and

(3) seal the certificate with the seal of office.

(c) The failure of a notary public to attach an official seal to a certificate of an acknowledgement or proof of a written instrument made outside this state but inside the United States or its territories renders the acknowledgement or proof invalid only if the jurisdiction in which the certificate is made requires the notary public to attach the seal.

(d) The application of an embossed seal is not required on an electronically transmitted certificate of an acknowledgement.

Acts 1985, 69th Leg., ch. 959, § 1, eff. Sept. 1, 1985. Amended by Acts 1995, 74th Leg., ch. 603, § 1, eff. June 14, 1995; Acts 2001, 77th Leg., ch. 95, § 1, eff. May 11, 2001.

§ 121.005. Proof of Identity of Acknowledging Person

(a) An officer may not take the acknowledgment of a written instrument unless the officer knows or has satisfactory evidence that the acknowledging person is the person who executed the instrument and is described in it. An officer may accept, as satisfactory evidence of the identity of an acknowledging person, only:

(1) the oath of a credible witness personally known to the officer;

(2) a current identification card or other document issued by the federal government or any state government that contains the photograph and signature of the acknowledging person; or

(3) with respect to a deed or other instrument relating to a residential real estate transaction, a current passport issued by a foreign country.

(b) Except in a short form certificate of acknowledgment authorized by Section 121.008, the officer must note in the certificate of acknowledgment that:

(1) he personally knows the acknowledging person; or

(2) evidence of a witness or an identification card or other document was used to identify the acknowledging person.

Acts 1985, 69th Leg., ch. 959, § 1, eff. Sept. 1, 1985. Amended by Acts 1997, 75th Leg., ch. 90, § 1, eff. Sept. 1, 1997; Acts 2011, 82nd Leg., ch. 1242 (S.B. 1320), § 2, eff. Sept. 1, 2011.

§ 121.006. Alteration of Authorized Forms; Definition

(a) An acknowledgment form provided by this chapter may be altered as circumstances require. The authorization of a form does not prevent the use of other forms. The marital status or other status of the acknowledging person may be shown after the person's name.

(b) In an acknowledgment form "acknowledged" means:

(1) in the case of a natural person, that the person personally appeared before the officer taking the acknowledgment and acknowledged executing the instrument for the purposes and consideration expressed in it;

(2) in the case of a person as principal by an attorney-in-fact for the principal, that the attorney-in-fact personally appeared before the officer taking the acknowledgment and that the attorney-in-fact acknowledged executing the instrument as the act of the principal for the purposes and consideration expressed in it;

(3) in the case of a partnership by a partner, partners, authorized officer, or agent acting for the partnership, that the partner, partners, authorized officer, or agent personally appeared before the officer taking the acknowledgment and acknowledged executing the instrument in the capacity stated, as the act of the partnership, for the purposes and consideration expressed in it;

(4) in the case of a corporation by a corporate officer or agent, that the corporate officer or agent personally appeared before the officer taking the acknowledgment and that the corporate officer or agent acknowledged executing the instrument in the capacity stated, as the act of the corporation, for the purposes and consideration expressed in it;

(5) in the case of a person acknowledging as a public officer, trustee, executor or administrator of an estate, guardian, or other representative, that the person personally appeared before the officer taking the acknowledgment and acknowledged executing the instrument by proper authority in the capacity stated and for the purposes and consideration expressed in it; and

(6) in the case of a limited liability company by a member, manager, authorized officer, or agent acting for the limited liability company, that the member, manager, authorized officer, or agent personally appeared before the officer taking the acknowledgment and acknowledged executing the instrument in the capacity stated, as the act of the limited liability company, for the purposes and consideration expressed in it.

(c) For purposes of Subsection (b), a person may personally appear before the officer taking the acknowledgment by:

(1) physically appearing before the officer; or

(2) appearing by an interactive two-way audio and video communication that meets the online notarization requirements under Subchapter C, Chapter 406, Government Code,[1] and rules adopted under that subchapter.

(d) The acknowledgment form provided by this chapter must include a space for an online notarization as defined by Section 406.101, Government Code, to indicate by which method described by Subsection (c) the acknowledging person appeared before the officer.

Acts 1985, 69th Leg., ch. 959, § 1, eff. Sept. 1, 1985. Amended by Acts 2017, 85th Leg., ch. 340 (H.B. 1217), § 1, eff. July 1, 2018; Acts 2019, 86th Leg., ch. 32 (H.B. 1159), § 1, eff. Sept. 1, 2019.

[1] V.T.C.A., Government Code § 406.101 et seq.

§ 121.007. Form for Ordinary Certificate of Acknowledgment

The form of an ordinary certificate of acknowledgment must be substantially as follows:

"The State of ________,

"County of ________,

"Before me ________ (here insert the name and character of the officer) on this day personally appeared ________, known to me (or proved to me on the oath of ________ or through ________ (description of identity card or other document)) to be the person whose name is subscribed to the foregoing instrument and acknowledged to me that he executed the same for the purposes and consideration therein expressed.

(Seal) "Given under my hand and seal of office this ________ day of ________, A.D., ________."

Acts 1985, 69th Leg., ch. 959, § 1, eff. Sept. 1, 1985. Amended by Acts 1997, 75th Leg., ch. 90, § 1, eff. Sept. 1, 1997.

§ 121.008. Short Forms for Certificates of Acknowledgment

(a) The forms for certificates of acknowledgment provided by this section may be used as alternatives to other authorized forms. They may be referred to as "statutory forms of acknowledgment."

(b) Short forms for certificates of acknowledgment include:

(1) For a natural person acting in his own right:

State of Texas

County of ________

This instrument was acknowledged before me on (date) by (name or names of person or persons acknowledging).

(Signature of officer)

(Title of officer)

My commission expires: ________

(2) For a natural person as principal acting by attorney-in-fact:

State of Texas

County of ________

This instrument was acknowledged before me on (date) by (name of attorney-in-fact) as attorney-in-fact on behalf of (name of principal).

(Signature of officer)

(Title of officer)

My commission expires: ________

(3) For a partnership acting by one or more partners, an authorized officer, or an agent:

State of Texas

County of ________

This instrument was acknowledged before me on (date) by (name of acknowledging partner, partners, authorized officer, or agent), (partner(s), authorized officer, or agent) on behalf of (name of partnership), a partnership.

(Signature of officer)

(Title of officer)

My commission expires: ________

(4) For a corporation:

State of Texas

County of ________

This instrument was acknowledged before me on (date) by (name of officer), (title of officer) of (name of corporation acknowledging) a (state of incorporation) corporation, on behalf of said corporation.

(Signature of officer)

(Title of officer)

My commission expires: ________

(5) For a public officer, trustee, executor, administrator, guardian, or other representative:

State of Texas

County of ________

This instrument was acknowledged before me on (date) by (name of representative) as (title of representative) of (name of entity or person represented).

(Signature of officer)

(Title of officer)

My commission expires: ________

(6) For a limited liability company:

State of Texas

County of ________

This instrument was acknowledged before me on (date) by (name of acknowledging member, manager, authorized officer, or agent), a (member, manager, authorized officer, or agent) of (name of limited liability company) on behalf of (name of limited liability company), a limited liability company.

(Signature of officer)

(Title of officer)

My commission expires: ________

Acts 1985, 69th Leg., ch. 959, § 1, eff. Sept. 1, 1985. Amended by Acts 2019, 86th Leg., ch. 32 (H.B. 1159), § 2, eff. Sept. 1, 2019.

§ 121.009. Proof of Acknowledgment by Witness

(a) To prove a written instrument for recording, at least one of the witnesses who signed the instrument must personally appear before an officer who is authorized by this chapter to take acknowledgments or proofs and must swear:

(1) either that he saw the grantor or person who executed the instrument sign it or that that person acknowledged in the presence of the witness that he executed the instrument for the purposes and consideration expressed in it; and

(2) that he signed the instrument at the request of the grantor or person who executed the instrument.

(b) The officer must make a certificate of the testimony of the witness and must sign and officially seal the certificate.

(c) The officer may take the testimony of a witness only if the officer personally knows or has satisfactory evidence on the oath of a credible witness that the individual testifying is the person who signed the instrument as a witness. If evidence is used to identify the witness who signed the instrument, the officer must note the use of the evidence in the certificate of acknowledgment.

Acts 1985, 69th Leg., ch. 959, § 1, eff. Sept. 1, 1985.

§ 121.010. Form of Certificate for Proof by Witness

When the execution of a written instrument is proved by a witness, the certificate of the officer must be substantially as follows:

"The State of ________

"County of ________.

"Before me, ________ (here insert the name and character of the officer), on this day personally appeared ________, known to me (or proved to me on the oath of ________), to be the person whose name is subscribed as a witness to the foregoing instrument of writing, and after being duly sworn by me stated on oath that he saw ________, the grantor or person who executed the foregoing instrument, subscribe the same (or that the grantor or person who executed such instrument of writing acknowledged in his presence that he had executed the same for the purposes and consideration therein expressed), and that he had signed the same as a witness at the request of the grantor (or person who executed the same.)

(Seal) "Given under my hand and seal of office this ________ day of ________, A.D., ________."

Acts 1985, 69th Leg., ch. 959, § 1, eff. Sept. 1, 1985.

§ 121.011. Proof of Acknowledgment by Handwriting

(a) The execution of an instrument may be established for recording by proof of the handwriting of persons who signed the instrument only if:

(1) the grantor of the instrument and all of the witnesses are dead;

(2) the grantor and all of the witnesses are not residents of this state;

(3) the residences of the grantor and the witnesses are unknown to the person seeking to prove the instrument and cannot be ascertained;

(4) the witnesses have become legally incompetent to testify; or

(5) the grantor of the instrument refuses to acknowledge the execution of the instrument and all of the witnesses are dead, not residents of this state, or legally incompetent or their places of residence are unknown.

(b) If the grantor or person who executed the instrument signed his name to the instrument, its execution must be proved by evidence of the handwriting of that person and at least one witness who signed the instrument. If the grantor or person who executed the instrument signed the instrument by making his mark, its execution must be proved by the handwriting of at least two of the witnesses who signed the instrument.

(c) Evidence taken for proof of handwriting must give the residence of the testifying witness. A testifying witness must have known the person whose handwriting is being proved and must be well acquainted with the handwriting in question and recognize it as genuine.

(d) Evidence offered for proof of handwriting must be given in writing by the deposition or affidavit of two or more disinterested persons. The evidence must satisfactorily prove to the officer each of the requirements provided by this section. The officer taking the proof must certify the witnesses' testimony. The officer must sign, officially seal, and attach this certificate to the instrument with the depositions or affidavits of the witnesses.

Acts 1985, 69th Leg., ch. 959, § 1, eff. Sept. 1, 1985.

§ 121.012. Record of Acknowledgment

(a) An officer authorized by law to take an acknowledgment or proof of a written instrument required or permitted by law to be recorded must enter in a well-bound book and officially sign a short statement of each acknowledgment or proof. The statement must contain the date that the acknowledgment or proof was taken, the date of the instrument, and the names of the grantor and grantee of the instrument.

(b) If the execution of the instrument is acknowledged by the grantor of the instrument, the statement must also contain:

(1) the grantor's mailing address;

(2) whether the grantor is personally known to the officer; and

(3) if the grantor is unknown to the officer, the name and mailing address of the person who introduced the grantor to the officer, if any.

(c) If the execution of the instrument is proved by a witness who signed the instrument, the statement must also contain:

(1) the name of the witness;

(2) the mailing address of the witness;

(3) whether the witness is personally known to the officer; and

(4) if the witness is unknown to the officer, the name and mailing address of the person who introduced the witness to the officer, if any.

(d) If land is charged or conveyed by the instrument, the statement must also contain:

(1) the name of the original grantee; and

(2) the name of the county in which the land is located.

(e) The statements of acknowledgment recorded by the officer are original public records, open for public inspection and examination at all reasonable times. The officer must deliver the book to his successor in office.

Acts 1985, 69th Leg., ch. 959, § 1, eff. Sept. 1, 1985. Amended by Acts 2017, 85th Leg., ch. 731 (S.B. 1098), § 2, eff. Sept. 1, 2017.

§ 121.013. Subpoena of Witness; Attachment

(a) On the sworn application of a person interested in the proof of an instrument required or permitted by law to be recorded, stating that a witness to the instrument refuses to appear and testify regarding the execution of the instrument and that the instrument cannot be proven without the evidence of the witness, an officer authorized to take proofs of instruments shall issue a subpoena requiring the witness to appear before the officer and testify about the execution of the instrument.

(b) If the witness fails to obey the subpoena, the officer has the same powers to enforce the attendance and compel the answers of the witness as does a district judge. Attachment may not be issued, however, unless the witness receives or is tendered the same compensation that is made to witnesses in other cases. An officer may not require the witness to leave his county of residence, but if the witness is temporarily present in the county where the execution of the instrument is sought to be proven for registration, he may be required to appear.

Acts 1985, 69th Leg., ch. 959, § 1, eff. Sept. 1, 1985.

§ 121.014. Action for Damages

A person injured by the failure, refusal, or neglect of an officer to comply with a provision of this chapter has a cause of action against the officer to recover damages resulting from the failure, refusal, or neglect of the officer.

Acts 1985, 69th Leg., ch. 959, § 1, eff. Sept. 1, 1985.

§ 121.015. Private Seal or Scroll Not Required

A private seal or scroll may not be required on a written instrument other than an instrument made by a corporation.

Added by Acts 1993, 73rd Leg., ch. 268, § 2, eff. Sept. 1, 1993.

§ 121.016. Effect of Other Law

To the extent that a provision of this chapter conflicts with Subchapter C, Chapter 406, Government Code, that subchapter controls with respect to an online notarization as defined by Section 406.101, Government Code.

Added by Acts 2017, 85th Leg., ch. 340 (H.B. 1217), § 2, eff. July 1, 2018.

CHAPTER 122. JUROR'S RIGHT TO REEMPLOYMENT

§ 122.001. Protection of Jurors' Employment; Juror's Right to Reemployment; Notice of Intent to Return

(a) An employer may not discharge, threaten to discharge, intimidate, or coerce any permanent employee because the employee serves as a juror or grand juror, or for the employee's attendance or scheduled attendance in connection with the service, in any court in the United States.

(b) An employee who is discharged, threatened with discharge, intimidated, or coerced in violation of this section is entitled to return to the same employment that the employee held when summoned for jury or grand jury service if the employee, as soon as practical after release from that service, gives the employer actual notice that the employee intends to return.

Acts 1985, 69th Leg., ch. 959, § 1, eff. Sept. 1, 1985. Amended by Acts 2019, 86th Leg., ch. 234 (S.B. 370), § 1, eff. Sept. 1, 2019; Acts 2019, 86th Leg., ch. 356 (H.B. 504), § 1, eff. Sept. 1, 2019.

Section 5 of Acts 2019, 86th Leg., ch. 356 (H.B. 504) provides:

"The change in law made by this Act applies only to an employer who terminates, threatens to terminate, penalizes, or threatens to penalize an employee on or after the effective date [Sept. 1, 2019] of this Act."

§ 122.002. Damages; Reinstatement; Attorney's Fees

(a) A person who is injured because of a violation of this chapter is entitled to reinstatement to the person's former position and to damages in an amount not less than an amount equal to one year's compensation nor more than an amount equal to five years' compensation at the rate at which the person was compensated when summoned for jury or grand jury service.

(b) The injured person is also entitled to reasonable attorney's fees in an amount approved by the court.

(c) An action for damages brought by a person under Subsection (a) must be brought not later than the second anniversary of the date on which the person served as a juror or grand juror.

Acts 1985, 69th Leg., ch. 959, § 1, eff. Sept. 1, 1985. Amended by Acts 1991, 72nd Leg., ch. 442, § 5, eff. Jan. 1, 1992; Acts 1999, 76th Leg., ch. 770, § 1, eff. Sept. 1, 1999; Acts 2019, 86th Leg., ch. 356 (H.B. 504), § 2, eff. Sept. 1, 2019.

Section 5 of Acts 2019, 86th Leg., ch. 356 (H.B. 504) provides:

"The change in law made by this Act applies only to an employer who terminates, threatens to terminate, penalizes, or threatens to penalize an employee on or after the effective date [Sept. 1, 2019] of this Act."

§ 122.0021. Criminal Penalty

(a) A person commits an offense if the person violates Section 122.001.

(b) An offense under this section is a Class B misdemeanor.

Added by Acts 1999, 76th Leg., ch. 770, § 2, eff. Sept. 1, 1999.

§ 122.0022. Contempt

In addition to and without limiting any other sanction or remedy available under this chapter or other law, a court may punish by contempt an employer who terminates, threatens to terminate, penalizes, or threatens to penalize an employee because the employee performs jury or grand jury duty.

Added by Acts 1999, 76th Leg., ch. 770, § 2, eff. Sept. 1, 1999. Amended by Acts 2019, 86th Leg., ch. 356 (H.B. 504), § 3, eff. Sept. 1, 2019.

Section 5 of Acts 2019, 86th Leg., ch. 356 (H.B. 504) provides:

"The change in law made by this Act applies only to an employer who terminates, threatens to terminate, penalizes, or threatens to penalize an employee on or after the effective date [Sept. 1, 2019] of this Act."

§ 122.003. Defense

(a) It is a defense to an action brought under this chapter that the employer's circumstances changed while the employee served as a juror or grand juror so that reemployment was impossible or unreasonable.

(b) To establish a defense under this section, an employer must prove that the termination of employment was because of circumstances other than the employee's service as a juror or grand juror.

Acts 1985, 69th Leg., ch. 959, § 1, eff. Sept. 1, 1985. Amended by Acts 1991, 72nd Leg., ch. 442, § 6, eff. Jan. 1, 1992; Acts 2019, 86th Leg., ch. 356 (H.B. 504), § 4, eff. Sept. 1, 2019.

Section 5 of Acts 2019, 86th Leg., ch. 356 (H.B. 504) provides:

"The change in law made by this Act applies only to an employer who terminates, threatens to terminate, penalizes, or threatens to penalize an employee on or after the effective date [Sept. 1, 2019] of this Act."

CHAPTER 123. INTERCEPTION OF COMMUNICATION

§ 123.001. Definitions

In this chapter:

(1) "Communication" means speech uttered by a person or information including speech that is transmitted in whole or in part with the aid of a wire or cable.

(2) "Interception" means the aural acquisition of the contents of a communication through the use of an interception device that is made without the consent of a party to the communication, but does not include the ordinary use of:

(A) a telephone or telegraph instrument or facility or telephone and telegraph equipment;

(B) a hearing aid designed to correct subnormal hearing to not better than normal;

(C) a radio, television, or other wireless receiver; or

(D) a cable system that relays a public wireless broadcast from a common antenna to a receiver.

Acts 1985, 69th Leg., ch. 959, § 1, eff. Sept. 1, 1985. Amended by Acts 2017, 85th Leg., ch. 1058 (H.B. 2931), § 3.02, eff. Jan. 1, 2019.

§ 123.002. Cause of Action

(a) A party to a communication may sue a person who:

(1) intercepts, attempts to intercept, or employs or obtains another to intercept or attempt to intercept the communication;

(2) uses or divulges information that he knows or reasonably should know was obtained by interception of the communication; or

(3) as a landlord, building operator, or communication common carrier, either personally or through an agent or employee, aids or knowingly permits interception or attempted interception of the communication.

(b) This section does not apply to a party to a communication if an interception or attempted interception of the communication is authorized by Title 18, United States Code, Section 2516.

Acts 1985, 69th Leg., ch. 959, § 1, eff. Sept. 1, 1985.

§ 123.003. Defense

(a) A switchboard operator or an officer, employee, or agent of a communication common carrier whose facilities are used in the transmission of a wire communication may intercept, disclose, or use a communication in the normal course of employment if engaged in an activity that is necessary to service or for the protection of the carrier's rights or property. A communication common carrier may not use service observation or random monitoring except for mechanical or service quality control checks.

(b) It is a defense to an action under Section 123.002 that an interception, disclosure, or use of a communication is permitted by this section.

(c) A defendant must establish by a preponderance of the evidence a defense raised under this section.

Acts 1985, 69th Leg., ch. 959, § 1, eff. Sept. 1, 1985.

§ 123.004. Damages

A person who establishes a cause of action under this chapter is entitled to:

(1) an injunction prohibiting a further interception, attempted interception, or divulgence or use of information obtained by an interception;

(2) statutory damages of $10,000 for each occurrence;

(3) all actual damages in excess of $10,000;

(4) punitive damages in an amount determined by the court or jury; and

(5) reasonable attorney's fees and costs.

Acts 1985, 69th Leg., ch. 959, § 1, eff. Sept. 1, 1985. Amended by Acts 2001, 77th Leg., ch. 1049, § 1, eff. Sept. 1, 2001.

CHAPTER 124. PRIVILEGE TO INVESTIGATE THEFT

§ 124.001. Detention

A person who reasonably believes that another has stolen or is attempting to steal property is privileged to detain that person in a reasonable manner and for a reasonable time to investigate ownership of the property.

Acts 1985, 69th Leg., ch. 959, § 1, eff. Sept. 1, 1985.

CHAPTER 125. COMMON AND PUBLIC NUISANCES

SUBCHAPTER A. SUIT TO ABATE CERTAIN COMMON NUISANCES

§ 125.001. Definitions

In this chapter:

(1) "Common nuisance" is a nuisance described by Section 125.0015.

(1–a) "Computer network" means the interconnection of two or more computers or computer systems by satellite, microwave, line, or other communication medium with the capability to transmit information between the computers.

(2) "Public nuisance" is a nuisance described by Section 125.062 or 125.063.

(3) "Multiunit residential property" means improved real property with at least three dwelling units, including an apartment building, condominium, hotel, or motel. The term does not include a single-family home or duplex.

(4) "Web address" means a website operating on the Internet.

Added by Acts 2003, 78th Leg., ch. 1202, § 1, eff. Sept. 1, 2003. Amended by Acts 2005, 79th Leg., ch. 1246, § 1, eff. Sept. 1, 2005; Acts 2017, 85th Leg., ch. 596 (S.B. 1196), § 1, eff. Sept. 1, 2017; Acts 2017, 85th Leg., ch. 858 (H.B. 2552), § 2, eff. Sept. 1, 2017.

Section 63(c) of Acts 2021, 87th Leg., ch. 807 (H.B. 1540) provides:

"The change in law made to Chapters 125 and 140A, Civil Practice and Remedies Code, by this Act applies only to a cause of action that accrues on or after the effective date [Sept. 1, 2021] of this Act. A cause of action that accrues before the effective date of this Act is governed by the law applicable to the cause of action immediately before the effective date of this Act, and that law is continued in effect for that purpose."

§ 125.0015. Common Nuisance

(a) A person who maintains a place to which persons habitually go for the following purposes and who knowingly tolerates the activity and furthermore fails to make reasonable attempts to abate the activity maintains a common nuisance:

(1) discharge of a firearm in a public place as prohibited by the Penal Code;

(2) reckless discharge of a firearm as prohibited by the Penal Code;

(3) engaging in organized criminal activity as a member of a combination as prohibited by the Penal Code;

(4) delivery, possession, manufacture, or use of a substance or other item in violation of Chapter 481, Health and Safety Code;

(5) gambling, gambling promotion, or communicating gambling information as prohibited by the Penal Code;

(6) prostitution as described by Section 43.02, Penal Code, solicitation of prostitution as described by Section 43.021, Penal Code, promotion of prostitution as described by Section 43.03, Penal Code, or aggravated promotion of prostitution as described by Section 43.04, Penal Code;

(7) compelling prostitution as prohibited by the Penal Code;

(8) commercial manufacture, commercial distribution, or commercial exhibition of obscene material as prohibited by the Penal Code;

(9) aggravated assault as described by Section 22.02, Penal Code;

(10) sexual assault as described by Section 22.011, Penal Code;

(11) aggravated sexual assault as described by Section 22.021, Penal Code;

(12) robbery as described by Section 29.02, Penal Code;

(13) aggravated robbery as described by Section 29.03, Penal Code;

(14) unlawfully carrying a weapon as described by Section 46.02, Penal Code;

(15) murder as described by Section 19.02, Penal Code;

(16) capital murder as described by Section 19.03, Penal Code;

(17) continuous sexual abuse of young child or disabled individual as described by Section 21.02, Penal Code;

(18) massage therapy or other massage services in violation of Chapter 455, Occupations Code;

(19) employing or entering into a contract for the performance of work or the provision of a service with an individual younger than 21 years of age for work or services performed at a sexually oriented business as defined by Section 243.002, Local Government Code;

(20) trafficking of persons as described by Section 20A.02, Penal Code;[1]

(21) sexual conduct or performance by a child as described by Section 43.25, Penal Code;

(22) employment harmful to a child as described by Section 43.251, Penal Code;

(23) criminal trespass as described by Section 30.05, Penal Code;

(24) disorderly conduct as described by Section 42.01, Penal Code;

(25) arson as described by Section 28.02, Penal Code;

(26) criminal mischief as described by Section 28.03, Penal Code, that causes a pecuniary loss of $500 or more;

(27) a graffiti offense in violation of Section 28.08, Penal Code; or

(28) permitting an individual younger than 18 years of age to enter the premises of a sexually oriented business as defined by Section 243.002, Local Government Code.

(b) A person maintains a common nuisance if the person maintains a multiunit residential property to which persons habitually go to commit acts listed in Subsection (a) and knowingly tolerates the acts and furthermore fails to make reasonable attempts to abate the acts.

(c) A person operating a web address or computer network in connection with an activity described by Subsection (a)(3), (6), (7), (10), (11), (17), (18), (19), (20), (21), or (22) maintains a common nuisance.

(d) Subsection (c) does not apply to:

(1) a provider of remote computing services or electronic communication services to the public;

(2) a provider of an interactive computer service as defined by 47 U.S.C. Section 230;

(3) an Internet service provider;

(4) a search engine operator;

(5) a browsing or hosting company;

(6) an operating system provider; or

(7) a device manufacturer.

(e) This section does not apply to an activity exempted, authorized, or otherwise lawful activity regulated by federal law.

Acts 1985, 69th Leg., ch. 959, § 1, eff. Sept. 1, 1985. Amended by Acts 1987, 70th Leg., ch. 959, § 1, eff. Sept. 1, 1987; Acts 1991, 72nd Leg., ch. 14, § 284(42), eff. Sept. 1, 1991; Acts 1993, 73rd Leg., ch. 857, § 2, eff. Sept. 1, 1993; Acts 1993, 73rd Leg., ch. 968, § 1, eff. Aug. 30, 1993; Acts 1995, 74th Leg., ch. 76, § 14.03, eff. Sept. 1, 1995; Acts 1995, 74th Leg., ch. 318, § 25, eff. Sept. 1, 1995; Acts 1995, 74th Leg., ch. 663, § 2, eff. Sept. 1, 1995; Acts 1997, 75th Leg., ch. 1181, § 1, eff. Sept. 1, 1997; Acts 1999, 76th Leg., ch. 1161, § 1, eff. Sept. 1, 1999. Redesignated from V.T.C.A., Civil Practice & Remedies Code § 125.001 and amended by Acts 2003, 78th Leg., ch. 1202, § 1, eff. Sept. 1, 2003. Amended by Acts 2005, 79th Leg., ch. 1246, § 2, eff. Sept. 1, 2005; Acts 2007, 80th Leg., ch. 593, § 3.04, eff. Sept. 1, 2007; Acts 2007, 80th Leg., ch. 1399, § 6, eff. Sept. 1, 2007; Acts 2009, 81st Leg., ch. 87, § 5.004, eff. Sept. 1, 2009; Acts 2011, 82nd Leg., ch. 1 (S.B. 24), § 3.02, eff. Sept. 1, 2011; Acts 2011, 82nd Leg., ch. 687 (H.B. 289), § 1, eff. Sept. 1, 2011; Acts 2017, 85th Leg., ch. 596 (S.B. 1196), § 2, eff. Sept. 1, 2017; Acts 2017, 85th Leg., ch. 775 (H.B. 2359), § 1, eff. Sept. 1, 2017; Acts 2017, 85th Leg., ch. 858 (H.B. 2552), § 3, eff. Sept. 1, 2017; Acts 2021, 87th Leg., ch. 79 (S.B. 315), § 5, eff. May 24, 2021; Acts 2021, 87th Leg., ch. 221 (H.B. 375), § 2.05, eff. Sept. 1, 2021; Acts 2021, 87th Leg., ch. 807 (H.B. 1540), § 33, eff. Sept. 1, 2021; Acts 2021, 87th Leg., ch. 942 (S.B. 766), § 6, eff. Sept. 1, 2021.

[1] This same provision was added by Acts 2011, 82nd Leg., ch. 1 (S.B. 24), § 3.02 as subsec. (a)(19).

Section 9 of Acts 2021, 87th Leg., ch. 79 (S.B. 315) provides:

"The changes in law made by this Act apply only to an offense committed on or after the effective date [May 24, 2021] of this Act. An offense committed before the effective date of this Act is governed by the law in effect on the date the offense was committed, and the former law is continued in effect for that purpose. For purposes of this section, an offense was committed before the effective date of this Act if any element of the offense was committed before that date."

Section 3.01 of Acts 2021, 87th Leg., ch. 221 (H.B. 375) provides:

"The change in law made by this Act applies only to an offense committed on or after the effective date [Sept. 1, 2021] of this Act. An offense committed before the effective date of this Act is governed by the law in effect on the date the offense was committed, and the former law is continued in effect for that purpose. For purposes of this section, an offense was committed before the effective date of this Act if any element of the offense occurred before that date."

Section 63(d) of Acts 2021, 87th Leg., ch. 807 (H.B. 1540) provides:

"Except as otherwise provided by this section, the changes in law made by this Act apply only to an offense committed on or after the effective date [Sept. 1, 2021] of this Act. An offense committed before the effective date of this Act is governed by the law in effect on the date the offense was committed, and the former law is continued in effect for that purpose. For purposes of this section, an offense was committed before the effective date of this Act if any element of the offense occurred before that date."

Section 9 of Acts 2021, 87th Leg., ch. 942 (S.B. 766) provides:

"The changes in law made by this Act apply only to an offense committed on or after the effective date [Sept. 1, 2021] of this Act. An offense committed before the effective date of this Act is governed by the law in effect on the date the offense was committed, and the former law is continued in effect for that purpose. For purposes of this section, an offense was committed before the effective date of this Act if any element of the offense was committed before that date."

§ 125.0017. Notice by Law Enforcement of Certain Activities

If a law enforcement agency has reason to believe an activity described by Section 125.0015(a)(6), (7), or (18) has occurred at property leased to a person operating a massage establishment as defined by Section 455.001, Occupations Code, the law enforcement agency may provide written notice by certified mail to each person maintaining the property of the alleged activity.

Added by Acts 2017, 85th Leg., ch. 858 (H.B. 2552), § 4, eff. Sept. 1, 2017. Amended by Acts 2021, 87th Leg., ch. 807 (H.B. 1540), § 5, eff. Sept. 1, 2021.

Section 63(d) of Acts 2021, 87th Leg., ch. 807 (H.B. 1540) provides:

"Except as otherwise provided by this section, the changes in law made by this Act apply only to an offense committed on or after the effective date [Sept. 1, 2021] of this Act. An offense committed before the effective date of this Act is governed by the law in effect on the date the offense was committed, and the former law is continued in effect for that purpose. For purposes of this section, an offense was committed before the effective date of this Act if any element of the offense occurred before that date."

§ 125.002. Suit to Abate Certain Common Nuisances; Bond

(a) A suit to enjoin and abate a common nuisance described by Section 125.0015(a) or (b) may be brought by an individual, by the attorney general, or by a district, county, or city attorney. The suit must be brought in the county in which it is alleged to exist against the person who is maintaining or about to maintain the nuisance. The suit must be brought in the name of the state if brought by the attorney general or a district or county attorney, in the name of the city if brought by a city attorney, or in the name of the individual if brought by a private citizen. Verification of the petition or proof of personal injury by the acts complained of need not be shown. For purposes of this subsection, personal injury may include economic or monetary loss.

(b) A person may bring a suit under Subsection (a) against any person who maintains, owns, uses, or is a party to the use of a place for purposes constituting a nuisance under this subchapter and may bring an action in rem against the place itself. A council of owners, as defined by Section 81.002, Property Code, or a unit owners' association organized under Section 82.101, Property Code, may be sued under this subsection if the council or association maintains, owns, uses, or is a party to the use of the common areas of the council's or association's condominium for purposes constituting a nuisance.

(c) Service of any order, notice, process, motion, or ruling of the court on the attorney of record of a cause pending under this subchapter is sufficient service of the party represented by an attorney.

(d) A person who violates a temporary or permanent injunctive order under this subchapter is subject to the following sentences for civil contempt:

(1) a fine of not less than $1,000 or more than $10,000;

(2) confinement in jail for a term of not less than 10 or more than 30 days; or

(3) both fine and confinement.

(e) If judgment is in favor of the petitioner, the court shall grant an injunction ordering the defendant to abate the nuisance and enjoining the defendant from maintaining or participating in the nuisance and may include in its order reasonable requirements to prevent the use or maintenance of the place as a nuisance. If the petitioner brings an action in rem, the judgment is a judgment in rem against the property as well as a judgment against the defendant. The judgment must order that the place where the nuisance exists be closed for one year after the date of judgment.

(f) Repealed by Acts 2007, 80th Leg., ch. 1023, § 3

(f–1) If the defendant required to execute the bond is a hotel, motel, or similar establishment that rents overnight lodging to the public and the alleged common nuisance is under Section 125.0015(a)(6) or (7), the bond must also be conditioned that the defendant will, in each of the defendant's lodging units on the premises that are the subject of the suit, post in a conspicuous place near the room rate information required to be posted under Section 2155.001, Occupations Code, a sign that includes:

(1) an operating toll-free telephone number of a nationally recognized information and referral hotline for victims of human trafficking; and

(2) the contact information for reporting suspicious activity to the Department of Public Safety.

(g) In an action brought under this chapter, other than an action brought under Section 125.0025, the petitioner may file a notice of lis pendens and a certified copy of an order of the court in the office of the county clerk in each county in which the land is located. The notice of lis pendens must conform to the requirements of Section 12.007, Property Code, and constitutes notice as provided by Section 13.004, Property Code. A certified copy of an order of the court filed in the office of the county clerk constitutes notice of the terms of the order and is binding on subsequent purchasers and lienholders.

(h) A person who may bring a suit under Subsection (a) shall consider, among other factors, whether the property owner, the owner's authorized representative, or the operator or occupant of the business, dwelling, or other place where the criminal acts occurred:

(1) promptly notifies the appropriate governmental entity or the entity's law enforcement agency of the occurrence of criminal acts on the property; and

(2) cooperates with the governmental entity's law enforcement investigation of criminal acts occurring at the property.

Acts 1985, 69th Leg., ch. 959, § 1, eff. Sept. 1, 1985. Amended by Acts 1987, 70th Leg., ch. 959, § 2, eff. Sept. 1, 1987; Acts 1991, 72nd Leg., ch. 14, § 284(42), eff. Sept. 1, 1991; Acts 2003, 78th Leg., ch. 1202, § 2, eff. Sept. 1, 2003; Acts 2005, 79th Leg., ch. 1246, § 3, eff. Sept. 1, 2005; Acts 2007, 80th Leg., ch. 258, § 16.03, eff. Sept. 1, 2007; Acts 2007, 80th Leg., ch. 849, § 6, eff. June 15, 2007; Acts 2007, 80th Leg., ch. 990, § 1, eff. June 15, 2007; Acts 2007, 80th Leg., ch. 1023, §§ 1, 3, eff. June 15, 2007; Acts 2017, 85th Leg., ch. 596 (S.B. 1196), §§ 4, 5, eff. Sept. 1, 2017; Acts 2017, 85th Leg., ch. 858 (H.B. 2552), § 5, 6, eff. Sept. 1, 2017; Acts 2021, 87th Leg., ch. 280 (H.B. 3721), § 3, eff. Sept. 1, 2021.

Section 10 of Acts 2021, 87th Leg., ch. 280 (H.B. 3721) provides:

"The change in law made by this Act to Section 125.002, Civil Practice and Remedies Code, applies only to a suit filed on or after the effective date [Sept. 1, 2021] of this Act. A suit filed before the effective date of this Act is governed by the law in effect immediately before that date, and that law is continued in effect for that purpose."

§ 125.0025. Suit to Declare Certain Common Nuisances

(a) A suit to declare that a person operating a web address or computer network is maintaining a common nuisance may be brought by an individual, by the attorney general, or by a district, county, or city attorney.

(b) Except as provided by Section 125.005, on a finding that a web address or computer network is a common nuisance, the sole remedy available is a judicial finding issued to the attorney general.

(c) The attorney general may:

(1) notify Internet service providers, search engine operators, browsing or hosting companies, or device manufacturers on which applications are hosted of the judicial finding issued to the attorney general under Subsection (b) to determine if the persons notified are able to offer technical assis-

tance to the attorney general in a manner consistent with 47 U.S.C. Section 230; or

(2) post the judicial finding issued to the attorney general under Subsection (b) on the attorney general's Internet website.

Added by Acts 2017, 85th Leg., ch. 596 (S.B. 1196), § 3, eff. Sept. 1, 2017; Acts 2017, 85th Leg., ch. 858 (H.B. 2552), § 7, eff. Sept. 1, 2017. Amended by Acts 2021, 87th Leg., ch. 807 (H.B. 1540), § 6, eff. Sept. 1, 2021.

Section 63(d) of Acts 2021, 87th Leg., ch. 807 (H.B. 1540) provides:

"Except as otherwise provided by this section, the changes in law made by this Act apply only to an offense committed on or after the effective date [Sept. 1, 2021] of this Act. An offense committed before the effective date of this Act is governed by the law in effect on the date the offense was committed, and the former law is continued in effect for that purpose. For purposes of this section, an offense was committed before the effective date of this Act if any element of the offense occurred before that date."

§ 125.003. Suit on Bond

(a) If a condition of a bond filed or an injunctive order entered under this subchapter is violated, the district, county, or city attorney of the county in which the property is located or the attorney general shall sue on the bond in the name of the state. In the event the attorney general originates the suit, the whole sum shall be forfeited as a penalty to the state. In the event the suit is originated by any office other than the attorney general, the whole sum shall be forfeited as a penalty to the originating entity. On violation of any condition of the bond or of the injunctive order and subsequent to forfeiture of the bond, the place where the nuisance exists shall be ordered closed for one year from the date of the order of bond forfeiture.

(b) The party bringing the suit may recover reasonable expenses incurred in prosecuting the suits authorized in Subsection (a) including but not limited to investigative costs, court costs, reasonable attorney's fees, witness fees, and deposition fees.

(c) A person may not continue the enjoined activity pending appeal or trial on the merits of an injunctive order entered in a suit brought under this subchapter. Not later than the 90th day after the date of the injunctive order, the appropriate court of appeals shall hear and decide an appeal taken by a party enjoined under this subchapter. If an appeal is not taken by a party temporarily enjoined under this article, the parties are entitled to a full trial on the merits not later than the 90th day after the date of the temporary injunctive order.

(d) Repealed by Acts 2021, 87th Leg., ch. 807 (H.B. 1540), § 62(2).

(e) Nothing herein is intended to allow a suit to enjoin and abate a common nuisance to be brought against any enterprise whose sole business is that of a bookstore or movie theater.

Acts 1985, 69th Leg., ch. 959, § 1, eff. Sept. 1, 1985. Amended by Acts 1987, 70th Leg., ch. 959, § 3, eff. Sept. 1, 1987; Acts 1993, 73rd Leg., ch. 822, § 1, eff. Sept. 1, 1993; Acts 2003, 78th Leg., ch. 1202, § 3, eff. Sept. 1, 2003; Acts 2021, 87th Leg., ch. 807 (H.B. 1540), § 62(2), eff. Sept. 1, 2021.

Section 63(d) of Acts 2021, 87th Leg., ch. 807 (H.B. 1540) provides:

"Except as otherwise provided by this section, the changes in law made by this Act apply only to an offense committed on or after the effective date [Sept. 1, 2021] of this Act. An offense committed before the effective date of this Act is governed by the law in effect on the date the offense was committed, and the former law is continued in effect for that purpose. For purposes of this section, an offense was committed before the effective date of this Act if any element of the offense occurred before that date."

§ 125.004. Evidence

(a) Proof that an activity described by Section 125.0015 is frequently committed at the place involved or that the place is frequently used for an activity described by Section 125.0015 is prima facie evidence that the defendant knowingly tolerated the activity.

(a–1) Proof in the form of a person's arrest or the testimony of a law enforcement agent that an activity described by Section 125.0015(a)(6) or (7) is committed at a place licensed as a massage establishment under Chapter 455, Occupations Code, or advertised as offering massage therapy or massage services, after notice was provided to the defendant in accordance with Section 125.0017, is prima facie evidence that the defendant:

(1) knowingly tolerated the activity; and

(2) did not make a reasonable attempt to abate the activity.

(a–2) Proof that an activity described by Section 125.0015(a)(18) is committed at a place maintained by the defendant, after notice was provided to the defendant in accordance with Section 125.0017, is prima facie evidence that the defendant:

(1) knowingly tolerated the activity; and

(2) did not make a reasonable attempt to abate the activity.

(a–3) For purposes of Subsections (a–1) and (a–2), notice is considered to be provided to the defendant the earlier of:

(1) seven days after the postmark date of the notice provided under Section 125.0017; or

(2) the date the defendant actually received notice under Section 125.0017.

(b) Evidence that persons have been arrested for or convicted of offenses for an activity described by Section 125.0015 in the place involved is admissible to show knowledge on the part of the defendant with respect to the act that occurred. The originals or certified copies of the papers and judgments of those arrests or convictions are admissible in the suit for injunction, and oral evidence is admissible to show that the offense for which a person was arrested or convicted was committed at the place involved.

(c) Evidence of the general reputation of the place involved is admissible to show the existence of the nuisance.

(d) Notwithstanding Subsections (a), (a–1), or (a–2), evidence that the defendant, the defendant's authorized representative, or another person acting at the direction of the defendant or the defendant's authorized representative requested law enforcement or emergency assistance with respect to an activity at the place where the common nuisance is allegedly maintained is not admissible for the purpose of showing the defendant tolerated the activity or failed to make reasonable attempts to abate the activity alleged to constitute the nuisance but may be admitted for other purposes, such as showing that a crime listed in Section 125.0015 occurred. Evidence that the defendant refused to cooperate with law enforcement or emergency services with respect to the activity is admissible. The posting of a sign prohibiting the activity alleged is not conclusive evidence that the owner did not tolerate the activity.

(e) Evidence of a previous suit filed under this chapter that resulted in a judgment against a landowner with respect to an activity described by Section 125.0015 at the landowner's property is admissible in a subsequent suit filed under this chapter to demonstrate that the landowner:

(1) knowingly tolerated the activity; and

(2) did not make a reasonable attempt to abate the activity.

Acts 1985, 69th Leg., ch. 959, § 1, eff. Sept. 1, 1985. Amended by Acts 1987, 70th Leg., ch. 959, § 4, eff. Sept. 1, 1987; Acts 1991, 72nd Leg., ch. 14, § 284(42), eff. Sept. 1, 1991; Acts 1993, 73rd Leg., ch. 857, § 3, eff. Sept. 1, 1993; Acts 1993, 73rd Leg., ch. 968, § 2, eff. Aug. 30, 1993; Acts 1995, 74th Leg., ch. 76, §§ 14.04 to 14.06, eff. Sept. 1, 1995; Acts 1995, 74th Leg., ch. 318, §§ 26, 27, eff. Sept. 1, 1995; Acts 1995, 74th Leg., ch. 663, §§ 3, 4, eff. Sept. 1, 1995; Acts 1997, 75th Leg., ch. 1181, § 2, eff. Sept. 1, 1997; Acts 2003, 78th Leg., ch. 1202, § 4, eff. Sept. 1, 2003; Acts 2005, 79th Leg., ch. 1246, § 4, eff. Sept. 1, 2005; Acts 2017, 85th Leg., ch. 858 (H.B. 2552), § 8, eff. Sept. 1, 2017; Acts 2017, 85th Leg., ch. 1135 (H.B. 240), § 2, eff. Sept. 1, 2017; Acts 2021, 87th Leg., ch. 807 (H.B. 1540), §§ 7, 8, 62(3), eff. Sept. 1, 2021.

Section 63(d) of Acts 2021, 87th Leg., ch. 807 (H.B. 1540) provides:

"Except as otherwise provided by this section, the changes in law made by this Act apply only to an offense committed on or after the effective date [Sept. 1, 2021] of this Act. An offense committed before the effective date of this Act is governed by the law in effect on the date the offense was committed, and the former law is continued in effect for that purpose. For purposes of this section, an offense was committed before the effective date of this Act if any element of the offense occurred before that date."

§ 125.005. Attorney's Fees and Costs in Action Under Chapter

In an action brought under this chapter, the court may award a prevailing party reasonable attorney's fees in addition to costs incurred in bringing the action. In determining the amount of attorney's fees, the court shall consider:

(1) the time and labor involved;

(2) the novelty and difficulty of the questions;

(3) the expertise, reputation, and ability of the attorney; and

(4) any other factor considered relevant by the court.

Added by Acts 2021, 87th Leg., ch. 807 (H.B. 1540), § 9, eff. Sept. 1, 2021.

Section 63(d) of Acts 2021, 87th Leg., ch. 807 (H.B. 1540) provides:

"Except as otherwise provided by this section, the changes in law made by this Act apply only to an offense committed on or after the effective date [Sept. 1, 2021] of this Act. An offense committed before the effective date of this Act is governed by the law in effect on the date the offense was committed, and the former law is continued in effect for that purpose. For purposes of this section, an offense was committed before the effective date of this Act if any element of the offense occurred before that date."

SUBCHAPTER B. SUIT TO ABATE CERTAIN PUBLIC NUISANCES [REPEALED]

§§ 125.021, 125.022. Repealed by Acts 2003, 78th Leg., ch. 1202, § 14, eff. Sept. 1, 2003

SUBCHAPTER C. ADDITIONAL NUISANCE REMEDIES

§ 125.041. Repealed by Acts 2003, 78th Leg., ch. 1202, § 14, eff. Sept. 1, 2003

§ 125.042. Request for Meeting

(a) The voters of an election precinct in which a common nuisance is alleged to exist or is alleged to be likely to be created, or the voters in an adjacent election precinct, may request the district attorney, city attorney, or county attorney having geographical jurisdiction of the place that is the subject of the voters' complaints to authorize a meeting at which interested persons may state their complaints about the matter. To be valid to begin proceedings under this section, the written request must be signed by at least:

(1) 10 percent of the registered voters of the election precinct in which the common nuisance is alleged to exist or is alleged to be likely to be created; or

(2) 20 percent of the voters of the adjacent election precinct.

(b) On receiving a written request for a meeting from the required number of persons, the district attorney, city attorney, or county attorney may appoint a person to conduct the meeting at a location as near as practical to the place that is the subject of the complaints.

Added by Acts 1987, 70th Leg., ch. 959, § 7, eff. Sept. 1, 1987. Amended by Acts 2003, 78th Leg., ch. 1202, § 5, eff. Sept. 1, 2003.

§ 125.043. Notice

The district attorney, city attorney, or county attorney receiving the request may:

(1) post notice of the purpose, time, and place of the meeting at either the county courthouse of the county or the city hall of the city in which the place that is the subject of the complaints is located and publish the notice in a newspaper of general circulation published in that county or city; and

(2) serve the notice, by personal service, to the owner and the operator of the place.

Added by Acts 1987, 70th Leg., ch. 959, § 7, eff. Sept. 1, 1987.

§ 125.044. Findings

(a) After the meeting, the person appointed to conduct the meeting shall report the findings to the district attorney, city attorney, or county attorney who appointed the person. The district attorney, city attorney, or county attorney, on finding by the attorney that a common nuisance exists or is likely to be created, may initiate appropriate available proceedings against the persons owning or operating the place at which the common nuisance exists or is likely to be created.

(b) In a proceeding begun under Subsection (a):

(1) proof that acts creating a common nuisance are frequently committed at the place is prima facie evidence that the owner and the operator knowingly tolerated the acts;

(2) evidence that persons have been arrested for or convicted of offenses involving acts at the place that create a common nuisance is admissible to show knowledge on the part of the owner and the operator with respect to the acts that occurred; and

(3) notwithstanding Subdivision (1), evidence that the defendant, the defendant's authorized representative, or another person acting at the direction of the defendant or the defendant's authorized representative requested law enforcement or emergency assistance with respect to an activity at the place where the common nuisance is allegedly maintained is not admissible for the purpose of showing the defendant tolerated the activity or failed to make reasonable attempts to abate the activity alleged to constitute the nuisance but may be admitted for other purposes, such as showing that a crime listed in Section 125.0015 occurred. Evidence that the defendant refused to cooperate with law enforcement or emergency services with respect to the activity is admissible.

(b–1) The posting of a sign prohibiting the activity alleged is not conclusive evidence that the owner did not tolerate the activity.

(c) The originals or certified copies of the papers and judgments of the arrests or convictions described by Subdivision (2) of Subsection (b) are admissible in a suit for an injunction, and oral evidence is admissible to show that the offense for which a person was arrested or convicted was committed at the place involved.

Added by Acts 1987, 70th Leg., ch. 959, § 7, eff. Sept. 1, 1987. Amended by Acts 2003, 78th Leg., ch. 1202, § 6, eff. Sept. 1, 2003; Acts 2005, 79th Leg., ch. 1246, § 5, eff. Sept. 1, 2005.

§ 125.045. Remedies

(a) If, after notice and hearing on a request by a petitioner for a temporary injunction, a court determines that the petitioner is likely to succeed on the merits in a suit brought under Section 125.002, the court:

(1) may include in its order reasonable requirements to prevent the use or maintenance of the place as a nuisance; and

(2) shall require that the defendant execute a bond.

(a–1) The bond must:

(1) be payable to the state at the county seat of the county in which the place is located;

(2) be in the amount set by the court, but not less than $5,000 or more than $10,000;

(3) have sufficient sureties approved by the court; and

(4) be conditioned that the defendant will not knowingly maintain a common nuisance to exist at the place.

(a–2) If the defendant required to execute the bond is a hotel, motel, or similar establishment that rents overnight lodging to the public and the alleged common nuisance is under Section 125.0015(a)(6) or (7), the bond must also be conditioned that the defendant will, in each of the defendant's lodging units on the premises that are the subject of the suit, post in a conspicuous place near the room rate information required to be posted under Section 2155.001, Occupations Code, an operating toll-free telephone number of a nationally recognized information and referral hotline for victims of human trafficking.

(b) If, after an entry of a temporary or permanent injunction, a court determines that a condition of the injunctive order is violated, the court may:

(1) order a political subdivision to discontinue the furnishing of utility services to the place at which the nuisance exists;

(2) prohibit the furnishing of utility service to the place by any public utility holding a franchise to use the streets and alleys of the political subdivision;

(3) revoke the certificate of occupancy of the place;

(4) prohibit the use of city streets, alleys, and other public ways for access to the place during the existence of the nuisance or in furtherance of the nuisance;

(5) limit the hours of operation of the place, to the extent that the hours of operation are not otherwise specified by law;

(6) order a landlord to terminate a tenant's lease if:

(A) the landlord and the tenant are parties to the suit; and

(B) the tenant has violated a condition of the injunctive order; or

(7) order any other legal remedy available under the laws of the state.

(c) If a condition of a bond filed or an injunctive order entered under this subchapter is violated, the district, county, or city attorney of the county in which the property is located or the attorney general may sue on the bond in the name of the state. In the event the attorney general originates the suit, the whole sum shall be forfeited as a penalty to the state. In the event the suit is originated by any office other than the attorney general, the whole sum shall be forfeited as a penalty to the originating entity.

Added by Acts 1987, 70th Leg., ch. 959, § 7, eff. Sept. 1, 1987. Amended by Acts 2003, 78th Leg., ch. 1202, § 6, eff. Sept. 1, 2003; Acts 2007, 80th Leg., ch. 258, § 16.04, eff. Sept. 1, 2007; Acts 2007, 80th Leg., ch. 849, § 7, eff. June 15, 2007; Acts 2007, 80th Leg., ch. 990, § 2, eff. June 15, 2007; Acts 2007, 80th Leg., ch. 1023, § 2, eff. June 15, 2007; Acts 2011, 82nd Leg., ch. 91 (S.B. 1303), § 27.001(1), eff. Sept. 1, 2011.

§ 125.046. Additional Remedies; Receiver

(a) If, in any judicial proceeding under Subchapter A,[1] a court determines that a person is maintaining a vacant lot, vacant or abandoned building, or multiunit residential property that is a common nuisance, the court may, on its own motion or on the motion of any party, order the appointment of a receiver to manage the property or render any other order allowed by law as necessary to abate the nuisance.

(b) A receiver appointed under this section may not be appointed for a period longer than one year.

(c) The court shall determine the management duties of the receiver, the amount to be paid the receiver, the method of payment, and the payment periods.

(d) A receiver appointed under this section shall continue to manage the property during the pendency of any appeal relating to the nuisance or the appointment of the receiver.

(e) A receiver appointed by the court may:

(1) take control of the property;

(2) collect rents due on the property;

(3) make or have made any repairs necessary to bring the property into compliance with minimum standards in local ordinances;

(4) make payments necessary for the maintenance or restoration of utilities to the properties;

(5) purchase materials necessary to accomplish repairs;

(6) renew existing rental contracts and leases;

(7) enter into new rental contracts and leases;

(8) affirm, renew, or enter into a new contract providing for insurance coverage on the property; and

(9) exercise all other authority that an owner of the property would have except for the authority to sell the property.

(f) Expenditures of monies by the receiver in excess of $10,000 under Subdivisions (3) and (5) of Subsection (e) shall require prior approval of the court.

(g) On the completion of the receivership, the receiver shall file with the court a full accounting of all costs and expenses incurred in the repairs, including reasonable costs for labor and subdivision, and all income received from the property.

Added by Acts 1995, 74th Leg., ch. 818, § 2, eff. Aug. 28, 1995. Amended by Acts 2003, 78th Leg., ch. 1202, § 7, eff. Sept. 1, 2003; Acts 2017, 85th Leg., ch. 775 (H.B. 2359), § 2, eff. Sept. 1, 2017.

[1] V.T.C.A., Civil Practice & Remedies Code § 125.001 et seq.

§ 125.047. Nuisance Abatement Fund

(a) In this section:

(1) "Fund" means a nuisance abatement fund.

(2) "Nuisance abatement" means an activity taken by a municipality to reduce the occurrences of a common or public nuisance.

(b) This section applies only to a municipality with a population of 1.5 million or more.

(c) A municipality shall create a fund as a separate account in the treasury of the municipality.

(d) The fund consists of:

(1) money awarded the municipality in an action under this chapter;

(2) money awarded the municipality under a settlement to an action under this chapter;

(3) fines resulting from code enforcement citations issued by the municipality for conduct defined as a common or public nuisance under this chapter;

(4) bonds forfeited to the municipality under this chapter; and

(5) donations or grants made to the municipality for the purpose of nuisance abatement.

(e) The money in the fund may be used only for the purpose of ongoing nuisance abatement. That purpose includes:

(1) regular and overtime compensation for nuisance abatement or enforcement personnel; and

(2) hiring additional personnel for nuisance abatement as needed.

Added by Acts 2003, 78th Leg., ch. 1202, § 8, eff. Sept. 1, 2003.

SUBCHAPTER D. MEMBERSHIP IN CRIMINAL STREET GANG

§ 125.061. Definitions

In this subchapter:

(1) "Combination" and "criminal street gang" have the meanings assigned by Section 71.01, Penal Code.

(2) "Continuously or regularly" means at least five times in a period of not more than 12 months.

(3) "Gang activity" means the following types of conduct:

(A) organized criminal activity as described by Section 71.02, Penal Code;

(B) terroristic threat as described by Section 22.07, Penal Code;

(C) coercing, soliciting, or inducing gang membership as described by Section 71.022(a) or (a-1), Penal Code;

(D) criminal trespass as described by Section 30.05, Penal Code;

(E) disorderly conduct as described by Section 42.01, Penal Code;

(F) criminal mischief as described by Section 28.03, Penal Code, that causes a pecuniary loss of $500 or more;

(G) a graffiti offense in violation of Section 28.08, Penal Code;

(H) a weapons offense in violation of Chapter 46, Penal Code; or

(I) unlawful possession of a substance or other item in violation of Chapter 481, Health and Safety Code.

Added by Acts 1993, 73rd Leg., ch. 968, § 3, eff. Aug. 30, 1993. Amended by Acts 1995, 74th Leg., ch. 76, § 14.10, eff. Sept. 1, 1995; Acts 1995, 74th Leg., ch. 318, § 31, eff. Sept. 1, 1995; Acts 2003, 78th Leg., ch. 1202, § 9, eff. Sept. 1, 2003; Acts 2005, 79th Leg., ch. 472, § 1, eff. Sept. 1, 2005; Acts 2011, 82nd Leg., ch. 91 (S.B. 1303), § 5.002, eff. Sept. 1, 2011; Acts 2011, 82nd Leg., ch. 976 (H.B. 1622), § 1, eff. Sept. 1, 2011.

§ 125.062. Public Nuisance; Combination

A combination or criminal street gang that continuously or regularly associates in gang activities is a public nuisance.

Added by Acts 1993, 73rd Leg., ch. 968, § 3, eff. Aug. 30, 1993. Amended by Acts 1995, 74th Leg., ch. 76, § 14.11, eff. Sept. 1, 1995; Acts 1995, 74th Leg., ch. 318, § 32, eff. Sept. 1, 1995; Acts 2003, 78th Leg., ch. 1202, § 9, eff. Sept. 1, 2003.

§ 125.063. Public Nuisance; Use of Place

The habitual use of a place by a combination or criminal street gang for engaging in gang activity is a public nuisance.

Added by Acts 1993, 73rd Leg., ch. 968, § 3, eff. Aug. 30, 1993. Amended by Acts 2003, 78th Leg., ch. 1202, § 9, eff. Sept. 1, 2003.

§ 125.064. Suit to Abate Nuisance

(a) A district, county, or city attorney, the attorney general, or a resident of the state may sue to enjoin a public nuisance under this subchapter.

(b) Any person who habitually associates with others to engage in gang activity as a member of a combination or criminal street gang may be made a defendant in the suit. Any person who owns or is responsible for maintaining a place that is habitually used for engaging in gang activity may be made a defendant in the suit.

(c) If the suit is brought by the state, the petition does not require verification.

(d) If the suit is brought by a resident, the resident is not required to show personal injury.

Added by Acts 1993, 73rd Leg., ch. 968, § 3, eff. Aug. 30, 1993. Amended by Acts 1995, 74th Leg., ch. 76, § 14.12, eff. Sept. 1, 1995; Acts 1995, 74th Leg., ch. 318, § 33, eff. Sept. 1, 1995; Acts 2003, 78th Leg., ch. 1202, § 10, eff. Sept. 1, 2003.

§ 125.065. Court Order

(a) If the court finds that a combination or criminal street gang constitutes a public nuisance, the court may enter an order:

(1) enjoining a defendant in the suit from engaging in the gang activities of the combination or gang; and

(2) imposing other reasonable requirements to prevent the combination or gang from engaging in future gang activities.

(b) If the court finds that a place is habitually used in a manner that constitutes a public nuisance, the court may include in its order reasonable requirements to prevent the use of the place for gang activity.

Added by Acts 1993, 73rd Leg., ch. 968, § 3, eff. Aug. 30, 1993. Amended by Acts 1995, 74th Leg., ch. 76, § 14.13, eff. Sept. 1, 1995; Acts 1995, 74th Leg., ch. 318, § 34, eff. Sept. 1, 1995; Acts 2003, 78th Leg., ch. 1202, § 11, eff. Sept. 1, 2003.

§ 125.066. Violation of Court Order

A person who violates a temporary or permanent injunctive order under this subchapter is subject to the following sentences for civil contempt:

(1) a fine of not less than $1,000 nor more than $10,000;

(2) confinement in jail for a term of not less than 10 nor more than 30 days; or

(3) both fine and confinement.

Added by Acts 1993, 73rd Leg., ch. 968, § 3, eff. Aug. 30, 1993.

§ 125.067. Continuation of Activities Pending Trial or Appeal; Appeal

(a) A person may not continue the enjoined activity pending trial or appeal on the merits of an injunctive order in a suit brought under this subchapter.

(b) Not later than the 90th day after the date of the injunctive order, an appropriate court of appeals shall hear and decide an appeal taken by a person enjoined under this subchapter.

(c) If an appeal is not taken by a person temporarily enjoined under this subchapter, the person is entitled to a trial on the merits not later than the 90th day after the date of the temporary injunctive order, unless otherwise ordered by the court.

Added by Acts 1993, 73rd Leg., ch. 968, § 3, eff. Aug. 30, 1993. Amended by Acts 2011, 82nd Leg., ch. 976 (H.B. 1622), § 2, eff. Sept. 1, 2011.

§ 125.0675. Injunction for Specified Period

In addition to any other order that may be issued under this subchapter or other law, a court of appeals or a trial court acting under Section 125.067(b) or (c) may issue an injunctive order under this subchapter stating that the injunction remains in effect during the course of the trial or until lifted by the court.

Added by Acts 2003, 78th Leg., ch. 1202, § 12, eff. Sept. 1, 2003.

§ 125.068. Repealed by Acts 2021, 87th Leg., ch. 807 (H.B. 1540), § 62(4), eff. Sept. 1, 2021

Section 63(d) of Acts 2021, 87th Leg., ch. 807 (H.B. 1540) provides:

"Except as otherwise provided by this section, the changes in law made by this Act apply only to an offense committed on or after the effective date [Sept. 1, 2021] of this Act. An offense committed before the effective date of this Act is governed by the law in effect on the date the offense was committed, and the former law is continued in effect for that purpose. For purposes of this section, an offense was committed before the effective date of this Act if any element of the offense occurred before that date."

§ 125.069. Use of Place; Evidence

In an action brought under this subchapter, proof that gang activity by a member of a combination or a criminal street gang is frequently committed at a place or proof that a place is frequently used for engaging in gang activity by a member of a combination or a criminal street gang is prima facie evidence that the proprietor knowingly permitted the act, unless the act constitutes conspiring to commit gang activity.

Added by Acts 1993, 73rd Leg., ch. 968, § 3, eff. Aug. 30, 1993. Amended by Acts 1995, 74th Leg., ch. 76, § 14.14, eff. Sept. 1, 1995; Acts 1995, 74th Leg., ch. 318, § 35, eff. Sept. 1, 1995; Acts 2003, 78th Leg., ch. 1202, § 13, eff. Sept. 1, 2003.

§ 125.070. Civil Action for Violation of Injunction

(a) In this section, "governmental entity" means a political subdivision of this state, including any city, county, school district, junior college district, levee improvement district, drainage district, irrigation district, water improvement district, water control and improvement district, water control and preservation district, freshwater supply district, navigation district, conservation and reclamation district, soil conservation district, communication district, public health district, and river authority.

(b) A criminal street gang or a member of a criminal street gang is liable to the state or a governmental entity injured by the violation of a temporary or permanent injunctive order under this subchapter.

(c) In an action brought against a member of a criminal street gang, the plaintiff must show that the member violated the temporary or permanent injunctive order.

(d) A district, county, or city attorney or the attorney general may sue for money damages on behalf of the state or a governmental entity. If the state or a governmental entity prevails in a suit under this section, the state or governmental entity may recover:

(1) actual damages;

(2) a civil penalty in an amount not to exceed $20,000 for each violation; and

(3) court costs and attorney's fees in accordance with Section 125.005.

(e) The property of the criminal street gang or a member of the criminal street gang may be seized in execution on a judgment under this section. Property may not be seized under this subsection if the owner or interest holder of the property proves by a preponderance of the evidence that the owner or interest holder was not a member of the criminal street gang and did not violate the temporary or permanent injunctive order. The owner or interest holder of property that is in the possession of a criminal street gang or a member of the criminal street gang and that is subject to execution under this subsection must show that the property:

(1) was stolen from the owner or interest holder; or

(2) was used or intended to be used without the effective consent of the owner or interest holder by the criminal street gang or a member of the criminal street gang.

(f) The attorney general shall deposit money received under this section for damages or as a civil penalty in the neighborhood and community recovery fund held by the attorney general outside the state treasury. Money in the fund is held by the attorney general in trust for the benefit of the community or neighborhood harmed by the violation of a temporary or permanent injunctive order. Money in the fund may be used only for the benefit of the community or neighborhood harmed by the violation of the injunctive order. Interest earned on money in the fund shall be credited to the fund. The attorney general shall account for money in the fund so that money held for the benefit of a community or neighborhood, and interest earned on that money, are not commingled with money in the fund held for the benefit of a different community or neighborhood.

(g) A district, county, or city attorney who brings suit on behalf of a governmental entity shall deposit money received for damages or as a civil penalty in an account to be held in trust for the benefit of the community or neighborhood harmed by the violation of a temporary or permanent injunctive order. Money in the account may be used only for the benefit of the community or neighborhood harmed by the violation of the injunctive order. Interest earned on money in the account shall be credited to the account. The district, county, or city attorney shall account for money in the account so that money held for the benefit of a community or neighborhood, and interest earned on that money, are not commingled with money in the account held for the benefit of a different community or neighborhood.

(h) An action under this section brought by the state or a governmental entity does not waive sovereign or governmental immunity for any purpose.

Added by Acts 2009, 81st Leg., ch. 1130, § 10, eff. Sept. 1, 2009. Amended by Acts 2021, 87th Leg., ch. 807 (H.B. 1540), § 10, eff. Sept. 1, 2021.

Section 63(d) of Acts 2021, 87th Leg., ch. 807 (H.B. 1540) provides:

"Except as otherwise provided by this section, the changes in law made by this Act apply only to an offense committed on or after the effective date [Sept. 1, 2021] of this Act. An offense committed before the effective date of this Act is governed by the law in effect on the date the offense was committed, and the former law is continued in effect for that purpose. For purposes of this section, an offense was committed before the effective date of this Act if any element of the offense occurred before that date."

CHAPTER 126. LOCAL RELIGIOUS CONGREGATIONS

SUBCHAPTER A. RECEIVERSHIP FOR LOCAL RELIGIOUS CONGREGATION

SUBCHAPTER B. TRUSTEES

SUBCHAPTER A. RECEIVERSHIP FOR LOCAL RELIGIOUS CONGREGATION

§ 126.001. Definition

In this subchapter, "religious congregation" does not include the religion or a denomination of the religion as a whole.

Acts 1985, 69th Leg., ch. 959, § 1, eff. Sept. 1, 1985. Amended by Acts 1987, 70th Leg., ch. 937, § 1, eff. Aug. 31, 1987.

§ 126.002. Appointment of Receiver

(a) The judge of a district court or another court of jurisdiction shall on application appoint a receiver for any religious congregation that:

(1) formerly maintained regular forms of work and worship in a given community at regular intervals; and

(2) has ceased to function as a religious congregation in those or similar capacities for at least one year.

(b) The judge shall hear and determine the application in term or in vacation.

(c) Before appointing a receiver, the judge shall apply to the secretary of state for a certified copy of the record of trustees required by this chapter.

Acts 1985, 69th Leg., ch. 959, § 1, eff. Sept. 1, 1985. Amended by Acts 1987, 70th Leg., ch. 937, § 1, eff. Aug. 31, 1987.

§ 126.003. Qualifications

(a) A person appointed receiver for the religious congregation need not be a member of an active religious congregation of like faith. If an organization is appointed receiver, the organization must be a recognized organization of like faith.

(b) If the organization of like faith has a state society or an organization similarly formed and named and the society or organization is authorized to act as receiver or trustee for the organization, the court may appoint the society or organization to serve as receiver.

Acts 1985, 69th Leg., ch. 959, § 1, eff. Sept. 1, 1985. Amended by Acts 1987, 70th Leg., ch. 937, § 1, eff. Aug. 31, 1987.

§ 126.004. Powers and Duties

(a) The receiver shall take charge of all property belonging to the religious congregation and administer that property under the direction of the court for the best interests of the religious congregation.

(b) If necessary to preserve the property, the receiver may sell it under order of the court.

(c) The court shall order the public or private sale of property belonging to a religious congregation that may not be revived or reorganized within a reasonable time. The proceeds of the sale shall be delivered to the receiver, who shall use them for a religious congregation of like faith.

Acts 1985, 69th Leg., ch. 959, § 1, eff. Sept. 1, 1985. Amended by Acts 1987, 70th Leg., ch. 937, § 1, eff. Aug. 31, 1987.

SUBCHAPTER B. TRUSTEES

§ 126.011. Record

(a) On receipt of $2.50, the secretary of state shall record the names of all trustees appointed by any state organization of a religious congregation in this state.

(b) The appointment must be duly authenticated by an officer authorized to acknowledge deeds in this state.

(c) The secretary of state shall keep the record in a well-bound book in the secretary of state's office.

Acts 1985, 69th Leg., ch. 959, § 1, eff. Sept. 1, 1985. Amended by Acts 1987, 70th Leg., ch. 937, § 1, eff. Aug. 31, 1987.

§ 126.012. Certified Copy to Court

(a) The secretary of state shall furnish a certified copy of the appointments to any court in this state on application by the judge or court clerk.

(b) If the certified copy is used in a proceeding, $1.50 shall be taxed as costs to be collected and paid as other costs.

Acts 1985, 69th Leg., ch. 959, § 1, eff. Sept. 1, 1985. Amended by Acts 1987, 70th Leg., ch. 937, § 1, eff. Aug. 31, 1987.

Repeal

Acts 2021, 87th Leg., ch. 472 (S.B. 41), § 5.01(a)(2) repeals this section effective Jan. 1, 2022.

§ 126.013. Change in Trustees

This chapter does not affect a religious congregation's right to change, appoint, or elect its trustees.

Acts 1985, 69th Leg., ch. 959, § 1, eff. Sept. 1, 1985. Amended by Acts 1987, 70th Leg., ch. 937, § 1, eff. Aug. 31, 1987.

CHAPTER 127. INDEMNITY PROVISIONS IN CERTAIN MINERAL AGREEMENTS

Section

§ 127.001. Definitions

In this chapter:

(1) "Agreement pertaining to a well for oil, gas, or water or to a mine for a mineral":

(A) means:

(i) a written or oral agreement or understanding concerning the rendering of well or mine services; or

(ii) an agreement to perform a part of those services or an act collateral to those services, including furnishing or renting equipment, incidental transportation, or other goods and services furnished in connection with the services; but

(B) does not include a joint operating agreement.

(2) "Joint operating agreement" means an agreement between or among holders of working interests or operating rights for the joint exploration, development, operation, or production of minerals.

(3) "Mutual indemnity obligation" means an indemnity obligation in an agreement pertaining to a well for oil, gas, or water or to a mine for a mineral in which the parties agree to indemnify each other and each other's contractors and their employees against loss, liability, or damages arising in connection with bodily injury, death, and damage to property of the respective employees, contractors or their employees, and invitees of each party arising out of or resulting from the performance of the agreement.

(4) "Well or mine service":

(A) includes:

(i) drilling, deepening, reworking, repairing, improving, testing, treating, perforating, acidizing, logging, conditioning, purchasing, gathering, storing, or transporting oil, brine water, fresh water, produced water, condensate, petroleum products, or other liquid commodities, or otherwise rendering services in connection with a well drilled to produce or dispose of oil, gas, other minerals or water; and

(ii) designing, excavating, constructing, improving, or otherwise rendering services in connection with a mine shaft, drift, or other structure intended for use in exploring for or producing a mineral; but

(B) does not include:

(i) purchasing, selling, gathering, storing, or transporting gas or natural gas liquids by pipeline or fixed associated facilities; or

(ii) construction, maintenance, or repair of oil, natural gas liquids, or gas pipelines or fixed associated facilities.

(5) "Wild well" means a well from which the escape of oil or gas is not intended and cannot be controlled by equipment used in normal drilling practice.

(6) "Unilateral indemnity obligation" means an indemnity obligation in an agreement pertaining to a well for oil, gas, or water or to a mine for a mineral in which one of the parties as indemnitor agrees to indemnify the other party as indemnitee with respect to claims for personal injury or death to the indemnitor's employees or agents or to the employees or agents of the indemnitor's contractors

but in which the indemnitee does not make a reciprocal indemnity to the indemnitor.

Acts 1985, 69th Leg., ch. 959, § 1, eff. Sept. 1, 1985. Amended by Acts 1989, 71st Leg., ch. 1102, § 1, eff. Sept. 1, 1989; Acts 1991, 72nd Leg., ch. 36, § 1, eff. April 19, 1991.

§ 127.002. Findings; Certain Agreements Against Public Policy

(a) The legislature finds that an inequity is fostered on certain contractors by the indemnity provisions in certain agreements pertaining to wells for oil, gas, or water or to mines for other minerals.

(b) Certain agreements that provide for indemnification of a negligent indemnitee are against the public policy of this state.

(c) The legislature finds that joint operating agreement provisions for the sharing of costs or losses arising from joint activities, including costs or losses attributable to the negligent acts or omissions of any party conducting the joint activity:

(1) are commonly understood, accepted, and desired by the parties to joint operating agreements;

(2) encourage mineral development;

(3) are not against the public policy of this state; and

(4) are enforceable unless those costs or losses are expressly excluded by written agreement.

Acts 1985, 69th Leg., ch. 959, § 1, eff. Sept. 1, 1985. Amended by Acts 1991, 72nd Leg., ch. 36, § 2, eff. April 19, 1991.

§ 127.003. Agreement Void and Unenforceable

(a) [1] Except as otherwise provided by this chapter, a covenant, promise, agreement, or understanding contained in, collateral to, or affecting an agreement pertaining to a well for oil, gas, or water or to a mine for a mineral is void if it purports to indemnify a person against loss or liability for damage that:

(1) is caused by or results from the sole or concurrent negligence of the indemnitee, his agent or employee, or an individual contractor directly responsible to the indemnitee; and

(2) arises from:

(A) personal injury or death;

(B) property injury; or

(C) any other loss, damage, or expense that arises from personal injury, death, or property injury.

Acts 1985, 69th Leg., ch. 959, § 1, eff. Sept. 1, 1985.

[1] So in enrolled bill. There is no subsec. (b).

§ 127.004. Exclusions

This chapter does not apply to loss or liability for damages or an expense arising from:

(1) personal injury, death, or property injury that results from radioactivity;

(2) property injury that results from pollution, including cleanup and control of the pollutant;

(3) property injury that results from reservoir or underground damage, including loss of oil, gas, other mineral substance, or water or the well bore itself;

(4) personal injury, death, or property injury that results from the performance of services to control a wild well to protect the safety of the general public or to prevent depletion of vital natural resources; or

(5) cost of control of a wild well, underground or above the surface.

Acts 1985, 69th Leg., ch. 959, § 1, eff. Sept. 1, 1985. Amended by Acts 1989, 71st Leg., ch. 1102, § 2, eff. Sept. 1, 1989.

§ 127.005. Insurance Coverage

(a) This chapter does not apply to an agreement that provides for indemnity if the parties agree in writing that the indemnity obligation will be supported by liability insurance coverage to be furnished by the indemnitor subject to the limitations specified in Subsection (b) or (c).

(b) With respect to a mutual indemnity obligation, the indemnity obligation is limited to the extent of the coverage and dollar limits of insurance or qualified self-insurance each party as indemnitor has agreed to obtain for the benefit of the other party as indemnitee.

(c) With respect to a unilateral indemnity obligation, the amount of insurance required may not exceed $500,000.

Acts 1985, 69th Leg., ch. 959, § 1, eff. Sept. 1, 1985. Amended by Acts 1989, 71st Leg., ch. 1102, § 3, eff. Sept. 1, 1989; Acts 1991, 72nd Leg., ch. 36, § 3, eff. April 19, 1991; Acts 1995, 74th Leg., ch. 679, § 1, eff. Aug. 28, 1995; Acts 1999, 76th Leg., ch. 1006, § 1, eff. Aug. 30, 1999.

§ 127.006. Insurance Contract; Workers' Compensation

This chapter does not affect:

(1) the validity of an insurance contract; or

(2) a benefit conferred by the workers' compensation statutes of this state.

Acts 1985, 69th Leg., ch. 959, § 1, eff. Sept. 1, 1985.

§ 127.007. Owner of Surface Estate

This chapter does not deprive an owner of the surface estate of the right to secure indemnity from a lessee, an operator, a contractor, or other person conducting operations for the exploration or production of minerals of the owner's land.

Acts 1985, 69th Leg., ch. 959, § 1, eff. Sept. 1, 1985.

§ 127.008. Repealed by Acts 1991, 72nd Leg., ch. 36, § 4, eff. April 19, 1991

CHAPTER 127A. DISCLOSURES REGARDING INDEMNIFICATION OBLIGATIONS AND INSURANCE COVERAGE REGARDING WELL OR MINE SERVICES PROVIDED BY CERTAIN SUBCONTRACTORS

Section

§ 127A.001. Definitions

In this chapter:

(1) "Temporary placement service" means an entity or other person that employs individuals or contracts with another entity or person to refer or assign personnel to the placement service's clients to support or supplement the clients' workforce in a special work situation, including:

(A) an employee absence;

(B) a temporary skill shortage;

(C) a seasonal or cyclical workload;

(D) work requiring uniquely skilled personnel; or

(E) a special assignment or project.

(2) "Temporary subcontractor" means an independent contractor who, in connection with performing well or mine services:

(A) is referred to or placed by a temporary placement service with the placement service's client; or

(B) has entered into an agreement with a temporary placement service to provide those services to the placement service's client.

(3) "Well or mine service" has the meaning assigned by Section 127.001.

Added by Acts 2021, 87th Leg., ch. 903 (H.B. 3416), § 1, eff. Sept. 1, 2021.

Section 2 of Acts 2021, 87th Leg., ch. 903 (H.B. 3416) provides:

"The change in law made by this Act applies only to an agreement entered into on or after the effective date [Sept. 1, 2021] of this Act."

§ 127A.002. Disclosure Regarding Temporary Subcontractor Indemnification Obligations and Insurance Coverage Requirements

(a) Before a temporary placement service refers or assigns a temporary subcontractor to the placement service's client to perform well or mine services, the placement service shall provide a written disclosure to the subcontractor that:

(1) describes the subcontractor's indemnification obligations, if any, to the placement service and to the placement service's client in connection with the services the subcontractor will provide to the client;

(2) describes any insurance policy, including the amount of coverage and any limits on coverage, that is provided for the benefit of the subcontractor by the placement service or the placement service's client, or both, in connection with the services the subcontractor will provide to the client; and

(3) expressly states whether and to what extent any insurance policy described by Subdivision (2) will cover the subcontractor's tort liability and contractual indemnity obligations arising out of the performance of the services by the subcontractor for the placement service's client or clients.

(b) The disclosure required under Subsection (a) may state that the disclosure does not alter, amend, or otherwise modify the terms of any agreement governing services provided by the temporary subcontractor or any insurance policy described by Subsection (a)(2), provided that the temporary placement service is responsible for the content of the disclosure.

(c) A temporary placement service shall:

(1) provide the disclosure required under Subsection (a) to a temporary subcontractor as a separate document from any agreement entered into with the subcontractor by the placement service or the placement service's client; and

(2) ensure that the disclosure is written in plain English and in a manner that is clear, concise, and designed to enable the temporary subcontractor to understand the subcontractor's contractual indemnity obligations, if any, and any insurance policy provided for the benefit of the subcontractor in connection with well or mine services to be performed by the subcontractor.

(d) A temporary placement service may satisfy the requirement to describe an insurance policy under Subsection (a)(2) by providing to the temporary subcontractor a certificate of insurance evidencing applicable coverage and limits.

Added by Acts 2021, 87th Leg., ch. 903 (H.B. 3416), § 1, eff. Sept. 1, 2021.

Section 2 of Acts 2021, 87th Leg., ch. 903 (H.B. 3416) provides:

"The change in law made by this Act applies only to an agreement entered into on or after the effective date [Sept. 1, 2021] of this Act."

§ 127A.003. Disclosure Requirements for Ongoing Insurance Policy

A temporary placement service that provides a disclosure to a temporary subcontractor under Section 127A.002 that states that an insurance policy described in that disclosure that is provided for the benefit of the temporary subcontractor remains in effect for a specified time period and with respect to a specified client or clients is not required to provide that subcontractor with an additional disclosure under Section 127A.002 for future services provided by the subcontractor to that client or those clients until:

(1) the insurance policy is no longer in effect; or

(2) the placement service is required to provide the subcontractor a new disclosure because of a change concerning the insurance policy as provided under Section 127A.004.

Added by Acts 2021, 87th Leg., ch. 903 (H.B. 3416), § 1, eff. Sept. 1, 2021.

Section 2 of Acts 2021, 87th Leg., ch. 903 (H.B. 3416) provides:

"The change in law made by this Act applies only to an agreement entered into on or after the effective date [Sept. 1, 2021] of this Act."

§ 127A.004. Notice Required for Certain Changes Related to Insurance Policy

A temporary placement service shall provide a temporary subcontractor who is provided a disclosure of a provided insurance policy under Section 127A.002 a separate written notice of a cancellation or nonrenewal of the policy or a material reduction in coverage under the insurance policy not later than the 30th day before the date the cancellation or nonrenewal of the policy or the material reduction in insurance coverage takes effect.

Added by Acts 2021, 87th Leg., ch. 903 (H.B. 3416), § 1, eff. Sept. 1, 2021.

Section 2 of Acts 2021, 87th Leg., ch. 903 (H.B. 3416) provides:

"The change in law made by this Act applies only to an agreement entered into on or after the effective date [Sept. 1, 2021] of this Act."

CHAPTER 128. LIMITATION ON SUITS AGAINST SPORT SHOOTING RANGE OR FIREARMS OR AMMUNITION MANUFACTURER, TRADE ASSOCIATION, OR SELLER

SUBCHAPTER A. SUIT BY GOVERNMENTAL UNIT

SUBCHAPTER B. CIVIL ACTIONS

A former Chapter 128, Unauthorized Use of Television Decoding and Interception Devices, consisting of §§ 128.001 and 128.002, was repealed by Acts 1995, 74th Leg., ch. 76, § 14.15, effective September 1, 1995 to conform to Acts 1993, 73rd Leg., ch. 900, § 1.01.

SUBCHAPTER A. SUIT BY GOVERNMENTAL UNIT

§ 128.001. Limitation on Right to Bring Suit or Recover Damages

(a) In this section:

(1) "Governmental unit" means:

(A) a political subdivision of the state, including a municipality or county; and

(B) any other agency of government whose authority is derived from the laws or constitution of this state.

(2) "Sport shooting range" has the meaning assigned by Section 250.001, Local Government Code.

(b) Except as provided by Subsections (c) and (f), a governmental unit may not bring suit against:

(1) a firearms or ammunition manufacturer, trade association, or seller for recovery of damages resulting from, or injunctive relief or abatement of a nuisance relating to, the lawful design, manufacture, marketing, or sale of firearms or ammunition to the public; or

(2) a sport shooting range, the owners or operators of a sport shooting range, or the owners of real property on which a sport shooting range is operated, for the lawful discharge of firearms on the sport shooting range.

(c) A governmental unit on behalf of the state or any other governmental unit may bring a suit described by Subsection (b) if the suit is approved in advance by the legislature in a concurrent resolution or by enactment of a law. This subsection does not create a cause of action.

(d) Nothing in this section shall prohibit a governmental unit from bringing an action against a firearms manufacturer, trade association, or seller for recovery of damages for:

(1) breach of contract or warranty as to firearms or ammunition purchased by a governmental unit;

(2) damage or harm to property owned or leased by the governmental unit caused by a defective firearm or ammunition;

(3) personal injury or death, if such action arises from a governmental unit's claim for subrogation;

(4) injunctive relief to enforce a valid ordinance, statute, or regulation; or

(5) contribution under Chapter 33, Civil Practice and Remedies Code.

(e) Nothing in this section shall prohibit the attorney general from bringing a suit described by Subsection (b) on behalf of the state or any other governmental unit. This subsection does not create a cause of action.

(f) Nothing in this section shall prohibit a governmental unit from bringing an action against a sport shooting range, the owners or operators of a sport shooting range, or the owners of real property on which a sport shooting range is operating if the sport shooting range began operation after September 1, 2011, and operates exclusively within the governmental unit's geographical limits, exclusive of the governmental unit's extraterritorial jurisdiction:

(1) for injunctive relief to enforce a valid ordinance, statute, or regulation; or

(2) to require the sport shooting range to comply with generally accepted standards followed in the sport shooting range industry in this state at the time of the sport shooting range's construction.

Added by Acts 1999, 76th Leg., ch. 597, § 1, eff. Sept. 1, 1999. Amended by Acts 2011, 82nd Leg., ch. 624 (S.B. 766), § 3, eff. Sept. 1, 2011.

§ 128.002. Repealed by Acts 1995, 74th Leg., ch. 76, § 14.15, eff. Sept. 1, 1995

SUBCHAPTER B. CIVIL ACTIONS

§ 128.051. Definitions

In this subchapter:

(1) "Claim" means any relief sought in a civil action, including all forms of monetary recovery or injunctive relief.

(2) "Claimant" has the meaning assigned by Section 41.001.

(3) "Expert" means a person who is:

(A) giving opinion testimony about the appropriate standard of care for a sport shooting range, an owner or operator of a sport shooting range, or the owner of real property on which a sport shooting range is operated, or the causal relationship between the injury, harm, or damages claimed and the alleged departure from the applicable standard of care; and

(B) qualified to render opinions on the standards and causal relationship described by Paragraph (A) under the Texas Rules of Evidence.

(4) "Expert report" means a written report by an expert that provides a fair summary of the expert's opinions as of the date of the report regarding applicable standards of care for operation of a sport shooting range, the manner in which a defendant failed to meet the standards, and the causal relationship between that failure and the injury, harm, or damages claimed.

(5) "Sport shooting range" has the meaning assigned by Section 250.001, Local Government Code.

Added by Acts 2011, 82nd Leg., ch. 624 (S.B. 766), § 4, eff. Sept. 1, 2011.

§ 128.052. Limitation on Civil Action and Recovery of Damages

(a) Except as provided by Subsection (b), a civil action may not be brought against a sport shooting range, the owner or operator of a sport shooting range, or the owner of the real property on which a sport shooting range is operated for recovery of damages resulting from, or injunctive relief or abatement of a nuisance relating to, the discharge of firearms.

(b) Nothing in this section prohibits a civil action against a sport shooting range, the owner or operator of a sport shooting range, or the owner of the real property on which a sport shooting range is operated for recovery of damages for:

(1) breach of contract for use of the real property on which a sport shooting range is located;

(2) damage or harm to private property caused by the discharge of firearms on a sport shooting range;

(3) personal injury or death caused by the discharge of a firearm on a sport shooting range; or

(4) injunctive relief to enforce a valid ordinance, statute, or regulation.

(c) Damages may be awarded, or an injunction may be obtained, in a civil action brought under this section if the claimant shows by a preponderance of the evidence, through the testimony of one or more expert witnesses, that the sport shooting range, the owner or operator of the sport shooting range, or the owner of real property on which the sport shooting range is operated deviated from the standard of care that is reasonably expected of an ordinarily prudent sport shooting range, owner or operator of a sport shooting range, or owner of real property on which a sport shooting range is operated in the same or similar circumstances.

Added by Acts 2011, 82nd Leg., ch. 624 (S.B. 766), § 4, eff. Sept. 1, 2011.

§ 128.053. Expert Report

(a) In a suit against a sport shooting range, an owner or operator of a sport shooting range, or the owner of real property on which a sport shooting range is operated, a claimant shall, not later than the 90th day after the date the original petition was filed, serve on each party or the party's attorney one or more expert reports, with a curriculum vitae of each expert listed in the report for each defendant against whom a claim is asserted. The date for serving the report may be extended by written agreement of the affected parties. Each defendant whose conduct is implicated in a report must file and serve any objection to the sufficiency of the report not later than the 21st day after the date the report is served or all objections are waived.

(b) If, as to a defendant, an expert report has not been served within the period specified by Subsection (a), the court, on the motion of the affected defendant, shall, subject to Subsection (c), enter an order that:

(1) awards to the affected defendant attorney's fees and costs of court incurred by the defendant; and

(2) dismisses the claim with prejudice with respect to the affected defendant.

(c) If an expert report has not been served within the period specified by Subsection (a) because elements of the report are found deficient, the court may grant one extension of not more than 30 days to the claimant in order to cure the deficiency. If the claimant does not receive notice of the court's ruling granting the extension until after the 90th day after the date the deadline has passed, then the 30-day extension runs from the date the plaintiff first receives the notice.

(d) Notwithstanding any other provision of this section, a claimant may satisfy any requirement of this section for serving an expert report by serving reports of separate experts regarding different defendants or regarding different issues arising from the conduct of a defendant, including issues of liability and causation. Nothing in this section shall be construed to mean that a single expert must address all liability and causation issues with respect to all defendants or with respect to both liability and causation issues for a defendant.

(e) A court shall grant a motion challenging the adequacy of an expert report only if it appears to the court, after a hearing, that the report does not represent an objective, good faith effort to comply with the requirements of an expert report.

(f) Until a claimant has served the expert report and curriculum vitae as required by Subsection (a), all discovery is stayed except that after a claim is filed all claimants, collectively, may take not more than two depositions before the expert report is served as required by Subsection (a).

Added by Acts 2011, 82nd Leg., ch. 624 (S.B. 766), § 4, eff. Sept. 1, 2011.

CHAPTER 129. AGE OF MAJORITY

Section

§ 129.001. Age of Majority

The age of majority in this state is 18 years.

Acts 1985, 69th Leg., ch. 959, § 1, eff. Sept. 1, 1985.

§ 129.002. Rights, Privileges, or Obligations

A law, rule, or ordinance enacted or adopted before August 27, 1973, that extends a right, privilege, or obligation to an individual on the basis of a minimum age of 19, 20, or 21 years shall be interpreted as prescribing a minimum age of 18 years.

Acts 1985, 69th Leg., ch. 959, § 1, eff. Sept. 1, 1985.

§ 129.003. Alcoholic Beverage Code Prevails

The minimum age provisions of the Alcoholic Beverage Code prevail to the extent of any conflict with this chapter.

Acts 1985, 69th Leg., ch. 959, § 1, eff. Sept. 1, 1985.

CHAPTER 129A. RELIEF FOR CYBERBULLYING OF CHILD

§ 129A.001. Definition

In this chapter, "cyberbullying" has the meaning assigned by Section 37.0832(a), Education Code.

Added by Acts 2017, 85th Leg., ch. 522 (S.B. 179), § 11, eff. Sept. 1, 2017.

§ 129A.002. Injunctive Relief

(a) A recipient of cyberbullying behavior who is younger than 18 years of age at the time the cyberbullying occurs or a parent of or person standing in parental relation to the recipient may seek injunctive relief under this chapter against the individual who was cyberbullying the recipient or, if the individual is younger than 18 years of age, against a parent of or person standing in parental relation to the individual.

(b) A court may issue a temporary restraining order, temporary injunction, or permanent injunction appropriate under the circumstances to prevent any further cyberbullying, including an order or injunction:

(1) enjoining a defendant from engaging in cyberbullying; or

(2) compelling a defendant who is a parent of or person standing in parental relation to an individual who is younger than 18 years of age to take reasonable actions to cause the individual to cease engaging in cyberbullying.

(c) A plaintiff in an action for injunctive relief brought under this section is entitled to a temporary restraining order on showing that the plaintiff is likely to succeed in establishing that the individual was cyberbullying the recipient. The plaintiff is not required to plead or prove that, before notice can be served and a hearing can be held, immediate and irreparable injury, loss, or damage is likely to result from past or future cyberbullying by the individual against the recipient.

(d) A plaintiff is entitled to a temporary or permanent injunction under this section on showing that the individual was cyberbullying the recipient.

(e) A court granting a temporary restraining order or temporary injunction under this section may, on motion of either party or sua sponte, order the preservation of any relevant electronic communication. The temporary restraining order or temporary injunction is not required to:

(1) define the injury or state why it is irreparable;

(2) state why the order was granted without notice; or

(3) include an order setting the cause for trial on the merits with respect to the ultimate relief requested.

Added by Acts 2017, 85th Leg., ch. 522 (S.B. 179), § 11, eff. Sept. 1, 2017.

§ 129A.003. Promulgation of Forms

(a) The supreme court shall, as the court finds appropriate, promulgate forms for use as an application for initial injunctive relief by individuals representing themselves in suits involving cyberbullying and instructions for the proper use of each form or set of forms.

(b) The forms and instructions:

(1) must be written in language that is easily understood by the general public;

(2) shall be made readily available to the general public in the manner prescribed by the supreme court; and

(3) must be translated into the Spanish language.

(c) The Spanish language translation of a form must:

(1) state:

(A) that the Spanish language translated form is to be used solely for the purpose of assisting in understanding the form and may not be submitted to the court; and

(B) that the English language version of the form must be submitted to the court; or

(2) be incorporated into the English language version of the form in a manner that is understandable to both the court and members of the general public.

(d) Each form and its instructions must clearly and conspicuously state that the form is not a substitute for the advice of an attorney.

(e) The attorney general and the clerk of a court shall inform members of the general public of the availability of a form promulgated by the supreme court under this section as appropriate and make the form available free of charge.

(f) A court shall accept a form promulgated by the supreme court under this section unless the form has been completed in a manner that causes a substantive defect that cannot be cured.

Added by Acts 2017, 85th Leg., ch. 522 (S.B. 179), § 11, eff. Sept. 1, 2017.

§ 129A.004. Inapplicability

(a) An action filed under this chapter may not be joined with an action filed under Title 1, 4, or 5, Family Code.[1]

(b) Chapter 27 does not apply to an action under this chapter.

Added by Acts 2017, 85th Leg., ch. 522 (S.B. 179), § 11, eff. Sept. 1, 2017.

[1] V.T.C.A., Family Code §§ 1.001 et seq., 71.001 et seq., 101.001 et seq.

§ 129A.005. Certain Conduct Excepted

This chapter does not apply to a claim brought against an interactive computer service, as defined by 47 U.S.C. Section 230, for cyberbullying.

Added by Acts 2017, 85th Leg., ch. 522 (S.B. 179), § 11, eff. Sept. 1, 2017.

CHAPTER 130. LIABILITY PROVISIONS IN CERTAIN CONSTRUCTION CONTRACTS

§ 130.001. Definition

In this chapter "construction contract" means a contract or agreement made and entered into by an owner, contractor, subcontractor, registered architect, licensed engineer, or supplier concerning the design, construction, alteration, repair, or maintenance of a building, structure, appurtenance, road, highway, bridge, dam, levee, or other improvement to or on real property, including moving, demolition, and excavation connected with the real property.

Added by Acts 1987, 70th Leg., ch. 167, § 3.14(a), eff. Sept. 1, 1987. Amended by Acts 2001, 77th Leg., ch. 351, § 2, eff. Sept. 1, 2001.

§ 130.002. Covenant or Promise Void and Unenforceable

(a) A covenant or promise in, in connection with, or collateral to a construction contract is void and unenforceable if the covenant or promise provides for a contractor who is to perform the work that is the subject of the construction contract to indemnify or hold harmless a registered architect, licensed engineer or an agent, servant, or employee of a registered architect or licensed engineer from liability for damage that:

(1) is caused by or results from:

(A) defects in plans, designs, or specifications prepared, approved, or used by the architect or engineer; or

(B) negligence of the architect or engineer in the rendition or conduct of professional duties called for or arising out of the construction contract and the plans, designs, or specifications that are a part of the construction contract; and

(2) arises from:

(A) personal injury or death;

(B) property injury; or

(C) any other expense that arises from personal injury, death, or property injury.

(b) A covenant or promise in, in connection with, or collateral to a construction contract other than a contract for a single family or multifamily residence is void and unenforceable if the covenant or promise provides for a registered architect or licensed engineer whose engineering or architectural design services are the subject of the construction contract to indemnify or hold harmless an owner or owner's agent or employee from liability for damage that is caused by or results from the negligence of an owner or an owner's agent or employee.

(c) Except as provided by Subsection (d), (e), or (f), a covenant or promise in, in connection with, or collateral to a construction contract for engineering or architectural services related to an improvement to real property is void and unenforceable to the extent the covenant or promise provides that a licensed engineer or registered architect must defend a party, including a third party, against a claim based wholly or partly on the negligence of, fault of, or breach of contract by the owner, the owner's agent, the owner's employee, or another entity over which the owner exercises control. A covenant or promise in, in connection with, or collateral to a contract for engineering or architectural services related to an improvement to real property may provide for the reimbursement of an owner's reasonable attorney's fees in proportion to the engineer's or architect's liability.

(d) Notwithstanding Subsection (c), an owner that is a party to a contract for engineering or architectural services related to an improvement to real property may require in the contract that the engineer or architect name the owner as an additional insured under any of the engineer's or architect's insurance coverage to the extent additional insureds are allowed under the policy and provide any defense to the owner provided by the policy to a named insured.

(e) Subsection (c) does not apply to a contract for services in which an owner contracts with an entity to provide both design and construction services.

(f) Subsection (c) does not apply to a covenant to defend a party, including a third party, for a claim of negligent hiring of the architect or engineer.

Added by Acts 1987, 70th Leg., ch. 167, § 3.14(a), eff. Sept. 1, 1987. Amended by Acts 2001, 77th Leg., ch. 351, § 3, eff. Sept. 1, 2001; Acts 2021, 87th Leg., ch. 686 (H.B. 2116), § 2, eff. Sept. 1, 2021.

Section 5 of Acts 2021, 87th Leg., ch. 686 (H.B. 2116) provides:

"(a) Section 130.002(c), Civil Practice and Remedies Code, as added by this Act, applies only to a covenant or promise in, in connection with, or collateral to a contract entered into on or after the effective date [Sept. 1, 2021] of this Act.

"(b) Sections 130.002(d) and 130.0021, Civil Practice and Remedies Code, as added by this Act, apply only to a contract entered into on or after the effective date of this Act."

§ 130.0021. Architect's or Engineer's Standard of Care

(a) A construction contract for architectural or engineering services or a contract related to the construction or repair of an improvement to real property that contains architectural or engineering services as a component part must require that the architectural or engineering services be performed with the professional skill and care ordinarily provided by competent architects or engineers practicing under the same or similar circumstances and professional license.

(b) If a contract described by Subsection (a) contains a provision establishing a different standard of care than the standard described by Subsection (a):

(1) the provision is void and unenforceable; and

(2) the standard of care described by Subsection (a) applies to the performance of the architectural or engineering services.

(c) Section 130.004 does not limit the applicability of this section.

Added by Acts 2021, 87th Leg., ch. 686 (H.B. 2116), § 3, eff. Sept. 1, 2021; Acts 2021, 87th Leg., ch. 838 (S.B. 219), § 3, eff. Sept. 1, 2021.

Section 5(b) of Acts 2021, 87th Leg., ch. 686 (H.B. 2116) provides:

"(b) Sections 130.002(d) and 130.0021, Civil Practice and Remedies Code, as added by this Act, apply only to a contract entered into on or after the effective date [Sept. 1, 2021] of this Act."

Section 6 of Acts 2021, 87th Leg., ch. 838 (S.B. 219) provides:

"(a) Except as provided by Subsection (c) of this section, the changes in law made by this Act apply only to a contract entered into on or after the effective date [Sept. 1, 2021] of this Act. A contract entered into before the effective date of this Act is governed by the law in effect when the contract was entered into, and the former law is continued in effect for that purpose.

"(b) An original contract for the construction or repair of an improvement to real property with the owner of an interest in real property that is entered into before the effective date of this Act, and a subcontract or purchase order for providing labor or materials associated with that original contract, whether the subcontract or purchase order is entered into before, on, or after the effective date of this Act, is governed by the law in effect when the original contract was entered into, and the former law is continued in effect for that purpose.

"(c) The changes in law made by this Act to Section 473.003, Transportation Code, as added by Chapter 382 (H.B. 2899), Acts of the 86th Legislature, Regular Session, 2019, are intended to clarify existing law and apply to a contract entered into before, on, or after the effective date of this Act."

§ 130.003. Insurance Contract; Workers' Compensation

This chapter does not apply to:

(1) an insurance contract; or

(2) a workers' compensation agreement.

Added by Acts 1987, 70th Leg., ch. 167, § 3.14(a), eff. Sept. 1, 1987.

§ 130.004. Owner of Interest in Real Property

(a) Except as provided by Section 130.002(b) or (c) or Section 130.0021,[1] this chapter does not apply to an owner of an interest in real property or persons employed solely by that owner.

(b) Except as provided by Section 130.002(b) or (c) or Section 130.0021,[2] this chapter does not prohibit or make void or unenforceable a covenant or promise to:

(1) indemnify or hold harmless an owner of an interest in real property and persons employed solely by that owner; or

(2) allocate, release, liquidate, limit, or exclude liability in connection with a construction contract between an owner or other person for whom a

construction contract is being performed and a registered architect or licensed engineer.

Added by Acts 1987, 70th Leg., ch. 167, § 3.14(a), eff. Sept. 1, 1987. Amended by Acts 2001, 77th Leg., ch. 351, § 4, eff. Sept. 1, 2001; Acts 2021, 87th Leg., ch. 686 (H.B. 2116), § 4, eff. Sept. 1, 2021; Acts 2021, 87th Leg., ch. 838 (S.B. 219), § 4, eff. Sept. 1, 2021.

[1] As amended by Acts 2021, 87th Leg., ch. 686 (H.B. 2116), § 4. Acts 2021, 87th Leg., ch. 838 (S.B. 219), § 4, inserted "or 130.0021" instead of "or (c) or Section 130.0021".

[2] As amended by Acts 2021, 87th Leg., ch. 686 (H.B. 2116), § 4. Acts 2021, 87th Leg., ch. 838 (S.B. 219), § 4, inserted "or 130.0021" instead of "or (c) or Section 130.0021".

Section 6 of Acts 2021, 87th Leg., ch. 838 (S.B. 219) provides:

"(a) Except as provided by Subsection (c) of this section, the changes in law made by this Act apply only to a contract entered into on or after the effective date [Sept. 1, 2021] of this Act. A contract entered into before the effective date of this Act is governed by the law in effect when the contract was entered into, and the former law is continued in effect for that purpose.

"(b) An original contract for the construction or repair of an improvement to real property with the owner of an interest in real property that is entered into before the effective date of this Act, and a subcontract or purchase order for providing labor or materials associated with that original contract, whether the subcontract or purchase order is entered into before, on, or after the effective date of this Act, is governed by the law in effect when the original contract was entered into, and the former law is continued in effect for that purpose.

"(c) The changes in law made by this Act to Section 473.003, Transportation Code, as added by Chapter 382 (H.B. 2899), Acts of the 86th Legislature, Regular Session, 2019, are intended to clarify existing law and apply to a contract entered into before, on, or after the effective date of this Act."

§ 130.005. Application of Chapter

This chapter does not apply to a contract or agreement in which an architect or engineer or an agent, servant, or employee of an architect or engineer is indemnified from liability for:

(1) negligent acts other than those described by this chapter; or

(2) negligent acts of the contractor, any subcontractor, any person directly or indirectly employed by the contractor or a subcontractor, or any person for whose acts the contractor or a subcontractor may be liable.

Added by Acts 1987, 70th Leg., ch. 167, § 3.14(a), eff. Sept. 1, 1987.

CHAPTER 131. VIOLATION OF COLLEGIATE ATHLETIC ASSOCIATION RULES

Another Chapter 131, Presumption of Death, consisting of §§ 131.001 to 131.003, was added by Acts 1987, 70th Leg., ch. 167, § 3.15(a). The chapter was redesignated as Chapter 133, consisting of V.T.C.A., Civil Practice & Remedies Code §§ 133.001 to 133.003 by Acts 1989, 71st Leg., ch. 2, § 16.01(4).

§ 131.001. Definitions

In this chapter:

(1) "National collegiate athletic association" means a national collegiate athletic association with one or more member institutions in 40 or more states, including Texas.

(2) "Person" does not include a government or governmental subdivision or agency.

(3) "Regional collegiate athletic association" means a regional collegiate athletic association with one or more of its member institutions in Texas.

(4) "Institution" means a public or private institution of higher education, including any senior college, university, community college, technical institute, or junior college.

Added by Acts 1987, 70th Leg., ch. 1065, § 1, eff. Sept. 1, 1987. Amended by Acts 1997, 75th Leg., ch. 279, § 1, eff. Sept. 1, 1997.

§ 131.002. Adoption of Rules

The rules of each national collegiate athletic association in effect on January 1, 1987, are adopted.

Added by Acts 1987, 70th Leg., ch. 1065, § 1, eff. Sept. 1, 1987.

§ 131.003. Cause of Action by Regional Collegiate Athletic Association

A person who violates a rule of a national collegiate athletic association adopted by this chapter is liable for damages in an action brought by a regional collegiate athletic association if:

(1) the person knew or reasonably should have known that a rule was violated; and

(2) the violation of the rule is a contributing factor to disciplinary action taken by the national collegiate athletic association against:

(A) the regional collegiate athletic association;

(B) a member institution of the regional collegiate athletic association; or

(C) a student at a member institution of the regional collegiate athletic association.

Added by Acts 1987, 70th Leg., ch. 1065, § 1, eff. Sept. 1, 1987.

§ 131.004. Cause of Action by Institution

A person who violates a rule of a national collegiate athletic association adopted by this chapter is liable for damages in an action brought by an institution if:

(1) the person knew or reasonably should have known that a rule was violated; and

(2) the violation of the rule is a contributing factor to disciplinary action taken by the national collegiate athletic association against the institution or a student at the institution.

Added by Acts 1987, 70th Leg., ch. 1065, § 1, eff. Sept. 1, 1987.

§ 131.005. Defenses

(a) It is a defense to an action under this chapter that, at the time of the violation of the rule:

(1) the rule was not a current rule of the national collegiate athletic association; or

(2) the rule had been substantially changed by the national collegiate athletic association.

(b) It is a defense to an action under Section 131.003 that, at the time of the violation of the rule, the defendant was:

(1) an employee of the national collegiate athletic association whose rule was violated;

(2) an employee of the regional collegiate athletic association;

(3) an employee of a member institution of the regional collegiate athletic association; or

(4) a student at a member institution of the regional collegiate athletic association.

(c) It is a defense to an action under Section 131.004 that, at the time of the violation of the rule, the defendant was:

(1) an employee of the national collegiate athletic association whose rule was violated;

(2) an employee of the regional collegiate athletic association of which the institution is a member;

(3) an employee of the institution; or

(4) a student at the institution.

Added by Acts 1987, 70th Leg., ch. 1065, § 1, eff. Sept. 1, 1987.

§ 131.006. Damages

Damages to a regional collegiate athletic association or institution may include lost television revenues and lost ticket sales of regular season and post-season athletic events.

Added by Acts 1987, 70th Leg., ch. 1065, § 1, eff. Sept. 1, 1987.

§ 131.007. Distribution of Damages

A regional collegiate athletic association that prevails in an action under Section 131.003 shall distribute the awarded damages to its member institutions in the same manner that it regularly distributes proceeds it receives in connection with athletic contests among member institutions.

Added by Acts 1987, 70th Leg., ch. 1065, § 1, eff. Sept. 1, 1987.

§ 131.008. Attorney's Fees and Costs

A regional collegiate athletic association or institution that prevails in an action under this chapter is entitled to an award of reasonable attorney's fees and costs.

Added by Acts 1987, 70th Leg., ch. 1065, § 1, eff. Sept. 1, 1987.

CHAPTER 132. UNSWORN DECLARATIONS

§ 132.001. Unsworn Declaration

(a) Except as provided by Subsection (b), an unsworn declaration may be used in lieu of a written sworn declaration, verification, certification, oath, or affidavit required by statute or required by a rule, order, or requirement adopted as provided by law.

(b) This section does not apply to a lien required to be filed with a county clerk, an instrument concerning real or personal property required to be filed with a county clerk, or an oath of office or an oath required to be taken before a specified official other than a notary public.

(c) An unsworn declaration made under this section must be:

(1) in writing; and

(2) subscribed by the person making the declaration as true under penalty of perjury.

(d) Except as provided by Subsections (e) and (f), an unsworn declaration made under this section must include a jurat in substantially the following form:

"My name is ____________, ____________, ____________,
(First) (Middle) (Last)
my date of birth is ____________, and my address is ____________, ____________, ____________, ____________,
(Street) (City) (State) (Zip Code)
and ____________. I declare under penalty of
(Country)
perjury that the foregoing is true and correct.

Executed in ____________ County, State of ____________, on the ______ day of ____________, ____________.
(Month) (Year)

____
Declarant"

(e) An unsworn declaration made under this section by an inmate must include a jurat in substantially the following form:

"My name is ____________, ____________, ____________,
(First) (Middle) (Last)
my date of birth is ____________, and my inmate identifying number, if any, is ____________. I am presently incarcerated in ____________
(Corrections unit name)
in ____________, ____________, ____________, ____________.
(City) (County) (State) (Zip Code)
I declare under penalty of perjury that the foregoing is true and correct.

Executed on the ______ day of ____________, ____________.
(Month) (Year)

____
Declarant"

(f) An unsworn declaration made under this section by an employee of a state agency or a political subdivision in the performance of the employee's job duties, must include a jurat in substantially the following form:

"My name is ____________, ____________, ____________,
(First) (Middle) (Last)
and I am an employee of the following governmental agency: ____________. I am executing this declaration as part of my assigned duties and responsibilities. I declare under penalty of perjury that the foregoing is true and correct.

Executed in ____________ County, State of ____________, on the ______ day of ____________, ____________.
(Month) (Year)

____
Declarant"

Added by Acts 1987, 70th Leg., ch. 1049, § 60, eff. Sept. 1, 1987. Amended by Acts 2009, 81st Leg., ch. 87, § 25.011, eff. Sept. 1, 2009; Acts 2011, 82nd Leg., ch. 847 (H.B. 3674), § 1, eff. Sept. 1, 2011; Acts 2013, 83rd Leg., ch. 515 (S.B. 251), § 1, eff. Sept. 1, 2013; Acts 2013, 83rd Leg., ch. 946 (H.B. 1728), § 1, eff. June 14, 2013.

§§ 132.002, 132.003. Repealed by Acts 2011, 82nd Leg., ch. 847 (H.B. 3674) § 2, eff. Sept. 1, 2011

CHAPTER 133. PRESUMPTION OF DEATH

Chapter 131, Presumption of Death, consisting of V.T.C.A., Civil Practice & Remedies Code §§ 131.001 to 131.003, was added by Acts 1987, 70th Leg., ch. 167, § 3.15(a). Acts 1989, 71st Leg., ch. 2, § 16.01(4) redesignated this chapter as Chapter 133, consisting of V.T.C.A., Civil Practice & Remedies Code §§ 133.001 to 133.003, effective August 28, 1989.

§ 133.001. Seven-Year Absence

Any person absenting himself for seven successive years shall be presumed dead unless it is proved that the person was alive within the seven-year period.

Added by Acts 1987, 70th Leg., ch. 167, § 3.15(a), eff. Sept. 1, 1987. Redesignated from V.T.C.A., Civil Practice & Remedies Code § 131.001 by Acts 1989, 71st Leg., ch. 2, § 16.01(4), eff. Aug. 28, 1989.

§ 133.002. Armed Services Certificate of Death

If a branch of the armed services issues a certificate declaring a person dead, the date of death is presumed to have occurred for all purposes as stated in the certificate. The certificate may be admitted in any court of competent jurisdiction as prima facie evidence of the date and place of the person's death.

Added by Acts 1987, 70th Leg., ch. 167, § 3.15(a), eff. Sept. 1, 1987. Redesignated from V.T.C.A., Civil Practice & Remedies Code § 131.002 by Acts 1989, 71st Leg., ch. 2, § 16.01(4), eff. Aug. 28, 1989.

§ 133.003. Restoration of Estate

(a) If an estate is recovered on a presumption of death under this chapter and if in a subsequent action or suit it is proved that the person presumed dead is living, the estate shall be restored to that person. The estate shall be restored with the rents and profits of the estate with legal interest for the time the person was deprived of the estate.

(b) A person delivering an estate or any part of an estate under this section to another under proper order of a court of competent jurisdiction is not liable for the estate or part of the estate.

(c) If the person recovering an estate on a presumption of death sells real property from the estate to a purchaser for value, the right of restoration under this section extends to the recovery of the purchase money received by the person, but does not extend to the recovery of the real property.

Added by Acts 1987, 70th Leg., ch. 167, § 3.15(a), eff. Sept. 1, 1987. Redesignated from V.T.C.A., Civil Practice & Remedies Code § 131.003 by Acts 1989, 71st Leg., ch. 2, § 16.01(4), eff. Aug. 28, 1989.

CHAPTER 134. TEXAS THEFT LIABILITY ACT

Section

§ 134.001. Short Title

This chapter may be cited as the Texas Theft Liability Act.

Added by Acts 1989, 71st Leg., ch. 2, § 4.05(a), eff. Aug. 28, 1989.

§ 134.002. Definitions

In this chapter:

(1) "Person" means an individual, partnership, corporation, association, or other group, however organized.

(2) "Theft" means unlawfully appropriating property or unlawfully obtaining services as described by Section 31.03, 31.04, 31.06, 31.07, 31.11, 31.12, 31.13, or 31.14, Penal Code.

Added by Acts 1989, 71st Leg., ch. 2, § 4.05(a), eff. Aug. 28, 1989. Amended by Acts 1999, 76th Leg., ch. 858, § 4, eff. Sept. 1, 1999; Acts 2013, 83rd Leg., ch. 10 (S.B. 953), § 2, eff. Sept. 1, 2013.

§ 134.003. Liability

(a) A person who commits theft is liable for the damages resulting from the theft.

(b) A parent or other person who has the duty of control and reasonable discipline of a child is liable for theft committed by the child.

Added by Acts 1989, 71st Leg., ch. 2, § 4.05(a), eff. Aug. 28, 1989.

§ 134.004. Suit

A suit under this chapter may be brought in the county where the theft occurred or in the county where the defendant resides.

Added by Acts 1989, 71st Leg., ch. 2, § 4.05(a), eff. Aug. 28, 1989.

§ 134.005. Recovery

(a) In a suit under this chapter, a person who has sustained damages resulting from theft may recover:

(1) under Section 134.003(a), from a person who commits theft, the amount of actual damages found by the trier of fact and, in addition to actual damages, damages awarded by the trier of fact in a sum not to exceed $1,000; or

(2) from a parent or other person who has the duty of control and reasonable discipline of a child, for an action brought under Section 134.003(b), the amount of actual damages found by the trier of fact, not to exceed $5,000.

(b) Each person who prevails in a suit under this chapter shall be awarded court costs and reasonable and necessary attorney's fees.

Added by Acts 1989, 71st Leg., ch. 2, § 4.05(a), eff. Aug. 28, 1989.

CHAPTER 134A. TRADE SECRETS

Section

§ 134A.001. Short Title

This chapter may be cited as the Texas Uniform Trade Secrets Act.

Added by Acts 2013, 83rd Leg., ch. 10 (S.B. 953), § 1, eff. Sept. 1, 2013.

§ 134A.002. Definitions

In this chapter:

(1) "Claimant" means a party seeking to recover damages under this chapter, including a plaintiff, counterclaimant, cross-claimant, or third-party plaintiff. In an action in which a party seeks recovery of damages under this chapter on behalf of

another person, "claimant" includes both that other person and the party seeking recovery of damages.

(1-a) "Clear and convincing" means the measure or degree of proof that will produce in the mind of the trier of fact a firm belief or conviction as to the truth of the allegations sought to be established.

(2) "Improper means" includes theft, bribery, misrepresentation, breach or inducement of a breach of a duty to maintain secrecy, to limit use, or to prohibit discovery of a trade secret, or espionage through electronic or other means.

(3) "Misappropriation" means:

(A) acquisition of a trade secret of another by a person who knows or has reason to know that the trade secret was acquired by improper means; or

(B) disclosure or use of a trade secret of another without express or implied consent by a person who:

(i) used improper means to acquire knowledge of the trade secret;

(ii) at the time of disclosure or use, knew or had reason to know that the person's knowledge of the trade secret was:

(a) derived from or through a person who used improper means to acquire the trade secret;

(b) acquired under circumstances giving rise to a duty to maintain the secrecy of or limit the use of the trade secret; or

(c) derived from or through a person who owed a duty to the person seeking relief to maintain the secrecy of or limit the use of the trade secret; or

(iii) before a material change of the position of the person, knew or had reason to know that the trade secret was a trade secret and that knowledge of the trade secret had been acquired by accident or mistake.

(3-a) "Owner" means, with respect to a trade secret, the person or entity in whom or in which rightful, legal, or equitable title to, or the right to enforce rights in, the trade secret is reposed.

(4) "Proper means" means discovery by independent development, reverse engineering unless prohibited, or any other means that is not improper means.

(5) "Reverse engineering" means the process of studying, analyzing, or disassembling a product or device to discover its design, structure, construction, or source code provided that the product or device was acquired lawfully or from a person having the legal right to convey it.

(6) "Trade secret" means all forms and types of information, including business, scientific, technical, economic, or engineering information, and any formula, design, prototype, pattern, plan, compilation, program device, program, code, device, method, technique, process, procedure, financial data, or list of actual or potential customers or suppliers, whether tangible or intangible and whether or how stored, compiled, or memorialized physically, electronically, graphically, photographically, or in writing if:

(A) the owner of the trade secret has taken reasonable measures under the circumstances to keep the information secret; and

(B) the information derives independent economic value, actual or potential, from not being generally known to, and not being readily ascertainable through proper means by, another person who can obtain economic value from the disclosure or use of the information.

(7) "Willful and malicious misappropriation" means intentional misappropriation resulting from the conscious disregard of the rights of the owner of the trade secret.

Added by Acts 2013, 83rd Leg., ch. 10 (S.B. 953), § 1, eff. Sept. 1, 2013. Amended by Acts 2017, 85th Leg., ch. 37 (H.B. 1995), § 1, eff. Sept. 1, 2017.

§ 134A.003. Injunctive Relief

(a) Actual or threatened misappropriation may be enjoined if the order does not prohibit a person from using general knowledge, skill, and experience that person acquired during employment.

(a-1) On application to the court, an injunction shall be terminated when the trade secret has ceased to exist, but the injunction may be continued for an additional reasonable period of time in order to eliminate commercial advantage that otherwise would be derived from the misappropriation.

(b) In exceptional circumstances, an injunction may condition future use upon payment of a reasonable royalty for no longer than the period of time for which use could have been prohibited. Exceptional circumstances include a material and prejudicial change of position before acquiring knowledge or reason to know of misappropriation that renders a prohibitive injunction inequitable.

(c) In appropriate circumstances, affirmative acts to protect a trade secret may be compelled by court order.

Added by Acts 2013, 83rd Leg., ch. 10 (S.B. 953), § 1, eff. Sept. 1, 2013. Amended by Acts 2017, 85th Leg., ch. 37 (H.B. 1995), § 2, eff. Sept. 1, 2017.

§ 134A.004. Damages

(a) In addition to or in lieu of injunctive relief, a claimant is entitled to recover damages for misappropriation. Damages can include both the actual loss caused by misappropriation and the unjust enrichment caused by misappropriation that is not taken into account in computing actual loss. In lieu of damages measured by any other methods, the damages caused by misappropriation may be measured by imposition of liability for a reasonable royalty for a misappropriator's unauthorized disclosure or use of a trade secret.

(b) If willful and malicious misappropriation is proven by clear and convincing evidence, the fact finder may award exemplary damages in an amount not exceeding twice any award made under Subsection (a).

Added by Acts 2013, 83rd Leg., ch. 10 (S.B. 953), § 1, eff. Sept. 1, 2013. Amended by Acts 2017, 85th Leg., ch. 37 (H.B. 1995), § 3, eff. Sept. 1, 2017.

§ 134A.005. Attorney's Fees

The court may award reasonable attorney's fees to the prevailing party if:

(1) a claim of misappropriation is made in bad faith;

(2) a motion to terminate an injunction is made or resisted in bad faith; or

(3) willful and malicious misappropriation exists.

Added by Acts 2013, 83rd Leg., ch. 10 (S.B. 953), § 1, eff. Sept. 1, 2013. Amended by Acts 2017, 85th Leg., ch. 37 (H.B. 1995), § 4, eff. Sept. 1, 2017.

§ 134A.006. Preservation of Secrecy

(a) In an action under this chapter, a court shall preserve the secrecy of an alleged trade secret by reasonable means. There is a presumption in favor of granting protective orders to preserve the secrecy of trade secrets. Protective orders may include provisions limiting access to confidential information to only the attorneys and their experts, holding in camera hearings, sealing the records of the action, and ordering any person involved in the litigation not to disclose an alleged trade secret without prior court approval.

(b) In an action under this chapter, a presumption exists that a party is allowed to participate and assist counsel in the presentation of the party's case. At any stage of the action, the court may exclude a party and the party's representative or limit a party's access to the alleged trade secret of another party if other countervailing interests overcome the presumption. In making this determination, the court must conduct a balancing test that considers:

(1) the value of an owner's alleged trade secret;

(2) the degree of competitive harm an owner would suffer from the dissemination of the owner's alleged trade secret to the other party;

(3) whether the owner is alleging that the other party is already in possession of the alleged trade secret;

(4) whether a party's representative acts as a competitive decision maker;

(5) the degree to which a party's defense would be impaired by limiting that party's access to the alleged trade secret;

(6) whether a party or a party's representative possesses specialized expertise that would not be available to a party's outside expert; and

(7) the stage of the action.

Added by Acts 2013, 83rd Leg., ch. 10 (S.B. 953), § 1, eff. Sept. 1, 2013. Amended by Acts 2017, 85th Leg., ch. 37 (H.B. 1995), § 5, eff. Sept. 1, 2017.

§ 134A.007. Effect on Other Law

(a) Except as provided by Subsection (b), this chapter displaces conflicting tort, restitutionary, and other law of this state providing civil remedies for misappropriation of a trade secret.

(b) This chapter does not affect:

(1) contractual remedies, whether or not based upon misappropriation of a trade secret;

(2) other civil remedies that are not based upon misappropriation of a trade secret; or

(3) criminal remedies, whether or not based upon misappropriation of a trade secret.

(c) To the extent that this chapter conflicts with the Texas Rules of Civil Procedure, this chapter controls. Notwithstanding Section 22.004, Government Code, the supreme court may not amend or adopt rules in conflict with this chapter.

(d) This chapter does not affect the disclosure of public information by a governmental body under Chapter 552, Government Code.

Added by Acts 2013, 83rd Leg., ch. 10 (S.B. 953), § 1, eff. Sept. 1, 2013.

§ 134A.008. Uniformity of Application and Construction

This chapter shall be applied and construed to effectuate its general purpose to make uniform the law with respect to the subject of this chapter among states enacting it.

Added by Acts 2013, 83rd Leg., ch. 10 (S.B. 953), § 1, eff. Sept. 1, 2013.

CHAPTER 135. DURABLE POWER OF ATTORNEY FOR HEALTH CARE [REDESIGNATED]

§§ 135.001 to 135.011. Redesignated as V.T.C.A., Health & Safety Code §§ 166.151 to 166.161 by Acts 1999, 76th Leg., ch. 450, § 1.05, eff. Sept. 1, 1999

§§ 135.012, 135.013. Deleted by Acts 1999, 76th Leg., ch. 450, § 1.05, eff. Sept. 1, 1999

§§ 135.014 to 135.018. Redesignated as V.T.C.A., Health & Safety Code §§ 166.162 to 166.166 by Acts 1999, 76th Leg., ch. 450, § 1.05, eff. Sept. 1, 1999

CHAPTER 136. PROOF OF MAILING

Section

§ 136.001. Certified Mail

(a) Except as provided by Subsection (b), a person may use certified mail with return receipt requested in any case in which registered mail is required by law. The mailing of a notice of hearing, citation, bid request, or other notice, information, or material by certified mail has the same legal effect as if sent by registered mail, if the receipt for the certified mail is validated with an official post office postmark.

(b) An article shall be sent by registered mail if registered mail is required by law to provide insurance against loss of the article.

Added by Acts 1993, 73rd Leg., ch. 268, § 3, eff. Sept. 1, 1993.

CHAPTER 137. DECLARATION FOR MENTAL HEALTH TREATMENT

Section

Section

§ 137.001. Definitions

In this chapter:

(1) "Adult" means a person 18 years of age or older or a person under 18 years of age who has had the disabilities of minority removed.

(2) "Attending physician" means the physician, selected by or assigned to a patient, who has primary responsibility for the treatment and care of the patient.

(3) "Declaration for mental health treatment" means a document making a declaration of preferences or instructions regarding mental health treatment.

(4) "Emergency" means a situation in which it is immediately necessary to treat a patient to prevent:

(A) probable imminent death or serious bodily injury to the patient because the patient:

(i) overtly or continually is threatening or attempting to commit suicide or serious bodily injury to the patient; or

(ii) is behaving in a manner that indicates that the patient is unable to satisfy the patient's need for nourishment, essential medical care, or self-protection; or

(B) imminent physical or emotional harm to another because of threats, attempts, or other acts of the patient.

(5) "Health care provider" means an individual or facility licensed, certified, or otherwise authorized to administer health care or treatment, for profit or otherwise, in the ordinary course of business or professional practice and includes a physician or other health care provider, a residential care provider, or an inpatient mental health facility as defined by Section 571.003, Health and Safety Code.

(6) "Incapacitated" means that, in the opinion of the court in a guardianship proceeding under Title 3, Estates Code,[1] or in a medication hearing under Section 574.106, Health and Safety Code, a person lacks the ability to understand the nature and consequences of a proposed treatment, including the

benefits, risks, and alternatives to the proposed treatment, and lacks the ability to make mental health treatment decisions because of impairment.

(7) "Mental health treatment" means electroconvulsive or other convulsive treatment, treatment of mental illness with psychoactive medication as defined by Section 574.101, Health and Safety Code, or emergency mental health treatment.

(8) "Principal" means a person who has executed a declaration for mental health treatment.

Added by Acts 1997, 75th Leg., ch. 1318, § 1, eff. Sept. 1, 1997. Amended by Acts 1999, 76th Leg., ch. 464, § 1, eff. June 18, 1999; Acts 2017, 85th Leg., ch. 324 (S.B. 1488), § 22.009, eff. Sept. 1, 2017.

[1] V.T.C.A., Estates Code § 1001.001 et seq.

§ 137.002. Persons Who May Execute Declaration for Mental Health Treatment; Period of Validity

(a) An adult who is not incapacitated may execute a declaration for mental health treatment. The preferences or instructions may include consent to or refusal of mental health treatment.

(b) A declaration for mental health treatment is effective on execution as provided by this chapter. Except as provided by Subsection (c), a declaration for mental health treatment expires on the third anniversary of the date of its execution or when revoked by the principal, whichever is earlier.

(c) If the declaration for mental health treatment is in effect and the principal is incapacitated on the third anniversary of the date of its execution, the declaration remains in effect until the principal is no longer incapacitated.

Added by Acts 1997, 75th Leg., ch. 1318, § 1, eff. Sept. 1, 1997.

§ 137.003. Execution and Witnesses; Execution and Acknowledgment Before Notary Public

(a) A declaration for mental health treatment must be:

(1) signed by the principal in the presence of two or more subscribing witnesses; or

(2) signed by the principal and acknowledged before a notary public.

(b) A witness may not, at the time of execution, be:

(1) the principal's health or residential care provider or an employee of that provider;

(2) the operator of a community health care facility providing care to the principal or an employee of an operator of the facility;

(3) a person related to the principal by blood, marriage, or adoption;

(4) a person entitled to any part of the estate of the principal on the death of the principal under a will, trust, or deed in existence or who would be entitled to any part of the estate by operation of law if the principal died intestate; or

(5) a person who has a claim against the estate of the principal.

(c) For a witness's signature to be effective, the witness must sign a statement affirming that, at the time the declaration for mental health treatment was signed, the principal:

(1) appeared to be of sound mind to make a mental health treatment decision;

(2) has stated in the witness's presence that the principal was aware of the nature of the declaration for mental health treatment and that the principal was signing the document voluntarily and free from any duress; and

(3) requested that the witness serve as a witness to the principal's execution of the document.

Added by Acts 1997, 75th Leg., ch. 1318, § 1, eff. Sept. 1, 1997. Amended by Acts 2017, 85th Leg., ch. 349 (H.B. 1787), §§ 1, 2, eff. Sept. 1, 2017.

§ 137.004. Health Care Provider to Act in Accordance With Declaration for Mental Health Treatment

A physician or other health care provider shall act in accordance with the declaration for mental health treatment when the principal has been found to be incapacitated. A physician or other provider shall continue to seek and act in accordance with the principal's informed consent to all mental health treatment decisions if the principal is capable of providing informed consent.

Added by Acts 1997, 75th Leg., ch. 1318, § 1, eff. Sept. 1, 1997.

§ 137.005. Limitation on Liability

(a) An attending physician, health or residential care provider, or person acting for or under an attending physician's or health or residential care provider's control is not subject to criminal or civil liability and has not engaged in professional misconduct for an act or omission if the act or omission is done in good faith under the terms of a declaration for mental health treatment.

(b) An attending physician, health or residential care provider, or person acting for or under an attending physician's or health or residential care provider's control does not engage in professional misconduct for:

(1) failure to act in accordance with a declaration for mental health treatment if the physician, provider, or other person:

(A) was not provided with a copy of the declaration; and

(B) had no knowledge of the declaration after a good faith attempt to learn of the existence of a declaration; or

(2) acting in accordance with a directive for mental health treatment after the directive has expired or has been revoked if the physician, provider, or other person does not have knowledge of the expiration or revocation.

Added by Acts 1997, 75th Leg., ch. 1318, § 1, eff. Sept. 1, 1997.

§ 137.006. Discrimination Relating to Execution of Declaration for Mental Health Treatment

A health or residential care provider, health care service plan, insurer issuing disability insurance, self-insured employee benefit plan, or nonprofit hospital service plan may not:

(1) charge a person a different rate solely because the person has executed a declaration for mental health treatment;

(2) require a person to execute a declaration for mental health treatment before:

(A) admitting the person to a hospital, nursing home, or residential care home;

(B) insuring the person; or

(C) allowing the person to receive health or residential care;

(3) refuse health or residential care to a person solely because the person has executed a declaration for mental health treatment; or

(4) discharge the person solely because the person has or has not executed a declaration for mental health treatment.

Added by Acts 1997, 75th Leg., ch. 1318, § 1, eff. Sept. 1, 1997.

§ 137.007. Use and Effect of Declaration for Mental Health Treatment

(a) On being presented with a declaration for mental health treatment, a physician or other health care provider shall make the declaration a part of the principal's medical record. When acting in accordance with a declaration for mental health treatment, a physician or other health care provider shall comply with the declaration to the fullest extent possible.

(b) If a physician or other provider is unwilling at any time to comply with a declaration for mental health treatment, the physician or provider may withdraw from providing treatment consistent with the exercise of independent medical judgment and must promptly:

(1) make a reasonable effort to transfer care for the principal to a physician or provider who is willing to comply with the declaration;

(2) notify the principal, or principal's guardian, if appropriate, of the decision to withdraw; and

(3) record in the principal's medical record the notification and, if applicable, the name of the physician or provider to whom the principal is transferred.

Added by Acts 1997, 75th Leg., ch. 1318, § 1, eff. Sept. 1, 1997. Amended by Acts 1999, 76th Leg., ch. 464, § 2, eff. June 18, 1999.

§ 137.008. Disregard of Declaration for Mental Health Treatment

(a) A physician or other health care provider may subject the principal to mental health treatment in a manner contrary to the principal's wishes as expressed in a declaration for mental health treatment only:

(1) if the principal is under an order for temporary or extended mental health services under Section 574.034, 574.0345, 574.035, or 574.0355, Health and Safety Code, and treatment is authorized in compliance with Section 574.106, Health and Safety Code; or

(2) in case of an emergency when the principal's instructions have not been effective in reducing the severity of the behavior that has caused the emergency.

(b) A declaration for mental health treatment does not limit any authority provided by Chapter 573 or 574, Health and Safety Code:

(1) to take a person into custody; or

(2) to admit or retain a person in a mental health treatment facility.

(c) This section does not apply to the use of electroconvulsive treatment or other convulsive treatment.

Added by Acts 1997, 75th Leg., ch. 1318, § 1, eff. Sept. 1, 1997. Amended by Acts 1999, 76th Leg., ch. 464, § 3, eff. June 18, 1999; Acts 2019, 86th Leg., ch. 582 (S.B. 362), § 1, eff. Sept. 1, 2019.

Section 28 of Acts 2019, 86th Leg., ch. 582 (S.B. 362) provides:

"The Health and Human Services Commission is required to implement a provision of this Act only if the legislature appropriates money specifically for that purpose. If the legislature does not appropriate money specifically for that purpose, the Health and Human Services Commission may, but is not required to, implement a provision of this Act using other appropriations available for that purpose."

§ 137.009. Conflicting or Contrary Provisions

(a) Mental health treatment instructions contained in a declaration executed in accordance with this chapter supersede any contrary or conflicting instructions given by:

(1) a medical power of attorney under Subchapter D, Chapter 166, Health and Safety Code;[1] or

(2) a guardian appointed under Title 3, Estates Code,[2] after the execution of the declaration.

(b) Mental health treatment instructions contained in a declaration executed in accordance with this chapter shall be conclusive evidence of a declarant's preference in a medication hearing under Section 574.106, Health and Safety Code.

Added by Acts 1997, 75th Leg., ch. 1318, § 1, eff. Sept. 1, 1997. Amended by Acts 2017, 85th Leg., ch. 324 (S.B. 1488), § 22.010, eff. Sept. 1, 2017.

[1] V.T.C.A., Health & Safety Code § 166.151 et seq.

[2] V.T.C.A., Estates Code § 1001.001 et seq.

§ 137.010. Revocation

(a) A declaration for mental health treatment is revoked when a principal who is not incapacitated:

(1) notifies a licensed or certified health or residential care provider of the revocation;

(2) acts in a manner that demonstrates a specific intent to revoke the declaration; or

(3) executes a later declaration for mental health treatment.

(b) A principal's health or residential care provider who is informed of or provided with a revocation of a declaration for mental health treatment immediately shall:

(1) record the revocation in the principal's medical record; and

(2) give notice of the revocation to any other health or residential care provider the provider knows to be responsible for the principal's care.

Added by Acts 1997, 75th Leg., ch. 1318, § 1, eff. Sept. 1, 1997. Amended by Acts 1999, 76th Leg., ch. 464, § 4, eff. June 18, 1999.

§ 137.011. Form of Declaration for Mental Health Treatment

The declaration for mental health treatment must be in substantially the following form:

DECLARATION FOR MENTAL HEALTH TREATMENT

I, ______________, being an adult of sound mind, wilfully and voluntarily make this declaration for mental health treatment to be followed if it is determined by a court that my ability to understand the nature and consequences of a proposed treatment, including the benefits, risks, and alternatives to the proposed treatment, is impaired to such an extent that I lack the capacity to make mental health treatment decisions. "Mental health treatment" means electroconvulsive or other convulsive treatment, treatment of mental illness with psychoactive medication, and preferences regarding emergency mental health treatment.

(OPTIONAL PARAGRAPH) I understand that I may become incapable of giving or withholding informed consent for mental health treatment due to the symptoms of a diagnosed mental disorder. These symptoms may include:

____

PSYCHOACTIVE MEDICATIONS

If I become incapable of giving or withholding informed consent for mental health treatment, my wishes regarding psychoactive medications are as follows:

_____ I consent to the administration of the following medications:

____

_____ I do not consent to the administration of the following medications:

____

_____ I consent to the administration of a federal Food and Drug Administration approved medication that was only approved and in existence after my declaration and that is considered in the same class of psychoactive medications as stated below:

____

Conditions or limitations: ______________

CONVULSIVE TREATMENT

If I become incapable of giving or withholding informed consent for mental health treatment, my wishes regarding convulsive treatment are as follows:

_____ I consent to the administration of convulsive treatment.

_____ I do not consent to the administration of convulsive treatment.

Conditions or limitations: ______________

PREFERENCES FOR EMERGENCY TREATMENT

In an emergency, I prefer the following treatment FIRST (circle one) Restraint/Seclusion/Medication.

In an emergency, I prefer the following treatment SECOND (circle one) Restraint/Seclusion/Medication.

In an emergency, I prefer the following treatment THIRD (circle one) Restraint/Seclusion/Medication.

_____ I prefer a male/female to administer restraint, seclusion, and/or medications.

Options for treatment prior to use of restraint, seclusion, and/or medications:

____

Conditions or limitations: ______________

ADDITIONAL PREFERENCES OR INSTRUCTIONS

____

Conditions or limitations: ______________

Signature of Principal/Date: ______________

SIGNATURE ACKNOWLEDGED BEFORE NOTARY PUBLIC

State of Texas
County of__________
This instrument was acknowledged before me on __________(date) by ______________(name of notary public).

____
NOTARY PUBLIC, State of Texas
Printed name of Notary Public:
____
My commission expires:
____

SIGNATURE IN PRESENCE OF TWO WITNESSES

STATEMENT OF WITNESSES

I declare under penalty of perjury that the principal's name has been represented to me by the principal, that the principal signed or acknowledged this declaration in my presence, that I believe the principal to be of sound mind, that the principal has affirmed that the principal is aware of the nature of the document and is signing it voluntarily and free from duress, that the principal requested that I serve as witness to the principal's execution of this document, and that I am not a provider of health or residential care to the principal, an employee of a provider of health or residential care to the principal, an operator of a community health care facility providing care to the principal, or an employee of an operator of a community health care facility providing care to the principal.

I declare that I am not related to the principal by blood, marriage, or adoption and that to the best of my knowledge I am not entitled to and do not have a claim against any part of the estate of the principal on the death of the principal under a will or by operation of law.

Witness Signature: ______________
Print Name: ______________
Date: ______________
Address: ______________
Witness Signature: ______________
Print Name: ______________
Date: ______________
Address: ______________

NOTICE TO PERSON MAKING A DECLARATION FOR MENTAL HEALTH TREATMENT

This is an important legal document. It creates a declaration for mental health treatment. Before signing this document, you should know these important facts:

This document allows you to make decisions in advance about mental health treatment and specifically three types of mental health treatment: psychoactive medication, convulsive therapy, and emergency mental health treatment. The instructions that you include in this declaration will be followed only if a court believes that you are incapacitated to make treatment decisions. Otherwise, you will be considered able to give or withhold consent for the treatments.

This document will continue in effect for a period of three years unless you become incapacitated to participate in mental health treatment decisions. If this occurs, the directive will continue in effect until you are no longer incapacitated.

You have the right to revoke this document in whole or in part at any time you have not been determined to be incapacitated. YOU MAY NOT REVOKE THIS DECLARATION WHEN YOU ARE CONSIDERED BY A COURT TO BE INCAPACITATED. A revocation is effective when it is communicated to your attending physician or other health care provider.

If there is anything in this document that you do not understand, you should ask a lawyer to explain it to you. This declaration is not valid unless it is either acknowledged before a notary public or signed by two qualified witnesses who are personally known to you and who are present when you sign or acknowledge your signature.

Added by Acts 1997, 75th Leg., ch. 1318, § 1, eff. Sept. 1, 1997. Amended by Acts 2017, 85th Leg., ch. 349 (H.B. 1787), § 3, eff. Sept. 1, 2017.

CHAPTER 138. PERSONAL RESPONSIBILITY FOR FOOD CONSUMPTION

Section

§ 138.001. Definitions

In this chapter:

(1) "Agricultural commodity" has the meaning assigned by Section 41.002, Agriculture Code.

(2) "Agricultural producer" means any producer of an agricultural commodity.

(3) "Food" has the definition assigned by Section 431.002, Health and Safety Code. "Food" does not include:

(A) a cosmetic, as defined by Section 321(i) of the Federal Food, Drug, and Cosmetic Act (21 U.S.C. Section 321 (i));

(B) a drug, as defined by Section 321(g) of the Federal Food, Drug, and Cosmetic Act (21 U.S.C. Section 321(g)), whether prescription or over-the-counter; or

(C) a dietary supplement, as defined by Section 321(ff) of the Federal Food, Drug, and Cosmetic Act (21 U.S.C. Section 321(ff)).

(4) "Livestock" has the meaning assigned by Section 1.003, Agriculture Code.

(5) "Livestock producer" means any producer of livestock.

(6) "Manufacturer" means a person lawfully engaged, in the regular course of the person's trade or business, in manufacturing a food.

(7) "Seller" means a person lawfully engaged, in the regular course of the person's trade or business, in marketing, distributing, advertising, or selling a food.

(8) "State" includes each state of the United States, the District of Columbia, the Commonwealth of Puerto Rico, the Virgin Islands, Guam, American Samoa, and the Commonwealth of the Northern Mariana Islands and any other territory or possession of the United States and any political subdivision of any of those places.

(9) "Trade association" means any association or business organization, whether or not incorporated under federal or state law, that is not operated for profit and two or more members of which are manufacturers, marketers, distributors, advertisers, or sellers of a food.

Added by Acts 2005, 79th Leg., ch. 906, § 1, eff. June 18, 2005.

§ 138.002. Civil Action Prohibited

(a) Except as otherwise provided by this section, a manufacturer, seller, trade association, livestock producer, or agricultural producer is not liable under any law of this state for any claim arising out of weight gain or obesity, a health condition associated with weight gain or obesity, or any other generally known condition allegedly caused by or allegedly likely to result from the long-term consumption of food, including:

(1) an action brought by a person other than the individual on whose weight gain, obesity, or health condition the action is based; and

(2) any derivative action brought by or on behalf of any individual or any representative, spouse, parent, child, or other relative of any individual.

(b) This section does not prohibit a person from bringing:

(1) an action in which:

(A) a manufacturer or seller of a food knowingly and wilfully violates a federal or state statute applicable to the manufacturing, marketing, distribution, advertisement, labeling, or sale of the food; and

(B) the violation is a proximate cause of injury related to an individual's weight gain or obesity or any health condition associated with an individual's weight gain or obesity; or

(2) an action brought:

(A) under Chapter 431, Health and Safety Code; or

(B) by the attorney general under Section 17.47, Business & Commerce Code.

(c) This section does not create a cause of action.

Added by Acts 2005, 79th Leg., ch. 906, § 1, eff. June 18, 2005.

§ 138.003. Pleadings

In an action described in Section 138.002(b)(1), the initiating petition must state with particularity:

(1) the federal and state statutes allegedly violated; and

(2) the facts that are alleged to have proximately caused the injury claimed.

Added by Acts 2005, 79th Leg., ch. 906, § 1, eff. June 18, 2005.

§ 138.004. Stay

(a) For an action described by Section 138.002(b), all discovery and other proceedings are stayed during the pendency of any motion to dismiss unless the court finds on motion of any party that particularized discovery is necessary to preserve evidence or to prevent undue prejudice to that party.

(b) During the pendency of any stay of discovery, unless otherwise ordered by the court, any party to the action with actual notice of the allegations contained in the petition shall treat all documents, data compilations, including electronically recorded or stored data, and tangible objects that are in the custody or control of the person and that are relevant to the allegations, as if they were the subject of a continuing request for production of documents from an opposing party under the applicable rules of civil procedure.

(c) A party aggrieved by the wilful failure of an opposing party to comply with this section may apply to the court for an order awarding appropriate sanctions.

Added by Acts 2005, 79th Leg., ch. 906, § 1, eff. June 18, 2005.

CHAPTER 139. PERSONAL INJURY TO CERTAIN PERSONS

SUBCHAPTER A. GENERAL PROVISIONS

SUBCHAPTER B. STRUCTURED SETTLEMENT OFFER

SUBCHAPTER A. GENERAL PROVISIONS

§ 139.001. Definitions

In this chapter:

(1) "Claimant" means a person described by Section 139.002 (1) or (2) who makes a claim to which this chapter applies.

(2) "Incapacitated person" has the meaning assigned by Section 1002.017, Estates Code.

Added by Acts 1999, 76th Leg., ch. 1228, § 1, eff. Sept. 1, 1999. Amended by Acts 2017, 85th Leg., ch. 324 (S.B. 1488), § 22.011, eff. Sept. 1, 2017.

§ 139.002. Scope of Chapter

This chapter applies only to a suit on a claim for damages arising from personal injury:

(1) to an incapacitated person; or

(2) in which the personal injury has resulted in the substantial disablement of the injured person.

Added by Acts 1999, 76th Leg., ch. 1228, § 1, eff. Sept. 1, 1999.

SUBCHAPTER B. STRUCTURED SETTLEMENT OFFER

§ 139.101. Written Offer Required

An offer of structured settlement made after a suit to which this chapter applies has been filed must be:

(1) made in writing; and

(2) presented to the attorney for the claimant.

Added by Acts 1999, 76th Leg., ch. 1228, § 1, eff. Sept. 1, 1999.

§ 139.102. Presentation to Claimant

(a) As soon as practicable after receiving the offer under Section 139.101, but not later than any expiration date that may accompany the quotation that outlines the terms of the structured settlement offered, the attorney receiving the offer shall present the offer to the claimant or the claimant's personal representative.

(b) To the extent reasonably necessary to permit the claimant or the claimant's personal representative to make an informed decision regarding the acceptance or rejection of a proposed structured settlement, the attorney shall advise the claimant or the claimant's personal representative with respect to:

(1) the terms, conditions, and other attributes of the proposed structured settlement; and

(2) the appropriateness of the structured settlement under the circumstances.

Added by Acts 1999, 76th Leg., ch. 1228, § 1, eff. Sept. 1, 1999.

CHAPTER 140. CONTRACTUAL SUBROGATION RIGHTS OF PAYORS OF CERTAIN BENEFITS

Acts 2013, 83rd Leg., ch. 180 (H.B. 1869), § 1 added this Chapter 140. Another Chapter 140, Civil Racketeering Related to Trafficking of Persons, added by Acts 2013, 83rd Leg., ch. 1066 (H.B. 3241), § 1, was redesignated as Chapter 140A by Acts 2015, 84th Leg., ch. 1236 (S.B. 1296), § 21.001(5).

Section

§ 140.001. Definitions

In this chapter:

(1) "Covered individual" means an individual entitled to benefits described by Section 140.002.

(2) "Payor of benefits" or "payor" means an issuer of a plan providing benefits described by Section 140.002 that:

(A) pays benefits to or on behalf of a covered individual as a result of personal injuries to the covered individual caused by the tortious conduct of a third party; and

(B) has a contractual right of subrogation described by Section 140.004.

Added by Acts 2013, 83rd Leg., ch. 180 (H.B. 1869), § 1, eff. Jan. 1, 2014.

§ 140.002. Applicability of Chapter

(a) This chapter applies to an issuer of a health benefit plan that provides benefits for medical or surgical expenses incurred as a result of a health condition, accident, or sickness, a disability benefit plan, or an employee welfare benefit plan, including an individual, group, blanket, or franchise insurance policy or insurance agreement, a group hospital service contract, or an individual or group evidence of coverage or similar coverage document, including:

(1) an insurance company;

(2) a group hospital service corporation operating under Chapter 842, Insurance Code;

(3) a fraternal benefit society operating under Chapter 885, Insurance Code;

(4) a stipulated premium insurance company operating under Chapter 884, Insurance Code;

(5) a reciprocal exchange operating under Chapter 942, Insurance Code;

(6) a health maintenance organization operating under Chapter 843, Insurance Code;

(7) a multiple employer welfare arrangement that holds a certificate of authority under Chapter 846, Insurance Code; or

(8) an approved nonprofit health corporation that holds a certificate of authority under Chapter 844, Insurance Code.

(b) Notwithstanding Section 172.014, Local Government Code, or any other law, this chapter applies to a risk pool providing health and accident coverage under Chapter 172, Local Government Code.

(c) Notwithstanding any other law, this chapter applies to an issuer of a plan or coverage under Chapter 1551, 1575, 1579, or 1601, Insurance Code.

(d) Notwithstanding any other law, this chapter applies to any self-funded issuer of a plan that provides a benefit described by Subsection (a).

(e) This chapter applies to any policy, evidence of coverage, or contract under which a benefit described by Subsection (a) is provided and:

(1) that is delivered, issued for delivery, or entered into in this state; or

(2) under which an individual or group in this state is entitled to benefits.

(f) This chapter does not apply to:

(1) a workers' compensation insurance policy or any other source of medical benefits under Title 5, Labor Code [1];

(2) Medicare;

(3) the Medicaid program under Chapter 32, Human Resources Code;

(4) a Medicaid managed care program operated under Chapter 533, Government Code;

(5) the state child health plan or any other program operated under Chapter 62 or 63, Health and Safety Code; or

(6) a self-funded plan that is subject to the Employee Retirement Income Security Act of 1974 (29 U.S.C. Section 1001 et seq.).

Added by Acts 2013, 83rd Leg., ch. 180 (H.B. 1869), § 1, eff. Jan. 1, 2014.

[1] V.T.C.A., Labor Code § 401.001 et seq.

§ 140.003. Conflicts With Other Law

In the event of a conflict between this chapter and another law, including a rule of procedure or evidence, this chapter controls to the extent of the conflict.

Added by Acts 2013, 83rd Leg., ch. 180 (H.B. 1869), § 1, eff. Jan. 1, 2014.

§ 140.004. Contractual Subrogation Rights Authorized

An issuer of a plan that provides benefits described by Section 140.002 under which the policy or plan issuer may be obligated to make payments or provide medical or surgical benefits to or on behalf of a covered individual as a result of a personal injury to the individual caused by the tortious conduct of a third party may contract to be subrogated to and have a right of reimbursement for payments made or costs of benefits provided from the individual's recovery for that injury, subject to this chapter.

Added by Acts 2013, 83rd Leg., ch. 180 (H.B. 1869), § 1, eff. Jan. 1, 2014.

§ 140.005. Payors' Recovery Limited

(a) If an injured covered individual is entitled by law to seek a recovery from the third-party tortfeasor for benefits paid or provided by a subrogee as described by Section 140.004, then all payors are entitled to recover as provided by Subsection (b) or (c).

(b) This subsection applies when a covered individual is not represented by an attorney in obtaining a recovery. All payors' share under Subsection (a) of a covered individual's recovery is an amount that is equal to the lesser of:

(1) one-half of the covered individual's gross recovery; or

(2) the total cost of benefits paid, provided, or assumed by the payor as a direct result of the tortious conduct of the third party.

(c) This subsection applies when a covered individual is represented by an attorney in obtaining a recovery. All payors' share under Subsection (a) of a covered individual's recovery is an amount that is equal to the lesser of:

(1) one-half of the covered individual's gross recovery less attorney's fees and procurement costs as provided by Section 140.007; or

(2) the total cost of benefits paid, provided, or assumed by the payor as a direct result of the tortious conduct of the third party less attorney's fees and procurement costs as provided by Section 140.007.

(d) A common law doctrine that requires an injured party to be made whole before a subrogee makes a recovery does not apply to the recovery of a payor under this section.

Added by Acts 2013, 83rd Leg., ch. 180 (H.B. 1869), § 1, eff. Jan. 1, 2014.

§ 140.006. Attorney's Fees in Declaratory Judgment Action

Notwithstanding Section 37.009 or any other law, if a declaratory judgment action is brought under this chapter, the court may not award costs or attorney's fees to any party in the action.

Added by Acts 2013, 83rd Leg., ch. 180 (H.B. 1869), § 1, eff. Jan. 1, 2014.

§ 140.007. Attorney's Fees in Recovery Action

(a) Except as provided by Subsection (c), a payor of benefits whose interest is not actively represented by an attorney in an action to recover for a personal injury to a covered individual shall pay to an attorney representing the covered individual a fee in an amount determined under an agreement entered into between the attorney and the payor plus a pro rata share of expenses incurred in connection with the recovery.

(b) Except as provided by Subsection (c), in the absence of an agreement described by Subsection (a), the court shall award to the attorney, payable out of the payor's share of the total gross recovery, a reasonable fee for recovery of the payor's share, not to exceed one-third of the payor's recovery.

(c) If an attorney representing the payor's interest actively participates in obtaining a recovery, the court shall award and apportion between the covered individual's and the payor's attorneys a fee payable out of the payor's subrogation recovery. In apportioning the award, the court shall consider the benefit accruing to the payor as a result of each attorney's service. The total attorney's fees may not exceed one-third of the payor's recovery.

Added by Acts 2013, 83rd Leg., ch. 180 (H.B. 1869), § 1, eff. Jan. 1, 2014.

§ 140.008. First-party Recovery

(a) Except as provided by Subsection (b), a payor of benefits may not pursue a recovery against a covered individual's first-party recovery.

(b) A payor of benefits may pursue recovery against uninsured/underinsured motorist coverage or medical payments coverage only if the covered individual or the covered individual's immediate family did not pay the premiums for the coverage.

Added by Acts 2013, 83rd Leg., ch. 180 (H.B. 1869), § 1, eff. Jan. 1, 2014.

§ 140.009. Construction of Chapter

This chapter does not create a cause of action. Nothing in this chapter shall be construed to prevent a payor of benefits from waiving, negotiating, or not pursuing any claim or recovery described by Section 140.004 or 140.005.

Added by Acts 2013, 83rd Leg., ch. 180 (H.B. 1869), § 1, eff. Jan. 1, 2014.

CHAPTER 140A. CIVIL RACKETEERING RELATED TO TRAFFICKING OF PERSONS

SUBCHAPTER A. GENERAL PROVISIONS

Acts 2013, 83rd Leg., ch. 1066 (H.B. 3241), § 1 added this Chapter as Chapter 140. Acts 2015, 84th Leg., ch. 1236 (S.B. 1296), § 21.001(5) redesignated the Chapter as Chapter 140A, effective September 1, 2015.

SUBCHAPTER A. GENERAL PROVISIONS

§ 140A.001. Definitions

In this chapter:

(1) "Acquire" means an act to:

(A) possess property;

(B) prevent another person from using that person's property or dictate the terms of use of that property;

(C) bring about or receive the transfer of any interest in property, whether to oneself or to another person; or

(D) secure performance of a service.

(1–a) "Attorney general" means the attorney general of Texas or any assistant attorney general acting under the direction of the attorney general of Texas.

(2) "Enterprise" means a legal entity, a group of individuals associated in fact, or a combination of entities and individuals.

(3) "Gain" means a benefit, an interest, or property, without reduction for expenses incurred in acquiring or maintaining the benefit, interest, or property or incurred for any other reason.

(4) "Proceeds" means an interest in property acquired or derived from, produced or realized through, or directly or indirectly caused by an act or omission, and the fruits of the interest, in any form.

(5) "Racketeering" means an act described by Section 140A.002.

Added by Acts 2013, 83rd Leg., ch. 1066 (H.B. 3241), § 1, eff. June 14, 2013. Redesignated from V.T.C.A., Civil Practice & Remedies Code § 140.001 by Acts 2015, 84th Leg., ch. 1236 (S.B. 1296), § 21.001(5), eff. Sept. 1, 2015. Amended by Acts 2015, 84th Leg., ch. 1236 (S.B. 1296), § 21.002(1), eff. Sept. 1, 2015; Acts 2017, 85th Leg., ch. 685 (H.B. 29), § 3, eff. Sept. 1, 2017.

Section 63(c) of Acts 2021, 87th Leg., ch. 807 (H.B. 1540) provides:

"The change in law made to Chapters 125 and 140A, Civil Practice and Remedies Code, by this Act applies only to a cause of action that accrues on or after the effective date [Sept. 1, 2021] of this Act. A cause of action that accrues before the effective date of this Act is governed by the law applicable to the cause of action immediately before the effective date of this Act, and that law is continued in effect for that purpose."

§ 140A.0015. Applicability of Provisions

(a) The provisions of this chapter are cumulative of each other and any other provision of law in effect relating to the same subject. The provisions of this chapter preserve the constitutional and common law authority of the attorney general to bring any action under state and federal law.

(b) If any of the provisions of this chapter are held invalid, the remainder of the provisions are not affected as a result and the application of the provision held invalid to persons or circumstances other than those as to which it is held invalid are not affected as a result.

Added by Acts 2017, 85th Leg., ch. 685 (H.B. 29), § 4, eff. Sept. 1, 2017.

§ 140A.002. Civil Racketeering

A person or enterprise commits racketeering if, for financial gain, the person or enterprise commits an offense under Chapter 20A, Penal Code (trafficking of persons).

Added by Acts 2013, 83rd Leg., ch. 1066 (H.B. 3241), § 1, eff. June 14, 2013. Redesignated from V.T.C.A., Civil Practice & Remedies Code § 140.002 by Acts 2015, 84th Leg., ch. 1236 (S.B. 1296), § 21.001(5), eff. Sept. 1, 2015. Amended by Acts 2021, 87th Leg., ch. 807 (H.B. 1540), § 11, eff. Sept. 1, 2021.

Section 63(d) of Acts 2021, 87th Leg., ch. 807 (H.B. 1540) provides:

"Except as otherwise provided by this section, the changes in law made by this Act apply only to an offense committed on or after the effective date [Sept. 1, 2021] of this Act. An offense committed before the effective date of this Act is governed by the law in effect on the date the offense was committed, and the former law is continued in effect for that purpose. For purposes of this section, an offense was committed before the effective date of this Act if any element of the offense occurred before that date."

§ 140A.003. Redesignated as V.T.C.A., Civil Practice & Remedies Code § 140A.101 by Acts 2017, 85th Leg., ch. 685 (H.B. 29), § 7, eff. Sept. 1, 2017

§ 140A.004. Redesignated as V.T.C.A., Civil Practice & Remedies Code § 140A.102 and amended by Acts 2017, 85th Leg., ch. 685 (H.B. 29), § 7, eff. Sept. 1, 2017

§ 140A.005. Redesignated as V.T.C.A., Civil Practice & Remedies Code § 140A.103 by Acts 2017, 85th Leg., ch. 685 (H.B. 29), § 7, eff. Sept. 1, 2017

§ 140A.006. Redesignated as V.T.C.A., Civil Practice & Remedies Code § 140A.104 by Acts 2017, 85th Leg., ch. 685 (H.B. 29), § 7, eff. Sept. 1, 2017

§ 140A.007. Redesignated as V.T.C.A., Civil Practice & Remedies Code § 140A.105 by Acts 2017, 85th Leg., ch. 685 (H.B. 29), § 7, eff. Sept. 1, 2017

§ 140A.008. Redesignated as V.T.C.A., Civil Practice & Remedies Code § 140A.106 by Acts 2017, 85th Leg., ch. 685 (H.B. 29), § 7, eff. Sept. 1, 2017

§ 140A.009. Redesignated as V.T.C.A., Civil Practice & Remedy Code § 140A.107 by Acts 2017, 85th Leg., ch. 685 (H.B. 29), § 7, eff. Sept. 1, 2017

§ 140A.010. Redesignated as V.T.C.A., Civil Practice & Remedies Code § 140A.108 and amended by Acts 2017, 85th

Leg., ch. 685 (H.B. 29), § 7, eff. Sept. 1, 2017

§ 140A.011. Redesignated as V.T.C.A., Civil Practice & Remedies Code § 140A.109 and amended by Acts 2017, 85th Leg., ch. 685 (H.B. 29), § 7, eff. Sept. 1 2017

§ 140A.012. Redesignated as V.T.C.A., Civil Practice & Remedies Code § 140A.110 by Acts 2017, 85th Leg., ch. 685 (H.B. 29), § 7, eff. Sept. 1, 2017

§ 140A.013. Redesignated as V.T.C.A., Civil Practice & Remedies Code § 140A.111 by Acts 2017, 85th Leg., ch. 685 (H.B. 29), § 7, eff. Sept. 1, 2017

SUBCHAPTER B. PROCEDURES AND EVIDENCE

§ 140A.051. Definitions

In this subchapter:

(1) "Civil investigative demand" means any demand issued by the attorney general under this subchapter.

(2) "Documentary material" means the original or a copy of any paper, contract, agreement, book, booklet, brochure, pamphlet, catalog, magazine, notice, announcement, circular, bulletin, instruction, minutes, agenda, study, analysis, report, graph, map, chart, table, schedule, note, letter, telegram, telephone recordings, or data compilations stored in or accessible through computer or other information retrieval systems, together with instructions and all other materials necessary to use or interpret the data compilations, and any product of discovery.

(3) "Person" has the meaning assigned by Section 311.005, Government Code.

(4) "Product of discovery" means:

(A) the original or a copy of a deposition, interrogatory, document, thing, result of inspection of land or other property, examination, or admission that is obtained by any method of discovery in a judicial or administrative proceeding of an adversarial nature;

(B) a digest, analysis, selection, compilation, or derivation of any item listed in Paragraph (A); and

(C) an index, instruction, or other aid or means of access to any item listed in Paragraph (A).

(5) "Racketeering investigation" means any inquiry conducted by the attorney general for the purpose of ascertaining whether any person is or has been engaged in or is actively preparing to engage in activities that may constitute a racketeering violation.

(6) "Racketeering violation" means any act or omission in violation of any of the prohibitions in Section 140A.002.

Added by Acts 2017, 85th Leg., ch. 685 (H.B. 29), § 5, eff. Sept. 1, 2017.

§ 140A.052. Civil Investigative Demand

If the attorney general has reason to believe that a person may be in possession, custody, or control of any documentary material or other evidence or may have any information relevant to a civil racketeering investigation, the attorney general may, before beginning a civil proceeding, issue in writing and serve on the person a civil investigative demand requiring the person to:

(1) produce any of the documentary material for inspection and copying;

(2) answer in writing any written interrogatories;

(3) give oral testimony; or

(4) provide any combination of civil investigative demands under Subdivisions (1)–(3).

Added by Acts 2017, 85th Leg., ch. 685 (H.B. 29), § 5, eff. Sept. 1, 2017.

§ 140A.053. Contents of Demand

(a) A civil investigative demand issued under Section 140A.052 must:

(1) describe the nature of the activities that are the subject of the investigation;

(2) state each statute the activity violates; and

(3) advise the person on whom the demand is served that the person has the right to object to the demand as provided for in this subchapter.

(b) A demand for production of documentary material must:

(1) describe the class of material to be produced with reasonable specificity so that the material demanded is fairly identified;

(2) prescribe a return date that provides a reasonable period of time within which the material is to be produced; and

(3) identify the individual to whom the material is to be made available for inspection and copying.

(c) A demand for answers to written interrogatories must:

(1) propound the interrogatories with definiteness and certainty;

(2) prescribe a date by which answers to the interrogatories must be submitted; and

(3) identify the individual to whom the answers should be submitted.

(d) Each demand for the giving of oral testimony must:

(1) prescribe a reasonable date, time, and place at which the testimony will begin; and

(2) identify the individual who will conduct the examination.

Added by Acts 2017, 85th Leg., ch. 685 (H.B. 29), § 5, eff. Sept. 1, 2017.

§ 140A.054. Service; Proof of Service

(a) Service of any civil investigative demand or petition filed under Section 140A.055 or 140A.060 may be made on any natural person by delivering a duly executed copy of the demand or petition to the person to be served or by mailing a copy by registered or certified mail, return receipt requested, to the person at the person's residence or principal office or place of business.

(b) Service of any demand or petition filed under Section 140A.055 or 140A.060 may be made on any person other than a natural person by delivering a duly executed copy of the demand or petition to a person to whom delivery would be appropriate under state law if the demand or petition were process in a civil suit.

(c) A verified return by the individual serving any demand or petition filed under Section 140A.055 or 140A.060 setting forth the manner of service is proof of service. In the case of service by registered or certified mail, the return must be accompanied by the return post office receipt of delivery of the demand or petition.

Added by Acts 2017, 85th Leg., ch. 685 (H.B. 29), § 5, eff. Sept. 1, 2017.

§ 140A.055. Petition for Order Modifying or Setting Aside Demand

(a) At any time before the return date specified in a civil investigative demand or not later than the 30th day after the date the demand was served, whichever period is shorter, the person who has been served, and in the case of a demand for a product of discovery the person from whom the discovery was obtained, may file a petition for an order modifying or setting aside the demand in the district court in the county of the person's residence or principal office or place of business or a district court of Travis County. The petition must specify each ground upon which the petitioner relies in seeking the relief sought. The petition may be based on any failure of a demand to comply with the provisions of this subchapter or on any constitutional or other legal right or privilege of the petitioner.

(b) The petitioner shall serve a copy of the petition on the attorney general in accordance with Section 140A.054. The attorney general may submit an answer to the petition.

(c) In ruling on the petition under this section, the court shall presume absent evidence to the contrary that the attorney general issued the demand in good faith and within the scope of the attorney general's authority.

Added by Acts 2017, 85th Leg., ch. 685 (H.B. 29), § 5, eff. Sept. 1, 2017.

§ 140A.056. Compliance with Demand

(a) A person on whom a civil investigative demand is served under this subchapter shall comply with the terms of the demand unless otherwise provided by court order.

(b) The time for compliance with the demand wholly or partly does not run during the pendency of any petition filed under Section 140A.055, provided that the petitioner shall comply with any portions of the demand not sought to be modified or set aside.

Added by Acts 2017, 85th Leg., ch. 685 (H.B. 29), § 5, eff. Sept. 1, 2017.

§ 140A.057. Documentary Material

(a) Any person on whom any civil investigative demand for the production of documentary material has been duly served under this subchapter shall make the material available to the attorney general for inspection and copying during normal business hours on the return date specified in the demand at the person's principal office or place of business or as otherwise may be agreed on by the person and the attorney general. The attorney general shall bear the expense of any copying. The person may substitute copies for originals of all or part of the requested documents if the originals are made available for inspection. The attorney general may elect to obtain or review information in an electronic format. The person shall indicate in writing which, if any, of the documents produced contain trade secrets or confidential information.

(b) The production of documentary material in response to any demand must be made under a sworn certificate in the form the demand designates by a natural person having knowledge of the facts and circumstances relating to the production to the effect that all of the requested material in the possession, custody, or control of the person to whom the demand is directed has been produced.

Added by Acts 2017, 85th Leg., ch. 685 (H.B. 29), § 5, eff. Sept. 1, 2017.

§ 140A.058. Interrogatories

(a) Each interrogatory in any civil investigative demand duly served must be answered separately and fully in writing, unless it is objected to, in which case the basis for the objection shall be set forth in lieu of an answer. The person shall indicate in writing which, if any, of the answers contain trade secrets or confidential information.

(b) Answers to interrogatories must be submitted under a sworn certificate in the form the related demand designates by a natural person having knowledge of the facts and circumstances relating to the preparation of the answers to the effect that all of the requested information in the possession, custody, control, or knowledge of the person to whom the demand is directed has been set forth fully and accurately.

Added by Acts 2017, 85th Leg., ch. 685 (H.B. 29), § 5, eff. Sept. 1, 2017.

§ 140A.059. Oral Examination

(a) The examination of any person pursuant to a civil investigative demand for oral testimony duly served must be taken before any person authorized to administer oaths and affirmations under the laws of this state or the United States. The person before whom the testimony is to be taken shall put the witness on oath or affirmation and shall personally or by someone acting under the person's direction and in the person's presence record the witness's testimony. At the expense of the attorney general, and except as provided by this subsection, the testimony must be taken stenographically and may be transcribed. The attorney general may take audio and video recordings of the testimony by providing notice to the person to be examined not later than the seventh day before the day the person is to be examined.

(b) The oral testimony of any person taken pursuant to a demand served must be taken within 100 miles of the county where the person resides, is found, or transacts business or in any other place agreed on by the person and the attorney general.

(c) Any person compelled to appear under a demand for oral testimony may be accompanied, represented, and advised by counsel. Counsel may advise the person in confidence, either on the request of the person or on the counsel's own initiative, with respect to any question arising in connection with the examination.

(d) The individual conducting the examination on behalf of the attorney general shall exclude from the place of examination all other persons except the person being examined, the person's counsel, the counsel of the person to whom the demand has been issued, the person before whom the testimony is to be taken, any stenographer taking the testimony, audiographer, videographer, and any person assisting the individual conducting the examination.

(e) During the examination, the person being examined or the person's counsel may object on the record to any question in accordance with Rule 199.5(e), Texas Rules of Civil Procedure. An objection may properly be made, received, and entered on the record when it is claimed that the person is entitled to refuse to answer the question on grounds of any constitutional or other privilege, including the privilege against self-incrimination. Neither that person nor the person's counsel may otherwise object to or refuse to answer any question or interrupt the oral examination. If the person refuses to answer any question, the attorney general may petition the district court in the county where the examination is being conducted for an order compelling the person to answer the question.

(f) After the testimony has been fully transcribed, the person before whom the testimony was taken shall promptly transmit the transcript of the testimony to the witness and a copy of the transcript to the attorney general. The witness must have a reasonable opportunity to examine the transcript and make any changes in form or substance accompanied by a statement of the reasons for the changes. The witness shall then sign and return the transcript. If the witness does not return the transcript to the person before whom the testimony was taken not later than the 20th day after the date the transcript was provided to the witness, the witness may be deemed to have waived the right to make changes. The officer shall then certify on the transcript that the witness was duly sworn and that the transcript is a true record of the testimony given by the witness and promptly transmit a copy of the certified transcript to the attorney general.

(g) On request, the attorney general shall furnish a copy of the certified transcript to the witness.

(h) The attorney general may provide the witness the same fees and mileage reimbursement that are paid to witnesses in the district courts of this state.

Added by Acts 2017, 85th Leg., ch. 685 (H.B. 29), § 5, eff. Sept. 1, 2017.

§ 140A.060. Failure to Comply with Demand Petition for Enforcement

If a person fails to comply with a civil investigative demand duly served on the person, the attorney general may file in the district court in the county in which the person resides, is found, or transacts business or in a district court of Travis County and may serve on the person a petition for an order of the court for enforcement. If the person transacts business in more than one county and the attorney general elects not to file the petition in Travis County, the petition must be filed in the county of the person's principal office or place of business in the state or in any other county as may be agreed on by the person and the attorney general.

Added by Acts 2017, 85th Leg., ch. 685 (H.B. 29), § 5, eff. Sept. 1, 2017.

§ 140A.061. Deliberate Noncompliance

(a) A person commits an offense if the person, with intent to avoid, evade, or prevent compliance with a civil investigative demand issued under this subchapter, knowingly removes from any place, conceals, withholds, destroys, mutilates, alters, or by any other means falsifies any documentary material or otherwise provides inaccurate information.

(b) An offense under this section is a misdemeanor punishable by:

(1) a fine of not more than $5,000;

(2) confinement in a county jail for not more than one year; or

(3) both a fine and confinement.

Added by Acts 2017, 85th Leg., ch. 685 (H.B. 29), § 5, eff. Sept. 1, 2017.

§ 140A.062. Disclosure and Use of Material and Information

(a) The civil investigative demand issued by the attorney general, any information obtained, maintained, or created in response to the demand, or any documentary material, product of discovery, or other record derived or created during an investigation from the information, is not subject to disclosure under Chapter 552, Government Code, and is not subject to disclosure, discovery, subpoena, or other means of legal compulsion for the release, except as described in Subsections (b) and (c).

(b) The attorney general may not release or disclose information that is obtained in response to a demand or any documentary material, product of discovery, or other record derived from the information except:

(1) by court order for good cause shown;

(2) with the consent of the person who provided the information to the attorney general;

(3) to an employee or other person under the direction of the attorney general;

(4) to an agency of this state, the United States, or another state or foreign country;

(5) to any party or person in accordance with Sections 140A.107 and 140A.108;

(6) to a political subdivision of this state; or

(7) to a person authorized by the attorney general to receive the information.

(c) The attorney general may use information obtained in response to a demand, or any documentary material, product of discovery, or other record derived or created from the information as the attorney general determines necessary in the enforcement of this chapter, including presentation before court.

Added by Acts 2017, 85th Leg., ch. 685 (H.B. 29), § 5, eff. Sept. 1, 2017.

§ 140A.063. Jurisdiction

If a petition is filed in the district court in any county, the court has jurisdiction to hear and determine the matter presented and to enter any order required to implement this chapter. Any final order is subject to appeal. Failure to comply with any final order entered by a court under this chapter is punishable by the court as contempt of the order.

Added by Acts 2017, 85th Leg., ch. 685 (H.B. 29), § 5, eff. Sept. 1, 2017.

§ 140A.064. Nonexclusive Procedures

Nothing in this chapter precludes the attorney general from using any procedure not specified in this chapter in conducting a racketeering investigation.

Added by Acts 2017, 85th Leg., ch. 685 (H.B. 29), § 5, eff. Sept. 1, 2017.

SUBCHAPTER C. ENFORCEMENT

§ 140A.101. Suit to Abate Racketeering

(a) The attorney general may bring suit in the name of the state against a person or enterprise for racketeering and may seek civil penalties, costs, reasonable attorney's fees, and appropriate injunctive relief.

(b) This chapter does not authorize suit by a person or enterprise that sustains injury as a result of racketeering.

(c) A suit under this chapter must be brought in a district court in a county in which all or part of the alleged racketeering offense giving rise to the suit occurred.

Added by Acts 2013, 83rd Leg., ch. 1066 (H.B. 3241), § 1, eff. June 14, 2013. Redesignated from V.T.C.A., Civil Practice & Remedies Code § 140.003 by Acts 2015, 84th Leg., ch. 1236 (S.B. 1296), § 21.001(5), eff. Sept. 1, 2015. Redesignated from V.T.C.A., Civil Practice & Remedies Code § 140A.003 by Acts 2017, 85th Leg., ch. 685 (H.B. 29), § 7, eff. Sept. 1, 2017.

§ 140A.102. Injunctive Relief; Other Remedies

(a) A court in which a proceeding is brought under this chapter may prevent, restrain, and remedy racketeering by issuing appropriate orders. The orders may include a temporary restraining order, a temporary or permanent injunction, the creation of a receivership, and the enforcement of a constructive trust in connection with any property or other interest, prejudgment writs of attachment under Chapter 61 for the purposes of freezing, preserving, and disgorging assets, or another order for a remedy or restraint the court considers proper.

(b) Following a final determination of liability under this chapter, the court may issue an appropriate order, including an order that:

(1) requires a person to divest any direct or indirect interest in an enterprise;

(2) imposes reasonable restrictions on the future activities or investments of a person that affect the laws of this state, including prohibiting a person from engaging in the type of endeavor or enterprise that gave rise to the racketeering offense, to the extent permitted by the constitutions of this state and the United States;

(3) requires the dissolution or reorganization of an enterprise involved in the suit;

(4) orders the recovery of reasonable fees, expenses, and costs incurred in obtaining injunctive relief or civil remedies or in conducting investigations under this chapter, including court costs, investigation costs, attorney's fees, witness fees, and deposition fees;

(5) orders payment to the state of an amount equal to:

(A) the gain acquired or maintained through racketeering; or

(B) the amount for which a person is liable under this chapter;

(6) orders payment to the state of a civil penalty by a person or enterprise found liable for racketeering, in an amount not to exceed $250,000 for each separately alleged and proven act of racketeering;

(7) orders payment of damages to the state for racketeering shown to have materially damaged the state; and

(8) orders that property attached under Chapter 61 be used to satisfy an award of the court, including damages, penalties, costs, and fees.

(c) In determining the amount of a civil penalty ordered under Subsection (b)(6), the court shall consider:

(1) the seriousness of the racketeering offense and the consequent financial or personal harm to the state or to any identified victim;

(2) the duration of the racketeering activity; and

(3) any other matter that justice requires.

(d) If any property attached under Chapter 61 is not necessary to satisfy an award of the court after a finding of liability for racketeering of the person or enterprise having an interest in the property, the court may order that the property be disgorged to the state to the extent of the person's or enterprise's interest. To be disgorged, the property must be acquired or maintained by the person or enterprise through racketeering.

(e) In determining the amount of damages ordered under Subsection (b)(7), the court shall consider:

(1) loss of tax revenue to the state;

(2) unpaid state unemployment taxes;

(3) unpaid state licensing and regulatory fees;

(4) medical and counseling costs incurred by the state on behalf of any victim of the racketeering; and

(5) other material damage caused to the state by the racketeering.

(f) Except as otherwise provided by this chapter, remedies and awards ordered by a court under this chapter, including costs and reasonable attorney's fees, may be assessed against and paid from money or property awarded under this chapter.

(g) This chapter is not intended to provide the exclusive remedy for the activity addressed by this chapter. A proceeding under this chapter may be brought in addition to or in the alternative of any other civil or criminal action available under the laws of this state.

(h) Notwithstanding any other provision in this chapter, Articles 59.13 and 59.14, Code of Criminal Procedure, apply to a remedy under this section.

(i) A remedy under this section may not impair a security interest in property subject to a bona fide lien.

Added by Acts 2013, 83rd Leg., ch. 1066 (H.B. 3241), § 1, eff. June 14, 2013. Redesignated from V.T.C.A., Civil Practice & Remedies Code § 140.004 by Acts 2015, 84th Leg., ch. 1236 (S.B. 1296), § 21.001(5), eff. Sept. 1, 2015. Redesignated from V.T.C.A., Civil Practice & Remedies Code § 140A.004 and amended by Acts 2017, 85th Leg., ch. 685 (H.B. 29), § 7, eff. Sept. 1, 2017. Amended by Acts 2021, 87th Leg., ch. 807 (H.B. 1540), § 12, eff. Sept. 1, 2021.

Section 63(d) of Acts 2021, 87th Leg., ch. 807 (H.B. 1540) provides: "Except as otherwise provided by this section, the changes in law made by this Act apply only to an offense committed on or after the effective date [Sept. 1, 2021] of this Act. An offense committed before the effective date of this Act is governed by the law in effect on the date the offense was committed, and the former law is continued in effect for that purpose. For purposes of this section, an offense was committed before the effective date of this Act if any element of the offense occurred before that date."

§ 140A.103. Constructive Trust

(a) A person or enterprise that, through racketeering, acquires property or prevents another person from receiving property that by law is required to be transferred or paid to that person is an involuntary trustee. The involuntary trustee or any other person or enterprise, other than a bona fide purchaser for value as described by Subsection (b), holds the property and the proceeds of the property in constructive trust for the benefit of any person entitled to remedies under this chapter.

(b) A bona fide purchaser for value who was reasonably without notice of unlawful conduct and who did not knowingly take part in an illegal transaction is not an involuntary trustee under Subsection (a) and is not subject to a constructive trust imposed under this chapter.

Added by Acts 2013, 83rd Leg., ch. 1066 (H.B. 3241), § 1, eff. June 14, 2013. Redesignated from V.T.C.A., Civil Practice & Remedies Code § 140.005 by Acts 2015, 84th Leg., ch. 1236 (S.B. 1296), § 21.001(5), eff. Sept. 1, 2015. Redesignated from V.T.C.A., Civil Practice & Remedies Code § 140A.005 by Acts 2017, 85th Leg., ch. 685 (H.B. 29), § 7, eff. Sept. 1, 2017.

§ 140A.104. Evidence

(a) In a proceeding under this chapter, the state bears the burden of proof by a preponderance of the evidence.

(b) A person convicted in a criminal proceeding is precluded, in a proceeding under this chapter, from subsequently denying the essential allegations of the criminal offense of which the person was convicted. For purposes of this subsection, a verdict or a plea, including a plea of nolo contendere, is considered a conviction.

(c) An individual may not be held liable under this chapter based on the conduct of another person unless the finder of fact finds by a preponderance of the evidence that the individual authorized, requested, commanded, participated in, ratified, or recklessly tolerated the unlawful conduct of the other person.

(d) An enterprise may not be held liable under this chapter based on the conduct of a person unless the finder of fact finds by a preponderance of the evidence that a director or high managerial agent performed, authorized, requested, commanded, participated in, ratified, or recklessly tolerated the unlawful conduct of the person.

(e) A bank or savings and loan association insured by the Federal Deposit Insurance Corporation, a credit union insured by the National Credit Union Administration, or the holder of a money transmission license as defined by Chapter 151, Finance Code, may not be held liable in damages or for other relief under this chapter, unless the finder of fact finds by a preponderance of the evidence that the person or agent acquiring or maintaining an interest in or transporting, transacting, transferring, or receiving the funds on behalf of another did so knowing that the funds were the proceeds of an offense and that a director or high managerial agent performed, authorized, requested, commanded, participated in, ratified, or recklessly tolerated the unlawful conduct of the person or agent.

Added by Acts 2013, 83rd Leg., ch. 1066 (H.B. 3241), § 1, eff. June 14, 2013. Redesignated from V.T.C.A., Civil Practice & Remedies Code § 140.006 by Acts 2015, 84th Leg., ch. 1236 (S.B. 1296), § 21.001(5), eff. Sept. 1, 2015. Redesignated from V.T.C.A., Civil Practice & Remedies Code § 140A.006 by Acts 2017, 85th Leg., ch. 685 (H.B. 29), § 7, eff. Sept. 1, 2017. Amended by Acts 2021, 87th Leg., ch. 807 (H.B. 1540), § 13, eff. Sept. 1, 2021.

Section 63(d) of Acts 2021, 87th Leg., ch. 807 (H.B. 1540) provides:

"Except as otherwise provided by this section, the changes in law made by this Act apply only to an offense committed on or after the effective date [Sept. 1, 2021] of this Act. An offense committed before the effective date of this Act is governed by the law in effect on the date the offense was committed, and the former law is continued in effect for that purpose. For purposes of this section, an offense was committed before the effective date of this Act if any element of the offense occurred before that date."

§ 140A.105. Limitations Period

A proceeding may be commenced under this chapter only if the proceeding is filed on or before the seventh anniversary of the date on which the racketeering offense was actually discovered. This section supersedes any conflicting provision establishing a shorter period of limitations for the same conduct.

Added by Acts 2013, 83rd Leg., ch. 1066 (H.B. 3241), § 1, eff. June 14, 2013. Redesignated from V.T.C.A., Civil Practice & Remedies Code § 140.007 by Acts 2015, 84th Leg., ch. 1236 (S.B. 1296), § 21.001(5), eff. Sept. 1, 2015. Redesignated from V.T.C.A., Civil Practice & Remedies Code § 140A.007 by Acts 2017, 85th Leg., ch. 685 (H.B. 29), § 7, eff. Sept. 1, 2017.

§ 140A.106. Special Docketing Procedures

The attorney general may file with the clerk of the district court in which a proceeding is brought under this chapter a certificate stating that the case is of special public importance. The clerk must immediately furnish a copy of the certificate to the administrative judge of the district court of the county in which the proceeding is pending. On receiving the copy of the certificate, the administrative judge shall immediately designate a judge to hear and determine the proceeding. The designated judge shall promptly assign the proceeding for hearing, participate in hearings, make determinations, and cause the action to be expedited.

Added by Acts 2013, 83rd Leg., ch. 1066 (H.B. 3241), § 1, eff. June 14, 2013. Redesignated from V.T.C.A., Civil Practice & Remedies Code § 140.008 by Acts 2015, 84th Leg., ch. 1236 (S.B. 1296), § 21.001(5), eff. Sept. 1, 2015. Redesignated from V.T.C.A., Civil Practice & Remedies Code § 140A.008 by Acts 2017, 85th Leg., ch. 685 (H.B. 29), § 7, eff. Sept. 1, 2017.

§ 140A.107. Notice to Local Prosecutor

(a) In a reasonable time before initiating suit or on initiating an investigation on racketeering, the attorney general shall provide notice to the district attorney, criminal district attorney, or county attorney with felony criminal jurisdiction that appears to have primary jurisdiction over the criminal prosecution of any target of an investigation under this chapter at the time of the notice concerning the attorney general's intent to file suit under this chapter or investigate racketeering, as applicable.

(b) The notices described by Subsection (a) must describe or otherwise identify the defendant to the suit or the suspect, as applicable.

Added by Acts 2013, 83rd Leg., ch. 1066 (H.B. 3241), § 1, eff. June 14, 2013. Redesignated from V.T.C.A., Civil Practice & Remedies Code § 140.009 by Acts 2015, 84th Leg., ch. 1236 (S.B. 1296), § 21.001(5), eff. Sept. 1, 2015. Redesignated from V.T.C.A., Civil Practice & Remedies Code § 140A.009 by Acts 2017, 85th Leg., ch. 685 (H.B. 29), § 7, eff. Sept. 1, 2017.

§ 140A.108. Cooperation with Local Prosecutor

(a) A district attorney, criminal district attorney, or county attorney with felony criminal jurisdiction that receives notice under Section 140A.107 may notify the attorney general of a related pending criminal investigation or prosecution.

(b) Notification to the attorney general under Subsection (a) must be in writing and describe or otherwise identify the defendant or suspect in the criminal investigation or proceeding.

(c) On receipt of notice described by Subsection (a), the attorney general shall coordinate and cooperate with the district attorney, criminal district attorney, or county attorney with felony criminal jurisdiction to ensure that the filing of a suit under this chapter does not interfere with an ongoing criminal investigation or prosecution. The attorney general shall update the district attorney, criminal district attorney, or county attorney with felony criminal jurisdiction on matters affecting the suit or the investigation.

Added by Acts 2013, 83rd Leg., ch. 1066 (H.B. 3241), § 1, eff. June 14, 2013. Redesignated from V.T.C.A., Civil Practice & Remedies Code § 140.010 by Acts 2015, 84th Leg., ch. 1236 (S.B. 1296), § 21.001(5), eff. Sept. 1, 2015. Amended by Acts 2015, 84th Leg., ch. 1236 (S.B. 1296), § 21.002(2), eff. Sept. 1, 2015. Redesignated from V.T.C.A., Civil Practice & Remedies Code § 140A.010 and amended by Acts 2017, 85th Leg., ch. 685 (H.B. 29), § 7, eff. Sept. 1, 2017.

§ 140A.109. Abatement of Suit

If the district attorney, criminal district attorney, or county attorney with felony criminal jurisdiction determines that a suit brought under this chapter would interfere with an ongoing criminal investigation or prosecution after notifying the attorney general of the investigation or prosecution under Section 140A.108, the district attorney, criminal district attorney, or county attorney with felony criminal jurisdiction may request, in writing, that the attorney general abate the suit. On receipt of this request, the attorney general shall abate the suit.

Added by Acts 2013, 83rd Leg., ch. 1066 (H.B. 3241), § 1, eff. June 14, 2013. Redesignated from V.T.C.A., Civil Practice & Remedies Code § 140.011 by Acts 2015, 84th Leg., ch. 1236 (S.B. 1296), § 21.001(5), eff. Sept. 1, 2015. Amended by Acts 2015, 84th Leg., ch. 1236 (S.B. 1296), § 21.002(3), eff. Sept. 1, 2015. Redesignated from V.T.C.A., Civil Practice & Remedies Code § 140A.011 and amended by Acts 2017, 85th Leg., ch. 685 (H.B. 29), § 7, eff. Sept. 1, 2017.

§ 140A.110. Disposition of Assets

(a) An award issued in an action brought under this chapter must be paid in accordance with this section.

(b) After a deduction of any costs of suit, including reasonable attorney's fees and court costs, 80 percent of the amount of the award remaining must be paid to the state, and the remaining 20 percent must be paid, on a pro rata basis, to each law enforcement agency, district attorney's office, criminal district attorney's office, and office of a county attorney with felony criminal jurisdiction found by the court to have assisted in the suit.

(c) The first $10 million, after any costs of suit described by Subsection (b), that is paid to the state under this chapter in a fiscal year shall be dedicated to the compensation to victims of crime fund described by Subchapter J, Chapter 56B, Code of Criminal Procedure.

Added by Acts 2013, 83rd Leg., ch. 1066 (H.B. 3241), § 1, eff. June 14, 2013. Redesignated from V.T.C.A., Civil Practice & Remedies Code § 140.012 by Acts 2015, 84th Leg., ch. 1236 (S.B. 1296), § 21.001(5), eff. Sept. 1, 2015. Redesignated from V.T.C.A., Civil Practice & Remedies Code § 140A.012 by Acts 2017, 85th Leg., ch. 685 (H.B. 29), § 7, eff. Sept. 1, 2017. Amended by Acts 2019, 86th Leg., ch. 469 (H.B. 4173), § 2.02, eff. Jan. 1, 2021.

§ 140A.111. Previously Seized Assets

Notwithstanding another provision of this chapter, no remedies provided by this chapter may be assessed against proceeds, contraband, or other property over which a law enforcement agency has previously asserted jurisdiction under Chapter 59, Code of Criminal Procedure, at the time a suit under this chapter was filed.

Added by Acts 2013, 83rd Leg., ch. 1066 (H.B. 3241), § 1, eff. June 14, 2013. Redesignated from V.T.C.A., Civil Practice & Remedies Code § 140.013 by Acts 2015, 84th Leg., ch. 1236 (S.B. 1296), § 21.001(5), eff. Sept. 1, 2015. Redesignated from V.T.C.A., Civil Practice & Remedies Code § 140A.013 from Acts 2017, 85th Leg., ch. 685 (H.B. 29), § 7, eff. Sept. 1, 2017.

CHAPTER 141. STRUCTURED SETTLEMENT PROTECTION ACT

Section

§ 141.001. Short Title

This chapter may be cited as the Structured Settlement Protection Act.

Added by Acts 2001, 77th Leg., ch. 96, § 1, eff. Sept. 1, 2001.

§ 141.002. Definitions

In this chapter:

(1) "Annuity issuer" means an insurer that has issued a contract to fund periodic payments under a structured settlement.

(2) "Court" means:

(A) the court of original jurisdiction that authorized or approved a structured settlement; or

(B) if the court that authorized or approved the structured settlement no longer has jurisdiction to approve a transfer of payment rights under the structured settlement under this chapter, a statutory county court, a statutory probate court, or a district court located in the county in which the payee resides.

(3) "Dependents" includes a payee's spouse, minor children, and all other persons for whom the payee is legally obligated to provide support, including alimony.

(4) "Discounted present value" means the present value of future payments determined by discounting the payments to the present using the most recently published Applicable Federal Rate for determining

the present value of an annuity, as issued by the United States Internal Revenue Service.

(5) "Gross advance amount" means the sum payable to the payee or for the payee's account as consideration for a transfer of structured settlement payment rights before any reductions for transfer expenses or other deductions to be made from the consideration.

(6) "Independent professional advice" means advice of an attorney, certified public accountant, actuary, or other licensed professional adviser.

(7) "Interested party" means, with respect to any structured settlement:

(A) the payee;

(B) any beneficiary irrevocably designated under the annuity contract to receive payments following the payee's death;

(C) the annuity issuer;

(D) the structured settlement obligor; and

(E) any other party that has continuing rights or obligations under the structured settlement.

(8) "Net advance amount" means the gross advance amount less the aggregate amount of the actual and estimated transfer expenses required to be disclosed under Section 141.003(5).

(9) "Payee" means an individual who is receiving tax-free payments under a structured settlement and proposes to transfer payment rights under the structured settlement.

(10) "Periodic payments" includes both recurring payments and scheduled future lump-sum payments.

(11) "Qualified assignment agreement" means an agreement providing for a qualified assignment within the meaning of Section 130, Internal Revenue Code of 1986 (26 U.S.C. Section 130), as amended.

(12) "Settled claim" means the original tort claim or workers' compensation claim resolved by a structured settlement.

(13) "Structured settlement" means an arrangement for periodic payment of damages for personal injuries or sickness established by settlement or judgment in resolution of a tort claim or for periodic payments in settlement of a workers' compensation claim.

(14) "Structured settlement agreement" means the agreement, judgment, stipulation, or release embodying the terms of a structured settlement.

(15) "Structured settlement obligor" means, with respect to any structured settlement, the party that has the continuing obligation to make periodic payments to the payee under a structured settlement agreement or a qualified assignment agreement.

(16) "Structured settlement payment rights" means rights to receive periodic payments under a structured settlement, whether from the structured settlement obligor or the annuity issuer, if:

(A) the payee is domiciled in or the domicile or principal place of business of the structured settlement obligor or the annuity issuer is located in this state;

(B) the structured settlement agreement was authorized or approved by a court located in this state; or

(C) the structured settlement agreement is expressly governed by the laws of this state.

(17) "Terms of the structured settlement" include, with respect to any structured settlement, the terms of the structured settlement agreement, the annuity contract, any qualified assignment agreement, and any order or other approval of the court.

(18) "Transfer" means any sale, assignment, pledge, hypothecation, or other alienation or encumbrance of structured settlement payment rights made by a payee for consideration, except that the term does not include the creation or perfection of a security interest in structured settlement payment rights under a blanket security agreement entered into with an insured depository institution, in the absence of any action to redirect the structured settlement payments to the insured depository institution, or its agent or successor in interest, or to enforce the blanket security interest against the structured settlement payment rights.

(19) "Transfer agreement" means the agreement providing for a transfer of structured settlement payment rights.

(20) "Transfer expenses" means all the expenses of a transfer that are required under the transfer agreement to be paid by the payee or deducted from the gross advance amount, including court filing fees, attorney's fees, escrow fees, lien recording fees, judgment and lien search fees, finders' fees, commissions, and other payments to a broker or other intermediary, except that the term does not include preexisting obligations of the payee payable for the payee's account from the proceeds of a transfer.

(21) "Transferee" means a party acquiring or proposing to acquire structured settlement payment rights through a transfer.

Added by Acts 2001, 77th Leg., ch. 96, § 1, eff. Sept. 1, 2001. Amended by Acts 2003, 78th Leg., ch. 578, § 1, eff. Sept. 1, 2003.

§ 141.003. Required Disclosures to Payee

At least three days before the date on which the payee signs a transfer agreement, the transferee shall provide to the payee a separate disclosure statement, in bold type at least 14 points in size, that states:

(1) the amounts and due dates of the structured settlement payments to be transferred;

(2) the aggregate amount of the payments;

(3) the discounted present value of the payments to be transferred, which shall be identified as the "calculation of current value of the transferred structured settlement payments under federal standards for valuing annuities," and the amount of the Applicable Federal Rate used in calculating the discounted present value;

(4) the gross advance amount;

(5) an itemized listing of all applicable transfer expenses, other than attorney's fees and related disbursements payable in connection with the transferee's application for approval of the transfer, and the transferee's best estimate of the amount of those expenses;

(6) the net advance amount;

(7) the amount of any penalties or liquidated damages payable by the payee in the event of any breach of the transfer agreement by the payee; and

(8) a statement that the payee has the right to cancel the transfer agreement, without penalty or further obligation, not later than the third business day after the date the agreement is signed by the payee.

Added by Acts 2001, 77th Leg., ch. 96, § 1, eff. Sept. 1, 2001.

§ 141.004. Approval of Transfers of Structured Settlement Payment Rights

No direct or indirect transfer of structured settlement payment rights shall be effective and no structured settlement obligor or annuity issuer shall be required to make any payment directly or indirectly to any transferee of structured settlement payment rights unless the transfer has been approved in advance in a final court order based on express findings by the court that:

(1) the transfer is in the best interest of the payee, taking into account the welfare and support of the payee's dependents;

(2) the payee has been advised in writing by the transferee to seek independent professional advice regarding the transfer and has either received the advice or knowingly waived the advice in writing; and

(3) the transfer does not contravene any applicable statute or an order of any court or other governmental authority.

Added by Acts 2001, 77th Leg., ch. 96, § 1, eff. Sept. 1, 2001.

§ 141.005. Effects of Transfer of Structured Settlement Payment Rights

Following a transfer of structured settlement payment rights under this chapter:

(1) the structured settlement obligor and the annuity issuer shall, as to all parties except the transferee, be discharged and released from any and all liability for the transferred payments;

(2) the transferee shall be liable to the structured settlement obligor and the annuity issuer:

(A) if the transfer contravenes the terms of the structured settlement, for any taxes incurred by the parties as a consequence of the transfer; and

(B) for any other liabilities or costs, including reasonable costs and attorney's fees, arising from compliance by the parties with the order of the court or arising as a consequence of the transferee's failure to comply with this chapter;

(3) the transferee shall be liable to the payee:

(A) if the transfer contravenes the terms of the structured settlement, for any taxes incurred by the payee as a consequence of the transfer; and

(B) for any other liabilities or costs, including reasonable costs and attorney's fees, arising as a consequence of the transferee's failure to comply with this chapter;

(4) neither the structured settlement obligor nor the annuity issuer may be required to divide any periodic payment between the payee and any transferee or assignee or between two or more transferees or assignees; and

(5) any further transfer of structured settlement payment rights by the payee may be made only after compliance with all of the requirements of this chapter.

Added by Acts 2001, 77th Leg., ch. 96, § 1, eff. Sept. 1, 2001.

§ 141.006. Procedure for Approval of Transfers

(a) An application under this chapter for approval of a transfer of structured settlement payment rights shall be made by the transferee and shall be brought in the court.

(b) At least 20 days before the date of the scheduled hearing on any application for approval of a transfer of structured settlement payment rights under Section 141.004, the transferee shall file with the court and serve on all interested parties a notice of the proposed transfer and the application for authorization, including with the notice:

(1) a copy of the transferee's application;

(2) a copy of the transfer agreement;

(3) a copy of the disclosure statement required under Section 141.003;

(4) a listing of each of the payee's dependents, together with each dependent's age;

(5) notice that any interested party is entitled to support, oppose, or otherwise respond to the transferee's application, either in person or by counsel, by submitting written comments to the court or by participating in the hearing; and

(6) notice of the time and place of the hearing and notification of the manner in which and the time by which written responses to the application must be filed to be considered by the court.

(c) Written responses to the application under Subsection (b)(6) must be filed on or after the 15th day after the date the transferee's notice is served.

(d) If the application under this chapter for approval of a transfer of structured settlement payment rights includes a written request by the payee to conceal from public inspection the personally identifiable information of the payee and the court and each interested party required to receive notice under Subsection (b) receive complete, unredacted copies of the application, other pleadings, and any order in the time provided by Subsection (b), as applicable:

(1) in any application, other pleadings, or any order filed or submitted, the court shall permit the full redaction of the name of the payee, the address of the payee, and other information that could reasonably be used to determine the identity or address of the payee, including the names of dependents, family members, and beneficiaries; and

(2) with respect to any order issued approving or denying the transfer of structured settlement payment rights:

(A) a copy of the order, with the information described by Subdivision (1) redacted, shall be filed as part of the public record;

(B) at the same time as the filing under Paragraph (A), an unredacted copy of the order shall be issued under seal and shall be provided to the transferee and each interested party entitled to notice under Subsection (b); and

(C) not earlier than six months after the date the order is issued, the court on its own initiative may, or on the motion of any person including a member of the general public shall, unseal the unredacted order and make the order part of the public record.

(e) Except as provided by this subsection, Rule 76a, Texas Rules of Civil Procedure, applies to all court proceedings and filings under this chapter. A party is not required to comply with that rule in order to redact the payee's personally identifiable information under Subsection (d)(1) or for the purpose of issuing an unredacted copy of the order under seal under Subsection (d)(2).

Added by Acts 2001, 77th Leg., ch. 96, § 1, eff. Sept. 1, 2001. Amended by Acts 2017, 85th Leg., ch. 802 (H.B. 3356), § 1, eff. June 15, 2017.

§ 141.007. General Provisions; Construction

(a) The provisions of this chapter may not be waived by any payee.

(b) Any transfer agreement entered into by a payee who resides in this state must provide that disputes under the transfer agreement, including any claim that the payee has breached the agreement, shall be determined in and under the laws of this state. The transfer agreement may not authorize the transferee or any other party to confess judgment or consent to entry of judgment against the payee.

(c) Transfer of structured settlement payment rights may not extend to any payments that are life-contingent unless, prior to the date on which the payee signs the transfer agreement, the transferee has established and agreed to maintain procedures reasonably satisfactory to the structured settlement obligor and the annuity issuer for:

(1) periodically confirming the payee's survival; and

(2) giving the structured settlement obligor and the annuity issuer prompt written notice in the event of the payee's death.

(d) A payee who proposes to make a transfer of structured settlement payment rights may not incur any penalty, forfeit any application fee or other payment, or otherwise incur any liability to the proposed transferee or any assignee based on any failure of the transfer to satisfy the conditions of this chapter.

(e) Nothing contained in this chapter may be construed to authorize any transfer of structured settlement payment rights in contravention of any law or to imply that any transfer under a transfer agreement entered into before the effective date of this chapter is valid or invalid.

(f) Compliance with the requirements in Section 141.003 and fulfillment of the conditions in Section 141.004 are solely the responsibility of the transferee in any transfer of structured settlement payment rights, and neither the structured settlement obligor nor the annuity issuer bear any responsibility for, or any liability arising from, noncompliance with the requirements or failure to fulfill the conditions.

Added by Acts 2001, 77th Leg., ch. 96, § 1, eff. Sept. 1, 2001.

CHAPTER 142. LIMITATION ON LIABILITY FOR HIRING CERTAIN EMPLOYEES

Section

§ 142.001. Definitions

In this chapter:

(1) "Employee" means a person other than an independent contractor who, for compensation, performs services for an employer under a written or oral contract for hire, whether express or implied.

(2) "Independent contractor" has the meaning assigned by Section 91.001, Labor Code.

Added by Acts 2013, 83rd Leg., ch. 287 (H.B. 1188), § 1, eff. June 14, 2013.

§ 142.002. Limitation on Liability for Hiring Employee Convicted of Offense

(a) A cause of action may not be brought against an employer, general contractor, premises owner, or other third party solely for negligently hiring or failing to adequately supervise an employee, based on evidence that the employee has been convicted of an offense.

(b) This section does not preclude a cause of action for negligent hiring or the failure of an employer, general contractor, premises owner, or other third party to provide adequate supervision of an employee, if:

(1) the employer, general contractor, premises owner, or other third party knew or should have known of the conviction; and

(2) the employee was convicted of:

(A) an offense that was committed while performing duties substantially similar to those reasonably expected to be performed in the employment, or under conditions substantially similar to those reasonably expected to be encountered in the employment, taking into consideration the factors listed in Sections 53.022 and 53.023(a), Occupations Code, without regard to whether the occupation requires a license;

(B) an offense listed in Article 42A.054, Code of Criminal Procedure; or

(C) a sexually violent offense, as defined by Article 62.001, Code of Criminal Procedure.

(c) The protections provided to an employer, general contractor, premises owner, or third party under this section do not apply in a suit concerning the misuse of funds or property of a person other than the employer, general contractor, premises owner, or third party by an employee if, on the date the employee was hired, the employee had been convicted of a crime that includes fraud or the misuse of funds or property as an element of the offense, and it was foreseeable that the position for which the employee was hired would involve discharging a fiduciary responsibility in the management of funds or property.

(d) This section does not create a cause of action or expand an existing cause of action.

Added by Acts 2013, 83rd Leg., ch. 287 (H.B. 1188), § 1, eff. June 14, 2013. Amended by Acts 2015, 84th Leg., ch. 770 (H.B. 2299), § 2.02, eff. Jan. 1, 2017.

CHAPTER 142A. LIMITATION ON LIABILITY FOR CERTAIN PROGRAMS

Section

§ 142A.001. Definitions

In this chapter:

(1) "Employee" means a person who, for compensation, performs services for an employer under a written or oral contract, whether express or implied.

(2) "Employee wellness program" means a program established by an employer that provides an incentive to an employee that promotes wellness or a healthy lifestyle.

Added by Acts 2015, 84th Leg., ch. 774 (H.B. 2390), § 1, eff. Sept. 1, 2015.

§ 142A.002. Limitation on Liability for Wellness Programs

(a) A civil action may not be brought against an employer for establishing, maintaining, or requiring participation in an employee wellness program unless:

(1) the program discriminates on the basis of a prior medical condition, gender, age, or income level; or

(2) the cause of action is based on intentional or reckless conduct.

(b) This section does not create a cause of action or expand an existing cause of action.

Added by Acts 2015, 84th Leg., ch. 774 (H.B. 2390), § 1, eff. Sept. 1, 2015.

CHAPTER 143. HARMFUL ACCESS BY COMPUTER

§ 143.001. Cause of Action

(a) A person who is injured or whose property has been injured as a result of a violation under Chapter 33, Penal Code, has a civil cause of action if the conduct constituting the violation was committed knowingly or intentionally.

(b) A person must bring suit for damages under this section before the earlier of the fifth anniversary of the date of the last act in the course of the conduct constituting a violation under Chapter 33, Penal Code, or the second anniversary of the date the claimant first discovered or had reasonable opportunity to discover the violation.

Added by Acts 1989, 71st Leg., ch. 306, § 5, eff. Sept. 1, 1989.

§ 143.002. Damages

A person who establishes a cause of action under this chapter is entitled to:

(1) actual damages; and

(2) reasonable attorney's fees and costs.

Added by Acts 1989, 71st Leg., ch. 306, § 5, eff. Sept. 1, 1989.

CHAPTER 143A. DISCOURSE ON SOCIAL MEDIA PLATFORMS

§ 143A.001. Definitions

In this chapter:

(1) "Censor" means to block, ban, remove, deplatform, demonetize, de-boost, restrict, deny equal access or visibility to, or otherwise discriminate against expression.

(2) "Expression" means any word, music, sound, still or moving image, number, or other perceivable communication.

(3) "Receive," with respect to an expression, means to read, hear, look at, access, or gain access to the expression.

(4) "Social media platform" has the meaning assigned by Section 120.001, Business & Commerce Code.

(5) "Unlawful expression" means an expression that is unlawful under the United States Constitution, federal law, the Texas Constitution, or the laws of this state, including expression that constitutes a tort under the laws of this state or the United States.

(6) "User" means a person who posts, uploads, transmits, shares, or otherwise publishes or receives expression, through a social media platform. The term includes a person who has a social media platform account that the social media platform has disabled or locked.

Added by Acts 2021, 87th Leg., 2nd C.S., ch. 3 (H.B. 20), § 7, eff. Dec. 2, 2021.

Section 1 of Acts 2021, 87th Leg., 2nd C.S., ch. 3 (H.B. 20) provides:

"The legislature finds that:

"(1) each person in this state has a fundamental interest in the free exchange of ideas and information, including the freedom of others to share and receive ideas and information;

"(2) this state has a fundamental interest in protecting the free exchange of ideas and information in this state;

"(3) social media platforms function as common carriers, are affected with a public interest, are central public forums for public debate, and have enjoyed governmental support in the United States; and

"(4) social media platforms with the largest number of users are common carriers by virtue of their market dominance."

Sections 8 and 9 of Acts 2021, 87th Leg., 2nd C.S., ch. 3 (H.B. 20) provide:

"Sec. 8. (a) Mindful of *Leavitt v. Jane L.*, 518 U.S. 137 (1996), in which in the context of determining the severability of a state statute the United States Supreme Court held that an explicit statement of legislative intent is controlling, it is the intent of the legislature that every provision, section, subsection, sentence, clause, phrase, or word in this Act, and every application of the provisions in this Act, are severable from each other.

"(b) If any application of any provision in this Act to any person, group of persons, or circumstances is found by a court to be invalid or unconstitutional, the remaining applications of that provision to all other persons and circumstances shall be severed and may not be affected. All constitutionally valid applications of this Act shall be severed from any applications that a court finds to be invalid, leaving the valid applications in force, because it is the legislature's intent and priority that the valid applications be allowed to stand alone.

"(c) If any court declares or finds a provision of this Act facially unconstitutional, when discrete applications of that provision can be enforced against a person, group of persons, or circumstances without violating the United States Constitution and Texas Constitution, those applications shall be severed from all remaining applications of the provision, and the provision shall be interpreted as if the legislature had enacted a provision limited to the persons, group of persons, or circumstances for which the provision's application will not violate the United States Constitution and Texas Constitution.

"(d) The legislature further declares that it would have enacted this Act, and each provision, section, subsection, sentence, clause, phrase, or word, and all constitutional applications of this Act, irrespective of the fact that any provision, section, subsection, sentence, clause, phrase, or word, or applications of this Act, were to be declared unconstitutional.

"(e) If any provision of this Act is found by any court to be unconstitutionally vague, the applications of that provision that do not present constitutional vagueness problems shall be severed and remain in force.

"(f) No court may decline to enforce the severability requirements of Subsections (a), (b), (c), (d), and (e) of this section on the ground that severance would rewrite the statute or involve the court in legislative or lawmaking activity. A court that declines to enforce or enjoins a state official from enforcing a statutory provision does not rewrite a statute, as the statute continues to contain the same words as before the court's decision. A judicial injunction or declaration of unconstitutionality:

"(1) is nothing more than an edict prohibiting enforcement that may subsequently be vacated by a later court if that court has a different understanding of the requirements of the Texas Constitution or United States Constitution;

"(2) is not a formal amendment of the language in a statute; and

"(3) no more rewrites a statute than a decision by the executive not to enforce a duly enacted statute in a limited and defined set of circumstances."

"Sec. 9. Chapter 143A, Civil Practice and Remedies Code, as added by this Act, applies only to a cause of action that accrues on or after the effective date [Dec. 2, 2021] of this Act."

§ 143A.002. Censorship Prohibited

(a) A social media platform may not censor a user, a user's expression, or a user's ability to receive the expression of another person based on:

(1) the viewpoint of the user or another person;

(2) the viewpoint represented in the user's expression or another person's expression; or

(3) a user's geographic location in this state or any part of this state.

(b) This section applies regardless of whether the viewpoint is expressed on a social media platform or through any other medium.

Added by Acts 2021, 87th Leg., 2nd C.S., ch. 3 (H.B. 20), § 7, eff. Dec. 2, 2021.

Section 1 of Acts 2021, 87th Leg., 2nd C.S., ch. 3 (H.B. 20) provides:

"The legislature finds that:

"(1) each person in this state has a fundamental interest in the free exchange of ideas and information, including the freedom of others to share and receive ideas and information;

"(2) this state has a fundamental interest in protecting the free exchange of ideas and information in this state;

"(3) social media platforms function as common carriers, are affected with a public interest, are central public forums for public debate, and have enjoyed governmental support in the United States; and

"(4) social media platforms with the largest number of users are common carriers by virtue of their market dominance."

Sections 8 and 9 of Acts 2021, 87th Leg., 2nd C.S., ch. 3 (H.B. 20) provide:

"Sec. 8. (a) Mindful of *Leavitt v. Jane L.*, 518 U.S. 137 (1996), in which in the context of determining the severability of a state statute the United States Supreme Court held that an explicit statement of legislative intent is controlling, it is the intent of the legislature that every provision, section, subsection, sentence, clause, phrase, or word in this Act, and every application of the provisions in this Act, are severable from each other.

"(b) If any application of any provision in this Act to any person, group of persons, or circumstances is found by a court to be invalid or unconstitutional, the remaining applications of that provision to all other persons and circumstances shall be severed and may not be affected. All constitutionally valid applications of this Act shall be severed from any applications that a court finds to be invalid, leaving the valid applications in force, because it is the legislature's intent and priority that the valid applications be allowed to stand alone.

"(c) If any court declares or finds a provision of this Act facially unconstitutional, when discrete applications of that provision can be enforced against a person, group of persons, or circumstances without violating the United States Constitution and Texas Constitution, those applications shall be severed from all remaining applications of the provision, and the provision shall be interpreted as if the legislature had enacted a provision limited to the persons, group of persons, or circumstances for which the provision's application will not violate the United States Constitution and Texas Constitution.

"(d) The legislature further declares that it would have enacted this Act, and each provision, section, subsection, sentence, clause, phrase, or word, and all constitutional applications of this Act, irrespective of the fact that any provision, section, subsection, sentence, clause, phrase, or word, or applications of this Act, were to be declared unconstitutional.

"(e) If any provision of this Act is found by any court to be unconstitutionally vague, the applications of that provision that do not present constitutional vagueness problems shall be severed and remain in force.

"(f) No court may decline to enforce the severability requirements of Subsections (a), (b), (c), (d), and (e) of this section on the ground that severance would rewrite the statute or involve the court in legislative or lawmaking activity. A court that declines to enforce or enjoins a state official from enforcing a statutory provision does not rewrite a statute, as the statute continues to contain the same words as before the court's decision. A judicial injunction or declaration of unconstitutionality:

"(1) is nothing more than an edict prohibiting enforcement that may subsequently be vacated by a later court if that court has a different understanding of the requirements of the Texas Constitution or United States Constitution;

"(2) is not a formal amendment of the language in a statute; and

"(3) no more rewrites a statute than a decision by the executive not to enforce a duly enacted statute in a limited and defined set of circumstances."

"Sec. 9. Chapter 143A, Civil Practice and Remedies Code, as added by this Act, applies only to a cause of action that accrues on or after the effective date [Dec. 2, 2021] of this Act."

§ 143A.003. Waiver Prohibited

(a) A waiver or purported waiver of the protections provided by this chapter is void as unlawful and against public policy, and a court or arbitrator may not enforce or give effect to the waiver, including in an action brought under Section 143A.007, notwithstanding any contract or choice-of-law provision in a contract.

(b) The waiver prohibition described by Subsection (a) is a public-policy limitation on contractual and other waivers of the highest importance and interest to this state, and this state is exercising and enforcing this limitation to the full extent permitted by the United States Constitution and Texas Constitution.

Added by Acts 2021, 87th Leg., 2nd C.S., ch. 3 (H.B. 20), § 7, eff. Dec. 2, 2021.

Section 1 of Acts 2021, 87th Leg., 2nd C.S., ch. 3 (H.B. 20) provides:

"The legislature finds that:

"(1) each person in this state has a fundamental interest in the free exchange of ideas and information, including the freedom of others to share and receive ideas and information;

"(2) this state has a fundamental interest in protecting the free exchange of ideas and information in this state;

"(3) social media platforms function as common carriers, are affected with a public interest, are central public forums for public debate, and have enjoyed governmental support in the United States; and

"(4) social media platforms with the largest number of users are common carriers by virtue of their market dominance."

Sections 8 and 9 of Acts 2021, 87th Leg., 2nd C.S., ch. 3 (H.B. 20) provide:

"Sec. 8. (a) Mindful of *Leavitt v. Jane L.*, 518 U.S. 137 (1996), in which in the context of determining the severability of a state statute the United States Supreme Court held that an explicit statement of legislative intent is controlling, it is the intent of the legislature that every provision, section, subsection, sentence, clause, phrase, or word in this Act, and every application of the provisions in this Act, are severable from each other.

"(b) If any application of any provision in this Act to any person, group of persons, or circumstances is found by a court to be invalid or unconstitutional, the remaining applications of that provision to all other persons and circumstances shall be severed and may not be affected. All constitutionally valid applications of this Act shall be severed from any applications that a court finds to be invalid, leaving the valid applications in force, because it is the legislature's intent and priority that the valid applications be allowed to stand alone.

"(c) If any court declares or finds a provision of this Act facially unconstitutional, when discrete applications of that provision can be enforced against a person, group of persons, or circumstances without violating the United States Constitution and Texas Constitution, those applications shall be severed from all remaining applications of the provision, and the provision shall be interpreted as if the legislature had enacted a provision limited to the persons, group of persons, or circumstances for which the provision's application will not violate the United States Constitution and Texas Constitution.

"(d) The legislature further declares that it would have enacted this Act, and each provision, section, subsection, sentence, clause, phrase, or word, and all constitutional applications of this Act, irrespective of the fact that any provision, section, subsection, sentence, clause, phrase, or word, or applications of this Act, were to be declared unconstitutional.

"(e) If any provision of this Act is found by any court to be unconstitutionally vague, the applications of that provision that do not present constitutional vagueness problems shall be severed and remain in force.

"(f) No court may decline to enforce the severability requirements of Subsections (a), (b), (c), (d), and (e) of this section on the ground that severance would rewrite the statute or involve the court in legislative or lawmaking activity. A court that declines to enforce or enjoins a state official from enforcing a statutory provision does not rewrite a statute, as the statute continues to contain the same words as before the court's decision. A judicial injunction or declaration of unconstitutionality:

"(1) is nothing more than an edict prohibiting enforcement that may subsequently be vacated by a later court if that court has a different understanding of the requirements of the Texas Constitution or United States Constitution;

"(2) is not a formal amendment of the language in a statute; and

"(3) no more rewrites a statute than a decision by the executive not to enforce a duly enacted statute in a limited and defined set of circumstances."

"Sec. 9. Chapter 143A, Civil Practice and Remedies Code, as added by this Act, applies only to a cause of action that accrues on or after the effective date [Dec. 2, 2021] of this Act."

§ 143A.004. Applicability of Chapter

(a) This chapter applies only to a user who:

(1) resides in this state;

(2) does business in this state; or

(3) shares or receives expression in this state.

(b) This chapter applies only to expression that is shared or received in this state.

(c) This chapter applies only to a social media platform that functionally has more than 50 million active users in the United States in a calendar month.

(d) This chapter applies to the maximum extent permitted by the United States Constitution and the laws of the United States but no further than the maximum extent permitted by the United States Constitution and the laws of the United States.

Added by Acts 2021, 87th Leg., 2nd C.S., ch. 3 (H.B. 20), § 7, eff. Dec. 2, 2021.

Section 1 of Acts 2021, 87th Leg., 2nd C.S., ch. 3 (H.B. 20) provides:

"The legislature finds that:

"(1) each person in this state has a fundamental interest in the free exchange of ideas and information, including the freedom of others to share and receive ideas and information;

"(2) this state has a fundamental interest in protecting the free exchange of ideas and information in this state;

"(3) social media platforms function as common carriers, are affected with a public interest, are central public forums for public debate, and have enjoyed governmental support in the United States; and

"(4) social media platforms with the largest number of users are common carriers by virtue of their market dominance."

Sections 8 and 9 of Acts 2021, 87th Leg., 2nd C.S., ch. 3 (H.B. 20) provide:

"Sec. 8. (a) Mindful of *Leavitt v. Jane L.*, 518 U.S. 137 (1996), in which in the context of determining the severability of a state statute the United States Supreme Court held that an explicit statement of legislative intent is controlling, it is the intent of the legislature that every provision, section, subsection, sentence, clause, phrase, or word in this Act, and every application of the provisions in this Act, are severable from each other.

"(b) If any application of any provision in this Act to any person, group of persons, or circumstances is found by a court to be invalid or unconstitutional, the remaining applications of that provision to all other persons and circumstances shall be severed and may not be affected. All constitutionally valid applications of this Act shall be severed from any applications that a court finds to be invalid, leaving the valid applications in force, because it is the legislature's intent and priority that the valid applications be allowed to stand alone.

"(c) If any court declares or finds a provision of this Act facially unconstitutional, when discrete applications of that provision can be enforced against a person, group of persons, or circumstances without violating the United States Constitution and Texas Constitution, those applications shall be severed from all remaining applications of the provision, and the provision shall be interpreted as if the legislature had enacted a provision limited to the persons, group of persons, or circumstances for which the provision's application will not violate the United States Constitution and Texas Constitution.

"(d) The legislature further declares that it would have enacted this Act, and each provision, section, subsection, sentence, clause, phrase, or word, and all constitutional applications of this Act, irrespective of the fact that any provision, section, subsection, sentence, clause, phrase, or word, or applications of this Act, were to be declared unconstitutional.

"(e) If any provision of this Act is found by any court to be unconstitutionally vague, the applications of that provision that do not present constitutional vagueness problems shall be severed and remain in force.

"(f) No court may decline to enforce the severability requirements of Subsections (a), (b), (c), (d), and (e) of this section on the ground that severance would rewrite the statute or involve the court in legislative or lawmaking activity. A court that declines to enforce or enjoins a state official from enforcing a statutory provision does not rewrite a statute, as the statute continues to contain the same words as before the court's decision. A judicial injunction or declaration of unconstitutionality:

"(1) is nothing more than an edict prohibiting enforcement that may subsequently be vacated by a later court if that court has a different understanding of the requirements of the Texas Constitution or United States Constitution;

"(2) is not a formal amendment of the language in a statute; and

"(3) no more rewrites a statute than a decision by the executive not to enforce a duly enacted statute in a limited and defined set of circumstances."

"Sec. 9. Chapter 143A, Civil Practice and Remedies Code, as added by this Act, applies only to a cause of action that accrues on or after the effective date [Dec. 2, 2021] of this Act."

§ 143A.005. Limitation on Effect of Chapter

This chapter does not subject a social media platform to damages or other legal remedies to the extent the social media platform is protected from those remedies under federal law.

Added by Acts 2021, 87th Leg., 2nd C.S., ch. 3 (H.B. 20), § 7, eff. Dec. 2, 2021.

Section 1 of Acts 2021, 87th Leg., 2nd C.S., ch. 3 (H.B. 20) provides:

"The legislature finds that:

"(1) each person in this state has a fundamental interest in the free exchange of ideas and information, including the freedom of others to share and receive ideas and information;

"(2) this state has a fundamental interest in protecting the free exchange of ideas and information in this state;

"(3) social media platforms function as common carriers, are affected with a public interest, are central public forums for public debate, and have enjoyed governmental support in the United States; and

"(4) social media platforms with the largest number of users are common carriers by virtue of their market dominance."

Sections 8 and 9 of Acts 2021, 87th Leg., 2nd C.S., ch. 3 (H.B. 20) provide:

"Sec. 8. (a) Mindful of *Leavitt v. Jane L.*, 518 U.S. 137 (1996), in which in the context of determining the severability of a state statute the United States Supreme Court held that an explicit statement of legislative intent is controlling, it is the intent of the legislature that every provision, section, subsection, sentence, clause, phrase, or word in this Act, and every application of the provisions in this Act, are severable from each other.

"(b) If any application of any provision in this Act to any person, group of persons, or circumstances is found by a court to be invalid or unconstitutional, the remaining applications of that provision to all other persons and circumstances shall be severed and may not be affected. All constitutionally valid applications of this Act shall be severed from any applications that a court finds to be invalid, leaving the valid applications in force, because it is the legislature's intent and priority that the valid applications be allowed to stand alone.

"(c) If any court declares or finds a provision of this Act facially unconstitutional, when discrete applications of that provision can be enforced against a person, group of persons, or circumstances without violating the United States Constitution and Texas Constitution, those applications shall be severed from all remaining applications of the provision, and the provision shall be interpreted as if the legislature had enacted a provision limited to the persons, group of persons, or circumstances for which the provision's application will not violate the United States Constitution and Texas Constitution.

"(d) The legislature further declares that it would have enacted this Act, and each provision, section, subsection, sentence, clause, phrase, or word, and all constitutional applications of this Act, irrespective of the fact that any provision, section, subsection, sentence, clause, phrase, or word, or applications of this Act, were to be declared unconstitutional.

"(e) If any provision of this Act is found by any court to be unconstitutionally vague, the applications of that provision that do not present constitutional vagueness problems shall be severed and remain in force.

"(f) No court may decline to enforce the severability requirements of Subsections (a), (b), (c), (d), and (e) of this section on the ground that severance would rewrite the statute or involve the court in legislative or lawmaking activity. A court that declines to enforce or enjoins a state official from enforcing a statutory provision does not rewrite a statute, as the statute continues to contain the same words as before the court's decision. A judicial injunction or declaration of unconstitutionality:

"(1) is nothing more than an edict prohibiting enforcement that may subsequently be vacated by a later court if that court has a different understanding of the requirements of the Texas Constitution or United States Constitution;

"(2) is not a formal amendment of the language in a statute; and

"(3) no more rewrites a statute than a decision by the executive not to enforce a duly enacted statute in a limited and defined set of circumstances."

"Sec. 9. Chapter 143A, Civil Practice and Remedies Code, as added by this Act, applies only to a cause of action that accrues on or after the effective date [Dec. 2, 2021] of this Act."

§ 143A.006. Construction of Chapter

(a) This chapter does not prohibit a social media platform from censoring expression that:

(1) the social media platform is specifically authorized to censor by federal law;

(2) is the subject of a referral or request from an organization with the purpose of preventing the sexual exploitation of children and protecting survivors of sexual abuse from ongoing harassment;

(3) directly incites criminal activity or consists of specific threats of violence targeted against a person or group because of their race, color, disability, religion, national origin or ancestry, age, sex, or status as a peace officer or judge; or

(4) is unlawful expression.

(b) This chapter may not be construed to prohibit or restrict a social media platform from authorizing or facilitating a user's ability to censor specific expression on the user's platform or page at the request of that user.

(c) This chapter may not be construed to limit or expand intellectual property law.

Added by Acts 2021, 87th Leg., 2nd C.S., ch. 3 (H.B. 20), § 7, eff. Dec. 2, 2021.

Section 1 of Acts 2021, 87th Leg., 2nd C.S., ch. 3 (H.B. 20) provides:

"The legislature finds that:

"(1) each person in this state has a fundamental interest in the free exchange of ideas and information, including the freedom of others to share and receive ideas and information;

"(2) this state has a fundamental interest in protecting the free exchange of ideas and information in this state;

"(3) social media platforms function as common carriers, are affected with a public interest, are central public forums for public debate, and have enjoyed governmental support in the United States; and

"(4) social media platforms with the largest number of users are common carriers by virtue of their market dominance."

Sections 8 and 9 of Acts 2021, 87th Leg., 2nd C.S., ch. 3 (H.B. 20) provide:

"Sec. 8. (a) Mindful of *Leavitt v. Jane L.*, 518 U.S. 137 (1996), in which in the context of determining the severability of a state statute the United States Supreme Court held that an explicit statement of legislative intent is controlling, it is the intent of the legislature that every provision, section, subsection, sentence, clause, phrase, or word in this Act, and every application of the provisions in this Act, are severable from each other.

"(b) If any application of any provision in this Act to any person, group of persons, or circumstances is found by a court to be invalid or unconstitutional, the remaining applications of that provision to all other persons and circumstances shall be severed and may not be affected. All constitutionally valid applications of this Act shall be severed from any applications that a court finds to be invalid, leaving the valid applications in force, because it is the legislature's intent and priority that the valid applications be allowed to stand alone.

"(c) If any court declares or finds a provision of this Act facially unconstitutional, when discrete applications of that provision can be enforced against a person, group of persons, or circumstances without violating the United States Constitution and Texas Constitution, those applications shall be severed from all remaining applications of the provision, and the provision shall be interpreted as if the legislature had enacted a provision limited to the persons, group of persons, or circumstances for which the provision's application will not violate the United States Constitution and Texas Constitution.

"(d) The legislature further declares that it would have enacted this Act, and each provision, section, subsection, sentence, clause, phrase, or word, and all constitutional applications of this Act, irrespective of the fact that any provision, section, subsection, sentence, clause, phrase, or word, or applications of this Act, were to be declared unconstitutional.

"(e) If any provision of this Act is found by any court to be unconstitutionally vague, the applications of that provision that do not present constitutional vagueness problems shall be severed and remain in force.

"(f) No court may decline to enforce the severability requirements of Subsections (a), (b), (c), (d), and (e) of this section on the ground that severance would rewrite the statute or involve the court in legislative or lawmaking activity. A court that declines to enforce or enjoins a state official from enforcing a statutory provision does not rewrite a statute, as the statute continues to contain the same words as before the court's decision. A judicial injunction or declaration of unconstitutionality:

"(1) is nothing more than an edict prohibiting enforcement that may subsequently be vacated by a later court if that court has a different understanding of the requirements of the Texas Constitution or United States Constitution;

"(2) is not a formal amendment of the language in a statute; and

"(3) no more rewrites a statute than a decision by the executive not to enforce a duly enacted statute in a limited and defined set of circumstances."

"Sec. 9. Chapter 143A, Civil Practice and Remedies Code, as added by this Act, applies only to a cause of action that accrues on or after the effective date [Dec. 2, 2021] of this Act."

§ 143A.007. User Remedies

(a) A user may bring an action against a social media platform that violates this chapter with respect to the user.

(b) If the user proves that the social media platform violated this chapter with respect to the user, the user is entitled to recover:

(1) declaratory relief under Chapter 37, including costs and reasonable and necessary attorney's fees under Section 37.009; and

(2) injunctive relief.

(c) If a social media platform fails to promptly comply with a court order in an action brought under this section, the court shall hold the social media platform in contempt and shall use all lawful measures to secure immediate compliance with the order, including daily penalties sufficient to secure immediate compliance.

(d) A user may bring an action under this section regardless of whether another court has enjoined the attorney general from enforcing this chapter or declared any provision of this chapter unconstitutional unless that court decision is binding on the court in which the action is brought.

(e) Nonmutual issue preclusion and nonmutual claim preclusion are not defenses to an action brought under this section.

Added by Acts 2021, 87th Leg., 2nd C.S., ch. 3 (H.B. 20), § 7, eff. Dec. 2, 2021.

Section 1 of Acts 2021, 87th Leg., 2nd C.S., ch. 3 (H.B. 20) provides:

"The legislature finds that:

"(1) each person in this state has a fundamental interest in the free exchange of ideas and information, including the freedom of others to share and receive ideas and information;

"(2) this state has a fundamental interest in protecting the free exchange of ideas and information in this state;

"(3) social media platforms function as common carriers, are affected with a public interest, are central public forums for public debate, and have enjoyed governmental support in the United States; and

"(4) social media platforms with the largest number of users are common carriers by virtue of their market dominance."

Sections 8 and 9 of Acts 2021, 87th Leg., 2nd C.S., ch. 3 (H.B. 20) provide:

"Sec. 8. (a) Mindful of *Leavitt v. Jane L.*, 518 U.S. 137 (1996), in which in the context of determining the severability of a state statute the United States Supreme Court held that an explicit statement of legislative intent is controlling, it is the intent of the legislature that every provision, section, subsection, sentence, clause, phrase, or word in this Act, and every application of the provisions in this Act, are severable from each other.

"(b) If any application of any provision in this Act to any person, group of persons, or circumstances is found by a court to be invalid or unconstitutional, the remaining applications of that provision to all other persons and circumstances shall be severed and may not be affected. All constitutionally valid applications of this Act shall be severed from any applications that a court finds to be invalid, leaving the valid applications in force, because it is the legislature's intent and priority that the valid applications be allowed to stand alone.

"(c) If any court declares or finds a provision of this Act facially unconstitutional, when discrete applications of that provision can be enforced against a person, group of persons, or circumstances without violating the United States Constitution and Texas Constitution, those applications shall be severed from all remaining applications of the provision, and the provision shall be interpreted as if the legislature had enacted a provision limited to the persons, group of persons, or circumstances for which the provision's application will not violate the United States Constitution and Texas Constitution.

"(d) The legislature further declares that it would have enacted this Act, and each provision, section, subsection, sentence, clause, phrase, or word, and all constitutional applications of this Act, irrespective of the fact that any provision, section, subsection, sentence, clause, phrase, or word, or applications of this Act, were to be declared unconstitutional.

"(e) If any provision of this Act is found by any court to be unconstitutionally vague, the applications of that provision that do not present constitutional vagueness problems shall be severed and remain in force.

"(f) No court may decline to enforce the severability requirements of Subsections (a), (b), (c), (d), and (e) of this section on the ground that severance would rewrite the statute or involve the court in legislative or lawmaking activity. A court that declines to enforce or enjoins a state official from enforcing a statutory provision does not rewrite a statute, as the statute continues to contain the same words as before the court's decision. A judicial injunction or declaration of unconstitutionality:

"(1) is nothing more than an edict prohibiting enforcement that may subsequently be vacated by a later court if that court has a different understanding of the requirements of the Texas Constitution or United States Constitution;

"(2) is not a formal amendment of the language in a statute; and

"(3) no more rewrites a statute than a decision by the executive not to enforce a duly enacted statute in a limited and defined set of circumstances."

"Sec. 9. Chapter 143A, Civil Practice and Remedies Code, as added by this Act, applies only to a cause of action that accrues on or after the effective date [Dec. 2, 2021] of this Act."

§ 143A.008. Action by Attorney General

(a) Any person may notify the attorney general of a violation or potential violation of this chapter by a social media platform.

(b) The attorney general may bring an action to enjoin a violation or a potential violation of this chapter. If the injunction is granted, the attorney general may recover costs and reasonable attorney's fees incurred in bringing the action and reasonable investigative costs incurred in relation to the action.

Added by Acts 2021, 87th Leg., 2nd C.S., ch. 3 (H.B. 20), § 7, eff. Dec. 2, 2021.

Section 1 of Acts 2021, 87th Leg., 2nd C.S., ch. 3 (H.B. 20) provides:

"The legislature finds that:

"(1) each person in this state has a fundamental interest in the free exchange of ideas and information, including the freedom of others to share and receive ideas and information;

"(2) this state has a fundamental interest in protecting the free exchange of ideas and information in this state;

"(3) social media platforms function as common carriers, are affected with a public interest, are central public forums for public debate, and have enjoyed governmental support in the United States; and

"(4) social media platforms with the largest number of users are common carriers by virtue of their market dominance."

Sections 8 and 9 of Acts 2021, 87th Leg., 2nd C.S., ch. 3 (H.B. 20) provide:

"Sec. 8. (a) Mindful of *Leavitt v. Jane L.*, 518 U.S. 137 (1996), in which in the context of determining the severability of a state statute the United States Supreme Court held that an explicit statement of legislative intent is controlling, it is the intent of the legislature that every provision, section, subsection, sentence, clause, phrase, or word in this Act, and every application of the provisions in this Act, are severable from each other.

"(b) If any application of any provision in this Act to any person, group of persons, or circumstances is found by a court to be invalid or unconstitutional, the remaining applications of that provision to all other persons and circumstances shall be severed and may not be affected. All constitutionally valid applications of this Act shall be severed from any applications that a court finds to be invalid, leaving the valid applications in force, because it is the legislature's intent and priority that the valid applications be allowed to stand alone.

"(c) If any court declares or finds a provision of this Act facially unconstitutional, when discrete applications of that provision can be enforced against a person, group of persons, or circumstances without violating the United States Constitution and Texas Constitution, those applications shall be severed from all remaining applications of the provision, and the provision shall be interpreted as if the legislature had enacted a provision limited to the persons, group of persons, or circumstances for which the provision's application will not violate the United States Constitution and Texas Constitution.

"(d) The legislature further declares that it would have enacted this Act, and each provision, section, subsection, sentence, clause, phrase, or word, and all constitutional applications of this Act, irrespective of the fact that any provision, section, subsection, sentence, clause, phrase, or word, or applications of this Act, were to be declared unconstitutional.

"(e) If any provision of this Act is found by any court to be unconstitutionally vague, the applications of that provision that do not present constitutional vagueness problems shall be severed and remain in force.

"(f) No court may decline to enforce the severability requirements of Subsections (a), (b), (c), (d), and (e) of this section on the ground that severance would rewrite the statute or involve the court in legislative or lawmaking activity. A court that declines to enforce or enjoins a state official from enforcing a statutory provision does not rewrite a statute, as the statute continues to contain the same words as before the court's decision. A judicial injunction or declaration of unconstitutionality:

"(1) is nothing more than an edict prohibiting enforcement that may subsequently be vacated by a later court if that court has a different understanding of the requirements of the Texas Constitution or United States Constitution;

"(2) is not a formal amendment of the language in a statute; and

"(3) no more rewrites a statute than a decision by the executive not to enforce a duly enacted statute in a limited and defined set of circumstances."

"Sec. 9. Chapter 143A, Civil Practice and Remedies Code, as added by this Act, applies only to a cause of action that accrues on or after the effective date [Dec. 2, 2021] of this Act."

CHAPTER 144. DESTRUCTION OF CERTAIN RECORDS

Section

§ 144.001. Definitions

In this chapter:

(1) "Former mental health patient" means an individual who:

(A) between January 1, 1986, and December 31, 1993, was admitted to a mental health facility that has pled guilty, or whose parent or affiliate corporation has so pled, to unlawfully conspiring to offer and pay remuneration to any person to induce that person to refer individuals for services to a mental health facility; and

(B) has been released from that mental health facility; but

(C) was not admitted to the facility on the basis of a court proceeding that included a commitment hearing that was on the record.

(2) "Record" means a medical record:

(A) that a federal statute or regulation does not require to be retained, maintained, or preserved; or

(B) for which the requirement under a federal statute or regulation to retain, maintain, or preserve the record has expired.

(3) "Court" means a district or statutory probate court.

Added by Acts 1997, 75th Leg., ch. 1295, § 1, eff. Sept. 1, 1997.

§§ 144.002 to 144.004. Expired

§ 144.005. Court Records Concerning Order

The court shall seal records concerning an order issued under this chapter and ensure that the court's records are not open for inspection by any person except the former mental patient or on further order of the court after notice to the former mental patient and a finding of good cause. The institution of a suit or bringing of a claim by or on behalf of the former mental patient or the former patient's assignee or insurer constitutes good cause.

Added by Acts 1997, 75th Leg., ch. 1295, § 1, eff. Sept. 1, 1997.

§ 144.006. Collateral Effects of Order

(a) A former mental health patient who successfully petitions for an order under this chapter and a facility or health care provider, or the owner, operator, parent, or affiliate of a facility or health care provider, that is subject to an order under this chapter may deny:

(1) the existence of any record subject to the order;

(2) the existence of the order itself;

(3) the occurrence of the former mental patient's admission to a mental health facility if the records of the admission are subject to the order; and

(4) the occurrence of any treatment related to the admission if the records of the admission are subject to the order.

(b) A former mental health patient who makes a denial under Subsection (a) or a facility or health care provider, or the owner, operator, parent, or affiliate of a facility or health care provider, that is subject to an order under this chapter and that makes a denial under Subsection (a) is not liable for a civil or criminal penalty for perjury.

Added by Acts 1997, 75th Leg., ch. 1295, § 1, eff. Sept. 1, 1997.

§ 144.007. Limitation on Certain Lawsuits

(a) Except as provided by Subsection (b), a former mental patient who successfully petitions a court for an order under this chapter or a person acting on the former mental patient's behalf may not file an action against a facility or health care provider, or the owner, operator, parent, or affiliate of a facility or health care provider, related to an event or activity that formed the basis of a record subject to the court's order.

(b) A juvenile former mental health patient whose records have been sealed under this chapter may file an action or complaint at any time before the records have been destroyed under Section 144.002(c).

(c) A finding made under this chapter is not admissible against any party in litigation to establish liability for damages, expenses, or other relief as an alleged result of any treatment or admission.

Added by Acts 1997, 75th Leg., ch. 1295, § 1, eff. Sept. 1, 1997.

§ 144.008. Disclosure of Information Subject to Order; Penalty

(a) A person commits an offense if the person:

(1) knows of a former mental patient's admission to a mental health facility;

(2) knows of a court order issued under this chapter that relates to that admission; and

(3) intentionally releases, disseminates, or publishes a record or index reference subject to that order.

(b) A person commits an offense if the person:

(1) knowingly fails to delete, seal, destroy, or present to the court a record or index reference subject to an order issued under this chapter; and

(2) knows or should know that the record or index reference is subject to that order.

(c) An offense under this chapter is a Class B misdemeanor.

(d) This chapter does not prohibit an attorney or insurer of a provider or patient from retaining or communicating confidentially about a privileged document as necessary to provide legal advice regarding an actual or potential claim or issue. The document or communication remains privileged and not subject to a subpoena.

Added by Acts 1997, 75th Leg., ch. 1295, § 1, eff. Sept. 1, 1997.

§ 144.009. Applicability of Other Law

This chapter supersedes other state law regarding the retention or destruction of patient records.

Added by Acts 1997, 75th Leg., ch. 1295, § 1, eff. Sept. 1, 1997.

§ 144.010. Repealed by Acts 2021, 87th Leg., ch. 915 (H.B. 3607), § 3.002, eff. Sept. 1, 2021

CHAPTER 145. LIABILITY FOR NEGLIGENT HIRING BY IN-HOME SERVICE COMPANIES AND RESIDENTIAL DELIVERY COMPANIES

§ 145.001. Definitions

In this chapter:

(1) "In-home service company" means a person who employs a person to enter another person's residence and for a fee repair:

(A) an appliance;

(B) the residence's heating, air-conditioning, and ventilation system;

(C) the residence's plumbing system; or

(D) the residence's electrical system.

(1–a) "Residence" means a person's principal or ordinary home or dwelling place and includes:

(A) any garage that is attached to the home or dwelling place; and

(B) any construction area that is attached to and accessible from the inhabited area or the attached garage of the home or dwelling place.

(2) "Residential delivery company" means a person who employs a person to, for a fee:

(A) deliver an item to another person's residence; and

(B) enter the residence to place, assemble, or install the item.

Added by Acts 2003, 78th Leg., ch. 228, § 1, eff. Sept. 1, 2003. Amended by Acts 2009, 81st Leg., ch. 751, § 1, eff. Sept. 1, 2009.

§ 145.0015. Short Title

This chapter may be cited as the Sue Weaver Act.

Added by Acts 2009, 81st Leg., ch. 751, § 2, eff. Sept. 1, 2009.

§ 145.002. Criminal History Background Check

Before associating with or hiring an officer, employee, or prospective employee in a position whose duties include entry into another person's residence, an in-home service company or residential delivery company shall:

(1) obtain from the Department of Public Safety or a private vendor all criminal history record information relating to an officer, employee, or prospective employee; or

(2) ascertain that the person holds in good standing an occupational license issued by a licensing authority in this state that has, before issuing or renewing the license, performed a criminal history background check.

Added by Acts 2003, 78th Leg., ch. 228, § 1, eff. Sept. 1, 2003. Amended by Acts 2009, 81st Leg., ch. 751, § 3, eff. Sept. 1, 2009.

§ 145.003. Presumption of No Negligence

(a) This section applies only to an action against an in-home service company or residential delivery company that:

(1) arises out of a criminal act or omission by an officer or employee of the company as to whom the company has obtained criminal history record information under Section 145.002(1);

(2) is brought by or on behalf of a person whose home the officer or employee entered while in the performance of the employee's job duties, without regard to where the criminal act or omission occurred; and

(3) seeks damages from the company for the negligent hiring of the officer or employee.

(b) In an action to which this section applies, an in-home service company or residential delivery company is rebuttably presumed to have not acted negligently if:

(1) at the time a person was hired, the company obtained criminal history record information regarding the officer or employee under Section 145.002(1); and

(2) the criminal history record information shows that, in the 20 years preceding the date the information was obtained for a felony or in the 10 years preceding the date the information was obtained for a Class A or Class B misdemeanor, the officer or employee had not been convicted of, or placed on deferred adjudication for:

(A) an offense in this state classified as:

(i) an offense against the person or the family;

(ii) an offense against property; or

(iii) public indecency; or

(B) an offense in another jurisdiction that would be classified in a category described by Paragraph (A) if the offense had occurred in this state.

(c) A residential delivery company or an in-home service company that sends two or more employees together into a residence shall be deemed to have complied with the requirement in Section 145.002 as long as at least one of those employees has been checked as described in Section 145.002 and, while they are in the residence, that employee accompanies and directly supervises any employee who has not been checked, and the residential delivery company or in-home service company maintains a record of the identity of any such nonchecked employee for at least two years.

Added by Acts 2003, 78th Leg., ch. 228, § 1, eff. Sept. 1, 2003. Amended by Acts 2009, 81st Leg., ch. 751, § 4, eff. Sept. 1, 2009.

§ 145.004. Presumption of No Negligence for Persons Utilizing a Residential Delivery Company or In-Home Service Company

A person who contracts with a residential delivery company to deliver an item or who contracts with an in-home service company to place, assemble, repair, or install an item referred to in Section 145.001(1), is rebuttably presumed to have not acted negligently in doing so if:

(1) the residential delivery company or in-home service company is in compliance with Section 145.003(b); or

(2) the person who contracts with the residential delivery company or in-home service company requests that the company obtain a criminal history background check described by Section 145.002 on any employee of the company being sent to deliver, place, assemble, repair, or install an item and the

person's request is in writing and is delivered to the company prior to the company's employee being sent. A copy of any such request shall be maintained for at least two years.

Added by Acts 2003, 78th Leg., ch. 228, § 1, eff. Sept. 1, 2003.

CHAPTER 146. CERTAIN CLAIMS BY HEALTH CARE SERVICE PROVIDERS BARRED

Section

§ 146.001. Definitions

In this chapter:

(1) "Health benefit plan" means a plan or arrangement under which medical or surgical expenses are paid for or reimbursed or health care services are arranged for or provided. The term includes:

(A) an individual, group, blanket, or franchise insurance policy, insurance agreement, or group hospital service contract;

(B) an evidence of coverage or group subscriber contract issued by a health maintenance organization or an approved nonprofit health corporation;

(C) a benefit plan provided by a multiple employer welfare arrangement or another analogous benefit arrangement;

(D) a workers' compensation insurance policy; or

(E) a motor vehicle insurance policy, to the extent the policy provides personal injury protection or medical payments coverage.

(2) "Health care service provider" means a person who, under a license or other grant of authority issued by this state, provides health care services the costs of which may be paid for or reimbursed under a health benefit plan.

Added by Acts 1999, 76th Leg., ch. 650, § 1, eff. Sept. 1, 1999.

§ 146.002. Timely Billing Required

(a) Except as provided by Subsection (b) or (c), a health care service provider shall bill a patient or other responsible person for services provided to the patient not later than the first day of the 11th month after the date the services are provided.

(b) If the health care service provider is required or authorized to directly bill the issuer of a health benefit plan for services provided to a patient, the health care service provider shall bill the issuer of the plan not later than:

(1) the date required under any contract between the health care service provider and the issuer of the health benefit plan; or

(2) if there is no contract between the health care service provider and the issuer of the health benefit plan, the first day of the 11th month after the date the services are provided.

(c) If the health care service provider is required or authorized to directly bill a third party payor operating under federal or state law, including Medicare and the state Medicaid program, the health care service provider shall bill the third party payor not later than:

(1) the date required under any contract between the health care service provider and the third party payor or the date required by federal regulation or state rule, as applicable; or

(2) if there is no contract between the health care service provider and the third party payor and there is no applicable federal regulation or state rule, the first day of the 11th month after the date the services are provided.

(d) For purposes of this section, the date of billing is the date on which the health care service provider's bill is:

(1) mailed to the patient or responsible person, postage prepaid, at the address of the patient or responsible person as shown on the health care service provider's records; or

(2) mailed or otherwise submitted to the issuer of the health benefit plan or third party payor as required by the health benefit plan or third party payor.

Added by Acts 1999, 76th Leg., ch. 650, § 1, eff. Sept. 1, 1999.

§ 146.003. Certain Claims Barred

(a) A health care service provider who violates Section 146.002 may not recover from the patient any amount that the patient would have been entitled to receive as payment or reimbursement under a health benefit plan or that the patient would not otherwise have been obligated to pay had the provider complied with Section 146.002.

(b) If recovery from a patient is barred under this section, the health care service provider may not recover from any other individual who, because of a family or other personal relationship with the patient, would otherwise be responsible for the debt.

Added by Acts 1999, 76th Leg., ch. 650, § 1, eff. Sept. 1, 1999.

§ 146.004. Disciplinary Action Not Authorized

A health care service provider who violates this chapter is not subject to disciplinary action for the violation under any other law, including the law under which the health care service provider is licensed or otherwise holds a grant of authority.

Added by Acts 1999, 76th Leg., ch. 650, § 1, eff. Sept. 1, 1999.

CHAPTER 147. YEAR 2000 COMPUTER DATE FAILURE

SUBCHAPTER A. GENERAL PROVISIONS

§ 147.001. Definitions

In this chapter:

(1) "Action" means a cause of action to which this chapter applies.

(2) "Claimant" means a party seeking recovery of damages or other relief, including a plaintiff, counterclaimant, cross-claimant, or third-party plaintiff.

(3) "Computer product" means a computer, computer network, computer program, computer software, computer system, microprocessor, embedded computer chip, semiconductor device, any component of any of those items, or a product that includes any of those items as a component of the product.

(4) "Computer service product" means the product of the use of a computer, including uses related to data processing and storage. The term includes information stored in the computer by personnel supporting the computer.

(5) "Defendant" means a party from whom a claimant seeks recovery of damages or other relief, including a counterdefendant, cross-defendant, or third-party defendant.

(6) "Good faith" means honesty in fact in the conduct or transaction concerned.

(7) "Recent consumer product" means a mass-marketed computer product, intended by the seller to be used for personal, family, or household purposes or by small businesses, that will manifest a computer date failure during its normal use and was last offered for sale by the manufacturer after January 1, 1997, and in the case of software, was offered for a retail price of $300 or less. The term does not include customized products.

(8) "Small business" means a legal entity, including a sole proprietorship, that:

(A) is formed for the purpose of making a profit;

(B) is independently owned and operated; and

(C) has fewer than 100 employees or less than $1 million in annual gross receipts.

(9) "Year 2000 Project Office website" means the Texas Year 2000 Project Office website administered by the Department of Information Resources. The Internet address of the website is www.dir.state.tx.us/y2k.[1]

Added by Acts 1999, 76th Leg., ch. 128, § 2, eff. May 19, 1999.

[1] The website is no longer active.

§ 147.002. Action for Computer Date Failure

Subject to Section 147.004 and regardless of the legal theory, statute, or cause of action on which the action is based, including an action based in tort, contract, or breach of an express or implied warranty, this chapter applies only to an action in which a claimant seeks recovery of damages or any other relief for harm caused by:

(1) a computer date failure as described by Section 147.003; or

(2) the failure to properly detect, disclose, prevent, report, correct, cure, or remediate a computer date failure as described by Section 147.003.

Added by Acts 1999, 76th Leg., ch. 128, § 2, eff. May 19, 1999.

§ 147.003. Computer Date Failure

A computer date failure is the inability to correctly process, recognize, store, receive, transmit, or in any way use date data:

(1) referring to the year 2000 or affected by the transition between the 20th and 21st century or between 1999 and 2000; or

(2) with years expressed in a two-digit or four-digit format.

Added by Acts 1999, 76th Leg., ch. 128, § 2, eff. May 19, 1999.

§ 147.004. Applicability

This chapter does not apply to an action:

(1) for death or bodily injury;

(2) to collect workers' compensation benefits under the workers' compensation laws of this state; or

(3) to enforce the terms of a written agreement, or to seek contractual remedies for breach of a written agreement, that specifically provides for liability and damages for a computer date failure.

Added by Acts 1999, 76th Leg., ch. 128, § 2, eff. May 19, 1999.

§ 147.005. Duty or Action Not Created

(a) This chapter does not create a duty.

(b) This chapter does not create a cause of action.

Added by Acts 1999, 76th Leg., ch. 128, § 2, eff. May 19, 1999.

§ 147.006. Immunity Not Affected

This chapter does not expand or limit the immunity of a person under any other law or statute providing immunity.

Added by Acts 1999, 76th Leg., ch. 128, § 2, eff. May 19, 1999.

§ 147.007. Insurance Coverage Not Affected

This chapter does not affect the coverage or benefits of parties under a contract of insurance.

Added by Acts 1999, 76th Leg., ch. 128, § 2, eff. May 19, 1999.

§ 147.008. Sovereign Immunity Not Waived

This chapter does not waive any immunity of the state or of a political subdivision of the state or any employee or officer thereof.

Added by Acts 1999, 76th Leg., ch. 128, § 2, eff. May 19, 1999.

§ 147.009. Manufacturer's Duty to Indemnify

This chapter does not relieve a manufacturer from the obligation, if any, to indemnify a seller for losses arising out of a product liability action for property damage under Section 82.002, subject to any defenses the manufacturer could have asserted at the time the action was filed.

Added by Acts 1999, 76th Leg., ch. 128, § 2, eff. May 19, 1999.

SUBCHAPTER B. PREREQUISITES TO BRINGING ACTION

§ 147.041. Limitations Period

(a) An action must be brought not later than two years after the date the computer date failure first caused the harm that is the subject matter of the action.

(b) This section does not extend the limitations period within which an action for harm caused by a computer date failure may be commenced under any other law or revive a claim that is barred by the operation of any other law.

Added by Acts 1999, 76th Leg., ch. 128, § 2, eff. May 19, 1999.

§ 147.042. Repose

(a) Except as provided by Subsection (b), a claimant must commence an action against a manufacturer or seller of a computer product or computer service product before the end of 15 years after the date of the sale by the defendant. If the computer product which caused the computer date failure is a component of another product and if the product and computer product were sold at different times, the 15-year period begins to run on the date the defendant sold the computer product.

(b) If a manufacturer or seller expressly represented that the computer product or computer service product would not manifest the computer date failure, this section does not apply.

(c) This section does not reduce a limitations period that applies to an action that accrues before the end of the limitations period under this section.

(d) This section does not extend the limitations period within which an action may be commenced under any other law.

Added by Acts 1999, 76th Leg., ch. 128, § 2, eff. May 19, 1999.

§ 147.043. Disability

Section 16.001 applies to the periods of limitation and repose established by this subchapter.

Added by Acts 1999, 76th Leg., ch. 128, § 2, eff. May 19, 1999.

§ 147.044. Notice

(a) A claimant may not commence an action unless the claimant gave notice to the defendant before the 60th day preceding the date the action commences.

(b) If the 60-day notice requirement under Subsection (a) would prevent commencing the action before the expiration of the period of limitation or repose, the claimant must give notice to the defendant before the 31st day after the date the action commences.

(c) If the action is a counterclaim, cross-claim, or third-party action, the claimant must give notice to the defendant before the 31st day after the date of service on the defendant.

(d) The notice must:

(1) be in writing;

(2) identify the claimant;

(3) describe in reasonable detail the computer date failure and the harm caused by the failure; and

(4) include a specific statement of the amount of the damages claimed or the remedy sought.

Added by Acts 1999, 76th Leg., ch. 128, § 2, eff. May 19, 1999.

§ 147.045. Notice Stays Proceedings

All proceedings in the action are stayed for 60 days following the date the defendant received the notice under Section 147.044.

Added by Acts 1999, 76th Leg., ch. 128, § 2, eff. May 19, 1999.

§ 147.046. Failure to Give Notice

(a) On motion of the defendant that the claimant did not give the notice under Section 147.044, the court shall:

(1) abate the action; and

(2) require the claimant to give the notice before the 31st day after the date of the order of abatement.

(b) The court shall dismiss the claimant's action if the claimant does not give notice as required by Subsection (a)(2).

Added by Acts 1999, 76th Leg., ch. 128, § 2, eff. May 19, 1999.

§ 147.047. Inspection

(a) A person receiving notice under Section 147.044 may inspect a computer product or computer service product that is subject to the claimant's control to assess the nature, scope, and consequences of the computer date failure.

(b) The inspection must be conducted in a reasonable manner and at a reasonable time and place.

Added by Acts 1999, 76th Leg., ch. 128, § 2, eff. May 19, 1999.

§ 147.048. Offer to Settle

(a) A defendant receiving notice under Section 147.044 may offer to settle the claim. The offer may include an offer to cure or correct the computer date failure.

(b) The offer must be accepted by the claimant not later than the 30th day after the date the offer is made or the offer is rejected.

(c) A defendant may file a rejected offer to settle with the court with an affidavit certifying its rejection.

(d) If the court finds that the amount tendered in a rejected offer to settle filed with the court is the same as, substantially the same as, or more than the damages found by the trier of fact, the claimant may not recover any amount in excess of the lesser of:

(1) the amount of damages tendered in the settlement offer; or

(2) the amount of damages found by the trier of fact.

(e) Subsection (d) does not apply if the court finds that the defendant making the offer:

(1) could not perform the offer when the offer was made; or

(2) substantially misrepresented the value of the offer.

(f) In this section, the term "damages" does not include attorney's fees or litigation expenses.

Added by Acts 1999, 76th Leg., ch. 128, § 2, eff. May 19, 1999.

SUBCHAPTER C. AFFIRMATIVE DEFENSES TO LIABILITY

§ 147.081. Affirmative Defense: Notice to Cure or Correct

(a) It is an affirmative defense to liability in an action if:

(1) the claimant was notified in the manner provided by Section 147.082 that the computer product or computer service product may manifest computer date failure;

(2) the claimant was offered a cure or correction for the computer date failure; and

(3) the offered cure or correction would have avoided the harm to the claimant caused by the computer date failure.

(b) In addition to the requirement of Subsection (a), to establish the affirmative defense provided by this section:

(1) if the claimant's action involves a recent consumer product, the defendant must prove that the charge, if any, for the cure or correction did not exceed the reasonable charges for the delivery and installation of the product or items needed to cure or correct the computer date failure; or

(2) if the claimant's action involves a computer product or computer service product that is not a recent consumer product, the defendant must prove that the charge, if any, for the cure or correction did not exceed the reasonable and necessary costs to develop, produce, deliver, and install the product or items needed to cure or correct the computer date failure.

(c) If the cure or correction described by Subsection (a) is designed to cure or correct a computer date failure for only a limited period of time, that cure or correction does not entitle a person to a defense to liability for harm caused by the computer date failure after the period of time expires.

Added by Acts 1999, 76th Leg., ch. 128, § 2, eff. May 19, 1999.

§ 147.082. Notice

(a) Notice under Section 147.081 must:

(1) identify the computer product or computer service product that manifests or may manifest a computer date failure;

(2) explain how a cure or correction to the computer product or computer service product may be obtained;

(3)(A) in the case of a recent consumer product, state that there is no additional charge for the cure or correction and state the amount that will be charged, if any, for delivering and installing the cure or correction, as authorized by Section 147.081(b)(1); or

(B) in the case of a product or service that is not a recent consumer product, state the amount that will be charged, if any, for the cure or correction, as authorized by Section 147.081(b)(2); and

(4) inform the recipient that the solution is offered to avoid harm to the recipient and that offering the cure or correction could affect the recipient's right to recover damages.

(b) Notice under Section 147.081 must be received by the claimant before the beginning of the longer of the following periods:

(1) the 90th day before the date the claimant suffers harm from the computer date failure; or

(2) the time needed to order, deliver, and install the correction to the product or service before the claimant suffers harm from the computer date failure.

(c) The defendant may satisfy the notice requirement under Section 147.081 by showing that:

(1) the defendant delivered notice within the period provided by this section; or

(2) the claimant actually received notice within the period provided by this section.

(d) There is a rebuttable presumption that notice has been delivered to a claimant if the Year 2000 Project Office website or toll-free telephone number established under Section 147.083(e) provides access to information from which a person may obtain the information required by this section relating to a cure or correction for the computer date failure. The presumption may be rebutted by credible evidence that the claimant did not receive notice.

Added by Acts 1999, 76th Leg., ch. 128, § 2, eff. May 19, 1999.

§ 147.083. Notice on Year 2000 Project Office Website

(a) A person who provides information to the Year 2000 Project Office website to satisfy the requirements of Section 147.082 is responsible for the accuracy of the person's information posted on the website.

(b) A person is not subject to the jurisdiction of the courts of this state solely on the basis that the person has provided information for posting on the Year 2000 Project Office website.

(c) The state is not liable for any damages arising from its Year 2000-related activities conducted by the Department of Information Resources, including:

(1) operation of the Year 2000 Project Office website;

(2) reliance on the accuracy of the information on the Year 2000 Project Office website; or

(3) operation and management of the toll-free telephone number established in accordance with Subsection (e).

(d) The Department of Information Resources in its Year 2000 Project Office website shall provide for the posting of information and the creating of links to other websites to facilitate the posting of notice.

(e) The Department of Information Resources shall establish a toll-free telephone number for persons who are unable to access the Internet to provide to those persons information relating to a cure or correction for computer date failure posted on or linked to the Year 2000 Project Office website. The Department of Information Resources may establish the toll-free telephone number either in cooperation with the General Services Commission or by contracting with a private vendor.

(f) Any contracts for goods or services between the Department of Information Resources and private vendors that may be necessary or appropriate to the fulfillment of the requirements of this section are exempt from the requirements of Subtitle D, Title 10, Government Code.[1] If the Department of Information Resources elects to contract with one or more private vendors, the vendors have no greater liability to third parties for their actions than the state would have had if it had provided the goods and services directly.

Added by Acts 1999, 76th Leg., ch. 128, § 2, eff. May 19, 1999.

[1] V.T.C.A., Government Code § 2151.001 et seq.

§ 147.084. Affirmative Defense: Reliance

(a) In an action for fraud, misrepresentation, disparagement, libel, or other similar action based on the alleged falsity or misleading character of a computer date statement or an express warranty, it is an affirmative defense to liability that:

(1) the defendant reasonably relied on the computer date statement or express warranty of an independent, upstream manufacturer or seller of the computer product or computer service product that the computer product or computer service product would not manifest computer date failure;

(2) the statement was false or misleading; and

(3) the defendant did not have actual knowledge that the statement or warranty was false or misleading.

(b) In this section, "computer date statement" means a material statement about a computer product or computer service product regarding the present or future ability of a computer product in relation to avoiding computer date failure, including a statement that a computer product or computer service product:

(1) is "Year 2000 Compliant" or a similar representation; or

(2) complies with a computer date standard established by a state or federal regulatory agency or by a national or international standards organization.

Added by Acts 1999, 76th Leg., ch. 128, § 2, eff. May 19, 1999.

§ 147.085. Admissibility of Statement Relating to Computer Date Failure

(a) The following are not admissible to prove liability for computer date failure:

(1) an offer to settle under Section 147.048;

(2) notice required under Section 147.081(a)(1);

(3) except as provided by Subsection (b), evidence of furnishing or offering or promising to furnish a correction or cure for a present or future computer date failure; or

(4) except as provided by Subsection (c), a statement made in the process of correcting, curing, or

attempting to correct or cure a present or future computer date failure.

(b) Evidence of furnishing or offering or promising to furnish a correction or cure for a present or future computer date failure is admissible to the extent it is evidence of a guarantee or warranty of the correction or cure and the claim is for breach of the guarantee or warranty.

(c) A statement made in the process of correcting, curing, or attempting to correct or cure a present or future computer date failure is admissible if:

(1) the statement is false;

(2) the statement is made with knowledge that it is false; and

(3) the claimant relied on the statement to the claimant's detriment.

Added by Acts 1999, 76th Leg., ch. 128, § 2, eff. May 19, 1999.

SUBCHAPTER D. DAMAGES

§ 147.121. Damage Limitations Apply Only if Defendant Shows Good Faith Effort to Cure or Correct

The limitations on the recovery of damages established by Section 147.122 apply to a claimant only if the defendant can show a good faith effort to cure, correct, avoid, or mitigate the claimant's possible computer date failure problem.

Added by Acts 1999, 76th Leg., ch. 128, § 2, eff. May 19, 1999.

§ 147.122. Damages Not Recoverable

(a) Subject to Section 147.121, a claimant may not recover the following damages in an action:

(1) damages for mental anguish, loss of consortium, or loss of companionship;

(2) exemplary or punitive damages unless the claimant proves by clear and convincing evidence that the conduct of the defendant was committed with fraud or malice;

(3) additional damages under Section 17.50(b)(1), Business & Commerce Code, unless the trier of fact finds the conduct of the defendant was committed with fraud or malice; or

(4) consequential damages, unless they were reasonably foreseeable.

(b) In this section:

(1) "Fraud" means fraud other than constructive fraud.

(2) "Malice" means a specific intent by the defendant to cause substantial injury to the claimant.

Added by Acts 1999, 76th Leg., ch. 128, § 2, eff. May 19, 1999.

§ 147.123. Mitigation of Damages

(a) In an action to which Chapter 33 applies, the court shall instruct the finder of fact regarding the determination of responsibility pursuant to Section 33.003 using the appropriate approved pattern jury charge which may be modified by the court as appropriate to the circumstances.

(b) In all actions not governed by Subsection (a), the court shall instruct the finder of fact regarding a claimant's duty to mitigate or avoid damages in a manner appropriate to the action using the appropriate approved pattern jury charge which may be modified by the court as appropriate to the circumstances.

Added by Acts 1999, 76th Leg., ch. 128, § 2, eff. May 19, 1999.

CHAPTER 148. LIABILITY DURING PANDEMIC EMERGENCY

§ 148.001. Definitions

In this chapter:

(1) "Pandemic disease" has the meaning assigned by Section 74.155.

(2) "Pandemic emergency" means a state of disaster declared by the governor under Chapter 418, Government Code, in response to a pandemic disease.

Added by Acts 2021, 87th Leg., ch. 528 (S.B. 6), § 3, eff. June 14, 2021.

Sections 4(c) and 5(a) of Acts 2021, 87th Leg., ch. 528 (S.B. 6) provides:

"[Sec. 4.] (c) For purposes of Section 74.155 and Chapter 148, Civil Practice and Remedies Code, as added by this Act, the legislature finds that while some settled expectations regarding claims to which this Act applies may be impaired by this Act, the Act serves a compelling public interest in establishing certain procedures and standards for addressing potential claims against individuals and entities faced with an unprecedented public health emergency that has had severe and adverse impacts on both the health and safety of individuals and the ordinary functioning of governmental entities, the judicial system, the health care delivery system, educational and religious institutions, businesses, nonprofit entities, and others whose daily lives have been upended by the emergency."

"[Sec. 5.] (a) Section 74.155 and Chapter 148, Civil Practice and Remedies Code, as added by this Act, apply only to an action commenced on or after March 13, 2020, for which a judgment has not become final before the effective date [June 14, 2021] of this Act. An action commenced before March 13, 2020, or an action for which a judgment has become final before the effective date of this Act is governed by the law applicable to the action immediately before the effective date of this Act, and that law is continued in effect for that purpose."

§ 148.002. Products Liability Actions Related to Pandemic Emergency

(a) This section applies only to the following products:

(1) clothing or equipment worn to minimize exposure to hazards of a pandemic disease that cause injury or illness;

(2) medical devices, equipment, and supplies used during a pandemic emergency or to treat individuals infected or suspected to be infected with a pandemic disease, including devices, equipment, and supplies used or modified for an unapproved use to treat or prevent the spread of the disease or used outside of their normal use to treat or prevent the spread of the disease;

(3) drugs, medicines, or vaccines used to treat or prevent the spread of a pandemic disease, including drugs, medicines, or vaccines prescribed, dispensed, or administered for an unapproved use in an attempt to treat or prevent the spread of the disease or used outside of their normal use in an attempt to treat or prevent the spread of the disease;

(4) tests to diagnose or determine immunity to a pandemic disease;

(5) commercial cleaning, sanitizing, or disinfecting supplies used to prevent the spread of a pandemic disease; or

(6) any component of a product described by this subsection.

(b) A person who designs, manufactures, sells, or donates a product described by Subsection (a) during a pandemic emergency is not liable for personal injury, death, or property damage caused by the product unless:

(1) the person:

(A) had actual knowledge of a defect in the product when the product left the person's control; or

(B) acted with actual malice in designing, manufacturing, selling, or donating the product; and

(2) the product presents an unreasonable risk of substantial harm to an individual using or exposed to the product.

(c) A person who designs, manufactures, labels, sells, or donates a product described by Subsection (a) during a pandemic emergency is not liable for personal injury, death, or property damage caused by a failure to warn or provide adequate instructions regarding the use of a product unless:

(1) the person acted with actual malice in failing to warn or provide adequate instructions regarding the use of the product; and

(2) the failure to warn or provide adequate instructions regarding the use of the product presents an unreasonable risk of substantial harm to an individual using or exposed to the product.

(d) A person is not liable for personal injury, death, or property damage caused by or resulting from the person's selection, distribution, or use of a product described by Subsection (a) during a pandemic emergency unless:

(1) the person:

(A) had actual knowledge of a defect in the product when the person selected, distributed, or used the product; or

(B) acted with actual malice in selecting, distributing, or using the product; and

(2) the product presents an unreasonable risk of substantial harm to an individual using or exposed to the product.

Added by Acts 2021, 87th Leg., ch. 528 (S.B. 6), § 3, eff. June 14, 2021.

Sections 4(c) and 5(a) of Acts 2021, 87th Leg., ch. 528 (S.B. 6) provides:

"[Sec. 4.] (c) For purposes of Section 74.155 and Chapter 148, Civil Practice and Remedies Code, as added by this Act, the legislature finds that while some settled expectations regarding claims to which this Act applies may be impaired by this Act, the Act serves a compelling public interest in establishing certain procedures and standards for addressing potential claims against individuals and entities faced with an unprecedented public health emergency that has had severe and adverse impacts on both the health and safety of individuals and the ordinary functioning of governmental entities, the judicial system, the health care delivery system, educational and religious institutions, businesses, nonprofit entities, and others whose daily lives have been upended by the emergency."

"[Sec. 5.] (a) Section 74.155 and Chapter 148, Civil Practice and Remedies Code, as added by this Act, apply only to an action commenced on or after March 13, 2020, for which a judgment has not become final before the effective date [June 14, 2021] of this Act. An action commenced before March 13, 2020, or an action for which a judgment has become final before the effective date of this Act is governed by the law applicable to the action immediately before the effective date of this Act, and that law is continued in effect for that purpose."

§ 148.003. Liability for Causing Exposure to Pandemic Disease

(a) A person is not liable for injury or death caused by exposing an individual to a pandemic disease during a pandemic emergency unless the claimant establishes that:

(1) the person who exposed the individual:

(A) knowingly failed to warn the individual of or remediate a condition that the person knew was likely to result in the exposure of an individual to the disease, provided that the person:

(i) had control over the condition;

(ii) knew that the individual was more likely than not to come into contact with the condition; and

(iii) had a reasonable opportunity and ability to remediate the condition or warn the individual of the condition before the individual came into contact with the condition; or

(B) knowingly failed to implement or comply with government-promulgated standards, guidance, or protocols intended to lower the likelihood of exposure to the disease that were applicable to the person or the person's business, provided that:

(i) the person had a reasonable opportunity and ability to implement or comply with the standards, guidance, or protocols;

(ii) the person refused to implement or comply with or acted with flagrant disregard of the standards, guidance, or protocols; and

(iii) the government-promulgated standards, guidance, or protocols that the person failed to implement or comply with did not, on the date that the individual was exposed to the disease, conflict with government-promulgated standards, guidance, or protocols that the person implemented or complied with; and

(2) reliable scientific evidence shows that the failure to warn the individual of the condition, remediate the condition, or implement or comply with the government-promulgated standards, guidance, or protocols was the cause in fact of the individual contracting the disease.

(b) Except as provided by Subsection (c), not later than the 120th day after the date a defendant files an answer to a claim to which Subsection (a) applies, the claimant shall serve on the defendant:

(1) a report authored by at least one qualified expert that provides a factual and scientific basis for the assertion that the defendant's failure to act caused the individual to contract a pandemic disease; and

(2) a curriculum vitae for each expert whose opinion is included in the report.

(c) The deadline for serving the report and curriculum vitae required by Subsection (b) may be extended by written agreement of the affected parties.

(d) A defendant must file an objection to the sufficiency of the report and serve the objection on the claimant not later than 21 days after the later of:

(1) the date the report is served on the defendant; or

(2) the date the defendant's answer to the claim is filed.

(e) If a court determines that a report served under Subsection (b) does not represent an objective, good faith effort to provide a factual and scientific basis for the assertion that the defendant's failure to act caused the injured individual to contract a pandemic disease, the court may grant the claimant, on one occasion, a 30-day period to cure any deficiency in the report.

(f) If a sufficient report is not timely served under this section, the court, on the defendant's motion, shall enter an order:

(1) dismissing the claim with respect to the defendant, with prejudice; and

(2) awarding to the defendant reasonable attorney's fees and costs of court incurred by the defendant in the action.

(g) Nothing in this section shall be construed to mean that a single expert must address all causation issues with respect to all defendants.

(h) A report served under this section:

(1) is not admissible in evidence by any party;

(2) may not be used in a deposition, trial, or other proceeding; and

(3) may not be referred to by any party during the course of the action, except in a proceeding to determine if a report is sufficient or timely.

(i) After a claim to which Subsection (a) applies is filed, all claimants, collectively, may take not more than two depositions before the expert report is served as required by Subsection (b).

(j) For purposes of Subsection (a)(1)(B), if an order, rule, or authoritative declaration promulgated by the governor, the legislature, a state agency, or a local governmental entity with jurisdiction over the person conflicts with a different government-promulgated standard, guideline, or protocol, a person may not be considered to fail to implement or comply with the government-promulgated standard, guideline, or protocol if, at the time of the injured individual's exposure to the pandemic disease during a pandemic emergency, the person is making a good faith effort to substantially comply with at least one conflicting order, rule, or declaration.

Added by Acts 2021, 87th Leg., ch. 528 (S.B. 6), § 3, eff. June 14, 2021.

Sections 4(c) and 5(a) of Acts 2021, 87th Leg., ch. 528 (S.B. 6) provides:

"[Sec. 4.] (c) For purposes of Section 74.155 and Chapter 148, Civil Practice and Remedies Code, as added by this Act, the legislature finds that while some settled expectations regarding claims to which this Act applies may be impaired by this Act, the Act serves a compelling public interest in establishing certain procedures and standards for addressing potential claims against individuals and entities faced with an unprecedented public health emergency that has had severe and adverse impacts on both the health and safety of individuals and the ordinary functioning of governmental entities, the judicial system, the health care delivery system, educational and religious institutions, businesses, nonprofit entities, and others whose daily lives have been upended by the emergency."

"[Sec. 5.] (a) Section 74.155 and Chapter 148, Civil Practice and Remedies Code, as added by this Act, apply only to an action commenced on or after March 13, 2020, for which a judgment has not become final before the effective date [June 14, 2021] of this Act. An action commenced before March 13, 2020, or an action for which a judgment has become final before the effective date of this Act is governed by the law applicable to the action immediately before the effective date of this Act, and that law is continued in effect for that purpose."

§ 148.004. Liability of Educational Institutions for Certain Actions During Pandemic Emergency

(a) In this section, "educational institution" means an institution or program that facilitates learning or the acquisition of knowledge, skills, values, beliefs, or habits. The term includes:

(1) a public or private preschool, child-care facility, primary or secondary school, college, or university;

(2) an institution of higher education, as that term is defined by Section 61.003, Education Code; and

(3) a private or independent institution of higher education, as that term is defined by Section 61.003, Education Code.

(b) An educational institution is not liable for damages or equitable monetary relief arising from a cancellation or modification of a course, program, or activity of the institution if the cancellation or modification arose during a pandemic emergency and was caused, in whole or in part, by the emergency.

Added by Acts 2021, 87th Leg., ch. 528 (S.B. 6), § 3, eff. June 14, 2021.

Sections 4(c) and 5(a) of Acts 2021, 87th Leg., ch. 528 (S.B. 6) provides:

"[Sec. 4.] (c) For purposes of Section 74.155 and Chapter 148, Civil Practice and Remedies Code, as added by this Act, the legislature finds that while some settled expectations regarding claims to which this Act applies may be impaired by this Act, the Act serves a compelling public interest in establishing certain procedures and standards for addressing potential claims against individuals and entities faced with an unprecedented public health emergency that has had severe and adverse impacts on both the health and safety of individuals and the ordinary functioning of governmental entities, the judicial system, the health care delivery system, educational and religious institutions, businesses, nonprofit entities, and others whose daily lives have been upended by the emergency."

"[Sec. 5.] (a) Section 74.155 and Chapter 148, Civil Practice and Remedies Code, as added by this Act, apply only to an action commenced on or after March 13, 2020, for which a judgment has not become final before the effective date [June 14, 2021] of this Act. An action commenced before March 13, 2020, or an action for which a judgment has become final before the effective date of this Act is governed by the law applicable to the action immediately before the effective date of this Act, and that law is continued in effect for that purpose."

§ 148.005. No Civil Cause of Action

This chapter does not create a civil cause of action.

Added by Acts 2021, 87th Leg., ch. 528 (S.B. 6), § 3, eff. June 14, 2021.

Sections 4(c) and 5(a) of Acts 2021, 87th Leg., ch. 528 (S.B. 6) provides:

"[Sec. 4.] (c) For purposes of Section 74.155 and Chapter 148, Civil Practice and Remedies Code, as added by this Act, the legislature finds that while some settled expectations regarding claims to which this Act applies may be impaired by this Act, the Act serves a compelling public interest in establishing certain procedures and standards for addressing potential claims against individuals and entities faced with an unprecedented public health emergency that has had severe and adverse impacts on both the health and safety of individuals and the ordinary functioning of governmental entities, the judicial system, the health care delivery system, educational and religious institutions, businesses, nonprofit entities, and others whose daily lives have been upended by the emergency."

"[Sec. 5.] (a) Section 74.155 and Chapter 148, Civil Practice and Remedies Code, as added by this Act, apply only to an action commenced on or after March 13, 2020, for which a judgment has not become final before the effective date [June 14, 2021] of this Act. An action commenced before March 13, 2020, or an action for which a judgment has become final before the effective date of this Act is governed by the law applicable to the action immediately before the effective date of this Act, and that law is continued in effect for that purpose."

CHAPTER 149. LIMITATIONS IN CIVIL ACTIONS OF LIABILITIES RELATING TO CERTAIN MERGERS OR CONSOLIDATIONS

Section

§ 149.001. Definitions

In this chapter:

(1) "Asbestos claim" means any claim, wherever or whenever made, for damages, losses, indemnification, contribution, or other relief arising out of, based on, or in any way related to asbestos, including:

(A) property damage caused by the installation, presence, or removal of asbestos;

(B) the health effects of exposure to asbestos, including any claim for:

(i) personal injury or death;

(ii) mental or emotional injury;

(iii) risk of disease or other injury; or

(iv) the costs of medical monitoring or surveillance; and

(C) any claim made by or on behalf of any person exposed to asbestos, or a representative, spouse, parent, child, or other relative of the person.

(2) "Corporation" means a corporation for profit, including:

(A) a domestic corporation organized under the laws of this state; or

(B) a foreign corporation organized under laws other than the laws of this state.

(3) "Successor asbestos-related liabilities" means any liabilities, whether known or unknown, asserted or unasserted, absolute or contingent, accrued or unaccrued, liquidated or unliquidated, or due or to become due, that are related in any way to asbestos claims that were assumed or incurred by a corporation as a result of or in connection with a merger or consolidation, or the plan of merger or consolidation related to the merger or consolidation, with or into another corporation or that are related in any way to asbestos claims based on the exercise of control or the ownership of stock of the corporation before the merger or consolidation. The term includes liabilities that, after the time of the merger or consolidation for which the fair market value of total gross assets is determined under Section 149.004, were or are paid or otherwise discharged, or committed to be paid or otherwise discharged, by or on behalf of the corporation, or by a successor of the corporation, or by or on behalf of a transferor, in connection with settlements, judgments, or other discharges in this state or another jurisdiction.

(4) "Successor" means a corporation that assumes or incurs, or has assumed or incurred, successor asbestos-related liabilities.

(5) "Transferor" means a corporation from which successor asbestos-related liabilities are or were assumed or incurred.

Added by Acts 2003, 78th Leg., ch. 204, § 17.01, eff. June 11, 2003.

For validity of this section, see Associated Machine Tool Technologies v. Doosan Infracore America, Inc., 2015 WL 13660130 (2015).

§ 149.002. Applicability

(a) The limitations in Section 149.003 shall apply to a domestic corporation or a foreign corporation that has had a certificate of authority to transact business in this state or has done business in this state and that is a successor which became a successor prior to May 13, 1968, or which is any of that successor corporation's successors, but in the latter case only to the extent of the limitation of liability applied under Section 149.003(b) and subject also to the limitations found in this chapter, including those in Subsection (b).

(b) The limitations in Section 149.003 shall not apply to:

(1) workers' compensation benefits paid by or on behalf of an employer to an employee under the Texas Workers' Compensation Act, Subtitle A, Title 5, Labor Code,[1] or a comparable workers' compensation law of another jurisdiction;

(2) any claim against a corporation that does not constitute a successor asbestos-related liability;

(3) an insurance corporation, as that term is used in the Insurance Code;

(4) any obligations under the National Labor Relations Act (29 U.S.C. Section 151 et seq.), as amended, or under any collective bargaining agreement;

(5) a successor that, after a merger or consolidation, continued in the business of mining asbestos or in the business of selling or distributing asbestos fibers or in the business of manufacturing, distributing, removing, or installing asbestos-containing products which were the same or substantially the

same as those products previously manufactured, distributed, removed, or installed by the transferor;

(6) a contractual obligation existing as of the effective date of this chapter that was entered into with claimants or potential claimants or their counsel and which resolves asbestos claims or potential asbestos claims;

(7) any claim made against the estate of a debtor in a bankruptcy proceeding commenced prior to April 1, 2003, under the United States Bankruptcy Code (11 U.S.C. Section 101 et seq.) by or against such debtor, or against a bankruptcy trust established under 11 U.S.C. Section 524(g) or similar provisions of the United States Code in such a bankruptcy proceeding commenced prior to such date; or

(8) a successor asbestos-related liability arising from a claim brought under Chapter 95, a common law claim for premises liability, or a cause of action for premises liability, as applicable, but only if the successor owned or controlled the premise or premises at issue after the merger or consolidation.

Added by Acts 2003, 78th Leg., ch. 204, § 17.01, eff. June 11, 2003.

[1] V.T.C.A., Labor Code § 401.001 et seq.

For validity of this section, see Associated Machine Tool Technologies v. Doosan Infracore America, Inc., 2015 WL 13660130 (2015).

§ 149.003. Limitations on Successor Asbestos-Related Liabilities

(a) Except as further limited in Subsection (b), the cumulative successor asbestos-related liabilities of a corporation are limited to the fair market value of the total gross assets of the transferor determined as of the time of the merger or consolidation. The corporation does not have any responsibility for successor asbestos-related liabilities in excess of this limitation.

(b) If the transferor had assumed or incurred successor asbestos-related liabilities in connection with a prior merger or consolidation with a prior transferor, then the fair market value of the total assets of the prior transferor, determined as of the time of such earlier merger or consolidation, shall be substituted for the limitation set forth in Subsection (a) for purposes of determining the limitation of liability of a corporation.

Added by Acts 2003, 78th Leg., ch. 204, § 17.01, eff. June 11, 2003.

For validity of this section, see Associated Machine Tool Technologies v. Doosan Infracore America, Inc., 2015 WL 13660130 (2015).

§ 149.004. Establishing Fair Market Value of Total Gross Assets

(a) A corporation may establish the fair market value of total gross assets for the purpose of the limitations under Section 149.003 through any method reasonable under the circumstances, including:

(1) by reference to the going concern value of the assets or to the purchase price attributable to or paid for the assets in an arm's-length transaction; or

(2) in the absence of other readily available information from which fair market value can be determined, by reference to the value of the assets recorded on a balance sheet.

(b) Total gross assets include intangible assets.

(c) Total gross assets include the aggregate coverage under any applicable liability insurance that was issued to the transferor whose assets are being valued for purposes of this section and which insurance has been collected or is collectable to cover successor asbestos-related liabilities (except compensation for liabilities arising from workers' exposure to asbestos solely during the course of their employment by the transferor). A settlement of a dispute concerning such insurance coverage entered into by a transferor or successor with the insurers of the transferor 10 years or more before the enactment of this chapter shall be determinative of the aggregate coverage of such liability insurance to be included in the calculation of the transferor's total gross assets.

(d) The fair market value of total gross assets shall reflect no deduction for any liabilities arising from any asbestos claim.

Added by Acts 2003, 78th Leg., ch. 204, § 17.01, eff. June 11, 2003.

For validity of this section, see Associated Machine Tool Technologies v. Doosan Infracore America, Inc., 2015 WL 13660130 (2015).

§ 149.005. Adjustment

(a) Except as provided in Subsections (b), (c), and (d), the fair market value of total gross assets at the time of a merger or consolidation increases annually at a rate equal to the sum of:

(1) the prime rate as listed in the first edition of the Wall Street Journal published for each calendar year since the merger or consolidation; and

(2) one percent.

(b) The rate in Subsection (a) is not compounded.

(c) The adjustment of fair market value of total gross assets continues as provided under Subsection (a) until the date the adjusted value is exceeded by the cumulative amounts of successor asbestos-related liabilities paid or committed to be paid by or on behalf of the corporation or a predecessor, or by or on behalf of a transferor, after the time of the merger or consolidation for which the fair market value of total gross assets is determined.

(d) No adjustment of the fair market value of total gross assets shall be applied to any liability insurance otherwise included in the definition of total gross assets by Section 149.004(c).

Added by Acts 2003, 78th Leg., ch. 204, § 17.01, eff. June 11, 2003.

For validity of this section, see Associated Machine Tool Technologies v. Doosan Infracore America, Inc., 2015 WL 13660130 (2015).

§ 149.006. Scope of Chapter

The courts in this state shall apply, to the fullest extent permissible under the United States Constitution, this state's substantive law, including the limitation under this chapter, to the issue of successor asbestos-related liabilities.

Added by Acts 2003, 78th Leg., ch. 204, § 17.01, eff. June 11, 2003.

For validity of this section, see Associated Machine Tool Technologies v. Doosan Infracore America, Inc., 2015 WL 13660130 (2015).

CHAPTER 150. LICENSED OR REGISTERED PROFESSIONALS

Section

§ 150.001. Definitions

In this chapter:

(1) "Certified municipal inspector" means an individual who is employed full-time by a political subdivision and is currently:

(A) certified by a national model code group; or

(B) licensed as a plumbing inspector, as defined by Section 1301.002, Occupations Code.

(1-a) "Claimant" means a party, including a plaintiff or third-party plaintiff, seeking recovery for damages, contribution, or indemnification.

(1-b) "Complaint" means any petition or other pleading which, for the first time, raises a claim against a licensed or registered professional for damages arising out of the provision of professional services by the licensed or registered professional.

(1-c) "Licensed or registered professional" means a licensed architect, licensed professional engineer, registered professional land surveyor, registered landscape architect, or any firm in which such licensed or registered professional practices, including but not limited to a corporation, professional corporation, limited liability corporation, partnership, limited liability partnership, sole proprietorship, joint venture, or any other business entity.

(1-d) "National model code group" means an organization consisting of industry and government fire and building safety officials that develops and promulgates a national model code, as defined by Section 214.217, Local Government Code.

(2) "Practice of architecture" has the meaning assigned by Section 1051.001, Occupations Code.

(3) "Practice of engineering" has the meaning assigned by Section 1001.003, Occupations Code.

Added by Acts 2003, 78th Leg., ch. 204, § 20.01, eff. Sept. 1, 2003. Amended by Acts 2005, 79th Leg., ch. 189, § 1, eff. May 27, 2005; Acts 2005, 79th Leg., ch. 208, § 2, eff. Sept. 1, 2005; Acts 2009, 81st Leg., ch. 789, § 2, eff. Sept. 1, 2009; Acts 2013, 83rd Leg., ch. 244 (H.B. 403), § 1, eff. June 14, 2013; Acts 2019, 86th Leg., ch. 661 (S.B. 1928), § 1, eff. June 10, 2019.

Section 3 of Acts 2019, 86th Leg., ch. 661 (S.B. 1928) provides:

"The change in law made by this Act applies only to an action or arbitration proceeding commenced on or after the effective date [June 10, 2019] of this Act. An action or arbitration proceeding commenced before the effective date of this Act is governed by the law in effect immediately before the effective date of this Act, and that law is continued in effect for that purpose."

§ 150.002. Certificate of Merit

(a) In any action or arbitration proceeding for damages arising out of the provision of professional services by a licensed or registered professional, a claimant shall be required to file with the complaint an affidavit of a third-party licensed architect, licensed professional engineer, registered landscape architect, or registered professional land surveyor who:

(1) is competent to testify;

(2) holds the same professional license or registration as the defendant; and

(3) practices in the area of practice of the defendant and offers testimony based on the person's:

(A) knowledge;

(B) skill;

(C) experience;

(D) education;

(E) training; and

(F) practice.

(b) The affidavit shall set forth specifically for each theory of recovery for which damages are sought, the negligence, if any, or other action, error, or omission of the licensed or registered professional in providing the professional service, including any error or omission in providing advice, judgment, opinion, or a similar professional skill claimed to exist and the factual basis for each such claim. The third-party licensed architect, licensed professional engineer, registered landscape architect, or registered professional land surveyor shall be licensed or registered in this state and actively engaged in the practice of architecture, engineering, or surveying.

(c) The contemporaneous filing requirement of Subsection (a) shall not apply to any case in which the period of limitation will expire within 10 days of the date of filing and, because of such time constraints, a claimant has alleged that an affidavit of a third-party licensed architect, licensed professional engineer, registered landscape architect, or registered professional land surveyor could not be prepared. In such cases, the claimant shall have 30 days after the filing of the complaint to supplement the pleadings with the affidavit. The trial court may, on motion, after hearing and for good cause, extend such time as it shall determine justice requires.

(d) The defendant shall not be required to file an answer to the complaint and affidavit until 30 days after the filing of such affidavit.

(e) A claimant's failure to file the affidavit in accordance with this section shall result in dismissal of the complaint against the defendant. This dismissal may be with prejudice.

(f) An order granting or denying a motion for dismissal is immediately appealable as an interlocutory order.

(g) This statute shall not be construed to extend any applicable period of limitation or repose.

(h) This statute does not apply to any suit or action for the payment of fees arising out of the provision of professional services.

Added by Acts 2003, 78th Leg., ch. 204, § 20.01, eff. Sept. 1, 2003. Amended by Acts 2005, 79th Leg., ch. 189, § 2, eff. May 27, 2005; Acts 2005, 79th Leg., ch. 208, § 2, eff. Sept. 1, 2005; Acts 2009, 81st Leg., ch. 789, § 2, eff. Sept. 1, 2009; Acts 2019, 86th Leg., ch. 661 (S.B. 1928), § 2, eff. June 10, 2019.

Section 3 of Acts 2019, 86th Leg., ch. 661 (S.B. 1928) provides:

"The change in law made by this Act applies only to an action or arbitration proceeding commenced on or after the effective date [June 10, 2019] of this Act. An action or arbitration proceeding commenced before the effective date of this Act is governed by the law in effect immediately before the effective date of this Act, and that law is continued in effect for that purpose."

§ 150.003. Liability for Services Rendered During Disaster

(a) This section applies only to a licensed or registered professional who provides architectural or engineering services if the services:

(1) are authorized, as appropriate for the professional, in:

(A) Chapter 1001, Occupations Code;

(B) Chapter 1051, Occupations Code;

(C) 22 T.A.C. Part 6 (Texas Board of Professional Engineers and Land Surveyors), Chapter 137 (Compliance and Professionalism); and

(D) 22 T.A.C. Part 1 (Texas Board of Architectural Examiners), Chapter 1 (Architects), Subchapter H (Professional Conduct);

(2) subject to Subsection (d), are provided voluntarily and without compensation or the expectation of compensation;

(3) are in response to and provided during the duration of a proclaimed state of emergency under Section 433.001, Government Code, or a declared state of disaster under Section 418.014, Government Code;

(4) are provided at the request or with the approval of a federal, state, or local public official acting in an official capacity in response to the proclaimed state of emergency or declared disaster, including a law enforcement official, public safety official, or building inspection official; and

(5) are related to a structure, building, roadway, piping, or other system, either publicly or privately owned.

(b) A licensed or registered professional who provides the services to which this section applies is not liable for civil damages, including personal injury, wrongful death, property damage, or other loss related to the professional's act, error, or omission in the performance of the services, unless the act, error, or omission constitutes:

(1) gross negligence; or

(2) wanton, wilful, or intentional misconduct.

(c) This section does not apply to a licensed or registered professional who is at the scene of the emergency to solicit business or perform a service for compensation on behalf of the professional or a person for whom the professional is an agent.

(d) The entitlement of a licensed or registered professional to receive compensation for services to which this section applies does not determine whether the services provided by the professional were provided voluntarily and without compensation or the expectation of compensation.

Added by Acts 2007, 80th Leg., ch. 132, § 1, eff. May 18, 2007. Amended by Acts 2019, 86th Leg., ch. 1232 (H.B. 1523), § 2.01, eff. Sept. 1, 2019.

§ 150.004. Liability for Services Rendered by Certified Municipal Inspector During Emergency or Disaster

(a) This section applies only to a certified municipal inspector who provides inspection services if the services:

(1) are authorized by the scope of the inspector's:

(A) national model code group certification; or

(B) plumbing inspector's license under Chapter 1301, Occupations Code;

(2) are provided voluntarily and without compensation or the expectation of compensation from any source;

(3) are in response to and provided during the duration of a proclaimed state of emergency under Section 433.001, Government Code, or a declared state of disaster under Section 418.014, Government Code;

(4) are provided at the request or with the approval of a federal, state, or local public official acting in an official capacity in response to the proclaimed state of emergency or declared disaster, including a law enforcement official, public safety official, or building inspection official; and

(5) are related to a structure, building, premises, piping, or other system, either publicly or privately owned.

(b) A certified municipal inspector who provides the services to which this section applies is not liable for civil damages, including personal injury, wrongful death, property damage, or other loss related to the inspector's act, error, or omission in the performance of the services, unless the act, error, or omission constitutes:

(1) gross negligence; or

(2) wanton, wilful, or intentional misconduct.

Added by Acts 2013, 83rd Leg., ch. 244 (H.B. 403), § 2, eff. June 14, 2013.

CHAPTER 150A. DISCOVERY BY GOVERNMENTAL UNIT

§ 150A.001. Definitions

In this chapter:

(1) "Governmental unit" has the meaning assigned by Section 101.001.

(2) "Religious organization" means an organization that qualifies as a religious organization under Section 11.20, Tax Code.

(3) "Religious worship" has the meaning assigned by Section 11.20, Tax Code.

Added by Acts 2017, 85th Leg., ch. 39 (S.B. 24), § 1, eff. May 19, 2017.

§ 150A.002. Sermons Privileged from Disclosure to Governmental Unit

A governmental unit may not, in any civil action or other civil or administrative proceeding to which the governmental unit is a party, compel the production or disclosure of a written copy or audio or video recording of a sermon delivered by a religious leader during religious worship of a religious organization or compel the religious leader to testify regarding the sermon.

Added by Acts 2017, 85th Leg., ch. 39 (S.B. 24), § 1, eff. May 19, 2017.

CHAPTER 150C. ENTITY NAME FALSELY IMPLYING GOVERNMENTAL AFFILIATION

§ 150C.001. Definition

In this chapter, "governmental unit" has the meaning assigned by Section 101.001

Added by Acts 2021, 87th Leg., ch. 658 (H.B. 1493), § 1, eff. Sept. 1, 2021.

§ 150C.002. Falsely Implying Governmental Affiliation

(a) A governmental unit is entitled to enjoin another person's use of an entity name that falsely implies governmental affiliation with the governmental unit.

(b) In an action brought under this section, the governmental unit is entitled to injunctive relief throughout the state.

(c) If the court finds that the person against whom the injunctive relief is sought wilfully intended to imply governmental affiliation with the governmental unit, the court, in the court's discretion, may award reasonable attorney's fees and court costs to the governmental unit.

Added by Acts 2021, 87th Leg., ch. 658 (H.B. 1493), § 1, eff. Sept. 1, 2021.

TITLE 7. ALTERNATE METHODS OF DISPUTE RESOLUTION

Acts 1989, 71st Leg., ch. 2, § 16.01(5) amended the title heading to conform to the heading as added by Acts 1987, 70th Leg., ch. 167, § 3.16. Title 7 heading as added by Acts 1987, 70th Leg., ch. 1121, § 1 had read "Alternative Methods of Dispute Resolution".

CHAPTER 151. TRIAL BY SPECIAL JUDGE

§ 151.001. Referral by Agreement

On agreement of the parties, in civil or family law matters pending in a district court, statutory probate court, or statutory county court, the judge in whose court the case is pending may order referral of the case as provided by this chapter and shall stay proceedings in the judge's court pending the outcome of the trial. Any or all of the issues in the cases, whether an issue of fact or law, may be referred.

Added by Acts 1987, 70th Leg., ch. 167, § 3.16(a), eff. Sept. 1, 1987. Amended by Acts 1989, 71st Leg., ch. 2, § 4.06(a), eff. Aug. 28, 1989; Acts 2005, 79th Leg., ch. 49, § 1, eff. Sept. 1, 2005.

§ 151.002. Motion for Referral

Each party to the action must file in the court in which the case is filed a motion that:

(1) requests the referral;

(2) waives the party's right to trial by jury;

(3) states the issues to be referred;

(4) states the time and place agreed on by the parties for the trial; and

(5) states the name of the special judge, the fact that the special judge has agreed to hear the case, and the fee the judge is to receive as agreed on by the parties.

Added by Acts 1987, 70th Leg., ch. 167, § 3.16(a), eff. Sept. 1, 1987.

§ 151.003. Qualifications of Judge

The special judge must be a retired or former district court, statutory county court, statutory probate court, or appellate court judge who:

(1) has served as a judge for at least four years in a district court, statutory county court, statutory probate court, or appellate court;

(2) has developed substantial experience in the judge's area of specialty;

(3) has not been removed from office or resigned while under investigation for discipline or removal; and

(4) annually demonstrates completion in the past calendar year of at least five days of continuing legal education in courses approved by the state bar or the supreme court.

Added by Acts 1987, 70th Leg., ch. 167, § 3.16(a), eff. Sept. 1, 1987. Amended by Acts 1989, 71st Leg., ch. 2, § 4.06(a), eff. Aug. 28, 1989; Acts 1989, 71st Leg., ch. 179, § 2(a), eff. Sept. 1, 1989; Acts 1991, 72nd Leg., ch. 33, § 1, eff. April 19, 1991; Acts 2015, 84th Leg., ch. 1049 (H.B. 1923), § 1, eff. Sept. 1, 2015.

§ 151.004. Referral Order Entered

An order of referral must specify the issue referred and the name of the special judge. An order of referral may designate the time and place for trial and the time for filing of the special judge's report. The clerk of the court shall send a copy of the order to the special judge.

Added by Acts 1987, 70th Leg., ch. 167, § 3.16(a), eff. Sept. 1, 1987. Amended by Acts 1989, 71st Leg., ch. 2, § 4.06(a), eff. Aug. 28, 1989.

§ 151.005. Procedure

Rules and statutes relating to procedure and evidence in the referring judge's court apply to a trial under this chapter.

Added by Acts 1987, 70th Leg., ch. 167, § 3.16(a), eff. Sept. 1, 1987. Amended by Acts 2005, 79th Leg., ch. 49, § 2, eff. Sept. 1, 2005.

§ 151.006. Powers of Special Judge

(a) A special judge shall conduct the trial in the same manner as a court trying an issue without a jury.

(b) While serving as a special judge, the special judge has the powers of the referring judge except that the special judge may not hold a person in contempt of court unless the person is a witness before the special judge.

Added by Acts 1987, 70th Leg., ch. 167, § 3.16(a), eff. Sept. 1, 1987. Amended by Acts 1989, 71st Leg., ch. 2, § 4.06(a), eff. Aug. 28, 1989; Acts 2005, 79th Leg., ch. 49, § 3, eff. Sept. 1, 2005.

§ 151.007. Representation by Attorney

A party has the right to be represented by an attorney at the trial held as provided by this chapter.

Added by Acts 1987, 70th Leg., ch. 167, § 3.16(a), eff. Sept. 1, 1987.

§ 151.008. Court Reporter Required

To maintain a record of the proceedings at the hearing, the special judge shall provide a court reporter who meets the qualifications prescribed by law for court reporters in the referring judge's court.

Added by Acts 1987, 70th Leg., ch. 167, § 3.16(a), eff. Sept. 1, 1987. Amended by Acts 1989, 71st Leg., ch. 2, § 4.06(a), eff. Aug. 28, 1989; Acts 2005, 79th Leg., ch. 49, § 4, eff. Sept. 1, 2005.

§ 151.009. Fees and Costs

(a) The parties, in equal shares, shall pay:

(1) the special judge's fee; and

(2) all administrative costs, including the court reporter's fee, related to the trial.

(b) A cost for a witness called by a party or any other cost related only to a single party's case shall be paid by the party who incurred the cost.

(c) The state or a unit of local government may not pay any costs related to a trial under this chapter.

Added by Acts 1987, 70th Leg., ch. 167, § 3.16(a), eff. Sept. 1, 1987.

§ 151.010. Restrictions

Unless otherwise ordered by the referring judge, a trial under this chapter may not be held in a public courtroom, and a public employee may not be involved in the trial during regular working hours.

Added by Acts 1987, 70th Leg., ch. 167, § 3.16(a), eff. Sept. 1, 1987. Amended by Acts 2009, 81st Leg., ch. 675, § 1, eff. Sept. 1, 2009.

§ 151.011. Special Judge's Verdict

The special judge's verdict must comply with the requirements for a verdict by the court. The verdict stands as a verdict of the referring judge's court. Unless otherwise specified in an order of referral, the special judge shall submit the verdict not later than the 60th day after the day the trial adjourns.

Added by Acts 1987, 70th Leg., ch. 167, § 3.16(a), eff. Sept. 1, 1987. Amended by Acts 2005, 79th Leg., ch. 49, § 5, eff. Sept. 1, 2005.

§ 151.012. New Trial

If the special judge does not submit the verdict within the time period provided by Section 151.011, the court may grant a new trial if:

(1) a party files a motion requesting the new trial;

(2) notice is given to all parties stating the time and place that a hearing will be held on the motion; and

(3) the hearing is held.

Added by Acts 1987, 70th Leg., ch. 167, § 3.16(a), eff. Sept. 1, 1987.

§ 151.013. Right to Appeal

The right to appeal is preserved. An appeal is from the order of the referring judge's court as provided by the Texas Rules of Civil Procedure and the Texas Rules of Appellate Procedure.

Added by Acts 1987, 70th Leg., ch. 167, § 3.16(a), eff. Sept. 1, 1987. Amended by Acts 2005, 79th Leg., ch. 49, § 6, eff. Sept. 1, 2005.

CHAPTER 152. ALTERNATIVE DISPUTE RESOLUTION SYSTEM ESTABLISHED BY COUNTIES

Section

§ 152.001. Definition

In this chapter, "alternative dispute resolution system" means an informal forum in which mediation, conciliation, or arbitration is used to resolve disputes among individuals, entities, and units of government, including those having an ongoing relationship such as relatives, neighbors, landlords and tenants, employees and employers, and merchants and consumers.

Added by Acts 1987, 70th Leg., ch. 167, § 3.16(a), eff. Sept. 1, 1987. Amended by Acts 2011, 82nd Leg., ch. 1090 (S.B. 1271), § 1, eff. June 17, 2011.

§ 152.002. Establishment

(a) The commissioners court of a county by order may establish an alternative dispute resolution system for the peaceable and expeditious resolution of disputes.

(b) The commissioners court may do all necessary acts to make the alternative dispute resolution system effective, including:

(1) contracting with a private nonprofit corporation, a political subdivision, a public corporation, or a combination of these entities for the purpose of administering the system;

(2) making reasonable rules relating to the system, including rules specifying whether criminal cases may be referred to the system; and

(3) vesting management of the system in a committee selected by the county bar association.

(c) The actions of a committee authorized by Subsection (b)(3) are subject to the approval of the commissioners court.

Added by Acts 1987, 70th Leg., ch. 167, § 3.16(a), eff. Sept. 1, 1987. Amended by Acts 2011, 82nd Leg., ch. 1090 (S.B. 1271), § 2, eff. June 17, 2011; Acts 2013, 83rd Leg., ch. 781 (S.B. 1237), § 1, eff. Sept. 1, 2013.

§ 152.003. Referral of Cases

(a) A judge of a district court, county court, statutory county court, probate court, or justice of the peace court in a county in which an alternative dispute resolution system has been established may, on motion of a party or on the judge's or justice's own motion, refer a civil or, if the system accepts criminal cases and on the request of an attorney representing the state, a criminal case to the system regardless of whether the defendant in the criminal case has been formally charged. Referral under this section does not prejudice the case.

(b) Before requesting a referral of a criminal case under this section, an attorney representing the state must obtain the consent of the victim and the defendant to the referral.

(c) A criminal case may not be referred to the system if the defendant is charged with or convicted of an offense listed in Article 42A.054(a), Code of Criminal Procedure, or convicted of an offense, the judgment for which contains an affirmative finding under Article 42A.054(c) or (d), Code of Criminal Procedure.

Added by Acts 1987, 70th Leg., ch. 167, § 3.16(a), eff. Sept. 1, 1987. Amended by Acts 1999, 76th Leg., ch. 509, § 1, eff. Sept. 1, 1999; Acts 2013, 83rd Leg., ch. 781 (S.B. 1237), § 2, eff. Sept. 1, 2013; Acts 2015, 84th Leg., ch. 770 (H.B. 2299), § 2.03, eff. Jan. 1, 2017.

§ 152.004. Financing

(a) To establish and maintain an alternative dispute resolution system, the commissioners court may set a court cost in an amount not to exceed $15 to be taxed, collected, and paid as other court costs in each civil case filed in a county or district court in the county, including a civil case relating to probate matters but not including:

(1) a suit for delinquent taxes;

(2) a condemnation proceeding under Chapter 21, Property Code; or

(3) a proceeding under Subtitle C, Title 7, Health and Safety Code. [1]

(b) The county is not liable for the payment of a court cost under this section.

(c) The clerks of the courts in the county shall collect and pay the costs to the county treasurer or, if the county does not have a treasurer, to the county officer who performs the functions of the treasurer, who shall deposit the costs in a separate fund known as the alternative dispute resolution system fund. The fund shall be administered by the commissioners court and may only be used to establish and maintain the system. The system shall be operated at one or more convenient and accessible places in the county.

Added by Acts 1987, 70th Leg., ch. 167, § 3.16(a), eff. Sept. 1, 1987. Amended by Acts 1989, 71st Leg., ch. 2, § 4.07(a), eff. Aug. 28, 1989; Acts 1999, 76th Leg., ch. 509, § 2, eff. Sept. 1, 1999; Acts 2005, 79th Leg., ch. 1192, § 1, eff. Sept. 1, 2005.

[1] V.T.C.A., Health & Safety Code § 571.001 et seq.

Repeal

Acts 2021, 87th Leg., ch. 472 (S.B. 41), § 5.01(a)(3) repeals this section effective Jan. 1, 2022.

§ 152.005. Additional Fee for Justice Courts

(a) To establish and maintain an alternative dispute resolution system, the commissioners court may, in addition to the court cost authorized under Section 152.004, set a court cost in an amount not to exceed $5 for civil cases filed in a justice court located in the county, but not including:

(1) a suit for delinquent taxes; or

(2) an eviction proceeding, including a forcible detainer, a forcible entry and detainer, or a writ of re-entry.

(b) A clerk of the court shall collect and pay the court cost in the manner prescribed by Section 152.004(c).

Added by Acts 1999, 76th Leg., ch. 509, § 3, eff. Sept. 1, 1999. Amended by Acts 2005, 79th Leg., ch. 1192, § 2, eff. Sept. 1, 2005.

Repeal

Acts 2021, 87th Leg., ch. 472 (S.B. 41), § 5.01(a)(3) repeals this section effective Jan. 1, 2022.

§ 152.006. Fee for Alternative Dispute Resolution Centers

An entity described by Section 152.002(a) or (b)(1) that provides services for the resolution of disputes may collect a reasonable fee set by the commissioners court.

Added by Acts 2005, 79th Leg., ch. 1192, § 3, eff. Sept. 1, 2005. Amended by Acts 2011, 82nd Leg., ch. 1163 (H.B. 2702), § 4, eff. Sept. 1, 2011; Acts 2013, 83rd Leg., ch. 781 (S.B. 1237), § 3, eff. Sept. 1, 2013.

§ 152.007. Participant Fee for Criminal Dispute Resolution

(a) An entity that provides services for the resolution of criminal disputes under this chapter may collect a reasonable fee set by the commissioners court from a person who receives the services, not to exceed $350, except that a fee may not be collected from an alleged victim of the crime.

(b) Fees collected under this section may be paid on a periodic basis or on a deferred payment schedule at the discretion of the judge, magistrate, or program director administering the pretrial victim-offender mediation program. The fees must be based on the defendant's ability to pay.

Added by Acts 2013, 83rd Leg., ch. 781 (S.B. 1237), § 4, eff. Sept. 1, 2013.

CHAPTER 154. ALTERNATIVE DISPUTE RESOLUTION PROCEDURES

SUBCHAPTER A. GENERAL PROVISIONS

Section

SUBCHAPTER B. ALTERNATIVE DISPUTE RESOLUTION PROCEDURES

Section

SUBCHAPTER C. IMPARTIAL THIRD PARTIES

SUBCHAPTER D. MISCELLANEOUS PROVISIONS

SUBCHAPTER A. GENERAL PROVISIONS

§ 154.001. Definitions

In this chapter:

(1) "Court" includes an appellate court, district court, constitutional county court, statutory county court, family law court, probate court, municipal court, or justice of the peace court.

(2) "Dispute resolution organization" means a private profit or nonprofit corporation, political subdivision, or public corporation, or a combination of these, that offers alternative dispute resolution services to the public.

Added by Acts 1987, 70th Leg., ch. 1121, § 1, eff. June 20, 1987.

§ 154.002. Policy

It is the policy of this state to encourage the peaceable resolution of disputes, with special consideration given to disputes involving the parent-child relationship, including the mediation of issues involving conservatorship, possession, and support of children, and the early settlement of pending litigation through voluntary settlement procedures.

Added by Acts 1987, 70th Leg., ch. 1121, § 1, eff. June 20, 1987.

§ 154.003. Responsibility of Courts and Court Administrators

It is the responsibility of all trial and appellate courts and their court administrators to carry out the policy under Section 154.002.

Added by Acts 1987, 70th Leg., ch. 1121, § 1, eff. June 20, 1987.

SUBCHAPTER B. ALTERNATIVE DISPUTE RESOLUTION PROCEDURES

§ 154.021. Referral of Pending Disputes for Alternative Dispute Resolution Procedure

(a) A court may, on its own motion or the motion of a party, refer a pending dispute for resolution by an alternative dispute resolution procedure including:

(1) an alternative dispute resolution system established under Chapter 26, Acts of the 68th Legislature, Regular Session, 1983 (Article 2372aa, Vernon's Texas Civil Statutes[1]);

(2) a dispute resolution organization; or

(3) a nonjudicial and informally conducted forum for the voluntary settlement of citizens' disputes through the intervention of an impartial third party, including those alternative dispute resolution procedures described under this subchapter.

(b) The court shall confer with the parties in the determination of the most appropriate alternative dispute resolution procedure.

(c) Except as provided by agreement of the parties, a court may not order mediation in an action that is subject to the Federal Arbitration Act (9 U.S.C. Sections 1–16).

Added by Acts 1987, 70th Leg., ch. 1121, § 1, eff. June 20, 1987. Amended by Acts 2009, 81st Leg., ch. 621, § 1, eff. June 19, 2009.

[1] Repealed; see now, V.T.C.A., Civil Practice and Remedies Code § 152.001 et seq.

§ 154.022. Notification and Objection

(a) If a court determines that a pending dispute is appropriate for referral under Section 154.021, the court shall notify the parties of its determination.

(b) Any party may, within 10 days after receiving the notice under Subsection (a), file a written objection to the referral.

(c) If the court finds that there is a reasonable basis for an objection filed under Subsection (b), the court may not refer the dispute under Section 154.021.

Added by Acts 1987, 70th Leg., ch. 1121, § 1, eff. June 20, 1987.

§ 154.023. Mediation

(a) Mediation is a forum in which an impartial person, the mediator, facilitates communication between parties to promote reconciliation, settlement, or understanding among them.

(b) A mediator may not impose his own judgment on the issues for that of the parties.

(c) Mediation includes victim-offender mediation by the Texas Department of Criminal Justice described in Article 56A.602, Code of Criminal Procedure.

Added by Acts 1987, 70th Leg., ch. 1121, § 1, eff. June 20, 1987. Amended by Acts 2001, 77th Leg., ch. 1034, § 12, eff. Sept. 1, 2001; Acts 2019, 86th Leg., ch. 469 (H.B. 4173), § 2.03, eff. Jan. 1, 2021.

Sections 4.01 and 4.02 of Acts 2019, 86th Leg., ch. 469 (H.B. 4173) provide:

"Sec. 4.01. This Act is enacted under Section 43, Article III, Texas Constitution. This Act is intended as a codification only, and no substantive change in the law is intended by this Act.

"Sec. 4.02. (a) Chapter 311, Government Code (Code Construction Act), applies to the construction of each provision in the Code of Criminal Procedure that is enacted under Section 43, Article III, Texas Constitution (authorizing the continuing statutory revision program), in the same manner as to a code enacted under the continuing statutory revision program, except as otherwise expressly provided by the Code of Criminal Procedure.

"(b) A reference in a law to a statute or a part of a statute in the Code of Criminal Procedure enacted under Section 43, Article III, Texas Constitution (authorizing the continuing statutory revision program), is considered to be a reference to the part of that code that revises that statute or part of that statute."

§ 154.024. Mini-Trial

(a) A mini-trial is conducted under an agreement of the parties.

(b) Each party and counsel for the party present the position of the party, either before selected representatives for each party or before an impartial third party, to define the issues and develop a basis for realistic settlement negotiations.

(c) The impartial third party may issue an advisory opinion regarding the merits of the case.

(d) The advisory opinion is not binding on the parties unless the parties agree that it is binding and enter into a written settlement agreement.

Added by Acts 1987, 70th Leg., ch. 1121, § 1, eff. June 20, 1987.

§ 154.025. Moderated Settlement Conference

(a) A moderated settlement conference is a forum for case evaluation and realistic settlement negotiations.

(b) Each party and counsel for the party present the position of the party before a panel of impartial third parties.

(c) The panel may issue an advisory opinion regarding the liability or damages of the parties or both.

(d) The advisory opinion is not binding on the parties.

Added by Acts 1987, 70th Leg., ch. 1121, § 1, eff. June 20, 1987.

§ 154.026. Summary Jury Trial

(a) A summary jury trial is a forum for early case evaluation and development of realistic settlement negotiations.

(b) Each party and counsel for the party present the position of the party before a panel of jurors.

(c) The number of jurors on the panel is six unless the parties agree otherwise.

(d) The panel may issue an advisory opinion regarding the liability or damages of the parties or both.

(e) The advisory opinion is not binding on the parties.

Added by Acts 1987, 70th Leg., ch. 1121, § 1, eff. June 20, 1987.

§ 154.027. Arbitration

(a) Nonbinding arbitration is a forum in which each party and counsel for the party present the position of the party before an impartial third party, who renders a specific award.

(b) If the parties stipulate in advance, the award is binding and is enforceable in the same manner as any contract obligation. If the parties do not stipulate in advance that the award is binding, the award is not binding and serves only as a basis for the parties' further settlement negotiations.

Added by Acts 1987, 70th Leg., ch. 1121, § 1, eff. June 20, 1987.

§ 154.028. Mediation Following Application for Expedited Foreclosure

(a) A citation for expedited foreclosure may be served in the manner provided by Rule 106 or 736, Texas Rules of Civil Procedure. Following the filing of a response to an application for an expedited foreclosure proceeding under Rule 736.5, Texas Rules of Civil Procedure, a court may, in the court's discretion, conduct a hearing to determine whether to order mediation. A court may not order mediation without conducting a hearing. The petitioner or respondent may request a hearing to determine whether mediation is necessary or whether an application is defective.

(b) A hearing under Subsection (a) may not be conducted before the expiration of the respondent's deadline to file a response.

(c) Subject to Subsection (d), a hearing under Subsection (a) may be conducted by telephone.

(d) Not later than the 10th day before the date of a hearing under Subsection (a), the court shall send notice of the hearing to the parties concerning whether the hearing will be conducted by telephone and, if applicable, instructions for contacting the court and attending the hearing by telephone.

(e) At a hearing under Subsection (a), the court must consider any objections to the referral of the case to mediation.

(f) If the court orders the case to mediation, the mediation must be conducted before the expiration of any deadline imposed by Rule 736, Texas Rules of Civil Procedure.

(g) If the parties to a case that has been ordered to mediation are unable to agree on the appointment of a mediator, the court may appoint a mediator. If a mediator is appointed by the court, the court shall provide all parties with the name of the chosen mediator at the mediation hearing if the parties are unable to agree to a mediator at that hearing.

(h) A mediator's fee shall be divided equally between the parties.

(i) The parties may agree to waive the mediation process.

(j) The court may not conduct a hearing under this section if the applicant has served the citation in compliance with Rule 106, Texas Rules of Civil Procedure, and a response to the application has not been filed before the deadline provided by Rule 736, Texas Rules of Civil Procedure.

(k) If a respondent fails to attend a mediation hearing after notice in accordance with Subsection (d), the court:

(1) may not order mediation; and

(2) shall grant or deny the petitioner's motion for default order under Rule 736.7, Texas Rules of Civil Procedure.

(*l*) If a respondent attends a hearing and mediation is ordered, any mediation must take place not later than the 29th day after the date the petitioner filed a motion for default order.

(m) Notwithstanding Section 22.004, Government Code, the supreme court may not amend or adopt rules in conflict with this section.

Added by Acts 2013, 83rd Leg., ch. 1044 (H.B. 2978), § 2, eff. June 14, 2013.

SUBCHAPTER C. IMPARTIAL THIRD PARTIES

§ 154.051. Appointment of Impartial Third Parties

(a) If a court refers a pending dispute for resolution by an alternative dispute resolution procedure under Section 154.021, the court may appoint an impartial third party to facilitate the procedure.

(b) The court may appoint a third party who is agreed on by the parties if the person qualifies for appointment under this subchapter.

(c) The court may appoint more than one third party under this section.

Added by Acts 1987, 70th Leg., ch. 1121, § 1, eff. June 20, 1987.

§ 154.052. Qualifications of Impartial Third Party

(a) Except as provided by Subsections (b) and (c), to qualify for an appointment as an impartial third party under this subchapter a person must have completed a minimum of 40 classroom hours of training in dispute resolution techniques in a course conducted by an alternative dispute resolution system or other dispute resolution organization approved by the court making the appointment.

(b) To qualify for an appointment as an impartial third party under this subchapter in a dispute relating to the parent-child relationship, a person must complete the training required by Subsection (a) and an additional 24 hours of training in the fields of family dynamics, child development, and family law, including a minimum of four hours of family violence dynamics training developed in consultation with a statewide family violence advocacy organization.

(c) In appropriate circumstances, a court may in its discretion appoint a person as an impartial third party who does not qualify under Subsection (a) or (b) if the court bases its appointment on legal or other professional training or experience in particular dispute resolution processes.

Added by Acts 1987, 70th Leg., ch. 1121, § 1, eff. June 20, 1987. Amended by Acts 2017, 85th Leg., ch. 195 (S.B. 539), § 1, eff. Sept. 1, 2017.

§ 154.053. Standards and Duties of Impartial Third Parties

(a) A person appointed to facilitate an alternative dispute resolution procedure under this subchapter shall encourage and assist the parties in reaching a settlement of their dispute but may not compel or coerce the parties to enter into a settlement agreement.

(b) Unless expressly authorized by the disclosing party, the impartial third party may not disclose to either party information given in confidence by the other and shall at all times maintain confidentiality with respect to communications relating to the subject matter of the dispute.

(c) Unless the parties agree otherwise, all matters, including the conduct and demeanor of the parties and their counsel during the settlement process, are confidential and may never be disclosed to anyone, including the appointing court.

(d) Each participant, including the impartial third party, to an alternative dispute resolution procedure is subject to the requirements of Subchapter B, Chapter 261, Family Code, and Subchapter C, Chapter 48, Human Resources Code.

Added by Acts 1987, 70th Leg., ch. 1121, § 1, eff. June 20, 1987. Amended by Acts 1999, 76th Leg., ch. 1150, § 29, eff. Sept. 1, 1999.

§ 154.054. Compensation of Impartial Third Parties

(a) The court may set a reasonable fee for the services of an impartial third party appointed under this subchapter.

(b) Unless the parties agree to a method of payment, the court shall tax the fee for the services of an impartial third party as other costs of suit.

Added by Acts 1987, 70th Leg., ch. 1121, § 1, eff. June 20, 1987.

§ 154.055. Qualified Immunity of Impartial Third Parties

(a) A person appointed to facilitate an alternative dispute resolution procedure under this subchapter or under Chapter 152 relating to an alternative dispute resolution system established by counties, or appointed by the parties whether before or after the institution of formal judicial proceedings, who is a volunteer and who does not act with wanton and wilful disregard of the rights, safety, or property of another, is immune from civil liability for any act or omission within the course and scope of his or her duties or functions as an impartial third party. For purposes of this section, a volunteer impartial third party is a person who does not receive compensation in excess of reimbursement for expenses incurred or a stipend intended as reimbursement for expenses incurred.

(b) This section neither applies to nor is it intended to enlarge or diminish any rights or immunities enjoyed by an arbitrator participating in a binding arbitration pursuant to any applicable statute or treaty.

Added by Acts 1993, 73rd Leg., ch. 875, § 1, eff. Sept. 1, 1993.

SUBCHAPTER D. MISCELLANEOUS PROVISIONS

§ 154.071. Effect of Written Settlement Agreement

(a) If the parties reach a settlement and execute a written agreement disposing of the dispute, the agreement is enforceable in the same manner as any other written contract.

(b) The court in its discretion may incorporate the terms of the agreement in the court's final decree disposing of the case.

(c) A settlement agreement does not affect an outstanding court order unless the terms of the agreement are incorporated into a subsequent decree.

Added by Acts 1987, 70th Leg., ch. 1121, § 1, eff. June 20, 1987.

§ 154.072. Statistical Information on Disputes Referred

The Texas Supreme Court shall determine the need and method for statistical reporting of disputes referred by the courts to alternative dispute resolution procedures.

Added by Acts 1987, 70th Leg., ch. 1121, § 1, eff. June 20, 1987.

§ 154.073. Confidentiality of Certain Records and Communications

(a) Except as provided by Subsections (c), (d), (e), and (f), a communication relating to the subject matter of any civil or criminal dispute made by a participant in an alternative dispute resolution procedure, whether before or after the institution of formal judicial proceedings, is confidential, is not subject to disclosure, and may not be used as evidence against the participant in any judicial or administrative proceeding.

(b) Any record made at an alternative dispute resolution procedure is confidential, and the participants or the third party facilitating the procedure may not be required to testify in any proceedings relating to or arising out of the matter in dispute or be subject to process requiring disclosure of confidential information or data relating to or arising out of the matter in dispute.

(c) An oral communication or written material used in or made a part of an alternative dispute resolution procedure is admissible or discoverable if it is admissible or discoverable independent of the procedure.

(d) A final written agreement to which a governmental body, as defined by Section 552.003, Government Code, is a signatory that is reached as a result of a dispute resolution procedure conducted under this chapter is subject to or excepted from required disclosure in accordance with Chapter 552, Government Code.

(e) If this section conflicts with other legal requirements for disclosure of communications, records, or materials, the issue of confidentiality may be presented to the court having jurisdiction of the proceedings to determine, in camera, whether the facts, circumstances, and context of the communications or materials sought to be disclosed warrant a protective order of the court or whether the communications or materials are subject to disclosure.

(f) This section does not affect the duty to report abuse or neglect under Subchapter B, Chapter 261, Family Code,[1] and abuse, exploitation, or neglect under Subchapter C, Chapter 48, Human Resources Code.[2]

(g) This section applies to a victim-offender mediation by the Texas Department of Criminal Justice as described in Article 56A.602, Code of Criminal Procedure.

Added by Acts 1987, 70th Leg., ch. 1121, § 1, eff. June 20, 1987. Amended by Acts 1999, 76th Leg., ch. 1150, § 30, eff. Sept. 1, 1999; Acts 1999, 76th Leg., ch. 1352, § 6, eff. Sept. 1, 1999; Acts 2001, 77th Leg., ch. 1034, § 13, eff. Sept. 1, 2001; Acts 2001, 77th Leg., ch. 1420, §§ 21.001(6), 21.002(3), eff. Sept. 1, 2001; Acts 2019, 86th Leg., ch. 469 (H.B. 4173), § 2.04, eff. Jan. 1, 2021.

[1] V.T.C.A., Family Code § 261.101 et seq.

[2] V.T.C.A., Human Resources Code § 48.101 et seq.

Sections 4.01 and 4.02 of Acts 2019, 86th Leg., ch. 469 (H.B. 4173) provide:

"Sec. 4.01. This Act is enacted under Section 43, Article III, Texas Constitution. This Act is intended as a codification only, and no substantive change in the law is intended by this Act.

"Sec. 4.02. (a) Chapter 311, Government Code (Code Construction Act), applies to the construction of each provision in the Code of Criminal Procedure that is enacted under Section 43, Article III, Texas Constitution (authorizing the continuing statutory revision program), in the same manner as to a code enacted under the continuing statutory revision program, except as otherwise expressly provided by the Code of Criminal Procedure.

"(b) A reference in a law to a statute or a part of a statute in the Code of Criminal Procedure enacted under Section 43, Article III, Texas Constitution (authorizing the continuing statutory revision program), is considered to be a reference to the part of that code that revises that statute or part of that statute."

CHAPTER 155. SETTLEMENT WEEKS

Section

§ 155.001. Settlement Weeks Required

In every county with a population of 150,000 or greater there shall be a settlement week during law week and judicial conference week each year or during any other two weeks as the administrative judge of each judicial district may designate. During these weeks the district courts, constitutional and statutory county courts, and the family law courts will facilitate the voluntary settlement of civil and family law cases.

Added by Acts 1989, 71st Leg., ch. 1211, § 1, eff. Aug. 28, 1989. Amended by Acts 2009, 81st Leg., ch. 87, § 5.005, eff. Sept. 1, 2009.

§ 155.002. Settlement Week Committee

The administrative judge of each judicial district shall appoint a committee of attorneys and lay persons to effectuate each settlement week. The committee may include the director of any established mediation or alternative dispute resolution center in the county and the chairperson of the local bar association's committee on alternative dispute resolution.

Added by Acts 1989, 71st Leg., ch. 1211, § 1, eff. Aug. 28, 1989. Amended by Acts 2009, 81st Leg., ch. 87, § 5.006, eff. Sept. 1, 2009.

§ 155.003. Attorney to Serve as Mediator

Any attorney currently licensed in the state may serve as mediator during the settlement weeks under such terms and conditions and with such training as may be determined by the administrative judge of the judicial district. Any such attorney so appointed by the court must meet the qualifications and will be governed by the rules of conduct set forth in Sections 154.052 and 154.053. Any attorney so requested by the administrative judge of the judicial district shall serve as a mediator during the settlement weeks.

Added by Acts 1989, 71st Leg., ch. 1211, § 1, eff. Aug. 28, 1989. Amended by Acts 2009, 81st Leg., ch. 87, § 5.007, eff. Sept. 1, 2009.

§ 155.004. Application of Certain Alternate Dispute Resolution Procedures

The provisions of Sections 154.021 through 154.023, 154.053, 154.054, and 154.071 through 154.073 shall apply to parties and mediators participating in settlement weeks held under this chapter.

Added by Acts 1989, 71st Leg., ch. 1211, § 1, eff. Aug. 28, 1989. Amended by Acts 2009, 81st Leg., ch. 87, § 5.008, eff. Sept. 1, 2009.

§ 155.005. Authority of Court

Each court participating in settlement weeks under this chapter shall have the authority to make orders needed, consistent with existing law, to implement settlement weeks and ensure any party's good faith participation.

Added by Acts 1989, 71st Leg., ch. 1211, § 1, eff. Aug. 28, 1989. Amended by Acts 2009, 81st Leg., ch. 87, § 5.009, eff. Sept. 1, 2009.

§ 155.006. Funding; Cooperation with Other Organizations

The administrative judge may use any available funding from funds regularly used for court administration to carry out the purpose and intent of this chapter. The administrative judge shall cooperate with the director of any established mediation or alternative dispute resolution center, the local bar, and other organizations to encourage participation and to develop public awareness of settlement weeks.

Added by Acts 1989, 71st Leg., ch. 1211, § 1, eff. Aug. 28, 1989. Amended by Acts 2009, 81st Leg., ch. 87, § 5.010, eff. Sept. 1, 2009.

CHAPTER 171. GENERAL ARBITRATION

Acts 1997, 75th Leg., ch. 165, § 5.01, effective September 1, 1997, revised Chapter 171, which formerly consisted of §§ 171.001 to 171.023, as Chapter 171, consisting of V.T.C.A., Civil Practice & Remedies Code §§ 171.001 to 171.098.

DISPOSITION TABLE

Showing where the subject matter of provisions contained in former Chapter 171 may be found in Chapter 171 as amended by Acts 1997, 75th Leg., ch. 165, § 5.01.

Former Section	Amended Section
171.001	171.001, 171.002, 171.022
171.002	171.021, 171.023 to 171.025
171.003	171.041
171.004	171.042
171.005	171.043 to 171.046
171.006	171.048
171.007	171.049 to 171.052
171.008	171.053
171.009	171.054
171.010	171.048, 171.055
171.011	171.081
171.012	171.082 to 171.086, 171.094 to 171.097
171.013	171.087
171.014	171.088 to 171.090
171.015	171.091
171.016	171.092
171.017	171.098
171.018	—
171.019	171.003
171.020	—
171.021	—
171.022	—
171.023	—

SUBCHAPTER A. GENERAL PROVISIONS

§ 171.001. Arbitration Agreements Valid

(a) A written agreement to arbitrate is valid and enforceable if the agreement is to arbitrate a controversy that:

(1) exists at the time of the agreement; or

(2) arises between the parties after the date of the agreement.

(b) A party may revoke the agreement only on a ground that exists at law or in equity for the revocation of a contract.

Amended by Acts 1997, 75th Leg., ch. 165, § 5.01, eff. Sept. 1, 1997.

§ 171.002. Scope of Chapter

(a) This chapter does not apply to:

(1) a collective bargaining agreement between an employer and a labor union;

(2) an agreement for the acquisition by one or more individuals of property, services, money, or credit in which the total consideration to be furnished by the individual is not more than $50,000, except as provided by Subsection (b);

(3) a claim for personal injury, except as provided by Subsection (c);

(4) a claim for workers' compensation benefits; or

(5) an agreement made before January 1, 1966.

(b) An agreement described by Subsection (a)(2) is subject to this chapter if:

(1) the parties to the agreement agree in writing to arbitrate; and

(2) the agreement is signed by each party and each party's attorney.

(c) A claim described by Subsection (a)(3) is subject to this chapter if:

(1) each party to the claim, on the advice of counsel, agrees in writing to arbitrate; and

(2) the agreement is signed by each party and each party's attorney.

Amended by Acts 1997, 75th Leg., ch. 165, § 5.01, eff. Sept. 1, 1997.

§ 171.003. Uniform Interpretation

This chapter shall be construed to effect its purpose and make uniform the construction of other states' law applicable to an arbitration.

Amended by Acts 1997, 75th Leg., ch. 165, § 5.01, eff. Sept. 1, 1997.

§§ 171.004 to 171.020. Deleted by Acts 1997, 75th Leg., ch. 165, § 5.01, eff. Sept. 1, 1997

SUBCHAPTER B. PROCEEDINGS TO COMPEL OR STAY ARBITRATIONS

§ 171.021. Proceeding to Compel Arbitration

(a) A court shall order the parties to arbitrate on application of a party showing:

(1) an agreement to arbitrate; and

(2) the opposing party's refusal to arbitrate.

(b) If a party opposing an application made under Subsection (a) denies the existence of the agreement, the court shall summarily determine that issue. The court shall order the arbitration if it finds for the party that made the application. If the court does not find for that party, the court shall deny the application.

(c) An order compelling arbitration must include a stay of any proceeding subject to Section 171.025.

Added by Acts 1997, 75th Leg., ch. 165, § 5.01, eff. Sept. 1, 1997.

§ 171.022. Unconscionable Agreements Unenforceable

A court may not enforce an agreement to arbitrate if the court finds the agreement was unconscionable at the time the agreement was made.

Added by Acts 1997, 75th Leg., ch. 165, § 5.01, eff. Sept. 1, 1997.

§ 171.023. Proceeding to Stay Arbitration

(a) A court may stay an arbitration commenced or threatened on application and a showing that there is not an agreement to arbitrate.

(b) If there is a substantial bona fide dispute as to whether an agreement to arbitrate exists, the court shall try the issue promptly and summarily.

(c) The court shall stay the arbitration if the court finds for the party moving for the stay. If the court finds for the party opposing the stay, the court shall order the parties to arbitrate.

Added by Acts 1997, 75th Leg., ch. 165, § 5.01, eff. Sept. 1, 1997.

§ 171.024. Place for Making Application

(a) If there is a proceeding pending in a court involving an issue referable to arbitration under an alleged agreement to arbitrate, a party may make an application under this subchapter only in that court.

(b) If Subsection (a) does not apply, a party may make an application in any court, subject to Section 171.096.

Added by Acts 1997, 75th Leg., ch. 165, § 5.01, eff. Sept. 1, 1997.

§ 171.025. Stay of Related Proceeding

(a) The court shall stay a proceeding that involves an issue subject to arbitration if an order for arbitration or an application for that order is made under this subchapter.

(b) The stay applies only to the issue subject to arbitration if that issue is severable from the remainder of the proceeding.

Added by Acts 1997, 75th Leg., ch. 165, § 5.01, eff. Sept. 1, 1997.

§ 171.026. Validity of Underlying Claim

A court may not refuse to order arbitration because:

(1) the claim lacks merit or bona fides; or

(2) the fault or ground for the claim is not shown.

Added by Acts 1997, 75th Leg., ch. 165, § 5.01, eff. Sept. 1, 1997.

SUBCHAPTER C. ARBITRATION

§ 171.041. Appointment of Arbitrators

(a) The method of appointment of arbitrators is as specified in the agreement to arbitrate.

(b) The court, on application of a party stating the nature of the issues to be arbitrated and the qualifications of the proposed arbitrators, shall appoint one or more qualified arbitrators if:

(1) the agreement to arbitrate does not specify a method of appointment;

(2) the agreed method fails or cannot be followed; or

(3) an appointed arbitrator fails or is unable to act and a successor has not been appointed.

(c) An arbitrator appointed under Subsection (b) has the powers of an arbitrator named in the agreement to arbitrate.

Added by Acts 1997, 75th Leg., ch. 165, § 5.01, eff. Sept. 1, 1997.

§ 171.042. Majority Action by Arbitrators

The powers of the arbitrators are exercised by a majority unless otherwise provided by the agreement to arbitrate or this chapter.

Added by Acts 1997, 75th Leg., ch. 165, § 5.01, eff. Sept. 1, 1997.

§ 171.043. Hearing Conducted by Arbitrators

(a) Unless otherwise provided by the agreement to arbitrate, all the arbitrators shall conduct the hearing. A majority of the arbitrators may determine a question and render a final award.

(b) If, during the course of the hearing, an arbitrator ceases to act, one or more remaining arbitrators appointed to act as neutral arbitrators may hear and determine the controversy.

Added by Acts 1997, 75th Leg., ch. 165, § 5.01, eff. Sept. 1, 1997.

§ 171.044. Time and Place of Hearing; Notice

(a) Unless otherwise provided by the agreement to arbitrate, the arbitrators shall set a time and place for the hearing and notify each party.

(b) The notice must be served not later than the fifth day before the hearing either personally or by registered or certified mail with return receipt requested. Appearance at the hearing waives the notice.

(c) The court on application may direct the arbitrators to proceed promptly with the hearing and determination of the controversy.

Added by Acts 1997, 75th Leg., ch. 165, § 5.01, eff. Sept. 1, 1997.

§ 171.045. Adjournment or Postponement

Unless otherwise provided by the agreement to arbitrate, the arbitrators may:

(1) adjourn the hearing as necessary; and

(2) on request of a party and for good cause, or on their own motion, postpone the hearing to a time not later than:

(A) the date set by the agreement for making the award; or

(B) a later date agreed to by the parties.

Added by Acts 1997, 75th Leg., ch. 165, § 5.01, eff. Sept. 1, 1997.

§ 171.046. Failure of Party to Appear

Unless otherwise provided by the agreement to arbitrate, the arbitrators may hear and determine the controversy on the evidence produced without regard to whether a party who has been notified as provided by Section 171.044 fails to appear.

Added by Acts 1997, 75th Leg., ch. 165, § 5.01, eff. Sept. 1, 1997.

§ 171.047. Rights of Party at Hearing

Unless otherwise provided by the agreement to arbitrate, a party at the hearing is entitled to:

(1) be heard;

(2) present evidence material to the controversy; and

(3) cross-examine any witness.

Added by Acts 1997, 75th Leg., ch. 165, § 5.01, eff. Sept. 1, 1997.

§ 171.048. Representation by Attorney; Fees

(a) A party is entitled to representation by an attorney at a proceeding under this chapter.

(b) A waiver of the right described by Subsection (a) before the proceeding is ineffective.

(c) The arbitrators shall award attorney's fees as additional sums required to be paid under the award only if the fees are provided for:

(1) in the agreement to arbitrate; or

(2) by law for a recovery in a civil action in the district court on a cause of action on which any part of the award is based.

Added by Acts 1997, 75th Leg., ch. 165, § 5.01, eff. Sept. 1, 1997.

§ 171.049. Oath

The arbitrators, or an arbitrator at the direction of the arbitrators, may administer to each witness testifying before them the oath required of a witness in a civil action pending in a district court.

Added by Acts 1997, 75th Leg., ch. 165, § 5.01, eff. Sept. 1, 1997.

§ 171.050. Depositions

(a) The arbitrators may authorize a deposition:

(1) for use as evidence to be taken of a witness who cannot be required by subpoena to appear before the arbitrators or who is unable to attend the hearing; or

(2) for discovery or evidentiary purposes to be taken of an adverse witness.

(b) A deposition under this section shall be taken in the manner provided by law for a deposition in a civil action pending in a district court.

Added by Acts 1997, 75th Leg., ch. 165, § 5.01, eff. Sept. 1, 1997.

§ 171.051. Subpoenas

(a) The arbitrators, or an arbitrator at the direction of the arbitrators, may issue a subpoena for:

(1) attendance of a witness; or

(2) production of books, records, documents, or other evidence.

(b) A witness required to appear by subpoena under this section may appear at the hearing before the arbitrators or at a deposition.

(c) A subpoena issued under this section shall be served in the manner provided by law for the service of a subpoena issued in a civil action pending in a district court.

(d) Each provision of law requiring a witness to appear, produce evidence, and testify under a subpoena issued in a civil action pending in a district court applies to a subpoena issued under this section.

Added by Acts 1997, 75th Leg., ch. 165, § 5.01, eff. Sept. 1, 1997.

§ 171.052. Witness Fee

The fee for a witness attending a hearing or a deposition under this subchapter is the same as the fee for a witness in a civil action in a district court.

Added by Acts 1997, 75th Leg., ch. 165, § 5.01, eff. Sept. 1, 1997.

§ 171.053. Arbitrators' Award

(a) The arbitrators' award must be in writing and signed by each arbitrator joining in the award.

(b) The arbitrators shall deliver a copy of the award to each party personally, by registered or certified mail, or as provided in the agreement.

(c) The arbitrators shall make the award:

(1) within the time established by the agreement to arbitrate; or

(2) if a time is not established by the agreement, within the time ordered by the court on application of a party.

(d) The parties may extend the time for making the award either before or after the time expires. The extension must be in writing.

(e) A party waives the objection that an award was not made within the time required unless the party notifies the arbitrators of the objection before the delivery of the award to that party.

Added by Acts 1997, 75th Leg., ch. 165, § 5.01, eff. Sept. 1, 1997.

§ 171.054. Modification or Correction to Award

(a) The arbitrators may modify or correct an award:

(1) on the grounds stated in Section 171.091; or

(2) to clarify the award.

(b) A modification or correction under Subsection (a) may be made only:

(1) on application of a party; or

(2) on submission to the arbitrators by a court, if an application to the court is pending under Sec-

tions 171.087, 171.088, 171.089, and 171.091, subject to any condition ordered by the court.

(c) A party may make an application under this section not later than the 20th day after the date the award is delivered to the applicant.

(d) An applicant shall give written notice of the application promptly to the opposing party. The notice must state that the opposing party must serve any objection to the application not later than the 10th day after the date of notice.

(e) An award modified or corrected under this section is subject to Sections 171.087, 171.088, 171.089, 171.090, and 171.091.

Added by Acts 1997, 75th Leg., ch. 165, § 5.01, eff. Sept. 1, 1997.

§ 171.055. Arbitrator's Fees and Expenses

Unless otherwise provided in the agreement to arbitrate, the arbitrators' expenses and fees, with other expenses incurred in conducting the arbitration, shall be paid as provided in the award.

Added by Acts 1997, 75th Leg., ch. 165, § 5.01, eff. Sept. 1, 1997.

SUBCHAPTER D. COURT PROCEEDINGS

§ 171.081. Jurisdiction

The making of an agreement described by Section 171.001 that provides for or authorizes an arbitration in this state and to which that section applies confers jurisdiction on the court to enforce the agreement and to render judgment on an award under this chapter.

Added by Acts 1997, 75th Leg., ch. 165, § 5.01, eff. Sept. 1, 1997.

§ 171.082. Application to Court; Fees

(a) The filing with the clerk of the court of an application for an order under this chapter, including a judgment or decree, invokes the jurisdiction of the court.

(b) On the filing of the initial application and the payment to the clerk of the fees of court required to be paid on the filing of a civil action in the court, the clerk shall docket the proceeding as a civil action pending in that court.

Added by Acts 1997, 75th Leg., ch. 165, § 5.01, eff. Sept. 1, 1997.

§ 171.083. Time for Filing

An applicant for a court order under this chapter may file the application:

(1) before arbitration proceedings begin in support of those proceedings;

(2) during the period the arbitration is pending before the arbitrators; or

(3) subject to this chapter, at or after the conclusion of the arbitration.

Added by Acts 1997, 75th Leg., ch. 165, § 5.01, eff. Sept. 1, 1997.

§ 171.084. Stay of Certain Proceedings

(a) After an initial application is filed, the court may stay:

(1) a proceeding under a later filed application in another court to:

(A) invoke the jurisdiction of that court; or

(B) obtain an order under this chapter; or

(2) a proceeding instituted after the initial application has been filed.

(b) A stay under this section affects only an issue subject to arbitration under an agreement in accordance with the terms of the initial application.

Added by Acts 1997, 75th Leg., ch. 165, § 5.01, eff. Sept. 1, 1997.

§ 171.085. Contents of Application

(a) A court may require that an application filed under this chapter:

(1) show the jurisdiction of the court;

(2) have attached a copy of the agreement to arbitrate;

(3) define the issue subject to arbitration between the parties under the agreement;

(4) specify the status of the arbitration before the arbitrators; and

(5) show the need for the court order sought by the applicant.

(b) A court may not find an application inadequate because of the absence of a requirement listed in Subsection (a) unless the court, in its discretion:

(1) requires that the applicant amend the application to meet the requirements of the court; and

(2) grants the applicant a 10-day period to comply.

Added by Acts 1997, 75th Leg., ch. 165, § 5.01, eff. Sept. 1, 1997.

§ 171.086. Orders That May Be Rendered

(a) Before arbitration proceedings begin, in support of arbitration a party may file an application for a court order, including an order to:

(1) invoke the jurisdiction of the court over the adverse party and to effect that jurisdiction by service of process on the party before arbitration proceedings begin;

(2) invoke the jurisdiction of the court over an ancillary proceeding in rem, including by attachment, garnishment, or sequestration, in the manner and subject to the conditions under which the proceeding may be instituted and conducted ancillary to a civil action in a district court;

(3) restrain or enjoin:

(A) the destruction of all or an essential part of the subject matter of the controversy; or

(B) the destruction or alteration of books, records, documents, or other evidence needed for the arbitration;

(4) obtain from the court in its discretion an order for a deposition for discovery, perpetuation of testimony, or evidence needed before the arbitration proceedings begin;

(5) appoint one or more arbitrators so that an arbitration under the agreement to arbitrate may proceed; or

(6) obtain other relief, which the court can grant in its discretion, needed to permit the arbitration to be conducted in an orderly manner and to prevent improper interference or delay of the arbitration.

(b) During the period an arbitration is pending before the arbitrators or at or after the conclusion of the arbitration, a party may file an application for a court order, including an order:

(1) that was referred to or that would serve a purpose referred to in Subsection (a);

(2) to require compliance by an adverse party or any witness with an order made under this chapter by the arbitrators during the arbitration;

(3) to require the issuance and service under court order, rather than under the arbitrators' order, of a subpoena, notice, or other court process:

(A) in support of the arbitration; or

(B) in an ancillary proceeding in rem, including by attachment, garnishment, or sequestration, in the manner of and subject to the conditions under which the proceeding may be conducted ancillary to a civil action in a district court;

(4) to require security for the satisfaction of a court judgment that may be later entered under an award;

(5) to support the enforcement of a court order entered under this chapter; or

(6) to obtain relief under Section 171.087, 171.088, 171.089, or 171.091.

(c) A court may not require an applicant for an order under Subsection (a)(1) to show that the adverse party is about to, or may, leave the state if jurisdiction over that party is not effected by service of process before the arbitration proceedings begin.

Added by Acts 1997, 75th Leg., ch. 165, § 5.01, eff. Sept. 1, 1997.

§ 171.087. Confirmation of Award

Unless grounds are offered for vacating, modifying, or correcting an award under Section 171.088 or 171.091, the court, on application of a party, shall confirm the award.

Added by Acts 1997, 75th Leg., ch. 165, § 5.01, eff. Sept. 1, 1997.

§ 171.088. Vacating Award

(a) On application of a party, the court shall vacate an award if:

(1) the award was obtained by corruption, fraud, or other undue means;

(2) the rights of a party were prejudiced by:

(A) evident partiality by an arbitrator appointed as a neutral arbitrator;

(B) corruption in an arbitrator; or

(C) misconduct or wilful misbehavior of an arbitrator;

(3) the arbitrators:

(A) exceeded their powers;

(B) refused to postpone the hearing after a showing of sufficient cause for the postponement;

(C) refused to hear evidence material to the controversy; or

(D) conducted the hearing, contrary to Section 171.043, 171.044, 171.045, 171.046, or 171.047, in a manner that substantially prejudiced the rights of a party; or

(4) there was no agreement to arbitrate, the issue was not adversely determined in a proceeding under Subchapter B,[1] and the party did not participate in the arbitration hearing without raising the objection.

(b) A party must make an application under this section not later than the 90th day after the date of delivery of a copy of the award to the applicant. A party must make an application under Subsection (a)(1) not later than the 90th day after the date the grounds for the application are known or should have been known.

(c) If the application to vacate is denied and a motion to modify or correct the award is not pending, the court shall confirm the award.

Added by Acts 1997, 75th Leg., ch. 165, § 5.01, eff. Sept. 1, 1997.

[1] V.T.C.A., Civil Practice & Remedies Code § 171.021 et seq.

§ 171.089. Rehearing After Award Vacated

(a) On vacating an award on grounds other than the grounds stated in Section 171.088(a)(4), the court may order a rehearing before new arbitrators chosen:

(1) as provided in the agreement to arbitrate; or

(2) by the court under Section 171.041, if the agreement does not provide the manner for choosing the arbitrators.

(b) If the award is vacated under Section 171.088(a)(3), the court may order a rehearing before the arbitrators who made the award or their successors appointed under Section 171.041.

(c) The period within which the agreement to arbitrate requires the award to be made applies to a rehearing under this section and commences from the date of the order.

Added by Acts 1997, 75th Leg., ch. 165, § 5.01, eff. Sept. 1, 1997.

§ 171.090. Type of Relief Not Factor

The fact that the relief granted by the arbitrators could not or would not be granted by a court of law or equity is not a ground for vacating or refusing to confirm the award.

Added by Acts 1997, 75th Leg., ch. 165, § 5.01, eff. Sept. 1, 1997.

§ 171.091. Modifying or Correcting Award

(a) On application, the court shall modify or correct an award if:

(1) the award contains:

(A) an evident miscalculation of numbers; or

(B) an evident mistake in the description of a person, thing, or property referred to in the award;

(2) the arbitrators have made an award with respect to a matter not submitted to them and the award may be corrected without affecting the merits of the decision made with respect to the issues that were submitted; or

(3) the form of the award is imperfect in a manner not affecting the merits of the controversy.

(b) A party must make an application under this section not later than the 90th day after the date of delivery of a copy of the award to the applicant.

(c) If the application is granted, the court shall modify or correct the award to effect its intent and shall confirm the award as modified or corrected. If the application is not granted, the court shall confirm the award.

(d) An application to modify or correct an award may be joined in the alternative with an application to vacate the award.

Added by Acts 1997, 75th Leg., ch. 165, § 5.01, eff. Sept. 1, 1997.

§ 171.092. Judgment on Award

(a) On granting an order that confirms, modifies, or corrects an award, the court shall enter a judgment or decree conforming to the order. The judgment or decree may be enforced in the same manner as any other judgment or decree.

(b) The court may award:

(1) costs of the application and of the proceedings subsequent to the application; and

(2) disbursements.

Added by Acts 1997, 75th Leg., ch. 165, § 5.01, eff. Sept. 1, 1997.

§ 171.093. Hearing; Notice

The court shall hear each initial and subsequent application under this subchapter in the manner and with the notice required by law or court rule for making and hearing a motion filed in a pending civil action in a district court.

Added by Acts 1997, 75th Leg., ch. 165, § 5.01, eff. Sept. 1, 1997.

§ 171.094. Service of Process for Initial Application

(a) On the filing of an initial application under this subchapter, the clerk of the court shall:

(1) issue process for service on each adverse party named in the application; and

(2) attach a copy of the application to the process.

(b) To the extent applicable, the process and service and the return of service must be in the form and include the substance required for process and service on a defendant in a civil action in a district court.

(c) An authorized official may effect the service of process.

Added by Acts 1997, 75th Leg., ch. 165, § 5.01, eff. Sept. 1, 1997.

§ 171.095. Service of Process for Subsequent Applications

(a) After an initial application has been made, notice to an adverse party for each subsequent application shall be made in the same manner as is required for a motion filed in a pending civil action in a district court. This subsection applies only if:

(1) jurisdiction over the adverse party has been established by service of process on the party or in rem for the initial application; and

(2) the subsequent application relates to:

(A) the same arbitration or a prospective arbitration under the same agreement to arbitrate; and

(B) the same controversy or controversies.

(b) If Subsection (a) does not apply, service of process shall be made on the adverse party in the manner provided by Section 171.094.

Added by Acts 1997, 75th Leg., ch. 165, § 5.01, eff. Sept. 1, 1997.

§ 171.096. Place of Filing

(a) Except as otherwise provided by this section, a party must file the initial application:

(1) in the county in which an adverse party resides or has a place of business; or

(2) if an adverse party does not have a residence or place of business in this state, in any county.

(b) If the agreement to arbitrate provides that the hearing before the arbitrators is to be held in a county in this state, a party must file the initial application with the clerk of the court of that county.

(c) If a hearing before the arbitrators has been held, a party must file the initial application with the clerk of the court of the county in which the hearing was held.

(d) Consistent with Section 171.024, if a proceeding is pending in a court relating to arbitration of an issue subject to arbitration under an agreement before the filing of the initial application, a party must file the initial application and any subsequent application relating to the arbitration in that court.

Added by Acts 1997, 75th Leg., ch. 165, § 5.01, eff. Sept. 1, 1997.

§ 171.097. Transfer

(a) On application of a party adverse to the party who filed the initial application, a court that has jurisdiction but that is located in a county other than as described by Section 171.096 shall transfer the application to a court of a county described by that section.

(b) The court shall transfer the application by an order comparable to an order sustaining a plea of privilege to be sued in a civil action in a district court of a county other than the county in which an action is filed.

(c) The party must file the application under this section:

(1) not later than the 20th day after the date of service of process on the adverse party; and

(2) before any other appearance in the court by that adverse party, other than an appearance to challenge the jurisdiction of the court.

Added by Acts 1997, 75th Leg., ch. 165, § 5.01, eff. Sept. 1, 1997.

§ 171.098. Appeal

(a) A party may appeal a judgment or decree entered under this chapter or an order:

(1) denying an application to compel arbitration made under Section 171.021;

(2) granting an application to stay arbitration made under Section 171.023;

(3) confirming or denying confirmation of an award;

(4) modifying or correcting an award; or

(5) vacating an award without directing a rehearing.

(b) The appeal shall be taken in the manner and to the same extent as an appeal from an order or judgment in a civil action.

Added by Acts 1997, 75th Leg., ch. 165, § 5.01, eff. Sept. 1, 1997.

CHAPTER 172. ARBITRATION AND CONCILIATION OF INTERNATIONAL COMMERCIAL DISPUTES

SUBCHAPTER A. GENERAL PROVISIONS

Acts 1997, 75th Leg., ch. 165, § 5.02, effective September 1, 1997, revised Chapter 172, which formerly consisted of §§ 172.001 to 172.310, as Chapter 172, consisting of V.T.C.A., Civil Practice & Remedies Code §§ 172.001 to 171.215.

DISPOSITION TABLE

Showing where the subject matter of provisions contained in former Chapter 172 may be found in Chapter 172 as amended by Acts 1997, 75th Leg., ch. 165, § 5.02.

Former Section	Amended Section
172.001	172.001, 172.003, 172.004, 172.031
172.002	172.002, 172.007, 172.033
172.003	172.005
172.004	172.006
172.005	172.171
172.006	172.054, 172.060, 172.061, 172.082
172.051	172.032
172.052	172.174
172.053	172.175
172.101	172.051

Former Section	Amended Section
172.102	172.052 to 172.055
172.103	172.056 to 172.058
172.104	172.059, 172.060
172.105	172.061, 172.064
172.106	172.062, 172.063
172.151	172.082
172.152	172.083
172.201	172.101
172.202	172.103, 172.104
172.203	172.106
172.204	172.107
172.205	172.108
172.206	172.109, 172.110
172.207	172.111 to 172.113
172.208	172.114, 172.115
172.209	172.116
172.210	172.105, 172.172, 172.173
172.251	172.102
172.252	172.081
172.253	172.117, 172.146
172.254	172.141 to 172.145
172.255	172.118
172.256	172.147 to 172.150
172.301	172.201 to 172.203
172.302	172.204
172.303	172.205
172.304	172.206
172.305	172.207
172.306	172.208 to 172.210
172.307	172.211
172.308	172.212
172.309	172.213
172.310	172.214, 172.215

SUBCHAPTER A. GENERAL PROVISIONS

§ 172.001. Scope of Chapter

(a) This chapter applies to international commercial arbitration and conciliation, subject to any agreement that is in force between the United States and another state or states.

(b) This chapter, except Sections 172.174 and 172.175, applies only to arbitration or conciliation in this state.

(c) Except as provided by Subsection (d), this chapter does not affect another state law under which a dispute:

(1) may not be submitted to arbitration; or

(2) may be submitted to arbitration only in accordance with law other than this chapter.

(d) Except as provided by this subsection, this chapter supersedes Subchapters B[1] and C,[2] Chapter 171, with respect to international commercial arbitration and conciliation. This chapter does not supersede Subchapter A[3] or D[4] of that chapter or Section 171.022.

Amended by Acts 1997, 75th Leg., ch. 165, § 5.02, eff. Sept. 1, 1997.

[1] V.T.C.A., Civil Practice & Remedies Code § 171.021 et seq.
[2] V.T.C.A., Civil Practice & Remedies Code § 171.041 et seq.
[3] V.T.C.A., Civil Practice & Remedies Code § 171.001 et seq.
[4] V.T.C.A., Civil Practice & Remedies Code § 171.081 et seq.

§ 172.002. Definitions

(a) In this chapter:

(1) "Arbitration" includes any arbitration without regard to whether it is administered by a permanent arbitration institution.

(2) "Arbitration agreement" means an agreement to arbitrate a dispute that has arisen or may arise between the parties concerning a defined legal relationship, without regard to whether the legal relationship is contractual. The term includes an arbitration clause in a contract or a separate agreement.

(3) "Arbitration award" means a decision of an arbitration tribunal on the substance of a dispute submitted to it and includes an interim, interlocutory, or partial award.

(4) "Arbitration tribunal" means a sole arbitrator or a panel of arbitrators.

(5) "Claim" includes a counterclaim.

(6) "Conciliation" includes any conciliation without regard to whether it is administered by a permanent conciliation institution.

(7) "Defense" includes a defense to a counterclaim.

(8) "Party" means a party to an arbitration or conciliation agreement.

(b) The meanings assigned by this section to "claim" and "defense" do not apply in Sections 172.114(a) and 172.118(b)(1).

Amended by Acts 1997, 75th Leg., ch. 165, § 5.02, eff. Sept. 1, 1997.

§ 172.003. International Agreement

(a) An arbitration or conciliation agreement is international if:

(1) the places of business of the parties to the agreement are located in different states when the agreement is concluded;

(2) any of the following places is located outside any state in which a party has a place of business:

(A) the place of arbitration or conciliation determined under the arbitration or conciliation agreement;

(B) a place where a substantial part of the obligations of the commercial relationship is to be performed; or

(C) the place with which the subject matter of the dispute is most closely connected;

(3) each party has expressly agreed that the subject matter of the arbitration or conciliation agreement relates to commercial interests in more than one state; or

(4) the arbitration or conciliation agreement arises out of a legal relationship that has another reasonable relation with more than one state.

(b) Subsection (a)(4) applies without regard to whether the legal relationship is contractual.

(c) For purposes of this section, the place of business of a party who has more than one place of business is the place that has the closest relationship to the arbitration or conciliation agreement. If a party does not have a place of business, the party's place of business is the party's habitual residence.

(d) For purposes of this section, the states of the United States and the District of Columbia are one state.

Amended by Acts 1997, 75th Leg., ch. 165, § 5.02, eff. Sept. 1, 1997.

§ 172.004. Commercial Agreement

An arbitration or conciliation agreement is commercial if it arises out of a relationship of a commercial nature, including:

(1) a transaction for the supply or exchange of goods or services;

(2) a distribution agreement;

(3) a commercial representation or agency;

(4) an exploitation agreement or concession;

(5) a joint venture or other related form of industrial or business cooperation;

(6) the carriage of goods or passengers by air, sea, rail, or road;

(7) a relationship involving:

(A) construction;

(B) insurance;

(C) licensing;

(D) factoring;

(E) leasing;

(F) consulting;

(G) engineering;

(H) financing;

(I) banking;

(J) professional services; or

(K) intellectual or industrial property, including trademarks, patents, copyrights, and software programs; or

(8) the transfer of data or technology.

Amended by Acts 1997, 75th Leg., ch. 165, § 5.02, eff. Sept. 1, 1997.

§ 172.005. Date Written Communications Received

(a) Except as agreed by the parties, a written communication is received on the day that it is delivered:

(1) to the addressee personally; or

(2) at the addressee's place of business, habitual residence, or mailing address.

(b) If a place described by Subsection (a) cannot be found after a reasonable inquiry, a written communication is received if it is sent to the addressee's last known place of business, habitual residence, or mailing address by registered mail or other means that provides a record of the attempt to deliver it.

(c) This section does not apply to a written communication relating to a court proceeding.

Amended by Acts 1997, 75th Leg., ch. 165, § 5.02, eff. Sept. 1, 1997.

§ 172.006. Waiver of Right to Object

(a) A party who proceeds with the arbitration knowing that a provision of this chapter or the arbitration agreement has not been complied with waives the right to object to the noncompliance unless the party states the objection:

(1) without undue delay; or

(2) if a period is provided for stating that objection, within that period.

(b) Subsection (a) applies only to a provision of this chapter as to which the parties may agree to act in a different manner.

Amended by Acts 1997, 75th Leg., ch. 165, § 5.02, eff. Sept. 1, 1997.

§ 172.007. Delegation of Certain Determinations

The parties may authorize a third party, including an institution, to determine any issue the parties may determine under this chapter, other than a determination under Section 172.102.

Added by Acts 1997, 75th Leg., ch. 165, § 5.02, eff. Sept. 1, 1997.

SUBCHAPTER B. ARBITRATION AGREEMENTS

§ 172.031. Arbitration Agreements Valid

(a) A written arbitration agreement is valid and enforceable if the agreement is to arbitrate a controversy that:

(1) exists at the time of the agreement; or

(2) arises between the parties after the date of the agreement.

(b) A party may revoke the agreement only on a ground that exists at law or in equity for the revocation of a contract.

Added by Acts 1997, 75th Leg., ch. 165, § 5.02, eff. Sept. 1, 1997.

§ 172.032. Requirements for Arbitration Agreement

(a) An arbitration agreement must be in writing. The agreement is in writing if it is contained in:

(1) a document signed by each party;

(2) an exchange of letters, telexes, telegrams, or other means of telecommunication that provide a record of the agreement; or

(3) an exchange of statements of claim and defense in which the existence of an agreement is alleged by one party and not denied by another.

(b) A contract reference to a document containing an arbitration clause is an arbitration agreement if the contract is in writing and the reference is sufficient to make that clause part of the contract.

Added by Acts 1997, 75th Leg., ch. 165, § 5.02, eff. Sept. 1, 1997.

§ 172.033. Rules Referred to in Agreement

An agreement of the parties under this chapter includes any arbitration or conciliation rules referred to by that agreement.

Added by Acts 1997, 75th Leg., ch. 165, § 5.02, eff. Sept. 1, 1997.

SUBCHAPTER C. ARBITRATORS

§ 172.051. Number of Arbitrators

An arbitration has one arbitrator unless the parties agree to additional arbitrators.

Amended by Acts 1997, 75th Leg., ch. 165, § 5.02, eff. Sept. 1, 1997.

§ 172.052. Nationality of Arbitrator

A person of any nationality may be an arbitrator.

Amended by Acts 1997, 75th Leg., ch. 165, § 5.02, eff. Sept. 1, 1997.

§ 172.053. Appointment of Arbitration Tribunal

(a) Subject to Sections 172.054(b), (c), and (d) and Section 172.055, the parties may agree on a procedure for appointing the arbitration tribunal.

(b) If an agreement is not made under Subsection (a), in an arbitration with three arbitrators and two parties, each party shall appoint one arbitrator, and the two appointed arbitrators shall appoint the third arbitrator.

Amended by Acts 1997, 75th Leg., ch. 165, § 5.02, eff. Sept. 1, 1997.

§ 172.054. Appointment by Court

(a) On request of a party, the district court of the county in which the place of arbitration is located shall appoint each arbitrator if:

(1) an agreement is not made under Section 172.053(a) in an arbitration with a sole arbitrator and the parties fail to agree on the arbitrator; or

(2) the appointment procedure in Section 172.053(b) applies and:

(A) a party fails to appoint an arbitrator not later than the 30th day after the date of receipt of a request to do so from the other party; or

(B) the two appointed arbitrators fail to agree on the third arbitrator not later than the 30th day after the date of their appointment.

(b) On request of a party, the district court of the county in which the place of arbitration is located may take necessary measures if under an appointment procedure agreed to by each party:

(1) a party fails to act as required under that procedure;

(2) the parties or two appointed arbitrators fail to reach an agreement expected of them under that procedure; or

(3) a third party, including an institution, fails to perform a function assigned to the party under that procedure.

(c) Subsection (b) does not apply if the agreement on the appointment procedure provides other means for securing the appointment.

(d) A decision of the district court under this section is final and not subject to appeal.

Added by Acts 1997, 75th Leg., ch. 165, § 5.02, eff. Sept. 1, 1997.

§ 172.055. Factors Considered

In appointing an arbitrator, the district court shall consider:

(1) each qualification required of the arbitrator by the arbitration agreement;

(2) any consideration making more likely the appointment of an independent and impartial arbitrator; and

(3) in the case of a sole or third arbitrator, the advisability of appointing an arbitrator of a nationality other than that of any party.

Added by Acts 1997, 75th Leg., ch. 165, § 5.02, eff. Sept. 1, 1997.

§ 172.056. Disclosure of Grounds for Challenge

(a) Except as otherwise provided by this chapter, a person who is contacted in connection with the person's possible appointment or designation as an arbitrator or conciliator or who is appointed or designated shall, not later than the 21st day after the date of the contact, appointment, or designation, disclose to each party any information that might cause the person's impartiality or independence to be questioned, including information that:

(1) the person:

(A) has a personal bias or prejudice concerning a party;

(B) has personal knowledge of a disputed evidentiary fact concerning the proceeding;

(C) served as an attorney in the matter in controversy;

(D) is or has been associated with another who has participated in the matter during the association;

(E) has been a material witness concerning the matter;

(F) served as an arbitrator or conciliator in another proceeding involving a party to the proceeding; or

(G) has a close personal or professional relationship with a person who:

(i) is or has been a party to the proceeding or an officer, director, or trustee of a party;

(ii) is acting or has acted as an attorney or representative in the proceeding;

(iii) is or expects to be nominated as an arbitrator or conciliator in the proceeding;

(iv) is known to have an interest that could be substantially affected by the outcome of the proceeding; or

(v) is likely to be a material witness in the proceeding;

(2) the person, individually or as a fiduciary, or the person's spouse or minor child residing in the person's household has:

(A) a financial interest in:

(i) the subject matter in controversy; or

(ii) a party to the proceeding; or

(B) any other interest that could be substantially affected by the outcome of the proceeding; or

(3) the person, the person's spouse, a person within the third degree of relationship to either of them, or the spouse of that person:

(A) is or has been a party to the proceeding or an officer, director, or trustee of a party;

(B) is acting or has acted as an attorney in the proceeding;

(C) is known to have an interest that could be substantially affected by the outcome of the proceeding; or

(D) is likely to be a material witness in the proceeding.

(b) Except as provided by this subsection, the parties may agree to waive the disclosure under Subsection (a). A party may not waive the disclosure for a person serving as:

(1) the sole arbitrator or conciliator; or

(2) the chief or prevailing arbitrator or conciliator.

(c) After appointment and throughout the arbitration or conciliation, an arbitrator or conciliator shall promptly disclose to each party any circumstance described by Subsection (a) that was not previously disclosed.

Added by Acts 1997, 75th Leg., ch. 165, § 5.02, eff. Sept. 1, 1997.

§ 172.057. Grounds for Challenge; Limitation

Except as provided by agreement of the parties or the rules governing the arbitration, a party may challenge an arbitrator only if circumstances exist that give rise to justifiable doubts as to the arbitrator's impartiality, independence, or possession of a qualification on which the parties have agreed.

Added by Acts 1997, 75th Leg., ch. 165, § 5.02, eff. Sept. 1, 1997.

§ 172.058. Challenge After Appointment

A party who appointed or participated in the appointment of an arbitrator may challenge that arbitrator only for a reason that the party becomes aware of after the appointment is made.

Added by Acts 1997, 75th Leg., ch. 165, § 5.02, eff. Sept. 1, 1997.

§ 172.059. Challenge Procedure

(a) The parties may agree on a procedure for challenging an arbitrator. A decision reached under that procedure is final.

(b) If there is not an agreement under Subsection (a), a party challenging an arbitrator shall send a written statement of the reason for the challenge to the arbitration tribunal. The party shall send the statement not later than the 15th day after the later date the party becomes aware of:

(1) the constitution of the tribunal; or

(2) a circumstance referred to in Section 172.057 or 172.058.

(c) Unless the arbitrator challenged under Subsection (b) withdraws from office or the other party agrees to the challenge, the arbitration tribunal shall decide the challenge.

Added by Acts 1997, 75th Leg., ch. 165, § 5.02, eff. Sept. 1, 1997.

§ 172.060. Appeal of Unsuccessful Challenge

(a) If a challenge under Sections 172.059(b) and (c) is unsuccessful, the challenging party, not later than the 30th day after the date the party receives notice of the decision rejecting the challenge, may request the district court of the county in which the place of arbitration is located to decide the challenge.

(b) The court shall sustain the challenge if the facts support a finding that grounds under Section 172.057 fairly exist.

(c) The decision of the court is final and not subject to appeal.

(d) While a request under Subsection (a) is pending, the arbitration tribunal, including the challenged arbitrator, may continue the arbitration and make an award.

Added by Acts 1997, 75th Leg., ch. 165, § 5.02, eff. Sept. 1, 1997.

§ 172.061. Failure or Impossibility to Act

(a) The mandate of an arbitrator terminates if the arbitrator:

(1) is unable to perform the arbitrator's functions or for another reason fails to act without undue delay; and

(2) withdraws from office or each party agrees to the termination.

(b) If there is a controversy concerning the termination of the arbitrator's mandate under Subsection (a), a party may request the district court of the county in which the place of arbitration is located to decide the termination. The decision of the court is not subject to appeal.

Added by Acts 1997, 75th Leg., ch. 165, § 5.02, eff. Sept. 1, 1997.

§ 172.062. Termination of Mandate

The mandate of an arbitrator terminates:

(1) on withdrawal from office;

(2) when the parties agree; or

(3) as provided by Section 172.059, 172.060, or 172.061.

Added by Acts 1997, 75th Leg., ch. 165, § 5.02, eff. Sept. 1, 1997.

§ 172.063. Substitution of Arbitrator

(a) When the mandate of an arbitrator terminates, a substitute arbitrator shall be appointed according to the rules that were applicable to the appointment of the arbitrator being replaced.

(b) Except as agreed by the parties:

(1) if the sole or presiding arbitrator is replaced, a hearing previously held shall be repeated; and

(2) if an arbitrator other than the sole or presiding arbitrator is replaced, a hearing previously held

may be repeated at the discretion of the arbitration tribunal.

(c) Except as agreed by the parties, an order or ruling of the arbitration tribunal made before the replacement of an arbitrator under this section is not invalid because there has been a change in the composition of the tribunal.

Added by Acts 1997, 75th Leg., ch. 165, § 5.02, eff. Sept. 1, 1997.

§ 172.064. Withdrawal of Arbitrator

The withdrawal of an arbitrator from office or the agreement of a party to the termination of the mandate of an arbitrator under Section 172.059(c) or Section 172.061 does not imply acceptance of the validity of a ground referred to in Section 172.057, 172.058, or 172.061.

Added by Acts 1997, 75th Leg., ch. 165, § 5.02, eff. Sept. 1, 1997.

SUBCHAPTER D. ARBITRATION TRIBUNAL

§ 172.081. Decision of Arbitration Tribunal

(a) Except as agreed by the parties or as provided by Subsection (b), in an arbitration with more than one arbitrator, a decision of the arbitration tribunal must be made by a majority of its members.

(b) If authorized by the parties or all the members of the arbitration tribunal, a presiding arbitrator may decide a procedural question.

Added by Acts 1997, 75th Leg., ch. 165, § 5.02, eff. Sept. 1, 1997.

§ 172.082. Determination of Jurisdiction of Arbitration Tribunal

(a) The arbitration tribunal may rule on its own jurisdiction, including an objection with respect to the existence or validity of the arbitration agreement. For that purpose, an arbitration clause that is part of a contract is an agreement independent of the other terms of the contract. A decision by the tribunal that the contract is void does not make the arbitration clause invalid.

(b) A party may not plead that the arbitration tribunal does not have jurisdiction after the submission of the statement of defense. A party is not precluded from pleading because the party has appointed or participated in the appointment of an arbitrator.

(c) A party may plead that the arbitration tribunal is exceeding the scope of its authority only when the matter alleged to be beyond the scope of its authority is raised during the arbitration.

(d) The arbitration tribunal may allow a plea after the period described by Subsection (b) or (c) if the tribunal considers the delay justified.

(e) The arbitration tribunal may rule on a plea described by Subsection (b), (c), or (d) as a preliminary question or in an award on the merits.

(f) If the arbitration tribunal rules as a preliminary question that it has jurisdiction, a party waives objection to the ruling unless the party, not later than the 30th day after the date the party receives notice of that ruling, requests the district court of the county in which the place of arbitration is located to decide the matter. The decision of the court is not subject to appeal.

(g) While a request under Subsection (f) is pending before the court, the arbitration tribunal may continue the arbitration and make an award.

Added by Acts 1997, 75th Leg., ch. 165, § 5.02, eff. Sept. 1, 1997.

§ 172.083. Interim Measures Ordered by Arbitration Tribunal

(a) Except as agreed by the parties, the arbitration tribunal, at the request of a party, may order a party to take an interim measure of protection that the tribunal considers necessary concerning the subject matter of the dispute.

(b) The arbitration tribunal may require a party to provide appropriate security in connection with the interim measure ordered.

Added by Acts 1997, 75th Leg., ch. 165, § 5.02, eff. Sept. 1, 1997.

SUBCHAPTER E. ARBITRATION PROCEEDINGS

§ 172.101. Equal Treatment of Parties

The arbitration tribunal shall:

(1) treat each party with equality; and

(2) give each party a full opportunity to present the party's case.

Amended by Acts 1997, 75th Leg., ch. 165, § 5.02, eff. Sept. 1, 1997.

§ 172.102. Substantive Rules

(a) The arbitration tribunal shall decide the dispute according to the rules of law designated by the parties as applicable to the substance of the dispute.

(b) Unless otherwise expressed, a designation by the parties of the law or legal system of a given state refers to the substantive law of that state and not to conflict-of-laws rules.

(c) If the parties do not make a designation under Subsection (a), the arbitration tribunal shall apply the law determined by the conflict-of-laws rules that the tribunal considers applicable.

(d) The arbitration tribunal shall decide ex aequo et bono or as amiable compositeur if each party has expressly authorized it to do so.

(e) In each case, the arbitration tribunal shall:

(1) decide in accordance with the terms of the contract; and

(2) take into account the usages of the trade applicable to the transaction.

Amended by Acts 1997, 75th Leg., ch. 165, § 5.02, eff. Sept. 1, 1997.

§ 172.103. Rules of Procedure

(a) The parties may agree on the procedure to be followed by the arbitration tribunal in conducting the arbitration, subject to this chapter.

(b) If the parties do not agree, the arbitration tribunal may conduct the arbitration in the manner it considers appropriate, subject to this chapter.

Amended by Acts 1997, 75th Leg., ch. 165, § 5.02, eff. Sept. 1, 1997.

§ 172.104. Rules of Evidence

The power of the arbitration tribunal under Section 172.103(b) includes the power to determine the admissibility, relevance, materiality, and weight of any evidence.

Amended by Acts 1997, 75th Leg., ch. 165, § 5.02, eff. Sept. 1, 1997.

§ 172.105. Subpoena

(a) The arbitration tribunal may issue a subpoena as provided by Section 171.051.

(b) Section 171.052 applies with respect to a subpoena issued under this section.

Amended by Acts 1997, 75th Leg., ch. 165, § 5.02, eff. Sept. 1, 1997.

§ 172.106. Place of Arbitration

(a) The parties may agree on the place of arbitration.

(b) If the parties do not agree, the arbitration tribunal shall determine the place of arbitration considering the circumstances of the case, including the convenience of the parties.

(c) Except as agreed by each party, the arbitration tribunal may meet at any place it considers appropriate for:

(1) consultation among its members;

(2) hearing of witnesses, experts, or the parties; or

(3) inspection of documents, goods, or other property.

Amended by Acts 1997, 75th Leg., ch. 165, § 5.02, eff. Sept. 1, 1997.

§ 172.107. Commencement of Arbitration

Except as agreed by the parties, the arbitration begins on the date a request for the dispute to be referred to arbitration is received by the respondent.

Added by Acts 1997, 75th Leg., ch. 165, § 5.02, eff. Sept. 1, 1997.

§ 172.108. Language

(a) The parties may agree on the language or languages to be used in the arbitration.

(b) If the parties do not agree, the arbitration tribunal shall determine the language or languages to be used in the arbitration.

(c) Except as provided by the agreement or determination, the agreement or determination applies to each:

(1) written statement by a party;

(2) hearing; and

(3) award, decision, or other communication by the arbitration tribunal.

(d) The arbitration tribunal may order that documentary evidence be accompanied by a translation into the selected language or languages.

Added by Acts 1997, 75th Leg., ch. 165, § 5.02, eff. Sept. 1, 1997.

§ 172.109. Statement of Claim or Defense

(a) Within the period agreed on by the parties or determined by the arbitration tribunal:

(1) the claimant shall state:

(A) the facts supporting the claim;

(B) the points at issue; and

(C) the relief or remedy sought; and

(C) administration fees of the institution supervising the arbitration; and

(2) the tribunal may specify:

(A) the party entitled to costs;

(B) the party required to pay costs;

(C) the amount of costs or method of determining that amount; and

(D) the manner in which the costs are to be paid.

Added by Acts 1997, 75th Leg., ch. 165, § 5.02, eff. Sept. 1, 1997.

§ 172.146. Award on Agreed Terms

(a) The arbitration tribunal shall make an award on agreed terms as provided by Section 172.117. An award on agreed terms must state that it is an arbitration award.

(b) An award on agreed terms has the same status and effect as any other arbitration award on the substance of the dispute.

Added by Acts 1997, 75th Leg., ch. 165, § 5.02, eff. Sept. 1, 1997.

§ 172.147. Correction and Interpretation of Awards

(a) Not later than the 30th day after the date of receipt of the arbitration award, unless another period has been agreed to by the parties, a party may request the arbitration tribunal to:

(1) correct in the award a computation, clerical, or typographical error or a similar error; and

(2) interpret a part of the award, if agreed by the parties.

(b) If the arbitration tribunal considers a request under Subsection (a) to be justified, it shall make the correction or give the interpretation not later than the 30th day after the date of receipt of the request. The interpretation or correction becomes part of the arbitration award.

(c) The arbitration tribunal may correct an error described by Subsection (a)(1) on its own initiative not later than the 30th day after the date of the arbitration award.

Added by Acts 1997, 75th Leg., ch. 165, § 5.02, eff. Sept. 1, 1997.

§ 172.148. Additional Award

(a) Except as agreed by the parties, a party may request, not later than the 30th day after the date of receipt of the arbitration award, that the arbitration tribunal make an additional award for a claim presented in the arbitration but omitted from the award.

(b) If the arbitration tribunal considers the request to be justified, the tribunal shall make the additional award not later than the 60th day after the date of receipt of the request.

Added by Acts 1997, 75th Leg., ch. 165, § 5.02, eff. Sept. 1, 1997.

§ 172.149. Extension of Time

The arbitration tribunal may, if necessary, extend the period within which it may make a correction, give an interpretation, or make an additional award under Section 172.147 or 172.148.

Added by Acts 1997, 75th Leg., ch. 165, § 5.02, eff. Sept. 1, 1997.

§ 172.150. Applicable Law

Sections 172.141, 172.142, 172.144, and 172.145 apply to:

(1) a correction or interpretation of an arbitration award under Section 172.147; or

(2) an additional award made under Section 172.148.

Added by Acts 1997, 75th Leg., ch. 165, § 5.02, eff. Sept. 1, 1997.

§§ 172.151, 172.152. Deleted by Acts 1997, 75th Leg., ch. 165, § 5.02, eff. Sept. 1, 1997

SUBCHAPTER G. JUDICIAL PROCEEDINGS

§ 172.171. Role of Court

A court may not intervene in a matter governed by this chapter except as provided by this chapter or federal law.

Added by Acts 1997, 75th Leg., ch. 165, § 5.02, eff. Sept. 1, 1997.

§ 172.172. Assistance in Taking Evidence

The arbitration tribunal or a party with the approval of the tribunal may request assistance from a district court in taking evidence, and the court may provide the assistance according to its rules on taking evidence. The tribunal or a party shall select the district court in the manner provided by Section 171.096.

Added by Acts 1997, 75th Leg., ch. 165, § 5.02, eff. Sept. 1, 1997.

§ 172.173. Consolidation

(a) If the parties to two or more arbitration agreements agree, in the respective arbitration agreements or otherwise, to consolidate the arbitrations arising out of the agreements, a district court, on application by a party with the consent of each other party to the agreements, may:

(1) order the arbitrations consolidated on terms the court considers just and necessary;

(2) if all the parties cannot agree on a tribunal for the consolidated arbitration, appoint an arbitration tribunal as provided by Section 172.055; and

(3) if all the parties cannot agree on any other matter necessary to conduct the consolidated arbitration, make any other order the court considers necessary.

(b) The arbitration tribunal or the party shall select the district court in the manner provided by Section 171.096.

(c) This section does not prevent the parties to two or more arbitrations from agreeing to consolidate those arbitrations and taking any step necessary to effect that consolidation.

Added by Acts 1997, 75th Leg., ch. 165, § 5.02, eff. Sept. 1, 1997.

§ 172.174. Stay of Court Proceedings

(a) On request of a party, a court in which a pending judicial proceeding is being brought by a party to an arbitration agreement to obtain relief with respect to a matter covered by the arbitration agreement shall:

(1) stay the judicial proceeding; and

(2) refer the parties to arbitration.

(b) A party may not make a request for a stay after the time the requesting party submits the party's first statement on the substance of the dispute.

(c) The court may not stay the proceeding if it finds that the agreement is void, inoperable, or incapable of being performed.

(d) An arbitration may begin or continue, and an arbitration tribunal may make an award, while an action described in this section is pending before the court.

Added by Acts 1997, 75th Leg., ch. 165, § 5.02, eff. Sept. 1, 1997.

§ 172.175. Interim Orders

(a) A party to an arbitration agreement may request an interim measure of protection from a district court before or during an arbitration.

(b) A party to an arbitration may request from the court enforcement of an order of an arbitration tribunal granting an interim measure of protection under Section 172.083. The court shall grant enforcement as provided by the law applicable to the type of interim relief requested.

(c) In connection with a pending arbitration, the court may take appropriate action, including:

(1) ordering an attachment issued to assure that the award to which the applicant may be entitled is not rendered ineffectual by the dissipation of party assets; or

(2) granting a preliminary injunction to protect a trade secret or to conserve goods that are the subject matter of the dispute.

(d) In considering a request for interim relief, the court shall give preclusive effect to a finding of fact of the arbitration tribunal in the arbitration, including a finding of fact relating to the probable validity of the claim that is the subject of the order for interim relief that the tribunal has granted, if the interim order is consistent with public policy.

(e) If the arbitration tribunal has not ruled on an objection to its jurisdiction, the court may not grant preclusive effect to the tribunal's finding until the court makes an independent finding as to the jurisdiction of the tribunal. If the court rules that the tribunal did not have jurisdiction under applicable law, the court shall deny the application for interim measures of relief.

Added by Acts 1997, 75th Leg., ch. 165, § 5.02, eff. Sept. 1, 1997.

SUBCHAPTER H. PROVISIONS RELATING ONLY TO CONCILIATION

§ 172.201. Policy

It is the policy of this state to encourage parties to an international commercial agreement or transaction that qualifies for arbitration or conciliation under this chapter to resolve disputes arising from those agreements or transactions through conciliation.

Amended by Acts 1997, 75th Leg., ch. 165, § 5.02, eff. Sept. 1, 1997.

§ 172.202. Appointment of Conciliator

The parties to an agreement or transaction may select or permit an arbitration tribunal or other third party to select one or more persons to serve as the conciliator or conciliators to assist the parties in an independent and impartial manner to reach an amicable settlement of the dispute.

Amended by Acts 1997, 75th Leg., ch. 165, § 5.02, eff. Sept. 1, 1997.

§ 172.203. Conduct of Conciliation

(a) A conciliator:

(1) shall be guided by principles of objectivity, fairness, and justice; and

(2) shall consider, among other things:

(A) the rights and obligations of the parties;

(B) the usages of the trade concerned; and

(C) the circumstances surrounding the dispute, including any previous practices between the parties.

(b) The conciliator may conduct the conciliation in a manner that the conciliator considers appropriate, considering the circumstances of the case, the wishes of the parties, and the desirability of a speedy settlement of the dispute.

(c) Except as provided by this chapter, a law of this state governing procedure, other than this chapter, does not apply to conciliation under this chapter.

Amended by Acts 1997, 75th Leg., ch. 165, § 5.02, eff. Sept. 1, 1997.

§ 172.204. Representation and Assistance

In a conciliation proceeding, each party may appear in person or be represented or assisted by a person of the party's choice.

Amended by Acts 1997, 75th Leg., ch. 165, § 5.02, eff. Sept. 1, 1997.

§ 172.205. Draft Conciliation Settlement

(a) At any time during the conciliation, the conciliator may prepare a draft conciliation settlement and send a copy to each party, stating the time within which each party must approve the settlement. The draft conciliation settlement may include the assessment and apportionment of costs between the parties.

(b) A party is not required to accept a proposed conciliation settlement.

Amended by Acts 1997, 75th Leg., ch. 165, § 5.02, eff. Sept. 1, 1997.

§ 172.206. Confidentiality

(a) Evidence of anything said or of an admission made in the course of a conciliation is not admissible in evidence, and disclosure of that evidence may not be compelled in an arbitration or civil action in which, under law, testimony may be compelled to be given.

(b) Except as provided by a document prepared for the purpose of, in the course of, or pursuant to the conciliation, the document or a copy of the document is not admissible in evidence, and disclosure of the document may not be compelled in an arbitration or civil action in which, under law, testimony may be compelled to be given.

(c) Subsection (a) does not limit the admissibility of evidence if each party participating in conciliation consents to the disclosure.

(d) If evidence is offered in violation of this section, the arbitration tribunal or the court shall make any order it considers appropriate to deal with the matter, including an order restricting the introduction of evidence or dismissing the case without prejudice.

Amended by Acts 1997, 75th Leg., ch. 165, § 5.02, eff. Sept. 1, 1997.

§ 172.207. Stay of Arbitration and Resort to Other Proceedings

(a) The agreement of the parties to submit a dispute to conciliation is an agreement of the parties to stay a judicial proceeding or arbitration from the beginning of conciliation until the termination of conciliation.

(b) Each applicable limitation period, including a period of prescription, is tolled or extended on the beginning of a conciliation under this chapter for each party to the conciliation until the 10th day following the date of termination of the conciliation.

(c) For purposes of this section, conciliation begins when a party requests conciliation of a dispute and each other party agrees to participate in the conciliation.

Amended by Acts 1997, 75th Leg., ch. 165, § 5.02, eff. Sept. 1, 1997.

§ 172.208. Termination of Conciliation

(a) A conciliation proceeding may be terminated as to each party by:

(1) a written declaration of each conciliator, after consultation with the parties, that further efforts at conciliation are not justified, on the date of the declaration;

(2) a written declaration of each party addressed to each conciliator that the conciliation is terminated, on the date of the declaration; or

(3) the signing of a settlement agreement by each party, on the date of the agreement.

(b) The conciliation proceedings may be terminated as to particular parties by:

(1) a written declaration of a party to each other party and each conciliator, if appointed, that the conciliation is terminated as to that party, on the date of the declaration; or

(2) the signing of a settlement agreement by some of the parties, on the date of the agreement.

Amended by Acts 1997, 75th Leg., ch. 165, § 5.02, eff. Sept. 1, 1997.

§ 172.209. Conflict of Interest

Except as provided by rules adopted for the conciliation or arbitration, a person who has served as conciliator may not be appointed as an arbitrator for or take part in an arbitration or judicial proceeding in the same dispute unless each party consents to the participation.

Amended by Acts 1997, 75th Leg., ch. 165, § 5.02, eff. Sept. 1, 1997.

§ 172.210. Participation Not Waiver of Rights

(a) A party by submitting to conciliation does not waive a right or remedy that party would have had if conciliation had not been initiated.

(b) Subsection (a) does not apply to the waiver of a right or remedy stated in a settlement resulting from the conciliation.

Amended by Acts 1997, 75th Leg., ch. 165, § 5.02, eff. Sept. 1, 1997.

§ 172.211. Enforceability

A conciliation agreement has the same force and effect as a final arbitration award if the agreement:

(1) settles the dispute;

(2) is in writing; and

(3) is signed by each conciliator and each party or a representative of each party.

Added by Acts 1997, 75th Leg., ch. 165, § 5.02, eff. Sept. 1, 1997.

§ 172.212. Costs

(a) On termination of the conciliation proceedings, the conciliator shall set the costs of the conciliation and give written notice of the costs to each party.

(b) The parties shall bear the costs equally unless the settlement agreement provides for a different apportionment. A party shall bear any other expense incurred by that party.

(c) In this section, "costs" includes only:

(1) a reasonable fee to be paid to each conciliator;

(2) travel and other reasonable expenses of each conciliator and each witness requested by the conciliator with the consent of each party;

(3) the cost of expert advice requested by the conciliator with the consent of each party; and

(4) any court cost.

Added by Acts 1997, 75th Leg., ch. 165, § 5.02, eff. Sept. 1, 1997.

§ 172.213. No Consent to Jurisdiction

A request for conciliation, a consent to participate or participation in the conciliation, or the entering into a conciliation agreement or settlement is not consent to the jurisdiction of a court in this state if conciliation fails.

Added by Acts 1997, 75th Leg., ch. 165, § 5.02, eff. Sept. 1, 1997.

§ 172.214. Not Subject to Service of Process

A conciliator, party, or representative of a conciliator or party, while present in this state to arrange for or participate in conciliation under this chapter, is not subject to service of process in a civil matter related to the conciliation.

Added by Acts 1997, 75th Leg., ch. 165, § 5.02, eff. Sept. 1, 1997.

§ 172.215. Conciliator Immune

A conciliator is not liable in an action for damages resulting from an act or omission in the performance of the person's role as a conciliator in a proceeding subject to this chapter.

Added by Acts 1997, 75th Leg., ch. 165, § 5.02, eff. Sept. 1, 1997.

CHAPTER 173. ARBITRATION OF CONTROVERSIES BETWEEN MEMBERS OF CERTAIN NONPROFIT ENTITIES

Section

§ 173.001. Purpose

The purpose of this chapter is to abrogate the common law arbitration rule prohibiting specific enforcement of executory arbitration agreements.

Added by Acts 1997, 75th Leg., ch. 165, § 5.03, eff. Sept. 1, 1997.

§ 173.002. Scope of Chapter

This chapter applies only to the arbitration of a controversy between members of an association or corporation that is:

(1) exempt from the payment of federal income taxes under Section 501(a) of the Internal Revenue Code of 1986 by being listed as an exempt organization under Section 501(c) of the code; or

(2) incorporated under the Texas Non-Profit Corporation Act (Article 1396–1.01 et seq., Vernon's Texas Civil Statutes).

Added by Acts 1997, 75th Leg., ch. 165, § 5.03, eff. Sept. 1, 1997.

§ 173.003. Agreement or Bylaw Provision Valid

(a) A written agreement to submit a controversy to arbitration at common law is valid and enforceable if the agreement is to arbitrate a controversy that arises between the parties after the date of the agreement.

(b) A party may revoke the agreement only on a ground that exists at law or in equity for the revocation of a contract.

(c) A provision in the bylaws of a nonprofit corporation incorporated under the Texas Non-Profit Corporation Act (Article 1396–1.01 et seq., Vernon's Texas Civil Statutes) that requires a member of the corporation to arbitrate at common law a controversy that subsequently arises between members is a valid, enforceable, and irrevocable agreement by a member of the corporation to arbitrate the controversy.

Added by Acts 1997, 75th Leg., ch. 165, § 5.03, eff. Sept. 1, 1997.

§ 173.004. Common Law Preserved

This chapter is cumulative of other law relating to common law arbitration. Except as specifically provided by this chapter, this chapter does not abrogate or repeal that other law.

Added by Acts 1997, 75th Leg., ch. 165, § 5.03, eff. Sept. 1, 1997.

INDEX TO
CIVIL PRACTICE AND REMEDIES CODE

References are Sections